COMMON KNOWLEDGE

COMMON KNOWLEDGE

Volume 25 | Issues 1–3

April 2019

IN MEMORIAM

STANLEY CAVELL (1926–2018)
Member of the *Common Knowledge*
Editorial Board

FROM THE EDITOR

Jeffrey M. Perl

The special issue of *Common Knowledge* that you are reading commences the journal's twenty-fifth volume. At least some readers, I hope, may remember that, a quarter century ago, we began with calls for papers issued by individual editors and members of the editorial board. The journal's name, after all, was not meant to imply that consensus prevailed among the founders and participants but, instead, to suggest our intention to build toward agreement over time. As a colleague and I observed in 2002, the name was also meant

to express unease with the term or slogan "local knowledge," made famous by [Clifford] Geertz, a member of *CK*'s founding editorial board. "Local knowledge" had been a shorthand for the contextualist premise of [Thomas] Kuhn and the many scholars in the many fields he influenced, that truth and meaning are goods obtainable solely inside a language game, a paradigm, an episteme, a coherent circle closed on the outside—that truth and meaning are, in other words, local, untranslatable, and incommensurable with any knowledge obtainable across frontiers, whether those be spatial, cultural, or temporal. The "local knowledge" argument arose to oppose the universalism of positivist and structuralist theories, but also to defend both living cultures against imperialism and long-ago cultures against condescension. The moral impetus of the argument, however, was belied by unethical applications.

The author wishes to thank Adir H. Petel for his suggestions about how to arrange this special issue and about how this foreword to it should be written.

Common Knowledge 25:1–3
DOI 10.1215/0961754X-7299018

The conversations that resulted in the founding of *CK* took place as the Cold War was winding down and the Balkan crisis heating up. It was a time when various champions of "local knowledge" contextualism were seeking to map commonalities among discrete communities, or at least—in the East bloc vernacular adapted by Richard Rorty—to achieve solidarity among them. *Common Knowledge* enmagazined that project.[1]

The "conversations that resulted in the founding of *CK*" have continued here since 1992, as a call for papers that Rorty issued in that year foretold:

The word *conversation* is a useful, relatively bland substitute for terms like *argument* and *dialectic* and *philosophy*. Many of our best conversations are with people whose books we have pondered but have never met, or met only in passing. Indeed, much of our inner lives consist of conversations with such people. I've been asked to call for papers, so: I call for papers from people who would like to write up fragments of their inner lives—fragments which consist of conversations with people from whom they have learned but who inspired in them interesting and important disagreement. I wonder, what have Feyerabend and Popper learned from one another? Fang Lizhi from Mao or Kolakowski from Marx? What would Geertz say he'd learned from Lévi-Strauss, Alasdair MacIntyre from Foucault, Kenner from Ellmann, Irigaray from Mailer, Quentin Skinner from Raymond Williams, or Derrida from Gadamer? The editors of *CK* have agreed to hoard responses to this call and publish them together in an issue devoted to conversation(s).[2]

We never did publish a single "issue devoted to conversation(s)." Instead, the entire quarter century became a conversation, or a set of conversations, of the sort that Rorty had called for. Perhaps the best example is the memorial tribute to Rorty himself by Alasdair MacIntyre. The cultural politics of those two could hardly have differed more. Still, MacIntyre, a Thomist moral philosopher and a radical critic of liberalism and secularism, wrote of the liberals' champion that "I learned more [from Rorty] in a shorter period, during lunchtime walks by the lake at Princeton, than I have ever done before or since."[3]

In our first series, of seven volumes, when the publisher of *Common Knowledge* was Oxford University Press, symposia consumed one issue each or were spread seriatim, one article at a time, across several issues—and in some numbers of the first series there were no symposia at all. In its second series, with Duke University Press, *Common Knowledge* has become a venue exclusively for symposia, and indeed of multipart symposia that, as I like to think, are of unprecedented

1. Perl and Isaacs, "Postscript on Method," 148.   3. MacIntyre, "Richard Rorty," 185.

2. Rorty, "Call for Papers XIV."

thoroughness. The symposium on xenophilia that this anniversary issue interrupts has taken four installments so far (23.2–24.2) and is likely to require three or four more to complete. Other multipart symposia in series 2 have been:

- "In the Humanities Classroom" (23.1, 24.3);
- "Peace by Other Means: Symposium on the Role of Ethnography and the Humanities in the Understanding, Prevention, and Resolution of Enmity" (20.3–22.2);
- "Experimental Scholarship, Revisited" (20.1, 2);
- "Fuzzy Studies: A Symposium on the Consequence of Blur" (17.3, 18.2–19.3);
- "Apology for Quietism: A *Sotto Voce* Symposium" (15.1–16.3);
- "Devalued Currency: Elegiac Symposium on Paradigm Shifts" (14.1–3);
- "A 'Dictatorship of Relativism'?: Symposium in Response to Cardinal Ratzinger's Last Homily" (13.2–3);
- "Unsocial Thought, Uncommon Lives" (12.2–13.1);
- "Imperial Trauma: The Powerlessness of the Powerful" (11.2–12.1);
- "Talking Peace with Gods: Symposium on the Conciliation of Worldviews" (10.3, 11.1); and
- "Peace and Mind: Symposium on Dispute, Conflict, and Enmity" (8.1–9.3).

Our single-issue and seriatim discussions have included:

- "Anthropological Philosophy: Symposium on an Unanticipated Conceptual Practice" (22.3);
- "The Warburg Institute: A Special Issue on the Library and Its Readers" (18.1);
- "Between Text and Performance: Symposium on Improvisation and Originalism" (17.2);
- "Comparative Relativism: Symposium on an Impossibility" (17.1);
- "Neo-Stoic Alternatives, c. 1400–2004: Essays on Folly and Detachment" (10.2);
- "The Disregardable 'Second World': Essays on the Inconstancy of the West" (10.1);
- "Outside the Academy: Papers from the Papal Symposia at Castelgandolfo and Vienna, 1983–1996" (7.3);
- "Experimental Scholarship" (5.3);
- "Countertransference and the Humanities" (5.1, 5.3, 6.1, 6.3);
- "Science out of Context: The Misestimate and Misuse of the Natural Sciences" (6.2);
- "A Taste for Complexity: Ten Nondisciples of Stanley Cavell" (5.2);

- "The Individual and the Herd: The Public Secret of Self-Fashioning" (4.3);
- "A Turn away from 'Language'?" (4.2);
- "Community and Fixation: Toward a New Type of Intellectual" (3.3);
- "The Unfinished Project of Humanism" (3.1);
- "Exit from the Balkans—The Commensuration of Alien Languages" (2.3);
- "Platonic Insults" (2.2);
- "Beyond Post-: A Revaluation of the Revaluation of All Values" (1.3); and
- "Ambivalence" (1.1–3, 2.2).

To commemorate the journal's quarter century, this issue consists of pieces from in- and outside those symposia, arranged, to fulfill our obligation to Rorty, in conversational groupings. Readers are invited to shift, from knot to knot, around a common room filled to bursting with lively colleagues, young and old, but also ghosts, whose words mean more and other, now, than when originally written. The dead and quick alike drift from one conversation to another, then some go off, like MacIntyre with Rorty, to walk by some lake in odd couples. The dramatis personae, as I say, are representative but only as far as carnivorous agents have allowed. Hence the absence of writers (Kertész, Carver, Sebald, Bolaño, Nádas, Quignard, Calasso, and Hadot among them) whose work a reader of *Common Knowledge* might expect to find reprinted on this occasion.[4] Still, with ventures of this kind, celebrations are best held on the fly and called for in accordance with their peculiar criteria of attainment. On one occasion, marking no milestone of survival, I prefaced the introduction to a symposium ("on the conciliation of worldviews") by calling for self-congratulation:

The introduction to this symposium consists in its first two contributions: a cosmopolitan proposal by Ulrich Beck for negotiating between worldviews, then a warning from Bruno Latour against presuming we know what a conflict of worldviews entails. I would like to point out, as a preface to that introduction, that whereas versions of this discussion used to center on questions of commensurability—are worldviews comparable, let alone reconcilable?—the discussion here centers on problems of commensuration. How is it to be done and who might accomplish it? From commensurability to commensuration is a long trek, and we should feel self-congratulatory at this juncture. Historic events have turned the Linguistic Turn guild from theory toward—if not practice, then at least talk of practice. The contributors to this first installment of our symposium would have been, let me hazard, Left Kuhnians back when that term meant anything. During the time of dispute over Thomas Kuhn and incommensurability, the Right Kuh-

4. Kertész, "The Last Inn" and "Someone Else"; Carver, "Carnations"; Sebald, "The Rings of Saturn"; Bolaño, "Nazi Literature in the Americas"; Nádas, "Burial"; Quig- nard, "In Front of My Hermitage"; Calasso, "The Repulsive Cult of *Bonheur*"; Hadot, "Isis Has No Veils."

nian position was that commensuration between discrete contexts does not occur. Whereas our contributors imply or state that commensuration is the most difficult of all things not impossible (emphasis on both "most" and "not"). . . . It is vital to our moment of self-congratulation to acknowledge that this symposium involves neither, on the one hand, idealist universalism nor, on the other hand, contextualism of the absolute kind. . . . The question, in other words, is [no longer] whether worldviews are commensurable. The question is whether we should do what it takes—all that it takes—to communicate and reconcile with those we fear. . . . But whoever—let us admit it—takes on the task is going to end up with dirty hands. This job is not one for contextualists in white gloves. . . . There is no clean methodology for reconciling worldviews at odds.[5]

By this time, fifteen years later, our hands are filthy, and our shoes unwearable indoors. We are now closer, as a group, to "revanchist optimism," because Trump, Putin, and other masters of the noble arts of casuistry and sophistry have turned them to the dark side. It has gone unnoticed, perhaps, by most readers (but not, I assure you, by any authors) that this journal, as a policy, avoids the word *fact* and the phrase *in fact*, except where demonstrable facts are involved, since *fact* and *in fact* are devices of rhetoric for bullying readers and listeners. Our authors regularly object to this policy, because composition is made more difficult when "the fact that" is ruled out as a tool for writing easy sentences. Few objected to our hygienic rule, in the old days, on epistemological grounds. These days, however, I hear, even from founding members of the editorial board, that our diffidence about facts feels like capitulation to Trump, who issues "alternative facts" for the credulous on a daily basis. The god-awful state of world affairs presently (things did appear hopeful in our first years of publication) has made the tasks that *Common Knowledge* set for itself a bit less difficult to achieve. Conciliation between parties not malicious seems less impossible to arrange. On the other hand, as I have recently discovered, the world's most powerful institution committed to friendship between former adversaries—I mean the Roman Catholic Church—stands not only against relativism, which one knew (we dedicated a special issue to the problem in 2007),[6] but stands also, even under the present pope, against "eirenism" or irenicism.[7] Let us talk, by all means; let us break bread together, the bishops say to Protestants, Muslims, and Jews with warmth

5. Perl, "Preface to an Introduction," 426–29, excerpts.

6. See "A 'Dictatorship of Relativism'?"

7. See, for example, Pius XII's encyclical *Humani Generis*, which rules that peace must not be an end in itself: "Another danger is perceived which is all the more serious because it is more concealed beneath the mask of virtue. There are many who, deploring disagreement among men and intellectual confusion, through an imprudent zeal for souls, are urged by a great and ardent desire to do away with the barrier that divides good and honest men; these advocate an 'eirenism' according to which, by setting aside the questions which divide men, they aim not only at joining forces to repel the attacks of atheism, but also at reconciling things opposed to one another in the field of dogma" (sec. 11).

and sincerity. But by no means let us worry whether, on questions that divide us, both you and we may be wrong. Let us, in other words, rethink nothing. Thus the white gloves of the episcopate are kept pristine.

Meanwhile, recalling a remark of Rorty's to Gianni Vattimo ("once Christianity is reduced to the claim that love is the only law, the ideal of purity loses its importance"),[8] I have taken as my editorial mantra the following arrhythmic, unrhyming couplet:

The world was never cleaner
than on the day Noah left the ark.

The difference between cleansing and obliteration is not trivial, but perfect purity is, in itself, nonexistence. When told that my buoyancy about Muslim worship in Christian churches was inappropriate—given that, I was informed, both the Muslims and the Christians involved were indifferent—I replied that

exopraxis and xenophilia are only our latest excuses to broach the topic of affects and attitudes that, although widely spurned, tend to have irenic outcomes. Over the past quarter century, in these pages, ambivalence, "antipolitics," quietism, stoicism, sophistry, casuistry, pharisaism, apathy, cosmopolitanism, "gnostic diplomacy," ecumenism, syncretism, "comparative relativism," anarchism, skepticism, perspectivism, constructivism, de-differentiation, "fuzzy logic," *pensiero debole* and *Verwindung*, "unsocial thought," detachment, humility, cowardice, *caritas*, and well-motivated obnubilation have all come in for cordial scrutiny. . . . If we conceive of indifference as in-difference—that is, a state or sensibility in which differences go unnoticed or, if noticed, are not cared about—then it is fair to say that indifference should rank higher than xenophilia in a hierarchy of irenic affects. No one ever has died a martyr for indifference. And I would like to think that, in some cases at least, a believer has come down from the scaffold, alive, in awareness that to die for Islam, Christianity, or Judaism, in its conflict with one of the other two, is to bear witness in blood to no more than a nest of ambiguities. Never mind the social and historical overlaps, links, yokes, and vector-overlays among the three traditions. There is also a theological knot so undisentangleable that Allah, the Christian Trinity, and the God of Israel are indifferentiable scholastically. However much the *feel* of belief in each differs from the *feel* of belief in the others, I cannot imagine an honest (as opposed to a parochial) formulation that could distinguish among them without undermining the bases of all three religions.[9]

On the same topic, in an earlier issue, "I volunteered that I knew a man in New York, a Catholic convert, originally Jewish, who used to read Sufi hymns

8. Rorty and Vattimo, *Future of Religion*, 79.

9. Perl, "Xenophilia, Difference, and Indifference," 234–35.

to himself during mass. He wanted to be Jewish, Christian, and Muslim simultaneously. My students laughed, so I added that the man in question was renowned in the art world for being ahead of his time."[10] The man was Lincoln Kirstein, who brought modernism and George Balanchine to America, cofounded the New York City Ballet, and issued caveats that felt like blessings when I asked him how to make *Common Knowledge* happen.[11] On its silver anniversary, it occurs to me that reading Sufi prayers, in a Catholic church, as an ethnic Jew, was a feat of modernist choreography, one from which we may learn a good deal about what are thought to be opposed beliefs. An essay on resistance to harmony makes the point on which this introduction concludes:

> David and Goliath may appear to be dueling, when observed from the bird's-eye perspective of theory. Viewed from up close, however, it may turn out that they are dancing, shifting positions over rocky ground, as each does what he feels he must to keep the only dance he knows from ending.[12]

References

"A 'Dictatorship of Relativism'?: Symposium in Response to Cardinal Ratzinger's Last Homily." *Common Knowledge* 13, nos. 2–3 (Spring–Fall 2007): 214–455.

Beyer, Judith, and Felix Girke. "Practicing Harmony Ideology: Ethnographic Reflections on Community and Coercion." *Common Knowledge* 21, no. 2 (April 2015): 196–235.

Bolaño, Roberto. "From *Nazi Literature in the Americas*." Translated by Chris Andrews. *Common Knowledge* 14, no. 2 (Spring 2008): 296–306.

Calasso, Roberto. "The Repulsive Cult of *Bonheur*." Translated by Ann Goldstein. *Common Knowledge* 10, no. 2 (Spring 2004): 286–313.

Carver, Raymond. "Carnations: A Play in One Act." *Common Knowledge* 2, no. 3 (Winter 1993): 152–59.

Hadot, Pierre. "Isis Has No Veils." Translated by Michael Chase. *Common Knowledge* 12, no. 3 (Fall 2006): 349–53.

Kertész, Imre. "Someone Else: A Chronicle of the Change." Translated by Tim Wilkinson. *Common Knowledge* 10, no. 2 (Spring 2004): 314–46.

———. "The Last Inn: An Excerpt." Translated by Tim Wilkinson. *Common Knowledge* 21, no. 3 (September 2015): 545–53.

MacIntyre, Alasdair. "Richard Rorty (1931–2007)." *Common Knowledge* 14, no. 2 (Spring 2008): 183–92.

10. Perl, "Introduction: Postscript to Brown," 31.

11. For more on my exchanges with Kirstein, see my review of 1995 (reprinted here) of his memoirs.

12. Beyer and Girke, "Practicing Harmony Ideology," 235.

Nádas, Péter. "Burial: Comedy without Intermission." Translated by Imre Goldstein. *Common Knowledge* 8, no. 1 (Winter 2002): 218–68.

Perl, Jeffrey M. Review of Lincoln Kirstein, *Mosaic: Memoirs*. In *Common Knowledge* 4, no. 2 (Fall 1995): 120. Reprint, *Common Knowledge* 25, nos. 1–3 (April 2019): 438–49.

———. "Preface to an Introduction" [to "Talking Peace with Gods: Symposium on the Conciliation of Worldviews, Part 1"]. *Common Knowledge* 10, no. 3 (Fall 2004): 426–29.

———. "Introduction: Postscript to Brown." *Common Knowledge* 24, no. 1 (January 2018): 26–33.

———. "Xenophilia, Difference, and Indifference: Dialogical Introduction II." *Common Knowledge* 24, no. 2 (April 2018): 234–38.

———, and Alick Isaacs. "Postscript on Method: Editorial Note." *Common Knowledge* 8, no. 1 (Winter 2002): 147–51.

Pius XII. *Humani Generis*, encyclical (1950). Vatican website, w2.vatican.va/content /pius-xii/en/encyclicals/documents/hf_p-xii_enc_12081950_humani-generis.html (accessed June 24, 2018).

Quignard, Pascal. "In Front of My Hermitage." Translated by Ann Jefferson. *Common Knowledge* 21, no. 3 (Fall 2006): 460–502.

Rorty, Richard. "Call for Papers XIV." *Common Knowledge* 1, no. 2 (Fall 1992): 9–10.

———, and Gianni Vattimo. *The Future of Religion*, edited by Santiago Zabala. New York: Columbia University Press, 2005.

Sebald, W. G. "The Rings of Saturn." Translated by Michael Hulse. *Common Knowledge* 6, no. 2 (Fall 1997): 177–86.

Solzhenitsyn, Alexander. "Two Hundred Years Together." Translated by Jamey Gambrell. *Common Knowledge* 9, no. 2 (Spring 2003): 204–27.

CALL FOR PAPERS

Kwame Anthony Appiah, Joseph Frank,
and Stanley N. Katz

I

We would like to see the publication—and if not in *Common Knowledge*, then where?—of a major theoretical article on multicultural studies that addresses the philosophical problems attendant upon crossing hermeneutic frontiers. The philosophical principles of incommensurability and indeterminacy of translation, were, one could argue, developed to protect non-Western cultures from intellectual invasion, arrogation, and distortion. All serious parents in the West, given that the globe is shrinking, want their nineteen-year-olds educated in the society, history, and literature of a globe's-worth of cultures and subcultures. But parents who have read anything published in philosophy since the Forties will also worry that what their sophomores learn about foreign cultures will be of necessity an isogetical distortion.

Once this theoretical piece is published, we suggest that *Common Knowledge* seek out a wide variety of case studies that demonstrate comparatist approaches that, while extending our intercultural understanding, are not theoretically naive. These studies should presuppose, in accordance with the principles of incommensurability and indeterminacy, that the context in which two cul-

Originally published in *Common Knowledge* 1.2 (Fall 1995):
1. © 1995.

Common Knowledge 25:1–3
DOI 10.1215/0961754X-7299030

tures may be understood together will be *constructed* rather than *discovered* by a scholar—though the scholar may find that explorers, lexicographers, traders, and especially navies have begun the construction before the hermeneuticist arrived.

COMMENSURABILITY AND THE ALIEN MIND

W. V. Quine

Variety is the spice of life. Variety in language and culture is the spice of cosmopolitan life. *Vivent les différences*. But let me venture some homely reflections on the nature and limits of such differences.

I begin, as is my wont, with the field linguist who is investigating a remote tribe and eliciting and codifying their strange language. He ends up with a manual of translation. What qualifies it as successful? That it determines an English equivalent for every native sentence? An empty answer; what counts as equivalent is the whole question. The real test of a manual of translation is simply successful communication, and the test of successful communication is smoothness of dialogue and success in negotiation.

I hold that two manuals of translation could be wholly successful and yet give conflicting translations. This is not merely to say that they could give different translations; phrasing and choices of words can vary without conflicting. The conflict that I picture is rather as follows. Each manual translates a given dialogue coherently, but the two manuals produce incoherence when used alternately sentence by sentence.

This would not happen as long as the sentences were mere reports of observable events, but it is always possible when what is translated is appreciably theory-laden.

Originally published in *Common Knowledge* 1.3 (Winter 1992): 1–2. © 1992.

Common Knowledge 25:1–3
DOI 10.1215/0961754X-7299042

This thesis of indeterminacy of translation is by no means a theory of untranslatability. There are good translations and bad, and the two conflicting manuals imagined are both good. However, there are also plenty of cases of untranslatable sentences, and they are commonplace even within our own language. A sentence about neutrinos admits of no translation into the English of 1900. Terms for newly postulated particles are adequately explained, but usually not to the point of providing a phrase that can simply supplant the word, nor even of providing paraphrases that can supplant the contexts of the word. Even if such full definition were devised, it would have to contain other theoretical words whose reduction to prior language would present the same problem.

We see from this example that failure of translatability is humdrum, and that it is not necessarily an obstacle to explanation and successful communication. On the other hand, there are doubtless plenty of cases, between radically different cultures, where failures of translation spell incomprehension in varying degrees.

A notion that has had some currency among philosophers of science is incommensurability of physical theories old and new. *Mass* for Newton and for Einstein had quite different meanings, they tell us, each intelligible only within the total physical theory in which it figures. The sticking point here is the weasel word *meaning*, a word that I avoided earlier when I appealed rather to success in dialogue and negotiation.

Surely two theories cannot be utterly incommensurable and still qualify as science. The distinctive feature of science, after all, is its responsiveness to checkpoints in predicted observation; and the sentences that directly report observation are the very sentences that are most clearly amenable to determinate translation if the language is translatable at all. At worst, then, scientific theories are commensurable through their checkpoints.

POTENTIALLY EVERY CULTURE IS ALL CULTURES

Paul Feyerabend

In Book 9 of the *Iliad*, Aias, Odysseus, and Phoenix, acting as messengers, ask Achilles to return to the Achaeans and to aid them in their battle against Troy. Achilles, offended by Agamemnon, had withdrawn and the situation of the Greeks had deteriorated. Now Agamemnon offers an enormous present and the hand of his daughter in marriage (114ff.). For the messengers, this is suitable compensation and they urge Achilles to relent. Achilles whines and splutters—and refuses. In a long speech, he tries to explain the reasons for his attitude. "Equal fate," he says, "befalls the negligent and the valiant fighter; equal honor goes to the worthless and the virtuous." Striving after honor no longer makes any sense.

The messengers fall "silent, dismayed at his word, for he had resisted in a stunning way" (430f.)—but they soon start arguing again. Phoenix points out that the gods whose powers far exceed those of humans can be reconciled by gifts and sacrifice (497ff.); Aias adds that even the murder of a brother or of a son has its blood price (632f.). This is how conflicts were resolved in the past and this is how Achilles should act now. Aias ascribes Achilles' resistance to cruelty (632). Achilles remains adamant.

Returning to the camp, Odysseus reports what has happened. Again the Greeks fall "silent, for he had spoken in a stunning way" (693f.). They explain

Originally published in *Common Knowledge* 3.2 (Fall 1994):
16–22. © 1994.

Common Knowledge 25:1–3
DOI 10.1215/0961754X-7299054

Achilles' attitude by his anger (679) and his pride (700). Then Diomedes suggests they forget about Achilles and start fighting without him (697ff.).

What we have here is a conflict of attitudes—contrariness and persistent anger on one side, surprise and a plea to be reasonable on the other. The parties try to justify their attitudes. The messengers seem close to common sense. Achilles sounds a little strange.

The episode is problematic, in a familiar and annoying but manageable way. The episode becomes profound and paradoxical when lifted out of its natural habitat and inserted into a model or theory. One theory that has become rather popular assumes that languages, cultures, stages in the development of a profession, a tribe, or a nation are closed, in the sense that certain events transcend their capacities. Languages, for example, are restrained by rules. Persons who violate the rules do not enter new territory; they leave the domain of meaningful discourse. Even facts in these circumstances dissolve, because they are shaped by the language and subjected to its limitations. Looking at the exchange in *Iliad* 9 with such ideas in mind, some scholars have turned it into a rather sinister affair. Thus Adam Parry writes: Achilles

> is the one Homeric hero who does not accept the common language. . . .
> {He} has no language with which to express his disillusionment. Yet he
> expresses it, and in a remarkable way. He does it by misusing the lan-
> guage he disposes of. He asks questions that cannot be answered and
> makes demands that cannot be met. . . . {He} can in no sense includ-
> ing that of language (unlike, say, Hamlet) leave the society which has
> become alien to him.[1]

Parry does not summarize the episode, he interprets it. And he does not interpret it in accordance with the poet's scenario, but provides a framework of his own. The framework is not arbitrary—it is based on an empirical study of the Homeric text—and that text has indeed certain regularities. However, the evidence for these regularities does not imply or suggest that they are never violated, or that they are necessary, or that they constitute meaning so that whoever violated them would be talking nonsense. Such an assumption not only goes beyond the text, it is inherently implausible. First, because texts, mathematical texts included, lack the required uniformity. (Parry, for example, has been criticized for his streamlining of Homer.)[2] Second, because ingenious individuals often give sensible answers to allegedly inexpressible questions. There are of course misunderstandings. Even ordinary events baffle some people, enrage others, and render still others speechless. But we also find people who can explain events

---

1. "The Language of Achilles," *Transactions and Proceedings of the American Philosophical Association* 87 (1956): 6f.

2. See Hugh Lloyd-Jones, "Becoming Homer," *The New York Review of Books*, 5 March 1992, 52ff.

Achilles says that honor and the rewards of honor are different things. According to Parry, such a separation does not make sense. Honor and the rewards of honor cannot be separated, not even "in principle."

Now it is indeed true that "the Homeric notion of honor," to use a phrase that often occurs in this connection, is a social and not a metaphysical notion. Honor is an aggregate of individual and collective actions and events. Some of the elements of the aggregate are: the role (of the individual possessing or lacking honor) in battle, in the assembly, during internal dissension; his place at public ceremonies; the spoils and gifts he receives when the battle is finished; and, naturally, his behavior on all these occasions. Honor is present when (most of) the elements of the aggregate are present, absent otherwise (*Il.* 12, 310ff.—Sarpedon's speech). An explanation of honor, accordingly, would use a list, not comprehensive concepts.[4] We may infer that a way of speaking that conflicts with these features will cause surprise, but we cannot assume that surprising speech is without meaning.

A brief look at the rest of the epic shows indeed that Achilles' remarks do not come out of the blue. They arise from a situation—the conflict between custom and Agamemnon's actions—that lies squarely within the common sense of the time. Sensitized by his anger, Achilles remembers that merit was disregarded not only in his case but in other cases as well, and he generalizes: Honor is an orphan (318f.). The starting point of this generalization (the description of Agamemnon's actions) conforms to the archaic notion of honor; so do the cases Achilles remembers. The traditional concept allowed for discrepancies and identified them by using a standard. The full generalization—honor and its rewards *always* diverge—severs the connection between the standard and the events that gave it substance, at least in the opinion of some scholars.

3. For examples, see Caro Ginzburg, *The Cheese and the Worms: The Cosmos of a Sixteenth-Century Miller*, trans. John and Anne Tedeschi (New York: Penguin Books, 1982; first published in Italian, *Il formaggio e i vermi: il cosmo di un mugnaio del '500* [Torino: G. Einaudi, 1976]), and Emmanuel Le Roy Ladurie, *Montaillou: The Promised Land of Error*, trans. Barbara Bray (New York: Vintage Books, 1979; first published in French, *Montaillou, village Occitan de 1294 à 1324* [Paris: Gallimard, 1975]). Already in 1552, Copernicanism was part of Florentine gossip, which found ways of diffusing arguments against it (details in Leonardo Olschki, *Gesshichte der neusprachlichen wissen-schaftlichen Literatur*, vol. 2, Vaduz: Krauz Reprint, 1965 [first published in 1992], 134ff.). Some aspects of Florentine public life during the quattrocento implied rather unusual views about personal identity. An example is Brunelleschi's joke on Manetto di Jacopo Ammanarini (analyzed by Decio Gioseffi in "Realtà e conoscenza nel Brunelleschi," *La Critica del Arte* 85 [March 1965]: 8ff.). People who accept the Resurrection, the Virgin Birth of Christ, who believe in the miracle stories of the *Legenda Aurta*, and who take the Bible literally, as did many outstanding British scientists of the nineteenth century, the young Darwin included, are not likely to be stopped by "linguistic boundaries."

4. Lists are not restricted to Homer. They occur in Babylonian science, in early Greek science, in commonsense thinking, and even in Plato: the first answers Socrates receives to his what-is questions are lists, not definitions.

Achilles goes further. He implies that the general injustice he notices lies in the nature of things. Using modern terms, we can formulate this implication by saying that the traditional standards are no longer parts of social practice. Yet they continue to play a role. This is the first indication of a dichotomy that was soon to assume considerable importance—the dichotomy between (rich, concrete, but misleading) appearances and a (simple, abstract, almost empty, but still very important) reality. And this is also the reason why some scholars say that Achilles' speech does not make sense: a general rift between appearance and reality does not fit into "the Homeric world view."

But Homeric thought was not unprepared for grand subdivisions. Divine knowledge and human knowledge, divine power and human power, human intention and human speech (an example mentioned by Achilles himself: 312f.) were opposed to each other in ways that resemble the distinction Achilles is using. One might say that having cut the social links of honor, Achilles strengthens the ties of honor to divine judgment, especially to the judgment of Zeus (607f.). Such ties already existed; the judgment of the gods always played an important social role. Even the exclusive relevance of divine judgment hinted at by Achilles was prepared by the eminence of the gods and the steadily increasing power of one particular divinity—Zeus—in whom "all lines converge."[5] Considered in retrospect, it seems that the situation described by Achilles was there all along, though buried in a complex net that tied divine actions to human actions and human actions to each other. Achilles identifies the situation, lifts it out of its surroundings, and simplifies it by trimming some social connections. Even this last action is not arbitrary, or "creative," for Achilles has "inductive evidence" for the weakness and, perhaps, irrelevance of the connections that he trims. Nor is he left without standards, for the judgment of the gods remains, both for him and his visitors. What we have, then, in Book 9, is a change of emphasis supported by reasons and driven by Achilles' anger. We are a long way from the disaster announced by Parry and systematized by the champions of incommensurability.

Still, we may ask if the change of focus corresponded to and was perhaps supported by some more general tendency. Had Achilles or the poet who composed his lines lived in the seventh or sixth centuries B.C., I could have answered: There was a relevant tendency, closely connected with social developments. By that period, abstract groups had replaced neighborhoods (and the concrete relationships they embodied) as the units of political action (Cleisthenes); money had replaced barter with its attention to context and detail; the relations between military leaders and their soldiers had become increasingly impersonal; local gods had merged in the course of travel, which increased their power but reduced their humanity; tribal and cultural idiosyncracies had been evened out by trade, politics, and other types of international exchange; important parts of life had become bland and colorless, and terms tied to specifics accordingly had lost in content, or in importance, or had simply disappeared.[6] I could have added that individual human actions (such as the actions of Solon, of Cleisthenes, of their associates) played a large role in the process, but not with these later results as their aim. Seen "from the outside," we have an adaptation of one "conspiracy"[7] ("Homeric Common Sense") to others (the newly emerging structures I have just described). Seen "from the inside," we have a discovery: important features of the world are being revealed.

But Achilles did not live in the seventh or sixth centuries. He spoke at a time when the developments I enumerated were in their infancy. They had started; they had not yet produced their more obvious results. Achilles' speech contributed to the development and thus contains an element of invention. The invented features were part of a slowly rising structure, which means that Achilles also made a discovery. Subjectivity certainly played a role; it was Achilles' anger that made him resonate to what others did not yet notice. What he saw in a sense was already there—the judgment of the gods was always more decisive than that of mortals—which means that Achilles' vision had an "objective core." But it is still "subjective," for the move towards increasing abstractness, and the related separation of reality and appearance, were not the only developments.

As becomes clear from funeral inscriptions, passages of comedy, sophistic debates, medical and historical treatises, from the unwanted lists Socrates received to his what-is questions, and from Aristotle's recommendation of precisely such lists (cf. *Pol.* 1260b24ff.), the view that things, ideas, actions, processes are aggregates of (relatively independent) parts and that giving an account means enumerating instances, not subsuming them under a single term, retained its popularity right into the classical age of Greece. Geometric thought was a seed without a well-defined genetic program; accompanied by an ever-increasing cacophony of political, philosophical, military, artistic debates, it grew into many different plants. Nowhere in this process do we find the breaks, the lacunae, the unbridgeable chasms suggested by the idea of closed domains of discourse.

Now if we drop the artifice of closed domains, as simple common sense advises, then we must also drop the artifice of precise meanings—words, state-

---

6. For the contraction of the rich spectra of perceptual terms, see chap. 1 of Bruno Snell, *Die Entdeckung des Geistes: Studien z. Entstehung d. europ. Denkens bei d. Griechen* (Göttingen: Vandenhoeck und Ruprecht, 1975).

7. "[A]ny language . . . is a conspiracy against experience in the sense of being a collective attempt to simplify and arrange experience into manageable parcels." Michael Baxandall, *Giotto and the Orators: Humanist Observers of Painting in Italy and the Discovery of Pictorial Composition, 1350–1450* (Oxford: Clarendon Press, 1971), 44.

ments, even principles are ambiguous and change with the situations in which they are being used. Interactions among cultures, linguistic domains, professional groups are going on all the time, and it is therefore absurd to speak either of objectivity or of relative sense within well-defined boundaries. Both objectivism (and the associated idea of truth) and relativism assume limits that are not found in practice and postulate nonsense wherever people are engaged in interesting though occasionally difficult forms of collaboration. Objectivism and relativism are chimeras.

A discourse consisting of clear and distinct propositions (actions, plans, and so forth) has a very short breath—and I agree that such a discourse will often be interrupted by "irrational" events and soon replaced by a new and "incommensurable" discourse. If the history of science or the wider history of cultural interactions depended on a discourse of this kind, then they would consist of an ocean of irrationality punctured by tiny islands of sense. If, on the other hand, the elements of an argument, a worldview, a culture, a theoretical framework (such as classical mathematics) are allowed some leeway, so that they either keep their identity through very drastic changes (in which case one could say that they have potential meanings that are actualized in various ways) or change their content without violating the worldview to which they belong, then we have no reason to assume that our ways of conveying meaning have any limits. On the contrary, we can now search for features that connect the "inside" of a language, or a theory, or a culture, with its "outside," and thus reduce conceptually induced blindness to the real causes of incomprehension, which are ordinary, normal, run-of-the-mill inertia, dogmatism, inattention, and stupidity. Differences between languages, art forms, customs are not being denied. But I would ascribe them to accidents of location and/or history, not to clear, unambiguous, and immobile cultural essences: *potentially every culture is all cultures.*

The argument I have presented in this rather abstract way is developed with passion, wit, and many examples in Renato Rosaldo's *Culture and Truth*, whose second edition has just appeared.[8] Rosaldo is describing classical objectivist anthropology, which not only postulates closed systems but also tries to clean them up: "Most anthropological studies of death eliminate emotions by assuming the position of the most detached observer." Aiming at the discovery of strict rules that guide behavior like a juggernaut, objectivist studies "make it difficult to show how social forms can be both imposed *and* used spontaneously." They fail to recognize "how much of life happens in ways that one neither plans or expects." Boundary problems, not central events, teach us about the full resources of a culture. At the boundaries, writes Gloria Andaluza, a Chicana lesbian whom Rosaldo quotes, a person

8. (Boston: Beacon Press, 1993).

copes by developing a tolerance for contradictions, a tolerance for ambiguity. She learns to be Indian in Mexican culture, to be Mexican from an Anglo point of view. She learns to juggle cultures. She has a plural personality, she operates in a pluralistic mode—nothing is thrust out, the good, the bad and the ugly, nothing rejected, nothing abandoned. Not only does she sustain contradictions, she turns the ambivalence into something else. (216)

Is it not clear that (Rosaldo speaking) "in the present postcolonial world, the notion of an authentic culture as an autonomous internally coherent universe no longer seems tenable, except perhaps as a 'useful fiction' or a revealing distortion?" (217).

The situation is no different in the sciences. Despite a persistent fog of objectivism and despite the relativistic tricks inspired by Kuhn's idea of a paradigm, many scientists have lived and are still living with ambiguity and contradiction. They could not possibly live in any other way. New problems need new approaches. But new approaches do not fall like manna from the heaven of creativity. Old ideas continue to be used, they are slowly twisted around until some orderly minds perceive an entirely new structure, with new limits of sense, and start doing what they do best—they nail it down. This, incidentally, is the reason why the presentation of scientific *results* differs so drastically from what happens during *research*, i.e., while people are still *thinking*, and gives such a misleading picture of it. Of course, ideas can get stuck; imagination can be dimmed by dogma, financial pressures, education, and boredom. If that happens, then the idea of a closed system with precise concepts and rules slavishly followed will appear to be the only correct representation of Thought. But that situation should be avoided, not praised.

To my mind, the most important consequence of the new attitude towards cultures that underlies Rosaldo's book is that practices that seem legitimate when referred to a closed framework cease to be sacrosanct. If every culture is potentially all cultures, then cultural differences lose their ineffability and become *special and changeable manifestations of a common human nature*. Authentic murder, torture, and suppression become ordinary murder, torture, and suppression, *and should be treated as such*. Feminism has tasks not only in the United States, but even more so in Africa, India, and South America. Efforts to achieve peace need no longer respect some alleged cultural integrity that often is nothing but the rule of one or another tyrant. And there is much reason to suspect some of the ingredients of the ideology of political correctness.

But, in making use of this new freedom of action, we must be careful not to continue old habits. Objective judgments are out; so is an abstract and ideology-driven protection of cultures. Drastic interventions are not excluded but should be made *only after* an extended contact, not just with a few "leaders," but with the populations directly involved. Having discarded objectivity and cultural separation and having emphasized intercultural processes, those who perceive medical, nutritional, environmental problems or problems of human or, more specifically, female rights have to start such processes on the spot *and with due attention to the opinions of the locals.* There exist movements that already proceed in this particularizing, nonobjective manner. Liberation theology and some approaches in the area of development are examples. Let us support these movements and learn from them instead of continuing old-style epistemologies and other "authentic" games.

EXCHANGING PERSPECTIVES

The Transformation of Objects into Subjects in Amerindian Ontologies

Eduardo Viveiros de Castro

My subject is the cosmological setting of an indigenous Amazonian model of the self.[1] I will examine two major contexts, shamanism and warfare, in which "self" and "other" develop especially complex relations. Shamanism deals with the relation between humans and nonhumans; and in warfare, a human other, an "enemy," is used to bring a "self" into existence. I will deliberately use a set of traditional dichotomies (I mean, in the tradition of modernity) as both heuristic instruments and foils: nature/culture, subject/object, production/exchange, and so forth. This very crude technique for setting off the distinctive features of Amazonian cosmologies carries the obvious risk of distortion, since it is unlikely that any nonmodern cosmology can be adequately described either by means of such conceptual polarities or as a simple negation of them (as if the only point of a nonmodern cosmology were to stand in opposition to our oppositions). But the technique does have the advantage of showing how unstable and problematic those polarities can be made to appear, once they have been forced to bear "unnatural" interpretations and unexpected rearrangements.

Originally published in *Common Knowledge* 10.3 (Fall 2004): 463–84, as part of "Talking Peace with Gods: Symposium on the Conciliation of World Views, Part 1." © 2004 by Duke University Press.

Common Knowledge 25:1–3
DOI 10.1215/0961754X-7299066

Perspectival Multinaturalism

If there is one virtually universal Amerindian notion, it is that of an original state of nondifferentiation between humans and animals, as described in mythology. Myths are filled with beings whose form, name, and behavior inextricably mix human and animal attributes in a common context of intercommunicability, identical to that which defines the present-day intrahuman world. Amerindian myths speak of a state of being where self and other interpenetrate, submerged in the same immanent, presubjective, and preobjective milieu, the end of which is precisely what the mythology sets out to tell. This end is, of course, the well-known separation of "culture" and "nature"—of human and nonhuman—that Claude Lévi-Strauss has shown to be the central theme of Amerindian mythology and which he deems to be a cultural universal.[2]

In some respects, the Amerindian separation between humans and animals may be seen as an analogue of our "nature/culture" distinction; there is, however, at least one crucial difference between the Amerindian and modern, popular Western versions. In the former case, the separation was not brought about by a process of differentiating the human from the animal, as in our own evolutionist "scientific" mythology. For Amazonian peoples, *the original common condition of both humans and animals is not animality but, rather, humanity.* The great separation reveals not so much culture distinguishing itself from nature as nature distancing itself from culture: the myths tell how animals lost the qualities inherited or retained by humans. Humans are those who continue as they have always been. *Animals are ex-humans (rather than humans, ex-animals).* In some cases, humankind is the substance of the primordial plenum or the original form of virtually everything, not just animals. As Gerald Weiss puts it:

Campa mythology is largely the story of how, one by one, the primal Campa became irreversibly transformed into the first representatives of various species of animals and plants, as well as astronomical bodies or features of the terrain. . . . The development of the universe, then, has been primarily a process of diversification, with mankind as the primal substance out of which many if not all of the categories of beings and

1. Hypotheses that I made ("Cosmological Deixis and Amerindian Perspectivism," *Journal of the Royal Anthropological Institute*, n.s., 4.3 [1998]: 469–88) are rehearsed here since they ground the argument of this article. I gave an early version of the present article, in English, at the Chicago meeting of the American Anthropological Association in November 1999, and that version was subsequently published in Italian as "La transformazione degli ogetti in sogetti nelle ontologie amerindiane," *Etnosistemi* 7.7

(2000): 47–58. The title of that paper (a version of which is the subtitle of this essay) pays homage to Nancy Munn, "The Transformation of Subjects into Objects in Walbiri and Pitjantjara Myth," in *Australian Aboriginal Anthropology*, ed. Ronald M. Berndt (Nedlands: University of Western Australia Press, 1970).

2. Claude Lévi-Strauss, *Mythologiques*, 4 vols. (Paris: Plon, 1964–71).

things in the universe arose, the Campa of today being the descendants
of those ancestral Campa who escaped being transformed.[3]

The fact that many "natural" species or entities were originally human
has important consequences for the present-day state of the world. While our
folk anthropology holds that humans have an original animal nature that must
be coped with by culture—having been wholly animals, we remain animals "at
bottom"—Amerindian thought holds that, having been human, animals must
still be human, albeit in an unapparent way. Thus, many animal species, as well
as sundry other types of nonhuman beings, are supposed to have a spiritual
component that qualifies them as "people." Such a notion is often associated
with the idea that the manifest bodily form of each species is an envelope (a
"clothing") that conceals an internal humanoid form, usually visible to the eyes
of only the particular species and of "transspecific" beings such as shamans.
This internal form is the soul or spirit of the animal: an intentionality or subjectivity formally identical to human consciousness. If we conceive of humans
as somehow composed of a cultural clothing that hides and controls an essentially animal nature, Amazonians have it the other way around: animals have
a human, sociocultural inner aspect that is "disguised" by an ostensibly bestial
bodily form.

Another important consequence of having animals and other types of
nonhumans conceived as people—as kinds of humans—is that the relations
between the human species and most of what we would call "nature" take on the
quality of what we would term "social relations." Thus, categories of relationship and modes of interaction prevailing in the intrahuman world are also in
force in most contexts in which humans and nonhumans confront each other.
Cultivated plants may be conceived as blood relatives of the women who tend
them, game animals may be approached by hunters as affines, shamans may
relate to animal and plant spirits as associates or enemies.

Having been people, animals and other species continue to be people
behind their everyday appearance. This idea is part of an indigenous theory
according to which the different sorts of persons—human and nonhuman (animals, spirits, the dead, denizens of other cosmic layers, plants, occasionally even
objects and artifacts)—apprehend reality from distinct points of view. The way
that humans perceive animals and other subjectivities that inhabit the world
differs profoundly from the way in which these beings see humans (and see
themselves). Under normal conditions, humans see humans as humans; they see

3. Gerald Weiss, "Campa Cosmology," *Ethnology* 11.2
(April 1972): 169–70.

animals as animals, plants as plants. As for spirits, to see these usually invisible beings is a sure sign that conditions are not normal. On the other hand, animals (predators) and spirits see humans as animals (as game or prey) to the same extent that game animals see humans as spirits or as predator animals. By the same token, animals and spirits see themselves as humans: they perceive themselves as (or they become) anthropomorphic beings when they are in their own houses or villages; and, most important, they experience their own habits and characteristics in the form of culture. Animals see their food as human food (jaguars see blood as manioc beer, vultures see the maggots in rotting meat as grilled fish); they see their bodily attributes (fur, feathers, claws, beaks) as body decorations or cultural instruments; they see their social system as organized in the same way as human institutions are (with chiefs, shamans, ceremonies, exogamous moieties, and whatnot).

The contrast with our conceptions in the modern West is, again, only too clear. Such divergence invites us to imagine an ontology I have called "multinaturalist" so as to set it off from modern "multiculturalist" ontologies.[4] Where the latter are founded on the mutually implied unity of nature and multiplicity of cultures—the former guaranteed by the objective universality of body and substance, the latter generated by the subjective particularity of spirit and meaning—the Amerindian conception presumes a spiritual unity and a corporeal diversity. For them, culture or the subject is the form of the universal, while nature or the object is the form of the particular.

To say that humanity is the original common condition of humans and nonhumans alike is tantamount to saying that the soul or spirit—the subjective aspect of being—is the universal, unconditioned given (since the souls of all nonhumans are humanlike), while objective bodily nature takes on an a posteriori, particular, and conditioned quality. In this connection, it is also worth noticing that the notion of matter as a universal substrate seems wholly absent from Amazonian ontologies.[5] Reflexive selfhood, not material objectivity, is the potential common ground of being.

To say, then, that animals and spirits are people is to say that they are persons; and to personify them is to attribute to nonhumans the capacities of conscious intentionality and social agency that define the position of the subject.[6] Such capacities are reified in the soul or spirit with which these nonhumans are

4. See Eduardo Viveiros de Castro, "Cosmological Deixis." For a generalization of the notion of "multinaturalism," see Bruno Latour, *Politiques de la nature* (Paris: La Dècouverte, 1999), and, of course, his contribution to this symposium.

5. But see Anne Osborn, "Comer y ser comido: Los animales en la tradicion oral U'wa (tunebo)," *Boletin del Museo del Oro* 26 (1990): 13–41.

6. Animals and other nonhumans are subjects not because they are human (humans in disguise); rather, they are human because they are subjects (potential subjects).

endowed. Whatever possesses a soul is capable of having a point of view, and every being to whom a point of view is attributed is a subject; or better, wherever there is a point of view, there is a "subject position." Our constructionist epistemology can be summed up in the Saussurean (and very Kantian) formula, "the point of view creates the object."[7] The subject, in other words, is the original, fixed condition whence the point of view emanates (the subject creates the point of view). Whereas Amerindian perspectival ontology proceeds as though *the point of view creates the subject*: whatever is activated or "agented" by the point of view will be a subject.

The attribution of humanlike consciousness and intentionality (to say nothing of human bodily form and cultural habits) to nonhuman beings has been indiscriminately termed "anthropocentrism" or "anthropomorphism." However, these two labels can be taken to denote radically opposed cosmological perspectives. Western popular evolutionism, for instance, is thoroughly anthropocentric but not particularly anthropomorphic. On the other hand, animism may be characterized as anthropomorphic but definitely not as anthropocentric: if sundry other beings besides humans are "human," then we humans are not a special lot (so much for "primitive narcissism").

Karl Marx wrote of man, meaning *Homo sapiens*:

In creating an objective world by his practical activity, in working-up inorganic nature, man proves himself a conscious species being. . . . Admittedly animals also produce. . . . But an animal only produces what it immediately needs for itself or its young. It produces one-sidedly, while man produces universally. . . . An animal produces only itself, whilst man reproduces the whole of nature. . . . An animal forms things in accordance with the standard and the need of the species to which it belongs, whilst man knows how to produce in accordance to the standards of other species.[8]

Talk about primitive narcissism. . . . Whatever Marx meant by the proposition that man "produces universally," I fancy he was saying something to the effect that man is the universal animal: an intriguing idea. (If man is the universal animal, then perhaps each animal species would be a particular kind of humanity?) While apparently converging with the Amerindian notion that humanity is the universal form of the subject, Marx's is in fact an absolute inversion of the notion. Marx is saying that humans can be any animal (we have more "being" than any other species), while Amerindians say that any animal can be human (there is more "being" to an animal than meets the eye). Man is the universal animal in

---

7. Ferdinand de Saussure, *Cours de linguistique générale* (1916; Paris: Payot, 1981), 23.

8. Karl Marx, *Economic and Philosophic Manuscripts of 1844* (Moscow: Foreign Languages Publishing House, 1961), 75–76.

two entirely different senses, then: the universality is anthropocentric for Marx; anthropomorphic, for Amerindians.

The Subjectification of Objects

Much of the Amerindians' practical engagement with the world presupposes that present-day nonhuman beings have a spiritual, invisible, prosopomorphic side. That supposition is foregrounded in the context of shamanism. By shamanism, I mean the capacity evinced by some individuals to cross ontological boundaries deliberately and adopt the perspective of nonhuman subjectivities in order to administer the relations between humans and nonhumans. Being able to see nonhumans as they see themselves (they see themselves as humans), shamans are able to take on the role of active interlocutors in transspecific dialogues and are capable (unlike lay persons) of returning to tell the tale. If a human who is not a shaman happens to see a nonhuman (an animal, a dead human soul, a spirit) in human form, he or she runs the risk of being overpowered by the nonhuman subjectivity, of passing over to its side and being transformed into an animal, a dead human, a spirit. A meeting or exchange of perspectives is, in brief, a dangerous business.

Shamanism is a form of acting that presupposes a mode of knowing, a particular ideal of knowledge. That ideal is, in many respects, the exact opposite of the objectivist folk epistemology of our tradition. In the latter, the category of the object supplies the telos: to know is to objectify—that is, to be able to distinguish what is inherent to the object from what belongs to the knowing subject and has been unduly (or inevitably) projected into the object. To know, then, is to *desubjectify*, to make explicit the subject's partial presence in the object so as to reduce it to an ideal minimum. In objectivist epistemology, subjects as much as objects are seen as the result of a process of objectification. The subject constitutes/recognizes itself in the objects it produces, and the subject knows itself objectively when it comes to see itself from the outside as an "it." Objectification is the name of our game; what is not objectified remains unreal and abstract. The form of the other is *the thing*.

Amerindian shamanism is guided by the opposite ideal. To know is to personify, to take on the point of view of that which must be known. Shamanic knowledge aims at something that is a someone—another subject. The form of the other is *the person*. What I am defining here is what anthropologists of yore used to call animism, an attitude that is far more than an idle metaphysical tenet, for the attribution of souls to animals and other so-called natural beings entails a specific way of dealing with them. Being conscious subjects able to communicate with humans, these natural beings are able fully to reciprocate the intentional stance that humans adopt with respect to them.

Recently, there has been a new surge of interest in animism.[9] Cognitive anthropologists and psychologists have been arguing that animism is an "innate" cognitive attitude that has been naturally selected for its attention-grabbing potential and its practical predictive value.[10] I have no quarrel with these hypotheses. Whatever the grounds of its naturalness, however, animism can also be very much cultural—that is, animism can be put to systematic and deliberate use. We must observe that Amerindians do not spontaneously see animals and other nonhumans as persons; the personhood or subjectivity of the latter is considered a nonevident aspect of them. It is necessary *to know how* to personify nonhumans, and it is necessary to personify them in *order to know*.[11]

Personification or subjectification implies that the "intentional stance" adopted with respect to the world has been in some way universalized. Instead of reducing intentionality to obtain a perfectly objective picture of the world, animism makes the inverse epistemological bet. True (shamanic) knowledge aims to reveal a maximum of intentionality or abduct a maximum of agency (here I am using Alfred Gell's vocabulary).[12] A good interpretation, then, would be one able to understand every *event* as in truth an *action*, an expression of intentional states or predicates of some subject. Interpretive success is directly proportional to the ordinal magnitude of intentionality that the knower is able to attribute to the known.[13] A thing or a state of affairs that is not amenable to subjectification—to determination of its social relation to the knower—is shamanistically uninteresting. Our objectivist epistemology follows the opposite course: it considers our commonsense intentional stance as just a shorthand

9. See especially Philippe Descola, "Constructing Natures: Symbolic Ecology and Social Practice," in *Nature and Society: Anthropological Perspectives*, ed. Descola and Gísli Pálsson (London: Routledge, 1996), 82–102; and Nurit Bird-David, "'Animism' Revisited: Personhood, Environment, and Relational Epistemology," *Current Anthropology* 40, supp. (February 1999): 67–91.

10. See Pascal Boyer, "What Makes Anthropomorphism Natural: Intuitive Ontology and Cultural Representations," *Journal of the Royal Anthropological Institute*, n.s., 2.1 (March 1996): 83–97; and Stewart Guthrie, *Faces in the Clouds: A New Theory of Religion* (New York: Oxford University Press, 1993).

11. "The same convention requires that the objects of interpretation—human or not—become understood as other persons; indeed, the very act of interpretation presupposes the personhood of what is being interpreted. . . . What one thus encounters in making interpretations are always counter-interpretations." Marilyn Strathern, *Property, Substance, and Effect: Anthropological Essays on Persons and Things* (London: Athlone, 1999), 239.

12. Alfred Gell, *Art and Agency: An Anthropological Theory* (Oxford: Clarendon, 1998).

13. I am referring here to Daniel Dennett's idea of *n*-order intentional systems: a second-order intentional system is one to which the observer must ascribe not only beliefs, desires, and other intentions, but beliefs (etc.) *about* other beliefs (etc.). The standard cognitive thesis holds that only humans exhibit second- or higher-order intentionality. My shamanistic "principle of abduction of a maximum of agency" runs afoul of the creed of physicalist psychology: "Psychologists have often appealed to a principle known as Lloyd Morgan's Canon of Parsimony, which can be viewed as a special case of Occam's Razor: it is the principle that one should attribute to an organism as little intelligence or consciousness or rationality or mind as will suffice to account for its behaviour." Daniel Dennett, *Brainstorms: Philosophical Essays on Mind and Psychology* (Harmondsworth, U.K.: Penguin, 1978), 274.

that we use when the behavior of a target-object is too complicated to be broken down into elementary physical processes. An exhaustive scientific interpretation of the world would for us be able ideally to reduce every action to a chain of causal events and to reduce these events to materially dense interactions (with no "action at a distance").[14]

If in the naturalist view a subject is an insufficiently analyzed object, in the Amerindian animist cosmology the converse holds: *an object is an incompletely interpreted subject.* The object must either be "expanded" to a full-fledged subject—a spirit; an animal in its human, reflexive form—or else understood as related to a subject (as existing, in Gell's terms, "in the neighbourhood" of an agent). But an important qualification must now be made: Amerindian cosmologies do not as a rule attribute personhood (or the same degree of personhood) to each type of entity in the world. In the case of animals, for instance, the emphasis seems to be on those species that perform key symbolic and practical roles, such as the great predators and the principal species of prey for humans. Personhood and "perspectivity"—the capacity to occupy a point of view—is a question of degree and context rather than an absolute, diacritical property of particular species.

Still, despite this qualification, what cannot be conceived as a primary agent or subject in its own right must be traced up to one:

"Social agents" can be drawn from categories which are as different as chalk and cheese . . . because "social agency" is not defined in terms of "basic" biological attributes (such as inanimate thing vs. incarnate person) but is relational—it does not matter, in ascribing "social agent" status, what a thing (or a person) "is" in itself; what matters is where it stands in a network of social relations. All that may be necessary for stocks and stones to become "social agents" . . . is that there should be actual human persons/agents "in the neighbourhood" of these inert objects.[15]

Though there are Amazonian cosmologies that deny to postmythical nonhuman species any spiritual dimension, the notion (widespread, as is well known, throughout the continent) of animal or plant "spirit masters" supplies the missing agency. These spirit masters, equipped with an intentionality fully equivalent to that of humans, function as hypostases of the species with which they are associated, thereby creating an intersubjective field for human/nonhuman relations even where empirical nonhuman species are not spiritualized. Moreover,

14. Cf. Lévi-Strauss, *La pensée sauvage* (Paris: Plon, 1962), 355: "La pensée sauvage est logique, dans le même sens et de la même façon que la nôtre, mais comme l'est seulement la nôtre quand elle s'applique à la connaissance d'un univers auquel elle reconnaît simultanément des propriétés physiques et des propriétés sémantiques."

15. Gell, *Art and Agency*, 123.

the idea that nonhuman agents experience themselves and their behavior in the forms of (human) culture plays a crucial role: translating culture into the terms of alien subjectivities transforms many natural objects and events into indices from which social agency is derivable. The commonest case is that of defining what to humans is a brute fact or object as an artifact or cultured behavior: what is blood to us is manioc beer to jaguars, a muddy waterhole is seen by tapirs as a great ceremonial house. Artifacts have this interestingly ambiguous ontology. They are objects that necessarily point to a subject; as congealed actions, they are material embodiments of nonmaterial intentionality. What is nature to us may well be culture to another species.

Perspectivism Is Not Relativism

The idea of a world comprising a multiplicity of subject positions looks very much like a form of relativism. Or rather, relativism under its various definitions is often implied in the ethnographic characterization of Amerindian cosmologies. Take, for instance, the work of Kaj Århem, the ethnographer of the Makuna. Having described the elaborate perspectival universe of this Tukanoan people of northwestern Amazonia, Århem observes that the notion of multiple viewpoints on reality implies that, as far as the Makuna are concerned, "every perspective is equally valid and true" and that "a correct and true representation of the world does not exist."[16] Århem is right, of course; but only in a sense. For one can reasonably surmise that as far as humans are concerned, the Makuna would say that there is indeed only one correct and true representation of the world. If *you* start seeing, for instance, the maggots in rotten meat as grilled fish, you may be sure that you are in deep trouble, but grilled fish they are from the *vultures'* point of view. Perspectives should be kept separate. Only shamans, who are so to speak species-androgynous, can make perspectives communicate, and then only under special, controlled conditions.

My real point, however, is best put as a question: does the Amerindian perspectivist theory posit, as Århem maintains that it does, a multiplicity of *representations* of the same world? It is sufficient to consider ethnographic evidence to see that the opposite is the case: all beings perceive ("represent") the world *in the same way*. What varies is the *world* that they see. Animals impose the same categories and values on reality as humans do—their worlds, like ours, revolve around hunting and fishing, cooking and fermented drinks, cross-cousins and war, initiation rituals, shamans, chiefs, spirits, and so forth. Being people in their

16. Kaj Århem, "Ecosofía Makuna," in *La selva humanizada: Ecología alternativa en el trópico húmedo colombiano*, ed. François Correa (Bogotá: Instituto Colombiano de Antropología; Fondo FEN Colombia; Fondo Editorial CEREC, 1993), 124.

own sphere, nonhumans see things just *as* people do. But the things *that* they see are different. Again, what to us is blood is maize beer to the jaguar; what to us is soaking manioc is, to the souls of the dead, a rotting corpse; what is a muddy waterhole to us is for the tapirs a great ceremonial house.

Another good discussion of Amazonian "relativism" can be found in a study of the Matsiguenga by France-Marie Renard-Casevitz. Commenting on a myth in which the human protagonists travel to villages inhabited by strange people who call the snakes, bats, and balls of fire that they eat by the names of foods ("fish," "agouti," "macaws") appropriate for human consumption, she realizes that indigenous perspectivism is quite different from relativism. Yet she sees no special problem:

> This setting in perspective [*mise en perspective*] is just the application and
> transposition of universal social practices, such as the fact that a mother
> and a father of X are the parents-in-law of Y. . . . This variability of the
> denomination as a function of the place occupied explains how A can be
> both fish for X and snake for Y.[17]

But applying the positional relativity that obtains in social and cultural terms to the difference between species has a paradoxical consequence: Matsiguenga preferences are universalized and made absolute. A human culture is thus rendered natural—everybody eats fish and nobody eats snake.

Be that as it may, Casevitz's analogy between kinship positions and what counts as fish or snake for different species remains intriguing. Kinship terms are relational pointers; they belong to the class of nouns that define something in terms of its relations to something else (linguists have special names for such nouns—"two-place predicates" and such like). Concepts like fish or tree, on the other hand, are proper, self-contained substantives: they are applied to an object by virtue of its intrinsic properties. Now, what seems to be happening in Amerindian perspectivism is that substances named by substantives like *fish, snake, hammock*, or *beer* are somehow used as if they were relational pointers, something halfway between a noun and a pronoun, a substantive and a deictic. (There is supposedly a difference between "natural kind" terms such as *fish* and "artifact" terms such as *hammock*: a subject worth more discussion later.) You are a father only because there is another person whose father you are. Fatherhood is a relation, while fishiness is a intrinsic property of fish. In Amerindian perspectivism, however, something is a fish only by virtue of someone else whose fish it is.

17. France-Marie Renard-Casevitz, *Le banquet masqué:*
Une mythologie de l'étranger chez les indiens Matsiguenga
(Paris: Lierre and Coudrier, 1991), 29.

But if saying that crickets are the fish of the dead or that mud is the hammock of tapirs is like saying that my sister Isabel's son, Miguel, is my nephew, then there is no relativism involved. Isabel is not a mother "for" Miguel, from Miguel's "point of view" in the usual, relativist-subjectivist sense of the expression. Isabel is the mother *of* Miguel, she is really and objectively Miguel's mother, just as I am really Miguel's uncle. This is a genitive, internal relation (my sister is the mother of someone, our cricket the fish of someone) and not a representational, external connection of the type "X is fish for someone," which implies that X is "represented" as fish, whatever X is "in itself." It would be absurd to say that, since Miguel is the son of Isabel but not mine, then Miguel is not a son "for me"—for indeed he is. He is my sister's son, precisely.

Now imagine that all Amerindian substances were of this sort. Suppose that, as siblings are those who have the same parents, conspecifics are those that have the same fish, the same snake, the same hammock, and so forth. No wonder, then, that animals are so often conceived, in Amazonia, as affinely related to humans. Blood is to humans as manioc beer is to jaguars in exactly the way that my sister is the wife of my brother-in-law. The many Amerindian myths featuring interspecific marriages and discussing the difficult relationships between the human (or animal) in-marrying affine and his or her animal (or human) parents-in-law, simply compound the two analogies into a single complex one. We begin to see how perspectivism may have a deep connection with exchange—not only how it may be a type of exchange, but how any exchange is by definition an exchange of perspectives.[18]

We would thus have a universe that is 100 percent relational—a universe in which there would be no distinctions between primary and secondary qualities of substances or between "brute facts" and "institutional facts." This distinction, championed by John Searle, opposes brute facts or objects, the reality of which is independent of human consciousness (gravity, mountains, trees, animals, and all "natural kinds") to institutional facts or objects (marriage, money, axes, and cars) that derive their existence, identity, and efficacy from the culturally specific meanings given them by humans.[19] In this overhauled version of the nature/culture dualism, the terms of cultural relativism apply only to cultural objects and are balanced by the terms of natural universalism, which apply to natural objects. Searle would argue, I suppose, that what I am saying is that for Amerindians all facts are of the institutional, mental variety, and that all objects, even trees and

18. See Strathern, *The Gender of the Gift: Problems with Women and Problems with Society in Melanesia* (Berkeley: University of California Press, 1988) and "Writing Societies, Writing Persons," *History of the Human Sciences* 5.1 (February 1992): 5–16.

19. John Searle, *The Construction of Social Reality* (London: Allen Lane, 1995).

fish, are like money or hammocks, in that their only reality (as money and hammocks, not as pieces of paper or of string) derives from the meanings and uses that subjects attribute to them. This would be nothing but relativism, Searle would observe—and an absolute form of relativism at that.

An implication of Amerindian perspectivist animism is, indeed, that there are no autonomous, natural facts, for what we see as nature is seen by other species as culture (as institutional facts). What humans see as blood, a natural substance, is seen by jaguars as manioc beer, an artifact. But such institutional facts are taken to be universal, culturally invariable (an impossibility according to Searle). Constructionist relativism defines all facts as institutional and thus culturally variable. We have here a case not of relativism but universalism—cultural universalism—that has as its complement what has been called "natural relativism."[20] And it is this inversion of our usual pairing of nature with the universal and culture with the particular that I have been terming "perspectivism."

Cultural (multicultural) relativism supposes a diversity of subjective and partial representations, each striving to grasp an external and unified nature, which remains perfectly indifferent to those representations. Amerindian thought proposes the opposite: a representational or phenomenological unity that is purely pronominal or deictic, indifferently applied to a radically objective diversity. One culture, multiple natures—one epistemology, multiple ontologies. Perspectivism implies multinaturalism, for a perspective is not a representation. A perspective is not a representation because representations are a property of the mind or spirit, whereas the point of view is located in the body. The ability to adopt a point of view is undoubtedly a power of the soul, and nonhumans are subjects in so far as they have (or are) spirit; but the differences between viewpoints (and a viewpoint is nothing if not a difference) lies not in the soul. Since the soul is formally identical in all species, it can only perceive the same things everywhere. The difference is given in the specificity of bodies.

This formulation permits me to provide answers to a couple of questions that may have already occurred to my readers. If nonhumans are persons and have souls, then what distinguishes them from humans? And why, being people, do they not regard us as people?

Animals see in the *same* way as we do *different* things because their bodies differ from ours. I am not referring to physiological differences—Amerindians recognize a basic uniformity of bodies—but rather to *affects*, in the old sense of dispositions or capacities that render the body of each species unique: what it eats, how it moves, how it communicates, where it lives, whether it is gregarious or solitary. The visible shape of the body is a powerful sign of these affectual differ-

20. See Latour, *Nous n'avons jamais été modernes* (Paris: La Découverte, 1991), 144.

ences, although the shape can be deceptive, since a human appearance could, for example, be concealing a jaguar affect. Thus, what I call "body" is not a synonym for distinctive substance or fixed shape; body is in this sense an assemblage of affects or ways of being that constitute a *habitus*. Between the formal subjectivity of souls and the substantial materiality of organisms, there is thus an intermediate plane occupied by the body as a bundle of affects and capacities. And the body is the origin of perspectives.

Solipsism or Cannibalism

The status of humans in modern thought is essentially ambiguous. On the one hand, humankind is an animal species among other such, and animality is a domain that includes humans; on the other hand, humanity is a moral condition that excludes animals.[21] These two statuses coexist in the problematic and disjunctive notion of "human nature." In other words, our cosmology postulates a physical continuity and a metaphysical discontinuity between humans and animals, the continuity making of humankind an object for the natural sciences and the discontinuity making of humanity an object for the humanities. Spirit or mind is the great differentiator: it raises us above animals and matter in general, it distinguishes cultures, it makes each person unique before his or her fellow beings. The body, in contrast, is the major integrator: it connects us to the rest of the living, united by a universal substrate (DNA, carbon chemistry) that, in turn, links up with the ultimate nature of all material bodies. Conversely, Amerindians postulate metaphysical continuity and physical discontinuity. The metaphysical continuity results in animism; the physical discontinuity (between the beings of the cosmos), in perspectivism. The spirit or soul (here, a reflexive form, not an immaterial inner substance) integrates. Whereas the body (here, a system of intensive affects, not an extended material organism) differentiates.[22]

This cosmological picture, which understands bodies as the great differentiators, at the same time posits their inherent transformability: interspecific metamorphosis is a fact of nature. Not only is metamorphosis the standard etiological

---

21. See Tim Ingold, "Becoming Persons: Consciousness and Sociality in Human Evolution," *Cultural Dynamics* 4.3 (1991): 355–78; and Ingold, ed., *Companion Encyclopedia of Anthropology: Humanity, Culture, and Social Life*, s.v. "Humanity and Animality."

22. The counterproof of the singularity of the spirit in modern cosmologies lies in the fact that when we try to universalize it, we are obliged—now that supernature is out of bounds—to identify it with the structure and function of the brain. The spirit can only be universal (natural) if it is (in) the body. It is no accident, I believe, that this movement of inscription of the spirit in the brain-body or in matter in general—AI, Churchland's "eliminative materialism," Dennett-style "functionalism," Sperberian cognitivism, etc.—has been synchronically countered by its opposite, the neophenomenological appeal to the body as the site of subjective singularity. Thus, we have been witnessing two seemingly contradictory projects of "embodying" the spirit: one actually reducing it to the body as traditionally (i.e., biophysically) understood, the other upgrading the body to the traditional (i.e., cultural-theological) status of "spirit."

process in myth, but it is still very much possible in present-day life (being either desirable or undesirable, inevitable or evitable, according to circumstances). Spirits, the dead, and shamans can assume animal form, beasts turn into other beasts, humans inadvertently turn into animals. No surprises here: our own cosmology presumes a singular distinctiveness of minds but not even for this reason does it hold communication to be impossible (albeit solipsism is a constant problem). Nor does our cosmology discredit the mental/spiritual transformations induced by such processes as education and religious conversion. Indeed, it is because the spiritual is the locus of difference that conversion becomes a necessary idea. Bodily metamorphosis is the Amerindian counterpart to the European theme of spiritual conversion. Shamans are transformers (and likewise, the mythical demiurges who transformed primal humans into animals are themselves shamans). Shamans can see animals in their inner human form because they don animal "clothing" and thus transform themselves into animals.

Solipsism and metamorphosis are related in the same way. Solipsism is the phantom that threatens our cosmology, raising the fear that we will not recognize ourselves in our "own kind" because, given the potentially absolute singularity of minds, our "own kind" are actually not like us. The possibility of metamorphosis expresses the fear—the opposite fear—of no longer being able to differentiate between human and animal, and above all the fear of seeing the human who lurks within the body of the animal that one eats. Our traditional problem in the West is how to connect and universalize: individual substances are given, while relations have to be made. The Amerindian problem is how to separate and particularize: relations are given, while substances must be defined.

Hence the importance, in Amazonia, of dietary rules linked to the spiritual potency of animals. The past humanity of animals is added to their present-day spirituality, and both are hidden by their visible form. The result is an extended set of food restrictions or precautions that declare inedible animals that were, in myth, originally consubstantial with humans—though some animals can be desubjectified by shamanic means and then consumed.[23] Violation of food restrictions exposes the violator to illness, conceived of as a cannibal counterpredation undertaken by the spirit of the prey (turned predator) in a lethal inversion of perspectives that transforms human into animal. Thus cannibalism is the Amerindian parallel to our own phantom—solipsism. The solipsist is uncertain whether the natural similarity of bodies guarantees a real community of spirit. Whereas the cannibal suspects that the similarity of souls prevails over real differences of body and thus that all animals eaten, despite efforts to desubjectivize them,

23. Desubjectification is accomplished by neutralizing the spirit, transubstantiating the meat into plant food, or semantically reducing the animal subject to a species less proximate to humans.

remain human. To say that these uncertainties or suspicions are phantoms haunting their respective cultures does not mean, of course, that there are not solipsists among us (the more radical relativists, for instance), nor that there are not Amerindian societies that are purposefully and more or less literally cannibalistic.

Exchange as Transformation

The idea of creation ex nihilo is virtually absent from indigenous cosmogonies. Things and beings normally originate as a transformation of something else: animals, as I have noted, are transformations of a primordial, universal humanity. Where we find notions of creation at all—the fashioning of some prior substance into a new type of being—what is stressed is the imperfection of the end product. Amerindian demiurges always fail to deliver the goods. And just as nature is the result not of creation but of transformation, so culture is a product not of invention but of transference (and thus transmission, tradition). In Amerindian mythology, the origin of cultural implements or institutions is canonically explained as a borrowing—a transfer (violent or friendly, by stealing or by learning, as a trophy or as a gift) of prototypes already possessed by animals, spirits, or enemies. The origin and essence of culture is acculturation.

The idea of creation/invention belongs to the paradigm of production: production is a weak version of creation but, at the same time, is its model. Both are actions in—or rather, upon and against—the world. Production is the imposition of mental design on inert, formless matter. The idea of transformation/transfer belongs to the paradigm of exchange: an exchange event is always the transformation of a prior exchange event. There is no absolute beginning, no absolutely initial act of exchange. Every act is a response: that is, a transformation of an anterior token of the same type. *Poiesis*, creation/production/invention, is our archetypal model for action; *praxis*, which originally meant something like transformation/exchange/transfer, suits the Amerindian and other nonmodern worlds better.[24] The exchange model of action supposes that the the subject's "other" is another subject (not an object); and subjectification is, of course, what perspectivism is all about.[25] In the creation paradigm, production is causally primary; and exchange, its encompassed consequence. Exchange is a "moment" of production (it "realizes" value) and the means of *re*production. In the transformation paradigm, exchange is the condition for production since, without the proper social relations with nonhumans, no pro-

24. From the point of view of a hypothetical Amerindian philosopher, I would say that the Western obsession with production reveals it as the last avatar of the biblico-theological category of creation. Humans were not only created in the likeness of God, they create after His own image: they "produce." Ever since God "died," humans have produced themselves after *their* own image (and that is what culture is about, I suppose).

25. See Strathern, "Writing Societies," 9–10.

duction is possible. Production is a type or mode of exchange, and the means of "reexchange" (a word we certainly do not need, for exchange is by definition reexchange). Production creates; exchange changes.

I would venture a further remark on this contrast: the idiom of material production, if applied outside the original domain of *poiesis*, is necessarily metaphorical. When we speak of the production of persons (social reproduction) or the production of "symbolic capital" as if we meant the production of subjects rather than simply of human organisms, we are being no less metaphorical than when we apply the idiom of *praxis* to engagements between humans and non-humans. To speak of the production of social life makes as much, or as little, sense as to speak of an exchange between humans and animals. Metaphorical Marx is not necessarily better than metaphorical Mauss.

I would speculate, further, that the emphasis on transformation/exchange (over creation/production) is organically connected to the predominance of affinal relations (created by marriage alliance) over consanguineal ones (created by parenthood) in Amerindian mythology. The protagonists of the major Amerindian myths are related agonistically as siblings-in-law, parents-in-law, children-in-law. Our own Old World mythology (Greek, Near Eastern, or Freudian) seems haunted, on the other hand, by parenthood and especially fatherhood. Not to put too fine a point on it: we had to steal fire from a divine father; Amerindians had to steal it from an animal father-in-law. Mythology is a discourse on the given, the innate. Myths address what must be taken for granted, the initial conditions with which humanity must cope and against which humanity must define itself by means of its power of "convention."[26] If such is the case, then in the Amerindian world, affinity and alliance (exchange) rather than parenthood (creation/production) comprise the given—the unconditioned condition.

The Cannibal Cogito

The analogy between shamans and warriors in Amerindian ethnographies has often been observed. Warriors are to the human world what shamans are to the universe at large: conductors or commutators of perspectives. That shamanism is warfare writ large has nothing to do with violence (though shamans often act as warriors in the literal sense). But indigenous warfare belongs to the same cosmological complex as shamanism, insofar as both involve the embodiment by the self of the enemy's point of view.[27] Accordingly, in Amazonia, what is intended in

---

26. See Roy Wagner, *The Invention of Culture* (Chicago: University of Chicago Press, 1981).

27. See Viveiros de Castro, *From the Enemy's Point of View: Humanity and Divinity in an Amazonian Society* (Chicago: University of Chicago Press, 1992).

ritual exocannibalism is incorporation of the subjecthood of a hypersubjectified enemy. The intent is not (as it is in hunting game animals) desubjectification.

The subjectification of human enemies is a complex ritual process. Suffice it to say, for our purposes here, that the process supposes a thorough identification of the killer with its victim, just as shamans become the animals whose bodies they procure for the rest of their group. Killers derive crucial aspects of their social and metaphysical identities from their victims—names, surplus souls, songs, trophies, ritual perogatives; but in order to do so, a killer must first *become* his enemy. A telling example is the Araweté war song in which a killer repeats words taught him by the spirit of the victim during the ritual seclusion that follows the deed: the killer speaks from the enemy's standpoint, saying "I" to refer to the enemy and "him" to refer to himself.[28] In order to become a full subject—for the killing of an enemy is often a precondition to adult male status—the killer must apprehend the enemy "from the inside" (as a subject). The analogy with the animist perspectival theory already discussed is clear: nonhuman subjectivities see humans as nonhumans (and vice versa). Here, the killer must be able to see himself as the enemy sees him—as, precisely, an enemy—in order to become "himself" or, rather, a "myself." It is relevant in this connection to recall that the archetypal idiom of enmity, in Amazonia, is affinity. Enemies are conceptualized as "ideal" brothers-in-law, uncontaminated by the exchange of sisters (which would "consanguinize" them—make them cognates of one's children—and thus less than pure affines).

In this idiom of enmity, then, neither party is an object. Enmity of this sort is a reciprocal subjectification: an exchange, a transfer, of points of view. It is a *ritual transformation of the self* (to use Simon Harrison's term) that belongs entirely to the "exchange" (not the "production") paradigm of action—though the exchange in this case is very extreme. Harrison describes the situation in a Melanesian context that closely resembles the Amazonian: "Just as a gift embodies the identity of its donor, so in Lowland warfare the killer acquires through homicide an aspect of his victim's identity. The killing is represented as either creating or expressing a social relationship, or else as the collapse of a social relation by the *merging of two social alters into one.*"[29] The synthesis of the gift relates subjects who remain objectively separated—they are divided by the relation.[30] The killing of an enemy and its symbolic incorporation by the killer, on the other hand, produces a synthesis in which all distance is suppressed: the relation is created by abolishing one of its terms, which is then introjected by

28. See Viveiros de Castro, "Le meurtrier et son double chez les Araweté: Un exemple de fusion rituelle," *Systèmes de Pensée en Afrique Noire* 14 (1996): 77–104.

29. Simon Harrison, *The Mask of War: Violence, Ritual, and the Self in Melanesia* (Manchester, U.K.: Manchester University Press, 1993), 130.

30. See Strathern, *Gender of the Gift.*

the other. The reciprocal dependence of exchange partners becomes insepara-bility here, a kind of fusion.

Ontological predation appears to be the crucial idiom of subjectification in Amazonia. The relative and relational status of predator and prey is fun-damental to the inversions in perspective that obtain between humans and nonhumans. Again, the Melanesian context, as Harrison describes it, presents striking parallels to that of Amazonia: "Aggression is conceived as very much a communicative act directed against the subjectivity of others, and making war required the reduction of the enemy, not to the status of a non-person or thing but, quite the opposite, to an extreme state of subjectivity."[31] Which means, Harrison concludes, that enmity in these societies "is conceptualised not as a mere objective *absence* of a social relationship but as a definite social relationship like any other" (128). This remark brings to mind a well-known passage from Lévi-Strauss:

Les observateurs ont été souvent frappés par l'impossibilité, pour les indigènes, de concevoir une relation neutre, ou plus exactement une absence de relation . . . l'absence de relation familiale ne définit pas rien, elle définit l'hostilité . . . il n'est pas davantage possible de se tenir en deçà, ou au delà, du monde des relations.[32]

"Pour les indigènes," no difference is indifferent and must immediately be invested with positivity. Enmity is a full-blown social relationship. Not, how-ever, a relationship like any other: I would go a bit farther than Harrison and say that the overall schema of difference in Amazonia is cannibalistic predation. At the risk of falling into allegorical excess, I would even venture to say that, in Amazonian cosmologies, the generic attributive proposition is a cannibal proposition. The copula of all synthetic a priori judgments, in a universe articu-lated by a "logic of sensory qualities," is carnivorous copulation. Let me insist: these predatory relations are fully and immediately social relations. We are dealing here with a mode of subjectification, internal to the *monde des relations* to which Lévi-Strauss refers. That world has nothing to do with production and objectification, modes of action that suppose a neutral relationship in which an active and exclusively human subject confronts an inert and naturalized object. In the *monde de relations*, the self is the gift of the other.

31. Harrison, *Mask of War*, 121.

32. Lévi-Strauss, *Les structures élémentaires de la parenté*, 2d ed. (1949; La Haye: Mouton, 1967), 552–53.

Some Conclusions

Our current notions of the social are inevitably polarized by the oppositions I have been evoking: representation/reality, culture/nature, human/nonhuman, mind/body, and the rest. In particular, the social presupposes the nonsocial (the natural). It is impossible to rethink the social without rethinking the natural, for in our cosmological vulgate, nature (always in the singular) is the encompassing term, and society (often used in the plural) is the term encompassed.

The contrast between our basic naturalism and Amerindian cosmologies can be phrased in the terms of our own polarities. Animism could be defined as an ontology that postulates a social character to relations between humans and nonhumans: the space between nature and society is itself social. Naturalism is founded on the inverse axiom: relations between society and nature are themselves natural. Indeed, if in the animistic mode the distinction "nature/culture" is internal to the social world, humans and animals being immersed in the same sociocosmic medium (and in this sense, nature is a part of an encompassing sociality), then in naturalist ontology, the distinction "nature/culture" is internal to nature (and in this sense, human society is one natural phenomenon among others). Animism has society, and naturalism has nature, as its unmarked pole: these poles function, respectively and contrastingly, as the universal dimension of each mode. This phrasing of the contrast between animism and naturalism is not only reminiscent of, or analogous to, the famous (some would say notorious) contrast between gift and commodity—I take it to be the *same* contrast, expressed in more general, noneconomic terms.[33] Likewise the distinction that I have made here between production/creation (naturalism) and exchange/transformation (animism).

In our naturalist ontology, the nature/society interface is natural: humans are organisms like all the rest—we are body-objects in ecological interaction with other bodies and forces, all of them ruled by the necessary laws of biology and physics. Productive forces harness, and thereby express, natural forces. Social relations—that is, contractual or instituted relations between subjects—can only exist internal to human society (there is no such thing as "relations of production" linking humans to animals or plants, let alone political relations). But how alien to nature—this is the problem of naturalism—are these social relations? Given the universality of nature, the status of the human and social world is unstable. Thus, Western thought oscillates, historically, between a naturalistic monism (sociobiology and evolutionary psychology being two of its current avatars) and

---

33. "If in a commodity economy things and persons assume the social form of things, then in a gift economy they assume the social form of persons." Chris A. Gregory, *Gifts and Commodities* (London: Academic, 1982), 41, as cited in Strathern, *Gender of the Gift*, 134.

an ontological dualism of nature and culture ("culturalism" and symbolic anthropology being two of its recent expressions).

Still, for all its being the polar opposite of naturalistic monism, the dualism "nature/culture" discloses the ultimate referential character of the notion of nature by revealing itself to be directly descended from the theological opposition between nature and the supernatural. Culture is the modern name for Spirit—I am thinking of the distinction between *Naturwissenschaften* and *Geisteswissenschaften*; or at least culture names the compromise between nature and grace. Of animism, I am tempted to say that the instability is of an opposite kind: there, the problem is how to administer the mixture of humanity and animality that constitutes animals, rather than, as is the case among ourselves, how to administer the combination of culture and nature that characterizes humans.

Amerindian perspectivism might be viewed as a radical polytheism (or rather, henotheism) applied to a universe that supports no dualism between created matter and Creator Spirit. I am led to ask whether our own naturalistic monism is not the last avatar of our monotheistic cosmology.[34] Our ontological dualisms derive ultimately from the fundamental difference between Creator and creature. Killing off the Creator, as some say we have done, has left us with a creature whose unity depends on the now-absent God. For God prepared science, and the transcendence of transcendence has created immanence.[35] This birthmark is visible on all modern efforts to dispose of dualisms. Our monistic ontologies are always derived from some prior duality—they consist essentially in the erasure of one of the terms or in the absorption (sometimes "dialectical") of the erased term by the remaining one. A genuine monism, anterior and exterior to the great divide between Creator and creature, seems beyond our reach. A lesson we can usefully draw from Amerindian perspectivism is that the relevant conceptual pair may be monism and *pluralism*: multiplicity, not mere duality, is the complement of the monism I am contemplating. Virtually all attacks on Cartesian and other dualisms consider that two is already too much—we need just one (one principle, one substance, one reality). As far as Amerindian cosmologies are concerned, it would appear that two is not enough.

My problem with the notion of relativism, or with the opposition between relativism and universalism, pertains to the concept that underwrites such categories and oppositions: the concept of representation. And my problem with representation is the ontological poverty it implies—a poverty characteristic of modern thought. The Cartesian break with medieval scholasticism produced a

34. The question is also posed in Latour, *Nous n'avons jamais été modernes*, and in Marshall Sahlins, "The Sadness of Sweetness: The Native Anthropology of Western Cosmology," *Current Anthropology* 37.3 (June 1996): 395–428—to mention only two recent works of anthropology.

35. Amos Funkenstein, *Theology and the Scientific Imagination from the Middle Ages to the Seventeenth Century* (Princeton, NJ: Princeton University Press, 1986).

radical simplification of European ontology by positing only two principles or substances: unextended thought and extended matter. Modern thought began with that simplification; and its massive conversion of ontological into epistemological questions (questions of representation) is still with us. Every mode of being not assimilable to obdurate matter has had to be swallowed up by mind. The simplification of ontology has led to the enormous complication of epistemology. Once objects or things have been pacified—retreating to the exterior, silent, and uniform world of nature—subjects begin to proliferate and chatter: transcendental egos, legislative understandings, philosophies of language, theories of mind, social representations, the logic of the signifier, webs of signification, discursive practices, politics of knowledge, and, yes, anthropology of course.

Anthropology is a discipline plagued since its inception by epistemological angst. The most Kantian of disciplines, anthropology is practiced as if its paramount task were to explain how it comes to know (to represent) its object—an object also defined as knowledge (or representation). Is it possible to know it? Is it decent to know it? Do we really know it, or do we see it (and ourselves) through a glass, darkly? There is no way out of this maze of mirrors, mire of guilt. Reification or fetishism is our major care and scare: we began by accusing savages of confusing representations with reality; now we accuse ourselves (or, rather, our colleagues).[36]

While philosophy has been obsessed with epistemology, ontology has been annexed by physics. We have left to quantum mechanics the task of making our most boring dualism, "representation/reality," ontologically dubious. (Though physics has questioned that dualism only in the confines of a quantum world inaccessible to intuition and representation.) Supernature has thus given way to subnature as our transcendent realm. On the macroscopic side, cognitive

36. Polarities and other "othering" devices have gotten bad press lately. The place of the other, however, can never remain vacant for long. As far as contemporary anthropology is concerned, the most popular candidate for the position appears to be anthropology itself. In the formative phase (never completely outgrown) of anthropology, it's main task was to explain how and why the primitive or traditional other was wrong: savages mistook ideal connections for real ones and animistically projected social relations onto nature. In the discipline's classical phase (which lingers on), the other is Western society/culture. Somewhere along the line—with the Greeks? Christianity? capitalism?—the West got everything wrong, positing substances, individuals, separations, and oppositions wherever all other societies/cultures rightly see relations, totalities, connections, and embeddings. Because it is both anthropologically anomalous and ontologically mistaken, it is the West, rather than "primitive" cultures, that requires explanation. In the post-positivist phase of anthropology, first Orientalism, then Occidentalism, is shunned: the West and the Rest are no longer seen as so different from each other. On the one hand, we have never been modern, and, on the other hand, no society has ever been primitive. Then who is wrong, what needs explanation? (Someone must be wrong, something has to be explained.) Our anthropological forebears, who made us believe in tradition and modernity, were wrong—and so the great polarity now is between anthropology and the real practical/embodied life of everyone, Western or otherwise. In brief: formerly, savages mistook (their) representations for (our) reality; now, we mistake (our) representations for (other peoples') reality. Rumor has it we have even been mistaking (our) representations for (our) reality when we "Occidentalize."

psychology has been striving to establish a purely representational ontology, a *natural* ontology of the human species inscribed in cognition, in our mode of representing things. The representational function is ontologized in the mind but in terms set by a simpleminded ontology of mind *versus* matter.

The tug of war goes endlessly on: one side reduces reality to representation (culturalism, relativism, textualism), the other reduces representation to reality (cognitivism, sociobiology, evolutionary psychology). Even phenomenology, new or old—and especially the phenomenology invoked these days by anthropologists—may be a surrender to epistemology. Is not "lived world" a euphemism for "known world," "represented world," "world real for a subject"? *Real* reality is the (still virtual) province of cosmologists, the theorists of quantum gravity and superstring theory. But listen to these custodians of real reality and it becomes obvious—it has been obvious, I might add, for more than seventy-five years—that at the heart of the matter, there is no stuff; only form, only relation.[37] There are "materialist ontologies" on offer as cures for epistemological hypochondria, but I do not know what to do with them. All I know is that we need richer ontologies and that it is high time to put epistemological questions to rest. No effort less strenuous and transformative and dangerously disorienting would make even disagreement with an animist warrior possible.

37. See Alfred North Whitehead, *Science and the Modern World* (1925; New York: Macmillan, 1948).

CALL FOR PAPERS

Stephen Toulmin

Anyone who has lived in the Anglo-American academic world for the last forty years will recognize how boneheaded you would have to be not to have changed your mind about important issues during that time. Speaking for myself, I regard my book *Reason in Ethics*—written in 1946–47 and first published in 1949—as the work of another person: it is not without merit, but I can no longer take responsibility for all its arguments. To go further, I would think it *unreasonable* for any critic to hold me responsible for ideas I worked out as a graduate student.

Many of my colleagues must, in their hearts, acknowledge the distance they have moved during the years since the 1950s. We could certainly learn from one another by comparing notes about these changes, and seeing how far we have been travelling along parallel paths.

Let us therefore reflect in a cool hour on the changes of mind that life and experience have imposed on us during our careers. Instead of committing ourselves to positions of ideological purity and rigidity, we shall illustrate our human candor by inviting others to share in our personal odysseys. I would like to see *Common Knowledge* dedicate, if the volume and sincerity of reply warrant, a full issue to articles that "take it back."

Originally published in *Common Knowledge* 1.1 (Spring 1992): 1. © 1992.

Common Knowledge 25:1–3

DOI 10.1215/0961754X-7299078

CALL FOR PAPERS

Cornelius Castoriadis, Stanley Cavell, and Steven Marcus

We call for papers that advance the psychoanalytic theory of ambivalence; we call for papers that collocate and annotate Freud's and other major analysts' remarks on ambivalence and on such related subjects as anxiety. *Common Knowledge* will be interested particularly in submissions that treat social conflict and intellectual struggle as expressions of ambivalence, or that explore the applicability of ambivalence theory to the writing of cultural history.

Originally published in *Common Knowledge* 1.1 (Spring 1992): 10. © 1992.

Common Knowledge 25:1–3
DOI 10.1215/0961754X-7299090

SELF-SUBVERSION

Albert O. Hirschman

We authors are touchy and insatiable for praise. When a reader sincerely wishes to show admiration and declares "I liked your book a lot," are we not slightly offended and do we not feel like asking, "Which one?"—meaning in effect: "And what about the others?" Similarly, when I am complimented by a reader for my antitheoretical posture, that is for my critique of the "Search for Paradigms," or of the "Quest for Parsimony" in economic or social science theory,[1] I tend to be once again ungracious and am liable to rebuff the tribute by exclaiming: "I am not, you know, all that much set against paradigms or theorizing." For I like to claim that I have come up with a few theoretical notions of my own, from the early distinction between the "supply effect" and the "influence effect" of trade in *National Power and the Structure of Foreign Trade* (1945), all the way to my last book, *The Rhetoric of Reaction* (1991), where I undertake to array all arguments against change or reform into the three newly created categories of perversity, futility, and jeopardy.

For reasons that will become evident, I shall quickly cite a couple of fur-

Originally published in *Common Knowledge* 3.2 (Fall 1994): 10–15. © 1994.

The author wishes to express his gratitude to Harry Frankfurt for detailed critical comments.

1. See my two articles, "The Search for Paradigms as a Hindrance to Understanding," *World Politics* (March 1970), also in *A Bias for Hope: Essays on Development and Latin America* (New Haven: Yale University Press, 1971); and "Against Parsimony; Three Easy Ways of Complicating Some Categories of Economic Discourse," in *Economics and Philosophy* 1 (1985), also in *Rival Views of Market Society and Other Recent Essays* (New York: Viking/Penguin, 1986; paperback ed., Cambridge: Harvard University Press, 1991).

Common Knowledge 25:1–3

DOI 10.1215/0961754X-7299102

ther instances of theory-building on my part. In spite of its title and of its origin in practical advisory work in Colombia, *The Strategy of Economic Development* (1958) was widely regarded as a contribution to development theory. A simple principle—"unbalanced growth" or the idea of maximizing induced decision-making—was here shown to yield suggestions on a wide range of development problems, from investment priorities to industrialization patterns, from inflation and balance-of-payments policies to new attitudes toward population growth, from the choice of technology to the role of the state in development. Among subsequent writings on development, I might also mention my "tunnel effect" paper, which dealt with the effect on political stability of a growth process that brings with it, as is often the case initially in market economies, increased income inequality. I drew a theoretical distinction between an early phase of political tolerance for this inequality and a subsequent phase of impatience. The resulting model helped to explain a variety of political developments in the Third World during the fifties and sixties, and lent itself to being translated into quite simple mathematics (in addition to its illustration through the two-lane tunnel metaphor).[2] Finally, my theoretical bent is perhaps best illustrated by my book *Exit, Voice, and Loyalty* (1970). In that volume and subsequent elaborations, I tried to show that these simple concepts and their interrelations can be used to throw new light on a vast range of seemingly disparate social, political, and economic situations—surely the hallmark of useful theory-building.

So I bristle a bit when I am pigeonholed as "atheoretical" or "antitheoretical" or even "institutional," and cannot wholly agree when I am portrayed—as Michael McPherson once did in a perceptive paper—as someone who is primarily interested in noticing and underlining what more systematically minded (theoretical) economists or social scientists have overlooked.[3] I do admit to having frequently a reaction, perhaps something approaching a reflex, to other people's theories, of the "It ain't necessarily so" kind. Skepticism toward *other* people's claims to spectacular theoretical discoveries is, of course, not a noteworthy trait. It is, however, more unusual to develop this sort of reaction to *one's own* generalizations or theoretical constructs. And this has become increasingly the characteristic of my writing, a characteristic that I wish to look at here.

In *National Power and the Structure of Foreign Trade*, I showed how relations of influence, dependence, and domination arise directly from those commercial transac-

2. See "The Changing Tolerance for Income Inequality in the Course of Economic Development," *Quarterly Journal of Economics* 87 (Nov. 1973): 544–65, with a mathematical appendix by Michael Rothschild; reprinted (without the appendix) in my collection, *Essays in Trespassing: Economics to Politics and Beyond* (Cambridge: Cambridge University Press, 1981).

3. Michael S. McPherson, "The Social Scientist as Constructive Skeptic: On Hirschman's Role," in Alejandro Foxley, Michael S. McPherson, and Guillermo O'Donnell, eds., *Development, Democracy, and the Art of Trespassing: Essays in Honor of Albert O. Hirschman* (South Bend, IN: University of Notre Dame Press, 1986), 305–16.

tions between sovereign nations that had long been pronounced "mutually beneficial" by the theory of international trade. Even if one agreed with the classical
theory on the economic gains from trade, it could be shown that the *political* effects
of foreign trade were likely to be *asymmetrical* and to favor, at least initially, the
larger and richer countries. This basic finding was one reason my book was "redis-
covered" in the sixties when a number of writers—such as Fernando Henrique Car-
doso, Osvaldo Sunkel, and Andre Gunder Frank—developed the so-called dependencia thesis. Actually I never felt comfortable being cast as a "forerunner" of this
group, whose economic and political analysis I often found excessively somber. In
1977, an occasion arose to explain my attitude toward the "dependencia" school
and I decided to do so by criticizing my own thesis of a quarter-century before.[4] I
tried to show that the very situation of dependence that a small, poor country may
experience initially as a result of trading with a large and rich country can give
rise to countertendencies, both economic and political, that in time would reduce
this dependence. For example, while trade between a powerful large country and
a small country makes initially for subordination of the latter, this circumstance
will lead to a reaction that has some chance of success on account of what I called
the "disparity of attention." The large country is unable and unlikely to focus its
attention on its relations with a small trading partner, at least not with the single-
mindedness that is available to, and characteristic of, the latter ("the [dependent]
country is likely to pursue its escape from domination more actively and energeti-
cally than the dominant country will work on preventing this escape").[5]

My propensity to self-subversion manifests itself again in my reaction to
my next book, *The Strategy of Economic Development.* One of its principal chapters
dealt with the characteristic features of the process of industrialization in less
developed countries. I pointed out that industrial development in these countries
typically proceeds by means of what I called backward linkages—an industry
supplying a good proven to be in demand through prior imports will be established first on the basis of imported inputs (such as semifinished materials and
machinery), and domestic manufacture of these inputs will then follow via backward linkage. This sequence is very different from the order of events in which
industry was established in the pioneering industrial countries where locally
made machinery and intermediate materials had to be available from the start.
But I celebrated the backward-linkage dynamic just because it followed a different
road and could qualify as an original discovery of the late industrializers.

Already in *Strategy* I made some cautionary remarks on the conceivable
drawbacks of the backward-linkage dynamic, particularly on the possibility that

4. "Beyond Asymmetry: Critical Notes on Myself as a
Young Man and on Some Other Old Friends," *Interna-
tional Organization* 32 (Winter 1978): 45–50, reprinted in
Essays in Trespassing, 27–33.

5. See n. 2, *Essays in Trespassing,* 30.

it may turn out not to be all that dynamic, with the interests of the early indus- trialists often being opposed (for various reasons) to the domestic production of inputs. In an article that was written ten years later, I expanded on this theme and have now come to see this industrialization as liable to "get stuck," or as an example of what I call the "getting-stuck syndrome" that seems to affect a num- ber of intended but potentially abortive sequences.[6]

An example fresh in my mind of my arguing against my own propositions concerns my recent attempt to understand the events that led to the downfall of the German Democratic Republic in 1989—with the help of the concepts of my 1970 book *Exit, Voice, and Loyalty.*[7] In that book I had explained at length how exit undermines voice and how the inability to exit can strengthen voice. What happened in the German Democratic Republic in the course of 1989 seemed to contradict this model: here the massive flight toward the West contributed powerfully to massive demonstrations against the communist regime, which was brought down by the combined blows inflicted by exit and voice. It was this unex- pected and effective collaboration of exit and voice that excited my interest and made me examine closely the sequence of events. In the process, I came upon some complications of the original model that, once introduced, made it quite easy to understand how exit and voice could work in unison rather than at cross- purposes. But, as I wrote, "the inventiveness of history was needed to suggest the complication and to reveal its importance."[8]

Finally, I come to my most recent book, *The Rhetoric of Reaction.* This is, for me, the most pronounced instance of my propensity to ferret, undermine, or stand in some tension to propositions I have already put forward—most pro- nounced, because I engage in this propensity *within the same book*, rather than some years or decades later in a separate publication. The book was largely writ- ten in the years 1986–89 "as a tract—properly learned and scholarly, but still a tract—against the then aggressive and would-be triumphant neo-conservative positions on social and economic policy making."[9] The major portion of the book is devoted to three arguments that I show to have been marshalled time and again against the principal proposals for change and reform over the past two centuries: the arguments of perversity (the proposed change for the better will actually backfire and make things worse), of futility (the proposed change will be wholly ineffective), and of jeopardy (the proposed change will endanger some earlier advance).

---

6. See my paper, *"The Rhetoric of Reaction*—Two Years Later," *Government and Opposition* 28 (Summer 1993): 292–314. I have argued along somewhat similar lines in "The Case Against One Thing at a Time," *World Develop- ment* 18 (Aug. 1990): 1119–22.

7. "Exit, Voice, and the Fate of the German Democratic Republic: An Essay in Conceptual History," *World Politics* 45 (Jan. 1993): 173–202.

8. Ibid., 178.

9. *"The Rhetoric of Reaction,"* 292–93.

But, as I explain at greater length in a recent paper,[10] it occurred to me, in the course of considering the last of these arguments, that the jeopardy thesis is easily turned around: countering the view that a new reform will endanger an earlier advance, the partisans of that reform will often assert that the proposed reform will complement and strengthen the earlier one. I then looked for other "progressive" arguments that would be similarly, if less obviously, related to the perversity and futility theses. As a result, I wrote a chapter I had not planned to write, "From Reactionary to Progressive Rhetoric," that shows in some detail how "[r]eactionaries have no monopoly on simplistic, peremptory, and intransigent rhetoric" (149). I do not believe that this chapter blunted the polemical thrust of my book. Still, the demonstration that progressives can be as given to arguing along doctrinaire and routine-ridden lines as are reactionaries modified my overall message and brought me to conclude the book, originally written in a combative mood, on a quite unintended constructive note.

In the follow-up article that I just mentioned, I characterize my chapter on "Progressive Rhetoric" as "self-subversive." *Self-subversion* may in fact be apt as a general term for the intellectual wanderings I have been describing here. Self-subversion is perhaps unusual. It may seem odd that anyone should repeatedly *wish* to demonstrate that a tendency or line of causation he or she has suggested earlier needs to be substantially reconsidered and qualified by attention to the opposite line, in the light of subsequent events or findings. A simple reason scientists (social and otherwise) are rarely self-critical to the point of engaging in self-subversion is that they invest much self-esteem and even some portion of their identity in the findings and propositions for which they have become known. In their further work, they are likely to explore, along Kuhnian "normal science" lines, all those domains where their original findings can be *confirmed*. In this way, much confirmatory evidence will be accumulated and resistance against self-subversion will mount.

Another reason why there is resistance is the continuing hold on our minds of certain basic conceptions about "the way things are" in the physical world and the analogies to the social world that we are apt to draw. Whether the sun turns around the earth or the earth circles around the sun, we are certain that both of these propositions cannot be true at the same time. We tend to forget that, in the social world, things are much more complicated and ambiguous. Here any connection we have established convincingly between events, as though it were a universally valid law, could be found simultaneously to hold and not hold (or to hold in a very different form) in various subsections of human society—for the simple reason that some underlying assumptions, previously implicit and thought to be general, apply in one subsection but not in another.

10. Ibid., 302–7.

Here lies also the reason why my exercises in self-subversion, while often experienced at first as traumatic, are eventually rewarding and enriching. The new dynamics I come upon in matters of dependence, linkages, exit-voice, and so on, do not in the end cancel out or refute the earlier findings; rather they define domains of the social world where the originally postulated relationships do not hold. Far from having to hang my head in shame on account of some egregious error that needs to be recanted, I can still land on my feet or "come out on top" as I celebrate the new complexities I have uncovered.[11]

In closing, I concur with Stephen Toulmin[12] and plead for us to overcome the normal resistance to self-subversion. I even wish to proclaim the virtues and attractions of indulging that activity. In the first place, I believe that what I have here called self-subversion can make a contribution to a more democratic culture in which citizens not only have the right to their individual opinions and convictions but, more important, are ready to question them in the light of new arguments and evidence. Furthermore, just as Bachelard said of Freudian repression that it is "a normal activity, a useful activity, better still, a joyful activity,"[13] so engaging in self-subversion can actually be a positive and even enjoyable experience. When I encounter a social situation where exit stimulates voice instead of undermining it, as I had long thought, I may well pass through a moment of perplexity and concern about my exit-voice theory having been "falsified." But past this moment, I feel genuinely more alive, since I now have new interrelations and complexities to explore. Wittgenstein is reported to have remarked that "he could feel really active only when he changed his philosophical position and went on to develop something new."[14] At some point in one's life, self-subversion may in fact become the principal means to self-renewal.

CODA

I recall being much moved, many years ago, by Camus and his wartime essay "The Myth of Sisyphus," and particularly by its last sentence: *"Il faut imaginer Sisyphe heureux."* Perhaps, as a result of my reflections on the uses of self-subversion, I can now go beyond the Camus formulation and propose instead, less elegantly but more radically: One must imagine Sisyphus himself on making the rock tumble down.

---

11. See "Exit, Voice, and the Fate of the German Democratic Republic," 202.

12. Stephen Toulmin, Call for Papers I, *Common Knowledge* 1 (Spring 1992) : 4.

13. Gaston Bachelard, *La Psychoanalyse du feu* (Paris: Gallimard, 1949), 164.

14. Ray Monk, *Ludwig Wittgenstein: The Duty of Genius* (New York: Penguin Books, 1990), 467.

THE ACHIEVEMENT OF AMBIVALENCE

Hanna Segal

Central to Freud's conceptualisation of mental life is the idea of psychic conflict—conflict between conscious and unconscious desires and realities, between conflicting desires. Equally central is the notion that such conflicts, when unresolved, undergo repression, become unconscious, and find expression and "compromises" in dreams, symptoms, and parapraxes. Among those conflicts in the evolution of Freud's work, that of ambivalence acquires increasing importance. Ambivalence is a term sometimes used loosely to denote any ambiguity, but as a psychoanalytical term it has come to mean, more precisely, a conflict between aggression and love. In the 1920s, in his final theory of instincts, Freud posits a conflict between the instincts of life and death. That conflict, and the ambivalence that results from it, underlies all the others and is reflected not only in pathology or dreams but in all human individual and group behaviour. The conflict between the life and death instincts is expressed in ambivalence towards primary objects. Ambivalence is not psychopathological; it is part of human nature.

Freud first uses the term "ambivalence," which he borrows from Bleuler, in 1912 in "The Dynamics of Transference,"[1] and it is significant that it is a paper on

Originally published in *Common Knowledge* 1.1 (Spring 1992): 92–103. © 1992.

1. See Sigmund Freud, "The Dynamics of Transference," 1912, vol. 2 of *The Standard Edition of the Complete Psychological Works of Sigmund Freud,* trans. James Strachey et al. (London: Hogarth Press, 1953).

Common Knowledge 25:1–3
DOI 10.1215/0961754X-7299114

transference. It is in the transference relationship that we can observe firsthand and in detail emotional states, and it is in the transference that basic relationships to primary objects are relived and reenacted. Freud uses the term for the first time in 1912, but, as is characteristic of Freud, the theoretical formulation lags behind because it springs from clinical work. In his case histories preceding his use of the term "ambivalence," particularly in the account of the analyses of Little Hans and the Rat Man (1909), ambivalence plays a crucial role. He describes in the Rat Man how "A battle between love and hate was raging in the lover's breast and the object of both those feelings was one and the same person."[2]

In "Mourning and Melancholia" (1917) Freud gives perhaps the best description of the central role of ambivalence. This is the paper which foreshadows his description of the superego and his theory of the life and death instincts. He differentiates between mourning the loss of an object (which necessitates a gradual detachment of the libido from the lost object) and the state of melancholia. In melancholia the work of mourning is impeded by an ambivalence towards the object, an ambivalence that continues in relation to this object even after it has been internalized, and results in a painful mutual hatred, which conflicts with love, between this internal object and the ego. That paper brings to light more vividly than any of the preceding ones the importance of ambivalence towards an *internal object*. The Oedipus complex—simultaneous love and hate toward both parental objects—Freud sometimes refers to as the ambivalent complex.[3] And it is the introjection of those ambivalently loved figures which forms the core of the superego.

In 1920, in *Beyond the Pleasure Principle*, Freud posited the existence of two opposing instincts. One is the life instinct, which desires life, aims at life, love, integration, and growth; the other is the death instinct, which is the desire to return to an inorganic state. Freud assumes that what he calls the "organism," in order to avoid death, deflects the death instinct outwards where it becomes aggression against objects. He comments that in clinical practice we never observe the death instinct—its work being done silently within the organism—but we see it only as fused with libido (the term "libido," which originally described sexual drives, Freud extended to denote the flow of the life instinct as a whole). However, in the case of psychosis, severe neurosis, or sadistic perversions, we can observe defusion and the appearance of naked forms of the deflected death instinct.[4]

In his wish to map the history of sexual development, Freud was searching for the point at which sadism originally made its appearance, and he first thought it was at the second anal stage—anal sadism. Abraham had placed it earlier—in

2. Freud, "Notes Upon a Case of Obsessional Neurosis," 1909, *Standard Edition* 10: 191.

3. See Freud, "Inhibitions, Symptoms and Anxiety," 1926, *Standard Edition* 10.

4. Freud, "Beyond the Pleasure Principle," 1920, *Standard Edition* 18.

the second part of the oral stage. He assumed the first oral stage was narcissistic and devoid of aggression—aggression and therefore ambivalence making their appearance in the second, cannibalistic, oral stage. However, if Freud was right about the life and death instincts being active from the beginning of life, ambivalence too could exist from the beginning.

In some of his later writings Freud expresses a regret that he had not paid sufficient attention to aggression earlier in his career. Melanie Klein, starting work in the 1920s, addressed herself to the problem of ambivalence and resulting guilt at very early stages of her work. This may have been due to two factors: (1) because she was familiar with Freud's post-1920 work, and, maybe more importantly, (2) because she started her psychoanalytic practice by psychoanalysing children, in whom at very early stages she saw conflicts of ambivalence and processes of projection and introjection which brought to her attention the overweening importance of conflicts in the internal world. From the beginning, she questioned that there could be an objectless state at any stage of the infant's life:

The hypothesis that a stage extending over several months precedes object relations implies that—except for the libido attached to the infant's own body—impulses, phantasies, anxieties and defences are not present in him, or are not related to an object, that is to say they would operate (in a vacuum) . . . there is no anxiety Situation, no mental process which does not involve objects external or internal . . . furthermore, love and hatred, phantasies, anxieties and defences are indivisibly linked to object relations.[5]

Thus, in Klein's view, the conflict between loving and destructive impulses would attach itself from the beginning to objects, primarily the maternal breast. She takes a new view of Abraham's pre-ambivalent state. It is pre-ambivalent in a certain way, not that the two drives are nonexistent, but that they are split from one another and therefore not *experienced* as ambivalence. In her view, it is not the "organism" that deflects the death instinct but the rudimentary ego, capable of experiencing anxiety and therefore using defence mechanisms such as deflection of a threatening inner drive. She sees this deflection as a projection into an object as well as an aggression directed against the object. This projection creates a "hateful" object; it is perceived as full of hatred as well as being hated. And split off from this, the life instinct searches for the object of need and partly also creates one by projection (Freud's hallucinatory wish-fulfillment). Bad experiences attach themselves to, and are attributed to, the bad object, and good experiences to the good one. Klein called this early stage paranoid-schizoid because

5. Melanie Klein, "The Origins of Transference," 1952, vol. 3 of *The Writings of Melanie Klein* (New York: Free Press, 1984), 52–53.

of the paranoid anxiety in relation to a bad object imbued also with the infant's projected destructiveness, and because of the schizoid split existing between idealised and persecutory experiences. Those of course are not the only characteristics of the paranoid-schizoid position, but are the main ones in relation to dealing with ambivalence.

As those projections get gradually withdrawn, and a more realistic picture is formed of the object, and of itself, the infant has to experience his or her own ambivalence. The infant begins to perceive his mother as a whole object, that is, not split into two or fragmented into parts, but one person both gratifying and frustrating. And the infant also realises that he is one person with conflicting feelings. This is the stage Klein called the depressive position because the realisation of ambivalence brings with it the threat of the loss of the object and depressive feelings of loss and guilt associated with it. Looked at from that angle, the capacity to experience ambivalence is a fundamental achievement, a major step in development. It is essential to integration of split objects and feelings, and to the recognition of reality, which is both gratifying and frustrating. It also brings with it a new range of feelings, such as fear of loss and guilt. Guilt replaces persecution, and this is of great importance because persecution has no resolution: Hatred brings persecution and persecution brings hatred. On the other hand, when ambivalence is recognised, aggression is felt as damaging an object that is also needed and desired, and brings in its wake not more hatred but, on the contrary, a mobilisation of loving impulses and the wish to repair and restore. This, in Klein's view, is the basis of constructive sublimation. However, the recognition of the ambivalence, guilt, and fear of loss is extremely painful, and powerful defences can set in—manic defences, paranoid defences, and others—all necessitating some degree of regression to more primitive forms of functioning. Klein recognises Freud's distinction between mourning and melancholia. But she disagrees with him in one respect: Freud confessed himself baffled as to why the work of mourning was so painful. Klein's view is that mourning is not free of ambivalence and guilt because any mourning reawakens the unconscious mourning for the original loved and hated primary object, but that the difference between normal mourning and pathological depression lies in what prevails in the ambivalence: whether it is the love or the hatred. In melancholia the hatred predominates and projection of hatred into the internal object; guilt is felt as a persecution. (After 1920 Freud described the superego of the melancholic as a "pure culture" of the death instinct.) In normal mourning there is also ambivalence and guilt, and the various defences against it, like manic denial or transient persecutory feelings; but, if love is stronger than the destructiveness, the reparative process sets in and (as is well known) both creativity and personality may be enriched by experiences of mourning:

On ne peut recréer ce qu'on aime le renonçant. [It is only by renouncing that we can recreate what we love.]—Proust

The depressive position brings about a fundamental reorientation to reality. With the withdrawal of projections the object is perceived more in accordance with the reality principle and so is the self. We begin to take responsibility for our own impulses. It is a step between psychotic and normal functioning. The acceptance of ambivalence plays a crucial role. Bleuler thought that ambivalence characterises severe neuroses and psychoses, and LaPlanche & Pontalis, in *The Language of Psychoanalysis,* appear to think that Freud shared this view.[6] However, Freud clearly stated, after 1920, that the ambivalence we see in neurotics we do not see in paranoids.

Thus ambivalence can be seen as a developmental achievement. We know, however, that unresolved ambivalence leads to mental illness, both psychotic and neurotic. It is psychotic when the flight from ambivalence brings about a regression to the most primitive mental mechanisms of the paranoid-schizoid position of denial, splitting, projection, and fragmentation. It is neurotic when the ego is strong enough not to regress completely, but uses a variety of defences, all of which necessitate some regression to primitive mechanisms, but which can confine the illness to neurotic symptomatology without totally destroying the personality.

So what is the resolution of ambivalence, and on what does it depend? I think it is essential to differentiate the existence of ambivalence that is there from the beginning from the achievement of knowing one's ambivalence, accepting it, and working through it (this working through being accomplished primarily through the recognition of guilt and of the fear of loss brought about by ambivalence and the capacity to mobilise restoration and reparation). This does not mean that aggression is absent; but it becomes proportional to the cause, as does the guilt attached to it. I think this basically depends on the balance of the life and death instincts. If, in the paranoid-schizoid position, good experiences and love are felt to be stronger than bad experiences and hatred, integration of the two is easier than it is if the bad object and destructiveness are felt to predominate. When bad feelings predominate and are projected, a powerful bad object is experienced, inducing more hatred, in a vicious circle. When good feelings predominate, one's aggression feels less dangerous, and there is less need to project it. Therefore the object is felt as less hateful, therefore less hated; and a more benevolent circle is established of diminishing hatred. Good and bad can then be more easily integrated without fear that the bad will annihilate the good. What

6. See Jean LaPlanche and J. B. Pontalis, *The Language of Psycho-analysis* (London: Hogarth Press, 1973).

is the fusion described by Freud? And what is defusion, in which sadism appears? I think that fusion could be seen as an integration. It is my view that if the life instinct predominates over the death instinct, fusion is under the aegis of the life instinct and becomes useful aggression used to protect life, which also means to protect one's love objects. When the death instinct predominates the reverse is true, and often sexuality, which is part of the life instinct, is used in the service of sadism or masochism derived from the death instinct. This is a simple example but this predominance of one or the other is reflected in the symptomatology of the neurotic as well. Destructiveness is split off and contained in symptoms but never resolved. The life instinct is strong enough to keep destructiveness at bay but not strong enough to overcome it and resolve conflicts.

For instance, in childhood phobias, the ambivalence is deflected onto the phobic object, and it is ambivalence because the phobic object is also an object of attraction. But the persecutory feelings predominate in that fusion, and the phobic object is feared. Herbert Rosenfeld speaks of such "psychotic islands" in otherwise well-functioning personalities. Obsessional neurosis is a classic example, in the obsessional ceremonials of doing and undoing, and such overt apparent ambivalence as in *folie de doute*.

I have in analysis a young man who is a case of typical obsessional neurosis. His presenting problem was that he did not know whether to change professions, though highly qualified in his present one. Soon after starting his analysis, he also could not decide whether to leave his wife and rejoin a former lover. Apparently he faced his ambivalence: it dominated him. But this was not quite the case. He presented the problem as a choice between wife and lover, and was not aware of the intensity of his hatred of both of them. Moreover, the ambivalence was deflected from the parental objects. What actually brought him to analysis was his beginning to become aware of his tremendous ambivalence towards his father, whom he had previously adored and idealised. The emergence into consciousness of that ambivalence brought about a fear of total breakdown. He spoke of a few short bouts of "catastrophic" feeling, and his anxiety about it was so high, and his description so vivid, that it made me think of Schreber's description of the end of the world. As the analysis began, gradually his ambivalence toward both his parents emerged more clearly, but any approach of ambivalence toward his idealised analyst would bring about this threat of catastrophe. In the catastrophic state, fear of the death instinct was very palpable. His dreams presented devastated landscapes, ruined houses, desolate emptiness, sometimes devastating storms. But his overt, chronic symptoms were also clearly dominated by a destructiveness of which he was unaware. He had an acute ambivalence toward his own thoughts. Whatever trend of thought he started, or whatever conclusion he came to about anything, another part of his mind would immediately attack it and with enormous savagery. No decision, however small, could be considered without bringing about an immediate devastating feeling of guilt or loss, of being "thrust into outer darkness." This presented a formidable obstacle in the analytic work. No insight could ever be maintained any length of time without being savagely attacked.

So the indecision itself, which seems to be a compromise between two equal forces, is not really between two equal forces in the effect, i.e., the paralysis of his mental functioning: it is the destructive impulses that win. In "The Dynamics of the Transference" Freud says that we find resistance to every move in the analysis. At that point he certainly does not connect resistance with the death instinct, a much later concept. There are many causes of resistance, fear of pain, shame, etc., but I think that at rock bottom, the deepest resistance derives from the operation of the death instinct. The life instinct aims at integration, growth, and change; the death instinct is against all movement and change.

This is so, of course, not only in the obsessional neurotic. Another patient of mine, with completely different symptomatology, had the following dream:

A woman had been saved by being locked in a mental hospital. She was restrained by force and tied to a bed—a procrustean bed.

The patient could not be sure if this incarceration was to save the woman from violent gangs or whether it was part of her own activities. The imprisoned woman had features which linked her with the patient's mother, with me, and also with the patient herself. This patient had powerful defences against her aggression and fear of madness: roaming violent gangs outside the hospital (obviously the analysis with its bed-couch). But the violence with which the patient was restrained, and the immobilisation of herself, me, and the psychoanalytical process, carry all the violence that in the dream she suspects come from the same source as the roaming gangs. Immobility and inertia, resistance to movement and change, are part of the same death-and-violence drive as the more noisy manifestations that are projected outwards.

From my description, it sounds as though I were ignoring problems of environment. This is not the case. The environment helps or hinders the resolution of the ambivalent conflict. Obviously good experiences increase love and bad experiences hinder it. And furthermore, how the parental objects deal with the infant's destructiveness or self-destructiveness is of fundamental importance in modulating it. This fact is of course crucial in psychoanalysis used as a therapeutic tool. The patient brings his infantile impulses and his internal objects to be reexamined in a different way, a different environment. (And I do not mean by that, as some analysts do, that the analyst has to become like an ideal parent. But that discussion would go beyond the scope of this article.)

I have dealt so far with individual psychology only, but the conflicts described are also expressed in our group behaviour. Man is a social animal and this is life promoting. We form groups to help one another and to face problems together. But at the same time groups contain and give expression to death drives which are a danger to themselves and to other groups. Freud addresses himself to the psychological elements of group formation and thus to the roots of civilisation. People form groups for reality reasons ("to combat the forces of nature") and also for instinctual reasons—

I may now add that civilisation is a process in the service of Eros, whose purpose is to combine single human individuals, and after that families, then races, peoples and nations, into one great unity, the unity of mankind. Why this has to happen, we do not know; the work of Eros is precisely this. These collections of men are to be libidinally bound to one another. Necessity alone, the advantages of work in common, will not hold them together.

—and also "to bind man's destructiveness to man."[7]

People's lives are governed by object relationships. Infants depend on, and love, the breast. As they grow and see their mothers and their fathers as whole people, their dependence and love are transferred to the whole family. Soon, their love also embraces other social units to which they belong. Groups of various kinds, including national groups, are like an extension of families. But in extending their love from their early objects to the group, they also extend to the group the ambivalent conflicts experienced with those objects:

But man's natural aggressive instinct, the hostility of each against all and of all against each, opposes this programme of civilisation. This aggressive instinct is the derivative and the main representative of the death instinct which we have found alongside of Eros and which shares world-dominion with it.[8]

And more: we protect our primary objects by turning to groups to help us handle our ambivalence. The groups may do it in a constructive way, helping us in joint work and endeavour, to overcome ambivalence. But only too often, groups resort, on the contrary, to the most primitive psychotic mechanisms to keep their internal cohesion by denying problems and ambivalence. It is well known that groups tend to be paranoid, self-idealising, and self-aggrandising. They deal with aggression by projecting it outwards and creating enemies. Someone defined the nation as a group of people joined only by their common hatred of all their neighbors. Freud noticed that in a group we merge our superegos into a group superego. This allows us to deal with guilt and we perpetrate atrocities in wars and revolutions which our personal guilt would never allow us to perpetrate in our personal life.

7. Freud, "Civilisation and Its Discontents," 1930, *Standard Edition* 21: 122. 8. Ibid.

Wilfred Bion, basing his theory on actual clinical work with groups, extended Freud's hypothesis.[9] According to him, a group fulfills two functions. One he called the work group (I prefer to call it the work *function*), which is the group function of realistic joint work. The other he called the basic-assumption group (or function), which is to handle psychotic anxiety. And it is psychotic, rather than neurotic, anxieties which we tend to project into the group because those are hardest to tolerate in oneself and by oneself. A basic assumption is a psychotic premise on which the group functions. Such psychotic premises underlie, for instance, our sense of superiority to other groups, megalomania, and our unwarrantable hostility or fear of them (paranoia). Our psychotic parts are merged into our group identity, and we do not feel mad since our views are sanctioned by the group. If the work function predominates in the group, psychotic features are kept in check and are expressed in a fairly innocuous way.

Members of a group brought together by work, of whatever kind, have a compatible individual and group interest. The security of both the individual and his group is bound up with the success of the work. Ambivalence and rivalries are unavoidable, but tempered by the need for survival and success of the work. The group itself can face rivalry with other groups and this too can take a sane form. But it can take an insane, destructive form, liable to destroy both parties.

The prevalence of psychotic versus work orientation in a group is a particular danger of political groupings, whether national, religious, or ideological. This may be so because the national or political group's work is less well defined. If a group of workers in other fields was dominated, not by the work function, but by psychotic assumptions, the actual work would suffer. The danger in political groupings may also obtain because these groupings have to do with the search for power, which in itself is a primitive aim. I do not remember who it was who said that the tragedy of democracies is that in order to get to the top you must have qualities which make you unfit to be at the top. And of course this is even more true of dictatorships.

Groups dominated by psychotic functioning tend to throw up leaders who represent best the psychotic traits. And that is not all, since the more we project omnipotence into our leaders the more helpless we become, and the more we push them into believing their own omnipotence and omniscience. We deepen their madness. Just before the Gulf War one could not help but think that the conflict was personal—a clash between narcissistic leaders.

Franco Fornari considers defences against mourning (and therefore ambivalence) to be a major factor in going to war.[10] A group unable to deal with mourning, which included guilt about aggression, can defend itself against mourning

9. See Wilfred R. Bion, *Experiences in Groups* (London: Tavistock, 1961).

10. See Franco Fornari, *The Psychoanalysis of War* (Bloomington and London: Indiana University Press, 1975).

by going to war. And this creates a vicious circle: aggression, leading to more intolerable guilt, leading to more aggression to defend against guilt.

To give a current example: it is widely held that there is a link between the Vietnam War and the Gulf War. The disaster of Vietnam left the United States with a feeling both of failure and of unbearable guilt. The statistics regarding suicide among Vietnam-era veterans are alarming. The Vietnam War left the United States with unresolved guilt and mourning, unresolved by reparation. Cambodia has been "bombed into the Stone Age," and nothing effective so far has been done to restore it. In relation to Vietnam, sanctions are still continued to this day. And in relation to their own veterans there is a constant complaint that they were neglected and not treated in a reparative way after the war.

The Gulf War, we were assured, was carried out with a promise of "NO MORE VIETNAMS," and indeed it was no Vietnam: a quick victory and no guilt, since we on the side of the angels destroyed a wicked dictator (whom of course we had installed and armed in the first place). The wicked dictator is still in power, but the whole Gulf area is, as we begin to know more and more, an unmitigated human and ecological disaster. We are not clear about the future. Shall we be sufficiently capable of admitting our part in this disaster, and genuinely try to repair the damage? Or shall we maintain our sense of physical and moral superiority and thereby sow the seeds of future wars?

A group unable to deal with its internal problems needs a war and an enemy.[11] Apart from this connection with Vietnam, the Gulf War is also, I believe, partly a necessity created by perestroika. Between wars we lived in a state of Cold War. Unconsciously, since Hiroshima, we have lived in a psychotic situation both of terror of annihilation and destructive omnipotence, the lure of annihilating power—the lure of the atomic bomb. This created an endless vicious circle between destructiveness and fear. This situation was accompanied by the usual schizoid defences: splitting and projection into the enemy, the Evil Empire; idealisation of our selves, denial, depersonalisation (the world could be destroyed at the press of a button), etc. A totally paranoid-schizoid world was established on both sides of the Iron Curtain. We lived in the world of MAD, Mutually Assured Destruction, called deterrence.

This system was undermined by perestroika. The paranoid structure could no longer be maintained. We lost the enemy. Perestroika was a time of hope, a possibility of change of attitude. But it was also a time of possible new dangers and a search for a new enemy. Giving evidence to the House Services Committee in December 1990, Edward Heath said:

11. See Vamik D. Volkan, "Nuclear Weapons and the Need to Have Enemies. A Psychoanalytic Perspective," *Psychoanalysis and the Nuclear Threat*, ed. H. B. Levin, D. Jacobs, and L. J. Rubin (Hillsdale, NJ: The Analytic Press, 1988).

Having got rid of the Cold War, we are now discussing ways in which NATO can be urged to rush to another part of the world in which there looks like being a problem, and saying "Right, you must just put it right; we don't like those people; or they don't behave as we do; and so on; and so we are going to deal with it."

NATO went in search of a new enemy to justify its continued military power.

George Kennan, the American ambassador to Russia years ago, was shocked to discover, when he was visiting Western capitals, that despite the disappearance of the supposed Soviet threat, our apparent reason for keeping a nuclear arsenal, the Western countries could not even conceive a nuclear disarmament, a world without the atom bomb. It was, he said, like an addiction. And though, apparently, much had changed with perestroika, one thing had not changed. Nuclear firepower was constantly increasing, in so-called modernisation.

So what was going on? We are familiar with those moments of hope clinically when a paranoid patient begins to give up his delusions, or when an addict begins to give up the drug and get better. The improvement is genuine. But as they get better they have to face psychic reality. With the diminishing of omnipotence (in the case of the addict, maintained by drugs) they have to face their dependence, possibly helplessness, and the fact that they are ill. With the withdrawal of projections they have to face their own destructiveness, their inner conflicts and guilt: they have to face their internal realities. Moreover, they often have to face very real losses in external reality—the devastation that their illness may have brought about: the loss of time, the loss of jobs, sometimes family, and, in the case of addicts, possibly organic damage. This is the most taxing moment in the course of an analysis. And patients need a lot of help to face this overwhelming task. And formidable manic defences can be mobilised in defence against this depressive pain, with a revival of megalomania and in its wake a return to paranoia. Similarly, socially, when we stopped believing in the evil empire we had to turn to our internal problems. We had to face our social problems: economic decline, unemployment, guilt about the Third World. In England and America in particular, we had to face the effect of our mismanagement of resources. And we had to face the guilt about the waste of resources on excessive, unnecessary, mad nuclear armaments—resources which could have been turned to education, health, industrial infrastructure, etc. The countries that prospered most after the 1939–45 war were Germany and Japan, which were not allowed to arm themselves.

Faced with that possibility of confronting our inner reality, we turned to manic defences: triumphalism. Perestroika was felt to be our triumph, an indication of our superiority. Our mentality did not change. The megalomaniac search for power, noticed by Heath, and the addiction to the bomb, noted by Kennan, were bound to create new enemies to replace Soviet Russia. Firstly, because in fact triumphalism creates new enemies; and, secondly, because we need a new evil empire into which to project our feelings of aggression.

Soon after perestroika began some members of the International Psycho-analytical Association Against Nuclear Weapons wrote papers pointing out that if we did not oppose this triumphalism we were in danger of finding a new enemy. We did not think that it would be Saddam Hussein, the pet of both East and West. We just warned against the danger of looking for a new enemy. But in some way this new enemy was very appropriate since he was in a similar position. The West has lost its enemy, the U.S.S.R.; Saddam has lost his enemy, Iran, probably to face intolerable social and economic tensions. We were as well matched with Saddam Hussein as Mrs. Thatcher was with Galtieri over the Falklands, each facing a restless situation at home. But now all this is on a terrifyingly larger scale.

I may have digressed somewhat from the theme of ambivalence. And yet the conflict between life and death forces within us and the defences against it are active not only in individuals but also in groups. Ambivalence is part of the human condition and the price of denying it is very high indeed, both in the individual and in groups. In our nuclear age, the price may even be the survival of the human race.

ARE THERE RATIONALLY UNDECIDABLE ARGUMENTS?

Manfred Frank

Translated by Ruth Morris and Barry Allen

Great importance attaches to the question of whether conflicts that are beyond rational resolution can occur in negotiations designed to achieve agreement. It was on the basis of this question that Jean-François Lyotard hoped to assess the fate of the modern age. For if conflicts are more and more becoming fundamentally irresolvable—as he believed—then reason no longer counts as the supreme mediating authority: we are entering the *condition postmoderne*. Jürgen Habermas has challenged this argument, countering that the lack of an expansive conception of reason does not necessarily lead to the dead end defined by Lyotard. One can, Habermas says, accept a classical (say, Kantian) definition of rationality—in which assertions (and their grounds) must be universally true or false—but also feel no need for a final authority (God, tradition, transcendental subject, or absolute spirit) on which to rely: the universal truth or falsehood of propositions can in any case be guaranteed by the peaceableness of the participants in any discourse. All that they need do is recognize procedural principles such as nonaggression, fair allocation of opportunities to speak, and so forth. Observing

Originally published in *Common Knowledge* 9.1 (Winter 2003): 119–31, as part of "Peace and Mind: Seriatim Symposium on Dispute, Conflict, and Enmity Part 4: Secret Accomplices." © 2003 by Duke University Press.

Common Knowledge 25:1–3

DOI 10.1215/0961754X-7299126

principles whose violation would contradict the participants' declared aim of a cooperative quest for truth is, according to Habermas, an uncomplicated condition, free of any suspicion of metaphysics.

In an essay ("Die Grenzen der Verständigung") that I wrote in 1988, I explained why Lyotard's plea for postmodernity—as a situation in which differences are irresolvable—is unpersuasive. I also showed how easy it would be for Habermas to dismiss that kind of objection. It has generally been supposed that, in reaching my conclusion, I wanted to subscribe to all the implications of Habermas's theory of consensus formation; but this is not the case. Rather, I believe that, in negotiations designed to achieve agreement, there can indeed be rationally undecidable conflicts, though it is my contention that Lyotard's "différend" and similar constructions provide a workable approach for resolving them.

I

Lyotard's *Le différend* (1983) advances the thesis that conflicts might be insoluble even under ideal conditions of discourse.[1] Lyotard's is a very strong claim, because it questions the mediating capacity of reason even when understood, in Habermasian postmetaphysical terms, as discursive intersubjectivity.

Lyotard's thesis is simple. In explicit accord with Wittgenstein, he denies the existence of a "*super*ordination" of language, claiming that there exists a diversity of language games that are not reducible to each other and that cannot be derived from a single linguistic supraconcept.[2] Within this diversity of rules for language use, Lyotard distinguishes, further, between rules for the use of sentences and rules for speech-acts. The latter are rules for the use of sentences relative to "transphrastic" and "pragmatic" actions, such as *narrating, giving a lecture, leading someone astray*, and so on. Lyotard views both speech-acts and the use of sentences as governed by rules that prescribe linguistic practices only generally. The transition between speech-events of one type and another remains untheorized—there is, after all, no universal suprarule to regulate usages that violate the rules. Thus occurs the dearth of validation that Lyotard calls a "tort": a wrong or evil that no mediating authority can remedy. Since the (nonexistent) suprarules of discourse are what the modern age has meant by "reason," conflicts between pragmatic rules cannot be mediated rationally; by nature, discourses tend to be agonistic. Darwin's imagery of the struggle for survival finds its way into the postmodern view of discursive exchange in the simile of language at war with itself. Like all wars, this one is carried out by means of naked power and without an arbiter.

---

1. Jean-François Lyotard, *Le différend* (Paris: Editions de Minuit, 1983).

2. Ludwig Wittgenstein, *Philosophical Investigations*, trans. G. E. M. Anscombe (Oxford: Blackwell, 1968), 44, no. 97.

Lyotard's view of the nature of discourse is brutally realistic but also (fortunately) incorrect, because it is self-contradictory on a number of levels. First, Lyotard's struggle against the fetishizing of *langue* as an unvarying and hard-as-steel governor over each individual case of *parole* is inconsistent. He has himself an equally fetishistic view of the ineluctable mandate of individual language games, and that is the only reason he is able to maintain the absurd idea that any shift from one system of rules to another—since the transition is achieved without suprarules anticipated a priori—is invalid. If we limit ourselves to the case of rational arguments, it is obvious to everyone that arguments do not compel the consent of partners in dialogue by appeal to sensory or intuitive evidence, nor even by the sheer overwhelming finality of the logic. Arguments do not obtain consent through involuntary reflexes (like a blow to the kneecap) but through rational motivation. To want to subject such motivation to rules would be tantamount to the kind of terrorism of which Lyotard accuses consensus theory.

Second, Wittgenstein himself derided the notion that we could derive speech-acts from rules: fetishistic belief in the *deductive necessity* of speech-acts is, he said, "a mythology." A transition between sentences, he told Friedrich Waismann, is not like the mortar between two bricks,[3] bonding them securely. To confuse the application of a rule with the unerring output of an ideally inflexible machine[4] is like dreaming of a rule that regulates its own application—a dream leading to infinite regress.[5] Lyotard too broke with the representationist paradigm (according to which words depict perceptions or representations); and it is precisely for this reason that Lyotard, like Wittgenstein, had to reconsider the prevailing agreement on how we schematize the world. We see the world as mediated by semantic rules that replace a shared perception of reality with a harmony among ways of talking. But if neither the paradigm of perceptual evidence nor that of deductive necessity can be applied to these semantic rules, then neither a shift between systems of rules, nor even the application of rules, can be regarded as necessary. Therefore, Lyotard's metaphorical shudder—his shudder at the lack of justification for any shift between sets of rules for the use of sentences or types of discourse—is a particularly defenseless example of the language fetishism that he appropriately criticizes as a typical example of the modern penchant for metaphysics.

Third, Lyotard's theory breaks down when explaining its basic subject: discursive conflict. For if, as he assumes, differends occur because there is no

---

3. Friedrich Waismann, *Wittgenstein and the Vienna Circle: Conversations Recorded by Friedrich Waismann*, ed. Brian McGuinness, trans. Joachim Schulte and Brian McGuinness (New York: Barnes and Noble, 1979), 154–55.

4. Wittgenstein, *Philosophical Investigations*, 78, nos. 193–94.

5. Waismann, *Wittgenstein and the Vienna Circle*, 154–55.

third linguistic protocol in sight extending over the two conflicting protocols and common to them both, then it would be utterly impossible for conflicts to occur. Discursive conflicts *presuppose* not only a common referent but also a mutual intention to reach an understanding. If even one of these conditions is not met, the result is at most a divergence of statements, but not a conflict. Conflicts presuppose a common, mutual reference, as *that about which* there is conflict. Someone who asserts nothing can moreover dispute nothing; a person who speaks about nothing does not really *speak*, and therefore his or her utterance may have any number of effects but cannot be part of a dispute. And since Lyotard's own utterances seek to be understood as assertions (and consequently as fallible, contestable claims), his argument becomes entangled in performative contradiction: he has to concede that, lacking universal rules of language, it is impossible to decide on claims to validity.

II

But what does such criticism of Lyotard's thinking say about the possibility of rationally undecidable, argumentation-based conflicts?[6] Simply: that the idea must be presented in a way different from that suggested by Lyotard (and by those theoretically close to him). The conclusion of a logically incoherent argument may be a correct conclusion, just as a system constructed in strictly logical terms may be the work of a paranoiac.

For in acts of communication, differends do indeed occur that must remain undecided. However, the undecidability of discursive conflicts does not depend, as Lyotard would have it, on the inconceivability of a metarule mediating between various speech-acts or between rules for the use of sentences. When conflicting arguments are beyond decision, it is because the claims to validity that they raise cannot be assessed by appealing to a transdiscursive (substantial, absolute) criterion of truth. Habermas must also accept this situation when he places himself—no less firmly than Lyotard—outside the traditional framework of so-called metaphysics. In Habermas's case, the absence of a transcendent criterion of truth is compensated for specifically by the intersubjective organization of the discourse. We must reach an understanding about the legitimacy of our claims to validity, not *although* but precisely *because* we cannot fall back on a criterion of verification authenticated by monologic evidence or logical conclusiveness. Sensory evidence, moreover, is only subjective evidence and does not ascend to the rank of a partial—and also disputable—truth, unless affirmed

---

6. I wish to restrict myself to this category—differences between other uses of language create no differends: they assert nothing and dispute nothing.

by a number of people in intersubjective speech. But then, proposed norms are dependent on interpretations by the individuals involved in the discourse. In the words of Schleiermacher:

> Now that language is an adequate guarantee for us of the identity of the process, i.e. that I am certain that someone who says the same word as I must also construct the same inner image and thereby form the same particular organic effects, admittedly only appears as a presupposition which must continually be proved and, by being proved, will be declared to be true. This must continually be tried out. . . . We are continually testing and so are also testing in the perception of the identity of construction. All communication about external objects is a constant continuation of the test as to whether all people construct their ideas in identical fashion.[7]

Put another way: if language can no longer be understood as reflecting things or events, on the one hand, and mental structures, on the other hand, then the identity of our semantic schematization—but no less, our agreement over claims to truth—can emerge only from a fundamentally unstable shaping of consensus. "Fundamentally unstable" should be understood as meaning: fundamentally subject to withdrawal and consequently devoid of any established, timeless validity. Since I cannot regulate my interpretation of another's meaning, nor even of the facts, by a timeless criterion of truth, I must make allowance for the other's interpretation of the world in my assertions. Doing so will lead to my leaving undecided a whole series of questions, even if I myself am more inclined to one interpretation than another. There thus opens up a field of veritable differends that in all respects satisfy the procedural requirements of consensus theory, though without obeying the Habermasian rhetoric of ideal agreement. Dissent is an authentic and even normal case, meriting respect, of a nonviolent discourse oriented toward achieving agreement (and democratically organized). Indeed, because individual (and hence fundamentally pluralistic) interpretations of the world are inescapable, dissent is more likely than consensus. And about consensus, I can in fact always be wrong: there is no absolute criterion for ascertaining the continued existence of consensus, "precisely because . . . misunderstanding will never entirely go away."[8]

It is to Romanticism that we owe the first consensus theory of meaning and truth. Friedrich Schleiermacher was the first to expound it, while studying the rules according to which a (semantic or argumentative) dispute between

7. Friedrich Schleiermacher, "Schematism and Language," in *Hermeneutics and Criticism and Other Writings*, trans. and ed. Andrew Bowie, Cambridge Texts in the History of Philosophy (Cambridge: Cambridge University Press, 1988), 273–74.

8. Schleiermacher, "Über den Begriff der Hermeneutik mit Bezug auf F. A. Wolfs Andeutungen und Asts Lehrbuch," in *Hermeneutik und Kritik*, ed. Manfred Frank (Frankfurt: Suhrkamp, 1977), 328.

partners in a dialogue can occur and be overcome. Disagreement may occur over the identification of objects (which Schleiermacher calls "the maximum of the dispute")[9] or in divergent qualifications of one and the same object. If I am unable to prove that the "formal rules" of proceeding discursively (Schleiermacher says, *dialectically*) have been infringed,[10] then I must take account of my partner's divergent view in whatever I assert as true; for I no longer have the option of dismissing its legitimacy. As Schleiermacher writes, "We renounce such universal validity not only because of the inadequacy of our resources," but also because linguistic unity would stifle the plurality of individual perspectives and thus the possibility of linguistic and cognitive innovation.[11] Hence every consensus contains a residual misunderstanding that will never altogether go away, and this is why no consensus as to either meaning or the interpretation of the world can ever be final or universally valid. In other words, the potential for dissent belongs insuperably to every effort at reaching a mutual understanding.

It must, however, be realized that the Romantic conviction of the insuperability of all disputes takes advantage of two premises, neither of which can be reconciled with Lyotard's theory of the differend. The first opposes the thought that an entire conscious life might assume the form of a system; the second questions the accessibility of the absolute to our knowledge. These two forms of skepticism are of course closely interwoven and can barely be distinguished.

It is striking that the majority of sources for early Romantic speculation are themselves fragmentary in form. Does this fact of style indicate an abandonment of the need for systematic coherence? Not at all; for fragments are not aphorisms, which can stand on their own, to be read and thought about independently. Fragments are by definition parts and hence imply a whole—but a whole that cannot be constructed or conveyed, bit by bit, in speculative reflection. The impossibility of presenting philosophy systematically is, however, justified systematically. The following fragment of Novalis is characteristic of this paradoxical tendency:

A true philosophical system must be all freedom and infinity or, to coin a conspicuous phrase, "unsystematicity reduced to a system." Only such a system can avoid the errors of systematicity and stand accused of neither injustice nor anarchy.[12]

We find an echo of this notion in a fragment that Friedrich Schlegel added to his friend's collection, *Blüthenstaub*:

9. Schleiermacher, "Allgemeine Einleitung zur Dialektik," in Frank, *Hermeneutik*, 429.

10. Schleiermacher, "Allgemeine Einleitung zur Dialektik," 440.

11. Schleiermacher, "Allgemeine Einleitung zur Dialektik," 422.

12. Novalis, *Schriften*, ed. Paul Kluckhohn and Richard Samuel, 5 vols. (Stuttgart: W. Kohlhammer, 1960–88), 2:288–89, no. 648.

Once ardor is rendered absolute and cannot be renounced, one has no way out but to contradict oneself constantly and to connect opposing extremes. This is inevitable when the principle of contradiction is involved, and one's only choice is whether to behave with a show of long-suffering or to ennoble necessity by acknowledging free choice.[13]

This fragment of Schlegel's contains, in abstract, the Romantic paradox: in the absence of an Archimedean point, philosophy cannot find a keystone for its edifice of ideas. But then, thinking remains open; conflicting proposals for the definitive understanding of the Supreme Being—as in Schleiermacher—can no longer be settled by reference to a final arbitration authority, nor reduced to one of two alternatives. Thus, contradiction between statements about what essentially holds the world together is preordained. Under such circumstances, the best way to remain loyal to the absolute is by practicing irony against every one-sided statement about it—that is, by making the contradicting elements cancel each other out. This procedure does not lead for the Romantics—as it does for Hegel—to a unique and true formula for interpreting the world, but rather, as Schlegel says about his own philosophy, to a "system of fragments and a progression of projects."[14]

But what is involved in the paradox of thought as at once unsystematic and insuperably systematic? The two claims are irreconcilable yet ineluctable. However greatly the fragmentary form may strive to detach itself from the fundamental error of a thought process that insistently defines and reifies—however greatly it strives to detach itself from metaphysics and its compulsive systematicity—even the fragment remains in thrall to the form of a system. If, as Novalis says, every system produces injustices, the opposite obstacle—anarchy: thinking under the influence of inspiration and caprice—must still be negotiated.[15] However, there is a more obvious reason why systematicity cannot be renounced: without an awareness of the whole from which it is detached and with which it should become integrated, a thought would not be a fragment, would not be a part. Nor could it, without reference to a common intent, enter into a relationship of contradiction to other interpretations of the absolute—for contradictions emerge only between statements that make incompatible attributions to the same object; and even noncontradictory judgments presuppose an identity of reference. As we have seen, it is precisely this elementary consideration that Lyotard's idea of an irreconcilable conflict-without-conciliating-norm disregards. If there were no such norm, then differentiated statements or rules about statements would

---

13. Novalis, *Schriften*, 2:423, no. 26.

14. Friedrich Schlegel, *Kritische Ausgabe*, ed. Ernst Behler, 35 vols. (Munich: Paderborn; Vienna: Schöningh, 1958–95), 15:160, no. 857.

15. Novalis is referring to a totalization of anything one-sided. Cf. Schlegel: "Once anything becomes a system, it is no longer absolute" (*Kritische Ausgabe*, 12:5); "any sentence, any book, as long as it does not contradict itself, is incomplete" (*Kritische Ausgabe*, 13:83, no. 647).

be utterly incapable of contradicting each other for lack of a common standard. The only genuine fragment is an unsuccessful whole. The objection that fragments make multiple perspectives-on-the-whole possible, and that each perspective consists of far more than a single point of view, entirely fails to contradict the fundamental Romantic idea that "only the whole . . . [is] *real*. Only that thing would be absolutely real that could never be part of anything else."[16]

Since, however, the idea of the whole remains merely regulative and cannot actually be realized,[17] the system of fragments must be missing its keystone: the unique perspective at the core. Several candidates for truth arrive on the scene and, for lack of a positively final and authoritative arbiter, none can be eliminated. Instead, each claim to be the sole truth must be regarded as decidedly ironic, and from this Schlegel concludes that all truth is relative and that all knowledge is only (in Kant's sense) symbolic:[18]

> The proposition that all truth is relative could easily lead to general skepticism. For example, if all truth is relative, then so too is the proposition that all truth is relative. . . . But that is not the end of the matter: one must acknowledge not only this proposition, but also that the entire system of philosophy is relative. All truth is relative—but together with that proposition another must be coordinated: *There is essentially no such thing as error.* (12:95)

This position sounds incredible, and apparently in direct contradiction of the fundamental postulate of transcendental philosophy: philosophy aims for the absolute and takes the form of absolute unity (12:4–5). However, Schlegel specifies that while philosophy begins with skepticism, which is *"a completely negative condition"* (12:4), skepticism cannot have the last word. For no matter what, the principle just quoted remains applicable: the true is the whole—only the whole is real, *"and the part is only in the whole"* (12:77). Truth is attained by destroying the error of the finite (12:6). An ironic or polemical method confronts a limited statement—precisely because of its limitation—with others, so that their finitude is revealed as mere appearance and thus overcome. At which point, it becomes possible to see the systematically coherent whole, though only as a regulative idea and not as an idea about which there can be intelligent dispute:

> The truth emerges when opposing errors neutralize each other. *Absolute truth cannot be acknowledged*; and it is this that bears witness to the freedom of thought and the mind [*Geist*]. Were absolute truth to be found, this would put an end to the vocation of the mind [*Geschäft des Geistes*], and it would perforce cease to be, since it exists only in [forever unfulfilled] activity. (12:93)

16. Novalis, *Schriften*, 2:242, no. 445; cf. Schlegel, *Kritische Ausgabe*, 12:78.

17. Novalis, *Schriften*, 2:252.

18. Schlegel, *Kritische Ausgabe*, 18:417, no. 1149.

This passage outlines the program of a Hegelianism devoid of its culmination in absolute knowledge—a tale of the unconstrained relativization of all merely individual convictions in favor of a whole that can never be understood as such. Hence *"all knowledge is symbolic"* (12:92–93), meaning that knowledge is related not demonstratively but allegorically to the absolute, since in its relativity knowledge merely hints allegorically at the tendency to absoluteness, without actually attaining it. In this hypothesis, Schlegel sees not humiliation but a freeing of the mind. A fixation on absolute, definitive knowledge is a kind of "mental gout" (18:221, no. 318), ossifying the perpetually lively mind, which develops by becoming aware of the narrowness of every position it attains on its never-ending path to the infinite. Without a tendency toward the absolute, the mind could of course not behave "polemically" vis-à-vis the finite; and for that reason, those who want the authentically radical modern (or even postmodern) age to begin with increasing detachment from the idea of the absolute are mistaken. Were there no orientation to a nonrelative One [*nicht-relatives Eins*], the various interpretations of it that appear throughout history would be unable, utterly, to contradict each other and hence demolish each other.

Thus, the fragmentary form of early Romantic philosophical writing is connected with the idea that philosophy is by nature inconclusive and, as a consequence, inevitably unsystematic. These qualities in turn feed on doubt about the cognitive accessibility of an Archimedean point beyond all relativity—a point that idealism called "the absolute" and that Lyotard calls "the metadiscourse above individual discourses."

III

In my view, the early Romantic paradigm makes it possible to propose a differend that avoids all the dead ends of Lyotard's work and nevertheless does justice to the basic inspiration (for instance) of neostructuralist philosophy of the recent past, with its love of difference and division. If it is no longer possible for claims to validity to be derived from a *fundamentum inconcussum* (metaphysical self-consciousness) or brought to a definitive conclusion by reference to absolute knowledge, then the last word remains with the interpretive community, with its never entirely harmonious attributions of meaning and validity. By way of conclusion, I want to illustrate this point using two examples from modern theory: Jacques Derrida's thoughts on *"différance"* (understood as the undecidability of interpretation) and the W. V. Quine–Donald Davidson thesis of the inscrutability of reference and the indeterminacy of meaning. Both of these, I would say, present genuine candidates for differends that, even within negotiations designed to achieve agreement, are discursively insuperable.

Derrida shares two basic convictions with Schleiermacher. The first is that reference to subjective (mental) phenomena can only occur through the mediation of signs. (Compare Saussure's well-known observation that the mind, prior to its articulation in language through the "*chaîne phonatoire*," is just as amorphous as the "*matière phonique*" itself,[19] acquiring a shape only through its precipitation in the "*unité pensée-son*.") But even then—this is the second of Derrida's points—signs can never perform a precise "identifying" function. Schleiermacher accounts for such a conviction by claiming that every sign whose meaning depends on the act of an individual nevertheless requires interpretation. Derrida justifies his proposition by thoroughly radicalizing Saussure's principle of difference, according to which signs, since they are not articulated by nature, derive their identity from relation to a whole corpus of signs. Thus the meaning of sign a would be conveyed by relations of "being-different-than" vis-à-vis signs $b, c, d, e, f,$ and so on. Now, there is no compelling reason to assume that the chain of oppositions would be finite. Consequently, the semantic identity of a term is a function of an open system of perpetual differentiation, excluding the possibility of any term's self-presence or self-identity. Following Derrida, this point can also be worded more dramatically: the meaning of every sign is separated from itself; the identity of the sign being thus split, any determination of its meaning becomes undecidable.

I consider this notion correct. And I consider it an ominous objection to the semantic optimism of the "code model of understanding," whereby signs are understood by recognizing, in spoken *output*, the identical form of an *input* to a rigidly closed grammar that has been internalized by learning.

If Derrida is right, then where the differend begins is not at the stage when claims to validity of statements or proposed norms are discussed, but earlier, when the understanding of those elements that comprise language systems is established. The meaning of a sign is beyond decision. It must be conceded, however, that Derrida goes too far: if what he calls *différance* were total, it would no longer be possible to say what he does say—namely, that meaning is always realized as difference—because even this formulation presupposes a minimum identity of meaning. In performative terms, it is contradictory to claim, in the form of a statement and with the purpose of being understood, that a sign can mean anything whatever at any time. However, it remains the case that no sign need maintain the specific interpretation that I, for historical and biographical reasons, attribute to it in a given interpretive context.

The Quine school's reflections on the indeterminacy of meaning present us with a scarcely less radical questioning of semantic optimism. "Comprehensi-

19. Ferdinand de Saussure, *Cours de linguistique générale*, 3–103, printed in *Cahiers Ferdinand de Saussure* 15 (1957): 37–38.

bility" is an elementary criterion of validity among the categories accredited by Habermasian "universal pragmatics." Hence an attack on the possibility of my inquiring into the reference of a given semantic sign seriously undermines the utility of my counterfactual assumption that my interlocutor assigns the same meaning to the sign as I do.

Quine made his case for the indeterminacy of translation (an indeterminacy that transpires not only between different languages, but even earlier, "at home") while also radicalizing his thesis on the underdetermination of empirical theories. The latter may be accounted for as a combination of two assumptions. The first is the suggestion of C. S. Peirce that we understand the meaning of a proposition as an inferential process that includes our interpretive ability and is dependent on its proving its worth. The meaning of a proposition is what is supported by the totality of statements substantiating its truth; and as this process of interpretation is empirically endless, it follows that meaning and information, language and theory, cannot be separated. The second assumption is Quine's so-called holism, which proposes that theories be tested against reality only as a whole, not in individual propositions. If a view of reality expressed in language is completely laden with theory (and hence dependent on interpretation—that is, if distinguishing between "the world as it really is" and "convenient, but metaphorical, ways of talking about the world" no longer makes sense),[20] then we cannot exclude the possibility that mutually incompatible theories can each appropriately interpret the same set of experimentally guaranteed, empirical results. "In a word, they [theories] can be logically incompatible and empirically equivalent."[21] On the basis of what criteria, then, may theories or languages be selected? Quine admits only pragmatic considerations of the greatest possible usefulness: theories are not representations of theory-independent reality, but "tools for handling reality." An example of such a pragmatic consideration would be a theory's simplicity and clarity.

This purely pragmatic criterion (of simplicity and usefulness) is also knocked out of hand as soon as we begin looking for criteria for the communication of insights from one language or theory to another. While in the earlier case, theory remained *under*determined by empirical data (which, at best, provide boundary conditions), in this instance theory is utterly *in*determinate. Just as the same stock of information is open to various theories or languages, so translating the interpretations of empirical findings can be performed according to various "translation manuals." But now, simplicity can no longer act as a guide on the path to the truth. Quine comments (in conversation):

20. Richard Rorty, "Non-Reductive Physicalism," in *Objectivity, Relativism, and Truth: Philosophical Papers*, vol. 1 (Cambridge: Cambridge University Press, 1991), 116.

21. W. V. Quine, "On the Reasons for Indeterminacy of Translation," *Journal of Philosophy* 67 (1970): 179.

The simplest mapping of language A into language B followed by the simplest mapping of B into language C does not necessarily give the same mapping of A into C as does the simplest direct mapping of A into C. Similarly, the simplest mapping of A into B followed by the simplest mapping of B into A does not necessarily map every item in A back onto itself.[22]

While the various possible theories or languages are underdetermined by experiential data, the criteria for choosing the best translation are not even limited by pragmatic considerations like simplicity. When translating a word or sentence—but, more basically, as early as the stage of understanding the sentence—we completely lose all contact with reality and do no more than compare two *empirically underdetermined* theories or languages with each other:

As Quine has put it in conversation, that there is nothing to be right or wrong about in translation means that several different translation manuals fit the same states and distributions of all elementary particles.[23]

Here once again, it seems to me, is a description of a genuine semantic differend. In his *Inquiries into Truth and Interpretation* (1985), Donald Davidson tries to tone down Quine's conclusion by introducing a "principle of charity." But, if I understand correctly, this principle plays, not an epistemic, but a purely pragmatic, role, similar to the Quinian preference for simplicity in theory or language, and so leads just as little out of the differend as Habermas's similarly motivated, but far more forcefully devised, principle of consensus. Both serve only as (unquestionably crucial) regulative principles for orienting our understanding—and a theory like Lyotard's must permit a remark of that kind to be made about it. If, however, I can show that negotiations designed to achieve agreement cannot manage without a few counterfactual presuppositions, I have in no way proven on that account that it is impossible for "semantic" and "veritative" differends, which are insoluble because they are beyond decision, to occur. On the contrary, it must be expected that they will occur, since the reality that confronts our conscious lives does not come with the lens required to read it.

Nor can I entirely defeat the hermeneutic underdetermination of reality by means of a cooperative search for truth, though it is true that I *must* contemplate consensus as the goal of dialogue. For reality, after all, is not only relatively indifferent to holistically conceived systems of language or theory. The latter intensify their underdetermination in the process of translation and mutual under-

22. Dagfinn Føllesdal reports this conversational observation in his plausible reconstruction of "Indeterminacy of Translation and Underdetermination of the Theory of Nature," *Dialectica* 27.3–4 (1973): 295.

23. Føllesdal, "Indeterminacy of Translation," 295.

standing. But actually, the indeterminacy of meaning begins "at home" (here Derrida is more radical than Quine, and even than Davidson as interpreted by Richard Rorty). For not only is there no guarantee of the correctness of translation between theories or languages; there are no absolutely applicable criteria for systematizing or constructing our reality—as Schleiermacher puts it—even within one and the same linguistic system. Every act of understanding alien speech implies the possibility of a different understanding, whose source is the individual. Just as reality is not of itself meaningful, so too the signs by means of which my neighbor tries to make him- or herself understandable to me do not of themselves signify or bear meaning. I must try to understand them by means of abductive inferences, in which process any command I may have of grammar and other conventionalities may serve me as a motive, but not as a ground or guarantee, of interpretation.

In this respect, semantic differends are intrinsically programmed into negotiations designed to achieve agreement; they are inevitable. However, they can never be total, for their very identification takes advantage of the possibility of some understanding, however incomplete. In this sense, it may well be true that the differend is the source of all innovation and the reason why our world sustains such diverse and individual nuances—why the shaping of consensus will never lead us to a uniform symbolism that everyone must make use of in the same way.

UNLOADING THE SELF-REFUTATION CHARGE

Barbara Herrnstein Smith

Philosophers, logicians, and those whom they have instructed demonstrate recurrently—in classrooms, at conferences, in the pages of professional journals—the "incoherence" of certain theoretical positions, for example, relativism, skepticism, perspectivism, constructivism, and postmodernism. They often do this by exposing to their audiences—students, colleagues, and readers—how such positions are self-refuting. The positions so exposed are generally those that diverge from the relevant philosophical orthodoxy. Though presumably not impossible, it is certainly not common to find a neo-Platonist or neo-Kantian charged with self-refutation. Defenses of orthodox positions are, to be sure, charged with hollow arguments, but the charge here is characteristically petitio principii, begging the question: that is, circular self-affirmation rather than specular self-refutation. The classic agents and victims of self-refutation, however, are Protagoras, the relativist; Hume, the epistemological skeptic; Nietzsche, the perspectivist; and, in our own era, postmodernists such as Kuhn, Feyerabend, Foucault, Derrida, Lyotard, Goodman, and Rorty, whose individual and collective incoherence,

Originally published in *Common Knowledge* 2.2 (Fall 1993): 81–95. © 1993.

An earlier version of this essay was delivered at a conference, "Self and Deception: An Interdisciplinary and Intercultural Exploration," East-West Center, Honolulu, August 1992.

Common Knowledge 25:1–3

DOI 10.1215/0961754X-7299138

self-contradiction, and self-refutation have been demonstrated by, among others, Davidson, Putnam, and Habermas.[1]

As the foregoing list suggests, the agents/victims of self-refutation are also usually philosophical innovators: that is, theorists who have articulated original substantive views on various matters of philosophical interest: knowledge, language, science, and so forth. When their self-refutation is being exposed, however, they are seen primarily in their role of negative critics of orthodox thought: that is, as deniers, rejecters, and abandoners of views that are widely experienced as intuitively correct and manifestly true. Indeed, even prior to and independent of any formal demonstration of their self-refutation, the views of such theorists tend to be experienced by disciplinary philosophers—and those whom they have instructed—as self-evidently absurd.

Because various elements of the orthodoxies in question—that is, those from which the views of the skeptic/relativist/postmodernist diverge—are also widely seen as sustaining important communal goods (e.g., the authority of law, the possibility of moral and aesthetic judgment, the progress of science) and as averting corresponding evils (e.g., social anarchy, moral paralysis, aesthetic decline, intellectual chaos), the questioning or denial of those elements is also widely seen as, at the least, communally perilous and often morally criminal as well. It is not surprising, then, that the theoretical innovators mentioned above have often been demonized. Nor is it surprising that much of the energy of disciplinary philosophy has been and continues to be devoted to demonstrating—as the self-refutation charge itself proclaims—that the apparently dangerous demons are actually impotent, self-deceived fools. That, in fact, seems to be the point of the self-refutation charge: to show, so to speak, that the devil is an ass.

What officially justifies the charge of self-refutation is a manifestly self-canceling, self-disabling statement: "All generalizations are false," "Relativism is (absolutely) true," "It is wrong to make value judgments," etc. What more commonly elicits the charge, however, is some set of analyses and arguments that is said to "come down to" such a statement or, duly paraphrased, to have the "logical form" of such a statement. The justice of the charge, in either case, may be more or less readily acknowledged by the person accused, who may then attempt to eliminate the problem through some appropriate self-qualification. For example, the relatively alarming "All generalizations are false" may be amended to the relatively unexceptionable "Most generalizations have exceptions." Or, more strik-

1. Individual instances are cited where discussed, below. For recent rehearsals, collections, and surveys, see Harvey Siegel, *Relativism Refuted: A Critique of Contemporary Epistemological Relativism* (Dordrecht: Reidel, 1987); Michael Krausz, ed., *Relativism: Interpretation and Confrontation* (South Bend: University of Notre Dame Press, 1989); and Larry Laudan, *Science and Relativism: Some Key Controversies in the Philosophy of Science* (Chicago: University of Chicago Press, 1990).

ingly, acknowledgment of the justice of the charge of self-contradiction has had important effects on the development of the sociology of science.[2]

Charges of self-refutation do not always, however, yield genial or self-transformative resolutions. On the contrary, although a particular charge may be manifestly on target from the perspective of many members of some immediate audience, it may also appear empty and irrelevant to the alleged agent/victim and to his or her partisans. Indeed, a charge of self-refutation is, often enough, a sign of head-on intellectual collision and also an occasion of mutually frustrating nonengagement or impasse. Accordingly, it provides an instructive illustration of what could be called the microdynamics of incommensurability.

Although I am sympathetic to many of the views of the unorthodox theorists mentioned above (and have developed some relatively unorthodox views myself[3]), my purpose here is not to defend any of them (theorists or views) per se or to "refute" any specific charges leveled against them. It is, rather, to examine the more general rhetorical and psychological operations of the charge itself and, to some extent, its institutional operations as well. Though necessarily limited, the examination will, I hope, illuminate some issues of broader current interest and, perhaps, make the charge of self-refutation, in some quarters, somewhat less *automatic.*

Tricks of Thought

In the dialogue that bears his name, the good-natured, mathematically precocious Theaetetus offers, in reply to Socrates' questions about the nature of knowledge, the teachings of Protagoras: "Man is the measure," and so on. Through cross-questioning, certain implications and difficulties of the doctrine are explored. Protagoras himself is imagined risen from the grave and arguing in his own defense. Other difficulties, notably an "exquisite" self-contradiction, are drawn out. These are acknowledged by Theaetetus, now delivered to better understanding.[4]

2. The crucial charge here has been tu quoque, that is, unwarranted self-exception and thus (if condemnations are involved) implicit self-condemnation. See Steve Woolgar, ed., *Knowledge and Reflexivity: New Frontiers in the Sociology of Knowledge*, (London: Sage, 1988); Malcolm Ashmore, *The Reflective Thesis: Writing Sociology of Scientific Knowledge* (Chicago: University of Chicago Press, 1989); Andrew Pickering, "From Science as Knowledge to Science as Practice," in *Science as Practice and Culture*, ed. Pickering (Chicago: University of Chicago Press, 1992), 1–28.

3. *Contingencies of Value: Alternative Perspectives for Critical Theory* (Cambridge: Harvard University Press, 1988).

4. Plato, *Theaetetus* (170a–172c, 177c–179b). The translation by M. J. Levett is appended to Myles Burnyeat's study of the text, *The Theaetetus of Plato* (Indianapolis: Hackett, 1990). I draw here also on the following: Edward N. Lee, "'Hoist with His Own Petard': Ironic and Comic Elements in Plato's Critique of Protagoras (Tht. 161–71)," in *Exegesis and Argument*, ed. Lee, A. P. D. Mourelatos, and R. M. Rorty (Assen: Van Gorcum, 1973), 225–61; Myles Burnyear, "Protagoras and Self-Refutation in Plato's Theaetetus," *The Philosophical Review* 85 (April 1976): 172–95; David Bostock, *Plato's Theaetetus* (Oxford: Clarendon Press, 1988); and Rosemary Desjardins, *The Rational Enterprise: Logos in Plato's Theaetetus* (Albany: State University of New York Press, 1990).

This is the archetypal exposure of self-refutation, both in its dramatic, triangular form—student, false teacher, true teacher—(to which I return below) and in the logical/rhetorical details of the turnabout. Through the explications and applications of subsequent commentators, Socrates' exposure of self-refutation becomes the authority for charging, and the model for exposing, the incoherence of latter-day Protagoreans.

Man is the measure of all things, says the Protagorean, or *Each thing is as it is perceived.* Thus he denies the possibility of (objective, absolute) truth and (objectively) valid knowledge. But then he cannot claim that his own doctrine is (objectively, absolutely) true or the product of (objectively valid) knowledge. Thus also he declares the (objective, absolute) truth of the views that disagree with his own. But, then, he acknowledges that what he says is false and worthless. His doctrine refutes itself.

These moves are simple enough. So also is the problem with them, namely that they hinge on dubious paraphrase and dubious inference. For the self-refutation charge to have logical force (as officially measured), the mirror reversal it indicates must be exact: What the self-refuter explicitly, wittingly denies must be the same as what she unwittingly, implicitly affirms. Accordingly, the charge fails to go off properly, and the supposed demonstration is declared a trick or an error, if the restatement diverges too obviously or too crucially from the original[5] or if the supposedly implied affirmation is itself questionable: if, for example, Protagoras had actually said *"It appears to me that* man is the measure of all things . . . ,"* or obviously meant his doctrine to be taken as only *relatively* true, or obviously meant to affirm only that each thing is as it is perceived *to those who perceive it that way.* Similarly, in the case of the related tu quoque charge, the trait evidently condemned by the self-refuter must be the same as that thereby exhibited, as in the (social-)scientific theory that claims: "Scientific theories are (mere) reflections of the social interests of those who produce and promote them." Here the charge fails if the supposed self-refuter disavows the "mere" and the presumably self-*excepting* claim is revealed as (or transformed into) an explicitly and flagrantly self-*exemplifying* one: "You charge my theory of the social interests of all theories with reflecting social interests? But *of course* it does: it could hardly prosper otherwise!" Thus, as in the schoolyard exchange, the target of the taunt ("You, too. So *there!*") turns the tables back again ("Me, too. So *what?*").

5. When the texts of fertile and original theorists (Nietzsche or Foucault, for example) are paraphrased as one-line "theses," "claims," or *"p's,"* the assumption is that specific analyses, examples, and counterproposals are irrelevant to the identity of a theoretical position, and also that particulars of verbal idiom—diction, voice, imagery, style, etc.—are irrelevant to its force, uptake, interest, and appropriability. This assumption, fundamental to the operations of formal logic, is implicitly contested by the rhetoricist/pragmatist line in contemporary theory. See, for example, Stanley Fish, *Doing What Comes Naturally: Change, Rhetoric, and the Practice of Theory in Literary and Legal Studies* (Durham: Duke University Press, 1989), and, of course, the works of Nietzsche and Foucault.

An error or perhaps trick of this kind—that is, dubious paraphrase and/or dubious inference—occurs, according to most classical scholars, in the course of Socrates' examination of Protagoras' doctrine in *Theaetetus*.[6] Almost all of those scholars, however, read the charge of self-refutation as redeemed—both there and more generally—on shifted grounds. Thus it is said that Protagoras *must* claim the *absolute* truth of his doctrine because all assertions are implicit claims of absolute truth and/or that otherwise there would be no point to anyone's listening to or believing him. One commentator, for example, after extensive consideration of the text, concludes that Protagoras' doctrine and "relativism" more generally are self-refuting "for reasons that go deep into the nature of assertion and belief."[7] "No amount of maneuvering with his relativizing qualifiers will extricate Protagoras from the commitment to truth absolute which is bound up with the very act of assertion. To assert is to assert that *p*— . . . that something is the case—and if *p*, indeed if and only if *p*, then *p* is true (period)."[8] Another commentator assures his readers, "'Relative rightness' is not rightness at all. . . . The relativist cannot regard her beliefs, or her relative truths, as warranted or worthy of belief."[9] Yet another, acknowledging Socrates' dubious paraphrase of Protagoras' thesis, insists on the ignominious outcome of the examination: for, he observes, "if what [Protagoras] says is right he has no claim on our attention."[10]

It will be noted that, in all these recuperations, the assumption is that the particular conceptions of "truth," "assertion," "rightness," etc., to which they appeal are not themselves contestable, that those concepts and also the discursive/conceptual ("logical") connections among them could not be seen, framed, or configured otherwise. I return to this matter below.

Logic is not my primary concern here, but one point deserves emphasis in view of its significance in contemporary debates and also because it opens into the more general questions of psychology and cognition that are my main interest here. In explications of *Theaetetus* and elsewhere, the supposed self-refutation often hinges on what is taken to be an *egalitarian* claim implied by the unorthodox doctrine at hand: that is, a claim seen as erasing all differences of (presumably inherent, objective) better and worse, superiority and inferiority. A commentator writes: ". . . [T]he point of Protagoras' theory which is to be attacked [in the dialogue] is its implication that no man is wiser than any other." This supposed

6. G. B. Kerferd, "Plato's Account of the Relativism of Protagoras," *Durham University Journal* 42 (1949): 20–26; Gregory Vlastos, ed., *Plato's Protagoras*, trans. B. Jowett (Indianapolis: Liberal Arts Press, 1956), intro. The trick or error is noted and discussed in all the commentaries cited in n. 4, above, and also by Siegel, *Relativism Refuted*.

7. Burnyeat, *Theaetetus of Plato*, 30.

8. Burnyeat, "Protagoras and Self-Refutation," 195. See Smith, *Contingencies*, 112–14, 205, for a (self-exemplifying) reply to this formulation and argument.

9. Siegel, *Relativism Refuted*, 8, 20.

10. Bostock, *Plato's Theaetetus*, 95. Lee, "'Hoist with His Own Petard,'" argues the same point as Bostock.

implication leads to a self-refutation because, "according to his own theory (Protagoras) cannot himself be any better judge of truth than the ignorant audience he mocks."[11] Indeed, the familiar image of "relativism" as a fatuous, sophomoric demonism and, accordingly, the rhetorical force of the epithet itself derive largely from a supposed implication of this kind: that is, the idea that, according to the (unorthodox) doctrine in question, everything—every opinion, every scientific theory, every artwork, every moral practice, and so on—is "just as good" as every other.

I discuss this general supposition and argument elsewhere as the Egalitarian Fallacy.[12] It is a fallacy because, if someone rejects the notion of validity in the classic sense, what follows is not that she thinks *all* theories (etc.) are *equally* valid but that she thinks *no* theory (etc.) is valid *in the classic sense*.[13] The non sequitur here is the product of the common and commonly unshakable conviction that differences of better and worse must be objective or could not otherwise be measured. When appealed to in the argument, the conviction is obviously question-begging. Thus, the supposed relativist could observe that her point is, precisely, that theories (etc.) can be and are evaluated in *other* non-"objective" ways. Not all theories are equal because they (including her own) can be, and commonly will be, found better or worse than others in relation to measures such as applicability, connectibility, stability, and so forth. These measures are not objective in the classic sense, since they depend on matters of perspective, interpretation, and judgment, and will vary under different historical conditions. Nevertheless, they appear to figure routinely, and operate well enough, in scientific, judicial, and critical practice.

Close kin to the Egalitarian Fallacy is the idea that any theory that does not ultimately affirm the "constraints" of "an objective reality" or "nature itself" implies that "anything"—any practice, any belief, etc.—"goes." The assumption here is that there can be no other explanation for why we do not all run amok or believe ridiculous things: that is, that no alternative accounts of the dynamics of social behavior and cognition are possible. The logic of "anything goes" is identical to that of "everything's just as good as everything else": Both depend on taking for granted as *unquestionable* the classic concepts that *are being questioned* in the theory at hand. Hence the recurrent (and technically proper) countercharge of question-begging; hence the recurrent deadlocks, nonengage-

11. Bostock, *Plato's Theaetetus*, 89 and 85.

12. Smith, *Contingencies*, 98–101, 150–52. For the related idea that a rejection of classic conceptions of objective validity amounts to a rejection/forswearing of all value judgments (and thus to moral/political paralysis or quietism), see Smith, "The Unquiet Judge: Activism Without Objectivism in Law and Politics," *Annals of Scholar-ship* 9 (1–2) (1992): 111–33. For the idea that relativists who observe circularities, fallacies, and non sequiturs in their adversaries' arguments are caught in a "performative" self-contradiction, see n. 39, below.

13. "Validity" is especially pertinent here, but the analysis applies to the rejection of any classic measure—truth, beauty, virtue, etc.—in an absolute or objectivist sense.

ments, and impasses[14]—or, one could say, incommensurabilities. Which brings us to what is, in my view, the heart of the matter.

The classical scholars cited above, though close readers and scrupulous interpreters, operate within the closures of traditional epistemology and philosophy of language. The confinement is reflected in the strenuously self-affirming and self-absolutizing formulations that recur in their arguments. We recall, from one, "the commitment to truth absolute which is *bound up* with *the very act* of assertion."[15] He cites in support Husserl: "The content of such {relativistic} assertions rejects what is *part of the sense* . . . of *every assertion*. . . ."[16] For another commentator, it is *"the very notion* of rightness" that is undermined by Protagoras and latter-day relativists.[17] He cites in support Hilary Putnam: ". . . it is a *presupposition* of *thought itself* that some kind of objective 'rightness' exists."[18] A passage in the recent work of Jürgen Habermas is relevant here, but I would note that his intricate arguments and far from epigrammatic prose make extraction difficult. In any case, he writes as follows: In the process of "convincing a person who contests the hypothetical reconstructions (of the *inescapable presuppositions* of argument) . . . that he is caught up in performative contradictions[,] . . . I must appeal to the *intuitive preunderstandings* that *every* subject competent in speech and action brings to a process of argumentation."[19]

Two related ideas are notable in these formulations. One is that certain meanings, contents, forces, claims, or commitments inhere in (or are "bound up with," or are "part of the sense of") particular terms (or "concepts") and strings of words per se. The other is that certain concepts, claims, and commitments are deeply connected with ("presupposed by" or "fundamental to the nature of") our mental and discursive activities. Both ideas are recurrent; both, in my view, are dubious; and both, I think, are the product of cognitive tendencies—tricks of thought—that may be (as *tendencies*) endemic.[20]

It appears from the formulations cited above and from the arguments in

14. Since those who assume the unquestionability of ideas such as "intrinsic value," "universal moral norms," and "constraints of an objective reality" foreclose the possibility of alternative—non-objectivist, non-axiological—accounts of judgment, motivation, and cognition, it is not surprising that they have great difficulty entertaining or, it could be said, grasping such accounts.

15. See Burnyeat, above (italics added).

16. Edmund Husserl, *Logical Investigations*, 2d ed. (1913), trans. J. N. Findlay (London: Routledge and Kegan Paul, 1970), 139 (italics added), cited by Burnyeat, *Theaetetus of Plato*, 30.

17. Siegel, *Relativism Refuted*, 4 (italics added); similarly, later: "'Relative rightness' is not rightness *at all*. . . . To defend relativisim relativistically is to fail to defend it *at all*," 8–9 (italics added).

18. Putnam, *Reason, Truth and History* (Cambridge: Cambridge University Press, 1981), 124.

19. Habermas, "Discourse Ethics: Notes on a Program of Philosophical Justification," in *Moral Consciousness and Communicative Action*, trans. Christian Lenhardt and Shierry Weber Nicholsen (Cambridge: MIT Press, 1990), 89–90 (italics added).

20. The emphasis here is meant to distinguish this suggestion from the idea of cognitive universals in a classic (e.g., Kantian) sense.

which they figure that the discursive/conceptual elements in question (concepts, meanings, claims, commitments) and also their interconnectedness are experienced introspectively by those who appeal to them as self-evident—intuitively right. This is not remarkable, I think, in view of the particular conceptual traditions in which, as philosophers, logicians, and classicists, they were presumably both formally educated and professionally disciplined, and in view also of the particular idioms with which, as scholars in those disciplines, they presumably operate more or less every day of their lives. What is worth remarking, however, is the move from *experiencing* one's own cognitive activities and their conceptual and discursive products (that is, one's own thought, beliefs, and linguistic usages) as self-evident or intuitively right to *positing and claiming* them as prior, autonomous, transcendentally presupposed, and (properly) universal.

It appears (on the evidence of, among other things, alternative introspections) that ideas such as "inescapable presuppositions," "intuitive preunderstandings," and "truth absolute" are neither universal nor inescapable. On the contrary, it is possible to believe—as I do, myself—that such concepts and the sense of their inherent meanings and deep interconnectedness are, rather, the products and effects of rigorous instruction and routine participation in a particular conceptual tradition and its related idiom. It is also possible to believe, accordingly, that instruction (more or less rigorous) in some other conceptual tradition, and familiarity with its idiom, would yield other conceptions and descriptions of "the fundamental nature" of "thought itself" and of what is "presupposed" by "the very act of assertion." Or—as I would myself be more inclined to say, in the alternative idiom of one such alternative tradition—a different personal intellectual/professional history would make other descriptions and accounts of the operations of human cognition and communication more cognitively comfortable and congenial.[21]

I pursue these points further below. First, however, a brief trip to the theater and to school, which are, in this neighborhood, not too far apart.

Theaters of Instruction

Foiled, exposed, and rejected, the devil in the old morality play exits stage left, muttering curses. The evocation of theater is not irrelevant here. The archetypal, exemplary self-refutation, *Theaetetus*, is, of course, dramatically scripted, and theatricality remains central to its re-productions. The dramatis personae are certainly among the most compelling in cultural history: the callow, showy,

---

21. Disciplinary instruction is not, of course, simply determinative. All education is complexly interactive and the effects of formal/professional education are always diversely mediated by personal temperament as well as by other aspects of personal history.

scoffing, hubristic truth-denier; the seasoned, gently ironic, ultimately martyred truth-deliverer; plus, as crucial parties to the scene, the mixed chorus of disciples and occasional interlocutors and, not insignificantly, the audience itself, motley representatives of the community at large.[22] The self-refuting skeptic recalls other self-deluded, self-destroying heroes and villains: Oedipus unwittingly condemning himself in his sentence on the killer of Laius; Rosencrantz and Gildenstern "hoist with their own petard"; [23] Satan, self-corrupted and self-damned, his engines of unholy warfare recoiling upon himself.

The structural principle of self-refutation is turnabout, reversal—in logic, *peritrope.* It is the counterpart of *peripeteia,* the turn of fortune that Aristotle thought most conducive to the effects of tragedy: fear, pity, catharsis. The emotional effects of both—classical tragedy and classic self-refutation—are complex: anxiety and satisfaction, as fear yields to pity and terror to relief; the pleasure of formal symmetry (revenge and justice coincide, the punishment both fits and mirrors the crime) joined with knowledge of a threat averted, an outlaw brought to book, order restored, orthodoxy vindicated. There is in self-refutation the satisfaction, too, of cognitive and pragmatic economy: the exposure and defeat of an adversary accomplished neatly, at his own cost. And, certainly, the frequency of suicides and self-mutilations in tragedy indicates that *self*-destruction has, as such, a certain frisson.

Self-refutation dramas—like all great artworks, or so we are told—can be experienced repeatedly without satiety. The effects are endlessly renewable here, perhaps, because the threat involved is itself so strong and ineradicable. Every orthodoxy is to some extent unstable, vulnerable. And the skeptic's denial or countertruth is appalling: "All is flux," "It is as each man perceives it," "No knowledge is certain," "God is dead," "There is nothing outside of the text." A thrill of horror: What if it's *right?* Everything would be lost—rational argument, objective knowledge, truth itself, *and my life's work for naught.* But also, perhaps, another thrill, closer to desire: What if it's *right?* Everything would be permitted— anarchy, murder, mayhem, *and I, free at last of my life's work.*

The full tragic effect, it has been said, requires the spectator's identification with the hubristic hero: at least a moment of sympathy with him—or her—in opposition to all those gods, seers, kings, courtiers, and choruses of the orthodox. It may be that, among the audiences of self-refutation dramas, even among the disciples themselves, there are flashes of identification with the skeptic, even,

22. We may recall, in *Theaetetus,* the figures Theodorus, senior mathematician and occasional participant in the dialogue, and Eucleides (142a–143c), its continuous witness and scrupulous recorder.

23. The appropriateness of Shakespeare's phrase to Protagoras is remarked by Lee, "'Hoist with His Own Petard.'" Lee reads *Theaetetus* as fundamentally comic and, via the supposed punishment-fits-the-crime image of Protagoras reduced to a cabbage-like vegetable, as related in impulse to the *Divine Comedy.*

sometimes, secret hopes for his triumph. Indeed, although the two lead figures described above—truth-denier and truth-deliverer—are familiar, their respective characterizations tend to blur (scoffer and ironist, tragic hero and martyr), and their respective roles can seem as reversible as the self-refuter's own argument. Thus Socrates can be seen as trickster and, perhaps, as the most radical of skeptics.[24]

Nor is it irrelevant here that the drama of self-refutation was originally produced as a pedagogic exercise for the betterment of the young. The "brilliant" (as he is called) but philosophically immature Theaetetus arrives in a state of enthrallment to dubious doctrines. He is delivered to better understanding—if not to the knowledge of knowledge itself—by witnessing and participating in the exposure of the self-refutation of those doctrines, thereby undergoing, through Socrates' midwifely ministrations, his own intellectual rebirth. The model is powerful and itself proves enthralling, the drama still re-produced, more than two millennia later, for the delivery of similarly bright, abashable seventeen- and eighteen-year-olds.[25] Are the doctrines not, after all, still the same, still seductive, and still false? Perhaps. In any case, the classic pedagogic exposure merges, along the way, with other stagings of demonic exposure and spiritual salvation, including exorcism.

As often observed, the enlightenment of the young in formal education operates through a process not dissimilar from other inductions into orthodoxy, from boot camp to monastery: a process of ordeal, alternating public punishment and public reward, that concludes with a welcoming by and incorporation into the special community. Given the institutional conditions under which this commonly occurs, that is, the regular convening in a theater of instruction of young men and women[26] in quasi-familial and semi-erotic relationships to—and rivalry with—both each other and the supervising master or mistress of the mysteries, it is not surprising that public humiliation has emerged as a favored technique. Moreover, in a company where status is measured by the development of intellectual prowess, there is probably no instrument of instruction more effective in that respect than the demonstration that one has unwittingly *refuted oneself*—the counterpart, no doubt, of the exposure, in other companies (athletic or military, for example), of more bodily self-disablings or self-foulings. It is no wonder, then,

24. The irony in *Theaetetus* is exceedingly complex. Commentators note that it concludes with its ostensible central question—what is knowledge?—unanswered. Desjardins *(Rational Enterprise,* 85–90) goes further, reading Socrates/Plato as ultimately endorsing the Protagorean thesis, appropriately interpreted.

25. See Hadley Arkes, *First Things: An Inquiry into the First Principles of Morals and Justice* (Princeton: Princeton University Press, 1986), 78–80, for an unself-conscious report of triumphs along these lines by a professor of philosophy at a small, elite college.

26. Mostly young men, of course, in disciplinary philosophy. For original and instructive discussions of the significance of that bias, see Michele Le Doeuff, *The Philosophical Imaginary* (London: Athlone Press; Stanford: Stanford University Press, 1989), and Andrea Nye, *Words of Power: A Feminist Reading of the History of Logic* (New York: Routledge, 1990).

that the effects of such exposures (however gently, subtly, wittily, or ironically administered) remain, for those who receive or witness them, so powerful and profound, or that fear of a charge of relativism can haunt the spirits and buckle the knees of grown men and women, even the most sophisticated of them, even the most otherwise unorthodox of them.

Dreams of Reason

Like the devil, the skeptic is never finally vanquished or finally triumphant. No matter how decisively her self-refutation is demonstrated, she does not acknowledge or indeed believe that she has refuted herself. Nor does the orthodox believer regard the skeptic's evasion of his charge as proper, or acknowledge the justice of her countercharge that he has begged all the questions.[27] Alternatively, of course, it could be said that skepticism triumphant *is* orthodoxy.

But the question may still be asked: If orthodoxy is that which is manifestly true, self-evidently right, and intuitively and universally preunderstood, then how is it that its truth and rightness elude the skeptic? The orthodox answer to this question is familiar: profound defects and deficiencies of intellect and character—an innate incapacity for logical thinking, unregenerate corruption by false (or French) doctrine, domination by personal resentment and political ideology, or unfamiliarity with the best work on the subject in analytic philosophy.

The explanatory asymmetry here—that is, the orthodox believer's conviction that he believes what he does because it is true while skeptics and heretics believe what they do because there is something the matter with them—is a general feature of defenses of orthodoxy: political, aesthetic, and scientific as well as philosophical (or religious). Its recurrence seems to reflect the cognitive tendencies alluded to above: that is, the tendency to experience one's own beliefs as self-evident and, sometimes, to posit them as prior, necessary, and properly universal. The failure to believe what is self-evident is self-evidently folly; the failure to believe what is necessarily presupposed is necessarily irrational—or perverse.

The tendency to experience one's own thinking as inevitable and to experience its products as prior and autonomous is, in the conceptual traditions and idioms I find congenial and cognitively comfortable, not a foundational intuition to be affirmed but a more or less intriguing phenomenon to be explained. To summarize all too briefly:

27. See James L. Battersby, "Professionalism, Relativism, and Rationality," *PMLA* 107 (January 1992): 63, for the (awkwardly stated) counter-counterargument that "self-refutation" (i.e., presumably, the charge) does not beg the question because it is (i.e., presumably, it appeals to) "a standard" that "belongs to the class of transparadigmatic criteria." Of course this re-begs the question, though at a more elevated level. Similarly, Siegel argues (*Relativism Refuted*, 187) that the charge by epistemological "naturalists" that the "incoherence argument" is question-begging "founders on the confusion . . . between truth and certainty," thus appealing (question-beggingly, as charged) to the classic conception of "truth" at issue.

Certain configurations of perceptual/behavioral tendencies ("beliefs") are strengthened and stabilized by our effective-enough and predictable-enough interactions with our environments (including other people and what they produce, e.g., institutions and discourses). To the extent that this occurs, we (human, social, cultural, verbal organisms) may experience and interpret those configurations reflexively as "referring to" or "being about" specific, determinate features of an autonomous reality: features, that is, seen as (simply) "out there," prior to, quite separate from, and quite independent of, our own interactions, past or current, with our environments. This experience, so interpreted, is not, I would say, either "illusion" or "delusion." Nevertheless, it could be *otherwise*—and, for some purposes, from some perspectives, more usefully, interestingly, coherently, and appropriably—described and interpreted.[28]

We recall that, with some disciplined effort (by, for example, mystics, Buddhists, and deconstructionists), the experience of an autonomous reality may be subjected to reflexive scrutiny and to temporary de-naturalization, de-stabilization, and dis-integration.[29] Descriptions of technologically induced "virtual reality" also make alternative interpretations of the experience easier to entertain. Subjects report that, after a certain amount of interactive feedback from computer-generated sensory stimuli—goggle-generated images that shift their shapes and size as the subject turns her head, glove-induced pressures that vary with the subject's hand motions—these modally diverse sensations will seem suddenly to integrate themselves and to surround the subject as a distinct and autonomous environment.[30] The cognitive dynamics of our ordinary experiences of "real" reality are, perhaps, not too different from the dynamics of such reported experiences of "virtual" reality.[31]

28. Whether or not "it" is the same when otherwise conceived and described is a puzzle of which much has been made. It figures, for example, in the "dualism of [variable] conceptual scheme and [fixed] empirical content" alleged by Donald Davidson to be "essential to"—and thus, perhaps, crucially damaging of—certain views of Kuhn and Feyerabend (Davidson, "On the Very Idea of a Conceptual Scheme," in *Inquiries into Truth and Interpretation* [Oxford: Clarendon Press, 1984], 189). Here as elsewhere, however, part of the issue is what sort of puzzle one thinks it is: whether "essentially" logical, as Davidson's term seems to indicate, or contingently discursive, conceptual, and rhetorical, as it could also be seen (and, accordingly, handled quite differently). Davidson's own position on the question appears ambivalent. It is certainly more elusive than is suggested by recurrent citations of this essay as decisive for debates over the epistemological claims of "conceptual relativism" and "postmodernism" and the implications of the idea of incommensurability (cf. S. P. Mohanty, "Us and Them: On the Philosophical Bases of Political Criticism," *Yale Journal of Criticism* 2 [1989]: 1–31, and Chris-

topher Norris, *What's Wrong with Postmodernism: Critical Theory and the Ends of Philosophy* [Baltimore: Johns Hopkins University Press, 1990], 186–87).

29. For descriptions of the effort among Buddhists, see Francisco Varela, Evan Thompson, and Eleanor Rosch, *The Embodied Mind: Cognitive Science and Human Experience* (Cambridge: MIT Press, 1991), 59–81.

30. Howard Rheingold, *Virtual Reality* (New York: Summit Books, 1991).

31. It should be stressed that "cognitive" is not confined here to activities above the neck (i.e., the entire organism is involved) and also that the stabilization and naturalization of belief are the product of interacting psychophysiological, social, political, and technological dynamics and practices. For recent discussions, see "Irreductions" in Bruno Latour, *The Pasteurization of France* (Cambridge: Harvard University Press, 1988), and Andrew Pickering, "The Mangle of Practice: Agency and Emergence in the Sociology of Science" (1993, unpub. ms.).

Human beings appear to have a tendency to protect their particular beliefs from destabilization, even in the face of what strike other people as clearly disconfirming evidence and arguments. I have termed this tendency *cognitive conservatism*.[32] Though it often operates in technically "irrational" ways (as assessed by, say, economists),[33] cognitive conservatism is better regarded, I think, not as a flaw or failing but, rather, as the *ambivalent* (some times/ways good, some times/ways bad) counterpart of an (also endemic and ambivalent) tendency to cognitive flexibility and responsiveness.[34]

For better and for worse, cognitive conservatism yields intellectual stability, consistency, reliability, and predictability; it also yields, for better and for worse, powerfully self-immuring, self-perpetuating systems of political and religious belief. At its extreme, when played out in specifically theoretical domains, it can become *absolute epistemic self-privileging*: that is, the conviction that one's convictions are undeniable, that one's assumptions are established facts or necessary presuppositions, that the entities one invokes are unproblematically real, that the terms one uses are transparent and the senses in which one uses them inherent in the terms themselves, and, ultimately, that no alternative conceptualizations or formulations are possible at all, at least no "adequate," "coherent," or "meaningful" ones—at least not for beings claiming to be "rational." Cognitive conservatism is an endemic tendency and a mixed blessing. Its hypertrophic development, epistemic self-privileging, is a human frailty, common among common folk—but, in rationalist philosophy, honed to a fine art.

For those well instructed in traditional foundational epistemology, everything—each concept, each opposition, each link, and each move—hangs together, comfortably and, it seems, self-evidently. It hangs together in part because, perhaps, that's the way human cognition works, but also because the major project and achievement of foundational epistemology is the maintenance, monitoring, and justification of precisely that interdependency: the rigorous interorganization of everything that fits and the vigorous rejection (and "refutation") of everything that doesn't. Indeed, disciplinary philosophy *as such* (I do not say every philosopher or every philosophical work) can be seen as the cultural counterpart and institutional extension of individual cognitive conservatism—again, for better and for worse.

The routines—rituals, habits—of rigorously taught, strenuously learned conceptual production and performance come to operate virtually automatically, to be experienced as necessary and autonomous, and, sometimes, to be posited

32. Cf. Smith, "Belief and Resistance: A Symmetrical Account," *Critical Inquiry* 18 (Autumn 1991): 125–39.

33. Cf. Daniel Kahneman, Paul Slovic, and Amos Tversky, eds., *Judgment Under Uncertainty: Heuristics, and Biases* (Cambridge: Cambridge University Press, 1982).

34. Cf. Joan S. Lockard and Delroy L. Paulus, eds., *Self-Deception: An Adaptive Mechanism?* (Englewood Cliffs, N.J.: Prentice-Hall, 1988).

as prior to and independent of the activities of any mortal human agent.[35] The resulting coherence and interdependency of concepts, connections, distinctions, and moves is what Derrida and others speak of, with regard to the history of Western philosophy, as "the closure of metaphysics."[36] It is not, however (as such theorists commonly stress), altogether closed, nor could any conceptual system ever be. Both individually and culturally, there is always noise and uncontrollable play in the system. Individually, our beliefs are heterogeneous and, though more or less effective and coordinated ad hoc, not globally coherent and always potentially conflicting. Moreover, there are always glitches in cultural transmission. We never learn our lessons perfectly. The rigorous training is never rigorous enough. There is always someone who missed class that day, or got distracted, or came from somewhere else, or heard something else that she liked better first, or just didn't care: the class misfit—outlaw, heretic, devil, skeptic, spoiler.

None of this is to say that the postmodern skeptic has "discovered the objective truth of the inherent wrongness" of traditional epistemology. To an epistemological traditionalist, any skeptic who claimed that would refute herself on the spot. To a postmodernist, any postmodernist who claimed such a thing would be a pretty problematic postmodernist.

The postmodern skeptic does not say or think that traditional epistemology is inherently wrong, an error, or a delusion. She observes and believes that the conceptual systems it sustains operate well enough for a good many people. Nevertheless, she also knows that those systems and that epistemology do not operate as well for her as other conceptual systems and theories of knowledge. That does not make them, in her eyes, all "equally valid" or "equally invalid." All are, and will be, measured and judged by, among other things, their applicability, connectibility, and stability. By such measures, different epistemologies and conceptual systems are found, and will be found, better or worse or, sometimes, congruent enough. But the measurements themselves, taken under differing conditions, interpreted from different perspectives, will vary. Equivalence and disparity, like commensurability and incommensurability, are, in her view, not absolute but contingent matters. As Protagoras might have put it, man is the measure of all the measures that man has.

The postmodern skeptic thinks that the interest and utility of all theoretical formulations are contingent. She is not disturbed, however, by the idea that, in order to be self-consistent, she must "concede" the "merely" contingent

35. Cf. Brian Rotman, *Ad Infinitum: The Ghost in Turing's Machine—Taking God out of Mathematics and Putting the Body Back In* (Stanford: Stanford University Press, 1993).

36. Cf. Jacques Derrida, *Positions*, trans. Alan Bass (Chicago: University of Chicago Press, 1981), 6–7, 13, 22. For relevant discussion of the idea, see Arkady Plotnitsky, *Reconfigurations: Critical Theory and General Economy* (Gainesville: University of Florida Press, 1992), 194–211.

interest and utility of her own theoretical formulations. Nor is she embarrassed by her similar "obligation" to "concede" the historicity—and thus instability and eventual replacement—of the systems and idioms that she finds preferable to traditional epistemology and that she would, and does, recommend to other people. She is not disturbed or embarrassed—or, to her own way of thinking, self-refuted—by these things because she believes, in comfortable accord with the conceptual systems and idioms she prefers, that that's the way all disciplinary knowledge—science, philosophy, literary studies, and so forth—evolves. And she also believes that, all told (as she tallies such matters), that's not a bad way for it to happen.

Although the postmodern skeptic is not affirming (self-contradictorily) "the (objective) truth of the (inherent) wrongness" of traditional epistemology, a traditionalist may hear her affirming it, just as if those words were coming right out of her mouth. That is because, by his logic, that is just what it means for someone to *deny* something. Thus, he hears her contradicting (and, in his terms, refuting) herself. By the postmodern skeptic's own logic, the traditionalist is mistaken. The traditionalist will not see his mistake *as* one so long as he remains a traditionalist. He may, however, become a postmodern skeptic himself—or, of course, the skeptic a born-again believer.[37]

This last point is significant: not the conversion (or corruption) of the believer (or the skeptic) per se, but, despite the reciprocal impasses indicated here, the general possibility of the transformation of belief. Nothing said here implies a permanent structure of deadlock.[38] On the contrary, what has been said explicitly and implied throughout is that no orthodoxy—or skepticism—can be totally stable, no theoretical closure complete, no incommensurability absolute.

By the same token, one cannot *interact* with a theoretical closure and remain totally "outside" of it, even if the interaction is skeptical or adversarial. Thus one disputes "logic" with logic (or logic with "logic"), neither identical but

37. "Traditionalism" and "postmodernism" (each of which comes in a variety of sizes and colors, not all represented here) are not, to be sure, the only stances possible. Numerous transcendences and via medias have been proposed (e.g., Richard J. Bernstein, *Beyond Objectivism and Relativism* [Philadelphia: University of Pennsylvania Press, 1983]; Hilary Putnam, *Realism with a Human Face* [Cambridge: Harvard University Press, 1990]; Joseph Margolis, *The Truth About Relativism* [Cambridge, MA: Basil Blackwell, 1991])—and one must not forget the multitudes of people who lead rich, full lives without any articulated positions whatsoever on issues of epistemology. It must be added, however, that the psychological and social/political dynamics that operate to stabilize beliefs seem also, under a wide range of conditions, to *polarize* them (cf. Howard Margolis, *Patterns, Thinking, and Cognition: A Theory of Judgment* [Chicago: University of Chicago Press, 1987], esp. 274–76, and William E. Connolly, *Identity/Difference: Democratic Negotiations of Political Paradox* [Ithaca: Cornell University Press, 1991]). Also, while some transcendences and via medias are, from the present perspective, more congenial or interesting than others, it seems that most of them strive to hunt with the hounds and run with the fox(es), i.e., to exhibit the solid home virtues of orthodoxy but seek credit for the cosmopolitanism (as it may be seen) of postmodernism. It is no coincidence that the pages in which they are developed are commonly strewn with charges of the "incoherence" and self-refutation of more unambivalently unorthodox positions.

38. Nor is it implied, more generally, by critiques of the traditional idea of ultimate "determinations" of which side is/was ("essentially," "objectively") right ("all along").

each, over time, shaped by the other.[39] The process—that is, skeptical, adversarial interactions with traditional conceptual systems—is both rhetorical and cognitive: played out in public theaters (classrooms, conference halls, the pages of journals) and also in the private theater of the mind, where the "self" takes all the roles—truth-deliverer and truth-denier, master and disciple, chorus of mixed voices and motley audience—and every self-refutation is, simultaneously, the self's triumph and transformation.

39. The quotation marks here distinguish what are commonly seen as the fixed canons of formal logic from what could otherwise be seen as contingently (though very broadly) effective discursive/conceptual practices. The parenthetical reversal acknowledges the claims of each of these logics to priority: "logical" priority for the traditionalist; pragmatic/historical/psychological priority for the postmodern skeptic. Habermas and Karl-Otto Apel, among others, would see in this disputing of logic with "logic" a "performative [self-]contradiction" and, accordingly, validation of the "inescapably presupposed rules of argumentation" (Habermas, "Discourse Ethics: Notes on a Program of Philosophical Justification") and of "reason itself" (Apel, "The Problem of Philosophical Foundations in Light of a Transcendental Pragmatics of Language," in *After Philosophy: End or Transformation?* ed. Kenneth Baynes, James Bohman, and Thomas McCarthy [Cambridge: MIT Press, 1987]). In a sequel to the present essay, I examine (as ["]rationally["] and ["]logically["] as seems necessary, under current conditions, to be persuasive) the questionable logical/rhetorical operations of such arguments.

"WEAK THOUGHT" AND THE REDUCTION OF VIOLENCE

A Dialogue with Gianni Vattimo

Gianni Vattimo and Santiago Zabala

Translated by Yaakov Mascetti

Santiago Zabala: In your book *The Vocation and Responsibility of the Philosopher*, you say that "philosophy is more an edifying discourse than a demonstrative one, more oriented toward the edification of humanity than toward the development of knowledge and progress." You say also that "the duty of the philosopher no longer corresponds to the Platonic agenda: the philosopher is no longer humanity's guide to understanding the Eternal; rather, he redirects humanity toward history." Are these the meaning and direction of what you have termed—in books, in articles, in public debates—"weak thought"?

Gianni Vattimo: I would say that "weak thought," *pensiero debole*, can now be defined in more precise terms. It is as you describe it, of course; but not only as you describe it. Its content is an *ontology* of weakness. "Weak thought" is by no

Originally published in *Common Knowledge* 8.3 (Fall 2002): 452–63, as part of "Peace and Mind: Seriatim Symposium on Dispute, Conflict, and Enmity Part 3: Diffidence, Humility, Weakness, and Other Strengths." © 2002 by Duke University Press.

Common Knowledge 25:1–3

DOI 10.1215/0961754X-7299150

means a weakness of thinking as such. It is just that, because thinking is no longer demonstrative but rather edifying, it has become in that restricted sense weaker.

Zabala: In which case, "strong" is a negative description. In *The End of Modernity*, published nearly twenty years ago, you say, in the context of discussing "weak thought," that we now require "a fictionalized experience of reality"—and that this experience "is also our only possibility of freedom." You have said too that, during the waning of modernity, our experience of unlimited interpretability has led to "the weakening of the cogent force of reality." In other words, what used to be considered facts are now taken as interpretations. Of course, many people, including many intellectuals, many philosophers, find this an alarming development. But it is a development of which you approve, and you have encouraged the development, to match it, of a style of thinking that is, in that same sense, "weak." But can we conceive of a *strong* "weak thought"? Do we not need one now?

Vattimo: I believe that we may. In a strong theory of weakness, the philosopher's role would not derive from the world "as it is," but from the world viewed as the product of a history of interpretation throughout the history of human cultures. This philosophical effort would focus on interpretation as a process of weakening, a process in which the weight of objective structures is reduced. Philosophy can consider itself neither as knowledge of the external, universal structures of being, nor as knowledge of the external, universal structures of episteme, for both of these are undone by the philosophical process of weakening. That is, after the critique of ideology, after the Nietzschean critique of the notion of "things as they are" . . .

Zabala: After Freud?

Vattimo: After Freud, we can no longer believe that "being," as a type of incontrovertible evidence, can be apprehended by us. With Marx, Nietzsche, and Freud, we are led to doubt all that appears to us the most obvious. If institutions like the papacy, an empire, newspapers, the media, define objective truths, philosophy must do precisely the opposite. It must show that truth is conversational. It is within conversational frameworks that preferences (as opposed to objective truths) can be delineated. It is in conversation that preferred interpretations can be proposed—and interpretations are always remarks about history . . .

Zabala: Does that kind of deconstruction—or, as you have called it, "destructuration"—apply also to the rhetoric of the deconstructors? Should we not regard "God is dead!"—Nietzsche's claim—as a description of things as they are?

Vattimo: "God is dead!" is an announcement, not a claim. It means, not that God does not exist, but that our experience has been transformed such that we no longer conceive ultimate objective truths, and now respond only to appeals, announcements. When Nietzsche calls for a multitude of gods, we can understand him as calling for a polytheism of values. The call is thus not for a society with no values but for a society without *supreme and exclusive* values. On this model, cultures are complex conversations among varying conceptions of the world. Such dialogue can, and must not, shift into a dogmatic clash between conflicting truths. When Hitler exterminated 6 million Jews, I find it hard to believe that he did so on the basis of an "opinion." His actions were, on the contrary, based on an "objective truth," a "scientific fact"—and when a conversation begins to deteriorate into a clash between objective dogmas, "weak thought" has its peculiar part to play.

Zabala: In which case, science apparently requires weakening. When Heidegger claims that "science does not think," has he achieved a weakening of science?

Vattimo: I think that Heidegger made that claim as a provocation. Nevertheless, there is something to it. Science is a discipline that does not itself pose the problem of historically determined truth. Science works within given historical contexts, its nature being to demonstrate or falsify propositions on the basis of criteria that it does not itself invent but simply improves, transforms. I am thinking, of course, of Kuhn's paradigms . . .

Zabala: Kuhn! Discussing Kuhn in *Common Knowledge*—that's carrying coals to Newcastle. Could we discuss another discipline—law—with respect to "weak thought"? In your essay "Fare Giustizia del Diritto," you outline a philosophy of law that is based on a nihilistic substratum. By means of interpretation, law becomes an instrument for weakening the original violence of justice. Could you please explain how, within the frame of "weak thought," you would suggest we regard justice and punishment? I ask especially because—in the aftermath of the events of September 11, 2001—the question has been repeatedly raised of how a "postmodern" thinker can conceive of evil, crime, and retribution.

Vattimo: *Fare giustizia del diritto* is an expression I used with the intention of exploiting a pun. The phrase means "to make law just," "to fashion law into justice." But it also means, though in a rather vague way, "to execute law"—to abolish the sacred aura, the ultimate and foundational authority, of justice. My argument began with an effort to reconceive law and justice outside the metaphysical framework in which judicial punishment is thought to reestablish a state of affairs defined as "right," a situation now troubled by crime. I was also determined not to consider law as the formulation of a set of precepts founded on some essential structure—as is the case, for example, of "natural law." The practitioner of "weak thought," the hermeneutic nihilist, "executes" law in the sense that, while he strips it of its sacred aura, he opens the way to more human considerations. The hermeneutic ontology that derives from Heidegger has primarily produced *critical, negative* perspectives and methods—Derridean deconstruction, for example. But in ethics, let alone in law, it seems to me urgent that we move beyond the state in which agreement is suspended—kept in a state of pure suspension. In any case, this aspect of deconstruction appears to derive primarily, not from hermeneutics, but from the influence of phenomenology (pure epoché seems to me pure Merleau-Ponty).

Zabala: But if we interpret justice against the background of nihilism, is the loss to justice not immense?

Vattimo: What we do lose in the dissolution of metaphysics is the idea that in nature there are a right and a wrong. Put it this way: given the dissolution of metaphysics, it seems to me that the only supreme principle to be propounded, both in ethics and in law, is *the reduction of violence.* According to Heidegger, metaphysics must be refused, not only because it produces a totalitarian and overly rationalist social structure, but also because the idea of *Grund,* of ultimate foundation, is an authoritarian idea. The notion of primeval evidence, of a *Eureka!,* of a moment in which I have reached bedrock, of a foundation at which no questions can or need be asked—that state, in which questions are lacking, is not the end product of violence, but its origin.

Zabala: Would that be your definition of violence?

Vattimo: I would say so. Philosophically, violence can only be defined as the silencing of questions. That may happen in brutal forms, but also in philosophical forms, as when a philosopher concludes that he has reached the origin of all problematics: an example is Descartes's *cogito.* Obviously, metaphysics has not always been the origin of violence; but it is the case that the moments of greatest violence in history have always been justified by well-structured metaphysical pretenses. Burning heretics was a form of violence defended, in metaphysical terms, by a religion that professed an ultimate truth. Even with regard to modern theories of natural rights, there has been a close relationship—at least, historically—between metaphysics and violence. If philosophers of natural law cannot accept that the only authentic right is the right to be consulted on matters that concern us, and if they keep defining natural rights and laws in objective terms, we may always be vulnerable to outbursts of violence. The only right I would fight for is the right to express my opinion when I want to take part in a dialogue. But if I go up to someone who is profoundly convinced that one can live perfectly well in a totalitarian society and I oblige him, by means of economic blackmail, to support democracy, what I am doing is violent; I must try to persuade him instead.

Zabala: And how, in that context, are we supposed to imagine justice?

Vattimo: I would say that the *unicuique suum* is a good basis for understanding justice, the one always used in law codes. I am not so sure, on the other hand, that there is a natural *suum*. Saying so would require reference to a specific idea of human nature, and that could lead to dangerous forms of violence. A typical example would be a case reported in Italy of a young drug addict who had been tied in a pigsty to prevent him from taking drugs. After having found him dead, his family claimed that they had tied him up for his own good. The individual's *suum* is, I would hold, his own freedom; or better, his capacity to determine his own sense of justice on the basis of an intelligible line of reasoning. The insane are a problem; the fetus, as yet unborn, is not a problem. Nevertheless, we must try resolving all such problems on the basis of forms of social tutelage. Let me explain myself: generally, we assume that a child, before attaining legal age, follows his parents' advice. Then we realize that the age shifts—once, the age was twenty-one, today it's eighteen, some day it will be sixteen. It is not so easy to settle who (and until when) must be protected from which others.

Zabala: Are there ways, in any case, to limit the violence inherent in making decisions on behalf of, or with respect to, others?

Vattimo: Of course. To put someone in prison, though, is always a form of violence, which is sometimes justified by the practical and procedural rationale that governs collective life. Law and justice don't always coincide completely. If justice means to give each what he or she deserves, we must admit that what each "deserves" is much more a historical than a natural determination. In other words, such determinations are closely related to, and due to, historical conditions and traditions. If one has inherited five castles, it is right that we recognize him as the legal owner of those castles, even if his ownership is due to the fact that his ancestors were stronger pirates than mine. The concept of *suum* thus has scant meaning, and it is important to bear in mind that the *suum* is historically conditioned; furthermore, that the *suum* is always pragmatic, an adjustment to the need for reducing violence as far as possible. A society in which the death penalty is in force, if it is regulated by precise laws and if the sentence may be appealed, is certainly less violent than a society in which the sentence of death is handed down by decree. Obviously, a society in which there is no death penalty is the least violent of all. I regard societies that lack the death penalty as more just, because they respect the idea that the individual has the right to self-determination. My not asking the condemned prisoner his opinion regarding the fact that I have sentenced him to death is certainly more disturbing than my not asking his opinion about my condemning him to twenty years in prison. In the latter case, I am allowing him to question himself about his actions—to repent, to analyze his life, to understand the significance of what he has done. The reduction of violence, and the resultant increase in justice, derive from the progressively wider application of the principle of consensus, reciprocity, consultation.

Zabala: Luigi Pareyson argues, along the lines of our discussion here, that "of truth there is nothing but interpretation and . . . there is nothing but interpretation of truth." If so, it becomes literally impossible, philosophically and juridically, for a judge to be absolutely impartial; and yet his or her responsibility is to apply the written law objectively. Should we conclude, then, that the existence of iniquitous laws is symptomatic of the law's actual incapacity to embody justice?

Vattimo: I can accept a version of that formula: the judge is obviously not God. Hence the multitude of safeguards in place at trials—sometimes there are too many and they become an obstacle. A point can be reached at which the guarantees are so numerous that the primary aim of the trial (a judgment) cannot be arrived at or is blocked.

Zabala: Let's take the case of the most recent American presidential election. Did not appealing the election results in Florida to the U.S. Supreme Court imply a need to ascertain divine truth?

Vattimo: Well, it certainly implied a *hunger* for absolute truth. But with reference to the case you mention, I would ask, rather, if all the legal procedures were properly followed. Justice is the respect for canonized, written law. If, in the case of traffic lights, I drive on red, am I violating the natural law? No. I am violating a law that regulates traffic, a law meant to prevent people from getting killed at intersections. The example of traffic lights, I would say, is representative of all legal systems. If, in the middle of a hot day in August, when the city is empty, I drive on red through an intersection, what I am doing is superimposing on the existing legal system a superior law, my own, that I believe comprehends the necessity and logic of existing traffic regulations. In New York, until not so long ago, people simply crossed streets when there were no cars; now, the police fine jaywalkers, because people came to understand that a respect for mere form reflects a more basic respect for elementary social law. Justice, in these examples, is a procedural system that exists in opposition to the potential chaos of individual choices. In the same way, we may ask: Is it possible to prevent judges from expressing, in their judgments, their own personal and political opinions? Well, we may do so by increasing the number of judges called to judge any particular case. There will be right-wing judges and left-wing judges—the result will be forms of democratic self-government in the judiciary. Decisions will differ, and . . .

Zabala: However we improve the courts, justice will always be a "human, all too human" affair?

Vattimo: In this case, the "too" can never be too much. There are differing instances and different forms of justice; they cannot be compared and reconciled on the basis of their correspondence to some objective truth. Indeed, the concept of objective truth itself has always been imprecise, unclear. Even in the case of a murder, the objective truth about the facts is not ascertainable. All that we can do is reconstruct the facts in a way that satisfies the family of the victim, or society as a whole. As for the latter, it is society that holds that, were the murderer not punished, the risk of further murders would increase—and thus punishment appears to be more a readjustment, an accommodation, than it is an assertion about the case. To apply justice to human affairs is basically to adjust things . . .

Zabala: Adjust? Or *reduce* . . . ?

Vattimo: Yes, reduce, compromise, adjust things, in order to evade complaints and protests from the differing sides involved: in order to arrive at some kind of solution that may be acceptable to everyone. This is not always easy to do, and it is necessary to have a third party, a witness, a judge—but the entire community, which has delegated the judge to apply the canonized laws, must respect both those laws and the judgment. A judgment thus made is clearly intersubjective and limited, but also valid. Take a man who wants to buy a suit: he is not sure if he wants a blue one or a green one. So he tries on several and, in the end, he makes his choice. He knows perfectly well that from the point of view of eternity his choice is probably not right; but since there really are no eternal standards with respect to green or blue suits, his choice is not predetermined.

Zabala: It is, of course, useful to put the labors of judges in context. Nevertheless, we insist—do we not?—that "the law is the same for all."

Vattimo: "Law," in your aphorism, is a *procedure* applicable to all. Equality before the law means that everyone is treated in the same way on the basis of the same behavioral norms. Do such regulations correspond to an eternal truth? I don't think so.

Zabala: You have written that to "execute law" means "to interpret—applying laws to real situations in order to amend them without violence, without imposing force." And you say that this "does not mean exposing the implicit violence at the origin [of justice], nor does it mean to hide that violence with ad hoc adjustments; it means to progressively reduce violence." Is that your notion of postmetaphysical justice?

Vattimo: When I mentioned the violent origins of justice and the desire to expose them, I was alluding primarily to an essay of Derrida's. Derridean deconstruction creates a situation of suspense, an *epoché* of the faith in law. The origin of law is arbitrary. At the origin stands a king who usurped power. Still, it seems to me that, following the logic of secularization, it is important to acknowledge primeval violence *just because* it enables my understanding of successive events as a progressive attempt to displace the original void. On the other hand, in deconstruction, as also in Foucaultian thought, the originary violence of justice is evoked as if acknowledging its existence were a means of rebelling against it, a means of preventing it from overpowering us. There are anarchical overtones. In practice, Derrida's or Foucault's suspension of the faith in law would leave humanity with no procedural clue, and it runs the risk of idealizing a pure (and thus never-to-be realized) justice. The origin of states has always been violent. But this does not mean that, to constitute a state, violence is *necessary*.

Zabala: For example?

Vattimo: Take the question of a European constitution. There are political groups objecting that the birth of a European constitution is illegitimate because it will necessarily be the fruit of economic accommodations among the stronger countries. An Italian citizen on his way to a demonstration in Nice against the constitution said that "constitutions grow out of rebellions . . . and not in parliaments." Does this mean that, in order to establish a constitution for the European Community, there has to be a traumatic event, a bloodletting? Arguments about the violent origins of law have ambiguous consequences. I tend to resist the idea that violence is a good solution; it is obviously preferable to follow procedures that can lead to the reduction of violence. Social groups can conceive of means for transforming the legal order that do not imply rebellion—there is the possibility of representational democracy. People can be represented and consulted. But once again, it is important to understand this point from the perspective of "ontological difference." If we understand ontological difference as suspending the validity of *what is*, we will produce a negative theology, the most radical of anarchies, corresponding in religion to the mystic state. The mystic's idea is that there is available to us a means of contact with the First Principle. Applied to justice, the result is antinomian: the fact of violence is taken to invalidate all laws.

In response, all I can do is oppose the violence or withdraw from the game completely (becoming, again, a monk or mystic). Or else, because canonical norms no longer correspond to the state of affairs, I can oppose those norms with violence of my own. It is important, in other words, that there be norms for the modification of norms. Constitutions must formalize processes that provide for the possibility of internal modification.

Zabala: Modification, yes. But then, deeper transformations are impossible?

Vattimo: Take the case of constitutional reform in Italy. Can we "transform" the first article of the constitution, "Italy is a democratic republic"? The Italian constitution does not provide a legal basis for a referendum in which citizens can choose again between a monarchy and a republic. At the origin of anything there is a series of short circuits, and the origin is not easily justifiable. Which is not to say that there is anything wrong with laws whose origin is arbitrary. But there are, therefore, always matters that are settled—and always something that could be improved.

Zabala: Or, in Freud's language: the patient will never completely resolve his problems but will rather attain, with the aid of analysis, a state of peaceful coexistence with himself.

Vattimo: Of course. He will attain a state of tranquility, and that is what "constructions in analysis" really means—the opposite of a total and radical revelation. What I am hinting at, metaphysically, are ways leading the individual to accept "being" as an *event*, and not as an originary *structure, given once and for all*. The point is worth making both in politics and in psychology.

Zabala: In your essay on law and justice, you quote Nietzsche to the effect that "the progressive knowledge of the origin increases the insignificance of the origin."

Vattimo: Yes. We can never efface the fact that the origin is violent; to do so, we would have to efface our finite nature. But we can secularize our origin, or consume it progressively. Think again of the notion of history as a process of weakening. Writing history is a process by which the peremptoriness of reality is reduced and in which reality becomes a set of shared images—a discourse. (Though, obviously, I do not believe that the role of the historian is limited to this process.)

Zabala: Let's move to the problem of the accused at a trial, of his opportunity for repentance, of his responsibility . . .

Vattimo: Somewhere in his *Philosophy of Law*, Hegel says that it is the right of a prisoner to be put to death, once the sentence of death has been issued. No one will ever convince me of the correctness of this proposition. The concept of punishment, of a judicial sentence, implies an imposition of suffering that I cannot accept unless it leads to religious repentance, unless its use goes beyond mere punishment. Is there such a thing as an authentic guilt that formal justice can succeed in exposing and condemning? I have quite a few doubts on this point. Take the case of fiscal justice—the game that a citizen is required to play in order to keep as much of his money as possible without violating any written law. Must I absorb the tax laws into my own personal moral duties? Why should I? Should I respect all the laws of my city unconditionally, as Greek ethics would require? Should I do so despite the fact that some laws were conceived in order to favor members of a specific social class? We may say that I respect the tax laws of my country in order to avoid legal problems; it is, though, entirely compatible with my ethics to take advantage of all existing ways to pay the least amount of tax. Or again, take the case of murder. I would not define myself as a murderer if someone were to steal into my house and I were to use my gun against him out of fear, thinking that he also has a gun. If the intruder were to get shot, I would not feel guilty, even though I would be, in law, an unintentional murderer. In the event, killing would be for me the best choice; I would have to defend myself. And so the question that I ask myself continually is this: Isn't evil simply guilt—a guilty feeling?

Zabala: How would you compare what you're saying with Schleiermacher's advice: that everyone should write his own Bible—that everyone, in other words, should continuously rewrite the law? Why not rewrite the whole law?

Vattimo: It is clearly impossible, and that is why societies institute legal systems. We are incapable of living alone. Man, *logon echon*, is he who possesses discourse (not he who possesses reason). This notion explains the limits of the legal system in which we live. I conform my behavior to the laws, not because I agree with them unconditionally, but because I prefer living in this society to living in another, more primitive one. Here, I have my friends, my personal things, and so forth. The concept of contingency is pertinent: I belong to a specific group historically, and not absolutely. Die for my country? I would fight to defend a historical and social order—if someone were to try exterminating all Italian speakers or destroying the Italian democratic system, I would defend my language and culture. On the other hand, if it seemed necessary, for the benefit of my country and its citizens, that Italy become the fifty-first American state, despite all the respect I have for my tradition and language, I would have no problem with that. I often say that I feel Italian only when the national soccer team plays or when I sit down to eat, because these things are part of my tradition.

Zabala: Are these attitudes of yours a product of multiculturalism?

Vattimo: I am thinking of Europe, which I believe in. I also believe in the idioms of local traditions. I would not, though, fight for the supremacy of the Piedmont dialect over those of the rest of Italy. I would be sorry if it were to disappear, or if Piedmont cuisine were overtaken by fast-food culture . . . but in a supranational state, one with stronger cohesion than that of the European Community today, dialects and local traditions will be able to survive. National languages and national traditions will become "regional" traditions of Europe also, and will survive as such.

Zabala: The more cohesion, the more flexibility? The more strength, the more weakness?

Vattimo: In order to be truly pluralistic, a democratic society has to leave space even for those who don't want to take part in the social conversation. Society must tolerate even those who don't share the common binding principles. A real democracy would make space for such individuals. They should respect the behavioral norms of society, but if they want to live on charity, we should give them as much as they want, for as long as they want. Why should we oblige them to take on the customs of the middle class, and comforts such as television and elevators, if they really want to live as marginal members of society?

Zabala: You appear to be endorsing what Nietzsche defined in terms of nihilism. Or should we conclude that ours is already a nihilistic society?

Vattimo: Of course we should. A society is nihilistic not only when it loses its faith, but also when it allows for the existence of many other faiths. When Nietzsche declares that God is dead, he doesn't only mean that there are no longer supreme values; he also means that a multitude of values has taken their place at the ruined foundation. I think that this point is of great importance. The conviction of a degree of unity was accompanied by a degree of monoculturalism—and this may be rational, but it is nonetheless "mono." Today we are aware that, in imposing this kind of universal monoculture, we do violence to others. We need to structure a humanity in which a multitude of deities may coexist. And from the juridical point of view, we need to recognize the strictly procedural (as opposed to natural and objective) character of law. We can still use the expression "natural law" with reference to behavioral norms that are historically natural. I find it quite natural to buy Christmas presents in December; but if I were to live in a society in which Christmas takes place in August, I would find it equally natural to buy presents in August. "Natural law" means those procedural regulations that a society considers natural for its uses and customs. Obviously, one can criticize the law and, when necessary, change it. In a weak conception of natural law, what proceeds on its own—automatically—is natural. When it no longer proceeds on its own, reasons must be found to modify it or confirm it.

Zabala: You have just presented, in your own terms, weak versions of "natural law," "justice," "evil." You have even redescribed "nihilism" in a way that isn't so potent; isn't unsettling. But isn't metaphysics the real challenge? Is it, can it ever be, weak?

Vattimo: Metaphysics tends to ask the question, "Why 'being' rather than nothingness?" Since there is no definitive answer, the question signifies a confutation of the very possibility and creates conditions for the suspension of metaphysics. "Being" lacks a reason. There is no reason sufficient to explain why "being" is—and discovering this weakens not only the question and not only metaphysics, but the discovery weakens "being" itself. If "being" had a strong reason to be, then metaphysics would have significance, would have strength. But as things are, "being"—which never permits us to answer the question "Why 'being' rather than nothingness?"—is historical and causal, happened and happening.

Zabala: Then wouldn't you agree with Derrida's notion that we should let go of "being"—that we should disrupt any and all talk of it?

Vattimo: Not at all. By no means.

Zabala: Why? Because that would be falling back into metaphysics?

Vattimo: Of course. It would be like announcing that the metaphysical problem is meaningless, while the announcement itself is a metaphysical dissolution of the problem. It's an apparently strong move whose result is, unsurprisingly, nothing. Nothing is typically the result of strength. An alternative is "weak thought"—or as I called it in a *Common Knowledge* article years ago, "optimistic nihilism."[1]

1. Gianni Vattimo, "Optimistic Nihilism," *Common Knowledge* 1.3 (Winter 1992): 37–44.

PEACE AND KNOWLEDGE POLITICS IN THE UPPER XINGU

Marina Vanzolini

Translated by Julia Sauma

The battle for *a truth* is something entirely different from the battle
for *truth*.
—*Nietzsche*, "On Truth and Lies in a Nonmoral Sense"

The multilingual cultural system known as the Upper Xingu—a community
of indigenous peoples that inhabit the Xingu River's headwaters, in central
Brazil—is typically defined by ethnologists as a hierarchical and pacifist regime.
These two features seem to distinguish Upper Xinguan social philosophy from
that of most other indigenous Amazonian peoples. Hierarchy is usually attributed
to a system of linear status transmission associated with the position of village
chief. The distinction is primarily an ethnological one and a topic for debate

Originally published in *Common Knowledge* 22.1 (January 2016): 25–42, as part of the symposium "Peace by Other Means, Part 5." © 2016 by Duke University Press.

The author wishes to thank the program in social anthropology of the University of São Paulo for help in financing this translation, and Jeffrey Perl for his careful reading of the text.

Common Knowledge 25:1–3

DOI 10.1215/0961754X-7299162

among ethnographers. Pacifism, however—the second concept that ethnographers mention in describing the Xinguan system—is invoked as well by the Xinguans themselves. Thus, for example, indigenous accounts of entry into the ritual exchange system that defines boundaries in the Xinguan complex emphasize the pacification of newcomers; that is to say, the Xinguans stress the transition from a propensity toward war to the adoption of an antiwar ethos that is associated with participation in the *kwarup* intercommunity ritual.[1]

Taken as a set, hierarchy and pacifism definitively exclude the Upper Xingu from Pierre Clastres's image of "forest peoples": if Xinguans do not live "for-war," they do not seem either to be a society "against-the-state."[2] But then, perhaps we should take more care with the terms we use to translate other peoples' ideas. As I have argued elsewhere, the imputation of hierarchy can obstruct development of a more refined description of what is really involved in indigenous conceptions of "chieftainship," "linearity," "kinship," and "mastery."[3] The concept of hierarchy, furthermore, can lead us either to ignore those against-the-state vectors that act counter to political centralization or to interpret them as mere symptoms of social disintegration. Although they may be present in many different contexts, it matters to know what place it is that against-the-state vectors—or *lines of flight*, if we read Clastres's idea through Deleuze and Guattari—occupy in any given world.[4] I believe not only that such vectors occupy a central place in indigenous political philosophy but also that they can be seen to function in the idea of chieftainship itself. The same type of criticism can be directed against use of the concept of pacifism to describe social life in the Upper Xingu; this term, too, must be ethnographically unpacked if we are to understand what it really involves. We

1. See Ellen Basso, *The Last Cannibals: A South American Oral History* (Austin: University of Texas Press, 1995); Thomas Gregor, "Uneasy Peace: Intertribal Relations in Brazil's Upper Xingu," in *The Anthropology of War*, ed. Jonathan Haas (New York: Cambridge University Press, 1992); and Michael Heckenberger, *The Ecology of Power: Culture, Place, and Personhood in the Southern Amazon, A.D. 1000–2000* (New York: Routledge, 2005).

2. Pierre Clastres had South American indigenous peoples in mind when he developed these concepts, which allowed him to define forest societies positively and no longer in relation to a scale of human social development. Rather than understanding those peoples as incapable of reaching an elevated level of political organization, Clastres proposed that we should recognize the absence of the state as an active refusal of coercive power. Thus, for Clastres, primitive society is not a stateless society (one that still has not developed a state) but a society that is against-the-state. Clastres's hypothesis has been broadly contested by subsequent Americanist ethnology; see, for example, Fernando Santos-Granero, "From Prisoner of the Group to Darling of the Gods: An Approach to the Issue of Power

in Lowland South America," *L'Homme* 33 (1993): 126–28, 213–30; and Carlos Fausto, "Donos Demais. Maestria e Dominio na Amazonia," *Mana* 14, no. 2 (2008): 329–66. It is broadly accepted as well, however, that Clastres touched on a point that became important for research conducted in Amazonia, especially from the 1990s onward, on the social productivity of war and, more generally, on relations with alterity in the constitution of the Amerindian *socius*; see Clastres, *A Sociedade contra o Estado* (1974; repr., São Paulo: Cosac Naify, 2003); Renato Sztutman, *O Profeta e o Principal: A Acão Política Ameríndia e Seus Personagens* (São Paolo: FAPESP, 2012); Eduardo Viveiros de Castro, "O intempestivo, ainda," afterword to *Arqueologia da Violência: Pesquisas de antropologia política* by Pierre Clastres (São Paulo: Cosac Naify, 2011).

3. See Marina Vanzolini, "Eleições na aldeia ou o Alto Xingu contra o Estado?," *Anuário Antropológico* (2011): 31–54.

4. See Gilles Deleuze and Félix Guattari, "Micropolítica e segmentaridade," in *Mil Platôs: Capitalismo e Esquizofrenia*, vol. 3 (1980; repr., Rio de Janeiro: Editora, 1996), 83–116.

must investigate those forms of violence that are often ignored in both the indigenous and the ethnological affirmations of Xinguan pacifism. Sorcery, a central feature of Xinguan sociality, as it is described by themselves, must be taken into account, given its relation to war and to the formative dynamics of the Xinguan multilingual system.

The way in which sorcery comes to be known in their society illuminates other Xinguan knowledge practices. My argument here is that the mechanism that controls violence in the Upper Xingu is probably less the result of an applied pacifist ideology—the rejection of war as the *socius*'s generative matrix—than the effect of a specific conception of knowledge, one that both reflects and produces the Xinguan world. Xinguans might be unfamiliar with extreme forms of violence not because of what distances them from other Amazonian peoples but precisely because of what they share. It is through the Xinguan rejection of a single truth, rather than through their rejection of war per se, that their logic is "good to think" through the question of peace.

Sorcery against the State

I approach the Xinguan world through the perspective of the Aweti, a Tupi-speaking group that has inhabited the Upper Xingu area for at least two centuries. The Aweti currently number about 250 people, divided into four villages, a population not as small as it sounds, considering that no more than thirty individuals survived the successive chicken pox and mumps epidemics that ravaged the region in the 1950s and 1960s. Like their neighbors, Carib speakers, Arawak speakers, and Trumai speakers (Trumai being an isolated language), the Aweti subsist mainly on fishing and manioc derivation and participate in an intense network of ceremonial and matrimonial exchanges. This network is characterized by shared ethical and aesthetic standards and relational codes. They also share a mythological corpus describing how the twins Sun and Moon created these different peoples simultaneously and how the demiurges then differentiated them by distributing distinct weapons and artifacts to each.

The Aweti describe sorcery as a terrible evil that they would like to be rid of, and they see the sorcerer as in opposition to the humanity and morality that distinguish the Upper Xinguan from other human and nonhuman subjects. The Aweti also recognize, however, that sorcery is as old and inherent to their way of life as the *kwarup*, the intercommunity funerary ritual that constitutes a central axis of ritual exchange on the Upper Xingu and thereby traces the boundaries of Xinguan social life. Upper Xinguans regard sorcery as a primary existential problem—all deaths in the region are credited to the action of sorcerers—and the theme appears in most of the regional ethnographies. Anthropologists writing about Upper Xinguan sorcery, however, tend to reproduce the native discourse without giving due attention to the ambiguity that it necessarily evokes and that is particularly evident when adequately close attention is paid to actual life histories.

If asked to identify sorcerers who might be in the vicinity, an Aweti would likely indicate people from other villages or, even more likely, from a different Xinguan linguistic group. The Aweti might identify someone from their own group as a sorcerer, but if so it would probably be someone who lives on the other side of the village, since families naturally tend to build their houses side by side. Aweti discourse about sorcery begins, in other words, by designating the other—no kin, no one close—as sorcerer. In practice, however, this statement is only partly true. The Aweti generically affirm that the sorcerer acts out of malice, yet they always seek explanations to justify any particular case of sorcery. These speculations make it clear that sorcery is expected to come from those who are sufficiently close to the victim to want him or her to suffer. A plate of food denied, revenge for suspected adultery, envy of someone's healthy children or vegetable garden, or jealousy over care given to someone other than the sorcerer are typical examples of how sorcery is explained. Acts and suspicions of sorcery also appear to follow the paths of previous quarrels. A matrimonial betrayal, followed by separation, might lead to the mother-in-law's bewitchment by her former son-in-law; a father's brother who always had been suspected of envy might be accused of bewitching his nephew. Given that in each Xinguan village, as in the Upper Xingu generally, everyone expects to recognize anyone they meet as in some way kin, we should probably say that the sorcerer is an other *only from a certain point of view*. Xinguans recognize the difference between "real" kin and those with whom kinship operates as a relational schema guiding mutual affairs (applying the logic that "if my father calls so-and-so 'nephew,' so I call him 'cousin'"), but in any of these contexts the sorcerer is a type of kin. In contrast to what seems to be common for other Amazonian peoples, the suspects in a case of sorcery in the Upper Xingu will always be *other Xinguans*.[5] After the fact, it is only natural that a social distance separating sorcerer and victim should be affirmed: if the sorcerer were not other, he or she would not wish harm on a relative.

There is a marked difference between this form of violence, coming from the interior of a social world—only *a posteriori* classified as external to it—and contexts in which magical aggression is equated with open war between recognized enemies. The difference between internal and external aggression seems to correspond to the opposition between war and sorcery that, in the ethnological literature and according to the Xinguans themselves, marks the difference

---

5. While the Aweti tend to make accusations of sorcery against other Aweti (or at least other Xinguans in their circle of relations), the non-Xinguans with whom they live tend to accuse Xinguans as well. When a Trumai chief moved into Kayapó land, following a number of misunderstandings in the Xingu Park, it was said that his greatest fear was that he would be executed by his new neighbors, who would accuse him of sorcery as soon as one of them became ill.

between Xinguans and Amazonian warrior peoples. Xinguan sorcery, however, puts in question the possibility of distinguishing in definite and absolute terms between insides and outsides. Xinguan pacifism, it is important to note, is basically directed inward: it defines relational morality between people who recognize each other as part of the same collectivity, but it does not cover those who are situated beyond it. As Aristóteles Barcelos Neto observes, warrior attacks involving the kidnap of women and children were common among Upper Xinguans and their neighbors until the mid-twentieth century, just after the permanent installation in the region of Brazilian government bases.[6] It is very likely, as Rafael Bastos argues, that, if white people had not established a state that set limits, fixed identities, determined territories, and assigned group names, the boundaries between the interior and exterior of what we currently recognize as the Xinguan system would have undergone significant changes during the last three-quarters of a century, just as they had done before the state imposed itself on the indigenous peoples.[7] If such changes had indeed taken place, our ability to define the territorial and conceptual limits of Xinguan pacifism would probably be much more limited than it is now.

Today, war is no longer an existential option available to any Amazonian people. War—at least in its indigenous mode, as defined by Clastres—is against-the-state, and the progressive inclusion of these peoples in the Brazilian government's sphere of influence has meant that the warrior philosophy previously guiding indigenous life has become impracticable anywhere. Obviously, it is not by choice, then, that most Amazonian peoples are peaceful today—which does not mean that they are pacifist or that they define their existential condition (as in the Xinguan case) with reference to the abdication of violence. What differentiates Xinguans, in this light, from other Amazonian peoples is less the contemporary or historical presence or absence of war than the significance assigned to war in different sociological regimes. Nowadays, Xinguans profess a horror of violence and describe the manner in which they adopted their current way of life as a process of pacification. For other Amazonian peoples, meanwhile, war was in the past central to their social life, since the constitution of persons was, for them, effected by acquiring qualities, taken from captured enemies, that became their own source of existential power.[8] I am not saying that enmity plays

---

6. Aristóteles Barcelos Neto, "De divinações xamânicas e acusações de feitiçaria: Imagens Wauja de agência letal," *Mana* 12, no. 2 (October 2006): 285–313.

7. See Rafael José de Menezes Bastos, "A festa da Jaguatirica: Uma partitura crítico-interpretativa" (PhD diss., Universidade de São Paulo, 1989). Thanks to the efforts of the indigenist brothers Orlando, Claudio, and Leonardo Villas-Boas, the Xingu National Park was established in 1961 and would later be transformed into the Xingu

Indigenous Park. This area includes the Xingu River's inlets, where the Upper Xinguans live, and it also follows the river's course up to the border with Pará state, an area inhabited by the Ikpeng (also known as Txicão), Kajabi, Yudjá (or Juruna), and Kisêdjê (Suyá).

8. See, for example, Bruce Albert, "Temps du sang, temps des cendres: Représentations de la maladie, système rituel et espace politique chez les Yanomami du sud-est (Amazonie brésilenne)" (PhD diss., Laboratoire d'ethnologie et

no positive role in Xinguan social life, but in that context it assumes controlled forms, for example in the opposition between various Xinguan peoples in the ritual fight known as *huka-huka*, which is the *kwarup* funerary ritual's central episode; in the lance duel of the *Jawari* intercommunity party; and in the marked alterity within dance pairs in diverse intercommunity rituals that always bring together women and men from different groups. The problem, of course, is that enmity always seems to threaten to break free from control.

It is important, in this context, to rethink the contrast that is conventionally made between the Xinguan and other Amazonian peoples. In the end, each regime works toward relational harmony within a given collectivity (perhaps a universal truism). Given that the Xinguans comprise a variety of linguistic families, it seems to be in the cosmopolitan nature of their collectivity that they differ most from their neighbors. While it is true that the ideological value or, more exactly, the creative potency of war varies for different Amerindian peoples, the contrast between them seems to be related less to the presence or absence of open hostility than to the stability of the boundaries that define the group. Recently, Xinguan cosmopolitanism has been interpreted, along the lines of a century-old hypothesis of Max Schmidt's, as a product of a specific Arawakan ethos, taken to be incorporative and hierarchical.[9] Thus, according to Schmidt, war among the Arawak-speaking peoples would be a matter of subjugating human labor, conquering territories, and acquiring primary resources for the making of agricultural instruments. Whereas, for some Amazonian peoples (as described by Amerindian ethnology much later), war was a means of appropriating the enemy's subjective qualities (through anthropophagic rituals, headshrinking, song acquisition, and other such means), Arawakan cultures would tend to subordinate rather than cannibalize their others. Discussing the merits of this thesis would require a very broad comparative study, so here I shall simply indicate those Xinguan dynamics that could add some needed complexity to this description. If we grant that the Upper Xingu system is an example of an Arawakan "cultural matrix," then the Arawakan singularity, in the Amazon setting, will require reassessment as much as the Xinguan case does.

de sociologie comparative, Université de Paris X, 1985); Aparecida Vilaça, *Comendo Como Gente. Formas de Canibalimso Wari'* (Rio de Janeiro: UFRJ, 1992); Philippe Descola, "Les affinités sélectives: Alliance, guerre, et prédation dans l'ensemble Jivaro," *L'Homme* 33, nos. 126–28 (1993): 171–90; Anne-Christine Taylor, "Les bons ennemis et les mauvais parents: Le traitement symbolique de l'alliance dans les rituels de chasse aux têtes des Jivaros de l'Equateur," in *Les Complexités de l'alliance, IV, Économie, politique et fondements symboliques de l'alliance*, ed. Elisabeth Copet-Rougier and Françoise Héritier-Augé (Paris: Editions des Archives Contemporaines, 1993), 73–105; Carlos Fausto, "Of Enemies and Pets: Warfare and Shamanism in Amazonia," *American Ethnologist* 26, no. 4 (1999), 933–56; and Eduardo Viveiros de Castro, *A inconstância da alma selvagem e outro Ensaios de antropologia* (São Paulo: Cosac Naify, 2002).

9. Max Schmidt, *Die Aruaken: Ein Beitrag zum Problem der Kulturverbreitung* (Leipzig: Veit, 1917). The idea of a typically Arawakan regime of relations to alterity appears as well (though substantially transformed) in Heckenberger's *Ecology of Power*. See also Jonathan D. Hill and Fernando Santos-Granero, *Comparative Arawakan Histories: Rethinking Language, Family, and Culture in Amazonia* (Chicago: University of Illinois Press, 2002), 1–25.

As we have seen, the pacifist ideology and cosmopolitanism of the Xinguans do not guarantee an absence of violence; indeed, these characteristics appear to favor an irruption of violence in the form of sorcery. The violence comes from within, from another Xinguan, and very frequently from a relative or someone living alongside the victim. While war is waged to capture names and generative potency and is therefore a fundamental means, in Amerindian contexts, of constructing relations, Xinguan sorcery *undoes kinship ties*. Xinguan cosmopolitanism may imply, as is argued, a propensity to incorporate the other as a (diminished, dominated) selfsame, but Xinguan sorcery *makes the selfsame into the other*. This type of violence among allies may be understood as an inherently cosmopolitan form of aggression. Rather than the result of an always progressing cultural expansionism, Xinguan cosmopolitanism is better thought of as the mutating effect of group inclusions in and exclusions from an allied set that, on account of sorcery and its dynamics, is persistently unstable. It seems very likely that in the past sorcery led to war and vice versa, in expression of a constant shift between relations of friendship and enmity among neighboring groups, a common dynamic among most Amazonian peoples.

The relation between war and sorcery is a recurrent theme among researchers working in the Xinguan context, since the aversion to hostility, while a defining trait of their way of life, according to the Xinguans themselves, has not led to the complete disappearance of violence; sorcery, which is violent and provokes violence, remains for them a significant force. On that point, Thomas Gregor argues that fear of the accusation of sorcery—the pressure to demonstrate peaceable behavior at all times—plays a positive role in the Xinguans' recoil from every form of aggression.[10] Gregor's hypothesis is problematic for a number of reasons. First, its validity depends on agreement among the Xinguans about the identity of sorcerers, and, as Gregor himself observes, in his monograph on the Mehinaku (Xinguan Arawak): "Every Mehinaku man was regarded as a witch by at least one informant, and two men were named as witches by every informant."[11] Second, if the fear of accusation were an efficient means of effecting moral control, we would expect to find few cases of bewitchment in the Upper Xingu, but the reverse is true. And finally, the accusations themselves tend to be understood as disruptive, antisocial acts. An alternative analysis, made by Marcela Coelho de Souza, is that sorcery is the means by which the Upper Xinguan network of political and ritual relations opens itself to and integrates strangers.[12] Sorcery,

10. See also Gertrude Dole, "Shamanism and Political Control among the Kuikuro," in *Beiträge zur Völkerkunde Südamerikas*, ed. Hans Becker (Hannover: Munstermann-Druck, 1964), 53–62; Dole, "Anarchy without Chaos: Alternatives to Political Control among the Kuikuro," in *Political Anthropology*, ed. Marc J. Swartz, Victor W. Turner, and Arthur Tuden (Chicago: Aldine, 1976), 73–88; and George Zarur, *Parentesco, ritual e economia no Alto Xingu* (Rio de Janeiro: Funai, 1975).

11. Thomas Gregor, *Mehinaku: The Drama of Daily Life in a Brazilian Indian Village* (Chicago: University of Chicago Press, 1977), 207.

12. Marcela Coelho de Souza, "Virando gente: Notas a uma história aweti," in *Os povos do Alto Xingu: História e cultura*, ed. Bruna Franchetto and Michael J. Heckenberger (Rio de Janeiro: Editoria de Universidad de Rio de Janeiro, 2001), 358–400.

according to Coelho de Souza, represents the dangerous and thus negative side of the introjection of others into a cosmopolitan relational network that, while presuming the maintenance of identity, also requires the maintenance of a coefficient of difference as the condition of possibility for ceremonial and matrimonial exchange. Coelho de Souza thus regards sorcery as a residue of the necessarily incomplete process of becoming Xinguan.

As previously mentioned, Xinguans always point, in generic comments, to "others" as sorcerers, even when they are other Xinguans. It is understandable, as well as consistent with some Upper Xinguan accounts of sorcery, that groups recently integrated into the peaceful exchange regime that defines the Xinguan universe are held responsible for deaths associated with sorcery. Even, however, if Xinguan sorcery can be associated with the internalization of enemy peoples over time, if from the Xinguan perspective sorcery is always triggered by everyday interactions—of the same kinds that define kin relations—it is also intimately associated with a constant internal production of enmity. It does not seem sufficient to say that sorcery is war by other means, or war disguised by the operation of pacifist morality. Xinguan sorcery is an irruption of violence that begins *at the center* of social life, a type of violence produced continuously by the dynamics of kinship. That Xinguan sorcery no longer slips into open warfare is arguably a consequence of the freeze imposed on group boundaries following *contact* (a word that reverberates as euphemism here).[13]

Sorcery, as a force for indeterminacy, seems fundamentally connected to the way in which it is known (or, rather, is unknowable) in the Xinguan world.[14] Ultimately, my topic here is the Xinguan knowledge regime—their conception of what can be known, and how—in relation to Xinguan pacifism. Describing a case of sorcery that I followed in the field might help to make clear how their knowledge regime connects to the assumptions that Xinguans make about the accusations of sorcery that they hear and produce.

Kuriti

Kuriti is the specific and apparently pan-Xinguan name for a special type of sorcery that the Aweti know both by that name and by the generic Aweti term *tupiat*,

---

13. This hypothesis is in line with that of Bastos (in *Festa da Jaguatirica*). On the other hand, Heckenberger (in *Ecology of Power*) suggests that colonization led to the disorganization of a more stable political system that had tended toward centralization. I suspect that the effect was, rather, to stabilize a system that might always have been characterized by unstable boundaries, even when it operated in a much larger population.

14. Bruce Kapferer's analysis of sorcery in Sri Lanka points in the same direction. Borrowing a conceptual image from Deleuze and Guattari, he writes about Sinhalese sorcery as the creation of a "smooth space" at a moment in which the sociopolitical distinctions of a "striated space" have been temporarily undone and can be reformed only through performance of a disenchantment ritual. See Kapferer, *The Feast of the Sorcerer: Practices of Consciousness and Power* (Chicago: University of Chicago Press, 1997).

which in its strictest sense refers to minuscule arrows that sorcerers are said to shoot surreptitiously at their victims or tie to corporeal residues, food, or stolen belongings. *Kuriti* actually involves a potion made with urucum and a vegetable substance that no one could identify for me (since revealing knowledge of the formula would be equivalent to admitting "ownership" of the charm and, thus, of being a sorcerer). I was told that the potion has the appearance of normal urucum paste and must be rubbed onto the victim's arm. Most commonly, the *kuriti* victim is a woman bewitched by a man, with the effect that she falls head over heels in love with the sorcerer. At first glance, *kuriti* appears to be a typical form of affinal sorcery that transforms potential spouses—close or distant cross cousins—into actual lovers.

The first case of *kuriti* that I observed during fieldwork did not seem to fit with this generic description, which different Aweti gave to me dozens of times. The case began one afternoon when we received news of a young woman's disappearance. She had left home to visit her sister in a neighboring Aweti village but never arrived. A number of hypotheses emerged about what could have happened. Search parties were formed and sent to look for her in the forest, while shamans smoked their long cigars in attempts to see where her soul was located and to determine whether any spells against her were operative in the surrounding area. People said that she had run away because her father had hit her when she refused to help her sister in the vegetable garden. They said that she had most likely been eaten by a jaguar on her way to the other village but that, if she were not dead, she could only be with sylvan, nonhuman beings (*kat*), eating fruit in the forest, with no chance of returning home. Some time later, a theory that her classificatory brother (her mother's sister's son) was the culprit began to circulate, since everyone knew that he was the girl's lover and had been so for many years. People began to say he had "placed *kuriti* for her." As they were first-degree parallel cousins, the young man was not a suitable companion for the girl, and the relationship between them had been harshly and universally condemned.[15] Some suggested that the girl had run away when her mother chastised her for her forbidden love. Eventually, a shaman found a *kuriti*, close to where the young woman normally slept, in the external part of the straw roof that covered the family home. I was told—this all happened far from the village where I lived at the time—that the charm consisted of a small anthropomorphic effigy made of wax and wood, a "human image" (*mo'at a'ang*). It was also said that a similar *kuriti* had been found

15. Among the Aweti, and the Xinguans more generally, parallel relatives from the same generation, when they are genealogically and geographically close, are "consanguines" (or unmarriable), becoming "affinizable" only as the distances increase. Whatever the kinship tie, whether close or distant, however, it must be continually reaffirmed in performance: it is necessary to act like a brother and, especially, to call someone "brother" in order for the relationship to be regarded as real. See Eduardo Viveiros de Castro, "Alguns aspectos da afinidade no dravidianato amazônico," in *Amazônia: Etnologia e história indígena*, ed. Manuel Carneiro da Cunha and Viveiros de Castro (São Paulo: NHII-USP/FAPESP, 1993).

somewhere along the path between the new and the old village, having been placed there to attract the girl off the path and into the forest. Whatever the technique employed, the expectation would have been that the *kuriti* would make its object lose her capacity for good judgment.

The young woman reappeared several days later. Some said that, after having spent time lost in the forest, she returned alone in the middle of the night, at the Funai outpost, very thin and injured, knocking on a relative's door.[16] Another version had it that a Kamayurá woman had seen her in perfect health during the day at the Funai outpost and that she had been in her unapproved lover's house the whole time (he also lived at the outpost). These two versions concurred that the young woman, on her return, seemed somehow lost: "She doesn't see well," everyone said. Even those claiming that she had spent the entire time hidden in her lover's house saw her as a victim: *kuriti* had made her lose her head. A girl who has a classificatory brother as a lover is as lost as someone gone astray in the forest. Even though the *kuriti* is a special modality of sorcery in the Xinguan context, the story exemplifies a recurrent process in that region: the accusation of sorcery between people who are reasonably close and, at the same time, opposed in terms, so to speak, of amorous or conjugal interests. It is significant that this case was not one of sorcery between affines but rather of "affinizing" sorcery: a classificatory sister (first degree mother's sister's daughter) was transformed into a lover by means of a sorcerer's spell. Given, however, that these young people were already lovers—and everyone seemed to agree on this point—we could say that the accusation itself was directed at an affine (or a type of affine) of the victim. The *kuriti* and the accusation reveal that difference was found where identity was expected: those who should have behaved as siblings were behaving as spouses. Also significant about this case is how it shows that a charm can involve diverse mediations: the human effigy could have worked as much to attract forest spirits and divert the young woman from her path as to make her lose her mind and go off to live with her lover.

Even if there is no certainty regarding the presence or absence of sorcery when a misfortune occurs, it is likely that people will react as if there were, and thus sooner or later accusations will begin to surface and then lead to open conflict. In this case, as in all the others I followed in the field, people never knew exactly what happened and continued to offer hypothetical explanations that they characterized as "attempts." As the Aweti explained to me many times, when I asked what they thought had *actually* happened, "we are just searching [for the truth]." Their characterization of their efforts as an unending search is the aspect of sorcery that I would like especially to underscore with this case: *the very*

---

16. Funai is the Fundação Nacional do Índio, or National Indian Foundation, a body of the Brazilian federal government.

form of the conversations taking place around the subject of sorcery presupposes that an accusation is always provisional. Even when the accusation is founded on a shamanic vision, it is treated as provisional, for the Aweti do not discount the possibility that shamans can sometimes get it wrong or might not be able to identify the sorcerers or recognize the trappings of sorcery. Accepting this possibility does not mean that accusations of sorcery do not have the force of truth but, rather, that the claims made are understood as *transient* truth acts.

Knowledge as Politics

Sorcery is a highly secretive phenomenon in the Upper Xingu; no one would ever admit to being a sorcerer, and in the past a recognized sorcerer was often executed by his victim's relatives, once they had formed a large enough group for an ambush. Even in such cases, however, it was rare for the verdict to correspond to collective opinion: the family of an executed man would defend his innocence and counteraccuse the accusers—of aggression, of gossip, of being bad people. Anyone accused of sorcery today would do the same. There is no universal mechanism for verifying guilt, and revenge by execution remains a family affair.[17] For an outsider like the ethnographer, it is impossible to determine who is and is not a sorcerer—doing so requires choosing a side, thereby defining to what group one belongs. From the outside, sorcery presents itself as a matter of perspective: what some call sorcery others perceive as revenge against an unjust accusation of sorcery (or even as the attack of a pathogenic spirit). For those directly involved, however, lives are at risk, and it is vital to determine what has occurred and is occurring.

Much of the anthropological literature on sorcery deals with accusations rather than with sorcery itself—an analytical conundrum that can have one or both of two possible explanations. First, there is the ethnographic material itself: in contexts, such as that of the Upper Xingu, in which sorcery can never be observed because there are no self-professed sorcerers, the ethnographer has available only accounts of sorcery, mostly in the form of accusations. The second possible explanation speaks to the ethnographer's preconceptions when describing foreign worlds. Starting from the assumption that sorcery does not exist and that it can be understood solely as a false explanation of an underlying social or biological reality, the anthropologist deals exclusively with the accounts and their social effects. From this perspective, it is only the accusations, never sorcery itself, that can have an effect on intimate relations.

My own material on sorcery among the Aweti is based, likewise, on what

---

17. Obviously, I disagree with Patrick Menget's conclusion that the punishment of sorcery is a function of chieftainship in the Upper Xingu. See Menget, "Les frontières de la chefferie: Remarques sur le système politique du Haut Xingu (Brésil)," *L'Homme* 33, nos. 126–28 (1993): 59–76.

the Aweti say about it, basically in the form of accusations. It was interesting to notice, then, that the impossibility of determining the identity of a sorcerer sometimes enjoined my using language tricks that the Aweti themselves employ to maintain the uncertainty surrounding accusations (they want to be able to recant if a new and better account is offered). When openly spoken in the village center, accusations of sorcery are expected to dissuade the sorcerer from further wrongdoing and, thus, can be ideally regarded as mechanisms of pacification. Accusations are usually thought, however, to be as damaging as sorcery itself. Hence it is regarded as normal to accuse one's neighbors in the face of tragic circumstances, such as the death of a relative or a serious illness, but it is considered wrong to prolong the accusation indefinitely. In due course, furthermore, the accused is expected to forgive his accusers, as long as they have acted with appropriate restraint. Still, in practice, accusers frequently take revenge on whoever they think has attacked them, or at least an accused sorcerer will blame a serious illness in his own family on those who have accused him of sorcery: "They're taking revenge, unjustly, for a murder that I did not commit," these people might reason. This sort of exchange involves an intricate game of overlapping assumptions, in which the problem is always what the other side imagines about what is imagined about them. In short, sorcery and the accusation of sorcery are different modes of the same phenomenon (and are distinguishable principally as forms of gendered aggression: only men cast spells, and women are sorcery accusers par excellence).

While observing heated conversations on controversial topics during fieldwork, my knowledge of the Aweti language was sufficient only to understand a few sentences here and there, so afterward I often found myself asking what so-and-so meant by such-and-such a statement. This linguistic incompetence only exacerbated my overall ignorance when discussions turned to people whom I did not know. Sometimes they involved people whom I did know but alluded to them only vaguely ("the one who's in that place"). It took me a while to notice, at any event, that my friends were embarrassed when I asked them to name people who had been accused of sorcery. The less they said, apparently, the easier it would be for my friends to drop the accusations, if necessary, and return to the status quo ante. Vagueness and allusiveness serve a significant function when facts are assumed liable to change as new interpretations are credited.

Accusations circulate essentially through gossip, unless they are made at the village center, in public, which is unusual behavior—indeed, a gesture of desperation. Gossip is not, however, a discursive object with a defined nature. The Aweti word for gossip (*tuĩ popy'i*, literally "well-disposed chin") designates the propensity to talk too much. Talking little and speaking carefully are signs of nobility in the Upper Xingu; they are important characteristics expected of a chief. Not only speaking little but also *listening* little is admired, as it means taking no note of what is said about one's own family. Gossip too, then, can be an object of accusation. To discredit a story told by another, one might say "he speaks too much." No one, however, is going to say "I speak too much." From the speaker's point of view, he or she is simply retelling a story, *tomowkap*, which is a term that also means "myth," although what we would regard as a myth the Aweti sometimes distinguish from gossip by calling it "the ancient people's story" (*mote mo'aza etomowkap*). As stories are accredited or discredited by the listener, not the speaker, there is no objective difference for the Aweti between myth and gossip. The implication of this attitude is profound, as it points to an intimate connection between the political effects of sorcery and the epistemological regime by which the Xinguans constitute their world.

The Aweti regard myths as a fundamental source of esoteric knowledge. When asked a question about celestial geography, for instance where the village of the dead is located, they are sure to retell the story of the man that followed his dead friend to the sky and returned to tell the tale. "I have never been there, I don't know how it is," a shaman once responded to my query, then immediately went on to recount the same myth, which I had already heard from other sources, though always in slightly different versions. By listening to myths told by elders (normally a grandparent, a parent, or even a parent-in-law) on a daily basis, the Aweti learn how the dead live, why one should not urinate in a vegetable garden, or why we should treat our mothers-in-law well. This process involves hearing the origin saga, in which the demiurge twins Sun and Moon are central characters, as well as numerous myths about the acquisition of cultural attributes and about how certain powers (such as the ability to produce immense quantities of manioc starch with a minimal amount of manioc) were lost in times immemorial.

In his analysis of mythological narrative context among the Piro, Peter Gow argues that Piro myths are never didactic or pedagogical but, rather, are told for the pure pleasure of narrating.[18] A like observation might be made about the Aweti, but just because Aweti myths are not explicitly intended to instruct children or explain contemporary realities to adults does not mean that the stories told do not operate in that way unintentionally. Indeed, the Aweti word *tomowkap* that I translate as *story* is formed by the root of the verb "to guide" (*mowka*) and the instrumentalizing suffix *p*. *Tomowkap* designates stories, transmitted down the generations, in which unknown elders are the protagonists, but the word is used as well to identify narratives about events that happened only moments before. A man who has information about an event is, like an expert myth teller, a "story owner" (*tomowkap itat*), the sole difference between them being that the former holds the position temporarily, while the latter may hold it over the long term. *Mowkatu*, "guidance," can refer equally to the daily speech that a chief gives in the village center, to a father's advice, or to one person's account of a

18. See Peter Gow, *An Amazonian Myth and Its History* (Oxford: Oxford University Press, 2001).

fishing trip. What these varieties of communication have in common is the sense that they are not just accounts of past happenings but are also guides for future action. The instructive character that the Aweti associate with their myths explains the moralistic effect that some stories—those, for instance, recalling that terrible cosmological troubles were the result of bad behavior among kin in ancient times—can have. The notion that myths substantiate rules of behavior and explain the world's current condition surfaced in many contexts during my fieldwork. In a conversation, for example, with a man about his father's explanations of alimentary restrictions associated with the corn and pequi harvests, my interlocutor insisted, perhaps anticipating some skepticism on my part: "It isn't a lie, it is story!" (*temo'em e'ym, tomowkap!*).

Claude Lévi-Strauss defined myth as a discourse about a time in which humans communicated with animals. To this classic definition, Eduardo Viveiros de Castro has added that the past recounted in myth is never finally transcended and can always be actualized in the present.[19] Clearly, not every event that is told as a *story* implies to the Aweti the rise of a new world order, but the difference between cosmogonic and other kinds of stories seems to be the degree of the events' and the characters' potency. This distinction is neither negligible nor absolute. It appears to correspond to the high degree of formal codification in ancestral stories (which are about "grandparents" and also come to us from them), as well as to the acknowledged importance of events retold down the generations. Even so, if it is true to say that a story about the demiurge twins is held to determine the Aweti way of life more than a story about the current Aweti generation's grandparents, the less momentous and more recent narrative still carries a warning: what has happened could happen again. The numerous stories about men attacked by jaguars in paths surrounding a village are examples. *Tomowkapwan ekozoko*, "you will become a story," is a typical remark made by one protagonist to another as their narrative concludes: the protagonist will become a model for *amyñeza*, "future people." This affirmation reminds the audience that every agent in an extraordinary event can "become a story" or "remain in history" and thus become the prototype that configures a future world.[20]

For the Aweti, those of their stories that we would consider myths are speech acts whose narrative form should be kept intact for all generations. Mythic narratives, however, are always subject to variation, uncertainty, and criticism. This inconsistency became evident during my fieldwork, on visits to Aweti families, as I began to hear negative comments on narratives that I had taped in the village. When playing the recordings, in various houses, I would often hear statements like "it's a lie," "he doesn't know," "that's not the Aweti story, that's

19. Eduardo Viveiros de Castro, "A floresta de cristal: Notas sobre a ontologia dos espíritos amazônicos," *Cadernos de Campo* 14/15 (2006): 319–38.

20. The impossibility of clearly distinguishing the concept of story from that of history is evidence for the point being made here.

the Kamayurá [another group of Tupi-xinguans] story." At first, I imagined that these comments emerged from a short circuit I had caused by changing the way in which the stories usually circulated. Little by little, however, I realized that such was not the case. Aside from being recounted by older men to their sons and grandsons, at home and at nightfall, myths are also frequently remembered in the village's central square by men from different households or in a casual conversation among neighbors. These versions are very frequently criticized when the listener recounts them at home, and it is common for someone to say, "So-and-so just told me that story, I don't know where he got that from," or "So-and-so was telling such-and-such a story in the center, he thinks he knows everything." Critical voices might question the existence of an entire sequence of actions in a mythic narrative or even question a whole myth ("I've never heard that before, I don't know what that story is about"). In that vein, a story about the Bat (Tati'a) told to me by one storyteller as part of the Sun and Moon twin saga was dismissed by another storyteller who claimed that he had never heard the sequence organized in that way. It is also noteworthy that these criticisms are often softened by a type of relativism, with reflections such as "that's his story, the story that his father used to tell," or "the story that I learned from my father-in-law is different, the story he tells is from the Mehinaku people [Arawak-Xinguans], told him by his grandfather." I shall return to this point.

When members of the storyteller's audience characterize a narrative as a "lie," they almost always refer to the incomplete or inappropriate execution of its formal elements, such as the characters' names, the exact sequence of events, how a song is remembered or forgotten, and so forth. The word used by the Aweti for "lie," *mo'em,* can designate both a deliberately deceptive account and an unintentional mistake or bad representation (for example, a poorly executed pattern of body paint or a half-told myth). Meanwhile, there is no word that we might translate as "truth" or "true." *Na ytoto,* which translates as "himself" or "the very same," is used by the Aweti to indicate veracity; but, as *ytoto* also means "a lot," it is evident that "the very same/true" is only a more complete version of "false"—a distinction in degree, rather than a definite opposition between what is and what is not. Like *pacifism* and *hierarchy,* terms that tell us little about Xinguan sociopolitics, *truth* and *lie* are unreliable notions for dealing with the Xinguan way of conceiving knowledge.

The word *mo'em* does not imply that "lying" is in any way immoral, for a drawing or a narrative may be "false" not from any intention to conceal the "truth" but as a result of the creator's ineptitude. A judgment of falsity thus indicates no more than a lack in the correspondence between a model and its representation. In the case of myths and body patterns, correspondence is expected between past and present designs, or between narratives told by ancestors and those heard today, but not between the details of a factual narrative—the "real story"—and a narrative that recalls them, or between an actual ant path and a body pattern bearing the same name. When an Aweti says that some narration of a myth is a lie, he or she means that it has not been reproduced perfectly; its transmission from the past is faulty. A myth that lies is one lacking the form, including the richness of detail, that a listener hoped to find. Knowing through stories is always about knowing someone else's knowledge; it is not about knowing the real world and its true history, hence the necessity in Aweti of using the evidential *ti* ("they say") in mythic narratives: a myth is an account of events that "they say" happened, in such and such a way—but who knows? Thus, even though some mythic narratives are considered bad or false, they are admissible as "others' stories" and are sometimes taken on board in a spirit of comprehensiveness, the premise being, apparently, that it is beneficial and even important to know new versions. The narrators of Aweti myths and their listeners are only sometimes motivated by political disputes, envy, or the love of gossip; often there is a genuine interest in simply knowing more about how others (including white people) think.

It would be misleading to characterize this way of thinking as relativistic, however, for when the social context is fraught—when it does not permit the free exchange of knowledge, or of food and goods—the Aweti assume the truth to be singular. At such times, it is only my relatives' version of events that counts. If this scenario holds true for mythic narratives in some contexts—as, for example, in a dispute about who could give the ethnographer the best version—it is more dramatically the case when the discourse relates directly and crucially to the lives of living people, as in cases of illness and sorcery. The question of truth becomes important to the Aweti only when choosing one or another version of a story, which is tantamount to choosing a side in a controversy involving family members. Ellen Basso argues that, in Upper Xinguan narrative contexts, truth is always "social truth," defined in the interaction between narrator and listener as an act of agreement.[21] While this ethnographic observation is confirmed by my field experience, I believe that the author has not fully explored its consequences.

Myth is more than a mode of knowing; myth configures the world as it is. If myths say something about the world, what they say is never essentialistic, any more than it is relativistic. Myth as a knowledge regime never presents the world as a given essence but rather as a product of particular stories that are always prone to reformulation: we know that the village of the dead is thus only because so-and-so went there and told us and not because what so-and-so said corresponds to an intrinsic or immutable truth. This observation does not contradict Lévi-Strauss's thesis that myths function to obliterate history.[22] Rather

21. Basso, *Last Cannibals*, 39.

22. Claude Lévi-Strauss, "Raça e história" (1952), in *Antropologia Estrutural II*, 4th ed. (Rio de Janeiro: Tempo Brasileiro, 1993), 328–63.

than contradiction, what we encounter here is a paradox that lies at the heart of mythical thinking. At the same time as myth postulates the permanence of a way of life, creating an illusion of continuity in the order of the world, it also seems to escape the problem of essence: it conceives the imminence of the new as a constant possibility. Both storytellers and listeners are aware that myths change and that they exist in differing and sometimes contradictory versions. The emergence of more new and plausible versions is a constant possibility. In this sense, mythical logic is radically historical, rather than cyclical or ahistorical, but the historicism of myth is neither dialectical nor linear. Still less does myth deal with history as a necessary development, beginning from a causal principle.

Although it would be a stretch to say that, for the Aweti, every story potentially determines the configuration of a new cosmic or social order, we could say that their knowledge regime presupposes the world's intrinsic openness to change and to reinterpretation. If nothing can be definitively known, that is because nothing is definitively given. Whether myth, history, or simply gossip, narratives create the world as variation.

Mythic variation is obviously not unique to the Aweti: Lévi-Strauss constructed a masterly comparison of numerous indigenous stories from North and South America to show that variations obey a strict logic of transformation.[23] What I learned from the Aweti is that these variations are not an object of interest solely for anthropologists but also a topic for debate among myth narrators and listeners. In this sense, these narratives reveal not only a transformational logic and a particular form of historicity, as Lévi-Strauss argues, but also a particular knowledge regime inseparable from a particular conception of the world.[24]

The Fight for *a* Truth

As we know, in the context of science, as well as that of myth, truths are constantly changing. But for scientists, however sophisticated their understanding of the relativity of each new discovery, the truths they arrive at tend to be treated—if only as a matter of commonsense—as definitive truths. To be more precise, we could say that the scientific horizon includes the possibility of a definitive truth, which encourages scientists to move ever forward. There is no novelty in my pointing to the relation between the ideal of a monolithic truth and the

23. Gow (*Amazonian Myth and Its History*) offers a particularly interesting example of the use of the Lévi-Straussian method in association with ethnography in Peruvian Amazonia. See also, for considerations of the theme, Oscar Calávia Saez, "A variação mítica como reflexão," *Revista de Antropologia* 45, no. 1 (2002): 7–36; and Daniel Pierri, "Como acabará essa terra? Reflexões sobre a cataclismologia Guarani-Mbya, à luz da obra de Nim-

uendajú," *Tellus* 13, no. 24 (January–June 2013): 159–88, bd.trabalhoindigenista.org.br/sites/default/files/24_5_Como%20acabar%C3%A1%20essa%20terra.pdf.

24. Claude Lévi-Strauss, "A Gesta de Asdiwal" (1973), in *Antropoligia Estructural II*, 152–205; "Raça e história"; and "A estructura de mitos" (1955), in *Antropologia Estructural I* (Rio de Janeiro: Tempo Brasileiro, 2003), 237–65.

ethnocentrism that permitted the exterminations of indigenous America to take place and to continue even today. The struggle over truth, whether scientific or religious, has legitimated ethnocide and genocide for many centuries.

In the Aweti world, truth takes a different course, if indeed the notion of truth makes any sense in that world at all. It would be absurd to say that the Aweti do not care about whether they truly know the identity of the sorcerer who has killed their cousin. On the contrary, his identity is almost all that is worth knowing, and the Aweti spend a considerable amount of time speculating about what other people think (much as we do, perhaps). Nevertheless, the Aweti have not developed protocols for fact verification and, moreover, do not seek to discover, in an absolute sense, how things and events are either physically or metaphysically determined. As we saw in the case of the girl bewitched with *kuriti*, every Aweti story has a multiplicity of versions that people can negotiate with ease. Even if what seemed true five minutes before no longer makes sense, the Aweti find in situations of this kind no logical scandal. We cannot measure the political effects of this Xinguan knowledge politics, but we can observe that the Xinguans have never produced violence on a scale at all comparable to that experienced in the West. In this world, the limit of violence seems to be set by the social limits on the prestige and reach of a truth that can never be the state's truth or that of any group. It is worth remembering that the execution of sorcerers in the Upper Xingu is not a matter of consensus and public decision. Every group's suspicions remain unverifiable, and no one outside the family is expected to accept the decision reached. Executing a sorcerer requires no more than convincing a restricted group of men to carry out the task in the name of the family whose relative was killed by sorcery: a group of people struggling to establish *a* (not *the*) truth. The violence stops with a single death, and village life returns to normal. We might consider whether this way of thinking, once taken as proof of so-called primitive irrationality, might not actually constitute the strength of indigenous logic.

CALL FOR PAPERS

Clifford Geertz

One of the things you learn if you stay in this business long enough, and especially if you stay in it too long, is that it is not your enemies but your friends that you should fear. John Searle may not be right in saying that Thomas Kuhn was a Scientific Realist from the start and has been, from the start, misinterpreted by theorists who regard themselves as Kuhn's allies. But it does seem true that Kuhn has found himself pressed in a Realist direction by some unwanted readings, and even more unwanted uses, of his work in recent years—even uses by members of the original Linguistic Turn circle. Kuhn, in fact many of us, have divided loyalties. But we share a desire not to underwrite the further extremes of "deep irrealism," nor of the "strong program" which reduces science to nothing but a social and cultural phenomenon. I would like to see members of the original Linguistic Turn circle reinterpret their own work in the light of how their work has been used. I would also like to see papers detailing the history of Kuhn's influence—good, bad, and indifferent—and papers that explore how *The Structure of Scientific Revolutions* became itself the basis for a paradigm shift.

Originally published in *Common Knowledge* 1.1 (Spring 1992): 4–5. © 1992.

Common Knowledge 25:1–3
DOI 10.1215/0961754X-7299174

LEFT-WING KUHNIANISM

Richard Rorty

Some years back I coined the term "left-wing Kuhnians" in order to have an expression denoting people who thought that *The Structure of Scientific Revolutions* had important implications unintended, and unappreciated, by its author. The analogy was to the Left Hegelians, who thought that Hegel's philosophy of history had such implications. Jeffrey Perl once suggested, semi-seriously, that *Common Knowledge* was a journal of left-wing Kuhnian opinion.

Those who have written about the impact of Kuhn on various disciplines usually agree that Kuhn accomplished at least two things. He palliated neurotic suffering about insufficient scientificity, and he helped free scholars up to write narratives, as opposed to arguments. He showed that, even in the hardest sciences, important changes sometimes occur not because people have succumbed to what Habermas calls "the force of the better argument," but because everybody wants to get on the bandwagon. This realization has permitted intellectual historians to offer detailed and useful narratives, describing how such bandwagons got going.

Kuhn disjoined the notion of rationality from that of method. Nobody thinks that it was irrational of scientists to get on such bandwagons as quantum physics and place tectonics, but fewer people now think that the rationality of

Originally published in *Common Knowledge* 6.2 (Fall 1997): 20–22. © 1997.

doing so can be analyzed as an application of methodological principles. Feyerabend's aggressive title *Against Method* was very much to the point. Some philosophers of science (for example, Philip Kitcher, in his *The Advancement of Science*) still try (unsuccessfully, in my opinion) to rehabiliate the notion of "methods," in the plural. But the presumption that all good scientists apply a single set of methodological rules has been chastened by the realization that any rules general enough to be applied both in paleontology and in microbiology are likely to be unhelpful platitudes.

The wave of accusations of irrationalism that initially swept over Kuhn has long since receded. It is now much easier to get away with saying that scientific theories change in the same complicated ways that political institutions do, without being charged, as Kuhn was, with reducing science to mob psychology. Philosophy of science has become commonsensically Kuhnian in a way that would have seemed impossible thirty years ago. Nevertheless, Kuhn is once again being viewed with suspicion.

This suspicion comes from those who fear that the politically aware students, or at least the ones who sympathize with leftist causes, are being brought up to despise the natural sciences. C. P. Snow's claim that professors of English are as naturally on the political right as physicists are naturally on the political left now seems even more ludicrous than when *The Two Cultures* was written. For in many countries (especially the U.S.) political leftism on campus is most intense in the English department. The physicists and biologists are beginning to suspect that leftist teachers of literature are having their revenge on Snow. They get it by telling the young that natural science is, at least nowadays, just one more branch of the military-industrial complex, or that it is a horrible example of western, colonialist, phallogocentric, technological rationality, or that it is otherwise complicit with the powers of darkness.

Kuhn is thought by some to have cleared the way for this kind of nonsense, but that is like suggesting that the *philosophes* cleared the way for the Jacobins. They did, in a way. But they can hardly be blamed for the Terror. Kuhn would have been happy to agree that what Snow called "the scientific culture" is one of the great achievements of civilization. He would have been the last to denigrate it.

It is one thing to say the positivists' press campaign for the moral superiority of the natural scientists over the humanists was silly. It was. The positivists should not have tried to make literary critics feel like sissies. Nor should they have suggested that social scientists must, on pain of undesirable softness, stand ready to provide verifiable, quantitatively statable, behavioral evidence for any claim they make. Putting an end to such insinuations has liberated people to write a lot of good books that they might not otherwise have felt free to write.

But it is another thing to start up a new press campaign, trying to do to the scientists what the positivists tried to do to the "literary culture." People who know as much about science as Kuhn and Bruno Latour would never dream of participating in such a campaign. Latour still gets a kick out of mocking the pretentiousness and vacuity of the old "triumph of rationality" accounts of scientific progress. But the kind of history and sociology of science that he, Steven Shapin, and other post-Kuhnian writers produce offers much more than just debunking. It permits the integration of the development of the various natural sciences into the overall history of culture in a way that those older accounts made impossible.

Someday, with luck, we shall see the end of press campaigns that denigrate one area of culture at the expense of another. Then we shall all be able to get on with our work without worrying about the status of that work. Questions about the "status" of a discipline—its place in a hierarchy of disciplines, its relation to something large and overarching (Truth, Reason, God's Plan, The Pressing Needs of Our Time)—will seem pointless.

DO SCIENTIFIC OBJECTS HAVE A HISTORY?

Pasteur and Whitehead in a Bath of Lactic Acid

Bruno Latour

Translated by Lydia Davis

But in the real world it is more important that a proposition be interesting than it be true. The importance of truth is, that it adds to interest.

It must be remembered that the phrase actual world is like yesterday and tomorrow, in that it alters its meaning according to standpoint.
—Alfred N. Whitehead, *Process and Reality*

In a recent issue of *Common Knowledge,*[1] I followed in some detail the progressive transformation of a tiny piece of Amazonian forest into scientific knowledge. To do so, I multiplied mediations, replacing the huge vertical gap between words and

Originally published in *Common Knowledge* 5.1 (Spring 1996): 76–90. © 1996.

1. "The 'Pédofil' of Boa Vista: A Photo-Philosophical Montage," *Common Knowledge* 4 (Spring 1995): 144–87.

Common Knowledge 25:1–3

DOI 10.1215/0961754X-7299198

world with a horizontal set of tiny translations from one representational medium to another. In that article, the main activity was from the human side, from the scientists and their instruments, from maps and diagrams and collections. No matter how many intermediary steps I unfolded, those steps were still portrayed by me as a way to gain access to the forest "out there." More exactly, even though the forest "out there" was reformatted in my paper as a thing circulating "inside" the network of science, this circulating thing could not be imagined otherwise than *passive*. The Boa Vista forest, in itself, was doing nothing.

It is this passivity that I want to try to overcome in this essay. At the risk of taxing the patience of the readers of *Common Knowledge*, I will consider another piece of hard science—borrowed this time, in honor of the centenary of his death, from the story of Pasteur and the history of fermentation. What has made so many modern philosophers and theorists shun realism is the impoverished role assigned by realist philosophers to objects of scientific discovery, which apparently had no other function, no other ontological life, than to wait silently in the dark before shutting the mouths of the human agents discussing them. This silent and silencing function was what irritated, and with good reason, those who could not believe in unmediated access to truth. In their eyes, science is interesting not because it offers unmediated access to the world, but rather another form of mediation, of transcendence, of truth warmly clothed.

The question I want to ask is whether it is possible to develop a sort of realism that would offer the agents of the world a more interesting role than that of passive object. Strangely, not many philosophers are interested in this metaphysical question. No matter whether they worship or hate science, most thinkers take for granted that scientific objects, accessible or not, behave as realists believe them to behave—that is, in a passive and indifferent manner, wholly impervious to human history. The only alternatives that most philosophers can imagine are animism and anthropomorphism, horrors to which they always prefer the canonical version of objects seen *sub specie scientiae*. A. N. Whitehead is one of the interesting exceptions, and it is his "historical realism," though largely out of fashion, that I want to use as my guide or goad for this exploration. But since I am only half a philosopher, I need an empirical site in order not to lose myself in questions that quickly become too deep for me: my project, then, will be to imagine how Whitehead would have accounted for Pasteur's understanding of the discovery of lactic-acid fermentation in 1858.

Some Recent Controversies in Science Studies

The simple notion of an enduring substance sustaining persistent qualities, either essentially or accidentally, expresses a useful abstract for many purposes of life. But whenever we try to use it as a fundamental statement of the nature of things, it proves itself mistaken. It arose from a mistake and has never succeeded in any of its applications.[2]

This critique of substantialism, so important for Whitehead, could be shared by numerous historians and sociologists of science, but for very different reasons. In an account of a discovery, one should *not*, according to students of science, refer to a substance external to the human work involved in order to explain its genesis.[3] Of course, like Kant, most contemporary historians, in order to avoid the extremes of idealism, do not deny the existence of such a substance, but they wish to emphasize the concrete attributes only of the mind that knows or, in more recent historiography, only of the practice of the scientific group that manipulates and demonstrates the substance within the closed and local precinct of the laboratory.[4] According to them, in order to criticise substantialism, one must quite simply *abstain from giving a role to nonhumans* in the story of a discovery and instead construct the account exclusively with reference to the practices, the places, the instruments, the authorities, the institutions, and the historical events furnished by the context. Such historians hope that a multitude of small determinations when added to one another will count for as much as the always-already-there substance of the old-fashioned accounts of discoveries. However, as Isabelle Stengers has clearly shown in a recent book,[5] there is something unlikely for the practicing scientist in this approach, something unrealistic, not only in the philosophical sense of the word but also in the common meaning of improbable. Something essential seems missing from the account. Is it precisely essence that is lacking? No, and it is Whitehead's interest to imagine a realism without substance, a radical historical realism ("The Castle Rock of Edinburgh exists from moment to moment, and from century to century, by reason of the decision effected by its own historic route of antecedent occasions.")[6]

It has seemed necessary to some of us to devise what we call in our jargon "principles of symmetry" in order to do justice—without falling back on essentialism—to the feeling scientists and common sense share that something is miss-

2. Alfred N. Whitehead, *Process and Reality: An Essay in Cosmology* (New York: Free Press, [1929] 1978), 79.

3. The canonical description of this principle can be found in Harry M. Collins, *Changing Order: Replication and Induction in Scientific Practice* (London: Sage, 1985).

4. The most developed examples can be found in Steven Shapin and Simon Schaffer, *Leviathan and the Air-Pump:*

Hobbes, Boyle and the Experimental Life (Princeton: Princeton University Press, 1985), and, more recently, Christian Licoppe, *La Formation de la pratique scientifique* (Paris: La Découverte, 1996).

5. Isabelle Stengers, *L'Invention des sciences modernes* (Paris: La Découverte, 1993).

6. Whitehead, 43.

ing from accounts of science that consider only the human side. The first principle of symmetry demanded that historians judge accounts of discovery fairly
by treating on terms of equality scientists who have been wrong and those who
have been right.[7] This principle, which is opposed to the French epistemological
tradition that demands one distinguish "out-of-date science" from "sanctioned
science,"[8] permitted nice effects of historical drama. The victories of Boyle over
Hobbes, of Newton over Descartes, or of Pasteur over Pouchet, no longer differed from the provisional victories of Napoleon over Tsar Alexander, or of Clinton over Bush. The history of science ceased to be distinguished from history
plain and simple.

   The price paid for this reunification was very high. The principle of limited
symmetry does not equalize the possibilities of the victors (rationality) and the
vanquished (irrationality) except in that the principle forbids both protagonists
access to the very phenomena that they both consider their only reason for being.
There is something heroic in this: nature, the symmetrical historians all say with
a yogi's asceticism, does not intervene in the interpretations we make with respect
to it.

   One can understand the motives of historians who are partisans of symmetry—they are reacting against the abuses of substantialists who are content
to explain that victors in the history of science won because they were more
rational or had better access to the nature of things. By insisting, for the first
time, on the difficulties of the experiment, on the uncertainties of the instruments, on the irremediable localization of the methods, on the ambiguity of
interpretations, on the importance of a community of more or less credible colleagues, the constructivist historians find it easy to ridicule those who believe
they benefit from immediate access to the real and who take social or cognitive
habits that date only from yesterday to be the permanent essence of things.

   It is important, however, to avoid pressing asceticism to the point of
anorexia, and this is where another, more general, principle of symmetry
becomes necessary.[9] No longer is it a matter of equalizing the possibilities for
success of the victors and the vanquished by evenhandedly forbidding both
groups access to the real but rather of equalizing by allowing all groups to
construct simultaneously and symmetrically both their natural reality and
their social reality. Like yogis who have been without food too long and forced

---

7. See David Bloor, *Knowledge and Social Imagery* (Chicago: University of Chicago Press, [1976] 1991). For a more
recent justification, see the preface to the second edition.

8. See Georges Canguilhem, *Ideology and Rationality in
the History of the Life Sciences*, trans. Arthur Goldhammer (Cambridge: MIT Press, [1968] 1988), for an extreme
example. See also, more recently, G. Canghuilhem, *A

Vital Rationalist: Selected Writings, trans. A. Goldhammer,
ed. François Delaporte (New York: Zone Books, 1994).

9. See Bruno Latour, *We Have Never Been Modern*, trans.
Catherine Porter (Cambridge; Harvard University Press,
1993), for a presentation of this principle and its consequences for anthropology.

to sleep too many nights on beds of nails, one finally allows victors and vanquished alike to gorge themselves on reality and sleep in featherbeds. This shift enables recovery from Kantianism since one no longer has to choose, in order to explain a discovery, between privileged access to the real and determination through thousands of small social or practical causes. One sees in effect that the real as a reserve or anchor against idealism had meaning only by contrast with the knowing mind (or the laboratory, or the paradigm). For every Copernican revolution, there is a counterrevolution and a half. Discoverers establish at once what they are, the world in which they are situated, and the numerous social, practical, and historical causalities compatible with the type of phenomena with which they are populating the collective. The differences among ontological, epistemological, and sociological questions become indistinct. The question becomes: In which socionatural world do we agree to live? The principle of generalized symmetry does not abolish the principle of limited symmetry, but extends it to questions about nature and about society, and thus allows a new object to appear—the *collective* of humans and nonhumans.[10]

This solution, however, does not have the metaphysics of its ambitions. While no longer anthropomorphic, it remains as fragile as the meaning given to the word *collective*. If one means by that word the demiurgic activity of researchers in engendering not only nature but also society and the history in which they are situated, one comes dangerously close to the tales of the absolute idealists that believed they could go "beyond Kant." Whereas if it is semiotic proliferation that endows humans, nonhumans (i.e., objects in circulation), enunciative positions, and the contexts inscribed in texts with certain properties, then we are awash in discourse, in a sea of positions without subjects, and we drift farther from the realism that we were aiming for. The "superman" of the first (the demiurgic) account is abruptly followed by the "death of man" in the second. In a third account the activity of researchers is a matter of allowing nonhumans to proliferate in society as subjects, in which case we run the risk of naturalizing the whole of history without any longer being able to endow objects with their uncertainty, their transcendence, their "tremolo." This third account relies on a will to power to anchor discourse and action in biology or in physics.

In order to be sure of escaping these three perils—being trapped in society, in language, or in nature—we must leave behind for a moment the ambiguity of the word *collective* and abandon the notions of actors, actions, subjects, objects, humans, and nonhumans that have provisionally served to enable our escape from Kantianism. Thus we must dare, like Whitehead, to have commerce with metaphysics despite the embargo declared against it by analytic philosophy as well as by constructivism.

10. See B. Latour, "On Technical Mediation," *Common Knowledge* 3 (Fall 1994): 29–64.

How Pasteur Stages His Own Discovery of the Lactic Acid Ferment

In 1858, sometime after having discovered the fermentation of brewer's yeast, Pasteur relates, in a celebrated report to the Académie des sciences, the discovery of a yeast peculiar to lactic acid.[11] Today, lactic fermentation is no longer an object of discussion, and one can order by mail any quantities of yeast for dairies, creameries, and cheese manufacturers the world over. But one has only to "place oneself in the conditions of the period" to measure the originality of Pasteur's report, and thus the reward he can claim for his pains. In the middle of the nineteenth century, in scientific circles influenced by Liebig's chemistry, the claim that a specific microorganism could explain fermentation amounted to a step backward, since it was through ridding itself of obscure vitalist explanations that chemistry had only just won its laurels.[12] Fermentation could and had been explained, without the intervention of any living thing whatsoever, in a purely chemical way by the degradation of inert substances. In any case, specialists in lactic fermentation had never seen microorganisms inseparably associated with the transformation of sugar:

Until now minute researches have been *unable to discover* the development of organized life. Observers who have identified some organisms have at the same time found that they were *accidental* and *detrimental* to *the process.*

The facts then seem *very favorable* to the ideas of Liebig or to those of Berzelius. In the eyes of the former a ferment is an unstable substance that decomposes and thereby excites fermentation in consequence of its alteration which communicates a disintegrating disturbance to the molecular group of the fermentable matter. According to Liebig, such is *the primary cause* of all fermentations and the origin of most contagious diseases. Berzelius believes that the chemical act of fermentation is to be referred to the action of contact. These opinions *gain more credit daily. . . .* These works all agree in *rejecting the idea of some sort of influence from organization and life* as a cause of the phenomena that we are considering. (*Emphasis added.*)

And Pasteur quietly adds: "I have been led to an entirely different point of view"![13] The discoverer will appear all the more involved in the process because

11. The English text is "Pasteur's Study of Fermentation" in *Harvard Case Histories in Experimental Science*, vol. 2, ed. James B. Conant (Cambridge: Harvard University Press, 1957), 453–60. A fuller semiotic analysis of Pasteur's report can be found in my "Pasteur on Lactic Acid Yeast: A Partial Semiotic Analysis," *Configurations* 1 (January 1993): 127–42. For a general presentation of Pasteur's career, the best source is now Gerald Geison, *The Private Science of Louis Pasteur* (Princeton: Princeton University Press, 1995). In this article, I am concentrating on the text in order to extract from it its various ontologies, and not concerning myself with other material (as I did for the Boa Vista forest; *Common Knowledge* 4:1, 144–87) that would connect me more securely to Pasteur's laboratory and method.

12. For a description of the chemists and their professional ideologies at the time, see Bernadette Bensaude-Vincent and I. Stengers, *Histoire de la chimie* (Paris: La Découverte, 1993).

13. J. B. Conant, 455.

he will have everyone against him, the unanimous opinion of the chemists as well as the scrupulous research of the specialists. The discoverer does not lift the veil behind which the yeast in lactic fermentation has always been hiding. Like the story of General de Gaulle rising from obscurity to triumph, the discoverer's story can be told as a tale of victory. But Pasteur's act was not the imposition of a framework or vision on powerless matter—though he later posed the problem to himself in these terms (as we shall see). He states, in fact, that he has been *led* to a point of view. His activity consists in allowing himself to be carried along by the "propensity of things," to adopt François Jullien's beautiful expression.[14] Even when Pasteur acts to cause the yeast to emerge, in opposition to the convictions of the rest of the world, he still allows himself to be led by things—thus mingling once again the fate of a subject and an object.

For political and military history, resources exist that allow one to weigh the respective roles of *longue durée*, opportunity, circumstances, chance, individual genius, and finally the attribution of responsibility to a few individual geniuses. However, when it is a matter of accounting for beings who have been invented or discovered, the historian of science becomes more timid, more hesitant than his colleagues. The historian of science accosts one monster more than the historian plain and simple: however great may be the heterogony of factors that history summons, it is never as great as in the history of science, where one must integrate the short life of Pasteur, the longer span of the Second Empire or of chemistry, the even longer existence of alcoholic or lactic fermentations (which go back to Neolithic times), and the existence, infinitely longer, absolutely longer, of lactic acid yeast, always already present. Once discovered by Pasteur in 1857, lactic acid yeast has always already been there, from Neolithic times in the gourds of homo sapiens to the present in the whey that is souring in all the dairies on earth. How should one go about historicizing the creation of a being that seems to overflow its historical framework immediately, to go back through the whole of time and spread through the whole of space? Historians are used to dealing with the *longue durée*, but how to deal with timelessness?

The only solution consists in bestowing historicity on all elements that enter into an account. Young Louis Pasteur of Lille counts as an episode in the destiny, in the essence, in the trajectory of lactic yeast: The absurdity of a premise like this, the scandal it may provoke, is brought home if, instead of to yeast, still close to the agitated history of living things, the premise is applied to gravitation or cosmology. Newton happened to universal gravitation? The European Center for Nuclear Research happened to the Big Bang?

14. Surprising resonances exist between Whitehead, *op. cit.*, and this admirable book on Chinese philosophy: François Jullien, *The Propensity of Things: Toward a History of Efficacy in China* (New York: Zone Books, 1995).

If, once again seeking refuge in the cozy Kantian framework, one were to speak only of *representation*, there would be no difficulty here. Pasteur would be said to transform the ideas that chemists and dairymen have formed "about" lactic fermentation, much as Newton modified our ideas about the action of distant celestial bodies. One would return more easily to history if one remained exclusively among humans with their representations, their visions of the world, their more or less passionate interests. The history of science, social or intellectual, could be deployed, like most of anthropology, with a boldness all the greater because it would be limited to representations alone, leaving the phenomena themselves out of reach. But, given generalized symmetry, we want to reach the phenomena, to emerge from the childhood home of idealism and rediscover, with realism, the risks of ontology without losing the uncertainties of history or the localization of methods.[15] We must therefore explore this path, however bizarre it may appear, and speak of Pasteur as an *event that occurs to lactic acid.*

Several Ontologies with Variable Geometries

What seemed absurd in a metaphysics of essence and attributes can become child's play for "an ontology of events and relations."[16] In Whitehead's vocabulary, Pasteur's laboratory appears to us an *occasion* offered to *trajectories* of entities that *inherit* preceding circumstances by *deciding* to persevere in a new way of being. Certain entities will travel through the laboratory as stabilized practices. This is the case of lactic acid itself:

Lactic acid was discovered by Scheele in 1780 in soured whey. His *procedure* for removing it from the whey is still today the best one can follow.

In a footnote, Pasteur adds:

First he *reduced* the whey to an eighth of its volume by evaporation. He *filtered* it and *saturated* it with lime to *precipitate* the phosphate of lime. The liquid was then *filtered* and *diluted* with three times its weight of water; into this he *poured* oxalic acid drop by drop to *precipitate* all the lime. He *evaporated* the liquid to the consistency of honey. . . . (*Emphasis added.*)

15. What is involved, in fact, is attributing to the following passage in Kuhn an ontology, where, in his understanding of it, it has a psychosocial meaning: "[T]hough the world does not change with a change of paradigm," he writes, "*the scientist afterward works in a different world.* Nevertheless, I am convinced that we must learn to make sense of statements that at least resemble theses. What occurs during a scientific revolution is not fully reduc-ible to a reinterpretation of individual and stable data." Thomas S. Kuhn, *The Structure of Scientific Revolutions* (Chicago: University of Chicago Press, [1962] 1970), 121.

16. I am borrowing these terms from the excellent article by John B. Cobb, "Alfred North Whitehead," in *Founders of Constructive Philosophy*, ed. David Ray Griffin (Albany: State University of New York Press, 1993).

Even here, the acid is not presented as a substance durable in time and defined by its attributes but rather by a collection of verbs referring to laboratory gestures. Acid is ultimately a *procedure*, a recipe, and is coextensive with a course of action. The fact that the list of operations is long hardly matters, since each of them is part of the routine of a well-equipped chemistry laboratory. The interlocking of the subprograms does not make the essence fragile because skillful chemists have no trouble understanding the gestures for filtering, evaporating, precipitating, and because they take their arrangement as monolithic.

The same is not true for the yeast that the entire scientific community found so dubious in 1857:

If one examines carefully an ordinary lactic fermentation, *there are cases* where one *can find* on top of the deposit of the chalk and nitrogenous material *spots* of a gray substance which sometimes form a layer on the surface of the deposit. At other times, this substance is found adhering to the upper sides of the vessel, where it has been carried by effervescence. Under the microscope, when one is not forewarned, it ts *hardly possible* to distinguish it from casein, disaggregated gluten, etc.; in short, *nothing indicates* that it is a separate material or that it originated during the fermentation. Its apparent weight always remains *very little* as compared to that of the nitrogenous material originally necessary for the carrying out of the process. Finally, *very often* it is *so mixed* with the mass of casein and chalk that there would be no reason to *suspect* its existence. It is nevertheless this substance that plays the principal role. (*Emphasis added.*)

The very existence of the yeast is in question, as that of lactic acid is not. There are no routinized gestures that would allow one to assure the regular presence of yeast. The entity is defined only by a "degree zero" of existence, appearing as "spots of a gray substance which sometimes form a layer on the surface of the deposit." One could scarcely exist less! The contrast appears all the stronger in the act of defiance with which the quotation above concludes. In opposition to Liebig and Berzelius, as we have seen, Pasteur was "led to an entirely different point of view." This thought process depends on a conversion by which a creature of whom one does not have "reason to suspect its existence" "nevertheless plays the principal role"!

In order to follow how the yeast—criticized by everyone, invisible, a poor spot at the bottom of a glass vessel—will soon become the "only thing responsible" for lactic fermentation, the expressions "subject" and "object" must become, as one may imagine, of little use. Pasteur plays his large part in this affair, as do the yeast, Liebig, and the dairymen. We do not observe a man endowed with faculties discovering a creature defined by attributes. We see a body with multiple and partial members seeking to bring about in its laboratory, through a series of trials, a regular succession of actions:

I am going to show, first of all, how to isolate it and prepare it in a pure state.

I extract the soluble part from brewer's yeast, by *treating* the yeast for some time with fifteen to twenty times its weight of water at the temperature of boiling water. The liquid, a complex solution of albuminous and mineral material, is carefully *filtered*. About fifty to one hundred grams of sugar are then dissolved in each liter, some chalk is *added*, and a trace of the gray material I have just mentioned extracted from a good, ordinary lactic fermentation is *sprinkled* in; then one *raises* the temperature to 30 or 35 degrees Centigrade. It *is also good* to *introduce* a current of carbonic acid in order to expel the air from the flask, which is fitted with a bent exit tube immersed under water. On the very next day a lively and regular fermentation *is manifest*. (*Emphasis added*.)

In the laboratory, the body of Pasteur, careful and skilled, serves as the occasion, the circumstance, the concrescence of the enduring establishment of lactic fermentation. Through gestures (filtering, dissolving, adding), ingredients (brewer's yeast, solution, chalk), fixtures (faucets, receptacles, ovens, tubes), instruments for measuring (thermometers, scales, thermostats), and little tricks of the profession, fermentation becomes visible and stable. At this stage of variation, the essence of fermentation is coextensive with the deployment of practical and local circumstances.

Granting historicity to the yeast, in this instance, goes much further than a simple return to the contingencies of the period in question. It is no longer a matter simply of going back to Pasteur, trembling in his laboratory with fear that he might lose his fermentation and that his yeast might not be a "correlative to life." The lactic fermentation is also trembling. This controlled manifestation, "lively and regular," has never happened before, since the world began, to yeast, anywhere. The small laboratory of the dean of the faculty of science at Lille also constitutes a decisive juncture in the trajectory of this fermentation since here it becomes visible and pure. It is no longer: only Pasteur who alters his "representation" of the fermentation, but the fermentation itself (in its being, in its history, in its ascents and descents) that modifies its manifestations.

If Pasteur hesitates, the fermentation is also hesitating. Ambivalence, ambiguity, uncertainty, and plasticity bother humans groping their way toward phenomena that are in themselves secure.[17] But ambivalence (etc.) also accompanies

17. It is the mistake of social constructivists to accord *interpretive flexibility* only to researchers actively engaged with the data. To introduce nonhumans would always amount, according to him, to silencing controversies. Inversely, Hacking has no difficulty giving a constructivist reading of social facts since it is understood, once and for all, that they can correspond to nothing but arbitrary, self-realizing prophecies. Ian Hacking, "World-Making by Kind-Making: Child Abuse for Example," in *How Classification Works: Nelson Goodman Among the Social Sciences*, ed. Nelson Goodman, Mary Douglas, and David L. Hull (Edinburgh: Edinburgh University Press, 1992), 180–237.

creatures to which the laboratory offers the possibility of existence, a historic opportunity. Fermentation has experienced other lives before now (1857) and elsewhere, but its new concrescence is a unique, dated, localized life made up in part of Pasteur—himself transformed by his second great discovery—and in part of the laboratory. By speaking of events defined in terms of their relations, I am sketching here the history of Pasteur and *his* yeast, of the yeast and *its* Pasteur.

From the Event to the Substance

By describing in this way the shared history of a researcher, a discipline, a laboratory, a fixture, a yeast, and a theory, one does not for all that lose the substance and its attributes, but the meaning of the word *substance* changes profoundly and becomes the gradual attribution of stable properties attached by an institution to a name lastingly linked to a practice, the whole circulating in a relatively standardized network. This transition from the event to the newly defined substance poses a formidable problem of description and interpretation from which Pasteur extricates himself through two apparent contradictions.

At the beginning of his report, the author does not yet know which properties to attribute to which essences. By the end, the yeast possesses the same solidity as that of brewer's yeast, recently discovered. The substance endowed with attributes offers a particular case of the event defined by its relations, a manner of summarizing, of routinizing, of stabilizing, of institutionalizing events. It is as though one began with attributes before coming to an essence. Let us take this transition, rarely studied, between two completely different ontological states summed up in two paragraphs of Pasteur's report:

> Let us consider now what are *the characteristics* of this *substance*, the production of which goes hand in hand with those phenomena that, taken together, we call lactic fermentation. *Viewed as a mass* it *looks* exactly *like* ordinary pressed or drained yeast. It is slightly viscous, and gray in color. *Under the microscope*, it appears to be *formed* of little *globules* or very short segmented filaments, isolated or in clusters, which form irregular flakes resembling those of certain amorphous precipitates. It can be *collected* and *transported* for great distances without *losing* its activity, which is *weakened only* when the material is *dried* or when it is *boiled* in water. *Very little* of this yeast is necessary to *transform* a considerable weight of sugar. . . .
>
> Here we find all the *general characteristics* of brewer's yeast, and these *substances* probably have organic structures that, in a natural *classification*, place them in neighboring *species* or in two connected *families*. (*Emphasis added.*)

In the first paragraph, the essence is defined only by various trials to which one submits the anonymous "special substance," recording responses that have recently become stable thanks to the care and skill of the scientist and to the laboratory's genius loci. Each trial brings a new surprise: "x" can be transported without weakening! So little "x" is needed to transform so much sugar! Still, attributes float without being able to attach themselves to a substratum. One senses in the text Pasteur's hesitations, scruples, shilly-shallying before a viscous, gray matter that resists dryness and boiling. The trial defines it in all its freshness, as though, to use the vocabulary of semiotics, one could induce *competences* only on the basis of troubling *performances*.

But in the next paragraph, the coalescence has taken place. The "special substance" no longer merely resembles brewer's yeast, it is no longer merely composed of globules, of irregular flakes. The yeast, now named, becomes a substance and occupies a clearly locatable position in a classification by family and by species. The attributes that floated randomly become the marks of an enduring essence—not simply of a stabilized routine like the lactic acid with which we began.

How can we explain the transition from a long series of hesitant trials to a being summed up in a name? The answer of those historians of science who are inspired by the first principle of symmetry leaves no doubt. Without presupposing an organism, Pasteur never could have reduced up the long list of trials into a single yeast. According to historians of science since Duhem, one has in fact always needed a theory, a prejudice, a presupposition, a conceptual framework, a paradigm, in order to organize data that one can never encounter face to face: the inevitable return to Kant and his sociologist followers. Curiously, Pasteur asks himself the same question and seems to espouse the constructivist thesis before contradicting himself a second time:

All through this memoir, I have *reasoned* on the basis of the hypothesis that the new yeast is organized, that it is a living organism, and that its chemical action on sugar corresponds to its development and organization. If someone were to tell me that in these conclusions I am going *beyond* that which the facts prove, I would answer that this is quite true, in the sense that *the stand I am taking is in a framework of ideas* that in rigorous terms cannot be irrefutably demonstrated. Here is *the way I see it*; whenever a chemist makes a study of these mysterious phenomena and has the good fortune to bring about an important development, he will *instinctively be inclined* to assign its primary cause to a type of reaction *consistent with* the general results of his own research. It is the *logical* course of the human mind in all controversial questions. (*Emphasis added*.)

In the purest (French) rationalist tradition, Pasteur insists on the necessity of a theory in order to make facts speak and, in the same breath, brings into play practical training in chemistry, instinctive inclinations, the "logical course" of the human mind, and personal perspective. He knows that one must follow reason to find the facts. But, in spite of the superficial resemblance to social constructivists, there is nothing in Pasteur's rhetoric to enchant them because, without fear of contradicting himself, Pasteur goes on to the most traditional realism, and tranquilly affirms:

And it is my opinion, at this point in the development of my knowledge of the subject, that *whoever* judges *impartially* the results of this work and that which I shall shortly publish *will recognize with me* that fermentation appears to be correlative to life and to the organization of globules, and not to their death or putrefaction. Any contention that fermentation is a phenomenon due to contact in which the transformation of sugar takes place in the presence of the ferment without giving up anything to it or taking anything from it, *is contradicted by experiment* as will be soon seen. (*Emphasis added.*)

Give me impartial colleagues, he says, and they will recognize what the experiment incontestably affirms—the same experiment that had required after-the-fact presuppositions without which the presence of microorganisms could not be demonstrated. Pasteur ignores this flagrant contradiction and moves from a realist to a constructionist epistemology in much the way that the yeast smoothly moves from event to substance.

Before reading Whitehead, I could not extricate myself from this dilemma. It seemed that we always had to choose between two evils: Whitehead opens a new possibility and allows us to understand why the contradiction is only apparent. Lactic-acid yeast changes its history upon contact with Pasteur and his laboratory. It is quite real, but its historical reality puts it on an equal footing with the researcher and the laboratory in which it is involved. Lactic acid has also changed. The yeast has taken the little push that Pasteur has given it as a historic opportunity to manifest itself by altering its entire trajectory. The yeast proposes, Pasteur disposes. Pasteur proposes, the yeast disposes. Pasteur has not imposed his views on an infinitely plastic form, nor tentatively discovered the resistance of an infinitely robust form; he has given a phenomenon its chance. This is why, writing his report, he sees no contradiction between his realist and constructivist rhetoric, though everything distinguishes them in the eyes of an epistemologist or a social historian. An ontology, even more counterintuitive than that of the social history of science, allows us to follow the common sense of a scientist:

The experimenter, a man of conquest over nature, finds himself cease-lessly at grips with facts that are not yet manifested and *exist, for the most part, only potentially in natural law.* The unknown in the possible and not in what has been—this is his domain. (*Emphasis added.*)[18]

Tested by Whitehead

Why does positing the historicity of all things, even though this solution may in the end be reconciled with common sense, appear at first sight so unlikely, so senseless? Because of our ideas about nature, about transcendence, and about causality, ideas that Whitehead allows, profoundly, to dismiss.

Suppose we were to calculate the ingredients that enter into the composi-tion of lactic yeast of 1857 in order to understand the coproduction of this scien-tific fact. Once the accounts of discovery in the old mode have been abandoned, along with the more recent accounts of social construction, we must draw up a heterogeneous list that includes, among many other factors, Pasteur, the Fac-ulty of Science at Lille, Liebig, cheesemongers, laboratory apparatus, brewer's yeast, sugar, and lactic yeast. There is no essentialism in this list since each entity is defined only by its relations. If the relations change, the definition changes similarly; the Faculty of Science with and without Pasteur is not exactly the same Faculty; sugar with and without lactic yeast is not quite the same sugar; lactic yeast after and before 1857 is not at all the same yeast.

But history cannot be defined by a simple rearrangement of factors. His-tory is not created from already made ingredients. To avoid the jangling of com-binations, the atomism of factors, we must thus recognize in every compound, in every concrescence, something more, some radical and unique capacity for innovation—and, to do so, we must accept the fact that events, to deserve their name, are in part without cause. As absurd as that appears, realism demands that one abandon the idea of causality as compulsory movement or as a displace-ment of forms. The discovery of lactic yeast in 1857 is not due to a dispersal of infinitesimal conditions that defy calculation but of which each, nevertheless, acts as a cause. For there to be history, the yeast-of-1857-at-Lille-with-Pasteur must in part be *causa sui*.[19]

Nowhere in the universe does one find a cause, a compulsory movement, that permits one to sum up any event in order to explain its emergence retro-spectively. If it were otherwise, one would not be faced with an event, with a difference, but only with the simple activation of a potential, the mere actual-

18. Louis Pasteur, *Oeuvres complètes*, trans. L. Davis, 7 vols. (Paris: Masson, 1939), 7:334.

19. All actual entities share with God this characteris-tic of self-causation. For this reason every actual entity also shares with God the characteristic of transcending all other actual entities, including God." Whitehead, 223.

ization of a cause.[20] Time would *do* nothing and history would be in vain. The discovery-invention-construction of lactic yeast requires that it be given the status of a mediation, that is, of an occurrence that is neither altogether a cause nor altogether a consequence, nor completely a means nor completely an end.

Pasteur can be understood as an event occurring to lactic yeast because he is unforeseen, external to the history that until then defined the "society" of the microorganism, its trajectory, its heritage. To find itself in a laboratory, there to be scattered, cultivated, redescribed, purified, diverts the yeast in an unpredictable way. At the same time, the lasting presence of a yeast associated with a fermentation, the chemical activity of a living creature, constitutes, for Pasteur, a decisive branching out of his career and identity. As for the chemists, by accepting Pasteur and his yeast, they become, through a decisive translation, biochemists. No ingredient, as we can see, enters into these relations without changing its nature.

As long as one made nature the kingdom of causes, to speak of a historicity of *things* seemed improbable: inventiveness, flexibility, hesitation, could only come from humans and their painful history. They alone could transcend the brutal realm of objects, affirm their freedom against the viscous constraints of the "practico-inert," to use Sartre's expression for the antipodes of freedom. By linking humans and nonhumans, the principle of generalized symmetry causes a small scandal, since it amounts to extending the notion of personhood to creatures of nature—panpsychism, hylozoism—or, on the other hand, to plunging human invention into the more or less predictable game of causes—mechanism, social engineering.[21]

What a difference it would make if all entities left behind, transcended, exceeded to some degree their causes, their histories, their ancestries! The objects of nature no longer offer as their only ontological model the stubborn, obstinate, headstrong, silent demand of substance. Nothing thus prevents us from granting them a role in the fabrication of the human world, and doing so does not require our returning to the old-style realism that social historians rightly fought, nor does it open us to the accusation of granting to nonhumans that intentional personality heretofore reserved for humans. Nature shares with society the same historicity, but the unified whole does not become either immanent or transcendent, impersonal or personal, animated or inanimate. The transcendence necessary to innovation is distributed through all the little uncouplings through which

20. This is also the argument of the most Whiteheadian French philosopher, Deleuze. See especially Gilles Deleuze, *Le Pli: Leibniz et le baroque* (Paris: Minuit, 1988), and the remarkable small book by François Zourabichvili, *Deleuze une philosophie de l'événement* (Paris: Presses Universitaires de France, 1994).

21. The transition from cause-and-effect analysis to a conception of order through disorder has curiously not changed this alternative, despite Ilya Prigogine and Isabelle Stengers, *Entre le temps et l'éternité* (Paris: Fayard, 1988). The notion of emergence, though very Whiteheadian, does not necessarily imply the symmetrical historicization of nature and society.

effects leave behind their causes. The history of science becomes once and for all an existentialism extended to *things*. Nature, by becoming historical,[22] becomes even more interesting, more realistic.

As for nature's contrary, culture, it is transformed even more thoroughly, and may be reconciled more completely with common sense. In culture, one is therefore not forever a prisoner of language, locked into conceptual frameworks, forever deprived of all access to things themselves, on which, as for Kant, we could only impose arbitrary categories. Our minds, our societies, our paradigms are no longer so many closed circles. Despite his hesitations, Pasteur does not dictate to the facts how they should speak. He *mingles* with them. He does not discover them any more than he fashions them.

Whitehead pleasantly makes fun of philosophers who believe our minds are connected to the world by the fragile footbridge of perception alone, as though a great city, until then open to the surrounding countryside, had decided to enclose itself gradually behind ramparts, permitting no passage except by way of a narrow postern gate and a shaky drawbridge. All philosophy of knowledge arises, he argues, from this *artificially* maintained fragility, as though the mind constantly risked losing its precious provisions. But if you demolish the ramparts, authorize other passages, open wide the city to the countryside, do away with city taxes, contacts between the mind and the world will not be lacking. There is no risk of an embargo on importations, since, no longer ascetics, we would no longer be obliged to deprive ourselves of summoning the things of nature, which would then be broadly accessible because transcendent like us, historical like us, heterogeneous like us.

By sharing transcendence with objects and gaining access to them through the thousand conduits of language, of practice, of social life, we are no longer bound to file items exclusively under the heading of nature or society or discourse. It is enough to place them in "networks"—but while that word used to be employed in a vague sense, it can have, thanks to Whitehead, the ontology of its ambitions. Every item or circumstance exactly fills, without supplement or residue, its unique spatiotemporal envelope. There exists nothing, not lactic yeast, not universal gravitation, that "would overflow" the historical conditions of its emergence—which does not mean, however, that everything is the result of human work alone, as social constructivists feel always obliged to conclude. Again, we do not have to choose between these two versions. In order for an item or circumstance to extend and thus give the impression of "overflowing,"

---

22. This historicity must not be confused with a transformation in time of particles or living creatures such as are discussed in cosmological or evolutionist accounts as, for instance, Stephen Jay Gould, *Wonderful Life: The Burgess Shale and the Nature of History* (New York: W. W. Norton, 1989). Inverting the anthropic principle causes scientists to enter the history of things. One not only recounts how the dinosaurs disappeared but also how paleontologists participate in the very history of the dinosaurs—two complementary but distinct historicities.

it requires other historical conditions, other vehicles, other mediations, other underpinnings—each partially causes of themselves.

We would not find this historicization difficult except that we make unconsidered use of the two pairs of adverbs *always/never* and *everywhere/nowhere*. Since the emergence in 1857 of lactic acid, we have concluded that it has *always* been there and that it acts equally *everywhere*. From the time of Pasteur's destruction of Liebig's theory about fermentation through degradation of substances, we have concluded that it has *never* been present, *anywhere*—a double exaggeration that makes the history of things coalesce and then obliges one to invent, by contrast, those accounts of discovery that I criticized at the opening of this essay. Because yeast has always existed, a fact unknown before 1857, Pasteur must necessarily have discovered it by lifting a veil that concealed it. But Pasteur, his colleagues, the cheesemongers, the dairies, the historians, must work hard in order to extend into the past the retrospective presence of lactic-acid yeast. Scientists and historians work like software companies that, for a modest sum, will replace version 2.1 of your program with the new version 2.2, retrofitting all the new advances without (so you hope) endangering your earlier programs. In the case of the lactic-acid yeast, enormous work is necessary also in space as well as time to extend to all dairies and cheese manufacturers the presence, soon "universal," of lactic yeast. Still more work must be done to eliminate Liebig's version from history and gradually eliminate it from scientific manuals—until the "discovery" of enzymes, later in the century, which newly reshapes fermentation, Pasteur, Liebig, and the retrospective history of biochemistry. Lactic yeast, in the course of its history, never exaggerates either its existence or nonexistence, its locality or universality. Like other entities, it perseveres in its being, however tiny, in certain places, for a certain time, on condition of existing in common with many others that also decline to acquiesce either to substance or nothingness, but "decide," at the turning points, on their history. Like fibers, lineages, trajectories, heritages, societies, rhizomes.

I hope that I have shown, as I promised, that Whitehead's metaphysics allows us to help the philosophy of the history of science—blocked for some time on the question of the role that ought to be given to nonhumans—to take a small step forward. It is perfectly possible to reconcile skepticism and realism, provided historicity be thoroughly granted to nonhumans as well. A little historicity spawns relativism, a great deal engenders realism.

ON NONSCALABILITY

The Living World Is Not Amenable to Precision-Nested Scales

Anna Lowenhaupt Tsing

There is something disturbingly beautiful about precision, even when we know it fails us. A century ago, people stood awestruck at the terrible precision of the factory; today it is the precision of the computer. Precision has mesmerized not just engineers but all kinds of designers, scholars, and observers. One arena where precision has gained a malevolent hegemony is the use of scale. As in digital media, with its power to make the great tiny and the tiny great in an effortless zoom, *scale* has become a verb that requires precision; to scale well is to develop the quality called *scalability*, that is, the ability to expand—and expand, and expand—without rethinking basic elements. Scalability is, indeed, a triumph of precision design, not just in computers but in business, development, the "conquest" of nature, and, more generally, world making. It is a form of design that has a long history of dividing winners and losers. Yet it disguises such divisions by blocking our ability to notice the heterogeneity of the world; by its design, scalability allows us to see only uniform blocks, ready for further expansion. This essay recalls attention to the wild diversity of life on earth through the argument that it is time for a theory of *nonscalability*.[1]

Originally published in *Common Knowledge* 18.3 (Fall 2012): 505–24, as part of the symposium "Fuzzy Studies, Part 3." © 2012 by Duke University Press.

1. An earlier version of this essay was presented at the "Conceptualizing the World" conference at the University of Oslo (September 2011). Conversations with colleagues there, as well as at the University of California,

Even as technologies of scalability advance, the charm of world-making scalability is unraveling in our times. Scalability spreads—and yet it is constantly abandoned, leaving ruins. We need a nonscalability theory that pays attention to the mounting pile of ruins that scalability leaves behind. Nonscalability theory makes it possible to see how scalability uses articulations with nonscalable forms even as it denies or erases them. Entrepreneurs have already taken great advantage of this feature of the contemporary political economy. So have the plants and animals we call weeds and pests, and indeed the great variety of life that thrives with human disturbance. Yet scholars lag behind, holding on to the aesthetic pleasures of scalable precision even when it projects only our fantasies. It is time for scholars to look out beyond our models to the continuing vitality of life, both terrible and wonderful.

Scalability and Expansion

Conceptualizing the world and making the world are wrapped up with each other—at least for those with the privilege to turn their dreams into action. The relationship goes both ways: new projects inspire new ways to think, which also inspire new projects. This essay concerns one historically significant link between conceptualizing and making the world: the naturalization of *expansion* as the way for humans to inhabit the earth. Why have people called expansion "growth" as if it were a biological process? I came to this question not only for historical reasons but also to consider contemporary challenges of how to live well with others—both other species and other cultures. European and North American elites have had trouble living with others, and not just because of prejudice. In the twentieth century, we became used to political ecologies of production— the production of stuff, the production of citizenship, and the production of knowledge—in which unauthorized others had no useful place. Others had no useful place because they got in the way of that expansion imagined as necessary for well-being; expansion was progress. Biological and cultural diversity were the enemies of progress. So it seems important to ask: What was that growth? What legacy has it left us with today?

Expansion reflects more than a will to power, although it may reflect that too. Expansion in the sense I am discussing is a technical problem, requiring considerable ingenuity in design. Ordinarily, things that expand change as they take on new materials and relationships. Let us say I expand my scholarly network to include colleagues in another country or another discipline. My scholarly outlook will change as I learn something new. This is not the kind of expansion I am discussing. The expansion that counted as progress did not allow changes in the nature of the expanding project. The whole point was to extend the project

Santa Cruz; Aarhus University; Leiden University; and the University of Wisconsin "Globalization and the   Humanities" conference (February 2010) have been most instructive.

without transforming it at all. Otherwise it would not have added to the universal prowess imagined as progress. This was a technical feat involving scale—that is, the relationship between the small and the large. Somehow, project elements had to be stabilized so that expansion added more elements without changing the program. My title calls this trick the "precision nesting" of scales, and the term works if applied to questions about design: the small is encompassed neatly by the large only when both are crafted for uniform expansion. Precision nesting must avoid the project-distorting effects of transformation. How do you keep project inputs standardized? How do you keep them self-contained, unable to form relationships? Relationships are potential vectors of transformation. Only without the indeterminacy of transformation can you nest scales—that is, move from small to large without redoing the design.

When small projects can become big without changing the nature of the project, we call that design feature "scalability." Scalability is a confusing term because it seems to mean something broader, the ability to use scale; but that is not the technical meaning of the term. Scalable projects are those that can expand without changing. My interest is in the exclusion of biological and cultural diversity from scalable designs. Scalability is possible only if project elements do not form transformative relationships that might change the project as elements are added. But transformative relationships are the medium for the emergence of diversity. Scalability projects banish meaningful diversity, which is to say, diversity that might change things.

Scalability is not an ordinary feature of nature. Making projects scalable takes a lot of work. Yet we take scalability so much for granted that scholars often imagine that, without scalable research designs, we would be stuck in tiny microworlds, unable to scale up. To "scale up," indeed, is to rely on scalability—to change the scale without changing the framework of knowledge or action. There are alternatives for changing world history locally and for telling big stories alongside small ones, and "nonscalability theory" is an alternative for conceptualizing the world. But before considering these alternatives, let me return to that familiar domain for experience with scalability: digital technology.

The digital technologies of the last fifty years have shown us the pleasures of the pixelated zoom: we move from tiny details to wide views with a few clicks. On our computers, we enlarge text and the alphabet looks just the same. Our digital photographs lend themselves to looking for details or panning for overviews. On the website "Paris 26 Gigapixels," we see all of Paris, or one room inside a window.[2] This wizard-like skill is scalability. In digital files, scalability is the ability to move across scales without changing the shapes of images, which is made possible by the stability of the pixel, the picture element. The digital image is made bigger or smaller by resizing the pixels. Of course, pixels must therefore

2. www.paris-26-gigapixels.com/index-en.html.

remain uniform, separate, and autonomous; they cannot bleed into each other or transform each other. Artists complain about pixelation, which fragments our vision of the world. Most of us do not care. But what made this technology so easy to imagine, I would argue, is the pixelated quality of the expansion-oriented world, which *is* something we ought to care about. To capture the vividness of the pixel, I will coin a parallel term. *Pixel* is an abbreviation of picture, "pix," and element, "el." Elements of the social landscape removed from formative social relations might be termed "nonsocial landscape elements" or, using the pixel formula, "nonso" plus "el" or *nonsoels*. How did we come to inhabit an expansionist world of nonsoels?

The term "scalability" had its original home not in technology but in business. Scalability in business is the ability of a firm to expand without changing the nature of what it does. "Economies of scale"—organizational practices that make goods cheaper because more are being produced—comprise one kind of business scalability. In contrast to digital technology, the point is not to zoom in; only expansion counts. Business scalability is about expansion for growth and profits: this was a tenet of twentieth-century progress. Under American hegemony, bigger was always better. Like business, development was supposed to scale up. The World Bank only funded village projects if they were already scalable; that is, if they could be spread to other villages without changing project elements. Indeed, the way you could tell if an institution was modern and developed, as opposed to backward, was if it was big. Bigness was progress.

Clifford Geertz went to study markets in Java at the height of this program, in the mid-twentieth century.[3] He was worried about what he saw: instead of scalable firms, Javanese traders based their businesses on *relationships* with buyers and other traders. Every time they expanded their networks, the business changed. Without scalable firms for expansion, Geertz argued, there could be no development. Javanese markets were hopelessly caught beyond the reach of progress. From our current perspective, Geertz's assessment tells us as much about the program of progress as it does about the Javanese.

Today, it is easy to look back with a critical eye on this twentieth-century program, because it has been challenged by changes in the global political economy. In the twenty-first century, the hegemony of economies of scale has crumbled before the advance of global supply chains in which economic activities are spread across many firms, in many places. Many powerful firms no longer strive just to be big; instead they use their "competencies" strategically. Competency here is one way of talking about privilege. Firms in powerful countries use their position to contract with firms in poor countries; and national elites, to contract

3. Clifford Geertz, *Peddlers and Princes: Social Development and Economic Change in Two Indonesian Towns* (Chicago: University of Chicago Press, 1968).

with their countries' disadvantaged. Competency is also a way of talking about cultural mobilization. Firms at every level save costs by getting workers to do their jobs for cultural reasons, rather than for wage-and-benefit packets. The turn to cultural niche making in the global economy is surprising from the perspective of twentieth-century ideals of scalability, which depended on the regularization and discipline of labor to drive expansion. Today, inventory is scalable, but both labor and natural-resource management are in retreat from scalability. Meanwhile, supply chains require attention to relationships among firms, rather than just expanding inputs; there is something here reminiscent of the progress-resisting practices of the Javanese traders Geertz described. All these developments allow us to look back at twentieth-century projects of scalability with an awareness of their limitations and failings, including their aversion to diversity and its consequence—imprecision.[4]

As for nonscalability theory: nonscalability is by no means better than scalability just by being nonscalable. The nonscalable aspects of the twenty-first century political economy do not represent an improvement over those of the twentieth century; indeed, they stimulate nostalgia for a moment when one could say "regulation" without politicians looking horrified. Both good and bad things can be nonscalable. Feudal service was a nonscalable form of labor but not commendable because of it. Cutting down a forest may be nonscalable but not, as a result, better than scientific forestry. At the same time, ecological complexity is nonscalable, and so is love; and we value these things. The difference between scalable and nonscalable designs cannot be placed a priori on a normative scale. The definition of nonscalability is in the negative: scalability is a distinctive design feature; nonscalability refers to everything that is without that feature, whether good or bad. But our not wanting something is no reason to ignore it. Nonscalability theory is an analytic apparatus that helps us notice nonscalable phenomena.[5]

Nonscalability theory allows scales to arise from the relationships that inform particular projects, scenes, or events. Many scale-making projects compete for the scholar or world-builder's attention; the trick is to trace or make relationships between projects. In that work, there are big stories as well as small ones to tell. There is no requirement that the scales nest or that one perform the

4. For additional discussion of supply-chain capitalism, see Anna Lowenhaupt Tsing, "Supply Chains and the Human Condition," *Rethinking Marxism* 21.2 (2009): 148–76.

5. In contrast, scalability theory asks how to make systems more scalable and takes the desirability of doing so for granted. Scalability theory is like nonscalability theory in tracking design problems that arise in making things scalable. (See, e.g., Martin Abbott and Michael Fisher, *The Art of Scalability* [Upper Saddle River, NJ: Addison-Wesley, 2010].) However, the point of scalability theory is not only to improve but also to *naturalize* scalability. In this framework, a system that works ought to be scalable, and nonscalable systems are understood to be flawed. The first step in building nonscalability theory is to denaturalize scalability, revealing its historicity and specifying alternatives.

wizardry of conversion from one to the other without distortion. Project scales jostle and contest each other. Because relationships are encounters across difference, they have a quality of indeterminacy. Relationships are transformative, and one is not sure of the outcome. Thus diversity-in-the-making is always part of the mix. Nonscalability theory requires attention to historical contingency, unexpected conjuncture, and the ways that contact across difference can produce new agendas. In earlier work, I have called these processes "friction."[6] This kind of friction is an important feature of nonscalability theory.

To demonstrate how scalability works through friction, let me begin to tell a nonscalable version of the history of scalability. One important model of scalability design was the plantation and, particularly, the European sugarcane plantations of the New World. These plantations developed the standardized and segregated nonsocial landscape elements, the "nonsoels," that showed how scalability might work to produce profit (and progress). Plantations gave us the equivalent of pixels for the land. But unlike pixels these plantations did not come into being through an already developed aesthetics of scalability. Instead they stumbled into history and only afterward became a model for further scalable designs. Attention to their stumbling—that is, the contingencies and conjunctures that informed their design—is the "nonscalable" approach I take to seeing where their plans failed to meet their own expectations. Scalability is never complete. If the world is still diverse and dynamic, it is because scalability never fulfills its own promises.

Nonscalability theory is of use even in recounting the highlights of scalability. Instead of taking scalability for granted as a necessary tool of progress, nonscalability theory attends to the work of contingency and failure. Nonscalability theory shows us scalability in action.

Plantations as Models for Scalability

Scalability, one might argue, came into being with the European colonial plantation, as it emerged between the fifteenth and seventeenth centuries. Sugarcane plantations can show us how.[7] Early plantations were not designed with modern blueprints, and there were many dead ends. When the Spanish first tried planting cane in the Caribbean, for example, they employed Native Americans and used their mound-planting methods.[8] The cane grew, but the results were ordinary; in

6. Anna Lowenhaupt Tsing, *Friction: An Ethnography of Global Connections* (Princeton, NJ: Princeton University Press, 2005).

7. A rich interdisciplinary literature—comprising anthropology, geography, art history, and historical agronomy, among other fields—has gathered around the history of the sugarcane plantation. See especially Sidney Mintz, *Sweetness and Power: The Place of Sugar in Modern History* (Harmondsworth, UK: Penguin, 1986) and *Worker in*

the Cane (New Haven, CT: Yale University Press, 1960); J. H. Galloway, *The Sugar Cane Industry* (Cambridge: Cambridge University Press, 1991); Jill Casid, *Sowing Empire* (Minneapolis: University of Minnesota Press, 2005); and Jonathan Sauer, *A Historical Geography of Crop Plants* (Boca Raton, FL: CRC Press, 1993).

8. Eric Wolf, *Europe and the People without History* (Berkeley: University of California Press, 1982).

other words, nonscalable. When the Spanish saw what the Portuguese were doing in Brazil, they gave up mounds and native peoples and copied the Portuguese. So it is to Portuguese experiments we might look to see how stable landscape elements were formed by contingency and friction.

Consider the nature of the cane itself, as Europeans knew it then: domestic sugarcane is not a proper species, not an interbreeding group of organisms. What Linneas called *Saccharum officinarum*, domestic sugarcane, is a group of vegetatively propagated clones.[9] Sugarcane was planted by sticking a cane in the ground and waiting for it to sprout. All plants were clones, and Europeans had no knowledge of how to breed this tropical species group. The interchangeability of planting stock was not a result of European intent but a characteristic of the cane. If Europeans had known how to choose new varieties, as Southeast Asians did, they would not have had to work so hard to grow the ones they had. But doing so forced them to experiment with new forms of land preparation, which led by chance to further forms of cane containment. In the New World, too, the cane had no history of either companion species or disease relations; it was isolated. Genetic isolates without interspecies ties: New World cane clones were the original nonsoels, landscape elements without transformative relationships. They made fields ready for expansion.

The original impetus for European sugarcane plantations was to obtain sugar not controlled by Muslims, but Europe was generally too cold to grow cane. When European voyages of discovery revealed warm new lands, investors raced to sponsor cane planting. By chance, one of the first Portuguese experiments was on the Atlantic island of Madeira, where a dry climate made the building of extensive irrigation works necessary, in the process remaking the landscape entirely.[10] The success of this experiment directed subsequent Portuguese efforts toward terraforming and irrigation, though neither was necessary to grow cane in the tropical New World, where flat and moist country was easily available. But it turned out that these technologies made a tighter *control* of cane growth possible, facilitating the interchangeability of elements and, thus, scalability. Irrigation helped to coordinate synchronized growth, facilitating the scalability of both resource management and labor. Meanwhile, colonial planters took control of native lands. Through doing away with native peoples and seizing their land, a

9. Many domestic sugarcane clones cannot reproduce sexually; breeders cannot develop new varieties with them. In the homeland of sugarcane in New Guinea and Southeast Asia, however, people have long produced new varieties through choosing useful hybrids of *Saccharum robustum* and *S. spontaneum*. Europeans came into this knowledge very late, only after they had finished conquering the world for sugar. Before the twentieth century, Europeans obtained new varieties only by getting samples from people who grew them. See Sauer, *Historical Geography of Crop Plants*, 236–50.

10. War captives were hung over cliffs to carve channels into the rock; many lost their lives in the process. Madeira's cane-preparation experiments thus also prefigured the use of unfree labor for scalable agribusiness. See Sidney Greenfield, "Madeira and the Beginnings of New World Sugar Cane Cultivation and Plantation Slavery: A Study in Institution Building," *Annals of the New York Academy of Sciences* 292 (1977): 536–52. Christopher Columbus went to check out Madeiran sugar and took Madeiran cane with him on his travels to the New World, where landscape reengineering for cane soon became the norm.

vast terrain for experimentation with nonsoels spread out before the European planters. As the geographer J. H. Galloway writes: "The vast plantations of Brazil presented a picture of abundant resources and profligate use that must have astonished anyone familiar with the careful husbandry of the tiny terraced fields of Madeira."[11] Despite the new terrain, planters followed the precedent established in Madeira by terraforming artificial cane-field modules. Brazil showed the potential of the Madeira experiment to create an expansion-oriented world through the replication of controlled field practices.

Portuguese cane growing came together with their newly gained power to extract enslaved people from Africa. As cane workers in the New World, enslaved Africans had great advantages from the growers' perspective: slaves had no local social relations and thus no easy place to run. Like the cane itself, they had been transplanted; and now they were isolated. They were on their way to becoming self-contained. Furthermore, the plantations were organized to foster alienation and thus enhance control. Once central milling operations were started, all operations had to run on the time frame of the mill. Workers had to cut cane as fast as they could, and with full attention, just to avoid injury. Under these conditions, workers became autonomous units.[12] Already considered commodities, they were given jobs made interchangeable by the monotonous regularity and coordinated timing engineered into the cane. Slaves were the next nonsoel, design elements engineered for expansion without change.

The success of the Brazilian experiment prompted Spanish, English, French, and Dutch versions in the Caribbean. Landscapes were transformed for the new, disciplined cane and its enslaved workforce. The art historian Jill Casid calls what they made "a hybrid agro-industrial landscape, a landscape machine," overseen by colonial grafting and drafting.[13] The Caribbean was just the start for this machine. When the abolition of the slave trade reduced the profits of the Atlantic exchange, growers took their terraforming machine to the Pacific. Coerced Asian labor took the place of Africans. Capital intensification resulted in fewer firms with more expensive milling technologies. Sugarcane production became increasingly tied to concentrated foreign capital. In Puerto Rico, the US occupation in 1901 signaled a new American sugar industry, controlled by a few giants that offered piecework and day wages. This is the industry that Sidney

---

11. Galloway, *Sugar Cane Industry*, 72.

12. Mintz described cane labor in the 1950s in Puerto Rico. Synchronized planting and harvesting of a single variety made attention to the growth of the plants unnecessary. Instead, discipline of humans and nonhumans was key. When harvest time was announced, the cane had to be cut and transferred to the factory in twenty-four hours, before any sugar was lost to fermentation. The coordination of time was of the essence. Workers were forced to use their full energy and attention to cut in synchrony and avoid injury. As Mintz's key informant put it, "I am really afraid of it. Especially when they are cutting cane heavy with trash [cane leaves], a machete can easily get entangled in the straw and incapacitate a man, what with so many people cutting at the same time." Mintz, *Worker in the Cane*, 202.

13. Casid, *Sowing Empire*, 44.

Mintz later described as producing a rural proletariat "doing battle" with the cane.[14] Replacing relations of care between farmers and crops, plantation designs led to alienation between workers and cane; cane was the enemy. At least in theory, such labor avoided transformative relationships and thus could not disturb system design. Human work and plant commodities each emerged as modules composed of stable and regularized units.

The experiment was a success: great profits were made in Europe, and most Europeans were too far away to see the effects. The project seemed, for the first time, scalable. Sugarcane plantations expanded and spread across the warm regions of the world. Their contingent components—cloned planting stock, unfree labor, and conquered, thus open, land to put them on—showed how making nonsoels could lead to unprecedented profits. This formula shaped a dream we have come to call modernity. Even now, we see a trace of the plantation in conditions we think of as modern. Modernity is, among other things, the triumph of technical prowess over nature. This triumph requires that nature be cleansed of transformative social relations; otherwise it cannot be the raw material of techne.[15] The plantation shows how: one must create *terra nullius*, nature without entangling claims. Native entanglements, human and not human, must be extinguished; remaking the landscape is a way to get rid of them. Then exotic workers and plants (or other project elements) can be brought in, engineered for alienation and control: nonsoels. Both work and nature are close to self-contained and interchangeable in relation to the project frame under these conditions, and thus the project is ready for expansion.

Expand it did. By the eighteenth century, Europeans thought that remaking the world as a plantation might be necessary to progress. They devised governance systems in which potential workers and natural resources were prepared for within-project interchangeability through administrative decree. They invented machines through which the interface between work and nature could be ever more tightly managed, facilitating scalable economic projects. Factories modeled themselves on plantations, building the segregation of work and nature, and the alienation of each, into their plans.[16] Meanwhile, with the enclosure of the peasant commons, a new kind of "free labor" appeared in cities. This displaced and already alienated labor could be set to work in factories with some of the same nonsoel control as enslaved labor. When Marx adapted the labor theory of value to talk about the factory, he proposed a history of the scalability of work. The commodification of "labor power" means that workers become interchangeable and self-contained elements of the factory, since only then are they able to sell

14. Mintz, *Worker in the Cane*, 16.

15. For a related analysis, see Bruno Latour, *We Have Never Been Modern*, trans. Catherine Porter (Cambridge, MA: Harvard University Press, 1993).

16. For discussion of sugar cane plantations as a model for factory discipline, see Mintz, *Sweetness and Power*, 47; also, Wolf, *Europe and the People without History*.

their abstract labor—that is, their ability to work in standardized conditions. The scalability of labor thus lies at the foundation of capitalism.[17] This point seemed so important that Marx hesitated to posit any constitutive "outside" within capitalism—any joints where scalability required articulations with nonscalable relations. Most Marxists have continued to treat the scalability of labor as limited only by the progress of the expansion of capitalism, itself a scalable project. As capitalism spreads, they argue, so too does scalability.

Investors have agreed. Thinking through scalability has allowed them to expand capitalism. By envisioning more and more of the world as the nonsoels of the plantation, they devised all kinds of new commodities, both material and virtual. Eventually, they posited that everything on earth—and beyond—might be scalable and thus exchangeable at market values. This was utilitarianism, which eventually congealed as neoclassical economics and contributed to forging more scalability. In contrast to Marxism, which considered the potential for radical change offered by scalability, neoclassical economics theorized the potential for scalability offered by even the most radical change.

What happened to diversity in the shadow of scalable projects? The free play of diversity was banished from the plantation and the factory. However, until the end of the nineteenth century, plantations and factories were islands of scalability in an ocean of nonscalable diversity. Only in the twentieth century did modernization and development spread scalability projects across the earth, shrinking what had been a diversity ocean into residual puddles. The twentieth-century advance of modernization succeeded, in part, through a chain of related projects in which government and industry formed joint-scalability pacts. In the beginning of the century, it was still colonial enterprise that formed the model. But as the century advanced, populist endorsements of scalability arose in the metropole. Both socialism and social democracy mobilized popular excitement about scalability: scalability was progress. For example, the New Deal in the United States enrolled unions and ignited popular sentiment in support of scalable business. By the mid-twentieth century, one role of government in the United States was to educate citizens for a role as interchangeable units of labor in industry. Another was to regulate natural resources, such as water and forests, to facilitate their use as scalable raw materials. Such arts of governance were supposed to build wealth and well-being by allowing economies of scale. Thus projects of training and regulation were spread around the world in the twentieth-century enthusiasm for global development. The new nations of the global south all wanted to remake their citizens and resources for scalability projects. Expansion was advancement.[18]

17. Karl Marx, *Capital: A Critique of Political Economy*, vol. 1, trans. Ben Fowkes (1976; Harmondsworth, UK: Penguin, 1992).

18. For a related analysis, see James Scott, *Seeing like a State* (New Haven, CT: Yale University Press, 1999).

In the last third of the century, critical social movements gathered steam. Minorities demanded rights. Environmentalists raged at nature's desecration. Indigenous people mobilized. By the 1990s, "diversity" as an issue had enough clout to acquire both lip service and co-optation from government and industry around the world. Yet by that time scalability seemed unstoppable. Many critics pointed to its problems: it did not stop for human needs. It did not stop at the destruction of nature. It knew no limits—only expansion. Widespread public realization of its horrors has not slowed it down. Perhaps, however, public notice has contributed to awareness of a different issue: scalability is always incomplete. Project elements are never fully under control. Even on the sugar plantation, enslaved workers slipped away to form maroon communities, and planting stock arrived with stowaway fungal rots that spread to the whole field. At best, scalable projects are articulations between scalable and nonscalable elements, in which nonscalable effects can be hidden from project investors. In the wake of nineteenth- and twentieth-century enthusiasms for scalability, the world today is crisscrossed by such articulations between the scalable and the nonscalable. Many projects for life—both human and otherwise—take place in the ruins of scalability designs.

From Sugar to Mushrooms

To illustrate the uses of nonscalability theory, it may be helpful to turn to a completely different example, drawn from my collaborative research on the global ecologies and commodity chains of matsutake.[19] Found in forests across the northern hemisphere, matsutake are expensive wild mushrooms of especially high value in Japan, and so a transcontinental trade in them has emerged.[20] As icons for scalability, matsutake and sugarcane occupy opposite ends of the spectrum. Sugarcane is grown as self-contained clones, nonsoels ready for expansion. Matsutake, in contrast, cannot live without transformative relations with other species; they refuse to become nonsoels. Matsutake mushrooms are the fruiting bodies of an underground fungus associated with certain forest trees. The fungus gets its carbohydrates from mutualistic relations with the roots of its host trees, for which it also forages. Matsutake make it possible for host trees to live in poor soils, without fertile humus. In turn, the fungi are nourished by the trees. This transformative mutualism has made it impossible for humans to cultivate matsutake. Japanese research institutions have thrown millions of yen into making

19. The Matsutake Worlds Research Group consists of Tim Choy, Lieba Faier, Michael Hathaway, Miyako Inoue, and Shiho Satsuka, as well as myself. Parts of our research were supported by grants from the Toyota Foundation and the UC Pacific Rim research initiative.

20. The term *matsutake* refers to mushrooms acceptable in the transnational trade, including *Tricholoma matsutake* from Eurasia, *T. magnivelera* from North America, and *T. caligatum* from North Africa.

matsutake cultivation possible, but so far without success. Matsutake resist the conditions of the plantation. They require the dynamic multispecies diversity of the forest.[21]

Just as sugarcane allowed me to tell a story about the advance of scalability projects through the reordering of the social-natural landscape, matsutake provoke a story about life in the ruins of scalability. In the United States, matsutake grow in the ruins of industrial forests—a scalability project gone awry. They allow us to consider the diversity of life in such ruins. They show us how human livelihoods are eked from nonscalable resource patches without the fanfare—or planning, or work—of making things scalable. And because matsutake pickers are something like the opposite of scalable labor, they allow us to consider the possibilities of forms of capitalism that wind in and out of scalability. Much of the world's economy looks more like this, I would argue, than conventional economic models (whether liberal or Marxist) show us. Expectations about scalability have blinded observers to the vitality of nonscalable worlds—and to the links between the scalable and nonscalable.

Consider the Pacific Northwest, the most concentrated area for twentieth-century scientific-industrial forestry in the United States. The Pacific Northwest attracted the timber industry after it had already destroyed midwestern forests and just as scientific forestry became a power in US administration. More recently, big timber moved on. The region's centrality as the crucible of timber policy and practice in the United States thus neatly spans the twentieth century. Private and public (and, later, environmentalist) forest interests battled it out in the Pacific Northwest; the scientific-industrial forestry on which they tenuously agreed was a creature of many compromises. Still, here is a place to see forests treated as much like scalable plantations as they might ever be. During the heyday of joint public-private industrial forestry in the 1960s and 1970s, model forests were monocrop, even-aged timber stands. Such management took a huge amount of work. Unwanted tree species, and indeed all other species, were sprayed with poison. Fires were absolutely excluded. "Superior" trees were planted by alienated work crews, sometimes prisoners. Thinning was brutal, regular, and essential. Proper spacing allowed maximum rates of growth as well as mechanical harvesting. Timber trees were a new kind of sugarcane: managed for uniform growth, without multispecies interference, thinned and

21. For matsutake biology, see Ogawa Makoto, *Matsutake no seibutsugaku (Biology of matsutake mushrooms)* (Tokyo: Tsukiji Shokan, 1991); David Hosford, David Pilz, Randy Molina, and Michael Amaranthus, "Ecology and Management of the Commercially Harvested American Matsutake Mushroom," USDA Forest Service General Technical Report PNW-412 (1997). For matsutake social worlds, see Matsutake Worlds Research Group, "A New Form of Collaboration in Cultural Anthropology: Matsutake Worlds," *American Ethnologist* 36.2 (2009): 380–403; Anna Lowenhaupt Tsing, "Beyond Economic and Ecological Standardization," *Australian Journal of Anthropology* 20.3 (2009): 347–68.

harvested by machines and anonymous work crews. They were nonsoels, units of controlled expansion.[22]

Despite its technological prowess, the project of turning forests into plantations worked out unevenly, at best. Earlier, timber companies had made a killing just by harvesting the most expensive trees; when US national forests were opened after World War II, they continued this policy of "high grading," dignified under standards that said mature trees were better replaced by fast-growing youngsters. Clear cutting, or "even-aged management," was introduced to move beyond the inefficiencies of such pick-and-choose harvesting. But the regrowing trees of scientific-industrial management were not so inviting, in terms of profit. In places where the great timber species had earlier been maintained by fire regimes, including Native American burning, it was difficult to reproduce the "right" species. Firs and spindly lodgepole pines grew up where great ponderosas had once held dominance. Meanwhile, the price of Pacific Northwest timber plummeted as Japan found cheaper Southeast Asian trees to import. Without the easy pickings of high grading, timber companies began to search elsewhere for cheaper trees. Without the political clout and funds of big timber, the regional Forest Service lost funding, and maintaining plantation-like forests became cost prohibitive. At this same time, environmentalists started going to the courts, asking for stricter conservation protections. The environmentalists were easily blamed for the crashing timber economy, but the timber companies—and most of the big trees—had already left.[23]

By the time I first wandered into the eastern Cascades, in 2004, fir and lodgepole had made great advances across what once were almost pure stands of ponderosa pine. The Forest Service had no funds for forest management except those generated by offering timber contracts; thus they had to give away their best timber just to thin the dense and fire-prone brush of regrowing lodgepole. Although signs along the highways still said "Industrial Timber," it was hard to imagine money rolling in. The landscape was covered with thickets of lodgepole and fir: too small for most timber users, not scenic enough for recreation. But something else had emerged in the regional economy: matsutake mushrooms. Although Japanese Americans began harvesting matsutake from the Cascades in the early twentieth century, most foresters and regional planners never noticed

22. My discussion of Pacific Northwest forestry draws particularly on William Robbins, *Landscapes of Conflict* (Seattle: University of Washington Press, 2004); Paul Hirt, *A Conspiracy of Optimism* (Lincoln: University of Nebraska Press, 1994); Richard Rajala, *Clearcutting the Pacific Rain Forest: Production, Science, and Regulation* (Vancouver: UBC Press, 1998).

23. For what went wrong, see Nancy Langston, *Forest Dreams, Forest Nightmares* (Seattle: University of Wash-

ington Press, 1996). For the eastern Cascades, see Mike Znerold, "A New Integrated Forest Resource Plan for Ponderosa Pine Forests on the Deschutes National Forest" (paper presented at the Ontario Ministry of Natural Resources workshop, "Tools for Site Specific Silviculture in Northwestern Ontario," Thunder Bay, Ontario, April 19–20, 1989).

matsutake: this was timber country.[24] Still, beneath official notice, matsutake nurtured timber. Some matsutake grow with ponderosa pine, the prime timber species. Shasta red fir is such a good host for matsutake that some pickers call it the "mushroom tree." Most strikingly, matsutake produce mushrooms especially well under mature lodgepoles, But these exist in prodigious numbers in the eastern Cascades only because of fire exclusion, the starting point of industrial forestry. Fire exclusion has made it more difficult for the ponderosas to reestablish their dominance after logging, and lodgepoles have spread. Despite their flammability, they are allowed a long maturity. Matsutake flourish only after forty to fifty years.[25] The abundance of matsutake may derive in part from the conditions of both making and abandoning industrial forests in the Pacific Northwest.

In this combination of changing ecologies and changing perspectival frames, the matsutake economy blossomed in the late 1980s. Japan's own changing ecology had made matsutake rare there by the 1970s; at the same time, its boom economy of the 1970s and 1980s made expensive imports possible. There was also ready labor—not only the discards of the logging industry in the Pacific Northwest, who were already familiar with the forest, but also a new migration of Southeast Asian refugees, fresh from experience with precarious survival. But this labor was totally different from that of the tree-planting and -thinning crews; it was impossible to recruit and impossible to discipline. It was unresponsive to authority. It self-mobilized.

Matsutake foragers in the Pacific Northwest work only for themselves. Most are there because they love mushroom picking—for the freedom of the forest, for the independent searching, and for the money, which they use to support themselves. Many are war survivors whose priority is living through their trauma in the forest, with its openness to both forgetting and remembering war.[26] Even though they work, matsutake foragers do not fit the requirements for capitalist labor: they receive no wages; they do not have standardized work practices that can be accounted for as "abstract labor"; they do not feel alienated from the work process. They are nothing like nonsoels. Since they come for their own reasons, it would be impossible to expand the work unit without transforming it. Anyone can join, for his or her own reasons. Workers from Mexico and Guatemala do not share ideals of forest work as war survival. Native Americans pick to revive their connections to the land. But whites and Southeast Asians looking for something they call "freedom" dominate the scene.[27]

24. In 2005, an impressive celebration of the Japanese American matsutake legacy was held at the Oregon Nikkei Legacy Center in Portland.

25. Forester Phil Cruz, personal communication, October 2004.

26. See Anna Lowenhaupt Tsing, "Free in the Forest: Popular Neoliberalism and the Aftermath of War in the

US Pacific Northwest," in States of (In)security, ed. Zeynep Gambetti and Marcial Godoy-Anatiria, forthcoming.

27. This concept of "freedom" touches neoliberal economic ideologies but is too much shaped by cultures of war survival to be synonymous. Matsutake pickers do not believe that they must become autonomous units of choice to be "free." Instead, "freedom" furthers communal cultural agendas of war survival. See Tsing, "Free in the Forest."

Mushrooms are foraged during the day and sold to independent buyers in the evening. Buyers sell to bulkers who sell to exporters who send the mushrooms on their way to Japan by early the next morning. Amazingly, by the time the mushrooms are in the belly of the plane, they have taken the form of scalable inventory: a capitalist commodity sorted by its maturity, size, and weight.[28] Expansion is suddenly easy for these packaged mushrooms; dissociated from the forest and the foragers, they are workable nonsoels. Here we have stumbled on another kind of articulation between the nonscalable and the scalable—not the ruins of scalability, but the recuperation of nonscalable forest resources for scalable inventory. Transformation from unscalable process to scalable inventory is what the contemporary capitalism of supply chains does best. Perhaps this return to scalability is a good place to turn back to general issues.

Pirates, or Nonscalability for Old Hands

Scalable projects are everywhere linked with nonscalable worlds. In one kind of link, scalability becomes riddled with nonscalability, just as weeds take over plantations every time the poison lets up. One might see the weeds as taking advantage of the hard work of making the plantation, from eradicating the original flora to providing water and fertilizers. Weeds here are "pirates" of scalability, reaping the rewards of plantation work. Matsutake in industrial forests are one kind of weed. Meanwhile, there is another kind of linking: scalable projects can reap the rewards of nonscalability. The pirates here are the sponsors of scalability, stealing from the work of transformative relations. For example, most grasses, including sugarcane, benefit from transformative associations with fungi. The fungi aid the plants' search for nutrients, while also protecting the plants from harmful bacteria.[29] But these are endomycorrhizal fungi, which are found entirely inside the plants. Until recently, European cane producers were entirely unaware that their sugarcane clones contained another species, a species that helped the sugarcane to grow. Plantations were designed with the idea that only one crop was relevant: the sugarcane. Yet plantation owners were pirates, reaping the rewards of the transformative work of sugarcane-fungal relations.

This kind of piracy is illustrative of an emergent form of global capitalism that I have called "supply-chain capitalism."[30] The name is supposed to be

28. See Anna Lowenhaupt Tsing, "Sorting Out Commodities," in *The Paradox of Value*, ed. Ton Otto and Rane Willerslev, forthcoming.

29. See, e.g., S. F. Jamal, Patrice Cadet, R. S. Rutherford, and C. J. Straker, "Effect of Mycorrhiza on the Nutrient Uptake of Sugarcane," *Proceedings of the South African Sugar Technology Association* 78 (2004): 343–47, www.sasta.co

.za/wp-content/uploads/ Proceedings/2000s/2004_jamal _EFFECT%20OF%20MYCORRHIZA%20ON%20THE .pdf.

30. See Tsing, "Supply Chains and the Human Condition." Making use of links between scalable projects and unscalable relations is not limited to supply-chain capital-

jarring: "supply chain" is the term used by enthusiasts, while "capitalism" is the term used by critics. I use it to describe the supply-chain-based political economy that, since the 1970s, has emerged with the rise of finance capital. At the heart of this system are links between scalable and nonscalable projects, which is why conventional social analysts have not been able to see it very clearly. The uneasiness of the name is intended to stimulate awareness. Japanese supply chains are a good place to start. In the 1960s and 1970s, general trading companies in Japan perfected the art of forging global supply chains. Since the nineteenth-century Meiji Restoration, Japanese have characterized their country as dependent on foreign resources, making international trade a key sector for national development. General trading companies were a post–World War II version of how to craft such ties.[31] Unlike American companies of that time, they had no interest (despite their vast wealth) in taking over production in the various countries from which they bought supplies. Japanese companies were traders: their goal was to turn products created in strange places and processes into inventory. Their secret of success was to imagine this practice as the work of sorting and translation; they dictated standards but allowed producers to obtain the products through any crazy means producers wanted. Thus, for example, to obtain cheap timber, the trading companies made deals with corrupt officials and vicious generals in Southeast Asia, who, in turn, bulldozed the forest territories of villagers. The traders were not responsible, and the wood was cheap.[32] (Hence the drop in prices that helped drive timber companies from the US Pacific Northwest, giving birth to that region's matsutake economy.)

In this model, production need not be scalable. In Southeast Asian forests, for instance, timber was obtained by merely cutting without replenishing: this is not scalability. But the same timber became scalable when it entered the inventory of Japanese traders. Its origins and the process of harvesting were erased; it was sorted and translated into size, wood quality, and weight. In transport, it became a nonsoel, ready for expansion. Inventory making, a project of scalability, reaped the benefits of a nonscalable process of forest destruction and indigenous displacement. Piracy of this sort makes supply-chain capitalism work.

The success of Japanese trading companies was one factor promoting the US "stockholders revolution" of the 1980s and 1990s, in which big companies were dismantled and replaced with supply chains. US investors were worried that the United States was losing its global power, and they thought it might be

ism, though the process is especially clear in that context.

31. See Alexander Young, *The Sogo Shosha: Japan's Multi-national Trading Companies* (Boulder, CO: Westview, 1979); Michael Yoshino and Thomas Lifson, *The Invis-*

ible Link: Japan's Sogo Shosha and the Organization of Trade (Cambridge: MA: MIT Press, 1986).

32. See Peter Dauvergne, *Shadows in the Forest: Japan and the Politics of Timber in Southeast Asia* (Cambridge, MA:

renewed by taking advantage of the leverage of American money.[33] The result was a cross continental supply-chain network that quickly dwarfed the Japanese experiment. The goals were, however, similar: to outsource costs and responsibility in order to reap inventory and profits. The key, again, is to allow producers to use any methods they want. Later the goods can be converted to inventory.

Much of the nonscalability exploited in this system is shocking. Instead of using alienated and disciplined labor, violence and intimidation can be used to recruit workers. Instead of even pretending to maintain resources, raw materials can be stolen, salvaged, or adulterated with cheap poisons. As I have been arguing, just because something is nonscalable does not mean it is good. US inventory behemoths, such as Walmart and Amazon, show the economics of pushing costs back to producers so that products can be sold at "everyday low prices." Producers must find a way to please such harsh masters, which usually means eliminating labor and environmental standards while churning out more junk.[34]

But the nonscalability exploited by supply-chain capitalism is not *necessarily* terrible. The point is to save costs, and cost saving is variable. The United States-to-Japan matsutake commodity chain is an example of a relatively benign form of supply-chain capitalism. There are no costs of labor recruitment and discipline, and no benefits. Matsutake pickers work for their own reasons. There are no costs of raw-material renewal. The mushrooms are foraged on national land. Traders do not try to control production; they merely turn these nonscalable production relations into scalable inventory. As pirates, they enjoy the assets of this conversion. And while the matsutake commodity chain is an unusually benign case, it also exemplifies two key principles of supply-chain capitalism: independent contracting as labor; and stealing, foraging, or salvaging as resource procurement. Independent contracting is supply-chain capitalism's signature form of labor; independent contractors recruit and discipline themselves with no cost or responsibilities for lead firms. And why do all the work of starting a plantation if you can take raw materials for free from public or common sources? These forms of nonscalability have become the lifeblood of supply-chain capitalism, from software to mining. Here scalable commodities are made through the exploitation (in the natural-resource sense) of nonscalable labor and environmental relations. Grab—and convert to inventory.

Why have scholars and pundits not described these features of supply chains? Why might knowledge workers be slow to notice what entrepreneurs— not to speak of weeds and fungi—have made use of for so long?

MIT Press, 1997); Michael L. Ross, *Timber Booms and Institutional Breakdowns in Southeast Asia* (Cambridge: Cambridge University Press, 2001).

33. See Chris Gregory, *Savage Money* (Amsterdam: Harwood, 1997); Karen Ho, *Liquidated* (Durham, NC: Duke University Press, 2009).

Nonscalability for Beginners

To pay attention to articulations between the scalable and the nonscalable requires rethinking our knowledge practices, which have been shaped within the history of remaking the world for scalability. To explain how requires returning to the design features of scalability.

Most modern science demands scalability, the ability to make one's research framework apply to greater scales without budging the frame. This kind of expansion is only possible when the research framework parses stable data elements—the nonsoels of science. Only data of the same sort can be added to the research without messing up the frame. Thus an economics research project that studies household income can expand to engulf data from many households, but if a data gatherer shows that households are not a unit of income in the place she is recording data, her data can only be discarded. It would destroy the frame of the research to include it. Only data that have been gathered to fit a particular standard allow the research to be expandable. The units of analysis must be stably defined across instances and interchangeable in their relationship to the research frame. Everything outside the nonsoels made by scalability projects is banished here and, with it, the free play of kinds from which diversity emerges. This kind of knowledge cannot see nonscalability, because of the constitutive scalability of its own practices.

The problems of diversity, and of living together with others, require other modes of knowledge. Nonsoels are not enough, whether for knowledge about humans or other species. Consider the global political economy. It seems to me a striking fact that scholars and journalists have conducted many, many studies of the diverse niches that are drawn into global capitalism today. We know about rug-making children and indigenous suppliers of supermarkets and stinking computer graveyards. But most scholars of the global economy as a whole, whether qualitative or quantitative, Marxist or liberal, angry or self-satisfied, are still stuck on scalability assumptions and thus rarely make use of this wealth of ethnographic data. Its anecdotes are isolated, kept outside their big stories. These stories are continuations of twentieth-century scalability stories; the transformative diversity of economic niches is missing. We need nonscalability theory to tell a different story, a story alert to the awkward, fuzzy translations and disjunctures inherent in global supply chains. There are many scale-making projects here, and they do not nest neatly. Nonscalability theory shows us the architecture of nonnesting, which is key to the (re)making of cultural diversity, capitalist and otherwise.

The problem is equally severe in thinking about biological diversity. Classic twentieth-century population genetics blocked attention to diversity-making processes, because it was a science of expansion. By taking scalability for granted, it asked how populations expand. Expansion was possible because each organism was thought to be autonomous, a nonsoel. Collaboration was not necessary for survival. Diversity was the current scoreboard of varied but similarly autonomous strategies of conquest. To see the *making* of diversity, we need something different. In recent years, the spark has come from a new combination of evolutionary, ecological, and developmental biology, which has studied interactions across species in the generation of multispecies life.[35] For humans, this field shows how much we need the bacteria in our guts and in our skin to become who we are. Note how this knowledge changes the scale-making project. Our units are transformative relations, not self-contained nonsoels. The question of emergence takes precedence over expansion and is, thus, an application of nonscalability theory.

Matsutake show us this kind of biological diversity. Matsutake are creatures of disturbed forests, where they live in relations with tree roots. They do not grow where soils are rich and full of nutrients, but rather where glaciers, volcanoes, drifting sand—or human activities—have deprived the land of nourishing humus. Most commercially collected matsutake grow in industrial forests or peasant forests. In these human-disturbed places, matsutake show us the forms of collaborative survival—the transformative social relations—that make life possible. The forests inhabited by matsutake are collaborations among many species, including humans. We need nonscalability theory to understand how such multispecies landscapes work. Rather than scalable science, the place to start is *critical description* of relational encounters across difference. But that topic is for another article. Here, it is time to rehearse my main points: the ease with which our computers zoom across magnifications lulls us into the false belief that both knowledge and things exist by nature in precision-nested scales. Scalability, again, is this ability to expand without distorting the framework. But it takes hard work to make knowledge, landscapes, and projects scalable. What I have tried to show is how that work, by its design, covers up and attempts to block the transformative diversity of social relations. From this perspective, the history of scalability must be considered in relation to both its moments of success and its sometimes-happy failures.

Projects that could expand through scalability were the poster children of modernization and development. Agribusiness expanded. Biological populations expanded. Scalable approaches to knowledge expanded. We learned to know the modern by its ability to scale up. Scalable expansion reduced a once surrounding ocean of diversity into a few remaining puddles. Project advocates thought that they had grasped the world. But they have been confronted with two problems: first, expandability has gotten out of control. Second, scalability has left ruins in its wake. Nonscalable effects that once could be swept under the rug have come to haunt us all.

34. Walmart's supply-chain practices are increasingly well documented; see, e.g., Nelson Lichtenstein, ed., *Walmart: The Face of Twenty-First-Century Capitalism* (New York: New Press, 2006).

How is scalability created? It is not a necessary feature of the world. People stumbled on scalable projects through historical contingencies. They cobbled together ways to make raw materials (for both goods and knowledge) self-contained and static, and thus amenable to expansion. In European sugarcane plantations, the natives were wiped out; exotic, coerced, and alienated plants and workers came to substitute for them. Profits were made because the general mess of extermination and slavery could be discounted from the books. Such historically indeterminate encounters formed models for later projects of scalability.

Do we live in a world of scalable nonsocial landscape elements—nonsoels? Yes and no. The great "progress" projects of the last several centuries have built on the legacy of the colonial plantation to make scalability work in business, government, and technology. But scalability has never been complete. In recent years, changes in global capitalism have challenged the assumption of scalability for labor and natural-resource management, and at least some theorists in the social sciences have pointed out the malevolent hegemony of precision. Meanwhile, critics of scalability have raised distress signals about the fate of biological and cultural diversity on earth. It is an important time to develop nonscalability theory as a way to reconceptualize the world—and perhaps rebuild it.

HISTORIANS AND STORYTELLERS

Keith Thomas

I once accompanied Carlo Ginzburg on a visit to Blackwells, Oxford's famous bookshop. He had no interest in seeing the large section devoted to history. Instead he made straight for the shelves containing works of anthropology, philosophy, and literary theory. At that moment I learned the difference between a mere historian and a European intellectual.

Threads and Traces: True False Fictive, Ginzburg's latest collection of translated essays on historiography and historical method, abounds in references to philosophers from Plato to Wittgenstein, anthropologists from Lafitau to Geertz, and literary figures from Homer to Proust.[1] The thoughts of Benedetto Croce, Erich Auerbach, Walter Benjamin, and Siegfried Kracauer are repeatedly invoked. *Threads and Traces* moves with equal ease from classical rhetoric to *The Protocols of the Elders of Zion*, and from fifth-century Minorca to fourteenth-century Venice. Ginzburg disarmingly confesses that the pleasure of mastering new subjects leads him into areas with which he is previously unacquainted. Like a gifted student, he can write a dazzling essay at the end of the week on a topic of which he had never heard at the beginning.

This intellectual restlessness has its disadvantages. Ginzburg dips into a subject, brilliantly illuminates some aspect of it, then darts away to something

Originally published in *Common Knowledge* 20.1 (Winter 2014): 9–10. © 2014 by Duke University Press.

1. Carlo Ginzburg, *Threads and Traces: True False Fictive*, trans. Anne C. Tedeschi and John Tedeschi (Berkeley: University of California Press, 2012).

entirely different. He suggests new questions to be asked but does not stay to answer them. His essays do not always pursue a consecutive argument, and their jerkiness and apparent lack of direction are exacerbated by his practice of dividing them into numbered paragraphs. Yet his combination of erudition and piercing intelligence is irresistible.

Much of this collection concerns the relationship between history and fiction. In company with most practicing historians, Ginzburg is hostile to postmodernist skeptics who deny the existence of any firm distinction between the two genres. Like Pierre Vidal-Naquet before him, he knows only too well that the Holocaust happened and that the writings of a witness like Primo Levi are not to be dismissed as mere literary texts that can never give us a window onto reality. Yet Ginzburg is also aware that histories are literary creations that compete with novels and poetry as ways of representing the past. He reminds us that, over the centuries, historians and storytellers have, by reciprocal borrowings, forced each other to raise their game. Early modern historians strengthened their claims to tell the truth about the past by ceasing to put imaginary speeches in the mouths of their dramatis personae and by drawing a firm distinction between "primary" and "secondary" sources. In response, the novelists tried to enhance the status of their art by pretending that the stories they told were indeed true histories. Later, they shed their sense of inferiority and went onto the offensive, claiming that fiction could illuminate areas of the past that historians had ignored. The authors of the *Athenian Letters* (1741) and *Le Voyage du jeune Anarchasis* (1788) invented documents that vividly evoked the ethnography of ancient Greece. Stendhal, Manzoni, Balzac, and Flaubert claimed to offer a fuller picture of life than that offered by historians who confined themselves to public affairs. Curiously, Ginzburg makes no reference to the essential contribution of Sir Walter Scott, the inventor of modern social history.

Threads and Traces abounds in striking aperçus on a variety of subjects, from the origins of Italian microhistory to the importance of reading documents against the grain. As Ginzburg remarks, every text contains uncontrolled elements, and all writers leave involuntary traces about themselves. Ginzburg leaves voluntary ones as well, for he is a highly self-conscious author who speculates freely about his own unconscious motivations. His distinctive voice stems from his Jewishness, his left-wing politics, and, above all, the impression made upon him by Tolstoy's "fierce disdain for the vacuous and conventional history of historians."

LOCAL KNOWLEDGE
AND MICROIDENTITIES

G. W. Bowersock

Local histories are nothing new in ancient history, but today's rampant globalization has inevitably attracted increased attention to the differences of places and peoples in an interconnected world. In *Local Knowledge and Microidentities in the Imperial Greek World*, Tim Whitmarsh introduces the papers from a conference in 2004 at Exeter by a superficially paradoxical comparison of Aelius Aristides's speech on Rome with the contemporary guidebook to Greece by Pausanias.[1] Aristides sees the Roman empire as a vast international community under the aegis of Rome, whereas Pausanias sees local differences everywhere inside mainland Greece. But the paradox only reflects the genres of both writers. Encomium and description inevitably produce different pictures, and Whitmarsh is right to step back from this paradox by observing that the idea of the local can only arise from a supralocal perspective. As he observes, people living in isolation on an island would not think of themselves as local. After all, Aristides, praising Rome, and Pausanias, describing Greece, both came from Asia Minor. What Whitmarsh and his colleagues tried to do was to broaden current interest in identity by investigating the strength of attachment to local places and traditions. These are the microidentities of their title.

Originally published in *Common Knowledge* 20.1 (Winter 2014): 137–38. © 2014 by Duke University Press.

1. Tim Whitmarsh, *Local Knowledge and Microidentities in the Imperial Greek World* (Cambridge: Cambridge University Press, 2010).

Common Knowledge 25:1–3
DOI 10.1215/0961754X-7299234

Five years after Whitmarsh's event at Exeter, two French scholars, Anna Heller and Anne-Valérie Pont, organized a conference at Tours on multiple citizenships in the imperial Greek world, and they thereby complicated the issue of microidentities, demonstrating that various identities could coexist. The title of their book of 2012, *Patrie d'origine et patries électives*, clearly exposes their theme.[2] Two of the contributors to Whitmarsh's volume also contributed papers to the recent Tours volume, Christopher Jones and Onno van Nijf. Jones develops his earlier work on kinship diplomacy to show how traditions of shared ancestors, heroes, and gods reinforced the continuity of local identities and the usable memory of the past. In the Tours volume, he directly approaches the question of multiple citizenship through an analysis of Dio Chrysostom's oration no. 38, which shows Dio as an adopted citizen of several Greek cities besides his own. By contrast, in writing for Whitmarsh, van Nijf dilates on the cemeteries of Pisidian Termessos in order to determine its local identity, but in the Tours volume he concentrates on Greek public competitions (*agônes*) and the citizenships conferred upon widely traveled athletes and performers. His conclusion that these minor celebrities transformed "the way that citizenship was experienced" hardly follows from the examples he adduces.

The emphasis on local identities in the Whitmarsh volume cuts deep into the social fabric of the Greek Roman empire, whereas the proliferation of multiple citizenships does little more than illustrate the international character of the age. Although the two books complement each other helpfully, the Exeter volume includes a dazzling essay by Maud Gleason on bicultural identity in the commemoration of Regilla by Herodes Atticus. Her essay makes the whole concept of microidentity seem hopelessly simplistic.

2. Anna Heller and Anne-Valérie Pont, eds., *Patrie d'origine et patries électives: les citoyennetés multiples dans le monde grec d'époque romaine* (Pessac, France: Institut Ausonius Scripta Antiqua 40, 2012).

THE HISTORIANS' PREPOSTEROUS PROJECT

Inga Clendinnen

In a recent *London Review of Books* (June 10, 2010), Keith Thomas began an essay by reflecting on the dangers of historians revealing their research methods: "Only too often, such revelations dispel the impression of fluent, confident omniscience; instead, they suggest that histories are concocted by error-prone human beings who patch together the results of incomplete research in order to construct an account whose rhetorical power will, they hope, compensate for gaps in the argument and deficiencies in the evidence." He went on to confess his own method: a pleasantly domestic business of relabeling used envelopes and stuffing them with clipped-out notes and quotes from his immense reading ("my aim is to go on reading until I can hear the people talking"). Then, with the reading done and the ghostly voices talking, the time has come to start writing: "I go through my envelopes, pick out a fat one and empty it out onto the table, to see what I have got. At this point a pattern usually forms" (and we wonder, briefly but poignantly, how).

Thomas quotes a reader's cheerful report on the manuscript of his own most recent book, *The Ends of Life*:

There is always a line of argument, but it tends to be both contained and artfully concealed in a great many references to and citations of a gener-

Originally published in *Common Knowledge* 18.3 (Fall 2012): 553–56. © 2012 by Duke University Press.

Common Knowledge 25:1–3
DOI 10.1215/0961754X-7299246

ous selection of (mostly printed) texts and documents. . . . According to strict and even censorious critical criteria, these materials cannot stand as proof of any argument, since the reader is in the hands of the author and of what he has chosen to serve up as, strictly speaking, illustrations of his own contentions, it being, in principle, always possible to build up a different picture with the aid of different examples.

As we read, we realize with discomfort that this insight was exactly the one behind the sequence of jujitsu throws that Hilary Mantel inflicted on the discipline in her brilliantly subversive "historical novel," *Wolf Hall*. And it is exactly at the point where we realize that "a different picture" is always possible by tweaking the evidence that questions of epistemology impose themselves on the historian. Yet, while claiming to admire "those who write tightly focused micro-studies of episodes or individuals," and also to be "impressed by the kind of quantitative history . . . which aspires to the purity of physics or mathematics," Thomas says that he remains "content to immerse [himself] in the past until [he knows] it well enough for [his] judgment of what is or is not representative to seem acceptable without undue epistemological debate." But why "undue"? Historians, he tells us, "are like reliable local guides. Ideally, they will know the terrain like the backs of their hands. . . . They may not have much sense of world geography and probably can't even draw a map. But if you want to know how to get somewhere, they are the ones to take you." One would not debate epistemology with a reliable local guide.

I understand what Thomas says about "representative" bits of evidence, but where do the patterns that he finds in them come from? He declares his subject to be "the historical ethnography of early modern England," which makes his close-to-total focus on written records surprising. Nor is there a conceptualization of "culture" in sight, presumably because that would incite more "epistemological debate." I am reminded that when, for example, E. P. Thompson beckons me into unfamiliar territory, I do not follow him because he "knows the terrain like the back of his hand," though often enough he does. I follow because he is alert to the epistemological precariousness of historians' preposterous project of discovering something of the thinking of people not personally known to them and moreover long dead—and this, when we have difficulty enough understanding not only the people around us but even ourselves. Yet, undeterred, we track changeful individuals; we struggle to retrieve changing contexts and relationships (including their material manifestations); we puzzle over episodes until we think we understand something of what particular dead people once (and maybe fleetingly) had "in mind."

Thomas proceeds to some acerbic comments on younger historians who favor computers and search engines over the serendipitous shuffling of envelopes and the pleasures of messing about with notes. These "modern researchers" have no cause to read whole books: "They have only to type a chosen word into the appropriate database to discover all the references to the topic they are pursuing. . . . much of what has taken me a lifetime to build up by painful accumulation can now be achieved by a moderately diligent student in the course of a morning." When I picked up Thomas's essay, I had just been reading the work of a young historian, born in 1970 in South Africa, educated and teaching in Australia, and presumably exploiting the full panoply of new technology; who knows many maps and can therefore pursue unobvious reverberations between countries and indeed between hemispheres; who reads much and closely; who deploys delicate retrieval-of-contexts and analysis-of-episodes research to reveal local "attitudes and assumptions . . . implicit in the evidence" as well as those "explicitly articulated at the time," which Thomas says are his own aims; who writes with grace, pace, wit, and lovely epistemological discretion.

Kirsten McKenzie's *A Swindler's Progress* offers us linked narratives, one concerning an intrepid con-man and ex-convict pursuing his disreputable trade in the new colony of Sydney.[1] The other concerns the struggle of an upstart clan out to deploy a West Indian fortune—made out of slaves, sugar, and rum—to gain entry into an "old" and consciously beleaguered aristocracy in England. "John Dow" had begun insisting (in a thick Scots accent) that he was Lord Edward Lascelles, a viscount, son of the earl of Harewood and heir to that same West Indian fortune, when actually Dow was on a convict ship taking him to penal servitude in Van Diemen's Land for an earlier imposture. His story was that he had been unjustly transported to preserve the family's reputation. (Fortuitously, the real Edward Lascelles had been banished from England by his father at about the same time, packed off to the Continent to conceal a "low" marriage.) After serving his time in Tasmania, Dow took himself and his noble identity to Sydney, where he persuaded a sequence of worthies that the unhappy viscount was now employed by the Crown to inquire, discreetly, into the treatment of assigned convicts and stood ready to receive board, lodgings, and other tokens of regard, for which payment would always be unaccountably delayed.

"John Dow" maintained his borrowed identity through to our last sight of him, in a Sydney courtroom in May 1835, rising superbly to the occasion before a raucously appreciative audience. McKenzie nobly resists the temptation to probe the mystery of his inner life and the sources of his élan. What is revealed is his thrilling refusal to "get into character" (his accent, his deplorable spelling, his democratic ways with his "servant"), relying instead on implacable aplomb and the obstinate credulity of his colonial marks. From the courtroom he vanishes

1. Kirsten McKenzie, *A Swindler's Progress: Nobles and Convicts in the Age of Liberty* (Cambridge, MA: Harvard University Press, 2010).

back into the obscurity of the Tasmanian convict system, initially "for the term of his natural life," mitigated to a conditional pardon in 1845: a pardon that would keep him in the colony but would give him the freedom (if he dared, on that narrow stage) to reinvent himself afresh.

It is unsurprising that remote colonies struggling to create ordered societies out of a convict past should be a breeding ground for beautiful, self-transforming lies. McKenzie persuades us by some beautiful history that the mother country, vibrant with economic, political, and philosophical change, was a playground for upstarts too, like the new-minted earl of Harewood himself, intent on winning a notable place in his home territory and choosing bruising, brawling Yorkshire politics to do it. McKenzie writes out of deep local knowledge of her localities, and her intertwined narratives enthrall (one Internet reviewer was so enthralled, she took this fine history to be a novel). My single regret is that McKenzie reserves her reflections on the making of *A Swindler's Progress* to a brief final chapter, which nonetheless provides a muscular counterpoint to Thomas's *LRB* essay. Here she reveals how she came to recognize (through a mix of determination and imagination that took her across oceans) that an "ostensibly isolated incident"—a glimpse of "John Dow" in creative action in Sydney—was "a chapter in a sprawling saga of opportunism and imposture which reached right across the British empire and linked the eighteenth and nineteenth centuries."

McKenzie's first book, *Scandal in the Colonies: Sydney and Capetown*, though on a related theme, was clumsy in comparison with this elegant new study. This time, she knows exactly what she is doing. Nestled among the mass of British and Australian material in her bibliography, there is a migrant from elsewhere: Natalie Zemon Davis's *The Return of Martin Guerre*. That lovely microstudy—that tender parsing of a dense episode in a particular locality penetrated by distant events—continues to shed its light far beyond itself.

MARTIN LUTHER, MARTIN GUERRE, AND WAYS OF KNOWING

Natalie Zemon Davis

Reading Keith Thomas's appreciative review of *History in the Making* by John Elliott not long ago, I laughed at Sir John's witty quip—as I had when I first heard it—that "something is amiss when the name of Martin Guerre threatens to become better known than that of Martin Luther."[1] But let us press this comparison further. Let us think of some of the ways in which each man might be known and the kinds of knowledge that might cluster around each man's name.

Much depends on the time, the place, the circle of knowers, and the information flow. In the 1560s in Languedoc, Martin Guerre and Martin Luther were both hot news for villagers and seigneurs, and topics for current quarrel: the impostor Arnaud du Tilh—the false Martin Guerre—had just been burned, and the teachings of Jean Calvin, and behind him Martin Luther, were being preached and fought over. Catholic polemicists in France and elsewhere might or might not have heard the Martin Guerre story, spread as it was in legal commentary and literary reference, but they were quite ready to extend to Martin Luther, as to other founders of heretical movements, the term "impostor." Protestants returned the compliment: in his *Histoires admirables* of 1600, Pastor Simon Gou-

Originally published in *Common Knowledge* 20.1 (Winter 2014): 4–8. © 2014 by Duke University Press.

1. Keith Thomas, "The Empires of Elliott," *New York Review of Books* 50, no. 3 (February 21, 2013): 30.

lart placed the "marvelous artifices" of Arnaud du Tilh in his section on "impostures," next to the claims of young Catholic women to live miraculously without food or drink. Naysayers were being accused of "heresy," until the women were exposed as liars.

In these examples, information was being circulated about contemporaries or near-contemporaries, and however different the peasant's story and the religious leader's story, one thread ran through them all: lying or truth telling about who one was and/or what powers one possessed.

John Elliott was commenting, however, on what is known about the past by present-day historians and students of history. Knowing about Martin Luther brings one the life of an extraordinary sixteenth-century clergyman, whose actions helped effect change in religious doctrine and social teachings, political organization and law, church organization and the clergy, and family structure and gender roles. Knowing about Martin Luther is part of knowing about the Protestant Reformation in Germany, an up-front central event, for which there is abundant evidence—some still to be discovered—and enduring need for interpretation.

Knowing about Martin Guerre brings one the lives of at least five peasant men and women in southwestern France—one of them, the pretend Martin Guerre, a remarkable sixteenth-century figure—and of at least one ennobled judge. Though Judge Jean de Coras was an innovator in his legal writings, the actions of the peasants here did not bring about historical change. Rather, discovering and interpreting these events open up important and slowly changing features of village family life and gender roles, social standing and local quarrel, and the possibilities for choice and maneuverability in a peasant world—for a young woman and young men.

Knowing Martin Guerre tells us about how peasants understood identity and its creation, and how they linked it to inheritance and succession. Following the fascination with Martin Guerre among lawyers, judges, literary men, and publishers, one catches sight of their own ambivalence as they rose in the world. And the secrets of the wife of Martin Guerre, both those she tried to keep and those left unexamined by judges and commentators of her day, add support to the worrisome power of women, even peasant women, to identify the father of their children.

Since direct evidence from peasants is scarce—most of them could not write—we are lucky when a case such as Martin Guerre's offers us an avenue into that rural realm and suggests new ways we might get at it.

And Martin Guerre's life has a great story line, culminating in his return on his wooden leg to unseat the almost triumphant impostor. So does the life of Martin Luther. Quite apart from the impact of Luther's doctrine, the mere chain of events of his life, as told by him and recounted by many a historian, is riveting: his abrupt decision to become a monk, his tests of the church's paths to salvation, his refusal to recant before the emperor at Worms, his marriage to the ex-nun Katharina van Bora. We have here another way to link inquiry about the peasant Martin Guerre with inquiry about Martin Luther. What makes a good narrative in the sixteenth century, a sequence of events that people like to tell, ponder, argue about, and marvel at?

Further, one can look at Martin Luther not only as a historical mover and shaker, but as an individual *example*, that is, as a source of evidence for a deep malaise, indeed a despair felt by many in his day, and for its spiritual solution. Luther, no matter how many times he confessed or performed pious works or imposed penances upon himself, was unable to see himself as anything but a sinner, threatened by the devil; and, no matter how hard he tried to love God, he was unable to regard him as anything but a wrathful judge. Luther's solution was to define a new self and conscience for the Christian believer in a changed relation to God.

This spiritual trajectory has been delicately traced in classical studies by the Reformation historian Roland Bainton, the theologian Karl Holl, and the psychoanalyst Erik Erikson, among others, and in a newer biography by the renowned Heiko Oberman.[2] None of them treat Luther as "representative," as typical or everyday. He was on a daring and often lonesome expedition: "[he] took upon himself the latent sadness of his age,"[3] in Erikson's phrase. And yet Luther's record of his spiritual exploration yielded clues about the response of those who found his message believable and those who found it diabolic.

In short, these scholars viewed Luther's inner journey from a perspective similar to that which Carlo Ginzburg brought to Menocchio and his Inquisitors and that I brought to Martin Guerre, Bertrande de Rols, and Arnaud du Tilh—that is, as a *telling and in some ways extreme case*, from which emerge suggestions for how to understand lives, thoughts, and feelings of other contemporaries.

Such an approach treats Martin Luther as a "microhistorical" subject, to use the term of Ginzburg and Giovanni Levi. Though an admirer of their works, I rarely find myself thinking about whether I'm doing "macrohistory" or "microhistory" at any given time. I simply feel I'm doing history *tout court*, adjusting my questions, my search for sources, and my interpretive mode depending on whether I'm tracking a single slave family or a few hundred gift transactions. Sometimes the perspective shifts within the same study.

Whatever the terminology, Martin Guerre and Martin Luther are both

2. Roland H. Bainton, *Here I Stand: A Life of Martin Luther* (Nashville: Abingdon-Cokesbury Press, 1950); Erik H. Erikson, *Young Man Luther: A Study in Psychoanalysis and History* (New York: Norton, 1958); Karl Holl, *What Did Luther Understand by Religion?*, trans. Fred W. Meuser and Walter R. Wietzke, ed. James Luther Adams and Walter F. Bense (1917; Philadelphia: Fortress Press, 1977); Heiko A. Oberman, *Luther: Man between God and Devil*, trans. Eileen Walliser-Schwarzbart (New Haven, CT: Yale University Press, 1989). The forthcoming biography of Luther by Lyndal Roper promises to be a major enrichment of this picture.

3. Erikson, *Young Man Luther*, 128.

necessary parts of a wide realm of historical inquiry. There is no zero-sum game going on here: knowing about villagers and their networks does not impede or subtract from knowing about the Reformer and his circle and audiences, and vice versa. On the contrary, they often must be talked about together, their spheres impinging upon each other. The Reformation threads its way through the Martin Guerre story, its main actors on opposite sides of the religious divide. And of course the Peasants' War was a turning point for Luther, arousing him to denounce the "murderous and plundering hordes of the peasants," who had misused his message. If no impostor husband crossed Luther's path, impostor prophets did in the form of Pastors Zwingli and Oecolampadius, whose view of the Lord's Supper Luther condemned as "fraud and humbug," "the teachings of Satan."[4] Not long after, biblical identities were assumed during the short-lived Anabaptist Kingdom of Münster, where one leader claimed to be the new Enoch, and a woman took herself to be Judith, in a failed attempt to assassinate the prince-bishop besieging the town. No complicated unmasking was needed, for Enoch was killed by the prince-bishop's troops and Judith was beheaded on his orders.

More deeply, what we now call questions of identity—of concealment and uncovering, of self-presentation and staying true—were in one form or another a salient issue in Western Europe in the sixteenth century.[5] In religious life, hypocrisy was the accusation that Reformers cast against monks and nuns, and that Catholics hurled against smug Protestant preachers. Was God the only one who could identify holiness, or could human beings truly tell its signs? At the same time, for Jews and Muslims forced to convert, pretense was an essential if dangerous tool for staying true, while some ecumenical Christians thought outward accommodation made no difference as long as inwardly one believed the right thing.

In the life of the court or any place where favor was sought, careers being advanced or marriages made, dissimulation was required to reach one's goals, even while its practice was being decried by observers as searching as the great Michel de Montaigne. And what about those beggars and vagabonds on the city streets, possibly lying about their infirmities and their woes: didn't they need to be cleaned up? In villages, a seemingly good neighbor might turn out to be a witch, and when she got to the trial court, the judges would have to decide how to extract truth from her.

4. Mark U. Edwards Jr. has told us much about Luther's rhetoric here in *Luther and the False Brethren* (Stanford, CA: Stanford University Press, 1975).

5. Recent books that have approached this issue are Moshe Sluhovsky, *Believe Not Every Spirit: Possession, Mysticism, and Discernment in Early Modern Catholicism* (Chi-cago: University of Chicago Press, 2007); Valentin Groebner, *Who Are You? Identification, Deception, and Surveillance in Early Modern Europe*, trans. Mark Kyburz and John Peck (New York: Zone Books, 2007); and Miriam Eliav-Feldon, *Renaissance Impostors and Proofs of Identity* (London: Palgrave Macmillan, 2012).

Meanwhile kings and town councils were everywhere fashioning documents of identity for those moving about or making claims—papers and tokens that could then be efficiently counterfeited by those who needed another name. If carnivals allowed a time of masking, there were some who wanted to make disguise a lifetime affair, whether in the form of returned peasant or prince or prophet. Truly Martin Guerre and Martin Luther both attest to that world in movement.

COMPARISON AS A MATTER OF CONCERN

Isabelle Stengers

We are all comparativists, and so probably are all animals. Comparison is an important part of any animal's equipment for dealing with its respective world. This symposium, however, is not about comparison as a matter of fact (I am using Bruno Latour's terminology here) but as a matter of concern. But comparison may be a matter for many kinds of concern. The concern that gathers around those of us who are haunted by the polemical opposition of relativism and universalism demands to be situated in order to avoid the trap of generality. More precisely, it may demand that those it gathers around speak about the situation that made it a matter of effective concern.

Do we impose comparison or are we authorized to compare by the subjects we address? I will not attempt to deal with this question as if from the outside — as if it were an epistemological or critical problem. To take it as such would be to enter, from the very beginning, into a polemical confrontation with those practices for which this question is already a matter of crucial concern: practices that in one way or another present themselves as inheritors of the Greek claim that to understand is to identify a *logos.* Both *logos* and the Latin *ratio* are an etymologi-

Originally published in *Common Knowledge* 17.1 (Winter 2011): 48–63, as part of the symposium "Comparative Relativism." © 2011 by Duke University Press.

cal source for terms such as *reason* and *account* but also *proportion*, which signifies an operation of comparison. The French word *rapport* has inherited this constellation of meanings, while its usual translation, "relation," has lost it. Everything may be described as related, but not everything entertains "rapports." My text will connect comparison with the creation/discovery of what I will describe as "rapport." The disturbing effects due to the idiomatic senses of the term in English are quite welcome since they will slow down readers at a very relevant point, avoiding the too easy connection between relation and relativism.

We know the mathematical origin of the classic *logos*, linking understanding and a rapport that authorizes comparison. To compare magnitudes such as weights or lengths is unproblematic, because comparison is the very point of defining measurements and inventing such measuring devices as scales for weight or the yardstick for length. But where to go from this unproblematic point? The quarrel may begin here and, if so, it will start with the claims associated with experimental sciences. The critical temptation could be to identify these sciences with an extension of the art of measurement. We would then directly arrive at the idea that they embody the methodological decision to identify reality and measurability—that is, at the "relativist" thesis that sciences discover only what they have first presupposed and then unilaterally imposed.

I intend to resist this move, not in order to defend these sciences but to dramatize cases that actually concern me, when comparison entails ethical and political challenges. Often the practitioners confronting such challenges will appeal to the experimental, "objective" sciences as a justification. They will claim that if science is to be possible it must obey and extend their example. It is this alignment, making experimental sciences a model to be approached by other sciences, that I wish to call into question. In order to do so, I first want to insist on the singularity of the achievements proper to experimental sciences, characterizing them as the production of situations that authorize them to claim that the subject matters that they address *lend themselves* to quantitative comparison.

This approach, by the way, marks me as a Whiteheadian. In *The Concept of Nature*, Whitehead remarked, in opposition to skeptical theories of knowledge, that such theories attack not just the claims of science but also "our immediate instinctive attitude towards perceptual knowledge." "We are instinctively willing to believe," he wrote, "that by due attention, more can be found in nature than that which is observed at first sight. But we will not be content with less."

I refuse to be content with any "relativist" claim about experimental scientists only "believing" that they discover in nature more than is observable at first sight. It may well be that those scientists' attention functions like a sieve or filter, but it does not follow that what they retain is only what they have already, unilaterally, defined as significant. The question is rather: "To what," in Whitehead's words, "do they pay due attention?" And the answer would be: to the distinction between measurements as usual, acting like a unilateral sieve, retaining only what can be measured, and measurements as related to the *creation* of a rapport or *logos*. A creation of this kind has the character of an event rather than of a methodological enterprise. It may be characterized in terms of "relevance" as a matter of crucial concern. But to speak about the discovery that phenomena may "lend themselves to" measurement is to insist on the rather particular meaning of relevance when an experimental achievement is concerned.

Such an achievement certainly needed more general conditions. Pierre Duhem can help us here. Duhem emphasized that Aristotle's understanding of nature in terms of qualitative opposites (warm and cold, for instance) precluded understanding the relevance of quantitative assessment. For Duhem, the conceptual event that made the modern sciences possible happened in the fourteenth century, when thinkers first defined qualities not in opposition to each other, but in terms of increasing or decreasing degrees of intensity. This new conceptual definition was necessary before Galileo could characterize the motion of heavy bodies in terms of increasing and decreasing degrees of velocity.

However, what Duhem pointed out was a necessary, not a sufficient, condition for modern science. For medieval thinkers, any quality could be redefined in terms of varying degrees; for instance, varying degrees of charity and sin during the course of a human life. If Galileo was able to compare the varying degrees of velocity of a body at determinate moments of its fall, it is because the inclined plane enabled him to do so. The inclined plane is the first experimental device, the first device the achievement of which is to create a very unusual kind of rapport: a rapport that authorizes claiming that what is measured lends itself to the measurement.[1] But such a rapport is never a general one. The inclined plane is obviously not relevant to all qualities, nor is it relevant to space-time motion in general. It identifies a quite specific kind of motion, that of what we may call Galilean bodies, which have no internal source of motion (as opposed to a car or a horse) and move in an ideally frictionless manner (as opposed to an avalanche).

Experimental sciences are not objective because they would rely on measurement alone. In their case, objectivity is not the name for a method but for an achievement, for the creation of a rapport authorizing the definition of an object. Each such creation is an event, the production of a new way to measure that the rapport itself specifies. The measurements created act as a sieve or filter, but what matters is the singularity of what is retained by the filter. When experimenters do find more in nature than is initially obvious, the due attention they pay encompasses the specificity of the rapport. "More" also means that what may appear to be secondary differences can come to matter a good deal. In the case of Galilean

1. See Isabelle Stengers, *The Invention of Modern Science*, trans. Daniel W. Smith (Minneapolis: University of Minnesota Press, 2000).

motion, for instance, the question of friction matters as the rapport refers to an ideally frictionless motion. It matters to such an extent that it occasioned the distinction between sets of professional concerns—those of the physicists, from Galileo to Hawking, who are still working with tools derived from "rational" mechanics, and those of the engineers, who deal with friction as constitutive of their subject matter—no machine works without friction.

Measurement in chemistry is another example. Here we deal with bodies that are not in any way Galilean. Since they cannot be submitted to the common reference of some uniform quality, like inertial motion, they do not respond to questions about the increasing or decreasing degrees of given qualities. Paying due attention in experimental chemistry requires addressing bodies as agents; that is, as capable of entering into correlated transformations with which the chemist must learn to play along. There is no equivalent of an inclined plane in chemistry.

I will limit myself here to eighteenth-century chemistry and, more specifically, to the labor of those eighteenth-century chemists who composed increasingly exhaustive tables of affinities or rapports. Such tables were organized by columns, headed by an element, followed by all the elements liable to combine with it, in the order determined by their mutual displacements. The starting point of this enterprise had been Newton's reasoning in the *Opticks*: "a solution of iron in aqua fortis dissolves the cadmium which is put into it, and abandons the iron," which means that "the acid particles of the aqua fortis are more strongly attracted by cadmium than by iron." Two chemical elements were thus compared in their "rapport" to a third one with which both could be associated; the one with the stronger affinity for the third would displace the other from such an association. The tables published by Torbern Bergman between 1775 and 1783 would bring together the results of thousands of chemical reactions organized in twin tables of forty-nine columns each, one for reactions in solution, one for dry reactions.

The affinity tables are now outmoded, but chemistry is still full of tables characterizing chemical agents. Like Galileo's measurements of velocity, such tables enact a non-Aristotelian definition. Chemistry is not a science of transformations; it deals with combinations of elements that conserve some identity while associating and dissociating. But while the tables follow from the idea of combination, they also conceive the combination event as effecting a comparison between two elements in relation to an unchanged third—that is, they endow elements with an agency that is both specific and relational.

The point I wish to emphasize with the two rather different cases I have touched on is the matter of concern that characterizes experimental scientists ever since: they should be able to claim that they benefit from states of affairs that they did not impose, that pertained to the phenomena studied, and that therefore could be turned successfully into tools for making comparisons. It is important to underscore that such claims, upon which the realism particular to the experimental sciences depends, are relative to the creation of a "rapport," such as the ones made possible by the inclined plane or by the use of chemical reactions to order affinities. The very specificity of this rapport is to authorize the "objective" definition of a state of affairs. As such, the event of its creation may be forgotten: the experimental practice then appears to follow from the objective definition. Underlining the event—the creation of a rapport—is however important when the abstract universal/relative dilemma is concerned. Experimental objectivity is relative to a very unusual concern. Neither the concern nor the exacting demands the experimental rapport must satisfy because of this concern are "universal." As a consequence, resisting the equation identifying experimental sciences with universality does not require our "deconstructing" realist claims. It is sufficient to know that any general extension of an experimental objective definition also means the loss of the legitimacy of such claims. "Experimental reality" only extends through the demanding and always situated exploration of the consequences of a new "rapport," which Imre Lakatos named a "research program" and Thomas Kuhn a "paradigm."

Kuhn's famous claim of incommensurability between rival paradigms has been widely thought to reevaluate the history of science, long understood to be a tale of reason and progress, as a succession of socially constructed frames of interpretation. As a result, for many critical thinkers, Kuhn is the first social constructionist, having shown that scientists impose a socially transmitted interpretive frame on what they study and have thus no special access to reality. This use of Kuhn, however, and the identification of his position as antirealist and relativist are questionable. Why, if Kuhn was describing the history of science as contingent, dependent upon socially accepted frames of interpretation, did so many physicists in his time agree with his description of paradigmatic revolutions? Why moreover was Kuhn himself so unhappy with the antirealist interpretation of his book? I would argue that the physicists who agreed with Kuhn were right. They understood an important feature of his account that social constructionists neglected, which is (yet again) the specific matter of concern shared by scientists engaging in the evaluation and comparison of rival paradigms.

Kuhn's claim about incommensurability means that there is no way that rival paradigms can agree on a single test that would reliably decide in favor of one against the other. But his claim does not mean that the reasons for deciding cannot be created. Kuhn indeed characterizes the period following the proposition of a new paradigm as dominated by critical discrimination, by the exploration of the diverging consequences of both paradigms. So the scientists involved work to develop whatever may enable them to compare and evaluate research paradigms. In other words, they work to produce and activate reasons for a decision the consequences of which matter for them.

Typically, they will imagine new experimental situations, for which the new paradigm B promises the possibility of new kinds of reliable experimental results, while paradigm E tells nothing about them in particular. In case of success, paradigm E will probably be able to produce, in one way or another, an interpretation of the new result. This is both the meaning of the incommensurability argument and the reason for Max Planck's famous remark that some scientists, insisting they have not been objectively defeated, will stand by their interpretation until death. Indeed; but it does not mean at all that the final decision will be irrational, devoid of "good" reasons. What defeats a paradigm is never an objective, disinterested comparison, but rather an active and interested one made by a collective that shares the same matter of concern and that privileges whatever can be associated with emergent questions and experimentally challenging consequences. As Lakatos argued (without recognizing that it was also Kuhn's point), defeat comes when a paradigmatic research program is forced to produce increasingly complicated and defensive interpretations, and this is precisely what protagonists pay due attention to.

I would conclude that if Kuhnian revolutions are not about arbitrary decision making, and still less about crowd psychology, it is because Kuhn wove them into a tale of competent and passionate hesitation in a matter of intense concern — which is to say, a matter on which researchers bet their careers and reputations, as well as the future of their fields. In other words, Kuhn described a situation in which comparison is made possible only by a common concern and by the concerned protagonists lending themselves and their work to comparison. Or, more precisely, the antagonists in such competitions are regarded by colleagues as required to lend themselves and their work to comparison and will be deemed defeated if they do not do so. Everyone involved knows that any attempt to play dirty or evade facing an objection will be considered an infraction of the rules of the game. Interpreting the position of a colleague as contingent upon philosophical or social factors — which is what critical constructionists freely do — is a possible but very dangerous move in this game. It means betting that the case is virtually closed and that any one still objecting is virtually defeated in the eyes of his or her colleagues. If well placed, such a move will herald the end of a controversy; but if not, it will endanger the position of whoever risks making it.

The famous tale of the three blind men and the elephant, one man recognizing a trunk, the second a snake, and the third a fly swatter, has sometimes been used to illustrate the workings of Kuhnian incommensurability. But this example misses the point about collective concern that, so I believe, must be associated with Kuhn's description. The blind men all investigate the elephant, but the diverging ways in which they characterize it appear as an end point. The divergence is not a matter of crucial concern to them. If it had been such, the story would not end when the blind men make their first contradictory assessments; they would next move around the elephant to explore the possibility of a coherent account that could turn outright contradictions into very interesting contrasted standpoints. In other words, the blind men would have lent themselves and their respective interpretations to active comparison, giving that which they all address the power to impose "due attention."

Let me be clear about the standpoint from which I am making these observations. I am dealing with paradigmatic sciences as seen from Kuhn's perspective, a perspective that ratifies the closure of scientific communities and ignores what those who operate within a research paradigm agree to think of as "outside." I would also underline that my point here is not Popperian. I would not characterize such scientists as having a special capacity or training enabling them to make comparative judgments about their colleagues' research, while, in the context of other practices, conflict would stubbornly prevail. What distinguishes paradigmatic sciences is the possibility of a collective game to bind colleagues. A paradigm is not a doctrine held in common. A paradigm follows from a special and exclusive kind of event or achievement: the production of facts the interpretation of which can resist the charge that they have been imposed on some mute reality. What binds practitioners is the continuation and reproduction of such very particular events when it can be claimed the interpretation is authorized by the way "reality" lends itself to experimental measurement.

I should add that what binds practitioners binds them just as long as it binds them (and no longer). Indeed the knowledge economy, so called, is in the process of destroying such bonds. Scientists, as they are directly mobilized by competing industrial interests, will no longer be mobilized by the duty to have their facts resisting their colleagues' objections and compelling their colleagues' agreement. Industrial interests do not need experimental reliability; they need claims that seem good enough for patenting, demonstrating promise, and stimulating the appetite of investors. Moreover, scientists under such conditions are bound to keep aspects of their work secret or to ignore questions the answer to which (given already existent patents) would be of no commercial interest. The collective game I have been describing, in which colleagues are welcome to object because reliability has no other meaning than resisting such objections, will probably soon be a thing of the past; and the general wisdom will prevail that one should not object much if the weakness of a scientific argument might lead to weakening the promise of a field. (You do not saw off the branch on which you and everyone else are sitting.) The parable of the three blind men would at this juncture become only too relevant.

Kuhn's "incommensurability argument" has been invoked by most of its advocates to resist the use and (mainly) abuse of the "scientific rationality" argument—and it may be said that, however important the bathwater, a crucial baby was thrown away; that is, the kind of event that has had scientists dancing in their labs and the achievement of which was the reason why they lent themselves to objections and comparisons. These advocates had no power other than to produce scientists' outrage and blind rhetorical retaliation. With the advent of the knowledge economy, the antirealist critiques may well be fully verified. Dancing in the lab is becoming a thing of the past. But critics have no cause for rejoicing since this verification will not make claims for objectivity, scientific rationality, and authority any weaker, only more arrogant and dangerous, having lost any connection with the kind of achievement that relates objections and reliability.

If experimental sciences are of interest in the much more general context of this symposium, it is in order to approach some aspects of the ethical and political challenges associated with comparison. I will effect the transition starting with the analogy that Kuhn offered between incommensurability and the practice of translation. Diverging paradigms means a breakdown in communication between protagonists, and there is no neutral language in which to restore it. But such a breakdown does not make it impossible for the protagonists in this crisis to learn how to translate each other's words. It is even the prerequisite to their designing experimental situations to challenge one another and put one another on the defensive. Kuhn's analogy is not about comparability in general; it concerns an art of comparison, the aim of which is as clear as the aim of the hunter who understands the behavior of his prey, in spite of the incommensurability of their experiences. Commensurability is created and it is never neutral, always relative to an aim. The ethical and political challenge begins with the aim. Does it, or does it not, require an agreement between the terms that are being compared?

Ethnologists tell us about hunting practices where the understanding of the hunter involves the agreement of the prey. The point that matters here is that these practices are effectively different, and the very fact of naming them with the same word we use for some of our own hunting practices is a very dubious and probably unilateral comparative operation. It is as dubious a comparison as the one assimilating scientists hesitating between rival paradigms to a mob hesitating between two rival leaders (choice as a matter of "mob psychology").

Agreeing is accepting a "rapport." And when the need for agreement is underscored, the creation of the rapport is no longer primarily a matter of legitimating knowledge or of deciding what may be compared with what. Comparison is now more like a contest—one with importance for both sides, one that requires that both sides accept as relevant the terms of the contest.

Charles Péguy's beautiful text *Note conjointe sur M. Descartes et la philosophie cartésienne* is a good place to begin outlining my approach.[2] In this text, Péguy defines *Polyeucte*, a tragedy of Corneille's, as a case of "perfect comparison." The

2. Charles Péguy, *Œuvres en prose complètes*, vol. 3 (Paris: Gallimard, 1992), 1278–1477, at 1367–75.

comparison is between the Christian martyr Polyeucte and Severus, a Roman knight whose character embodies all the virtues of the pagan world. Péguy underscores that the contest between the two men is a fair one. Each appears, and is concerned to appear, in his particular full force. They share the idea that who will win does not depend on them. What depends on them is that the one who wins will not have won by having managed to weaken the other. Any foul play would abase their respective causes. In other words, they actively lend themselves to the comparison—which is why, according to Péguy, *Polyeucte* had to display the full greatness of the pagan civilization that Christianity would eventually destroy.

Péguy's proposition is very demanding and, as such, very interesting. His implication is that no comparison is legitimate if the parties compared cannot each present his own version of what the comparison is about; and each must be able to resist the imposition of irrelevant criteria. In other words, comparison must not be unilateral and, especially, must not be conducted in the language of just one of the parties. To take a prime example, the contrast between mythological and rational or scientific discourse is of Greek origin and belongs to what is now called the Euro-American traditions of thought. In a comparative inquiry involving East and West, or North and South, words such as *myth* and *science*, if we follow Péguy, should be ruled radically out of order. As the word *nature* should be. What do we mean by *nature*? A term that covers neutrinos, pigs, and tornadoes has nothing obvious about it. As Geoffrey Lloyd has argued, the existence of the category *nature*, which did not exist in ancient China, cannot be dissociated from the polemical maneuver that, in Greece, counterposed the new proponents of "rationality" (as they themselves called it) both against the tales and gossip related by travelers about wonderful distant lands and against the many deities that inhabited Greek rivers, mountains, and caves. Nature as consistent and intelligible has nothing neutral about it. It appears as the ally of the polemicist, as what lends itself to rational inquiry and rewards it. Following Péguy, I thus would characterize any comparison involving or implying the nature/culture opposition as foul play—definable here as a play in relation to which the Euro-American protagonist is both a participant and the arbiter. I should perhaps mention in this context that the deliberately oxymoronic term *multinature* (as employed by Eduardo Viveiros de Castro, Bruno Latour, and others) may be ill protected from foul play of this kind. The term's use could well lead to undue extensions of their own concern about the ruling disconnection between "nature" and "culture," taking the others as witnesses to a question that perhaps does not interest them.

Finally, the abusive consequences of our routine opposition between so-called natural and supernatural causations should be reason enough not to retain the Greek polemical apparatus or its Christian continuation. The crucial question of the existence of "supernatural beings" is a heritage of the Christian missionary past, though it was raised later against the Christian God itself, along with a demand that whatever exists demonstrate its existence against "the critique." This demand, when pressed, leads straight to what Péguy denounces as unfair comparisons. The mode of existence of experimental beings, such as electrons and neutrinos—which indeed exist only because they have satisfied such a demand—is taken as the yardstick (when it is not itself the target of critique). A being of faith, the Blessed Virgin for example, is precluded from revealing her own particular force. Typically she is relegated to a category such as the famous "efficacy of the symbolic": a very wide and reassuring category that includes all that is efficacious but does not exist. Symbolic entities do not, that is, have the power to trouble our distinction between what exists and what does not.

Worse yet arrives when, at Lourdes and other miracle sites, the church hierarchy awaits, before confirming a miracle, the verdict of physicians empowered to decide if a healing can be explained away in terms of hypothetical "natural causes." Thus the only (and very poor) definition of a "supernatural intervention" is the impossibility of explaining away an event in terms of natural causes, where *natural* means, foremost, exclusion of the *super*natural. The brilliance of this feat indicates that it is polemics, rather than relevance, that shapes the whole scene.

My point here is not about universalism versus relativism so much as about what really concerns me: the poverty of our ruling definitions—and the point is widely applicable. Another example is found in sociobiology, with its definition of society in terms of altruistic self-sacrifice. Once again, this rather strange definition has emerged from a polemical scene, requiring that two causes be compared in terms favorable to one of them. Sociobiology casts individual selection and group selection as rival causes whose relative power must be compared. To do so demands a clear-cut separation between the rivals: social behavior must be defined as anything that cannot be explained in terms of individual interest (this definition is the real scandal of sociobiology). Likewise in the case of clinical testing, when the efficacy of a drug is compared with that of a placebo. This comparison is a legitimate one only if it concerns a drug that claims to work no matter what the patient feels, thinks, or understands. To impose this criterion on all drugs using healing practices frames a significant issue in (yet again) polemical terms, since it is not analytically the case that the healing arts must disqualify the imagination as a therapeutically effective force. That modern medicine does so, that it ignores the healing rapport, is one result of a polemically informed choice to draw and enforce an artificial distinction between the charlatan (with his or her ointments, mixtures, or herbs) and the certified practitioner of medical science.[3]

The examples I have offered are of unilateral, one-sided definitions that impose on others categories that do not concern them—categories the appar-

3. See Isabelle Stengers, "Le Médecin et le charlatan," in Tobie Nathan and Stengers, *Médecins et Sorciers* (Paris: Le Plessis-Robinson-Synthélabo, 1995).

ent objectivity of which only recalls that the general idea of objectivity itself can never be dissociated from an overpowering determination to silence or eradicate storytellers, teachers of popular creeds and customs, and other inadequately credentialed claimants to knowledge. Ethnologists may well discover the destructive character of "Euro-American" categories when applied elsewhere. I would underscore that in Europe, where they were born, these categories have always been used to dismember, eradicate, or appropriate. I would thus avoid saying, as a European, that they are "ours," rather that they "happened" to us first.

The problem is not with comparison and the operation making commensurability possible. The problem is not that some such operations get forgotten, the matter of concern being turned into a matter of fact. The problem begins with the imperative "comparison *must* be possible." This imperative may be justified in terms of objective knowledge to be mastered, or in the name of rational governance, or because progress means to crush illusion. The imperative always means the imposition of a standard that presupposes and enacts silence, the impossibility of objecting or of demanding due attention. This silencing power affects both terms it enrolls. For instance, science as it has been enrolled in order to determine what must be recognized as "really existing" has produced sad inquisitors, bad metaphysicians, or fearless explorers of the "beliefs of others."

The ethical and political challenge associated with comparativism makes itself felt here. I selected my examples so as to recall that this challenge concerns us in the modern West as much as it does our distant others. And it now urgently concerns "us" academics—that is, the contributors and readers of such texts as mine. Technoscience is in the process of redefining our own worlds in terms that make them available for its comparative operations. The relative passivity of the academic world in facing the ranking systems and "objective" productivity comparisons that are reshaping academic life radically is sufficient to demonstrate how simple it is, even for people who are not naive or easily impressed or overpowered, to submit to questions that are not only irrelevant but that indeed sound the death knell for all that matters most to them.

As academics, we belong now to worlds on the brink of defeat, as so many worlds have been before ours. Péguy's characterization of the contest between paganism and Christianity is (as all of his work is) the cry of a defeated man. The experience of defeat, that of Christianity, however, gave him the vigor to fabulate and create. I would like our own imminent defeat to give me the strength to do so as well. I want our fate to sound like destruction, not like the logical outcome of a process that would finally demonstrate what we really served beyond our illusions. Daring to speculate will not likely save us, but it may provide words that disentangle us from this process and that affirm our closeness with those who have already been destroyed in the name of rationality, objectivity, and the great divide between nature and culture. Affirming closeness, in this sense, is not the same as affirming similarity. It is not a question of comparison. What relates modern practices and the many practices and forms of life that were already destroyed is that all are equally subject to eradication.

Eradication may, as is the case with the knowledge economy, preserve the appearances of continuity, appear as a mere "adaptation" to new conditions. We will still have specialists busying themselves in their laboratories. What will have been destroyed, however, is what I call *divergence*. Hence I would take the term *practice* in a rather unusual sense, as denoting any form of life that is bound to be destroyed by the imperative of comparison and the imposition of a standard ensuring equivalency, because what makes each one exist is also what makes it diverge.

It is crucial here not to read "diverge from others," as doing so would turn divergence into fuel for comparison. Divergence is not between practices; it is not relational. It is constitutive. A practice does not define itself in terms of its divergence from others. Each does have its own positive and distinct way of paying due attention; that is, of having things and situations matter. Each produces its own line of divergence, as it likewise produces itself. Experimental sciences are practices, because what matters for experimenters, the creation of a rapport that authorizes an "objective" definition, is an event. And it is an event that cannot be separated from the community for which it crucially matters and which is to test it and to imagine and verify its consequence. To describe this divergence as a divergence *from* other practices is a trap. Such a trap has been laid by scientific propaganda since Galileo: "we diverge because objectivity is what matters for us." As if what is called objectivity in this case were not a name for the event the possibility of which is what makes the experimental practice exist! What if pilgrims going to a miracle site were to affirm: "we diverge from science because the transformative force of the Blessed Virgin's gaze upon us matters"?

Some years ago, I introduced the idea of an "ecology of practices" to emphasize both the divergence and the possibility of destruction that characterize what I have called *practice*.[4] I use *ecology*, as a transversal category, to help define relational heterogeneity—by which I mean situations that relate heterogeneous protagonists. Situations in natural ecology induce naturalists to define their subject matter not in general terms, but rather in the quite specific terms of how the *ethos*—that is, the needs, behaviors, habits, and crucial concerns—of each protagonist diverges positively (and not from the others). Using the term *ecology* is meant to indicate as well that practices should be characterized in terms that do not dissociate the *ethos* of a practice from its *oikos*—the way it defines its environment (including other environing practices).

4. See Isabelle Stengers, "Introductory Notes on an Ecology of Practices," *Cultural Studies Review* 11.1 (2005): 183–96.

The simplest situation for ecologists is defined in terms of predator/prey relations. It may be said that a predator/prey ecology obtains wherever the criteria associated with terms like *objectivity* and *rationality* are universally applied, since practices that maintain stronger definitions of objectivity will freely define others as potential prey; and all sciences will define as prey whatever is not scientific. The gain in clarity of the usage *predator/prey* over the more usual term for the same set of phenomena—*naturalism*—is palpable.

Another interest of the recourse to ecology is that it has no point of contact with the ideal of harmony, peace, and goodwill (in which all parties are asked to bow down to some general interest). The idea of ecology is incompatible, moreover, with neutrality: in an ecological situation, there is no neutral position from which an arbiter could assess rights and duties, nor is there any central and highest position from which a ruler could assign to each protagonist its part in a harmonious whole. Whatever the pretensions of rationality or (good) governance, the comparative operations they authorize are describable as an ecological catastrophe. It is not people who will die, obviously; and it is always possible to speak of practices as flexibly transforming themselves. What will have been eradicated, though, are all the diverging, practical attachments standing in the way of systemic flexibility—attachments that determine what matters for each practice, what motivates its practitioners to think, feel, and (if need be) resist.

Still, ecology is not about predators and prey only, but also about connecting-events, such as symbiosis, that positively relate heterogeneous terms even as the terms diverge. Symbiotically related beings go on diverging, go on defining in their own manner what matters for them. Symbiosis means that these beings are related by common interests, but *common* does not mean having the same interest in common, only that diverging interests now need each other. Symbiotic events are a matter of opportunity, of partial connection, not of harmony. It is as such that they are these days taken to be the very source of innovation in the history of life. And they may also indicate a way out of the "either/or" that haunts us: either universality (meaning that all practices have something in common) or else relativism (meaning that each practice has its own incommensurable standpoint and that practices are thus blindly indifferent to each other, except insofar as they destroy or are destroyed by each other).

As it is the case with many an either/or, this one has nothing neutral about it. It demands that we choose universality, and it can even be said that universality is nothing other than what must be postulated in order to escape the relativist menace. It is the very rhetoric whereby commensurability and equivalence are imposed as conditions for science, governance, or the need to identify charlatans. Alternative to all this commonplace thinking is the interest in the many kinds of rapport that symbiosis may bring about. The importance of symbiotic events is suggested by William James's idea of a *pluriverse*. Unsatisfied with the choice on offer in metaphysics between, on the one hand, a *universe*, with its ready-made oneness, justifying efforts at overcoming discordance, and, on the other hand, a *multiverse*, made of disconnected parts indifferent to each other, James proposed that the world is a pluriverse *in the making*. Connections are in the making, breaking indifference but bringing no encompassing unity. Plurality means divergences that communicate, but partially, always partially. What I called the creation of a "rapport," whatever its meaning (experimental, religious, therapeutic, or otherwise), then participates in James's pluriverse in the making. Each such creation is an event to be celebrated as adding a new dimension to the whole and having it "rise in value." This vision is the inverse of the unthinking dream of eradication—the dream of a world improved by a universal agreement among its denizens about what matters. James's pluriverse may be related to Donna Haraway's idea of "situated standpoints," in which each standpoint, in situating itself, becomes able to assert the legitimacy of other diverging standpoints.

If the making of the pluriverse that James celebrates is to be thought in terms of symbiotic events, the connection between heterogeneous ways of life or being as such, it also demands that we not accept settled ways of life or being as given, with survival or eradication as their only prospect. Such was for me the very hypothesis that developed into an "ecology of practices."[5] If experimental practices, the invention of which marked the birth of what we call "modern science," are to survive eradication, they will not be by trying to defend some sad remains of their past autonomy. Rather than lament over the loss of this autonomy, it may be well to consider its price. Science as the famous goose that lays golden eggs claimed that it should be unconditionally fed because of its contribution to general progress. But it also meant that scientists would be free to try and interest allies that could turn the "eggs" into gold while proclaiming utter nonresponsibility for the eventual outcome. Allies that fed public scientific research have now decided to turn a deaf ear to the goose's warning that she should not be killed. However, others still need scientific research to be reliable and would furthermore welcome scientists learning to present what they know in as demanding a way when they deal with nonscientists as when they deal with colleagues. It may well be that the only possibility for scientists to keep their divergence, their very specific way of having what they learn from matter, alive, is to betray their role as consensual proponents of reason and progress. Connection with groups needing their cooperation and expertise to formulate relevant arguments against the technoscientific transformation of our world(s) would be a "symbiotic event," the creation of a new kind of demanding "rapport," a contribution to the Jamesian pluriverse. And it may well be that here some ethnologists

5. See Isabelle Stengers, *Cosmopolitics I*, trans. Robert Bonomo (Minneapolis: University of Minnesota Press, 2010).

and sociologists show the way, as they struggle to create connections that allow them to learn and also allow those they learn from to learn as well, and for their own sakes. The point in this case is not to learn from the others "as they are," but to learn from them as they become able to produce relevant ways of resisting what defines them as prey.

It may be objected that what would be learned in this case cannot be called "science," since there is no way to disentangle what is learned from the situation. The answer, "such is also the case in the creation of experimental rapport," is insufficient, because what is lacking in our case is the "research program," the succession of "but then . . . ," "what if . . . ," "why did it not work?" that both extends and tests the scope of the rapport. In other words, the rapport does not authorize a dynamics of inventive consequences that clearly disentangles the scientists from what answers their questions.

It may well be that accepting this difference is the crucial point, the one that may free us from any nostalgia for academic research institutions, invented as they were around the generalization of research programs. It may well be that these institutions were never good places for learning what science means when addressed to sentient beings, beings who enter a rapport for their own reasons. Whatever the case, I want, in closing, to be clear that my reference to James's pluriverse does not imply an impending utopia of universal peace. While everything is always related to everything else, the creation of a rapport is always a local, precarious event and, more crucially (I agree utterly with Donna Haraway), never an innocent one.

This is the ultimate interest of our reference to ecology. Ecology understands conflicting interests as being a general rule. Ecological, symbiotic events, the creation of rapport between divergent interests as they diverge, mean novelty, not harmony. From an ecological viewpoint, the questions raised by a creation of rapport are not epistemological, but rather political, pragmatic, and (again) never innocent ones. Who is, or will be, affected, and how? The answer to such questions ought to be a matter of collective concern and accountability. Rather than critical reflexivity, our answering requires that, collectively, we learn the art of situating knowledge, which involves learning how to pay due attention to situations and consequences. Relativism, then, is not the debunking of universalistic claims, but an affirmation that there is no "innocent" knowledge because there is no knowledge without a creation of rapport. If a debunking there must be, it should be directed at the many ways in which the production of rapports may evade the challenge of considering the consequences fully.

Returning to comparativism as a method of learning, I would conclude that there is only one general rule, which may be derived from both Péguy and the experimenters, as in both cases what matters is that rapports be created between terms in their "full force," with no "foul play" weakening one and ensuring the position of the other. This is why, when those one wishes to learn from are what we call "humans," common humanity is a trap, since it defines divergence as secondary. Those you address must be empowered to evaluate the relevance of your interest, to agree or refuse to answer, and even to spit in your human, too human, face. This demands that you present yourself in terms of your own divergence—of what matters to you, and how. "Learning from" requires encountering, and encountering may indeed imply comparison, but there is no comparison if the encountered others are defined as unable to understand the point of the comparison. We are returned here to the Latin etymology of "comparison": *compar* designates those who regard each other as equals—that is, as able to agree, which means also able to disagree, object, negotiate, and contest.

RETHINKING "NORMATIVE CONSCIENCE"

The Task of the Intellectual Today

Julia Kristeva

It is common knowledge that the "intellectual" is an Enlightenment figure whose prototypes date back to the French encylopedists Rousseau, Voltaire, and Diderot. In the aftermath of the crisis of religion to which these names are connected, the nineteenth and twentieth centuries gave rise to new forms of thought that were to become the "human and social sciences" or, more simply, the "humanities." These disciplines progressively filtered into the university, notably the American university, though there remain "media personality" intellectuals outside the academy committed to the same radical overhaul of thought. In taking over from theology and philosophy, the humanities replaced the "divine" and the "human" with new objects of investigation: social bonds, the structures of kinship, rites and myths, the psychic life, the genesis of languages, and written works. We have by these means acquired an unprecedented understanding—one that disturbs complacency and hence meets with resistance and censorship—of the richness and risks of the human mind. Still, as promising as these territories are, thus constituted they fragment human experience; heirs to metaphysics,

Originally published in *Common Knowledge* 13.2–3 (Spring 2007): 219–26, as part of the symposium "A 'Dictatorship of Relativism'?" © 2007 by Duke University Press.

they keep us from identifying new objects of investigation. Crossing boundaries between compartmentalized fields does not in itself suffice to construct the intellectual life that we need now. What matters is that from the outset the thinking subject should connect his thought to his being in the world through an affective "transference" that is also political and ethical. In my own case, the clinical practice of psychoanalysis, the writing of novels, and work in the social domain are not "commitments" additional to my theoretical and scholarly work. Rather, these activities are an extension of a mode of thinking at which I aim and which I conceive as an *energeia* in the Aristotelian sense: thought as act, the actualization of intelligence.

In my experience—to take the most relevant instance—the interpretation of texts and behavior, notably in the light of psychoanalysis, opens up a new approach to the world of religion. The discovery of the unconscious by Freud showed us that far from being "illusions"—while nevertheless being illusions—religions, beliefs, and other forms of spirituality shelter, encourage, or exploit specifiable psychic movements that allow the human being to become a speaking subject and a source of culture or, conversely, a source of destruction. The reverence for law, the celebration of the paternal function, and the role of maternal passion as the child's sensorial and prelinguistic support are examples of this process at work. My analytic practice has convinced me that when a patient comes for psychoanalysis, he is asking for a kind of forgiveness, not to ease his malaise but to find psychic or even physical rebirth. The new beginning made possible through transference and interpretation I call *for-giveness*: to give (and to give not just to oneself) a new self, a new time, unforeseen ties. In this context, we recognize the complexity of the internal experience that religious faith cultivates, but we also bring to light the hate that takes the guise of lovers' discourse, as well as the death drive channeled to merciless wars and political vengeance.

A new conception of the human is in the process of being constituted out of contributions from fields in the humanities where transcendence is considered immanent. The new conception is of the human as synonymous with the desire for meaning, and of that desire as inseparable from pleasure, which is rooted in sexuality and which decrees both the sublimity of culture and the brutality of "acting out." The intellectual today is confronted with a difficult, historic task commensurate with our now-difficult juncture in the history of civilization. The task is neither more nor less than to coax this new type of knowledge to emerge progressively. In order to do so, we use the technical terms of our specific fields but without reducing them to their strict meaning, which is always too narrow. By positioning ourselves at the interface of the diverse disciplines of the humanities, we give ourselves the opportunity to clarify, even if only a little, the enigmas we have still to comprehend: psychosis, murderous hate, the war of male and female, maternal madness, nihilism, passion, sublimation, and belief.

An Intellectual Countercurrent: Böckenförde, Habermas, Ratzinger

Of what specific relevance are my remarks about the task of the intellectual at the present time to the theme of this symposium? The homily of Cardinal Ratzinger's that is our topic here forms part of an intellectual current that runs counter to the radical overhaul of thought that I have been describing. Two of the most prestigious spokesmen for this countercurrent are Joseph Ratzinger and Jürgen Habermas, who recently (though before Ratzinger's election as pope) became collaborators in each other's projects. Having remarked the failure of rationalist humanism to avert or cope with twentieth-century totalitarianism—and having predicted that it would yet fail to prevent the economic and biological automatization threatening the human species in the new century—Ratzinger and Habermas jointly diagnosed the problem as confusion on the part of modern democracies in the absence of a reliable "higher" authority to regulate the frenetic expansion of liberty.[1] This joint declaration by the theologian and the philosopher implies that a return to faith is the only way possible to establish the moral stability required for us to face the risks of freedom. In other words, since constitutional democracies need "normative presuppositions" to found "rational law"—and since the secular state does not provide an intrinsically "unifying bond" (Ernst-Wolfgang Böckenförde)—it is imperative that we constitute a "conservative conscience": a normative conscience that would be either fueled by faith (Habermas) or by a "correlation between reason and faith" (Ratzinger).

To counterbalance this hypothesis, let me suggest that we are already confronted, notably in advanced democracies, with prepolitical and transpolitical experiences that render obsolete any appeal for a normative conscience or for a return to the reason/revelation duo. For these pre- and transpolitical experiences head us toward a reconstruction (without recourse to the irrational) of the humanism derived from *Aufklärung*. The Freudian discovery of the unconscious, and the literary experience that is inseparable from theoretical thought, are positioned at this key point in modern development. Their respective contributions—contributions to bringing greater complexity and sophistication to Enlightenment humanism—are not yet understood. In their pre- and transpolitical effects, Freud's discovery and those of literary theory, are likely to found the "unifying bond" that secular, political rationality has until now lacked. In any case, it is on the basis of this hypothesis that, I believe, we should conceive and develop our alternative to the arguments offered us by the trio of Böckenförde, Habermas, and Ratzinger.

Our fundamental problems may be religious, as this trio claims, but the clash of religions about which so many are now so concerned is merely a surface

---

1. Joseph Ratzinger and Jürgen Habermas, "Les fondements pré-politiques de l'Etat démocratique," *Esprit* 306 (July 2004): 5–28.

phenomenon. The real problem that we face at the beginning of this new millennium is not one of religious wars, but rather of a rift that divides those who want to know that God is unconscious from those who prefer not to know. Our globalized media have bought into the preference for being pleasured by God's existence, fueling the show that affirms his existence with the whole of their imaginary and financial economies. The media have joined in not wanting to know, in order to better enjoy the virtual—to take pleasure in hearing promises, and being satisfied with promises, of goods guaranteed by the promise of a superior Good. This situation, due to the globalization of denial, which is integral to it, appears without precedent in human history. Saturated with enterprises, seductions, and disappointments, our televisual civilization is propitious for belief and encourages the revival of religions.

Nietzsche and Heidegger warned us: modern man experiences "the absence of a sensible and supersensible world with the power to oblige." The annihilation of divine authority, and with it all authority, be it state or political, does not necessarily lead to nihilism. Nor does it lead to the systemic flip side of nihilism, which is fundamentalism with its attack on infidels. Hannah Arendt long ago remarked that, by making the divine a value, even a "supreme value," transcendentalists arrive, themselves, at a nihilistic utilitarianism. I would say that the alternative to the nonchoice between mounting religiosity and its counterpart, narrow nihilism, can be found in the vast continent of the human sciences, which we should try not to occupy but to vivify.

This task is one for specialists in every humanities discipline. In studying literature, for instance, the specialist will experience how language transverses sexual, gender, national, ethnic, religious, and ideological identities. Students of literature, whether open or hostile to psychoanalysis, elaborate a risky, singular, yet shareable understanding of the desire for meaning anchored in the sexual body. The study of literature, of writing, upsets the metaphysical duo *reason versus faith*. Those involved in the literary experience, and in a different but complicit manner, those who are involved in the psychoanalytical experience, or who are attentive to its issues, know that the oppositions *reason/faith* and *norm/liberty* are no longer sustainable if the speaking being that I am no longer thinks of myself as dependent on the supratangible world, and even less on the tangible world, "with the power to oblige." We also know that this *I* who speaks reveals himself as he is constructed in a vulnerable bond with a strange object or an ek-static, ab-ject other: this is the "sexual thing" (others will say: the object of the sexual drive of which the "carrier wave" is the death drive). This vulnerable bond *with* the sexual thing and *within* it—by which the social or sacred bond is shored up—is none other than the heterogeneous bond, the very fold, between biology and meaning on which our languages and discourses depend and through which they are modified so that, in turn, they modify the sexual bond itself.

In this understanding of the human adventure, literature and art do not constitute aesthetic decor (nor can philosophy and psychoanalysis claim to bring salvation). But each of these experiences, in its diversity, offers itself as a laboratory for new forms of humanism — or rather, for the new conception of the human that, as I have said, we have pursued and must continue to pursue. Understanding and accompanying the speaking subject in his bond to the sexual thing gives us an opportunity to face up to the new barbarisms of automatization, without seeking recourse in the safeguards upheld by infantilizing conservatism, and free of the short-term idealism with which a mortifying rationalism deludes itself. And yet, if the project I am depicting, undertaken within the human sciences, suggests an overhaul or even reconstruction of humanism, putting the project to work and dealing with its consequences can only be, in Sartre's words, "cruel and long drawn out."

I was part of the generation that objected to soft humanism with its vague idea of "man," emptied of his substance, and its utopian fraternity harkening back to the Enlightenment and the postrevolutionary social contract. Today it seems to me not only important but also possible to approach these ideals in a new, more positive manner. For I am persuaded that modernity, which we too often disparage, is a decisive phase in the history of thought. Modern thought, which is neither hostile nor indulgent toward religion, may be our one good option as we face, on the one hand, mounting obscurantism and, on the other, the technological management of the human species.

To plead for the reconstructive role that the humanities can play in the highly threatened social and political realm is, to say the least, difficult. I insist, however, on our need to plead. Intellectuals must fight against the temptation to give into depression. The case that we in the humanities have been making that normative conscience, normative presuppositions, utilitarian nihilism, and the supposed need of democracies for authority are based on obsolete and discredited assumptions must be heard in public spheres. And so we must participate courageously and appropriately in the "democracy of opinion" that our society of the spectacle has become. This symposium might be viewed as an example.

Ideality: An Adolescent Malady

As my contribution, I would like to outline here the sort of response that an intellectual in the human and social sciences can make to the kind of dilemmas that tend to call up statements of reproach and retrenchment from Ratzinger, Habermas, and other apostles of normative conscience. Thinking especially of the rioting and arson in French suburbs during 2005, I want to discuss something that concerns me as a parent, writer, psychoanalyst, and intellectual: namely, the "malady of ideality" specific to adolescents.

The "polymorphous perverse" child wants to know where babies come from and constructs himself as a "theoretician"; the adolescent, on the other hand, is starving for ideal models that will allow him to tear himself from his parents and meet the ideal partner, get the ideal job, and "turn himself into" an ideal being. Seen from this angle, the adolescent is a *believer*. Paradise is an adolescent invention with its Adams and Eves, Dantes and Beatrices. We are all adolescent believers when we dream about the ideal couple or the ideal life. The novel as a genre was built on adolescent figures: enthusiastic idealists smitten with the absolute but devastated by the first disappointment, depressed or perverse, sarcastic "by nature"—eternal believers and therefore perpetually rebellious, potentially nihilists. You know them: they have been chiming their credo from the courtly novel to Dostoevsky and Gombrowicz. This "malady of ideality" confronts us with a prereligious and prepolitical form of belief: it is a matter of needing an ideal that contributes to the construction of the psychic life but that, because it is an absolute exigency, can easily turn itself into its opposite: disappointment, boredom, depression, or even destructive rage, vandalism, all the imaginable variants of nihilism that are all just appeals to the ideal.

Civilizations commonly referred to as primitive have long used initiation rites, including initiatory sexual practices, to assert symbolic authority (whether religious for the invisible world, or political for the visible) while justifying what today would qualify as perverse behaviors. Medieval Christianity, among other religions, used mortification rituals and excessive fasting to channel the anorectic and sadomasochistic behaviors of adolescents and, in doing so, either downplayed or glorified them. Modern society, which is entirely incapable of understanding the structuring need of ideality, combines its destruction of the family fabric and weakening of authority with a failure to deal innovatively with adolescence. This incapacity and failure are blatant in the French crisis involving adolescents of North and West African descent—adolescents who are victims not only of broken families and the devaluing of authority, but also of social misery in its various kinds, including discrimination. How could we in France have imagined that they would "enter the established order" without first satisfying the structuring need of ideality? How can we imagine restoring order by repressing these tattered psyches? Certainly those who led in the expressions of social unrest, as well as the younger participants, need to be sanctioned. However, for the authority of law to be acknowledged, the legal code must address psychic lives capable of integrating it. These immigrant adolescents need urgent help in reconstructing their psychic lives, beginning with their recognizing that beneath their own vandalism is a long-neglected need to believe.

This malaise of immigrant adolescents is widespread, but especially worrisome in France because there it arises from a quite radical depth. Although we should not underestimate the manipulation of religion by the pyromaniacs, or the communal reflex underlying the need for recognition expressed by destruction, the unrest in French suburbs did not bespeak a religious conflict. Nor did these reckless acts constitute a backlash against the law forbidding "the wearing of religious signs" in public spaces. France's religious authorities disapproved of the violence; immigrant parents in no way condoned their children's delinquent behavior. Here was not a case of violence between ethnicities and religions (such as we do see elsewhere). All parties concerned strongly denounced the failure of integration, to which the immigrants aspired. The objects burned were envied symbols: cars, supermarkets, warehouses full of merchandise—so many signs of "success" and "wealth," so many things valued by families and friends. As for the schools, day care centers, and police stations set on fire—these were and remain signs of the social and political authority of which these adolescents would like to be a part. Is it Secular France that one wants to destroy when booing its (previously adulated) minister of the Interior? Is it Christianity that is attacked when one burns a church? The blogs said "Fuck France" in a frenzy of sexual desire that illumined no program or discourse or concrete complaint. On the political side, the need for an ideal, for recognition and respect, has crystallized in a single struggle, an enormous one judging by the suffering it has exposed and by the extent of the changes it necessitates: the struggle against discrimination.

Can it be that we have not yet arrived at the supposedly looming "clash of religions"? Or that our adolescent pyromaniacs are as yet incapable of donning the cloak of religion to satisfy their need for ideality? Those who promote these notions go so far as to indict French secularism for abolishing religious norms that serve as safeguards. Clearly, I do not share this opinion. It is a view based on belief in normative conscience, a belief that, as I have said, we must undertake difficult intellectual labors to get beyond. The crimes of our "underprivileged teens" disclose a more radical phase of nihilism, a phase whose arrival is made known only after or beneath the "clash of religions." This kind of violence is more serious than religious violence because it seizes the moving forces of civilization at an even deeper level, in the *prereligious* need to believe, constitutive of psychic life with and for the other. It is to this space that the parent, teacher, and intellectual are being called. While insisting on pragmatism and generosity from the political spheres, we ourselves must come up with ideals adapted to modern times and the multiculturality of souls. It is up to us to do so. For adolescent nihilism makes it abruptly apparent that, from now on, any religious treatment of such revolt will find itself discredited, ineffective, and unfit to ensure the paradisiacal aspiration of these paradoxical believers, these nihilistic believers—yes, necessarily nihilistic now. We are confronting a crisis whose source is *pre*religious (though it is a crisis of belief, of ideals) and *pre*political (though it affects the foundation of human bonds)—a crisis that, contra Joseph Ratzinger and Jürgen Habermas, who have made clear they understand the crisis, no religion or established moral order or ideal of normative conscience will ever resolve. Resolution will demand understanding of *and for* the human soul, along with a generosity that free intellectuals can acquire but that standards of normative conscience are intended to extinguish.

THE WOMAN WITH THE PEARL NECKLACE

Caroline Walker Bynum

In April of 2001 I went to the Metropolitan Museum of Art to see the exhibit *Vermeer and the Delft School.* I was tired after a hectic week of teaching, but fearing that the spring would slip away and I wouldn't get to the exhibit at all, I determined to squeeze in a visit to the museum on a Friday night just at the dinner hour when, I hoped, the galleries would be emptying. The rooms were, however, crowded. And the early parts of the show, devoted as they were to the Delft context, frustrated me in a way they would not have done had I been less tired. I wanted to see Vermeers. One or two of the Fabritiuses came as a revelation, and I have always liked de Hooch. Nonetheless, I didn't see what the *New Yorker* called "the Met at its best: a stately procession of masterpieces." There were too many people, too many paintings, too many objects, too much text to read. Until I came to *The Woman with the Pearl Necklace.*

    I have spent much time in Berlin and know exactly where the painting usually hangs in the Gemäldegalerie. Not only the *Woman* herself but also her setting mean a great deal to me, for I can remember the city (not so many years ago) when there was no Gemäldegalerie in the Kulturforum, when the collections were divided, when some of what one most wanted to view took visas and police

Originally published in *Common Knowledge* 8.2 (Spring 2002): 280–83. © 2002 by Duke University Press.

Common Knowledge 25:1–3

DOI 10.1215/0961754X-7299294

checks and sealed subway trains to reach. I never see her in her Berlin setting, where the rooms are quiet, the floors polished, and the light is gray, pearl-like, almost Vermeer's, without rejoicing that I can see her there. To find her in the Met show gave me a moment of peace, and I stood for a long time before her upraised arms, her earnest innocent look, and the Vermeer light that pours over her. For a moment the crowds fell away.

When I returned home, I mentioned to my husband what I had enjoyed most about the exhibit and then turned to other pressing matters. My brief report to him is important because it confirms what I saw.

Two weeks later, on a Saturday morning, I got up early, having decided to be at the Met when it opened. I wanted to go immediately to the end of the exhibit (as I often do) and work my way back against the crowd to see more of the paintings in peace. I was less tired; it was the weekend; the crowds lined up on the steps outside the Met were there to see the dresses of "Jackie O," not Vermeer. I could anticipate leisurely viewing.

But *The Woman with the Pearl Necklace* was not there. Slowly I turned back through the exhibit, looking. I counted the Vermeers. The reviews had said there were fifteen, possibly sixteen if one accepted a disputed attribution. I counted fifteen, without the *Woman*.

In something approaching terror, I then went quietly, deliberately, room by room, studying the labels. There was a painting from Berlin, but it was *The Glass of Wine*—busier, more orange and elegant. In it, the woman has always seemed to me to hold a glass to her face forever, hiding in it, shielded by it, her male companion foppish, supercilious, ever so slightly threatening. One cannot imagine anything there ever moving. But the *Woman* with her yellow ribbon and pearls, her lips slightly open, seems to me caught in the movement of thinking itself. The two paintings are completely different. I could not have confused one with the other. Where then was the *Woman*?

I went into the alcove where catalogues of the exhibit were displayed and began to read. Perhaps the *Woman* had been included only in the early weeks of the show. But my obsessive scrutiny established only that she had never been there. The sort of middle-aged panic one feels when one cannot remember a name or date or earlier event swept over me. But this was no "senior moment." I was not failing to remember what I HAD seen. I was remembering something that hadn't happened.

I am not given to prayer or meditation in any formal sense, nor am I a believer in the parapsychological, although I am inclined to think there is much about presence and absence that we do not fully understand. I am, however, quite certain that I saw *The Woman with the Pearl Necklace* in New York on an evening in April, that I stood before her when I was tired and in need of refreshment and felt the crowded room drop away. I remember being there and seeing; and I remember the intensity of the silence.

What happened?

I was exhausted, and the petty strains of a workweek can leave one as needy as do far more imperative and weighty demands. The *Woman* herself is associated for me with the complex happinesses of foreign travel (hence escape) and of discovery (hence learning, even power); she carries with her a little of my younger self, a self that grew and explored, that stretched itself, through seeing her. Yet she is not a mirror or projection. She is Vermeer. To see her again is both to be the earlier self that saw her once in a different place and to make a step forward into new seeing. I can only hypothesize that I must have deeply needed a moment out of ordinary time. And in the frustration born of the claustrophobic crowding of the galleries, something—a label, a glimpse of another painting from Berlin, another yellow, the glow of a pearl in another painting—triggered a memory so visceral that I saw it outside myself.

The medieval people I study "saw things," as my students put it. And those same students frequently ask me what I think they saw. Scholars are accustomed to answer that we, like good phenomenologists, "bracket" that question; we read the texts; we study what the mystics and visionaries say they saw and don't bother ourselves overmuch with whether it was really there. But the students are right to ask the question.

Medieval thinkers had their own theories and explanations. Augustine had argued, as is well known, that there were three categories of vision: corporal vision or the ordinary seeing of our bodily sense; spiritual vision, in which the person's "spirit" sees "images" or "semblances" or "phantasms" of bodies; and intellectual vision, in which the mind contemplates eternal truths without any mental images or representations. Dreams, like ghosts and apparitions, were visions of the second category. They were seen, but what was seen was not necessarily, to Augustine, "really there." It could be caused in the mind by God or devils—or by indigestion. Hence in his psychologically astute *De cura pro mortuis gerenda*, Augustine comforted a grieving woman by arguing that images of her dead son did not mean he was really present, demanding burial or retribution, any more than a dream of a distant friend means he is inside one's head.

Later theologians continued to espouse Augustine's theories, arguing that such things as werewolves, flying witches, and ghosts were only the manipulations by demons of visual material in our minds. The pious in the later Middle Ages probably did not quite agree. When they saw ghosts and beat off werewolf attacks, they probably thought the threat was more than a manipulation within the brain. And when the spiritually gifted, whether in religious houses, hermit cells, or bourgeois chambers, saw or heard Christ and the saints, they often wrote about the experience as more tactile and immediate than words such as *simulacra* would suggest. Moreover, when medieval people said that they "saw," they meant as wide a range of visual experiences as we claim today: from metaphorical to crudely physical. Fourteenth-century English villagers "saw" and ran from bales of hay that turned into demons; Peter the Venerable "saw" a murdered friend in a dream and wept real tears that he had not brought the murderer to justice; Angela of Foligno and Rupert of Deutz "saw" and embraced a physical body hanging on an altar cross; Margery Kempe "saw" Christ's suffering when a fellow townsman beat a mule or a child. These people would not have claimed that their visions were all the same; whatever the theorists wrote, Augustine's tripartite division was probably not sufficient to describe or explain them all. Moreover, there were, by the fourteenth century, theorists such as Nicole Oresme who argued that many so-called apparitions were mere natural illusions, a trick of the light, a paranoid reaction to shadows or the dark. Nonetheless, there seems to have been, in the Middle Ages, a wide range of experiences that would fit Augustine's second category, whether or not his explanation of its causes is the correct one. Whether God or angels, devils or grief or an upset stomach, caused them, people said that they "saw" the dead, the saints, werewolves, and God. I think I must tell my students that they did.

As I saw *The Woman with the Pearl Necklace*.

DECREATION

How Women Like Sappho, Marguerite Porete,
and Simone Weil Tell God

Anne Carson

This is an essay about three women and will have three parts. Part One concerns Sappho, a Greek poet of the seventh century BC, who lived on the island of Lesbos, wrote some famous poetry about love and is said to have organized her life around worship of the God Aphrodite. Part Two concerns Marguerite Porete, who was burned alive in the public square of Paris in 1310 because she had written a book about the love of God which the papal inquisitor deemed heretical. Part Three concerns Simone Weil, the twentieth-century French classicist and philosopher whom Camus called "the only great spirit of our time."

Part One
What if I were to begin an essay on spiritual matters by citing a poem that will not at first seem to you spiritual at all? Fragment 31 of Sappho says:

He seems to me equal to gods that man
whoever he is who opposite you
sits and listens close

Originally published in *Common Knowledge* 8.1 (Winter 2002): 188–203. © 2002 by Duke University Press.

to your sweet speaking
and lovely laughing—oh it
puts the heart in my chest on wings
for when I look at you, even a moment, no speaking

is left in me
no: tongue breaks and thin
fire is racing under skin
and in eyes no sight and drumming
fills ears

and cold sweat holds me and shaking
grips me all, greener than grass
I am and dead—or almost
I seem to me.

But all is to be dared, because even a person of poverty. . . . [1]

This poem has been preserved for us by the ancient literary critic Longinus, who quotes four complete Sapphic stanzas and then the first line of what looks like a fifth stanza and then breaks off, no one knows why. But the first four stanzas seem to compose a unit of music and thought; let's consider the thought. It comes to us bathed in light but this is the weirdly enclosed light of introspection. Sappho is staging a scenario inside the little theater of her mind. It appears to be an erotic scenario but the characters are anonymous, their interrelations obscure. We don't know why the girl is laughing, nor what the man is doing there, nor how Sappho's response to them makes sense. Sappho seems less interested in these characters as individuals than in the geometric figure that they form. This figure has three lines and three angles. One line connects the girl's voice and laughter to a man who listens close. A second connects the girl to Sappho. Between the eye of Sappho and the listening man runs a third. The figure is a triangle. Why does Sappho want to stage this figure? Common sense suggests it is a poem about jealousy. "Lovers all show such symptoms as these," says Longinus. So let's think about what the jealousy of lovers is.

The word comes from ancient Greek *zelos* meaning "zeal" or "hot pursuit." A jealous lover covets a certain location at the center of her beloved's affection only to find it occupied by someone else. If jealousy were a dance it would be a pattern of placement and displacement. Its emotional focus is unstable. Jealousy is a dance in which everyone moves.

Sappho's poem sets the stage for jealousy but she does not dance it. Indeed she seems to forget the presence of her dancing partners entirely after the first stanza

---

1. *Sappho et Alcaeus: Fragmenta*, ed. E. M. Voigt (Amsterdam: Athenaeum-Polak and Van Gennep, 1971). All sub- sequent references are to this edition and are cited in the text.

and shifts the spotlight onto herself. And what we see in the spotlight is an unexpectedly spiritual spectacle. For Sappho describes her own perceptual abilities (visual, aural, tactile) reduced to dysfunction one after another; she shows us the objects of outer sense emptying themselves; and there on the brightly lit stage at the center of her perception appears her own Being:

I am . . .

she says at verse 15 ("greener than grass I am").

This is not just a moment of revealed existence: it is a spiritual event. Sappho enters into ecstasy. "I am greener than grass," she says, predicating of her own Being an attribute observable only from outside her own body. This is the condition called *ekstasis*, literally "standing outside oneself," a condition regarded by the Greeks as typical of mad persons, geniuses, and lovers, and ascribed to poets by Aristotle.

Ecstasy changes Sappho and changes her poem. She herself, she says, is almost dead. Her poem appears to break down and stop. But then, arguably, both of them start up again. I say arguably because the seventeenth (last) verse of the poem has a puzzling history and is regarded with suspicion by some scholars, although it appears in Longinus and is corroborated by a papyrus. Let us attempt to see its coherence with what goes before.

"All is to be dared because even a person of poverty. . . ," says verse 17. It is a new thought. The content of the thought is absolute daring. The condition of the thought is poverty. I don't want to give the impression that I know what verse 17 is saying or that I see where the poem is headed from here; I don't. Overall this poem leaves me wondering. Sappho sets up a scenario of jealousy but that's not what the poem is about, jealousy is just a figure. Sappho stages an event of ecstasy but that's not what the poem is about either, ecstasy is just a means to an end. Unfortunately we don't reach the end, the poem breaks off. But we do see Sappho begin to turn toward it, toward this unreachable end. We see her senses empty themselves, we see her Being thrown outside its own center where it stands observing her as if she were grass or dead. At which point a speculation occurs to me: granted this is a poem all about love, do we need to limit ourselves to a reading of it that is merely or conventionally erotic? After all, Sappho is believed by some historians to have been not just a poet of love and a worshiper of Aphrodite on Lesbos but also a priestess of Aphrodite's cult and a teacher of her doctrines. Perhaps Sappho's poem wants to teach us something about the metaphysics or even the theology of love. Perhaps she is posing not the usual lovesong complaint, *Why don't you love me?* but a deeper spiritual question, *What is it that love dares the self to do?* Daring enters the poem in the seventeenth verse when Sappho uses the word *tolmaton*: "is to be dared."

This word is a verbal adjective expressing a mood of ability, possibility, or potential. Sappho says it is an *absolute* potential:

pan tolmaton: all is to be dared.

Moreover she consents to it—or seems to be on the point of consenting when the poem breaks off. Why does she consent? Her explanation no longer exists. So far as it goes, it leads us back to her ecstatic condition. For when an ecstatic is asked the question *What is it that love dares the self to do?* she will answer:

Love dares the self to leave itself behind, to enter into poverty.

Part Two

Marguerite Porete was burned at the stake in 1310 for writing a book about the absolute daring of love. *The Mirror of Simple Souls* is a theological treatise and also a kind of handbook for people seeking God. Marguerite Porete's central doctrine is that a human soul can proceed through seven different stages of love, beginning with a period of "boiling desire" (chap. 118), to an ecstasy in which the soul is carried outside her own Being and leaves herself behind. This departure from her own center is not passive. Like Sappho, Marguerite first discovers in reality a certain absolute demand and then she consents to it. Like Sappho, she sees herself split in two by this consent and experiences it as a kind of "annihilation." Marguerite's reasoning is severe: she understands the essence of her human self to be in her free will and she decides that free will has been placed in her by God in order that she may give it back. She therefore causes her will to depart from its own will and render itself back to God with nothing left over. Here is how she describes this event:

. . . a ravishing expansion of the movement of divine Light is poured into the Soul and shows to the Will [the rightness of what is . . . in order to move the Soul] from the place where it is now and ought not to be and render it back to where it is not, whence it came, there where it ought to remain. Now the Will sees . . . that it cannot profit unless it departs from its own will. And thus the Soul parts herself from this will and the Will parts itself from such a Soul and then renders itself and gives and goes back to God, there where it was first taken, without retaining anything of its own. . . . [2]

2. Marguerite Porete, *The Mirror of Simple Souls*, trans. Ellen L. Babinsky (New York: Paulist, 1993), chap. 118. I have altered Babinsky's translation slightly. All subsequent references are to this edition and are cited in the text.

Now it is noteworthy, in light of Sappho's account of ecstasy and its consequences, that Marguerite Porete twice refers to herself at the moment when God's abundance overflows her as:

I who am in the abyss of absolute poverty. (chap. 38)

She also describes her impoverishment as a condition of physical and metaphysical negation:

Now such a Soul is nothing, for she sees her nothingness by means of the abundance of divine understanding, which makes her nothing and places her in nothingness. (chap. 118)

Throughout *The Mirror* she speaks of herself as null, worthless, deficient, deprived, and naked. But at the same time she recognizes her poverty as an amazing and inexpressible kind of repletion; and of this absolute emptiness which is also absolute fullness she speaks in erotic language, referring to God as "overflowing and abundant Lover" (chap. 38) or as "the Spouse of my youth" (chap. 118). Even more interesting for our analogy with Sappho, Marguerite Porete twice proposes jealousy as a figure for her relationship with God. Thus she refers to God as "the most high Jealous One" and speaks of God's relation to her Soul in this way:

Jealous he is truly! He shows it by his works which have stripped me of myself absolutely and have placed me in divine pleasure without myself. And such a union joins and conjoins me through the sovereign highness of creation with the brilliance of divine being, by which I have being which is being. (chap. 71)

This is an unusual erotic triangle consisting of God, Marguerite, and Marguerite. But its motions have the same ecstatic effect as the three-person situation in Sappho's poem. Marguerite feels her self pulled apart from itself and thrown into a condition of poverty, to which she consents. Her consent takes the form of a peculiarly intense triangular fantasy:

. . . and I pondered, as if God were asking me, how would I fare if I knew that he preferred me to love another more than himself? And at this my sense failed me and I knew not what to say. Then he asked me how would I fare if it could happen he should love another more than me? And here my sense failed me and I knew not what to say. . . . Beyond this, he asked me what would I do and how would I fare if it

See also "The Mirror of Simple Souls," trans. Edmond Colledge, in *Notre Dame Texts in Medieval Culture*, vol. 6 (Notre Dame, IN: University of Notre Dame Press, 1999), chap. 118; and *Le mirouer des simples ames anienties et qui seulement demourent en vouloir et desir d'amour*, ed. Romana Guarnieri, *Archivio Italiano per la storia della Pietà* 4 (1965): 513–635.

could be he preferred another to love me more than he. . . . And there
I fainted away for I could say nothing to these three things, nor refuse,
nor deny. (chap. 131)

Notice how Marguerite turns the fantasy this way and that, rotating its personnel and reimagining its anguish. Jealousy is a dance in which everyone moves. It is a dance with a dialectical nature. For the jealous lover must balance two contradictory realities within her heart: on the one hand, that of herself at the center of the universe and in command of her own will, offering love to her beloved; on the other, that of herself off the center of the universe and in despite of her own will, watching her beloved love someone else. Naked collision of these two realities brings the lover to a sort of breakdown, as we saw in Sappho's poem, whose effect is to expose her very Being to its own scrutiny and to dislodge it from the center of itself. It would be a very high test of dialectical endurance to be able to, not just recognize, but consent to this breakdown. Sappho seems to be entering on a mood of consent when her poem stops. Marguerite faints three times before she can manage it. But then, with a psychological clarity as amazing as Sappho's, Marguerite pushes open the implications of her own pain. Here is her analysis of what she sees when she looks inside Marguerite:

And so long as I was at ease and loved myself "with" him, I could not at
all contain myself or have calm: I was held in bondage by which I could
not move. . . . I loved myself so much along "with" him that I could not
answer loyally. . . . Yet all at once he demanded my response, if I did not
want to lose both myself and him. . . . I said to him that he must want to
test me in all points. (chap. 131)

Marguerite reaches rock bottom here when she faces the fact that loyalty to God is actually obstructed by her love of him because this affection, like most human erotic feeling, is largely self-love: it puts Marguerite in bondage to Marguerite rather than to God. Her reasoning uses the figure of jealousy in two ways. She sees jealousy as an explanation of her own feelings of inner division; she also projects jealousy as a test of her ability to decenter herself, to move out of the way, to clear her own heart and her own will off the path that leads to God. For in order to (as she says) "answer God loyally" she cannot stay one with her own heart or with her own will, she cannot love her own love or love herself loving or love being loved. And insofar as she can "annihilate" all these—her term—she can resolve the three angles of the dance of jealousy into a single nakedness and reduce her Being from three to two to one:

Now this Soul . . . has left three and has made two one. But in what does
this one consist? This one is when the soul is rendered into the simple
Deity, in full knowing, without feeling, beyond thought. . . .

Higher no one can go, deeper no one can go, more naked no human
can be. (chap. 138)

Part Three

Simone Weil was also a person who wanted to get herself out of the way so as to
arrive at God. "The self," she says in one of her notebooks, "is only a shadow projected by sin and error which blocks God's light and which I take for a Being." She
had a program for getting the self out of the way which she called "decreation."
This word is a neologism to which she did not give an exact definition nor a consistent spelling. "To undo the creature in us" is one of the ways she describes its
aim.[3] And when she tells of its method she uses language that may sound familiar.
Like Marguerite Porete she expresses a need to render back to God what God has
given to her, that is, the self:

We possess nothing in this world other than the power to say "I." This
is what we must yield up to God. (GG, 71; PG, 35)

And like Marguerite Porete she pictures this yielding as a sort of test:

God gave me Being in order that I should give it back to him. It is like
one of those traps whereby the characters are tested in fairy tales. If I
accept this gift it is bad and fatal; its virtue becomes apparent through
my refusal of it. God allows me to exist outside himself. It is for me to
refuse this authorization. (GG, 87; PG, 48)

And also like Marguerite Porete she feels herself to be an obstacle to herself
inwardly. The process of decreation is for her a dislodging of herself from a center
where she cannot stay because staying there blocks God. She speaks of a need "to
withdraw from my own soul" and says:

God can love in us only this consent to withdraw in order to make way
for him. (GG, 88; PG, 49)

But now let us dwell for a moment on this statement about withdrawal and consent. Here Simone Weil enters upon a strangely daring and difficult negotiation
that seems to me to evoke both Marguerite Porete and Sappho. For Simone Weil
wants to discover in the three-cornered figure of jealousy those lines of force that
connect a soul to God. She does not, however, fantasize relationships with ordinary human lovers. The erotic triangle Simone Weil constructs is one involving
God, herself, and the whole of creation:

3. Simone Weil, *Gravity and Grace*, trans. Arthur Wills
(Lincoln: University of Nebraska Press, 1997), 81, hereafter cited in the text as *GG* = *La pesanteur et la grâce*, ed.
Gustave Thibon (Paris: Plon, 1948), 43, hereafter cited in
the text as *PG*.

All the things that I see, hear, breathe, touch, eat; all the beings I meet—
I deprive the sum total of all that of contact with God, and I deprive God
of contact with all that insofar as something in me says "I."

I can do something for all that and for God—namely, retire and
respect the *tête-à-tête*. . . .

I must withdraw so that God may make contact with the beings whom
chance places in my path and whom he loves. It is tactless of me to be
there. It is as though I were placed between two lovers or two friends. I
am not the maiden who awaits her betrothed but the unwelcome third
who is with two betrothed lovers and ought to go away so that they can
really be together.

If only I knew how to disappear there would be a perfect union of love
between God and the earth I tread, the sea I hear. . . . (*GG*, 88; *PG*, 49)

If only she could become what Marguerite Porete calls an "annihilated soul," if
only she could achieve the transparency of Sappho's ecstatic condition "greener
than grass and almost dead," Simone Weil would feel she had relieved the world
of an indiscretion. Jealousy is a dance in which everybody moves because one of
them is always extra—three people trying to sit on two chairs. We saw how this
extra person is set apart in Marguerite Porete's text by a canny use of quotation
marks—remember her plaintive observation: I loved myself so much along "with"
him that I could not answer loyally. When I read this sentence the first time, it
seemed odd to me that Marguerite Porete puts the quotation marks around the
"with" rather than around one of the pronouns. But Marguerite knows what
she is doing: the people are not the problem here. Withness is the problem. She
is trying to use the simplest language and the plainest marks to express a profoundly tricky spiritual fact, viz. that I cannot go toward God in love without
bringing myself along. And so in the deepest possible sense I can never be alone
with God. I can only be alone "with God."

To catch sight of this fact brings a wrench in perception, forces the perceiver to
a point where she has to disappear from herself in order to look. As Simone Weil
says longingly:

If only I could see a landscape as it is when I am not there. But when
I am in any place I disturb the silence of heaven by the beating of my
heart. (*GG*, 89; *PG*, 50)

As we saw, Marguerite Porete found a way to translate the beating of her own
heart into a set of quotation marks around the word "with." And Sappho found
a way to record the beating of her heart while imagining its absence—for surely
this is the function performed in her poem by "the man who opposite you sits and

listens close." This man, Sappho tells us, is "equal to gods"; but can we not read him as her way of representing "the landscape as it is when I am not there"? It is a landscape where joy is so full that it seems to go unexperienced. Sappho does not describe this landscape further but Marguerite Porete offers an amazing account of a soul in some such condition:

Such a Soul . . . swims in the sea of joy—that is in the sea of delights
flowing and streaming from the Divinity, and she feels no joy for
she herself is joy, and swims and floats in joy without feeling any joy
because she inhabits Joy and Joy inhabits her. . . . (chap. 28)

It seems consistent with Simone Weil's project of decreation that, although she too recognizes this kind of joyless joy, she finds in it not an occasion of swimming but one of exclusion and negation:

Perfect joy excludes even the very feeling of joy, for in the soul filled by
the object no corner is left for saying "I." (*GG*, 77; *PG*, 40)

Part Four

Inasmuch as we are now entering upon the fourth part of a three-part essay, we should brace ourselves for some inconsequentiality. I don't feel the cause of this inconsequence is me. Rather it originates with the three women we are studying and the cause of it is the fact that they are writers. When Sappho tells us that she is "all but dead," when Marguerite Porete tells us she wants to become an "anni-hilated soul," when Simone Weil tells that "We participate in the creation of the world by decreating ourselves," how are we to square these dark ideas with the brilliant self-assertiveness of the writerly project shared by all three of them, the project of telling the world the truth about God, love, and reality? The answer is we can't. It is no accident that Marguerite Porete calls her book a *Mirror*. To be a writer is to construct a big, loud, shiny center of self from which the writing is given voice and any claim to be intent on annihilating this self while still continu-ing to write and give voice to writing must involve the writer in some important acts of subterfuge or contradiction.

Which brings us to contradiction and its uses. Simone Weil speaks plainly about these:

Contradiction alone is the proof that we are not everything. Contradiction is our badness and the sense of our badness is the sense of reality.
For we do not invent our badness. It is true. (*GG*, 148; *PG*, 100)

To accept the true badness of being human is the beginning of a dialectic of joy for Simone Weil:

If we find fullness of joy in the thought that God is, we must find the same fullness in the knowledge that we ourselves are not, for it is the same thought. (*GG*, 84; *PG*, 46)

Nothing and something are two sides of one coin, at least in the mind of a dialectician. As Marguerite Porete puts it:

Nothing is nothing. Something is what it is. Therefore I am not, if I am something, except that which God is. (chap. 70)

She also says:

Lord you are one goodness through opened out goodness, absolutely in you. And I am one badness through opened out badness, absolutely in me. (chap. 130)

Marguerite Porete's vision is dialectical but it is not tragic: she imagines a kind of chiastic immersion or mutual absorption by means of which these two absolute opposites—God and the soul—may ultimately unite. She uses various images of this union, for example iron which when placed in the furnace actually becomes fire (chap. 25); or a river which loses its name when it flows into the sea (chap. 82). Her common images carry us beyond the dialectical account of God and soul. For dialectic is a mode of reasoning and an application of the intellectual self. But the soul that has been driven by love into God, the soul consumed as into fire, dissolved as if into water—such a soul has no intact intellect of the ordinary human kind with which to construe dialectical relationships. In other words such a soul passes beyond the place where she can *tell* what she knows. To tell is a function of self.

This situation is a big problem for a writer. It is more than a contradiction, it is a paradox. Marguerite Porete broaches the matter, early in her *Mirror*, with her usual lack of compromise:

For whoever talks about God . . . must not doubt but must know without doubt . . . that he has never felt the true kernel of divine Love which makes the soul absolutely dazzled without being aware of it. For this is the true purified kernel of divine Love which is without creaturely matter and given by the Creator to a creature *and takes away absolutely the practice of telling*. (chap. 18; emphasis added)

Marguerite delivers herself of a writerly riddle here. No one who talks about God can have experienced God's love, she asserts, because such Love "takes away absolutely the practice of telling." She reinforces this point later by arguing that, once a soul has experienced divine Love, no one but God ever understands that soul again (chaps. 19 and 20). We might at this point be moved to question what Marguerite Porete thinks she is doing in the remaining chapters of her book, which number 139 in all, when she gives a step-by-step account of the soul's progress toward annihilation in God. We might wonder what all this telling is about. But we are unlikely to receive an answer from Marguerite Porete herself. Nor I think will any prudent writer on matters of God and soul venture to nail such things down. Quite the contrary, to leave us in wonder is just what such a writer feels compelled to do. Let us look more closely at how this compulsion works. We have said that telling is a function of self. If we study the way these three writers talk about their own telling, we can see how each of them feels moved to create a sort of dream of distance in which the self is displaced from the center of the work and the teller disappears into the telling.

Let's begin with Simone Weil who was a practical person and arranged for her own disappearance on several levels. Among other things, she is believed to have hastened her own death from tuberculosis in 1943 by a regime of voluntary self-starvation undertaken out of sympathy for people in France who didn't have enough to eat. However that may be, when her parents insisted on fleeing France for America in 1942 she briefly and reluctantly accompanied them, leaving behind in the hands of a certain Gustave Thibon (a farmer in whose vineyard she had been working) about a dozen notebooks of personal reflection (which now form a substantial part of her published work). She told him in a letter to use the thoughts in the notebooks however he liked:

So now they belong to you and I hope that after having been transmuted within you they will one day come out in one of your works. . . . I should be very happy for them to find a lodging beneath your pen, whilst changing their form so as to reflect your likeness. . . .

In the operation of writing, the hand which holds the pen and the body and soul attached to it are things infinitely small in the order of nothingness. (*GG*, 11)

Gustave Thibon never saw Simone Weil again, nor did he follow the instructions of this letter, to transmute her ideas into his own—at least not explicitly. Instead he went through the notebooks, extracted punchy passages, grouped these under headings like The Self, The Void, The Impossible, Beauty, Algebra, Luck, The Meaning of the Universe, and published them as a book whose English title is *Gravity and Grace by Simone Weil with Introduction by Gustave Thibon* (London

1952). That is, he made a serious effort to force her back into the center of herself, and the degree to which she nonetheless eludes this reinstallation is very hard for readers like you or me to judge from outside. But I admire the final, gentle piece of advice that she gives to him at the close of her letter of 1942:

I also like to think that after the slight shock of separation you will not
feel any sorrow about whatever may be in store for me and that if you
should happen sometimes to think of me you will do so as one thinks of
a book read in childhood . . . (GG, 12)

When I think of books read in childhood they come to my mind's eye in violent foreshortening and framed by a precarious darkness, but at the same time they glow somehow with an almost supernatural intensity of life that no adult book could ever effect. I remember a little book of The Lives of the Saints that was given to me about age five. In this book the various flowers composing the crowns of the martyrs were so lusciously rendered in words and paint that I had to be restrained from eating the pages. It is interesting to speculate what taste I was expecting from those pages. But maybe the impulse to eat pages isn't about taste. Maybe it's about being placed at the crossing-point of a contradiction, which is a painful place to be and children in their natural wisdom will not consent to stay there, but mystics love it. So Simone Weil:

Man's great affliction, which begins with infancy and accompanies him
till death, is that looking and eating are two different operations. Eternal beatitude is a state where to look is to eat. (GG, 153; PG, 105)

Simone Weil had a problem with eating all her life. Lots of women do. Nothing more powerfully or more often reminds us of our physicality than food and the need to eat it. So she creates in her mind a dream of distance where food can be enjoyed perhaps from across the room merely by looking at it, where desire need not end in perishing, where the lover can stay, at the same time, near to and far from the object of her love.

Food and love were analogous contradictions for Simone Weil. She did not freely enjoy either of them in her life and was always uneasy about her imaginative relationship to them. But after all, eternal beatitude is not the only state where to look is to eat. The written page can also reify this paradox for us. A writer may *tell* what is near and far at once.

And so, for example, in Marguerite Porete's totally original terminology the writ-er's dream of distance becomes an epithet of God. To describe the divine Lover who feeds her soul with the food of truth, Marguerite Porete invents a word: *le*

Loingprés in her Old French, or *Longe Propinquus* in the Latin translation: English might say "the FarNear." She does not justify this word, simply begins using it as if it were self-evident in chapter 58 of her book, where she is telling about annihilation. At the moment of its annihilation, she says, God practices upon the soul an amazing act of ravishing. For God opens an aperture in the soul and allows divine peace to flow in upon her like a glorious food. And God does this in his capacity as *le Loingprés*, the FarNear:

> For there is an aperture, like a spark, which quickly closes, in which one cannot long remain. . . . The overflowing from the ravishing aperture makes the Soul free and noble and unencumbered [and its] peace lasts as long as the opening of the aperture. . . . Moreover the peace is so delicious that Truth calls it glorious food. (chap. 58)

> . . . And this aperture of the sweet movement of glory that the excellent FarNear gives is nothing other than a glimpse which God wants the soul to have of her own glory that she will possess without end. (chap. 61)

Marguerite Porete's concept of God as "the excellent FarNear" is a radical invention. But even more radical is the riddle to which it forces her:

> . . . where the Soul remains after the work of the Ravishing FarNear, which we call a spark in the manner of an aperture and fast close, *no one could believe . . . nor would she have any truth who knew how to tell this.* (chap. 58; emphasis added)

Inside her own telling, Marguerite Porete sets up a little ripple of disbelief—a sort of distortion in the glass—as if to remind us that this dream of distance is after all just a dream. At the end of her book she returns to the concept one last time, saying simply:

> His Farness is the more Near. (chap. 135)

I have no idea what this sentence means but it gives me a thrill. It fills me with wonder. In itself the sentence is a small complete act of worship, like a hymn or a prayer. Now hymns and prayers are the conventional way for lovers of God to mark God's farnearness, for prayer lays claim to an immediate connection with this Being whose absence fills the world. But Marguerite Porete was a fairly unconventional lover of God and did not engage in prayer or credit its usefulness. Simone Weil, on the other hand, although she was never a Christian herself, had a profound attachment to that prayer which Christians call The Our Father. During the summer of 1941 when she worked in the vineyard of Gustave Thibon she found herself repeating this prayer while she worked. She had never prayed before, she acknowledges in her notebook, and the effect was ecstatic:

The very first words tear my thoughts from my body and transport it to
a place outside space . . . filling every aspect of this infinity of infinity.[4]

Prayer seems to have been for her an experience of spatial contradiction—or perhaps a proof of the impossible truth of God's motion. In another passage she returns to The Lord's Prayer and its impossible truth:

Our Father who art in heaven. There is a sort of humour in that. He is your Father, but just try going to look for him up there! We are quite as incapable of rising from the ground as an earthworm. And how should he for his part come to us without descending? There is no way of imagining a contract between God and man which is not as unintelligible as the Incarnation. The Incarnation explodes unintelligibility. It is an absolutely concrete way of representing impossible descent. Why should it not be the truth? (*GG*, 148; *PG*, 100)

Why should the truth not be impossible? Why should the impossible not be true? Questions like these are the links from which prayers are forged. Here is a prayer of Sappho's which will offer us one final example of the dream of distance in which a writer tells God:

. . . . [come] here to me from Krete
to this holy temple where is
your graceful grove of apple trees and altars
smoking with frankincense.

And in it cold water makes a clear sound through apple branches
and with roses the whole place
is shadowed and down from radiant-shaking leaves
sleep comes dropping.

And in it a horse meadow has come into bloom
with spring flowers and breezes
like honey are blowing. . . .

In this place you Kypris having taken up
in gold cups delicately
nectar mingled with festivities:
pour.
(frag. 2)

4. *The Simone Weil Reader*, ed. George A. Panichas (New York: Mckay, 1977), 492.

This fragment was scratched on a shard of pottery by a careless hand in the third century BC. The text is corrupt and incomplete. Nonetheless we can identify it as a hymn of the type called " kletic," a calling hymn, an invocation to God to come from where she is to where we are. Such a hymn typically names both of these places, setting its invocation in between in order to measure the difference—a difference which it is the function of the hymn to *decreate*—not to destroy, but to decreate. Among the remarks on decreation in Simone Weil's notebooks is the statement:

God can only be present in creation under the form of absence. (*GG*, 162; *PG*, 112)

For the writer of a kletic hymn God's absence is something tricky, perhaps impossible, to tell. This writer will have to invoke a God who arrives bringing her own absence with her—a God whose Farness is the more Near. It is an impossible motion possible only in writing. Sappho achieves it by various syntactic choices: for example, suppression of the verb in the first stanza of her poem. In the English translation I have tentatively supplied an imperative "Come!" in square brackets as the first word of the poem, and the sense may seem to require this, but the Greek text has no such verb. It begins with the adverb "Here." In fact the imperative verb for which the entire poem, with its slow and onomatopoeically accumulating clauses, seems to be waiting does not arrive until the very last word of our text: "Pour!" The effect of this suspension is uncanny: as if the whole of creation is depicted waiting for an action that is already perpetually *here*. There is no clear boundary between far and near; there is no climactic moment of God's arrival. Sappho renders a set of conditions which at the beginning depend on Aphrodite's absence but by the end include her presence. Sappho imitates the distance of God in a sort of suspended solution—and there we see Divine Being as a dazzling drop that suddenly, impossibly saturates the world.

To sum up. Each of the three women we've been considering had the nerve to enter a zone of absolute spiritual daring. Each of them undergoes there an experience of decreation, or so she tells us. But the telling remains a bit of a wonder. Decreation is an undoing of the creature in us—that creature enclosed in self and defined by self. But to undo self one must move through self, to the very inside of its definition. We have nowhere else to start. This is the parchment on which God writes his lessons, as Marguerite Porete says.

Marguerite's parchment burned in 1310. To us this may seem an outrage or a mistake. Certainly the men who condemned her thought she was all wrong and referred to her in the proceedings of her trial not only as "filled with errors and heresies" but as *pseudo-mulier* or "fake woman."

Was Marguerite Porete a fake woman?

Society is all too eager to pass judgments on the authenticity of women's ways of being but these judgments can get crazy. As a case in point, the book for which Marguerite Porete was burned in 1310 was secretly preserved and copied after her death by clerics who transmitted the text as an anonymous devotional work of Christian mysticism, until 1946 when an Italian scholar reconnected *The Mirror* with the name of its author. At the same time, it is hard to commend moral extremism of the kind that took Simone Weil to death at the age of thirty-four; saintliness is an eruption of the absolute into ordinary history and we resent that. We need history to be able to call saints neurotic, anorectic, pathological, sexually repressed, or fake. These judgments sanctify our own survival. By the same token, Sappho's ancient biographers tried to discredit her seriousness by assuring us she lived a life of unrestrained and incoherent sexual indulgence, for she invented lesbianism and then died by jumping off a cliff for love of a young man. As Simone Weil says:

Love is a sign of our badness. (*GG*, 111; *PG*, 68)

Love is also a good place to situate our mistrust of fake women. What I like best about the three women we've been studying is that they know what love is. That is, they know love is the touchstone of a true or a false spirituality; that is why they play with the figure of jealousy. As fake women they have to inhabit this figure gingerly, taking a position both near and far at once from the object of their desire. The truth that they tell from this paradoxical position is also fake. As Marguerite says briskly:

For everything that one can tell of God or write, no less than what one can think, of God who is more than words, is as much lying as it is telling the truth. (chap. 119)

So in the end it is important not to be fooled by fake women. If you mistake the dance of jealousy for the love of God, or a heretic's Mirror for the true story, you are likely to spend the rest of your days in terrible hunger. No matter how many pages you eat.

REGARDING CHANGE AT ISE JINGŪ

Jeffrey M. Perl

There is something—two or three things, actually—provincial about the idea
of paradigm shifts. In its heyday, the notion of incommensurable paradigms
was useful in defense of local cultures against encroachments from the outside.
Anthropologists and historians in particular took to the notion as support for
the happy thought that outlandish systems of belief could not be judged with
reference to any universal standard. The leading candidate for universal standard
(Science) was understood as itself a province—a remote island continent, with its
uniquely intimidating language, hermetic concepts, and incomparably fastidious
manners. In the sense most relevant to this symposium, the idea of paradigm
shifts is provincial in that it relates to a quintessentially modern and Western
experience of continuity as monotony. Kuhn argued that changes so basic can
ensue during a shift in paradigm that "what were ducks . . . before the revolution
are rabbits afterwards."[1] He is not talking about a change in mere nomenclature
(the shift is from *duck* to *rabbit*). Notice also the tense and mood: "*were* ducks," not
"*seem to have been* ducks." Expelled from scientific memory, ducks migrate from
the textbooks of science to those of metadisciplines—history of science, philosophy of science—on the opposite side of campus. In its way of seeing the world

Originally published in *Common Knowledge* 14.2 (Spring
2008): 208–220, as part of "Devalued Currency: Elegiac
Symposium on Paradigm Shifts, Part 2." © 2008 by Duke
University Press.

1. Thomas Kuhn, *The Structure of Scientific Revolutions*,
2nd ed. (1962; Chicago: University of Chicago Press,
1970), 111.

Common Knowledge 25:1–3
DOI 10.1215/0961754X-7299318

Figure 1. *The Lost Samurai* (1895), woodblock-print triptych by Toshikata Mizuno (1866–1908). Courtesy of Japan Print Gallery, London.

and its way of doing business, one science or another has been transformed. It is hard to imagine a theory better suited to a culture so impatient with continuity.

Other cultures, I hope and believe, regard and manage change differently. As a student of modernist drama and art, which are deeply indebted to those of Japan, I have learned something about Japanese attitudes toward and ways of dealing with major change and have found them difficult to parse in Western terms. Take the shift, apparently revolutionary, from the way things were organized under the Tokugawa shogunate to the way things got reorganized after the accession of Emperor Meiji in 1867. My subject here is art rather than politics, so let Exhibit A be a triptych of the Meiji era (fig. 1). "The Lost Samurai," a set of three woodblock prints designed by Toshikata Mizuno and published in 1895, is said in an online gallery description to picture a warrior who, "hoping to obtain directions, spots a person in a small hut deep in the mountains." But the lost samurai does not look especially hopeful; nor does he appear the kind of samurai who, even if lost, would ask for directions at a pastoral hut. With his hands in mail mittens—one gripping a sword; the other, a stick fully his height—the samurai glowers with what looks to be impotent menace. Certainly, the contrast that Toshikata has drawn between samurai and hermit could not be more stark. The former is wearing regalia and colorful armor (in blue, brown, red, orange, and yellow layers, plus a headdress in black, fixed to his brow with a fussy white bow)—all detailed in the style of kabuki prints, including gesture and facial expression. The hut with its thatched little roof, the little bridge over the little stream, and the iconographically correct misty landscape are done cursorily in black ink and wash, as required by classic *sumi-e* style. The latter originated in seventh-century China (Tang dynasty) and migrated, under Zen auspices, to Japan in the mid-fourteenth century. *Sumi-e* is thus referred to by some as "Zen style," but its context is not necessarily Buddhist.

Two characteristically Japanese styles of pictorial art—one understated, one hyperbolic—are posed here as in conflict, and the conflict is represented as if self-evidently clear. The warrior is portrayed as if indignant at the countryfolk. Had their backward, colorless, tradition-bound modesty given comfort to the emperor in his determination to lose the shogunate and samurai? Somehow I doubt it. But a lively, passionate, and chivalric era had come to an end—or so it was said—in the name of a prior and more naturally Japanese order. Hence the term for this apparent shift in paradigm: the Meiji Restoration. But it is unclear, to me anyway, what it was that needed restoring. The proper order of Japan, it was an axiom of Shinto belief, had been continuous from the seventh century BCE, when Kamuyamato Iwarebiko, a descendant of Amaterasu, sun goddess of Nippon (Land of the Rising Sun), became its first emperor under the name of Jimmu. Emperor Meiji (born Mutsuhito) was one-hundred-twenty-second in descent from Jimmu. The first fourteen emperors in the official lineage are thought by historians to be legendary, and so the relevant clause in the emperor's title ("seated on the throne occupied by the same dynasty changeless through ages eternal") is regarded as slightly fanciful. But it is accepted that Ojin, who ascended the throne in 270 CE, is a historical personage and that the line of descent from him to Emperor Meiji is as straight as a line ever gets.

On the other hand, the shogunate too was ancient, by no means a late imposition on imperial governance. The title *sei-i taishōgun* (roughly "supreme commander, conqueror of barbarians") was held by military commanders-in-chief from the eighth to twelfth centuries; and the institution, the shogunate per se, was established in 1192. The Tokugawa (or Edo) shogunate was, at its founding around 1600, only the latest in a series, each led by another clan of the military aristocracy; though the shogunate at Edo was the most tenacious, lasting more than one-third of a millennium. Further, the historically verifiable samurai date back perhaps as far as historically verifiable emperors do. Both shogun and samurai had been, throughout their known history, subordinate, at least nominally, to the emperor; emperors of the one dynasty had reigned virtually without interruption (there were regencies) but rarely governed, their powers assumed by ministers of state; and, in any case, there had never been—not really—an emperor of Japan. The seventh-century titles translated, since Meiji's time, as *emperor* are *tennô* (heavenly sovereign) and *tenshi* (son of heaven). Japan was not an empire but a collection of contiguous islands, and its sovereign was a demigod and chief priest (or perhaps shaman) of the national religion Shinto, but not the holder of a political office. It does seem that the Meiji emperor held more direct authority of political and military kinds than most of his predecessors. Still, his government and military were run by bureaucrats (though of a class different and lower than those who had exercised power before). Moreover, the samurai themselves had long since been transformed, under the Tokugawa, from soldiers into bureaucrats; and not a few of the Buddhists among them put down their swords and became monks.

Then why is the Meiji Restoration so called? Perry's "opening" of Japan to the West occurred when the prince who would be Meiji was about a year old, and Japanese elites absorbed the basics of Western history. France had had its Bourbon Restoration under Louis XVIII and Charles X, the British under Charles II had had their Stuart Restoration—and at the same time as Japanese nationalists decided that Nippon had always been an empire and its *tennô* an emperor, they determined that Japan, like these Western powers, had undergone the restoration of an interrupted order. But what happened constitutionally in Japan after 1867 seems, from a perspective not so far above sea level, rather limited. The court of the *tennô* relocated from Kyoto to the seat of de facto power at Edo. Samurai armies were disbanded and their social class in principle abolished, but the samurai of the time had not much in common with the warriors celebrated or lampooned in Meiji era prints like Toshikata's. And while the ruling shogun was dismissed and the institution of the shogunate abolished, even the emperor who had signed the decrees reigned more than he ruled over Japan. The same three institutions—reigning sovereign, ruling vizier, and military aristocracy—that had been in place, in one arrangement or another, "changeless through ages eternal," remained, at least structurally, in place. Did anyone in Japan believe otherwise?

Or better: what did Toshikata believe? It should be possible to approach an answer in stylistic terms. The kabuki milieu of the warrior in "The Lost Samurai" was thriving when Meiji took the throne but was fading out by 1895 when Toshikata made parodic use of it. Paradoxically, kabuki style in visual art is associated both with the Meiji Restoration and with the samurai of history and legend, though it is hard to imagine either the Meiji or samurai elites in attendance at performances.[2] Kabuki, unlike Noh drama, was a popular genre, as were kabuki woodblock prints; and conceivably, the contorted features of Toshikata's samurai reflect resentment that the ancient, noble class into which he was born had been co-opted for such pedestrian use. We may imagine that his grimace is, moreover, defiant. No matter what the historical time in which the triptych may be set, it was printed one generation after Meiji had decreed that samurai (a) could no longer wear swords in public or (b) execute commoners who evinced disrespect. The warrior whom Toshikata pictures in full armor (including the customary two blades and a glare threatening violence against a commoner's shack) is a figure of the indeterminate past, or else he is in violation of imperial edicts. Not impossibly, since he is lost (like a sailor marooned without news of Japan's surrender to MacArthur), this samurai is in violation unawares. Either way, it is reasonable to suppose that his glare is directed, in some part, at the *sumi-e* style

2. However, a kabuki performance was given for the emperor himself on April 21, 1887.

of the landscape in which he appears so out of place. *Sumi-e* is immemorial, time-less—as immemorial and timeless, let us say, as the natural ancient order of Japan that Meiji partisans suppressed the samurai and shogunate in order to "restore." At another level, presumably—I mean the level at which it is the samurai of legend, merely, who appear as characters in kabuki plays—the actual samurai, those who served as bureaucrats under the Tokugawa, would have had contempt for most genres of woodblock print and have preferred to acquire for their homes traditional scrolls brushed in modest *sumi-e* style.[3]

The samurai in Toshikata's triptych may be clueless, but the artist was evidently mindful of what was happening beyond his woodblock; and mindful, too, of the mindfulness of his audience. At best, I am an amateur of this art form, but it seems clear that Toshikata's piece is remarking on the shift—the supposed shift—in paradigm that had left the samurai wandering without place or role in Meiji Japan. Did that shift, the image prompts us to ask, restore an order even more ancient than that of the samurai? Was the shift, in other words, as it had been made out to be by the shifters? Given the increasingly noticeable presence of foreigners, and also the Westernization of the Japanese military and even monarchy, had there not been, rather than a restoration, a leap forward into the future? Or a fall sideways into the present day of an alien culture? Did not the Meiji Restoration have more to do with Commodore Perry than with Amaterasu Omikami? If such was Toshikata's conclusion, then the basic black-and-white landscape of his triptych, signaling continuity with immemorial tradition, would have to have been a kind of joke. More likely, I think, the artist saw that two ways of understanding the recent developments in Japan were being offered simultaneously and that there was little to choose between them. Both paradigms may have seemed to him fishy, shallow, or wrong. In which case, "The Lost Samurai" should be read as ironic.[4]

3. Unfortunately, I have not found, in any language that I can read, a persuasive account of the sociology of nineteenth-century Japanese prints and drama. It is clear, though, that the condescension among the upper classes and cognoscenti in Japan to woodblock prints is, even today, palpable. As for the artistic preferences of the late Edo and Meiji eras, there was one genre of woodblock print that at least some aristocrats admired: *surimono*. These are small-edition, small-sized, deluxe prints to order, often bearing extensive calligraphy (mostly of poems); and these embody a low-key but powerful aesthetic all their own. European Impressionists and van Gogh were collectors of Hiroshige and Hokusai; Picasso's interest was mainly in the erotic genre called *shunga*. Frank Lloyd Wright, however, was an important collector and promoter of *surimono*: see Joan B. Mirviss and John T. Carpenter, *The Frank Lloyd Wright Collection of Surimono* (Trumble, CT: Weatherhill, 1995).

4. I am hesitant to find irony in this picture, or any other picture, of this tradition. My hesitation comes from an experience of interpretive failure with a Kuniyoshi print confronting the viewer with three unreadable faces. One is the face of an *oiran* (a highest-class courtesan), the most haughty and sophisticated that I have seen portrayed in art. Cowering behind her is a sumptuously dressed child, presumably illegitimate, looking with what seems to be fear at a point off the right side of the image. The courtesan is looking at that point as well, though what feelings or thoughts her look indicates are (to me) obscure. In any case, the *oiran*'s look is not welcoming. She is more sumptuously dressed even than the child, but at just the spot on her kimono where she would be seated (she is standing, in the image) is a third face, embroidered or painted on the fabric—the face, unmistakably, of Daruma, the founder of Zen Buddhism. When she sits, it will be on the Zen master's face. Daruma too is looking at the point, off the print's right side, that has riveted the attentions of

I do not mean that the moral of Toshikata's piece is *plus ça change, plus c'est la même chose*—nothing so jaded (or French). Look again at the lost samurai's face. He has a strong feeling to express, apparently, and is doing so. Still, an expression not dissimilar can be found on the face or makeup "mask" of nearly any major figure at the climax of almost any kabuki play. That histrionic look is an iconographic sign. I have seen famously serene monks, in kabuki prints, wearing expressions like the lost samurai's face. Is the emotion a skit? These are theatrical prints, stylistically, but their subject matter would seem to carry historical and political significance. Was the Meiji Restoration, for Toshikata and his audience, a skit or in-joke? Did history (revolutions, restorations, changes of capital cities) seem to them histrionic—a performance? And what of change itself—another skit?

I will hazard this much in answer to my rhetorical questions: it is not inconsistent with the evidence of nineteenth-century political history in Japan, or the evidence of Japanese woodblock prints of the same period, that reconstitutions and restorations and overthrows are validly understood in theatrical terms. It would not be the first time that a modern Asian polity was so interpreted.[5] More consistent, however, might be to construe the performance of Japanese politics in terms of another ritual—a ritual of the state religion whose function may be to obviate fundamental change. The *tennô*'s court at Kyoto transferred to Edo, displacing the shogun from his own capital and abolishing the shogunate—a momentous historical event surely, a shift in political paradigm—but how different was it from the once-per-generation destruction and reconstruction of the shrines of Ise Jingū? As home of the imperial *kami* Amaterasu, Ise is the chief sanctuary of Shinto and Japan. In the ritual of *shikinen sengu*, the sixty-some shrine buildings of Ise (as well as the Uji Bridge leading to them over the Isuzu River) are demolished, then rebuilt, exactly, to the last detail, on the *kodenchi*, the

---

the *oiran* and child, but his features seem to me paralyzed with shock—as in: Where am I? What am I doing *here*? The only readings of this image that make sense to me are ironical. I can interpret the piece as saying, "Here is what we have come to as a society, where the *oiran* of some aristocrat wears the greatest of Zen masters on the seat of her gown." Or else, I could interpret it to say, "Here is where Buddhist disdain for *ukiyo-e* belongs—between a prostitute and a floor cushion." *Ukiyo-e* means "art of the floating world," the floating world being what a Buddhist knows as *samsara*—the burdensomely trivial realm of pleasures, events, relationships, and mere things—from which, with strenuous effort of spirit, one can be freed. Thus, either reading might be valid; but I suspect that both are wrong and that it is my Western attunement to irony that prevents my understanding properly. There is a print by Toshikata (made several decades later) on a related theme: in "Beauty and Daruma Reverse Roles," which was the frontispiece for a novel, the Zen master wears the kind

of ladies' kimono worn by the *oiran* in Kuniyoshi's print. He is sitting opposite a "beauty" (the *bijn* is a basic thematic category of prints) who is dressed in a plain Buddhist robe and holding a *hossu*—the Zen fly-swatter that is an iconographic attribute of Daruma himself. I know of at least one *ukiyo-e* print depicting a "Courtesan as Daruma Crossing the Sea on a Reed" (by Suzuki Harunobu, 1766–67). I have also seen a scroll painting (artist unknown) from about 1930, in which Daruma towers over a doll-like *bijn* whose kimono is decorated with what appear to be images of hell (a demon, a skeleton, etc.). In any of these cases, what the viewer is to make of the relationship between Zen master and *bijn* is unobvious, though I sense that "ironic" would not do the relationship justice.

5. See, for instance, Clifford Geertz, *Negara: The Theatre State in Nineteenth-Century Bali* (Princeton, NJ: Princeton University Press, 1980), and Jonathan D. Spence, *Return to Dragon Mountain* (New York: Viking, 2007).

Figure 2. *Kodenchi*, empty site for the reconstruction of Ise shrines immediately adjacent. © Jingū-shicho

vacated site of the last disassembled shrine (fig. 2). As Arata Isozaki, known for masterpieces of architecture in the West as well as in Japan, explains the procedure:

Each building in the shrine complex has an identical double, one of which is in use while the other is disassembled, then rebuilt. The period of rebuilding is officially set at 20 years. This ritualistic and performative rebuilding has persisted, it is said, since 685 C.E. (i.e., the fourteenth year of the reign of Emperor Tenmu). It is believed that the period of 20 years is predicated on the life span of buildings whose pillars are sunk directly into the ground, without foundation; or it may be the time needed for passing down the necessary carpentry techniques; or there may be another, more mysterious reason. Completion of the next rebuilding is scheduled for the year 2013.[6]

There have been sixty-one such unbuildings and rebuildings, historically verifiable, over the past 1,300 years, and the official line of Shinto is that this ritual

6. Arata Isozaki, *Japan-ness in Architecture*, trans. Sabu Kohso, ed. David B. Stewart (Cambridge, MA: MIT Press, 2006), 323 n. 1. Pages 117–69 of this book comprise a brilliant commentary on the architecture of Ise Jingū.

Figure 3. First fence, with main gate, surrounding the *shōden*, inner precinct of the enshrined *kami* Amaterasu at Ise. © Jingū-shicho

has been going on for about two millennia, ever since the *kami* left the emperor's palace at Yamato and found a home that she preferred in Ise. Since that time, her residence has been the small *shōden* in Ise's most sacred inner precinct, which is enclosed by four rows of fences, beyond even the first of which only descendants of Amaterasu are admitted, bearing gifts (fig. 3).

Imagine a ritual of this kind conducted every twenty years in the Vatican—tearing down and rebuilding St. Peter's Basilica—or conducted at the Al Aqsa Mosque and Dome of the Rock in Jerusalem. Imagine Jews celebrating, as a scheduled ritual occurrence (rather than mourning, in daily prayer, at three annual fasts, and even at the climax of wedding ceremonies), the destruction of the Jerusalem Temples. To picture any of these possibilities, you need first to imagine that monotheists in the West had come to reject their architectural, as well as ontological, foundationalism; had got beyond their addiction to real estate (NB *real*); had abandoned their ideals of solidity, permanence, or grandeur; and had embraced notions of artistic beauty demanding radical simplification (and efficient deconstruction). The Ise shrines are architecturally granaries of linear shape, built, without nails, of cypress, and with thatched gabled roofs comprised of miscanthus reeds; the only other materials used are gold and copper for the

7. The rebuilding process takes eight years of the twenty-year cycle, requires 14,000 pieces of timber, 25,000 sheaves of miscanthus reeds, and 122,000 specialist carpenters. Over sixty structures are rebuilt, and moreover

Figure 4. Detail of roof construction and balustrade, main sanctuary, Ise.
© Jingū-shicho

hardware (fig. 4).[7] These characteristics have had incalculable effect on the way the Japanese have built their buildings for many centuries—though it is forbidden to reproduce the Ise style of architecture elsewhere and, besides, only the imperial elite and their carpenters know how the insides of the buildings look.

Even more influential on Japanese culture, we may surmise, has been the effect of each generation's understanding that their most ancient and revered structures are always in process of intentional destruction and reconstruction. The buildings are thirteen (perhaps twenty) centuries old but never develop, are not permitted to develop, the patina of age. They are primeval but not old. As one of the early Western commentators on Ise Jingū put it:

> The Parthenon ... is aesthetically the greatest and most sublime building in stone, as are the Ise shrines in wood. But still there is a great difference. Even if the Parthenon had not been blown to ruins it would today still be only a monument of ancient times, as life is missing from it. How very different are the shrines at Ise! Not only are the religious rites and the everlasting stream of worshippers a living presence, the shrines have yet another vital quality, which is entirely original in its

all vestments and sacred treasures (supplied by the imperial family) are replaced (in all: 1,576 articles in 125 categories). Preparing each of these articles requires specialist skills and knowledge dating back numerous centuries. See the entry "Shikinensengū" in *The Encyclopedia of Shinto*, available online at eos.kokugakuin.ac.jp/modules/xwords (accessed November 26, 2007).

Figure 5. Aerial view of the "divine forest" surrounding Ise Jingū, Mie prefecture.
© Jingū-shicho

effect, intention, and perception. This is the fact that the shrines are
always new.[8]

The purity of the shrines is thought to depend on a renewal consisting of replacement and shifting. I use that gerund not only to recall us to our subject, shifts in
paradigm, but also because there is no other word for what happens at Ise Jingū.
Each structure in the complex has immediately at its side an empty space that is
constantly in preparation for shifting the *kami*'s treasures from one set of structures to fresh duplicates. Until the eighth century, "whenever a new emperor
ascended the throne, the capital had been moved" as well—and I suppose the
shifting of Emperor Meiji's court from Kyoto to Edo was, in this sense at least,
the restoration of a lapsed tradition.[9] At the *shōden* in Ise, it is the tutelary *kami*
of the emperor and nation who shifts, though only back and forth between contiguous sites. If the *kami* is regarded as herself a paradigm, then yes, there is a
paradigm shift at Ise. It takes place in the darkness of night, unwatched, deep
inside the "divine forest," on schedule, every twenty years (fig. 5). This paradigm
shifts but never ages, and *it does not change*. At Ise Jingū, as in Western science, the
only paradigm shift—the only truly revolutionary change—would be no longer
to shift at all.

8. Bruno Taut, *Houses and People of Japan* (Tokyo: San-   9. Isozaki, *Japan-ness in Architecture*, 131.
deidō, 1937), 139.

Postscript

It was learning about the *shikinen sengu* ritual that enabled me to understand, insofar as I do, the curious experience of the Western amateur in the market for *ukiyo-e* prints. Advice to new collectors is not hard to come by, much of it alarming and all of it confusing. One useful piece of advice is: look twice at the name, the full name, of any print's designer. Japanese dealers may offer a Hiroshige print without specifying that the Hiroshige in question is not Hiroshige I, also called Hiroshige Utagawa, also called Hiroshige Ando, also called Hiroshige Ichiyusai. His closest disciple (and eventual son-in-law) received the name Hiroshige II from Hiroshige I (and there are also a Hiroshige III and IV). Kunisada (a contemporary and collaborator of Hiroshige I and II) often signed Toyokuni III as his name (Toyokuni I being Kunisada's teacher)—but there are also successive Kunisadas with art-dynasty numbers following the name. Myself, I have not found that Japanese dealers or galleries conceal anything that they consider important from potential buyers. Hiroshige II often worked on woodblock designs with Hiroshige I and developed (as was expected of disciples) a derivative style. If that style is what the collector seeks to collect, well—Hiroshige is the style's name.

A second piece of advice, more alarming, is not to buy *ukiyo-e* prints at all except from a handful of galleries worldwide—galleries where each item sold is museum quality and its provenance clearly established. It is museum people who mostly give this advice (and then hint that a gift to the collections they oversee would, in the fullness of time, be welcome). What you are warned against in particular is that irresponsible dealers will sell you a posthumous "restrike" print, made with original but worn-down and repaired woodblocks. Or worse, they may sell you an image printed, using expertly recarved blocks, on authentically handmade (but cunningly aged) *washi* paper. It is true that I have noticed suspect items of the kind on auction occasionally but always offered at opening bids very far below what a posh gallery would ask for a first-edition print. The larcenous dealer is by no means getting rich quick. Japanese and Western dealers, posh or otherwise, are all happy, in my experience, to discuss the ontological status of their prints for sale. It is just that Japanese ontology (as Roland Barthes explained in *L'Empire des signes*) differs radically from the one involved with the Western art market. Ontologically speaking, an *ukiyo-e* print is called an original when it comes from the first edition approved by the artist. But what do "original" and "the artist" mean in a context (a) where a minimum of three artists (designer, woodblock carver, and printer) are involved from the beginning; (b) where the designer's signature and seal (if any) are carved in a woodblock, not added by hand; (c) where the designer hands the carver a colorfree cartoon (later destroyed, presumably without regret) as a guide for making the print; and (d) where it is never certain who chose and then mixed the colors? Moreover, *ukiyo-e* prints were unnumbered and were published, often, in editions of a thousand or more. How different, then, is a good print of a restrike edition—if the woodblocks are expertly repaired—from a print of the first-edition strike or, for that matter, from an outstandingly well-done print of a posthumous edition? There is no original (no "artist's proof" or color cartoon) with which to compare any of them.

The original and the unique are not especially valued in this ontology—Plato was not Japanese—and the recarving of important woodblock designs can be national events in Japan. The prints that result are not thought of as facsimiles, in the Western derogatory sense; they are originals of a fresh edition of an old, well-loved design. Virtually every skilled woodblock carver and printer in Tokyo during the years from 1998 to 2004 took part in preparing a complete, new edition of the *One Hundred Famous Views of Edo* series, designed in the 1850s by Hiroshige (that's Hiroshige I—though among the designs is one entirely the work of Hiroshige II). The paper in this new edition differs from that of the first edition in that *washi* is now somewhat differently made (though still made by hand and still, I am told, by artisans of the same family), and the pigments differ in that they are more durable now and less susceptible to fading. It is assumed that this latest edition will be the last recarved printing, ever, of this series, because the skills demanded are likely to die out with the present generation.[10] Each print in this "200th anniversary edition" costs around two hundred dollars and looks about as close as anything could, not to an 1850s original as it looks today, but to an early printing from the first edition *in the year of its initial release*.[11] For the thousands of additional dollars that you would pay for an 1850s (rather than twenty-first century) print from this series, you would be acquiring a prestige wholly un-Japanese, plus what is called patina—consisting, in the case at hand,

10. On the other hand, a Canadian, David Bull, got himself trained as a traditional woodblock carver in Tokyo and has busied himself there, for decades, producing not only expertly recarved editions of *ukiyo-e* prints but elaborating on all the old values of Japanese artists. These he defends, online and in the media, with polemical force and charm. He will, for instance, not sell you an individual print—you must "subscribe" to a full year's worth of ten, though he charges barely $60 each for them. He refuses to number prints or to limit editions—printing can continue as long as the woodblocks for a given print last and there is demand for more. He objects to any "attempt to maintain an artificially high price for a commodity by restricting the supply available. When people in other fields try tricks like this, they are castigated by society, and perhaps even find themselves in trouble with the law. How on earth is it that the world of prints has allowed itself to be caught up in this ridiculous practice? A practice that ultimately, over a century of incremental subversion, completely destroyed the world of printmaking. . . . What kind of value would a printmaker want his prints

to have? Should he really care what financial value they have? Should he want people to collect his prints as investments? If so, then he should sell stock certificates, not prints. I make prints because I like using my skills to make beautiful objects out of beautiful materials—cherry wood, fluffy paper, and soft pigments. Both the process and the result give me great pleasure." Bull moreover asks buyers not to frame his prints, since traditionally Japanese lovers of *ukiyo-e* do not do so. Woodblock prints, he maintains, are for holding in the hand—just so—in a natural light that permits viewing them as three-dimensional works (which indeed they are). For Bull's views on Japanese woodblock prints and printmaking, see especially woodblock.com/surimono/atgallery01.html (and /atgallery02.html) (accessed November 26, 2007), as well as www.asahi-net.or.jp/~xs3d-bull/feedback/brickbats .html (accessed November 26, 2007).

11. The standard price for a complete set of the "anniversary edition" is around $24,000—a price that one could well pay for a single, faultless print from the first edition.

of repaired wormholes and other insect damage, repaired tears, cleaned-off stains and surface dirt, undoable smears and centerfolds, trimmed margins, wrinkles, toning, foxing, and fading. My impression is that Japanese lovers of *ukiyo-e* prefer to acquire prints from painstakingly made editions of their own time and not simply in order to save money. They prefer to have their Hiroshige, Hokusai, or Utamaro clean, fresh, pure, and lacking in patina, but with the design and colors replicated to the exacting standards of the woodblock artists' guilds. If this idea makes a Western conservator or curator's skin crawl, it should be recalled that the Japanese also prefer to tear down their version of St. Peter's Basilica and rebuild it, clean, every twenty years.

It was, I have come to think, while studying the noble arts of Japan (or while studying Ernest Fenollosa's studies of them) that Ezra Pound came up with his motto for modernism: "make it new." But even Pound did not have what it would take to import the mentality of Ise into Western fine arts. His *Cantos* may be a riff on Homer and Dante, but not a facsimile of either's work. Whereas we in the West go in fear of replication, pay dearly for originals (however defined), number our print editions to make sure almost nobody but ourselves enjoys the same designs—the Japanese, by tradition, regard originality and uniqueness as untoward ideas, and think of patina as dirt.[12] "New" can mean "the same, but clean." In this context, I have lost track of what *paradigm shift* means or could mean, because I am uncertain of the meanings of four basic terms we require to define it. What are paradigm shifts in theory, and do they occur in practice? To answer that question, we need more thoughtfully to define *old* and *new*, *continuity* and *change*.

12. On the "fabricated origin" of Ise Jingū—which is the origin of "Japan-ness" itself—see Isozaki, *Japan-ness in Architecture*, 159–69.

PUNITIVE SCHOLARSHIP

Postwar Interpretations of Shinto and Ise Jingū

Michiko Urita

On September 2, 1945, Foreign Minister Mamoru Shigemitsu signed the Japanese Instrument of Surrender aboard the USS *Missouri*, Emperor Hirohito having already announced the acceptance of surrender terms in a radio address (known as the *Gyokuon-Hōsō*, or Jewel Voice Broadcast) on August 15. The Allied occupation force on December 15 issued SCAPIN 448, the so-called Shinto Directive, whose full title is "Abolition of Governmental Sponsorship, Support, Perpetuation, Control, and Dissemination of State Shinto." The directive, drafted by naval lieutenant William K. Bunce, the American military's expert on Japanese culture and religion, made clear in article 1 that its purpose was to end "the perversion of Shinto theory and beliefs into militaristic and ultranationalistic propaganda, designed to delude the Japanese people and lead them into wars of aggression." While "state Shinto" was categorically abolished, what the directive terms "shrine Shinto" was to be "recognized as a religion if its adherents so desire," although only after it had "been divorced from the state and divested of its militaristic and ultranationalistic elements." Beginning in the 1970s, the consensus view of scholars, especially outside but also to an extent inside Japan, has amounted to a more sweeping abolition of Shinto than the one effected in

Originally published in *Common Knowledge* 21.3 (September 2015): 484–509, as part of the symposium "Peace by Other Means, Part 4." © 2015 by Duke University Press.

Common Knowledge 25:1–3

DOI 10.1215/0961754X-7299330

accordance with the 1945 Allied directive. It has not been enough that Shinto was disestablished as the state religion of Japan. The scholarly consensus has insisted, in addition, that Shinto be understood as an invention of the Meiji Restoration (1867–68), devised in support of centralization, modernization, militarization, expansionism, and emperor worship. Thus defined, Shinto can be of no great age and not even authentically a religion. In other words, for these scholars, Japan has had no indigenous religious tradition, and the one that its people claim as their own was simply a device of the central government, then in alliance with Nazi Germany, to ensure solidarity with its military ambitions in Asia and the Pacific region.

This reinterpretation of Japanese religious history commenced in Japan with Marxist critics of state Shinto, in particular, Toshio Kuroda and Shigeyoshi Murakami.[1] The consensus widened and intensified in the 1980s in the wake of the Marxist historian Eric Hobsbawm's argument that " 'traditions' which appear or claim to be old are often quite recent in origin and sometimes invented"; moreover, he contended, the phenomenon of nationalism, which he regarded as essentially modern, "cannot be adequately investigated without careful attention to the 'invention of tradition.' "[2] Most recently, the British scholar John Breen and the Dutch scholar Mark Teeuwen attempt, in *A New History of Shinto* (2010), to show that Shinto did not develop historically as a religion distinct from Buddhism.[3] For Breen, Teeuwen, and other scholars in the West (notably, the American Helen Hardacre), Shinto has had a sporadic presence throughout Japan's history but cannot be said to constitute a discrete and continuous tradition.[4] Like the other Axis powers, Germany and Italy, Japan is said to have come to national consciousness only in the nineteenth century, at which point it required a myth of organic unity reinforced by a mythical state religion.

The problem with this type of analysis is so evident that its adoption is understood best as a war reparation that these scholars feel the Allied occupation force neglected to impose on Japan in 1945. In 701 CE, the Code of the Taihō was promulgated, and, as a part of its restructuring of the Japanese central government, in a section of the code called the Jingiryō, it made provision for both

1. For Toshio Kuroda, see Kuroda, "Shinto in the History of Japanese Religion," trans. James C. Dobbins and Suzanne Gay, *Journal of Japanese Studies* 7, no. 1 (1981): 1–21, and "The Legacy of Kuroda Toshio," special issue of *Journal of Japanese Religious Studies* 23, nos. 3–4 (Fall 1996). For Shigeyoshi Murakami, see: Murakami, *Kokka shintō* (Tokyo: Iwanami Shoten, 1970), and *Japanese Religion in the Modern Century*, trans. H. Byron Earhart (Tokyo: University of Tokyo Press, 1980). On Murakami, see also Shimazono Susumu, "State Shinto and Emperor Veneration," in *The Emperors of Modern Japan*, ed. Ben-Ami Shillony (Leiden: Brill, 2008), 53–78.

2. Eric Hobsbawm, "Introduction: Inventing Traditions," in *The Invention of Tradition*, ed. Hobsbawm and Terence Ranger (Cambridge: Cambridge University Press, 1983), 1, 14.

3. John Breen and Mark Teeuwen, *A New History of Shinto* (Chichester, UK: Wiley-Blackwell, 2010), 20.

4. See Helen Hardacre, *Shinto and the State, 1868–1968* (Princeton, NJ: Princeton University Press, 1989).

Buddhism and the worship of the traditional nature gods of Japan—the *kami*. It is this latter form of worship that is known as Shinto. The code established the Jingikan (the central government's bureau of *kami*) to ensure that the gods were properly worshipped. In other words, the connection between the state and Shinto worship is as old as the earliest written records in Japan. More than three thousand Shinto shrines were recorded in 737. Records kept at the most revered of these, the Grand Shrine at Ise (Ise Jingū), began to be collected by the central administration as early as 804. The two basic reference works for the rituals conducted at Ise, the *Kōtai Jingū gishikichō* and the *Toyukegū gishikichō*, were moved from the Ise shrine to the Jingikan in that year. The documentary evidence is that the shrine has been in operation since not later than 690. Some historians date it back to 685, and the mythology dates the key rituals practiced at Ise Jingū back some two millennia.

The most curious part of the effort to deny Shinto its temporal continuity is that the rituals of its central shrine are *about* continuity—or rather, as Jeffrey Perl has argued in these pages, the rituals at Ise are meant to show that change and even time are illusory.[5] Perl regards this feature of Shinto, moreover, as the most characteristically Japanese thing about the religion. Breen, Teeuwen, and Hardacre, among others, would have the Meiji Restoration set in motion a political revolution that would create Shinto as the state religion. But far from finding reasons to interpret Japanese religion in political terms, Perl redescribes the Meiji Restoration as a "performance," one in emulation of the most dramatic religious ritual performed at Ise. Perl's essay asks the crucial question and supplies a provocative but, to me, compelling answer. Emperor Meiji's court at Kyoto, Perl writes, was

transferred to Edo, displacing the shogun from his own capital and abolishing the shogunate—a momentous historical event surely, a shift in political paradigm—but how different was it from the once-per-generation destruction and reconstruction of the shrines of Ise Jingū? As home of the imperial *kami* Amaterasu, Ise is the chief sanctuary of Shinto and Japan. In the ritual of *shikinen sengu*, the sixty-some shrine buildings of Ise (as well as the Uji Bridge leading to them over the Isuzu River), are demolished, then rebuilt, exactly, to the last detail, on the *kodenchi*, the vacated site of the last disassembled shrine. . . . The purity of the shrines is thought to depend on a renewal consisting of replacement and shifting. I use that gerund not only to recall us to our subject, shifts in paradigm, but also because there is no other word for what happens at Ise Jingū. Each structure in the complex has immediately

5. Jeffrey M. Perl, "Regarding Change at Ise Jingū" (introduction to part 2 of "Devalued Currency: Symposium on Paradigm Shifts"), *Common Knowledge* 14, no. 2 (Spring 2008): 208–20.

at its side an empty space that is constantly in preparation for shifting the *kami*'s treasures from one set of structures to fresh duplicates. Until the eighth century, "whenever a new emperor ascended the throne, the capital had been moved" as well—and I suppose the shifting of Emperor Meiji's court from Kyoto to Edo was, in this sense at least, the restoration of a lapsed tradition. At the *shōden* in Ise, it is the tutelary *kami* of the emperor and nation who shifts, though only back and forth between contiguous sites. If the *kami* is regarded as herself a paradigm, then yes, there is a paradigm shift at Ise. It takes place in the darkness of night, unwatched, deep inside the "divine forest," on schedule, every twenty years. This paradigm *shifts* but never ages, and *it does not change*.[6]

My own archival and ethnographic fieldwork at Jingū confirms Perl's conclusion. I made twelve short visits, a few weeks in duration each, to Ise between 2008 and March 2012 and then conducted intensive research there, much of it involving interviews with the Jingū priests, from September 2012 to January 2013 and then, again, from June 2013 to June 2014. I was at Ise Jingū during the most recent performance of *shikinen sengū* in October 2013. I can add to Perl's interpretation of this rite that the priests understand it in terms of the Shinto concept of *tokowaka*, which means "forever young." By renewing all of the shrine buildings and treasures—including *tori'i* gates and fences, combs, six-string zither, swords, arrows, handlooms, as well as Naikū (the Inner Shrine), Gekū (the Outer Shrine), and fourteen auxiliary shrines—the vitality and strength of the sun goddess are renewed as well. Even the materials out of which the old shrine buildings were constructed are renewed and reused: they are donated to other shrines—to one-hundred-sixty-nine local shrines in 1993—and recycled for use in repair work throughout Japan. Thus, the materials live on at other shrines, in a process that not only symbolizes but actually effects continuity with the deep history of shrine Shinto.

Postwar interpreters of Shinto, whether Japanese or Western, are right in saying that Buddhism and Taoism are tied in Japan to worship of the national *kami*, but the understanding of the rites is not the same from one religious context to another. For example, a scholar of Japanese religion, Tetsuo Yamaori, suggests, from his Buddhist perspective, that the act of transferring the deity and reconstructing her shrine at Ise is analogous to death and rebirth,[7] but the Jingū priests strongly object to this view on the grounds that gods never die.[8] As one former senior priest told me, "Applying the idea of rebirth to *shikinen sengū*

6. Perl, "Regarding Change at Ise Jingū," 213–14, 217.

7. Tetsuo Yamaori, "Nihon kara ōmono ga kieta: Ise Jingū no kokoro to Aku Yū san" (A Great Man Is Lost to Japan: The Heart of Ise Jingū and Mr. Yū Aku), *Shokun* 39, no. 10 (2007): 24–33.

8. Shin'nyo, Kawai, *Tokowaka no shisō: nihon jin to Ise Jingū* (The Concept of "Forever Young": The Japanese and Ise Jingū) (Tokyo: Shōdensha, 2013).

is wrong. We humans get one year older every year. If you are twenty years old, then next year you will be twenty-one years old. It is not death." In other words, however young the shrines at Ise forever look, they have been the same—their identity and design have not changed—for more than thirteen hundred years. As for Taoism, Hiroko Yoshino, for example, has argued that the two adjacent sites for each of the Jingū shrines comprise a symbol for the unity of *ying-yang*.[9] She interprets *shikinen sengū*, then, in Chinese philosophical terms. While Buddhists and Taoists are welcome as pilgrims at the shrines and may cherish their own conceptions of the *kami* and how they are worshipped, these two religions are discrete and distinguishable from one another and from Shinto. Not death and rebirth but transfer and renewal—which is to say, continuity—are the watchwords of the Jingū priesthood. Masayuki Nakanishi, a scholar and former Jingū priest, understands *shikinen sengū* in the Shinto way as a device for storing memory so that, despite the inevitability of change elsewhere in Japanese society, an unchanging relationship with the gods can be passed on to the next generation. *Shikinen sengū*, in his view, is *sokei no saien*—the "repetition [literally, 'recurrent performance'] of the prototype"—by which he means that Japanese tradition descends from a divine gift that has been nurtured and transferred by emperors and priests in an unbroken line since the nation began in antiquity.[10]

My own view is that this divine gift is simply rice, the staff of life in Japan, and that Ise Jingū is basically a rice sanctuary; certainly rice is the most significant element in all rituals performed at the shrines (Fig. 1). The inner sanctuary building is, raised-floor style, in the form of a traditional Japanese granary. The most secret and hidden object, a wooden pillar called *shin no mihashira*, is buried in the center under the floor of the inner sanctuary. The cutting of this pillar, the first ritual in preparation for transferring the *kami* to a new shrine, is conducted secretly eight years prior to the year of *shikinen sengū* (Fig. 2). That this most hidden treasure is kept in the small sacred granary shrine, called *mishine no mikura*, for eight years, suggests the crucial importance of rice for Jingū. The *kannamesai*, the harvest festival for rice, is held at Ise in October, when rice harvested from Jingū's rice field as well as donated to Jingū by the emperor, who grows rice on imperial palace land, is offered to the *kami* in gratitude for this gift, and *shikinen sengū* is held in the same month. Indeed, the Jingū priests refer to the rite of *shikinen sengū* as *dai-kannamesai* (the "great rice-harvest festival"). In these ways, then, rice is shown to be sacred and is revealed as the epitome of Japanese culture and the Japanese ethos, of which Jingū is the imperial storehouse.

It is for this reason, I assume, that Breen and Teeuwen did not choose Ise Jingū as the subject of their case study when discussing shrine Shinto. Likewise,

9. Hiroko Yoshino, *Kakusareta kamigami* (Hidden Deities) (Tokyo: Kōdansha, 1975), 136–38.

10. Masayuki Nakanishi, *Jingū saishi no kenkyū* (Research on Jingū Rituals) (Tokyo: Kokushokankōkai, 2007), 281–85.

Figure 1. A group of priests and employees from Ise Jingū harvest a small amount of rice from sacred paddies during early September in preparation for the largest annual Shinto ceremony, the harvest ritual called *kannamesai*, held in October. All pictures were taken by the author except where otherwise indicated.

although they mention periodic mass pilgrimages to Ise, they exclude this subject too from their analysis, because it substantiates a cult of Jingū having nothing to do with Meiji political ideology or its subsequent ultranationalist development.[11] Hardacre likewise excludes the mass pilgrimage to Jingū, given its minimal relation to state Shinto, from her analysis; the pilgrimage, as she acknowledges, was "in large part a popular phenomenon."[12] In other words, these three scholars discard nonpolitical phenomena from the scope of their studies despite the significance of these phenomena in Japanese religious history. The spontaneous mass pilgrimage to Jingū is known as *okage mairi*, which means "thanksgiving pilgrimage." The tradition began in 1650, after the Tokugawa shogunate had made the roadways at last safe for travel, and continued for about two centuries. Professional *onshi*, Shinto priest-agents who owned their own halls of sacred music and dance, supplied religious and lodging services to pilgrims on these occasions. By the time that Meiji was enthroned in 1867, at which point *okage mairi* was abolished during the government's reformation of shrine Shinto, there were 309 houses of *onshi* in the area of Naikū and 550 in the area of Gekū.[13] The pilgrimages occurred only in years when *shikinen sengū* was conducted but not on every such occasion; the interval between them tended to be about sixty years,

11. See Breen and Teeuwen, *New History of Shinto*, 58.

12. Hardacre, *Shinto and the State*, 16.

13. Junichi Kamada, *Jingūshi gaisetsu* (Discourse on the History of Jingū) (Tokyo: Jinja Shinpōsha 2003), 127.

Figure 2. *Mishine no mikura* is a small sacred granary where harvested rice from Ise Jingū's field is kept to be offered to Amaterasu at the three major annual rituals. The enshrined deity protects both the granary and the rice stored there. A sacred pillar called *shin no mihashira* (the pillar of the heart) is buried under the center of the main sanctuary, where it is kept for eight years prior to the transfer of Amaterasu to the new sanctuary.

and it was an element of popular belief that every Japanese should visit Jingū at least once during his or her lifetime, hence the enormous numbers of pilgrims. After the first such pilgrimage in 1650, others occurred in 1705, 1771, and 1830, each time drawing several million people to Ise.

One can see why a government that was set on the centralization of power, such as the one that replaced the shogunate, might regard spontaneous gatherings in the millions as a threat and decide to put an end to them. "As for the *okage mairi*," Masatami Nishikawa explains,

most people who were connected to *onshi* used to be *jōmin*, or commoners, and the *okage mairi* was not a pilgrimage of the type that becomes popular under strong military leadership. People's reverence toward Jingū was quietly and steadily cultivated over a span of time. It is this kind of inwardness, characteristic of the common people, that is the basis of Japanese culture. It resists theoretical interpretation and continues to develop even now, without being much influenced by social change.[14]

14. Masatami Nishikawa, *Kindai no Jingū* (Jingū in the Modern Period) (Ise: Jingū Shichō, 1988), 16.

The phenomenon of the spontaneous mass pilgrimage to Ise is evidence, in other words, that the cult of Jingū among the common people was unrelated to the political agenda of the shogunate. And the imperial government under Meiji, in forbidding the pilgrimage, was acknowledging that shrine Shinto had been a popular religion over which the state had been remiss in not asserting its control.

Daijōsai: The Rite of Imperial Succession

Despite the separation of religion and state under the shogunate, there was no separation during those centuries between shrine Shinto and the emperors. It must be remembered, as Perl emphasizes in his essay about Ise Jingū, that

> there had never been—not really—an emperor of Japan. The seventh-century titles translated, since Meiji's time, as *emperor* are *tennô* (heavenly sovereign) and *tenshi* (son of heaven). Japan was not an empire but a collection of contiguous islands, and its sovereign was a demigod and chief priest (or perhaps shaman) of the national religion Shinto, but not the holder of a political office. . . . Then why is the Meiji Restoration so called? Perry's "opening" of Japan to the West occurred when the prince who would be Meiji was about a year old, and Japanese elites absorbed the basics of Western history. France had had its Bourbon Restoration under Louis XVIII and Charles X, the British under Charles II had had their Stuart Restoration—and at the same time as Japanese nationalists decided that Nippon had always been an empire and its *tennô* an emperor, they determined that Japan, like these Western powers, had undergone the restoration of an interrupted order. But what happened constitutionally in Japan after 1867 seems, from a perspective not so far above sea level, rather limited.[15]

The politicization of religion about which Breen and Teeuwen write emerged only with the determination by the nationalists supporting Meiji that, with his becoming the 122nd *tennô* in descent from Jinmu, Japan "had undergone the restoration of an interrupted order." The problem with Breen and Teeuwen's history of Shinto is that, while it contends that the nationalists were wrong, it does not acknowledge that, if so, then the order of Japanese society had indeed gone uninterrupted, at least until the Meiji Restoration.

Breen and Teeuwen argue that the definition of *daijōsai* as the ritual that effects the accession of a new emperor is part of the modern ultranationalist effort to deify the sovereign, deepen his claim on the obedience of the people, and make the powers of his government absolute. But *daijōsai* was established during the time of Emperor Tenmu, who reigned from 673 to 686, about twelve-

---

15. Perl, "Regarding Change at Ise Jingū," 210–11.

hundred years before Emperor Meiji's accession. Tsunetada Mayumi and Takeshi Matsumae find the first reference to *daijōsai* in the *Nihonshoki* (the Chronicles of Japan), compiled in 720.[16] The narrative to which both these scholars point concerns Jinmu and the way in which he defeats his enemies by conducting a ritual based on instructions that, in a dream, he has received from the god. To prepare, Jinmu takes earth from within the shrine of Heavenly Mount Kagu and, with it, makes jars and platters in which he cooks sacred rice. He offers the rice to one of the Three Creating Deities, Takami musubi no mikoto ("High-August-Growth"), who then possesses Jinmu. He becomes a *yorimashi*, a vessel, for the god, and it is as the god that Jinmu consumes the sacred rice. A ritual of this kind, in which the worshipper is transformed into the god he worships, is termed *utsushiiwai*. After performing it, Jenmu succeeds in uniting Japan and becomes its first sovereign. Mayumi reads this narrative as referring to *daijōsai*, the ritual in which the emperor consumes sacred rice and, by doing so, embodies the *kunitama*, the soul of all Japan. *Daijōsai* has two standard English translations, "rite of imperial succession" and "rite of the great tasting," and clearly it is both. In Mayumi's view, the transformation of a worshipper into the god worshipped is characteristic of the oldest Japanese rituals—it is common, certainly, to the rituals of the imperial court and those performed at Shinto shrines—and its antiquity may well be why Breen and Teeuwen do not mention *utsushiiwai* at all in their analysis of *daijōsai*, which they want to claim is a modern invention in the service of militant ultranationalism.[17]

After the *daijōsai*, the emperor performs the same actions every autumn, in a ceremony known as *niinamesai*—which is to say that it is the performance of this agricultural rite that makes him emperor. But there is nothing political about his role or these rites: the emperor, like Japan itself, is bound up with the sacredness of the rice plant. Before the modern era, most Japanese made their living at tasks related to the farming of rice, and the basic imperial myth tells how the sun goddess Amaterasu supplied rice to Japan, from her sacred rice field in heaven, through the agency of her grandson Ninigi no mikoto. Through Ninigi no mikoto, the first emperor's great-grandfather, she also transmitted her knowledge of both rice farming and nation building. The emperor's highest function is neither political nor military; it is to offer gratitude to the gods, on behalf of Japan, for a good crop and to pray for a good harvest and for peace in the year ahead. He also prays for unbroken continuity of the imperial succession. The apolitical role that the emperor has played since Hirohito announced the surrender of Japan is more a renewal of tradition, one might venture, than the

---

16. See Tsunetada Mayumi, *Daijōsai* (The Ritual of Imperial Succession) (Tokyo: Gakusei sha, 1988), 121–24, and *Matsumae Takeshi chosakushū* (Collected Works of Takeshi Matsumae), vol. 6 (Tokyo: Ōfū, 1997), 57–61.

17. See Mayumi, *Daijōsai*, 124.

Figure 3. Prince Akishinomiya, second son of the present emperor, visits Ise Jingū to observe rituals of *shikinen sengū* as the representative of the imperial household (October 6, 2013).

Meiji Restoration, which deepened the *tennō*'s involvement in political matters. Those functions had almost always been left to the military aristocracy, while the emperor embodied the spirit of Japan, performed agricultural rites at the imperial palace shrine, and prayed on behalf of the nation to his divine ancestor (Fig. 3).

Gokaisei: The Jingū Reformation

On the other hand, it must be said that Meiji's reign (1867–1912) possessed something vital in common with that of his ancestor Tenmu (673–86), and archival evidence suggests that, at least in matters of religion, Meiji did effect a kind of restoration and that it was his own decision to do so. In the seventh century, many neighboring countries were tributaries of the Chinese emperor, and to maintain its independence Japan wanted to demonstrate equal status with China. In the nineteenth century, European nations colonized most countries in Asia and Africa; in response, Japan in the Meiji era moved swiftly to establish a centralized, unified, modernized, industrialized, and militarily competitive state on a par with the empires of the West. Both reigns saw religious reforms as well. It was Tenmu, as chief priest, who first organized and regularized the Shinto rites conducted at the thousands of shrines throughout Japan, and likewise Tenmu who elevated the status of Ise Jingū to that of imperial grand shrine. In a self-consciously parallel way, Meiji oversaw reform of the shrine system: the shrines were declared national institutions in 1871, the hereditary priesthood of the Arakida and Watarai families was abolished, and the number of priests was greatly reduced.

Between the Tenmu and Meiji eras, the reign of Emperor Reigen (1663–87) saw the restoration of *daijōsai* and other important rites that had been disrupted by civil war. Desuetude and restoration have always been elements of continuity in the history of Shinto.

The standard argument, by this time, is that what is called the Jingū reformation (*Jingū Gokaisei*) was an innovation imposed on the Ise grand shrine and its priesthood by the central government under Emperor Meiji. Examination of imperial and shrine archives, however, makes it clear, first, that the priests themselves petitioned the emperor for the reforms that were then made; second, that it was Meiji himself, as chief priest, rather than his government, who was most involved in discussions with the Jingū priesthood; third, that the reforms requested and made had begun during the reign (1846–66) of Meiji's father, Emperor Kōmei, who in the tumultuous last years of the Tokugawa shogunate had what he considered urgent reasons for pursuing them; and finally, that the reforms, far from inventing a new religion or even initiating a new phase of an old one, brought the rituals at Ise, after careful study of their historical development, back to the ancient traditions of Jingū.

From 1853, when Commodore Perry and his four black ships came to Uraga, until 1864, Emperor Kōmei sent an envoy to Ise Jingū seven times to pray on his behalf for peace and for the protection of Japan from foreign threats.[18] Although there was no precedent for such a visit, Kōmei decided as well to pray at Jingū himself for the continuing independence of Japan. The Jingū priests began preparations to receive the emperor. Kiyonao Mikanagi (1812–94), a hereditary priest of Gekū (the Outer Shrine of Jingū), was sent to Kyoto in August 1863 to discuss the "ancient practices of Ise Jingū," in which Kiyonao was especially "well versed."[19] In the end, the emperor's visit to the shrine was canceled, and Kiyonao returned to Ise. Kōmei's strong interest in "ancient practices," at both Jingū and the imperial court, resulted in Kiyonao's continuing research into lapsed traditions and in their reimplementation. After a consultation with Kōmei in 1864, the ceremony of the emperor's offering silk at *kannamesai* was restored in 1865 at Ise Jingū. But Kiyonao had a more consequential restoration in mind as well. In a study ("Kannamesai gyoyū kōjitsu") of ritual music and dance at *kannamesai*, he detailed continuities between the ritual music performed at Jingū and that performed at the imperial court, with an eye to making them even more consistently the same:

The performing of ritual music during *kannamesai* at the two main sanctuaries was established [at Ise] based on the *daijōsai* and *niinamesai*

---

18. See Kiyondo Mori, ed., *Mikotonori* (Imperial Edicts) (Tokyo: Kinseisha, 2002).

19. Kiyonao Mikanagi, "Mikanagi Kiyonao Ouden" (Biography of Kiyonao Mikanagi), in *Jingū shinji kōshō kōhen* (Studies on Jingū Rituals), vol. 3 (Tokyo: Yoshikawakōbunkan, 2007), 1–14.

conducted at the imperial palace. During *daijōsai*, there is the *yamato-mai* dance performed by [palace] chamberlains and officials in charge of rituals, while at Ise Jingū there is the *yamatomai* dance performed by an [imperial] envoy and his attendants. There is a women's dance called *gosechimai* performed during *daijōsai*, while there is *gosechimai* performed by the court ladies of the *saiō* [the imperial princess serving at Ise Jingū]. There is the *kumemai* dance during *daijōsai*, while there is the *tonagomai* dance at Ise Jingū. Similarly, there are *ōnaobiuta* during *daijōsai* [at the palace] and *mikeuta* at the shrine; *ōuta* during *daijōsai* and *iseuta* at the shrine. While dancers, singers, and the players of zither and flute are gifted with ritual costumes at *daijōsai*, performers of *tonagomai*—the lead singer and the players of zither and flute—are given ritual costumes at the shrine. We should study the history of the music and rituals of Ise Jingū with the understanding that the music and rituals at the shrine do not differ from those of the imperial court.[20]

In the same document, Kiyonao presents his expert opinion on the origin of the ritual music and dance performed at Ise Jingū:

The origin of the *yamatomai* dance performed at the shrine is found in *Kogoshūi* [Gleanings from Ancient Narratives]. According to *Kogoshūi*, the [perhaps legendary] emperor [Sujin], while reigning [97 BCE–30 CE] at the Mizugaki Palace in Shiki, began to fear living under the same roof with Amaterasu and to feel overwhelmed by her divine presence. He instructed his daughter Toyosuki-iri-hime-no-mikoto to remove the sacred objects—the mirror and the sword—from the palace and to enshrine them in Kasanui-no-mura village in Yamato province. On the evening after the divine emblems were enshrined, all the courtiers gathered and entertained [the goddess] throughout the night, singing: "miyabito no ohoyosugarani isatohoshi yukinoyoroshimo ohoyosuga-rani." This song is still sung in a modified version, as follows: "miyabi-tono ohoyosogoromo hisatohoshi yukinoyoroshimo ohoyosogoromo." So says the *Kogoshūi*. The song and dance performed at this feast is the origin of the *yamatomai* dance. The performance of music and dance dedicated to Amaterasu began at that time.[21]

It is more usually said, based on what is called the "rock-cave myth," that Shinto ritual music and dance originated with the dance performed by Amanouzume-no-mikoto to encourage Amaterasu to emerge from the darkness of her cave. Instead, Kiyonao associates ritual music with that performed at Kasanui-no-mura village after the sacred mirror housing Amaterasu was transferred and reen-shrined outside the palace (Fig. 4).

20. Kiyonao Mikanagi, "Kannamesai gyoyū kōjitsu," [Study of the Ritual Music of *Kannamesai*], in *Jingū shinji kōshō zenpen* (Studies on Jingū Rituals), vol. 2 (Tokyo: Yoshikawakōbunkan, 2006), 759.

21. Kiyonao, "Kannamesai gyoyū kōjitsu," 761.

Figure 4. Maidens of Ise Jingū offer a dance to the enshrined deity, on October 8, 2013, in celebration of the completion of *shikinen sengū*. The music is based on *waka* poetry by Kazuko Takatsukasa (1929–89), the eldest sister of the present emperor and former *saishu* or highest priestess of Ise Jingū.

Emperor Kōmei's deep concern for the peace and permanent independence of Japan appears connected to his conviction that Shinto practice at the imperial palace and at Jingū should be restored to their ancient forms (Fig. 5). Perhaps, under threat of invasion, he aspired to closer contact with Japan's tutelary deity. Conceivably, he had read and been moved by Kiyonao's account of how the tenth emperor, Sujin, had transferred the deity from his palace but arranged for her intimate entertainment on her first day and night in her new home. We do know that Prince Asahiko, a close adviser on religious matters to Emperor Kōmei, studied Kiyonao's writings on the ancient practices of Jingū. Beginning in 1861, Kōmei took upon himself the performance of the *wagon*, a kind of Japanese zither, for the rite of *mikagura* at Amaterasu's shrine (*naishidokoro*) in the palace.[22] In lieu of visiting Ise, one may venture, he offered his prayer for the peace of Japan and its people by performing the *wagon*, in his own home, for his divine ancestor. On the night of December 11, 1886, Kōmei played the *wagon* for the *kagura* song "Sakaki" at *mikagura* and then died two weeks later, on December 25. Prince Asahiko became *saishu*, the supreme celebrant of rituals of Ise Jingū in 1875,

22. Mastering the musical instruments required for sacred rites has been part of the training for emperors for many centuries. Details can be found in *Kinpishō*, the practical guide to imperial events and regulations written by Emperor Juntoku (r. 1210–21).

Figure 5. In this painting, a dancer and court nobles perform *kagura* songs for Amaterasu at the ritual of sacred music held in 1866, during the reign of Emperor Kōmei, in front of the imperial palace shrine.

under Emperor Meiji, and was clearly the main guarantor and conduit of continuity between Shinto under the Tokugawa shogunate and Shinto under the Jingū reformation.

On May 1, 1893, Sanetsune Tokudaiji, the grand chamberlain of the imperial court, notified the grand master of ceremonies "unofficially" of Emperor Meiji's "wish" and "command" that the transmission of *kagura* (literally, "god entertainment") to future generations be assured. Tokudaiji recorded these, in his diary, as the emperor's own words:

Both *kagura taikyoku* [the great song] and *hikyoku* [the secret song] used to be transmitted by hereditary court nobles who specialized in vocal court music. As the system of transmission by hereditary noble families has been eliminated, however, . . . I am afraid that the transmission of *kagura taikyoku* and *hikyoku* will eventually die out. For the rite of reconstruction of Jingū and for other occasions as well, the performance of these private songs will be needed. Thus, it is necessary to transmit both types of song either to the descendants of hereditary nobles or to low-rank court musicians who are especially skilled at *gagaku*.[23]

23. *Tokudaiji Sanetsune nikki* (The Diary of Tokudaiji Sanetsune), May 1, 1893, Kunaichō (Imperial Household Archives) C1–149 *fuku* [facsimile edition] 3463.

This exchange took place twenty-five years after the Meiji Restoration and twenty-two years into the Jingū reformation. It seems likely that the emperor felt that the reformation had in some respects gone too far and that the principle of restoration should be more zealously applied than so far it had been to the Shinto rites of Ise Jingū and the imperial court.

Before the Jingū reformation, after the October rice festival (*kannamesai*), a feast called *naorai* was enjoyed by imperial envoys and high-ranking priests. The feast is mentioned as early as 804 in *Kōtaijingū gishikichō*, as well as in *Kōtaijingū nenjūgyōji*, on the basis of which Masayuki Nakanishi explains the accompanying music and dance:

At the main three rituals including *kannamesai* held annually at Jingū, people of local villages such as Shirota and Tanabegōrokkamura used to sing and play the flutes and the zithers to accompany the *tonagomai* dance performed by their children wearing *aozuri* or blue rubbed dyed robes. The written manuals of this folk ritual dance and music scores were lost during the pre-modern wars of the medieval era. However, the *tonagomai* was resurrected during the pre-modern period. The name of *tonagomai* originated in the *Tokoyo no naganakidori* or roosters of Heaven based on the myth of the rock-cave, and child dancers imitated the roosters and danced the *tonagomai*.[24]

In 1871, as a part of the Jingū reformation, these performances were prohibited. The reason, according to Nakanishi, may have been the failure to submit the old documents and texts describing the dance forms and music when, in response to an order of the Meiji government, Jingū officials did research on the origins and historical development of *tonagomai*.[25] In my view, even if Jingū officials could have found the records and identified the origin of these performances, *tonagomai* would not have survived at Jingū. The *tonagomai* dancers were children, and the dance belonged to the picturesque variety of folk tradition that the Meiji government considered unseemly for performance at the central religious shrine of a modern nation.

Instead, the government decreed that *gagaku*, the traditional music of the imperial court, be adapted to rituals at the grand shrine, but there were no musicians at Ise in 1871 able to perform it. Thus, twelve musicians from Jingū were sent to learn *gagaku* from court musicians.[26] In 1872, the ministry of religious education (Kyōbushō) sent eight court musicians to Jingū for *kannamesai*, where they performed *kagura* songs while sacred food was brought and taken away during *kannamesai*.[27] Since *kagura* songs were native in origin

24. Nakanishi, *Jingū saishi no kenkyū*, 49.

25. Nakanishi, *Jingū saishi no kenkyū*, 49–50.

26. *Mizugaki* (Jingū Journal) 116 (1978): 92.

27. Norifumi Shimazu, "Jingū saishi no gagaku dōnyū nitsuite" (Adoption of Gagaku to Jingū Rituals), *Shinto shūkyō* (Journal of Shinto Studies) 161 (1995): 97.

Figure 6. Sayako Kuroda, a daughter of the present emperor, serves in the role of priestess at one of the three major annual rituals at Ise Jingū (December 16, 2012).

and had been performed at the imperial court since the sixth century, they were highly regarded as ritual music by the Meiji government in its earliest years.[28] This performance was a formative event at Jingū: it inspired priests to perform *kagura* songs on their own in future years. It is easy to see how a scholar of Japanese religion unsympathetic to Shinto, on account of its association with emperor worship in the era of World War II, would regard this development of the music at Jingū as evidence that Shinto is a modern invention. It should be easy as well, however, to see how a scholar dedicated foremost to historical accuracy would regard such innovations as no more than changes of a kind that all traditions, without exception, undergo in every culture.

After all, the music added to the ritual at Jingū was added on the emperor's command, and Jingū is in the most literal way the emperor's own shrine. The most important rites there are performed by members of the imperial family (Fig. 6), and it is facing Ise that the emperor prays to Amaterasu every morning from the palace in Tokyo. Emperor Meiji's decision to lend more gravity and a more national (rather than a local or folk) spirit to the ceremonies at Ise is anything but a sign of discontinuity. One might say more aptly that it represents an increase in ceremonial dignity, intensity, and perhaps authenticity; moreover, it represents

28. Yasuko Tsukahara, *Meiji Kokka to Gagaku: Dentō no Kindaika/Kokugaku no Sōsei* (The Meiji Nation and *Gagaku*: The Modernization of Tradition and the Formation of a National Music) (Tokyo: Yūshisha, 2009), 79.

direct continuity between the religious policies of the Kōmei and Meiji eras. Emperor Kōmei, as I have already shown, began the process of restoring the most ancient and dignified practices for Shinto rites at both Jingū and the imperial court. As the ethnomusicologist Robert Garfias writes of the sacred music that Meiji preferred, "In the Gagaku tradition, the oldest and best documented form of vocal music is the sacred Kagura song cycle."[29] In the same vein, Tsukahara emphasizes that *kagura* "is the only genre of gagaku of native origin that has continued without any break of transmission."[30]

By "the sacred Kagura song cycle," Garfias means specifically *mikagura no gi*, the music that court musicians had performed, once a year for more than a millennium, at the *naishidokoro*, the shrine in the imperial palace where Amaterasu is worshipped. When *mikagura no gi* came eventually to be performed at Jingū as well, it was at the ardent request of the Jingū priesthood and musicians. With the government's approval, *mikagura no gi* was performed in 1889 for the first time at the fifty-sixth *shikinen sengū*, and then again at *kannamesai* in 1890. Since Jingū musicians had not yet mastered the full repertoire of *kagura* songs—the entire performance of which takes about six hours—court musicians performed at Jingū on these two occasions and continued to perform *mikagura no gi* at *kannamesai* every year until Jingū musicians had learned the song cycle well enough to conduct the music ritual at *kannamesai* on their own. (The Jingū musicians' first performance of the cycle came in 1932, twenty years after Meiji's death.)[31] One could also argue that the result of the changes at Ise Jingū was a kind of democratization, since it was through the replication of music and rituals until then exclusively performed at the imperial palace that the common people of Japan came to know them at all. After the prohibition in 1871 of all *onshi* activities, Jingū promptly constructed a *kagura* hall for pilgrims in Naikū, ready for use in 1873.[32] In that year, Jingū musicians were learning *gagaku* of foreign origin and performed them at the *kagura* hall in response to pilgrims' requests. Despite the government's insistence on removing folk music from Jingū rituals, music (though now, sacred music exclusively) was quickly returned to the shrine, and pilgrims were provided a place in which to hear it at the shrine itself, rather than outside under the unofficial auspices of *onshi*.[33] That common pilgrims are well satisfied with this arrangement, now almost a century and a half old, is confirmed by attendance records at the shrine. In 2010, Jingū received 8.6 million visitors (a new record), many of whom asked to attend performances of ritual music in

29. Robert Garfias, *Music of a Thousand Autumns: The Tōgaku Style of Japanese Court Music* (Berkeley: University of California Press, 1975), 136.

30. Tsukahara, *Meiji Kokka to Gagaku*, 79.

31. Shimazu, "Jingū saishi no gagaku dōnyū nitsuite," 107–8.

32. Jingū Shichō, *Jingū shi nenpyō* (Chronicle Roll of Jingū) (Tokyo: Ebisukōsyō, 2005), 215.

33. See Yasuji Honda, *Honda Yasuji chosakushū: Nihon no dentōgeinō* (Collected Works of Yasuji Honda), vol. 7, *Kagura VII* (Tōkyō: Kinseisha, 1993).

Figure 7. Senior priests carry the sacred mirror, in which the sun goddess Amaterasu is believed to reside, from the old shrine to the new shrine at Ise Jingū. They walk down a path that connects the shrines. To conceal and protect the deity, a white silk "fence" carried by other priests surrounds the group of the priests carrying the mirror. © Jingū-shichō

the *kagura* hall. To accommodate the requests, 24,346 such performances were given in 2010.[34]

If the aim of the Jingū reformation was to engage the tutelary deity of Japan by restoring the most intimate rituals of contact with her—in an effort, again, to secure her support for the country's peace and independence—then the culmination of the changes made was the bringing of *hikyoku* from the imperial court to Ise. *Hikyoku* is a voiceless and so-called secret song performed soundlessly *in camera* for Amaterasu alone. For our purpose here, I will translate *hikyoku* as "private serenade." *Hikyoku* is performed only once every twenty years at Ise Jingū, during *shikinen sengū*, and only once during the reign of each new emperor at the imperial palace. Its performance at Ise comes the day after Amaterasu is transferred, at night, to the newly built main sanctuary: the sacred music ritual including *hikyoku* is the final step in the rite of reconstruction (Fig. 7). Among *gagaku* repertoires, it is only *hikyoku* that has remained secret because access to the scores and the site of performance is limited strictly to the actual performers on each occasion. When the private serenade is scheduled for performance, the board of ceremonies selects five court musicians (a flute player, a *hichiriki* player, a *wagon* or Japanese zither player, a lead singer, and an assistant singer), and then the grand master of ceremonies distributes one score, kept locked in a safe at all other times, to each musician. These scores are never available to scholars or to anyone else not directly involved in performance.

Access to any performance of *hikyoku* is strictly limited as well. *Hikyoku* is performed in the middle of the sacred music ritual. When the first half is completed, all court musicians and priests leave the hall of performance, after which only the five performers of *hikyoku* enter the hall. The rest of the musicians and priests, including the supreme celebrant, must wait outside the hall for some thirty minutes until the private serenade of Amaterasu is concluded; the imperial envoy is not admitted either. Strikingly, it is a court musician rather than the envoy or a priest who recites the prayer with which the performance of the serenade ends. I came to know of the existence of this prayer only by reading a Shinto newspaper article in 2013 about the former chief court musician Toshiharu Tohgi.[35] He refers there to a prayer that he had recited during the sacred music ritual at Ise Jingū in 1993. Although he does not specify when, during the ritual, he recited the prayer, I was able to determine, by comparative analysis of historical manuscripts of the seventeenth and early twentieth centuries, that it concludes the silent performance of *hikyoku*. The relationship of the three ceremonies performed in Ise at twenty-year intervals—*shikinen sengū*, the sacred music ritual of which *hikyoku* is a part, and the prayer with which *hikyoku* concludes—is like that of Russian dolls, each contained and hidden within the next. The innermost and least open of these rites is the musician's nighttime prayer to the sun goddess.

Until the Jingū reformation, sacred music was transmitted from generation to generation among hereditary court nobility of high rank. When this system of transmission was terminated in 1870, the scores and related manuscripts were transferred from the nobility to the imperial court and were placed under government control. These documents are preserved, under sixteen subheadings, at the National Archives, under the title *Kagura hikyoku denjyu shorui* [Documents of Transmitted *Kagura* Secret Music].[36] A document titled "Mototakakyō shimeshisōrō kagura ryōkyoku" [The Two *Kagura* Songs That Sir Mototaka Displayed] records the following valuable details:

Taikyoku [the great song] refers to "Yudate."
Hikyoku [the secret song] refers to "Hirume."
Both songs were fixed during the reign [986–1011] of Emperor Ichijō.
Minister Sanehiro Tōin transmitted both songs to Lord Aritoshi
Ayanokōji on Eikyō 10.12.20 [December 20, 1438].
After the *fue*, the *hichiriki*, and the *wagon*, a song begins.[37]

35. See the interview with Toshiharu Tohgi in the *Jinja shinpō* newspaper of March 7, 2011.

36. *Kagura hikyoku denjyu shorui*, National Archives of Japan, 199-0442, nos. 1–16.

37. "Mototakakyō shimeshisōrō kagura ryōkyoku," National Archives of Japan, 199-0442, no. 15.

This document also includes the lyrics and score of "Hirume." Very likely it is because Hirume, another name for Amaterasu, is directly invoked that this lyric came to be classified as secret:

Hirume motokata: Ikabakari yokiwazashiteka
Suekata: Amateruya hirumenokamio
Shiriage motokata: Shibashi todomen, oke

After inviting Amaterasu and entertaining her,
how much more god-music and dance would it take
to induce her to remain here? *Oke*

The bisyllabic *oke* is used to mark the end of various *kagura* songs, including "Sakaki" and "Hayakarakami" as well as "Hirume," in something like the way that *amen* and *selah* mark the conclusion or the ends of sections of Hebrew psalms and other prayers.

The document that I have been quoting contains the lyrics and score of "Yudate" as well as "Hirume" and provides some information about their transmission. The record shows that Aritoshi Ayanokōji (b. 1419) received this material from Sanehiro Tōin (1409–59) on December 20, 1438. The lyrics and notation were transmitted from Mototaka Jimyōin (1520–1611) to Yukinaka Itsutsuji (1558–1626), who wrote the entire document in 1593. Aritoshi Ayanokōji belonged to a family of grand masters of *kagura* songs. The reason that he learned from Sanehiro Tōin—the son of Aritoshi's father's disciple—is that Aritoshi had lost his father when he was only nine and thus was not ready yet for instruction.[38] In a National Archives document titled "Taikyoku hikyoku denju azukarisōrō chūko iraino nintei," there is a list, beginning with Arisuke Ayanokōji (1204–72), of sixteen people (nine from the Ayanokōji family, six from the Jimyōin family, and one from the Itsutsuji family) who transmitted "Yudate" and "Hirume."[39] Only one person on the list, Yukinaka Itsutsuji, was not from a family of grand masters of *kagura*. Four years after Yukinaka's master, Mototaka Jimyōin, died, his adopted son Motohisa (1584–1615) fell in the Summer Siege of Osaka in 1615, and Motohisa's son Motomasa likewise died young.[40] Due to the loss of the present head of the family and the next in line as well, the Jimyōin faced a crisis of continuity as a family of grand masters of *kagura*. Yukinaka Itsutsuji restored the line of succession of the Jimyōin by inserting himself as a transitional figure until

38. "Tōin Sanehiro shinji hikyoku Aritoshi e denjūjō utsushi" (Copy of the Certification that Tōin Sanehiro Transmitted the *Kagura* Secret Song to Ayanokōji Aritoshi), National Archives of Japan, 199-0442, no. 4, states that to "Ayanokōji Aritoshi was transmitted all the contents of the *kagura* secret song 'Hirume' on Eikyō 10.12.20 [December 20, 1438]."

39. See "Taikyoku hikyoku denju azukarisōrō chūko irai no nintei," National Archives of Japan, 199-0442, no 10.

40. See *Jimyōin* (Genealogy of the Jimyōin), National Archives of Japan, 155-0001.

Motosada (1607–67), who married Motohisa's daughter, was allowed to inherit and continue the family line.

As for the Ayanokōji family, during the time of Yukinaka Itsutsuji the line had already terminated. The family name of the Ayanokōji was revived through adoption of Yukinaka's son Taka'ari.[41] Another National Archives document, titled "Kagura saibara sosen irai no den" [People to Whom Kagura and Saibara Have Been Transmitted], says that Taka'ari had transmitted to him "*kagura* great and secret songs from Yukinaka Itsutsuji."[42] In short, Yukinaka Itsutsuji maintained continuity in the transmission of the sacred music repertoire by restoring the lines of succession in both the Jimyōin and Ayanokōji families of *kagura* grand masters. In order to prevent any interruption in the conduct of *mikagura*, the sacred music ritual, noble families other than these two had to participate in the transmission of *kagura*, but as a result the scores and lyrics of "Yudate" and "Hirume" that had been handed down to Aritoshi Ayanokōji were transmitted from generation to generation, over a period of more than four centuries, until they were delivered to the Meiji government during the Jingū reformation.

According to the manuscripts that I have consulted, it was Aritoshi Ayanokōji who, in the fifteenth century, first began to sing *hikyoku* soundlessly. The technique of silent performance is called *bion* in Japanese. *Bi* means subtle, hidden, secretive; *on* means sound. The present score of *hikyoku* is a modernized version based primarily on seventeenth-century manuscripts that contain texts from still earlier times. The manuscripts also provide a type of musical notation called *hakase*. Without appropriate and strenuous training, it is impossible to sing by reading *hakase*. The present chief court musician, Hiroaki Tohgi, has said that, "if you have performed *kagura* songs for more than thirty or forty years, you can understand how you sing *hikyoku* with the score." *Hikyoku* has both instrumental and vocal parts. First, there are preludes of flute, *hichiriki*, and *wagon*, which are played, respectively, one after the other. While *hichiriki* is usually played loudly, it is also played softly for *kagura* songs, and it makes no sound at all for *hikyoku*. Likewise, the other instruments play soundlessly for the private serenade. Among these instruments, only the *wagon* (the Japanese zither) accompanies the lead singer, because it is regarded as the musical instrument with the closest link to the gods. A specially made *wagon* is kept, for serenading Amaterasu, in the main sanctuary of Jingū. Both the lead and the assistant singer play a pair of wooden clappers in a call-and-response sequence, but in such a way as to make no sound. The lead singer performs just as he would if he were singing *kagura* songs aloud, but the only sound that he produces is the sound of his breathing. Toward the end of *hikyoku*, there is a brief moment when sound is finally produced: the *wagon*

41. See "Ayanokōji Arikazu sashidashi" (Document Written by Ayanokōji Arikazu), Historiographical Institute, University of Tokyo, 00059840.

42. See "Kagura saibara sosen irai no den," National Archives of Japan, 199-0442, no. 6.

plays six strings in one regular quick stroke, which sounds like *barang*. It follows the lead singer's singing of "oke" in full volume. Those sounds mark the end of *hikyoku*, at least as the seventeenth-century manuscript describes it. Jingū priests tell me that, during the performance in 2013, they heard both the *barang* of the *wagon* and the sound of "oke" while waiting outside the hall in the main sanctuary complex.

Why is the serenade performed silently, and why have I put such emphasis on it and on the details of its historical transmission? *Hikyoku* is so sacred that even the performers are not allowed to hear it. It is performed exclusively for Amaterasu, who alone can hear the music and lyrics through the silence. Just as she needed to be reconciled by music to her new home when Emperor Sujin transferred her from the imperial palace to Ise, so again, by means of a serenade for her alone to hear, she must be reconciled to a new home when, once per generation, her sanctuary is disassembled and constructed identically anew. In the face of inevitable change, the divine protector of Japan must be comforted with an ancient, unchanging ritual, performed *in camera* exclusively for her. Even so, however inevitable change in general may be, the changes made at Jingū follow a wholly predictable schedule, a rigidly normative pattern, and depend on scrupulously recorded systems of transmission that, even when occasionally they falter, have never failed. In the same spirit, the prayers offered to the sun goddess in Ise and at the imperial palace shrine are for continuity of the imperial line and for the peace and prosperity of her people, who live in what is, after all, not only the Land of the Rising Sun but also a land that is subject, more than most, to devastating earthquakes and other natural, as well as unnatural, disasters. My point is that Shinto is tailor-made for the needs of Japan and that, therefore, the religion seems obviously to be the most indigenous feature of the islands' complex culture. Whether or not my readers agree with this conclusion, I hope I have demonstrated that, contrary to prevailing currents of scholarship about Japanese cultural history, Shinto is ancient, discrete, coherent, and as self-identical over time as any religious tradition can possibly be.

An Appeal

A concept of importance in Shinto is *kotoagesezu*: the avoidance of verbal expression about rituals and about the gods for whom they are performed. Jingū priests do not preach; they do not express their beliefs; they do not explain the meaning of rituals even to devoted pilgrims. When I first went to Jingū, the priests were extremely unapproachable. I have gradually attained their trust, I believe, by returning regularly. But even now, they do not speak among themselves, let alone to me, of the wooden pillar buried in the inner sanctuary. I can say of it that, in ancient Shinto tradition, trees were believed to be places that deities would pos-

Figure 8. Atsuko Ikeda (b. 1931), the *saishu* or highest priestess—an elder sister of the present emperor—marches in a procession during a *shikinen sengū* ritual. She carries branches of a type of tree regarded as sacred into the new sanctuary, on the day following the transfer of the sacred mirror (October 6, 2013). She has been serving as the *saishu* of Ise Jingū since 1988.

sess temporarily when invoked and invited. A wooden pillar and a tree are common images for the cosmic center in Asian shamanic traditions, of which Shinto is one (Fig. 8). I can also say that every Jingū priest, including the one of highest rank, is tested one day before each of the three important annual rites at the Grand Shrine to see if he is qualified to conduct them (Fig. 9). The test is a ritual of divination known as *miura*. It is documented in the *Kōtai-Jingū gishikichō*, and it continues to this day. The procedure is conducted by three selected priests. The first of the three calls a potential celebrant by his given name. The second whistles by inhaling. Then, the third priest makes a sound by striking a wooden board with a wooden stick. Jingū priests call this wooden board *kotoita* (a zither-board). If these three actions happen smoothly, then the priest who was called by his given name bows. He has passed the test. The next priest is then called by his given name, and the procedure is repeated until all the priests have been tested. If a name is skipped and not called, or if no sound is produced by whistling or by the wooden stick on the wooden board, that priest is considered unqualified to serve and must go home.[43] Needless to say, the priests being tested are tense. To Jingū priests, the presence of the *kami* is real. They feel it, one can tell, but they

43. Ken'ichi Yano, *Ise Jingū: Shirarezaru Mori no Uchi* (The Ise Grand Shrine: Inside the Unknown Sacred Forest Shrine) (Tokyo: Kadokawa sensho, 2006), 91–92.

Figure 9. A group of priests sits in silence, on May 31, 2012, during a purification ceremony called *ōharai*, in which one priest will recite a Shinto prayer on behalf of all. *Ōharai* is held on the last day of the months of January, April, May, June, September, October, November, and December to prepare priests for conducting major rituals of the month that follows.

do not indulge in talking about gods. They are engaged in their assigned tasks. They prepare sacred food every day for the gods without ever striking a match to set a fire for cooking. They rub wooden sticks to make their fires with frictional heat. They are allergic to innovation, wholehearted in their belief and service, and genuinely concerned lest Shinto and its Grand Shrine become implicated ever again in politics.

Still, one senior Jingū priest whom I interviewed told me that, "if there were no Shinto shrines and no emperor in Japan, then Japan is not Japan anymore." I have not asked priests about their views of this relationship, but over time I have developed a sense of their thinking and their feelings. In November 2009, a senior priest said in conversation that the priesthood has been "entrusted with Jingū by the emperor. Jingū is the shrine of the emperor. We are humbly looking after Jingū for him with this in our mind: that one day a time will come to return Jingū to the emperor." Somewhere in that sentiment, it appears, is an interpretation of the spatial separation that Emperor Sujin put between himself and his divine ancestor Amaterasu and of how, someday, a descendant of Sujin's may bridge and resolve it. In Japanese, the priest's word that I have translated as "entrusted" is *oazukarishiteiru*, a humble form of *azukaru* ("to look after," "to keep"). Since having that conversation, I have heard this same usage at Jingū occasionally and have learned that the priest's view is commonly shared. In March 2012, during

Figure 10. Emperor Akihito and Empress Michiko wave to people welcoming them to Ise on March 27, 2014. During March 25–28, the emperor and empress visited Mie prefecture for private visits to the newly rebuilt shrines of Ise Jingū.

an interview with an associate priest in his midfifties, I was told that "there are things that priests of younger generations at Jingū do not know much." I asked whether he meant "something like *oazukarishiteiru*." He looked surprised and said, "Yes, you know something that is not known [by visitors to Jingū]. These days, [even] young priests are not much aware of it, so I need to teach them." He meant, of course, his need to teach them that the priesthood looks after Ise Jingū for the emperor (Fig. 10). But he may have meant also that we all need to learn that Shinto is about continuity, renewal, and restoration in the face of disastrous change.

And so, I wonder, is it too much to ask that scholars, seventy years after Victory in Japan Day, take seriously, at last, what Shinto has offered for many centuries, in its reverent silence, to Japan? Let me conclude, in the spirit of this symposium, by recalling advice to historians about their responsibilities, written by a great British historian a few years before the outbreak of World War II:

If the historian can rear himself up like a god and judge, or stand as the official avenger of the crimes of the past, then one can require that he shall be still more godlike and regard himself rather as the reconciler than as the avenger; taking it that his aim is to achieve the understanding of the men and parties and causes of the past, and that in this understanding, if it can be complete, all things will be ultimately reconciled. . . . Studying the quarrels of an ancient day he can at least seek to understand both parties to the struggle and he must want to understand them better than they understood themselves; watching them entangled in the net of time and circumstance he can take pity on them—these men who perhaps had no pity for one another; and, though he can never be perfect, it is difficult to see why he should aspire to anything less than taking these men and their quarrels into a world where everything is understood and all sins are forgiven.[44]

44. Herbert Butterfield, *The Whig Interpretation of History* (1931; repr., London: Norton, 1965), 2–3.

EXCELLENCE IS BY NO MEANS ENOUGH

Intellectual Philanthropy and the Just University

Stanley N. Katz

Last year, a valued former student bludgeoned me into agreeing to be keynote speaker for a celebration at the university where he now teaches. The colloquium, called to mark a special founding anniversary, was to be entitled "Higher Education in and for a Just Society." With not a clue what I would talk about, I foolishly submitted my own title: "What Would It Mean to Be a 'Just' University?" I had planned to write the speech over the summer but of course did not. I was, though, fortunate to have a brilliant research assistant who would read selected texts on justice and on universities for me and let me know which would be worth my time. So, just after Labor Day in September, I ruminated on the texts he recommended and set about to write.

I took the photocopied texts with me on a train to Washington, D.C., that left my hometown—Princeton, New Jersey—at 6:45 A.M. on September 11, 2001. I intended to read on the way down and to begin writing on my laptop on the way back from a day-long meeting at the Urban Institute, a meeting about research on the subject of philanthropy. Like everyone else, I was mugged around

Originally published in *Common Knowledge* 8.3 (Fall 2002): 427–38. © 2002 by Duke University Press.

Common Knowledge 25:1–3
DOI 10.1215/0961754X-7299342

9:10 A.M.—just as I reached a friend's office in Dupont Circle. I spent about an hour watching the world fall apart on television before it dawned on me that I should try to get home to Princeton before Washington shut down. I was, of course, already too late. When I arrived at Union Station (having taken the Metro against my friend's advice) about 10:30 A.M., I found the station in the process of closing. I was forced into the plaza in front of the station, where I seemed to be the only person without a cell phone—and for the first time I felt hopelessly isolated without this technology. I walked back to Dupont Circle, had lunch with my friends, then checked into a hotel so I could continue to watch American life implode. I discovered that trains would start up again at 4 P.M. and took the Metro (nearly empty) to Union Station, where I caught the first Amtrak heading north.

Imagine yourself trying to write about justice and universities and what they have to do with each other on that train on that day. I could not write a word. I spent the trip asking myself if there was anything in my religious or philosophical repertoire that could sustain the concept of justice. As of 6:30 P.M., when the train stopped to let me off at Princeton Junction (and me alone—the crew was responding to individual requests for service), I could not come up with a thing. I still cannot, really; and I suppose that, for me, this is the most profound damage of September 11th. My moral universe was rendered dysfunctional, and has been slow to recover. I envy those who seem to have come through the experience with renewed confidence in justice, humankind, God, and the United States. My friend David Halberstam wrote a beautiful prose poem in praise of the United States as a nation and published it in *Vanity Fair*. I admired the writing but did not share his affirmation. My mood—despair, uncertainty, irresolution—is closer to the dark thoughts of my colleague Toni Morrison, whose memorial statement, delivered at a Princeton service for the victims of the September 11th attacks, appeared in the same issue as David's essay.

But the speech I had to deliver was not going away. The things that I had thought I might say seemed inadequate under the circumstances. It was more than a week before I was able to set pen sensibly to paper. When I finished a first draft, a colleague asked what I was writing about and I told him my topic: the Just University. His immediate response was, "Well, I guess we have to put that off for the moment." Though attempts to recover from my own sense of despair have been at best partial, I would like to argue that we should not set aside consideration of what justice, the university, and intellectual life generally have to do with each other, not even for a moment. What would have been a complete answer to the problem a year ago would no longer be complete today. What I want to do, then, is deal both with the ways in which the answer is the same and with the ways in which the answer must be different now.

The Just University

What would it mean to be a just university? is a question that might have two inflections. First, it could be taken as a question about what it would mean for the processes and practices within a university to take place justly. I think that it is fairly clear that in order for it to be just, a university, as a social institution, has to ensure that the way it behaves satisfies the minimal threshold of justice that we expect of all our social institutions. Consider, simply, that the university is a place where the process of employment takes place. Just as for any other employer, it would be unjust for a university to discriminate on the basis of race, ethnicity, gender, or religion against faculty and staff in its practices of hiring and promotion. It would be unjust of a university not to ensure a work environment free from sexual harassment and threats. It would be unjust for a university to refuse adequate health benefits to its employees. We in the United States demand just behavior, in this way, of corporations, and there is no reason to exempt universities from these demands. The university is, after all, legally a corporation, though of a very special sort, and at the least it must be a just corporation.

Or consider that universities are frequented by all sorts of people, some with disabilities. It would be unjust for universities not to make reasonable efforts to allow the disadvantaged full access to their facilities: there is no reason to exempt universities from a demand we make of city buses. Or finally, consider the equally uncontroversial notion that a university is a locus of research. It would be unjust for a university to allow its researchers to conduct experiments on human subjects without informing them of the risks they run—there is no reason to exempt universities from a demand we make even of tobacco companies.

There is, in other words, a minimal level of justice that universities must satisfy, as must all other social institutions in civilized societies. This way of interpreting the question focuses on what one might call a procedural notion of justice in the university. A good example is the campaign waged by university students against the sale of insignia apparel manufactured in sweatshops. The movement had its beginnings in 1996 and 1997, when the problem came to public notice after the revelation that Kathie Lee Gifford's line of clothing was made in Honduran sweatshops and after Thai immigrants were discovered working under substandard conditions in California. In July 1998, students from about thirty universities established the United Students Against Sweatshops, which described itself as "an informal but cohesive international coalition of campuses and individual students working on anti-sweatshop and Code of Conduct campaigns." Numerous universities responded positively to student pressure. Texas A&M University, for instance, went on record that it "recognizes that all people have rights at work, including the right to be treated with respect and dignity, the right to be recognized and rewarded fairly for performance, and the right to a work environment free from discrimination and harassment. The university is committed to these rights. All people at Texas A&M University are expected to treat each other in accordance with these rights."[1] In another example of student concern with procedural justice, protests reminiscent of those in the late sixties and early seventies have been staged recently in the United States in order to urge universities to treat their lowest-paid employees better. At Princeton, where I teach, the Workers' Rights Organizing Committee mounted a campaign to secure "respect, a fair wage, an end to outsourcing and casualization, and the provision of fair and affordable benefits for all of Princeton's employees." At Harvard, students pointed out that workers "can't eat prestige," and the students struggled alongside employees to encourage the university to pay the minimum living wage (calculated at $10.25 per hour in the Cambridge area).

Both of these movements have had an impact. On several campuses, students have managed to persuade university administrators to make public the names of companies producing insignia clothing and even to implement codes of conduct requiring these companies to disclose information about their employment practices. (About two years ago, Duke University ended contracts with twenty-eight companies that did not fulfill the terms of its code of conduct.) At Harvard, it took three weeks of sitting-in at venerable Massachusetts Hall, but by May 2001, student protesters had forced the university to endorse a $10.25 minimum wage. Admittedly, selling clothing and employing nonacademic workers are not central to what universities do in the way that teaching and research are, but universities should do such things justly nonetheless. I would add that universities need to be vigilant in determining what it means for a process or practice to take place justly and, moreover, in expanding the range of processes and practices that must be governed by precepts of minimal procedural justice. Universities should be held to a higher standard than that to which corporations, and perhaps even governments, are held. It is this notion that Princeton's former president Harold Shapiro was indirectly giving voice to when he wrote in January 1999 that "one aspect of a student's moral education lies not in the curriculum but in the behavior of the faculty, staff, and administration and in the policies of the institution. Students will observe . . . how the University treats its employees. . . . Students will be smart enough to discern if the University remains a symbol of enlightenment or an institution whose defining ambition is to sustain the status quo and its own special privileges."[2]

1. "Our Statement of Vision and Values," in *About Texas A&M University*, available at www.tamu.edu/oo/data /about.html.

2. Harold Shapiro, "Liberal Education, Moral Education: Can—and Should—a University Teach Its Students to Be Better Citizens and Better People?" *Princeton Alumni Weekly*, January 27, 1999.

Justice and/or Excellence

I have just noted that we expect universities to be fairer than other institutions, but even so, this procedural approach does not do much to distinguish universities from other social institutions or to explain the special resonance that the question *What would it mean to be a just university?* has for us. Most of us associated with universities believe that they are special institutions, with a unique role and unique virtues. We believe so because we think that the university is in manifold ways the provider of common benefits and the doer of social good. These thoughts suggest a second question, or a second inflection of the first: *What sorts of things would it be just for a university to do in pursuit of its basic mission?* Or, as Aristotle might have put it, *What would it mean to do justly those things that are inherent in the very nature of a university?* I now want to take, in other words, a substantive (as opposed to procedural) approach of justice in the university. I want to ask what sorts of things it would be normatively just for a university to do.

This second approach presupposes that the just university's role is to help in the achievement of social goals and thus requires that we consider what our societies need done in order to survive and prosper and progress. Society needs a strong economy; let universities give people the skills to build it and make the technological advances it depends on for expansion. Society needs to cure diseases; let universities investigate their causes and find cures for them. Society needs affordable energy; let universities discover how to provide it. The production of such public goods is probably the demand of universities most commonly heard, though not everyone is as blunt about it as Frances D. Ferguson, speaking at a 1988 panel titled "Keeping America Competitive: The Role of Education." "A liberal arts education," Ferguson said, "emphasizes the creative thinking needed to produce new technologies and marketing strategies, the global perspective that explains the cultural differences costing America its competitive edge, and the ethical responsibility that will help companies produce products to meet human needs."[3] As Arthur Cohen has observed, such claims are double-edged:

Higher education's requests for continually increased funding rest on a combination of premises: direct contributions to the economy, enhanced productivity yielded by trained workers, and progress toward an equitable society by providing everyone with opportunity to advance. Its weakest arguments from an economic perspective are that it should be supported because of the intrinsic educational value that its students gain. Education for its own sake is perceived as a consumption item. Institutions and programs showing measurable economic and social

---

3. Quoted in Mortimer R. Kadish, *Toward an Ethic of Higher Education* (Stanford, CA: Stanford University Press, 1991), 191 n. 3.

benefits are much easier to defend than are those claiming to have value in and of themselves. Many scholars have contended that higher education is more than an engine of economic activity, that it is the home of ideas, the archive of a people's culture. But those arguments have few friends in the legislatures.[4]

For me, the larger and more important point, one Cohen hints at but does not fully develop, is that higher education, in the United States and elsewhere, has gone too far in the direction of such functionalism. The most powerful recent critique of this trend has been the late Bill Readings's brilliant and eccentric book *The University in Ruins* (1996). Readings begins by arguing that "the wider social role of the University as an institution is now up for grabs. It is no longer clear what the place of the University is within Society nor what the exact nature of that Society is [so that] the changing institutional form of the University is something that intellectuals cannot afford to ignore." His basic argument is that the university has become "a transnational bureaucratic corporation" and that the "current crisis of the University in the West proceeds from a fundamental shift in its social role and internal systems, one which means that the centrality of the traditional humanistic disciplines to the life of the University is no longer assured." The result is what Readings calls the University of Excellence: "Excellence exposes the pre-modern traditions of the University to the force of market capitalism. . . . This classic free-market maneuver guarantees that the only criterion of excellence is performativity in an expanded market." Readings contends that all that the new educational system requires "is for activity to take place, [for] the empty notion of excellence refers to nothing other than the optimal input/output ratio in matters of information." It would be easy to reject Readings as a very radical critic of Western higher education, but I think he is fundamentally correct in his identification of the problematic character of the University of Excellence. For me, as for Readings, the problem is one of reconceiving the university "once the story of liberal education has lost its organizing center—has lost, that is, the idea of culture as the object . . . of the human sciences."[5]

The problematic University of Excellence requires further attention, but I want to return for now to the functionality of the university. Even a utilitarian understanding of what it would mean to be a just university does not necessarily imply that universities can furnish society with all its needs and solve all its problems. Much is simply beyond the university's capacity; and what it cannot do, it should not be accused of injustice for not doing. Nevertheless, a university

4. Arthur M. Cohen, *The Shaping of American Higher Education: Emergence and Growth of the Contemporary System* (San Francisco: Jossey-Bass, 1998), 432–33.

5. Bill Readings, *The University in Ruins* (Cambridge: Harvard University Press, 1996), 2, 3, 10, 38, 39.

will be a minimally just one to the extent that it does what it can to serve its society. And on the whole, universities accept this assessment of their role.

There is a second and quite different way to fulfill the university's obligation of substantive justice. Those taking this second approach explicitly reject the idea that a university should serve its community in anything like the direct way I have so far been outlining. Kenneth Minogue puts this rejection with particular force:

It is of the essence of public discussion that, beginning with some such entity as the state or the nation, it takes the form of fitting whatever it deals with into some larger harmony. The very form of the discussion impels us to regard as fundamental the question: what is the function (or place, role, or purpose) of the university? We begin, in other words, by preparing a Procrustean bed for the luckless object of our thought. And the result is that universities are required to fit a variety of functions sponsored by a variety of political and cultural interests: advocacy or prediction has recently taken them to be powerhouses of industrial society, institutions of "social criticism," promoters of the rate of industrial growth, "society's response to its troubled sense of something profoundly wrong," and much else.[6]

Therefore, Minogue concludes, "to treat universities simply as institutions which provide educational services for society is like treating a Ming vase as a cut glass flower bowl: plausible, but crass."[7] In a similar vein, my late friend Edward Shils denounced as a dangerous mistake the attempt of universities "to be all things to all men, more pleasing and accommodating to the external world, or more preoccupied with changing or abolishing the condition of the external society."[8] Both these positions are recognizably of the 1970s, taken up in reaction against what Minogue and Shils saw as perversions of the fundamental role of the university by antiwar and social activists—by those supporting diversity in every facet of university life and advocating the conversion of the university into a self-conscious promoter of radical social change. But more recent agendas for social action on the part of students have mainly focused on internal, procedural justice in the university; recently we have seen less pressure on universities to be active politically outside their institutional walls. *The Closing of the American Mind* seems out of date, even quaint, with respect to American universities at the beginning of the twenty-first century.

It may be that the more helpful question to ask at this troubled point in our history is not what it would mean for a university to be just, but rather

6. Kenneth R. Minogue, *The Concept of a University* (Berkeley: University of California Press, 1973), 1–2.

7. Minogue, *Concept of a University*, 78.

8. Edward A. Shils, *The Order of Learning: Essays on the Contemporary University*, ed. Philip G. Altbach (New Brunswick, NJ: Transaction, 1997), 68.

what it would mean for a university to be good—not *good* in Readings's sense of excellent but good or virtuous in the Greek philosophical sense of fulfilling well the inherent purpose of the institution. For Shils, academic goodness would be "improving the stock of ordered knowledge and rational judgment."[9] For Minogue, goodness would be full acceptance that, "in the academic world, the only relevant criterion is that of truth or falsity." "Effectiveness" would no longer be the academic norm:

> Truth is very frequently a part of effectiveness, but by no means the only part (or indeed, in many cases, the main part). In practice, it is often worthwhile to judge a statement as mean or generous, consoling or hurtful, reactionary or progressive, helpful or harmful: academically speaking, such things are irrelevant. If this is so, then there will be many circumstances in which it will be beside the point—"academic" is the word commonly used—to spend time arguing about the falsity of a belief that obviously serves us perfectly well.[10]

For Minogue and Shils, universities must centrally concern themselves with those practices that lead to their being derisively called "ivory towers": teaching for the sake of passing on what is already known and doing research for the sake of disinterestedly learning more. John Rawls has observed that "justice is the first virtue of social institutions, as truth is of systems of thought."[11] But in the view of academic conservatives, Rawls is wrong: truth—its pursuit and acquisition—is the first (and possibly the only) virtue in the university context.

I am aware, of course, that I have caricatured these two approaches to the question of substantive justice and the university. Sophisticated defenders of either position will concede something to those holding the other one, and all would probably accept in theory that universities should meet the standards of procedural justice that I outlined earlier. But what are we to do with this broad divergence in approaches? One answer would be to split the difference, and I would hazard the guess that most educators would like to do so. That a just university is one that plays a role in serving its society appears to be self-evidently right, though the tasks demanded and tasks undertaken have varied historically. When universities have refused to discharge some alleged social responsibility, the refusal has generally been to perform specific actions—such as undertaking classified government research or training students for military service—that those universities believe to be at odds with their specific institutional sense of substantive justice. Universities, especially the research universities with which I am mostly concerned here, can only do so much in the name of justice before they cease to be universities and become something else. There are some demands

9. Shils, *Order of Learning*, 68.

10. Minogue, *Concept of a University*, 84.

11. John Rawls, *A Theory of Justice*, rev. ed. (Cambridge: Harvard University Press, 1999), 3.

made of universities, typically in the name of someone's version of social justice, that, if fully satisfied, would either deform the shape of the university and distort its mission or expose it to political reaction and ultimately render it incapable of serving society at all. We all believe in this red line, even if we disagree as to where it must be drawn. Universities must tread the fine line between the giving of themselves that makes them just and the reserving of themselves that keeps them universities.

Educational Justice

Demands made for universities to be more just often come from students, and tend to deal either with research on the part of academic staff or with the business practices of administrators. But the university is also a teaching institution, and the shift of emphasis in universities from undergraduate to graduate teaching should be on the agenda for anyone concerned with our subject. The shift in emphasis is, I think, basically a consequence of the rise of the University of Excellence. But Julie Reuben makes the historical point that higher education, at least in America, lost its commitment to the place of values in the education of undergraduates a long time ago. She argues that, in the transition from the moral education of nineteenth-century colleges to the scientific-utilitarian education of twentieth-century universities, the

> separation of fact and value became both a powerful and a problematic concept in twentieth-century intellectual life. It has often been invoked as a normative guide for scholars. Its normative status is reinforced by the structure of modern higher education, which makes the separation of morality and knowledge seem a "natural" part of intellectual life.[12]

But it is not just that the moral-religious purpose of higher education has all but disappeared from secular universities. The fundamental focus of the enterprise has shifted from the instruction of the young to the creation of useful knowledge.

Matters need not have been so. In his inaugural address to the University of St. Andrews in 1867, John Stuart Mill asserted that there is "a tolerably general agreement about what an University is not. It is not a place of professional education." Mill believed that the university was a place of liberal education, a site where literature and science could both flourish, a training ground for the elite, "a system of education . . . not intended for the many [since] it has to kindle

12. Julie A. Reuben, *The Making of the Modern University: Intellectual Transformation and the Marginalization of Morality* (Chicago: University of Chicago Press, 1996), 268.

the aspirations and aid the efforts of those who are destined to stand forth as thinkers about the multitude." It was a place that fostered moral and religious values, he said, though "the moral or religious influence which an University can exercise, consists less in any express teaching, than in the pervading tone of the place." And Mill continued:

The proper business of an University [is] not to tell us from authority what we ought to believe, and make us accept the belief as a duty, but to give us information and training, and help us form our own belief in a manner worthy of intelligent beings, who seek for truth at all hazards, and demand to know all the difficulties, in order that they may be better qualified to find, or recognize, the most satisfactory mode of resolving them.[13]

A more recent gloss on the same idea is reflected in Donald Kennedy's praise of Edward Shils:

A clearly discernible theme in Shils's book is that the primary ethical test is the teacher's capacity to put the student's interests first. Its basis is the presumption, which I believe is beyond argument, that members of the professoriate are following a calling in which the central purpose is generational improvement. The university is an institution that exists to advance the culture, both by acquiring new knowledge and by disseminating received knowledge in ways that inspire young people to use it—both creatively and constructively. In that way professors are agents for making society better than it was, generation by generation.[14]

I hope my point begins to come clear. If we are to be just in our substantive educational purposes, our first responsibility is to be just in our teaching of students, especially undergraduates, and to inculcate in them the capacity to determine what, by their own lights, justice is. This kind of educating is, however, precisely what the University of Excellence does not do well, and without the recovery of this essential tradition in higher education, I think that we will fail in our basic commitment to justice. But the failure to educate, however fearful the prospect of it, is not the only such failure that I dread. Moreover, no education, however poor, will impede a secular saint, and no depth of moral education will inexorably occasion one. The passages following are culled from Albert Schweitzer's autobiography:

Even while I was a boy at school it was clear to me that no explanation of the evil in the world could ever satisfy me; all explanations, I felt, ended

13. John Stuart Mill, *Inaugural Address Delivered to the University of St. Andrews* (London: Routledge, 1994), 5, 65, 76, 80.

14. Donald Kennedy, *Academic Duty* (Cambridge: Harvard University Press, 1997), 68.

in sophistries, and at bottom had no other object than to minimize our sensitivity to the misery around us.

But however concerned I was with the suffering in the world, I never let myself become lost in brooding over it. I always held firmly to the thought that each one of us can do a little to bring some portion of it to an end.

I am also pessimistic about the current world situation. . . . I feel that we are on a fatal road, that if we continue to follow it, it will bring us into a new "Dark Ages." I see before me, in all its dimensions, the spiritual and material misery to which mankind has surrendered.

And yet I remain optimistic. . . . I am confident that the spirit generated by truth is stronger than the force of circumstances. In my view no other destiny awaits mankind than that which, through its mental and spiritual disposition, it prepares for itself. Therefore I do not believe that it will have to tread the road to ruin right to the end.[15]

Call for Projects

These passages from Schweitzer lead us, inevitably after September 11th, beyond the academy's protective walls. To this point in my exposition, I have made it seem that the academy is a place for the pursuit of righteousness, though within limits we have not as a community thoroughly explored. Now, I want to suggest that making our universities just is no longer enough. Partly I am responding to, and partly in agreement with, Jeffrey Perl's temperate indictment, in these pages (8.1: 2–5), of justice—or the fixation on justice—as itself an impediment to peace. But mostly I am suggesting that what is demanded of us as academics may be less than what is demanded of us as intellectuals. There has been, again since September 11th, a series of appeals in print for something new under the sun: "intellectual philanthropy" could be a tentative name for it. Lorraine Daston has argued in the *London Review of Books* that our public problems are now hermeneutic more than technical and has expressed the hope that "students of the symbolic" will now deal with "enormously complex problems" of commensuration that we have been ignoring and can no longer ignore. Keith Thomas has lectured the British Academy on "the need for scholars to dispel mutual incomprehension," a need that he traces historically but that he goes on to assert is at the present time more pressing than ever. Similar assessments have come from journalists like Flora Lewis in the *Herald-Tribune* and (in a rather less embraceable way) Peter Beinart in the *New Republic*. Universities cannot in themselves be

15. Albert Schweitzer, *Out of My Life and Thought: An Autobiography*, trans. Antje B. Lemke (New York: Henry Holt and Company, 1990), 279–80.

expected to take on tasks such as those defined by these writers, but intellectuals without frontiers—working together through journals, centers, and ad hoc associations—can certainly do so, and must.

There is a tradition in *Common Knowledge* of editors and editorial board members writing calls for papers that are signed and intensely personal. I would like to take that tradition a step further and offer a call for *projects* in the same spirit but with perhaps a more urgent tone. I would like to call on the *Common Knowledge* community—a group that includes superb hermeneuts—to take the lead and act now to clear away as many *specifically intellectual* obstacles to commensuration, communication, and comprehension as is humanly plausible. Scholars in the humanities and human sciences have particular skills, much as the physicians who volunteer for Médecins sans Frontières do, to offer in times of crisis. Scholars are less uniquely talented at solving public problems than at clarifying what a problem (as opposed to a pseudo-problem) is and what counts as a solution. Our task, then, is to find and fund limited and well-defined projects that will apply our theoretical training and experience to urgent problems whose full complexities have as yet gone untended. My hope is that readers of this journal will respond with more or less detailed proposals that the editors and members of the editorial board can assist them in developing to fruition. For if we do not undertake these vital hermeneutic tasks today, who will do so and when?

THE LATEST FORMS OF BOOK-BURNING

G. Thomas Tanselle

The present time will be regarded in the future as an age of book destruction. And the irony is that this destruction is being accelerated by those whose intention is to preserve books or facilitate their use. The danger arises from two sources: the effort to microfilm (and thus "save") brittle books, and the desire to convert texts to electronic form (and thus supposedly make them more convenient to examine). Both goals, which have their laudable aspects, have generally been promoted by persons who assume that "information" (that is, verbal texts) can be transferred without loss to alternative media. They often speak, for example, of "reformatting" texts, as if one "format" can simply be exchanged for another. The result of this attitude is that the original physical form in which a text appeared is not valued; once the transfer to another form is made, the book—so the thinking goes—can be discarded. Thousands of copies of books have already been destroyed as a consequence, and many millions may face the same fate in the near future. What is shocking about this destruction is that deliberate policy decisions have brought it about. Book-burnings of the past were small compared to the potential this one has.

Originally published in *Common Knowledge* 2.3 (Winter 1993): 172–77. © 1993.

Common Knowledge 25:1–3

DOI 10.1215/0961754X-7299354

Of course, the brittle and crumbling paper in a large proportion of books printed after 1850 is rightly a matter of concern. In 1986 the Commission on Preservation and Access was established in Washington to study the problem and take some action. Since then, supported by large amounts of public and private money, the commission has coordinated the microfilming of about half a million volumes. This achievement is not an unalloyed blessing, however, because the copies microfilmed generally do not survive the process. Normally the first step of the procedure is to chop off the spines ("guillotining"), leaving a stack of loose leaves, since the books are frequently too brittle to be opened flat without the leaves cracking at the gutter. Libraries do not usually wish to retain the mutilated fragments, which are therefore thrown away. Some of the copies that vanish in this way were in poor condition before being sent for microfilming; others, though on acidic paper, were in relatively good condition and, if not in high demand for research, might have remained in good condition for a long time. But in any case the destruction of these copies has been speeded up by the process; they are sacrificial offerings in the name of "textual preservation." The term "preservation" in the title of the Commission on Preservation and Access was never intended to refer to preservation of physical objects containing texts, but only to texts abstracted from objects; and in practice this "preservation" has been an agent of destruction for the objects. *Slow Fires* is the title of the commission's widely publicized film about the self-destruction of books containing acidic paper; the copies used in the commission's program of microfilming, however, are doomed to a much swifter conflagration.

Why this situation is undesirable, and how its severity could have been mitigated (indeed, still can be), I shall comment on in a moment. But first I think it is useful to note the other—and analogous—source of danger for books, computerization. The frequently adduced vision of the bookless (or relatively bookless) library of the future is based not only on the notion that most new verbal texts will be disseminated in machine-readable form but also on the prediction that many book texts of the past will be incorporated into immense data bases. There is no question about the convenience of such data bases, which would bring texts to readers' computer terminals (however far away the books containing those texts happened to be located) and would make the texts more readily searchable than even the best-indexed books. But many librarians, as well as the users of libraries, may be misled by this convenience into believing that the books from which the texts come are no longer necessary and can be disposed of. The administration of the Library of Congress now apparently thinks of a library's stacks simply as a "passive warehouse"; one member of the LC staff dreams of a future Library of Congress "emptied of most routine books and magazines and other routine paper" and believes that those who are concerned about physical books are worshiping false "idols."[1] (And the space saved by disposing of books is often seen as a desirable by-product; for this reason some librarians may not wish to retain books that have been microfilmed or re-keyboarded even if they are in usable condition.) Not only the movement to microfilm brittle books, therefore, but also the interest in converting the text of any book—brittle or not—to electronic form poses a threat to the survival of the massive book stock now filling thousands of miles of shelving.

Both these dangers arise from the assumption that books are mere containers for texts, which can be repackaged with no loss. What is required to counteract the pressure for disposing of books is a broader recognition that the artifactual evidence of books has its own story to tell—that books as objects (and not just their so-called contents) are "texts" from the past. Even some of the people who have argued along these lines have failed to present the full implications of their position. The argument one often hears for saving books after their texts are transferred to another form is that bookmaking and book design are significant categories of craft or of visual art and that books as objects—like other artifacts—must be included in any attempt to understand the culture of an age. Another argument frequently made is that the shape, the weight, the feel, even the smell, of old books are significant elements in the effort to recapture the past. These points are certainly correct, but they provide justification only for a relatively small number of "museums of the book" that would preserve representative examples of the craft of book production. They do not touch on the reasons why every copy of every book ought theoretically to be saved. One understands, of course, that it is unrealistic to expect all copies of books to survive—for the various vicissitudes of physical existence are bound to take their toll on all categories of artifacts. But there are reasons to lament the loss of any copy of a book and to advocate the preservation of as many copies as possible.

One reason is that books, like other physical objects, contain clues for reconstructing their own manufacturing history. And the details of that history are relevant not simply to the study of printing and publishing practices but also to the examination of textual accuracy (however one defines this concept). Analytical bibliographers have been demonstrating for at least a century the ways in which the processes of book production have affected the texts in books; and many of the evidences of the production process (such as shifts in paper stock, the structure of the gatherings, the substitution of one leaf for another) are available only in the original and not in any form of reproduction. Furthermore, copies of

1. See Robert Zich, "Idols in the Library," in *Research Collections in the Information Age*, ed. John Y. Cole (Washington: Library of Congress, 1990), 10–14. Linton Weeks, in "Brave New Library," *Washington Post Magazine*, 26 May 1991, 10–17, 27–31, quotes Zich as saying (irrelevantly) that in the future there will be technology that "duplicates all the virtues of the book." Among the relatively rare complaints in Grace Palladino's comment that the Library of Congress has "room enough for tourists but not books" ("Library of Congress Poses New Threats to Scholarships," *Chronicle of Higher Education*, 2 June 1993, A40; cf. the correspondence of 23 June, B3).

the same edition, or even of a single printing of an edition, cannot be assumed to be identical. Developments in printing-shop practices over the years have caused the primary kinds of variations among copies to differ from one period to another, but the general principle remains valid for all periods. Books are in this respect no different from other objects, for one can never take for granted the identity of any two manufactured objects, even if their producers intended them to be identical; and a cardinal rule of analytical bibliographers is that generalizations cannot responsibly be drawn about an edition until a large number of copies of that edition have been examined. Thus whenever a book is destroyed, no matter how many other copies of the edition still exist, there is the possibility that a unique source of evidence relating to its text is being lost.

This class of reasons for saving books stems from the usefulness of physical characteristics that the producers of books did not mean for readers to pay any attention to. But there is another kind of reason that emerges from a consideration of features intended to be noticed. The elements of book design—such as the quality of the paper, the size and shape of the leaves, the layout of the text on the pages, the style and size of the typefaces (or handwriting), and the material and design of the bindings—all convey meaning to the readers of books and play a role in the process of reading. Even when some of these features are partially recoverable from "reformatted" texts, the full impact of the original is lost—as when, in a microfilm or an electronically scanned image of a printed book, the texture of the inked type impressions and the paper are not recoverable, despite the fact that the text has been reproduced visually rather than re-keyboarded. Because verbal works employ an intangible medium, language, the characteristics of the tangible objects that serve to transmit verbal texts are not normally a part of the works themselves—though of course they can be, for sometimes authors create mixed-media works by combining words with visual effects. But even when a work is intended to be purely verbal, and its physical presentation not integral to it, that presentation often plays a role in readers' responses to the work. Any historical study of reading, therefore, or of literary production in its social setting, must take the whole physical object of the book into account (an observation as true of scroll and codex manuscripts as of printed books). And this kind of study has indeed aroused increasing interest in recent decades—a fact symbolized by the formation of a Society for the History of Authorship, Reading, and Publishing.

It is clear from both these lines of reasoning that the physical evidence in books is directly related to the effort to understand the texts in books. Most people who are attracted to books at all are interested in reading them, in deriving a "meaning" from their "contents"; and the only way to make large numbers of people concerned about saving books in their original forms is to make them aware of the intimate connections between the physical and the intellectual aspects of books. Readers in general do seem to recognize chat literature is not a tangible art form, since they know that verbal works are separable from any one of their physical manifestations. But what they conclude from this fact, all too often, is that one appearance of a text is as good as another, instead of realizing that the intangibility of verbal works makes imperative the scrutiny of every detail of the objects conveying verbal texts, for every detail is potentially a clue to the authenticity and interpretation of those texts. And if physical details are essential to reading, their preservation in as many copies as possible contributes to the goal of widespread textual "access"—an obvious desideratum proclaimed by all the microfilming, keyboarding, and scanning projects.

The practical question that follows is how to educate the reading public about this matter. The first step is to educate persons in positions of authority in the book world, persons whom the public understandably expects to have an enlightened view concerning the future of books. The prime group in this regard is librarians; but librarians, caught up in the excitement of planning for the electronic future, have not as a whole given adequate thought to the function of old books in that future. The point is not to wish them any less enthusiastic about computers; many of the changes computers are bringing, and will continue to bring, to the world of intellectual endeavor ought to be eagerly welcomed. There should be no regret, for instance, over the disappearance of the codex form for the publication of encyclopedias and other large reference works; in such a form as CD-ROM, they can be more easily searched and more efficiently kept up to date. What form other verbal works will take is an open question, and not one I am concerned with here. Most of the talk about a bookless future, or the death of the codex, has focused on new works, without much cognizance of the difference between new and old works. Whatever forms new works take will automatically become their historic forms, the original published sources for evidence about their texts (sources that must therefore be preserved for future use); but earlier works that first appeared in book form can never be fully divorced from that form, and the books must remain (by virtue of past action) the original published sources, with all their unique potential for revealing textually relevant information. If librarians, in planning for the future, were to make clear that the book stacks of the present must be maintained (indeed, treated with the same care now given "rare" books), alongside the machinery for increased electronic access to data bases, they would be helping not only to preserve the books but also—and in a powerful way—to educate the public. Librarians should of course be joined by the larger scholarly world in this effort, and it is a hopeful sign that the Modern Language Association of America (representing over thirty thousand literary scholars) has established an Ad Hoc Committee on the Future of the Print Record.

Another way in which the library and scholarly community could contribute generally to this educational process is by advocating the retention of brittle books after microfilming, regardless of their condition. Publicizing such a recommendation would help to make the point that the microfilming of books does not fully extract the useful information from them; yet it would not detract from the importance of taking some action to deal with the possibility that texts on brittle paper may disappear completely. It can hardly be denied that a microfilmed book is better than no book at all. But to state the dilemma in those terms grossly oversimplifies it. For example, the determination of the order in which books are selected for microfilming reminds one of the troubling issues raised by book-burnings in the past—though ironically complicated here by questions of technology, since the books not given top priority for microfilming may benefit, when their turn comes, from the development of less destructive procedures. A recent instance is the advent of the Gottschalk prismatic camera, which can photograph the facing pages of a book opened at an angle of only sixty degrees; if widely used, it would significantly reduce the damage inflicted by microfilming. But whatever state a book is in—even a pile of loose and mutilated leaves, with large parts of the text missing—it still retains some bibliographical evidence not available in the microfilm, and conceivably not available in any other copy. (The only copy of the first American edition of *Moby-Dick* so far known to have the prefatory page of "Etymology" backed up by the second, not the first, page of "Extracts " happens to be the copy guillotined to produce loose leaves for use in typesetting the Hendricks House edition of 1952; fortunately the stack of loose leaves was saved.)

The Commission on Preservation and Access, with its enormous influence, could have served an important educational function if it had insisted, from the outset, that all microfilmed copies be saved—and had reinforced this demand by providing a warehouse in which such copies could be kept in retrievable order if the libraries that owned them did not wish to retain them. This action would have dramatized the importance of the original books and might have convinced some librarians to keep them after microfilming. In any case, it would have constituted an emphatic statement that microfilmed books are not the equivalent of original books; and it might have caused a few librarians to turn additional mutilated books over to the established repository and might have made others feel guilty for not doing so (and might have spurred the establishment of such warehouses in other countries). Although it is a pity that the commission did not make such a repository a part of its plan, it is not too late to establish one now, either under the commission's auspices or as an independent undertaking. In view of the vast sums of money that have been spent on microfilming, it does not seem unreasonable to allocate some funds, modest by comparison, for taking care of the important residue left behind by the project.

By one current estimate (in an NEH press release of 24 February 1993), eighty million books are "in peril" in the United States. As attention is paid to saving the texts in them, let us not forget the following simple propositions: Books are for reading. Book-reading is the activity of reconstructing the texts of intangible works from the physical evidences for them found in books. Every physical characteristic of every copy of every edition is potentially relevant for the activity of reading. Saving the texts of books is therefore only part of the task of saving the verbal heritage of the past; the objects themselves must also be saved.

Book-burning, in one form or another, will always be with us; but if we wish the future to thank us, we should not be satisfied until we have done everything we possibly can to counteract the process in all its forms.[2]

2. For elaboration of some of the points taken up here, see my "Reproductions and Scholarship," *Studies in Bibliography* 42 (1989): 25–54; *A Rationale of Textual Criticism* (Philadelphia: University of Pennsylvania Press, 1989); and *Libraries, Museums, and Reading* (New York: Book Arts Press, Columbia University [now Book Arts Press, University of Virginia], 1991). These pieces contain numerous references to other discussions.

PUBLISHING MATTERS

Hugh Kenner

Oxford, wrote Henry James, ". . . a kind of dim and sacred ideal of the western intellect." And the Oxford University Press? Its coat of arms saying *Dominus Illuminatio Mea,* The Lord My Light, surely a sacred light if not a dim one. Oxford dates "appointment of a printer to the University" from 1584, which is much closer to the start of the Gutenberg Era than to now. (The Press as something more than a print shop—as a publishing body—was chartered in 1636.) And at Oxford, last June, they took pains to remind Bill Clinton that the building he stood in to receive a token degree had been completed 120 years before George Washington was inaugurated.

So much by way of placing in perspective the American university press, an entity still largely undefined. Narrative details differ vastly. According to a wonderfully readable memoir, August Frugé's *A Skeptic Among Scholars,*[1] the pattern—first Printer, then Publisher—was exactly mapped out near Berkeley, though the two dates were—well, fuzzed: there was a printing plant pre-1870, an "editorial committee" by 1885, lists of scholarly publications by 1893, but not a *publishing* house until 1933. August, by the way, was the director who presided while the Cal Press changed from a print shop with a monograph sideline into a major academic publishing force.

Originally published in *Common Knowledge* 4.1 (Spring 1995): 89–94. © 1995.

1. *A Skeptic Among Scholars: August Frugé on University Publishing* (Berkeley: University of California Press, 1993).

That slow sidle toward being regarded as a real publisher was normal. The University of Toronto Press, when I was an undergraduate at Toronto in the early '40's, was still essentially a printing house. One of the things it printed was a massive two-volume anthology called *Representative Poetry*, edited by several Toronto faculty members and guaranteed fiscal viability thanks to the number of Toronto undergraduates who, year after year, were sternly required to buy it. Not exactly Publishing, no, not by Oxbridge tradition; still, a step up from job printing, assuming that any direction toward curricular needs is "up."

At California, guided by the Frugé memoir, we may discern a response to a more complex need. Monographs—"intensive studies of small but worthwhile topics," e.g., the Tasmanian Bandicoot, or some surviving American Indian language—were of lasting value to scholars "in fields that could make good use of publication in discrete segments—geology, the several life sciences, linguistics, some kinds of anthropology" (Frugé, 67–68). That was especially true at a very large university scattered among far-flung campuses. There were some forty series of monographs, and of the thousand-odd copies of each item printed, about half went to libraries on exchange. The rest sold, slowly, to experts who wanted them; maybe some nascent experts were graduate students.

As more and more *books* got added to California's list, the monographs came to look more and more like a side-issue. Eventually they ceased to be printed by letterpress; authors were asked to supply cleanly typed copy for offset printing of those library exchange copies. By 1994, after the advent of what is called desktop publishing, we can identify a pattern that has long been emerging. If profitable sales can't be envisaged—in general, if we're stuck with a rather small press run—good computer software and the laser printer make possible a product whose professional look can belie its low cost. "Cleanly typed copy," after all, looks like just what it is: typescript. But Times Roman pages, justified and hyphenated and complete with italics and boldface and different sizes for body-text and quotations, are now within the reach of anyone who can call up software and operate a keyboard. And it's possible, next, to argue that the author of such a document doesn't need a publisher at all. Such an author likely knows who and where the audience is, likely possesses a mailing list. But I anticipate. . . .

Something else that's important: a university press is generally, by definition, nonprofit. That means, no income tax; which in turn spells the importance, for university presses, of the 1980 *Thor Power Tool* decision of the Supreme Court. The Court was affirming an IRS policy about "inventory value;" concerning which we'd best cite a definition:

The "inventory value" of a new book is simply the capital investment you made to put that book into the warehouse—where it retains that value until it is sold or discarded. The total of the accumulated inventory values of all the books in your warehouse (or on consignment to distributor—but still legally "yours") at any given time is a major asset on your balance sheet (which reflects the "book value" of your publishing house . . . frequently quite different from its "fair market value").

—*The Huenefeld Guide Book to Publishing*, 343

For "book" substitute any manufactured and warehousable artifact and you'll glimpse the relevance of Thor Power Tools. A manufacturer of items like electric drills had been challenged by IRS over a common habit: depreciating, at intervals, the value of warehoused stock on the assumption that it was obsolescing by stages. (Publishers did that too.) But IRS held that "writing down" an inventory value, then taking a tax deduction for the loss, was all too easy a game. You're not entitled to claim a loss, said the ticky taxfolk, until you've actually lost the money, whether by selling the items for less than their inventory value, or else by discarding or destroying them, poof.

When the Court upheld that notion, then suddenly, over at Knopf, Simon & Schuster, Macmillan, Prentice-Hall, the cost of maintaining a backlist skyrocketed. Backlists correspondingly shrank. If it's not selling at a healthy rate, then remainder it—fast; claim the lost value as a tax deduction. (You've noticed books becoming unobtainble eighteen months after they were published? That's one reason why.) And several university presses—California and Duke were two—saw their opportunity. Being not-for-profit, hence not income-taxable, they could afford to maintain a backlist of titles that might command steady sales, on and on, albeit sales too small, in any given year, to give a for-profit publisher's accountant comfort. For example? For example, the Collected Works of an important, aging poet whose day would yet come.

That's one reason California took on Louis Zukofsky's forbidding life-work, the long poem called "*A.*" A New York publisher—Grossman—had been issuing installments in pressruns (doubtless) just big enough to gratify current curiosity. But the 826-page totality, the forty-year monster: that might well sell, yes, but down the road, and not quickly. A long-term backlist item? Not something for Grossman. California's beautifully produced volume is dated 1978; Louis almost lived to see it. Later, his lynx-eyed widow sent me a list of errata. She'd found exactly ten. Given the textual peculiarities of "*A,*" that's as nigh perfection as book production can likely come.

But in California's current catalogue you'll not find "*A.*" No; they've been clearing out what gets defined as "dead" stock, apparently not distinguishing a truly dead monograph (to invent an example, *The Reception of Swedish Literature in Upper Bosnia, 1870–90*) from a book like "*A*" that may find its market in another twenty years. Though not a university press book, *Finnegans Wake* may serve as an instance of the latter. It's a steady seller today, and a Penguin I have within reach lists sixteen printings of the precursor Viking Compass paperback in the fourteen years 1959–75. Anyone who'd predicted such a record at the time of the first edition, 1939, would have been certified insane. So would anyone who'd thought that a steady strong seller at New Directions would one day be, lo!—the hardcovered eight-hundred-page *Cantos* of Ezra Pound. But a staple of the list it now is, thanks to publisher James Laughlin, who stubbornly kept it in print during long-ago years when it hardly sold at all. Moral: be careful how you prune your backlist.

A pruned backlist isn't peculiar to California. In general, university presses are under severe pressure to hold expenses down, and backlists can be expensive when we factor in the cost of warehouse space. The pressure comes, of course, from a university that pays subsidies, may even underwrite losses. Corrected for enrollment and inflation, university budgets are characteristically down. Meanwhile, publishing costs per copy mount and mount. A letter from John G. Ryden, director of the Yale University Press, puts it like this:

> {Sales of scholarly books} have been declining relentlessly since federal support for library purchases stopped in 1970. Yale and every other university press in America has seen the sale of the scholarly monograph, for example, decline by two-thirds. Where we once expected to sell perhaps 2500, we now sell 8–900. Over the years smaller print runs pushed up costs and therefore prices in an ongoing spiral. Scholars virtually stopped buying books. Library budgets declined in the 70s; in the 80s they dropped again and serial purchases cut deeply into funds available to buy books. Sales of most reference works, documentary and literary editions, and other staples of university publishing declined comparably. During the 1980s paperback sales, upper level textbook sales, and sales to the trade—that is, the small top end of the general reading public to which some university press titles sell, remained buoyant. A sagging economy and declining student enrollment, especially in the humanities, have since hurt these formerly strong areas.

—J. G. R. to H. K., 9 June 1994

That puts the situation pretty plainly; and Stan Holwitz, an editor at California, confirms that the U.C. Press is constantly being urged from on high to liquidate all that stuff that isn't selling. On the other hand, Jack Goellner, director of the Johns Hopkins Press, claims that he's never eliminated backlist titles save for self-evident deadwood items that have sold zero copies for, say, three years. Warehousing costs, though, he confirms, are real, and *pruning* the inventory is a valid option. (He mentioned a book the stocked warehouse life of which, at the current rate of sale, could be measured in millennia.) So offer some surplus copies at a heavy discount, watch a sector of the warehousing costs plummet, but don't be in a hurry to purge the book from your list. Goellner thinks it's easy to over-estimate the burden of warehouse costs. You sell a few copies of a warehoused book, and you've made perhaps a few hundred dollars you didn't expect. Discontinue the book? You discontinue that kind of opportunity.

The University of California Press, by the way, is *huge.* Johns Hopkins is *small.* That does make comparisons tricky. It's a fair guess that the big place gets more of those flaky submissions than the small one; statistically likely, too, that some of the flakes get published. That complicates questions about a slow-moving backlist.

And, adds Mr. Ryden at Yale, "We publish twice as many books as we did a dozen years ago—80 then, 165 now. We try to make the list pay for itself, not each book, just the sum of them including the backlist. Without the backlist built over the last 85 years we couldn't pay our own way. Younger and smaller presses can't possibly pay their own way."

"Pay our own way": was that what he said? Yes. "We are paying our own way. Nothing new about that. We've been doing it for a couple of generations. The University has never supported this press, or underwritten losses."

"The University has never supported this press, or underwritten losses." I don't know if that's unique to Yale or not, but it's the only instance I've heard of. And notice that, regarding the clout of the backlist, Mr. Ryden stresses the 85 years it's been a-building: i.e., since a year when Mark Twain was still alive. Something else he goes on to stress is that no publisher who had to turn a profit and pay shareholders could afford a list like Yale's. But at Yale, "We meet the payroll, we pay suppliers, we generate next year's working capital, all from revenues from licenses and sales."

Meanwhile, he adds, commercial publishers "become more and more bottom-line oriented as they conglomerate. . . . Every one of the bigger university presses publishes books today . . . that a short generation ago would have been published by a leading commercial publisher." Such as? Oh, Atheneum, Scribner's, Harper & Bros., Macmillan. And today? Atheneum and Macmillan are no more; Scribner's is a sub-imprint of a conglomerate that goes under various names, most recently Viacom. But Harper?

"In the 1950s Harper & Bros. published Heidegger's *Being and Time,* and it was reviewed in the *N.Y. Times* and the *Herald-Tribune.* I doubt that the publisher at HarperCollins, the successor company owned by Rupert Murdoch, has ever heard of Heidegger. They'd never publish *Being and Time* today, and if they did, the papers wouldn't review it."

Back away from the catbird seat occupied by Yale, where something seems to be being done right and lo, a turbulent weather-map on which university presses are mere details. I have in front of me a letter that urges an extreme proposition: "Scholarly publishing must be isolated even from the scholarly market."

(That's because the scholarly market gets corrupted by political corruptness: "A book on James will sell only if 'cross-dressing' appears in the title.") So university presses "should be endowed, heavily subsidized, whatever, on the principle that scholarship . . . is a gargoyle meant for the eye of Heaven alone. The point of academic publishing shouldn't be to sell copies, but to place one copy each in the L. of C., the BL, and Bodley."

But an author equipped with desktop publishing technology could generate those three copies with three button-presses, then shoot them off by certified mail to Washington, London, Oxford, where they'd be acknowledged and likely discarded. No, it's not the manufacturing of copies that's in question; it's having "the imprint" to assure a client of the L. of C. or the BL that responsible people, engaged in a respectable process, have certified the book as worth attention. "We control," Ralph Rader would say, "The Imprint"; that was when he was a Chairman of the University of California Press Editorial Committee, a role in which I was privileged to succeed him; he'd emphasize the formality of The Imprint by a downward punch with an invisible Great Seal. Yes, control of The Imprint amounted to far more than control of the pressroom technology, never mind that many presses, like California, had begun as printing plants. It was important because the people who mattered Out There—readers, buyers, librarians—all trusted The Imprint.

I'll guess we're in for a generation of chaos, as the role of libraries gets redefined, and that of publishers, even that of printed paper. Today library catalogues are becoming on-line resources; it gets less important for your local library to have the book, now that a few keypresses can locate it in the next city. And—especially if it's a reference book—it gets less important for you to hold a printed copy in your hands once you can call up the entry you need on-screen.

I've written too many books to feel pressured toward downplaying them. But the role of books does get more and more specialized. Molly Bloom (1904) read herself to sleep with *Ruby: Pride of the Ring.* Today her great-granddaughter is likely getting a similar result from TV: one less job for the book. Today, too, only a few junk authors prosper; you know who they are, and they sell by the hundred thousand. Yet in Molly Bloom's time, junk authors were more numerous than even TV weatherpersons today. Thus, while bookstores bulge as always, the net count of salable authors decreases. So: more books than ever, also more that don't matter at all.

So the commercial picture. As for the academic one: it's inconceivable that it will be much longer dominated by Publish or Perish. As journals proliferate, it gets hard to point to anyone who can't get published. That will before long be as routine as was, once, combing one's hair. And communication? Once, those monographs were efficacious, notably in the sciences. How else register what was known about the Bandicoot? Today, in the sciences, books cease to matter. Communication on a fastbreaking front is quick and often electronic. The books come later. They are cribs, for latecomers, i.e., students.

Finally: once the twentieth century began, Authors Who'd Matter got more numerous, decade by decade, than they'd ever been before: start with Conrad and James and keep counting . . . and Sam Beckett was with us till nearly the century's last decade. You're empowered, now, to rephrase all the above propositions with respect to academic authors; also junk academic authors, who've been known, like the author of *Ruby*, to give their beneficiaries sleep.

UNE MACHINE À PENSER

Carlo Ginzburg

An engine that helps you to think; an engine to think with, to think about. But what else, one could ask, are research libraries for? May we say that there is something special about the Warburg Library?

I

I entered the Warburg for the first time in the summer of 1960. My mentor, Delio Cantimori, who was spending some time in London doing research, offered me a tour of the Library, commenting upon its peculiar arrangement. Before leaving the building we met Gertrud Bing (at the time, she was the Institute's director), who exchanged a few words with Cantimori.

They were old friends. Cantimori's connection with the Warburg went back to the thirties. In 1937 he had published an essay ("Rhetoric and Politics in Italian Humanism") in the first issue of the *Journal of the Warburg Institute* and had contributed to the *Bibliography of the Survival of the Classics*, also published by the Institute.[1] For many years he had been traveling across Europe, visiting

Originally published in *Common Knowledge* 18.1 (Winter 2012): 79–85. © 2012 by Duke University Press.

1. *A Bibliography of the Survival of the Classics*, vol. 2, *The Publications of 1932–1933* (London: Warburg Institute, 1938). Cantimori contributed forty entries, which are

not included in the bibliography of his writings found in Giovanni Miccoli, *Delio Cantimori. La ricerca di una nuova critica storiografica* (Torino: G. Einaudi, 1970). See also Delio Cantimori, "Rhetoric and Politics in Italian Humanism," trans. Frances Yates, *Journal of the Warburg Institute* 1.2

libraries and archives, looking for traces left by sixteenth-century Italian heretics. The outcome of this long, painstaking work was an epoch-making book (*Eretici italiani del Cinquecento*, 1939). It is not surprising that this highly impressive young historian (he was born in 1904) attracted the attention of the Warburgians (Gertrud Bing as well as, I presume, Edgar Wind). But Cantimori's allegiance to fascism in the thirties would have made this relationship complicated, if not utterly impossible. It must be noted that Cantimori's writings dealing with contemporary Italian and German politics, including his deep interest in the work of Carl Schmitt (whom he introduced to the Italian public), were not unrelated to his scholarly work.[2] Cantimori's essay "Rhetoric and Politics," for instance, was obviously inspired by his interest in contemporary propaganda, and vice versa.[3] After a tortuous and painful trajectory, he became close to, then a member of, the Italian Communist Party, which he left in 1956. His wife, Emma Cantimori Mezzomonti, had been an underground member of the Communist Party in the thirties. She later translated into Italian a selection of Aby Warburg's essays, with an introduction (her last essay) by Gertrud Bing.[4]

This relationship with the Warburg—a largely unexplored chapter of Cantimori's controversial biography—would repay closer scrutiny, but my concern here is different. Retrospectively, I am inclined to think that my first encounter with the Warburg Institute and its Library oriented (in many ways, mostly unconscious) my later involvement with them. At that time (May–June 1960), Cantimori had just published in *Annales* a long review of *Au coeur religieux du XVIème siècle*: a collection of essays by Lucien Febvre, the journal's former director and cofounder.[5] Cantimori opened his review with some autobiographical recollections, followed by a series of remarks, one of which drew a parallel between Febvre and Aby Warburg. Those two scholars and their respective scholarly traditions were (Cantimori noted) very different and nearly ignored each other, but they shared a rejection of traditional disciplinary boundaries, an impulse to convey the meaning of larger historical realities through significant details, and the art ("l'arte") of rescuing articulate human voices from apparently marginal documents.[6]

(October 1937): 83–102. A longer, unpublished Italian version is included in Cantimori, *Eretici italiani del Cinquecento*, ed. Adriano Prosperi (Torino: G. Einaudi, 1992): 485–511. Prosperi's preface is the best available introduction to Cantimori.

2. Carl Schmitt, *Principii politici del nazionalsocialismo*, ed. Delio Cantimori (Florence: Sansoni, 1935), 1–42; "Note sul nazionalsocialismo," *Archivio di studi corporativi* 5 (1934): 291–328. See also Cantimori, *Politica e storia contemporanea. Scritti 1927–1942*, ed. Luisa Mangoni (Torino: G. Einaudi, 1991); Mangoni's introduction, "Europa sotterranea," is of fundamental importance. The debate over Cantimori's politics in the thirties is still very much alive.

3. Delio Cantimori, "Appunti sulla propaganda," *Civiltà fascista* 7 (1941): 37–56. Cf. Cantimori, *Politica*, 683–99.

4. Gertrud Bing, "A. M. Warburg," *Journal of the Warburg and Courtauld Institutes* 26 (1965): 299–313 (intro. to Aby Warburg, *La rinascita del paganesimo antico*, trans. E. Cantimori Mezzomonti [Florence: La Nuova Italia, 1966]).

5. *Annales E.S.C.* 15.3 (May–June 1960): 556–68. A longer, unpublished Italian version is included in Cantimori, *Eretici*, 551–62.

6. Cantimori, *Eretici*, 555–56.

In his comments on Febvre's essay "Sorcellerie: Sottise ou révolution mentale?" Cantimori evoked witchcraft trials like those preserved in the State Archive of Modena, as well as astrological tracts like those analyzed by Warburg and preserved in the Library he had created.[7]

This review (which I read in an offprint bearing Cantimori's signature and a handwritten dedication) affected me in many ways. The year before, since I had decided to work on witchcraft trials, Cantimori had directed me toward the Inquisition trials preserved in the Modena archives. Now I realized that my interest in witchcraft trials could be inscribed in a constellation that was familiar and, at the same time, unexpected. Cantimori introduced the parallel between Febvre and Warburg in a somewhat apologetic tone: "One should not regard as extravagant. . . ." Nowadays one may not realize that in 1960 the name of Warburg was scarcely known to historians (though it was well known to art historians, of course) while Febvre and *Annales*, the journal he had founded in 1929 with Marc Bloch, were at the very center of history as a discipline. In his review, Cantimori dismissed the center/periphery dichotomy (along with the notion of disciplinary boundaries) as meaningless. But at the same time he gave his readers (including myself) a map to move into that unknown territory, the Warburg Library.

II

Unknown, and possibly full of traps. In commenting on Aby Warburg's work on astrological tracts, Cantimori recalled the diffusion of magic and astrology in Nazi Germany. This remark did not entirely surprise me. I was aware that the research topic I had begun to work on—witchcraft and related issues—required a critical distance that had to be kept under control.

That distance was a fundamental concern for Gertrud Bing. She was deeply committed to preserving and developing Warburg's intellectual legacy, but her approach was different from his. The difference emerges in the obituaries published after her death. "On the one hand," Arnaldo Momigliano wrote, "Saxl and Bing were less committed to exorcising demons which had been for Warburg a daily experience; on the other, they were less sure that such an exorcising was possible." What happened in between was, on a personal level, Warburg's lapse into madness, which lasted for many years; and on a historical level, Nazism and its appeal to the irrational. "Preoccupation with the irrational worried her [Bing]," D. J. Gordon crisply remarked.[8] Cantimori once referred to the War-

7. Cantimori, *Eretici*, 561.

8. D. J. Gordon, *Gertrud Bing (1892–1964)* (London: Warburg Institute, 1965), 26: "Saxl e Bing erano da un lato meno impegnati in questa esorcizzazione di demoni che per Warburg erano stati una realtà quotidiana, ma d'altro lato erano meno sicuri che l'esorcizzazione fosse possibile" (Arnaldo Momigliano).

burgians as "highly rational salamanders," able to pass through fire without burning themselves. But Warburg himself got burned.

III

Any interaction with reality (as I learned most effectively from Ernst Gombrich's writings) implies filters. My encounter with the Warburg Library had been mediated by Cantimori and, more indirectly, by his relationship with the Warburgians—first of all, Bing. Cantimori and Bing were responding to Aby Warburg's own work (and Bing, to his personality as well). Moreover, both were responding, as so many others have done since then, to the Library and its arrangement.

Ernst Cassirer's comment after his first visit to the Library is famous. According to Fritz Saxl, who had walked him through the Library (at that time Warburg was a patient in Binswanger's clinic in Kreuzlingen), Cassirer said: "This library is dangerous. I shall either have to avoid it altogether or imprison myself here for years. The philosophical problems involved are close to my own, but the concrete historical material which Warburg has collected is overwhelming."[9] Some years later, Cassirer pointed out that the historical problem addressed by the Warburg Library was the survival (*Nachleben*) of antiquity. Philosophical perspective and historical specificity come together in the title of the bibliography published in Germany in 1934, immediately after the transfer of the Warburg Bibliothek from Hamburg to London: *Kulturwissenschaftliche Bibliographie zum Nachleben der Antike.*[10] In the title of the second volume (*A Bibliography of the Survival of the Classics*), the adjective *Kulturwissenschaftlich* disappeared—a symptom of the Institute's effort to adjust to the English intellectual landscape and also, perhaps, to overcome an unresolved tension within Warburg's own thinking.[11] But that tension did not affect the physiognomy of the Warburg Institute Library, whose scope includes not only the survival of the classics in a broad sense, but also the much broader space that Aby Warburg regarded as his own,

9. Fritz Saxl, "Ernst Cassirer," in *The Philosophy of Ernst Cassirer*, ed. Paul Arthur Schilpp, 2nd ed. (1949; New York: Tudor, 1959), 47–51, esp. 48; Cassirer, "Der Begriff der symbolischen Form im Aufbau der Geisteswissenschaften," *Vorträge der Bibliothek Warburg* 1 (1921–22): 11–39, esp. 11–12. This and other versions of Cassirer's visit to the Library are discussed in Salvatore Settis's essential essay, "Warburg *continuatus*: Descrizione di una biblioteca," *Quaderni storici* 58 (1985): 5–38, esp. 7–11.

10. The title continues as follows: *Erster Band. Die Erscheinungen des Jahres 1931 in Gemeinschaft mit Fachgenossen bearbeitet von Hans Meier, Richard Newald, Edgar Wind, herausgegeben von der Bibliothek Warburg* (Leipzig: Teubner, 1934). Fritz Saxl, "The History of Warburg's Library

(1886–1944)," in *Aby Warburg: An Intellectual Biography*, ed. Ernst Hans Gombrich (London: Warburg Institute, 1970), 336, mentions an attack (which I have not seen) in the Nazi magazine *Völkischer Beobachter* on Edgar Wind's introduction to the *Kulturwissenschaftliche Bibliographie*.

11. See Michael Baxandall's remark in Allan Langdale, "Art History and Intellectual History: Michael Baxandall's Work between 1963 and 1985" (PhD diss., University of California, Santa Barbara, 1995), 358. On the tension within Warburg's thought, see Settis, "Warburg *continuatus*," as well as (with respect to a specific issue) my introduction to *Peur, révérence, terreur: Quatre essais d'iconographie politique* (Dijon: Presses du Réel, 2011).

defined by image and word and their relationship.[12] In this sense, the current Library, notwithstanding its continuous expansion, still preserves the skeleton of Warburg's private library. This biological metaphor might convey the continuity with Warburg's original project, legitimizing his claim that the Library, through its arrangement, would offer, hidden on a shelf, a book that would provide an answer to a vital question related to the reader's research project.

IV

Many scholars from different disciplines and various parts of the world have undergone this experience. What follows is my own limited testimony.

In the summer of 1964, I was invited to spend one month at the Warburg Institute. To my great surprise, I was given a key to the building, which allowed me to spend extra hours in the Library. It was an unforgettable time. Some years before, I had begun to work on a research project based on a group of sixteenth- and seventeenth-century Inquisition trials I had come across first in Venice, then in Udine. They dealt with men and women who called themselves *benandanti*, "good-walkers." The men claimed to fight in spirit, four times a year, during the Ember Days, against the witches; the women claimed to see in spirit, four times a year, also during the Ember Days, the procession of the dead. All of this looked like a definite Friulian phenomenon: even the trial I came across by chance in the State Archive in Venice involved a Friulian cowherd. My attempts to put the trial into a larger comparative perspective had not gone beyond vague parallels. The Warburg Library seemed to be the ideal place to deepen my search.

Indeed it was. Besides a large amount of evidence related to my project, the Library offered me the opportunity to make a real breakthrough, condensed into one page and a half of the book I ultimately wrote: *I benandanti* (1966).[13] "The evidence which bears the closest resemblance to the Friulian is Bavarian," my paragraph began. What followed relied upon an offprint from a local Bavarian journal, *Oberstdorfer Gemeinde- und Fremdenblatt*. Even the title of the essay, by Karl Hofmann, conveyed some local flavor: "Oberstdorfer 'Hexen' auf dem Scheiterhaufen: Ein finsteres Kapitel aus der Geschichte unserer Heimat mit einem kurzen Ueberblick über den Verlauf der Hexenprozesse im Allgemeinen" ("'Witches' from Oberstdorf at the stake: A dark chapter from the history of our native country, with a short overall view of the history of witch-trials in general"),

---

12. See Settis, "Nota final. 1995," in *Warburg* continuatus: *Descripción de una biblioteca* (Barcelona: Ediciones de La Central, 2010), 71–88.

13. Carlo Ginzburg, *I benandanti* (Torino: G. Einaudi, 1966). The paragraph in question is on pp. 52–53 of the English translation: *The Night Battles*, trans. John and Anne Tedeschi (London: Routledge and Kegan Paul, 1983).

Oberstdorf 1931. The documents discovered by Hofmann dealt with a shepherd named Chonradt Stöcklin. In 1586, Chondradt told the Oberstdorf judges that, some years before, a dead person from the same town had appeared to him. Since that time, Chonradt would fall periodically into a swoon, followed by a journey in spirit into the beyond. He denied being a witch: as a member of the "nocturnal band," he was asked to pray 30,000 Ave Marias during the Ember Days. Later, pressed hard by the judges, he confessed that he had gone many times to the witches' sabbath. He died at the stake with the women he had accused of being witches.

Hofmann's essay is unsatisfactory.[14] But the case he discovered provides a piece of precious evidence—a nearly perfect parallel with the women *benandanti* put on trial by inquisitors in the same years on the other side of the Alps. For me, this was the beginning of a long comparative journey from Friulian *benandanti* to Siberian shamans.[15]

V

Could I have come across Hofmann's essay in another library? "To the best of my knowledge," I wrote in my book, "[these Oberstdorf documents] have not been analysed, or even cited, by other scholars."[16] I had no clues whatsoever that would have directed me to Hofmann's essay. Today, checking the word *Hexen* in the online catalog of the Bayerische Staatsbibliothek, I would indeed come across the title of Hofmann's essay: a precious (although, at first sight, not especially promising) needle buried in a haystack amounting to 1,463 entries. But in 1964, online catalogs did not exist. Only an open-stack library would have offered me the opportunity to come across that essay, and even then only a library whose shelves included one or more labeled "Witchcraft" or "Witch trials" or, perhaps, "Magic."

Today, Hofmann's offprint (classmark FDB 125) is located in the Warburg Library near Wolfgang Behringer's more recent book (FDB 125.B23), putting Chonrad Stoeckhlin's case in a different, and much broader, perspective, as is clear even from the title of the English translation: *Shaman of Oberstdorf*.[17] On the same shelf, one can find other books—some of them bearing Aby Warburg's *ex libris*—related to witchcraft and witch persecution. Only a short walk separates the section on "Magic" from the section on "Science": a contiguity that played a

14. Ginzburg, *Night Battles*, 191 n. 59.

15. Carlo Ginzburg, *Storia notturna: Una decifrazione del sabba* (Torino: G. Einaudi, 1989), translated into English as *Ecstasies: Deciphering the Witches' Sabbath*, trans. Raymond Rosenthal (London: Hutchinson Radius, 1990).

16. Ginzburg, *Night Battles*, 191 n. 59.

17. Wolfgang Behringer, *Shaman of Oberstdorf: Chonrad Stoeckhlin and the Phantoms of the Night*, trans. H. C. Erik Midelfort (Charlottesville: University of Virginia Press, 1998).

central role in Warburg's approach. It was marginal, however, in mine. But that difference did not impede my research: any library will interact with its readers, and also the other way around. In the case of the Warburg Library, the interaction, both conscious and unconscious, with its arrangement is a fundamental part of the readers' experience.

Une machine à penser: it was not by chance that Fritz Saxl dreamt of Le Corbusier (or Gropius) as a possible architect for the Warburg Library in Hamburg.[18]

18. Gertrud Bing, *Fritz Saxl (1890–1948): A Biographical Memoir . . . Reprinted on the Fiftieth Anniversary of His Death* (London: Warburg Institute, 1998), 12; Karen Michels, "Ein Versuch über die K. B. W. als Bau der Moderne," in *Porträt aus Büchern: Bibliothek Warburg und Warburg Institute, Hamburg-1933–London* (Hamburg: Dölling und Galitz, 1993), 71–81.

A TURNING-POINT
IN POLITICAL THOUGHT

Isaiah Berlin

I Preliminary Platitudes

I ought first to say something about what I consider a turning-point to be. I do not know how it is in the natural sciences—empirical ones like physics and biology, or formal ones like logic and mathematics. There, perhaps, revolutions occur when a central hypothesis or system of hypotheses is undermined or exploded by a discovery that leads to new hypotheses or laws which account for the new discovery and are incompatible with the central doctrines of the old system. The method is one of clean refutation: Galileo, Newton, Lavoisier, Darwin, Einstein, Planck and perhaps Bertrand Russell and Freud literally refuted earlier theories, made them obsolete, altered the methods by which new knowledge was gained, so that the interest of the superseded methods and theories is now largely historical, and those who persist in adhering to them are regarded as eccentric and are left out of account in serious circles of recognised experts.

This is conspicuously not the case in the great fields of imprecise knowledge—history, philosophy, scholarship, criticism—ideas about the arts and about the lives of men. Plato's physics or his mathematics may be obsolete, but both

Originally published in *Common Knowledge* 7.3 (Winter 1998): 187–214. Reproduced with permission of Curtis Brown Group Ltd., London, on behalf of the Estate of Isaiah Berlin. © Isaiah Berlin 1998.

Common Knowledge 25:1–3

DOI 10.1215/0961754X-7299390

Plato's and Aristotle's moral and political ideas are still capable of stirring men to violent partisanship. Karl Popper would not attack Plato's social theories with such fury and indignation if these ideas had no more life to them than, say, Plato's conception of the sun and the fixed stars, or Aristotle's doctrine that some bodies have weight and other bodies have lightness. I know of no one who feels outraged by medieval notions of cosmology or chemistry, or Descartes' physics, or phlogiston theory. But St. Augustine's views on the treatment of heretics or on slavery, or St. Thomas's view of political authority, or the doctrines of Rousseau or Hegel, cause violent reactions, intellectual and emotional, in those who look on the empirical or logical theories of these thinkers with comparative equanimity.

There is obviously some sense in which the criteria of truth and falsehood, tenability and untenability, operate in the case of certain disciplines, and do not operate so obviously or gain such universal assent in the case of other regions of thought. There is a sense in which some studies, such as the empirical sciences and mathematics and logic, progress by parricide, by killing off their ancestors to general satisfaction, and in which some subjects do not progress, at least in the same sense, so that it is difficult to enumerate, say, philosophical propositions or systems which are by universal consensus either dead beyond recall or established on firm foundations, at any rate so far as modern knowledge is concerned,

This is a paradox which I cannot investigate more deeply at present—it is a crucial and obscure subject in itself and deserves greater attention than has been lavished upon it. But I should like to say something about these imprecise disciplines, where we are dealing not so much with specific propositions, or great systems of them, as with what nowadays are called ideologies: attitudes, more exactly conceptual systems, frameworks that consist of interrelated categories through which and by means of which we judge periods. Perhaps it is best to describe them as central models, models drawn from some field that seems to a thinker clear and well established, and which he applies in a manner which seems to him to explain and illuminate a field that is less clear. Bertrand Russell once observed that to understand a thinker one must understand and grasp the basic pattern, the central idea which he is defending. The thinker's cleverness is usually expended in inventing arguments with which to fortify this central idea, or, still more, to repel attacks, refute objections; but to understand all this reasoning, however cogent and ingenious, will not lead one to grasp the thought of a philosopher, a historian, a critic unless one penetrates through these sophisticated defences upon his bastions to what he is really defending—the inner citadel itself, which is usually comparatively simple, a fundamental perception which dominates his thought and has formed his view of the world. Plato's application of a geometrical pattern to the life of society, eternal a priori axioms obtained by intuitive means from which all knowledge and all rules of life can be deduced; Aristotle's biological model of every entity as developing towards its own perfection and inner goal, in terms of which alone it can be defined or understood; the great medieval pyramid that stretches from God to the lowest amoeba; the mechanical structure of Hobbes; the image of the family and its natural relationships that runs through the political structures of Bodin, Burke, the Christian socialists of the West, and the Russian Slavophils; the genetic, biological and physical patterns that are the heart of nineteenth- and twentieth-century sociological doctrines; the legal notion of the social contract: these central models are not refuted by mere aspects of experience which are altered by some historical change or intellectual discovery. New models appear, throw light over dark areas, liberate men from the chains of the old constricting framework, and either extrude them completely or sometimes half blend with them into a new pattern. These new models in their turn fail to explain and answer questions which they themselves bring into being. The concept of man as an atom at first offered liberation from a constricting a priori theocratic model, and then in its turn proved inadequate. Man as an organic cell, man as a creator, man as a producer, as a creature seeking union with nature, or as a Promethean hero-martyr seeking to subdue her—these are all models that obscure and illuminate.

II

The great moments are those when one world dies and another succeeds it. This is marked by a change in the central model. Great moments of transformation occurred, for example, when the cyclical laws of the Greeks were succeeded by the ascending straight line, the historical teleology, of the Jews and Christians; or when teleology, in its turn, was overthrown by the causal-mathematical model of the seventeenth century; or when a priori constructions yielded to methods of empirical discovery and verification. There are those who, like Condorcet or Hegel, Buckle or Marx, Spengler or Toynbee, claim to be able to perceive a single pattern of development in this succession of human perspectives. I do not wish to maintain that such ambitious efforts to reduce the vast variety of conscious human experience to one enormous dominant pattern are necessarily doomed to failure; I confine myself to saying merely that the three great crises which I shall discuss are not satisfactorily explained by the hypotheses of any of these thinkers, and that this naturally reduces the value of these hypotheses in my eyes. I do not wish to condemn those who answer their own questions for failing to answer mine, but I cannot help having a certain prejudice in favour of those writers who are more modest and cautious, whose reflections attempt a good deal less and, whether or not for this reason, achieve, for me, a good deal more. History, Tolstoy once remarked, is like a deaf man who answers questions no one has asked. I do not think that this is true of historical writers, but it may not be entirely unjust about a good many philosophers of history who, in the name of science, seek to squeeze the multiplicity of phenomena into one simple cosmic scheme—the "terrible simplifiers" in matters of both theory and practice against whom Montesquieu warned us more than two centuries ago.

III

The three crises in Western political theory, when at least one central category was transformed beyond redemption, so that all subsequent thought was altered, occurred in the fourth century B.C., during the Renaissance in Italy, and towards the end of the eighteenth century in Germany.

Classical Western political theory may be likened to a tripod—that is, it rests on three central assumptions. These, of course, do not represent the totality of beliefs on which this central tradition rests, but they are amongst its most powerful pillars, so that the collapse or weakening of any of them is bound to affect the tradition and, indeed, change it to a considerable degree.

1. The first assumption is that questions about values, about ends or worth, about the rightness or desirability of human action, including political action, are genuine questions; genuine questions being those to which true answers exist, whether they are known or not. These answers are objective, universal, eternally valid and in principle knowable. To every genuine question only one answer can be true, all the other answers being necessarily false—either false in varying degrees, at various distances from the truth, or false absolutely, according to the logical doctrine adopted. The route to the truth has historically been a subject on which there have been the most profound disagreements among men. Some have believed that solutions were to be discovered by reason, others by faith or revelation, or empirical observation, or metaphysical intuition. Some have thought that the truth was, at least in principle, open to all if only they pursued the correct method—by reading sacred books, or communion with nature, or rational calculation, or looking within their own innermost heart; others have thought that only experts could discover the answer, or persons in certain privileged states of mind, or at certain times and in certain places. Some have thought that these truths could be discovered in this world; to others they would be revealed fully only in some future life. Some have supposed that these truths were known in a golden age in the remote past, or would be known in a golden age in the future; according to some they are timeless, according to others revealed progressively; according to some they can in principle be known to men, according to others to God alone.

Profound though these differences are, and the source at times of violent conflict, not only intellectual but social and political, they are differences within the agreed belief that the questions are genuine questions, and the answers to them, like hidden treasure, exist whether they have been found or not; so that the problem is not whether these answers exist at all, but only what is the best means of finding them. Values may differ from facts or from necessary truths in the way that Aristotle or the Fathers of the Church, or Hume or Kant or Mill, thought that they differed; but the propositions that assert or describe them are no less objective, and obey a logical structure no less coherent and rigorous, than propositions asserting facts—whether empirical or a priori or logical—and mathematical truths. This is the first and deepest assumption that underlies the classical form of political theory.

2. The second assumption is that the answers, if they are true, to the various questions raised in political theory do not clash. This follows from the simple logical rule that one truth cannot be incompatible with another. Many questions of value are bound to arise in the course of political enquiry: questions such as "What is justice and should it be pursued?" "Is liberty an end to be sought after for its own sake?" "What are rights, and under what circumstances may they be ignored or, to the contrary, asserted against the claims of utility or security or truth or happiness?" The answers to these questions, if they are true, cannot collide with each other. According to some views they harmonise with one another; according to other views they form an interrelated single whole, and mutually entail and are entailed by one another, so that denial of any one of them leads to incoherence or contradictions within the system. Whichever of these views is correct, the minimum assumption is that one truth cannot possibly logically conflict with another. Hence it follows that, if all our questions were answered, the collection or pattern or logically connected system of the true answers would constitute a total solution of all problems of value—of the questions of what to do, how to live, what to believe. This would be, in short, the description of the ideal state of which all actual human conditions fall short.

This may be called the jigsaw-puzzle view of ethics and politics and aesthetics. Since all true answers fit with one another, the problem is merely to arrange the fragments with which we are presented in everyday experience, or in moments of illumination, or at the end of some strenuous, but successful, intellectual investigation—to arrange these fragments in the unique way in which they compose the total pattern that is the answer to all our wants and perplexities.

Again the problem arises whether any man can do this, or only some—the experts or the spiritually privileged or those who happen to be in the right place for the completion of the solution to the puzzle. Is the answer vouchsafed to any man who uses correct methods, or only to a particular group in a peculiar favourable position—a particular Church or culture or class? Is the answer static, unaltered wherever and whenever it may be discovered, or dynamic—that is, once it is discovered by the progressive, perfecting searcher after the truth, who has made every serious effort to find it, then although it may not be final in the form in which he gives it, does it facilitate the process of transformation required by the continuing search for the final solution? The assumption here is that there is a final solution, that if all the answers to all the questions could *per impossibile* be found and properly related to one another, this would be a total answer—the necessary acceptance of which by those who had found it would solve all questions, both of theory and of practice, once and for all. Whether this answer is discoverable on Earth or not, all attempts to answer such questions can then be represented as being so many paths towards this central totality, adequate or inadequate, in direct proportion to the inner coherence and the comprehensiveness of the answers proposed.

3. The third assumption is that man has a discoverable, describable nature, and that this nature is essentially, and not merely contingently, social. There are certain attributes which belong to man as such, for example, the capacity for thought or communication; for a creature who does not think or communicate could not be called a man. Communication is by definition a relationship with others, and therefore relationship with other men of a systematic kind is not merely a contingent fact about men, but part of what we mean by men, a part of the definition of human beings as a species. If this is so, then political theory, which is the theory of how men do or should behave towards one another, and especially why anyone should obey anyone else rather than do as he likes (this raises all the questions of authority and sovereignty, of types of government and the foundations of obligation—these questions are necessarily raised whenever any questions about the nature or purposes of men are brought up)—is not a doctrine or a particular technique that men can use or not use, like the theory of navigation (men need not, after all, use ships if they do not wish to), but rather more like theories of thinking (which they cannot help doing), or theories of growth or history, or theories that deal with other inalienable attributes of human beings. Hence the traditional divisions of philosophy which deal with permanent, irremovable characteristics of human life: logic, metaphysics, epistemology, ethics, politics, aesthetics.

Each of these pillars on which political theory rests has been attacked. They have been attacked, historically, in order of mounting importance, in the reverse order from that in which I have stated them. The view of man as an intrinsically social being, and of political theory as consisting of questions that penetrate to the heart of what human beings are, was attacked at the end of the fourth century. The proposition that all values are compatible with one another, and that in principle there is a total solution of human problems, if only we could discover it—there must, at any rate, be a method of searching for it—was questioned by Machiavelli, questioned to such effect that the old confidence which had lasted for more than two thousand years never returned. The proposition that there may, in principle, exist no final solution to human problems, and that some values may be incompatible with others, entails considerations which few men are capable of facing without growing altogether too upset. Finally, the claim that questions of value are genuine questions and capable of solution, at least in principle, and that politics is a branch of intellectual enquiry capable of yielding propositions which can be true or false, was compromised by the German romantics toward the end of the eighteenth century with results of a very violent, revolutionary kind. The consequences are with us still; they have destroyed the foundations of the old beliefs and, whether as causes or as symptoms, they mark the most violent political and moral upheavals of our own day.

I shall discuss these three great crises one by one. I begin with the first—the question of man as a social being.

IV

It is by now a well-worn commonplace that the Greeks of the classical period, and in particular Athens and Sparta in the fifth century B.C., conceived of human beings in essentially social terms. The evidence for this need scarcely be adduced. Attic tragedy and comedy in the fifth century, and the historians Herodotus and Thucydides, take for granted that the natural life of men is the institutionalised life of the *polis*. The notion of resistance to it—in the name of individual liberty or even peaceful retreat from the marketplace into private life—is scarcely conceived. *Idiotes* means just "private citizen," but insofar as such a person is concerned with his own private affairs at the expense of those of the city, it can be a pejorative term, like the modern word etymologically related to it. As for the philosophers—those who consciously examined the presuppositions of commonly accepted notions and enquired about the ends of life—if we are to take the two great masters whose works dominate Greek, and all subsequent, thought—Plato and Aristotle—the emphasis on social values is overwhelming in their works. "One should say not that a citizen belongs to himself," says Aristotle, "but that all belong to the *polis:* for the individual is a part of the *polis.*"[1]

This simple statement could stand as a formula that summarises the attitude of all major thinkers of classical Athens. Aristotle cautiously qualifies this thesis: there can be such a thing as too much uniformity in the city. The citizens must not be crushed, differences of character and attitude must always be given adequate room in which to realise themselves. The virtues that Aristotle discusses are largely the characteristics of human beings in their intercourse with each other within a social context: the ideal figure of the generous, distinguished, rich, public-spirited man with a wide liberal outlook, great dignity and sweep, raised above the heads of the ordinary middle-class citizen, is not conceivable save

---

1. Aristotle *Politics* 1337a27; compare also *Nicomachean Ethics* 1180a24–29 and *Metaphysics* 1075a19.

in terms of a well-organised, ordered society. "Man has been created by nature to live in a *polis*."[2] This sentiment is central in the classical texts of Greek art and thought that have survived. No argument seems needed to establish this proposition, for it is evidently something that all sane men believe without question, it is part of the general notion of man. Solitude can be endured only by a god or a beast: it is subhuman or superhuman.

This too is the general attitude of Plato, for all his disgust with Athenian democracy. Some Platonists suppose him to be more interested in the well-ordered individual soul or mind than in social and political organisation. Occasionally he makes remarks to the effect that "no evil can befall a good man either in his lifetime or after his death"[3]—and this is, in effect, repeated in the *Republic*.[4] Both Plato and Aristotle speak of the contemplative life as the highest that a man can lead. Their vision is of the ultimate goal which all things seek, the answer to the question why things are as they are and seek to be what they seek to be: *that* is the fulfilment of the quest for truth, both in theory and practice. To return to the cave and the world of illusion, where men pursue false ends, and struggle and squabble and fret and lead foolish and vicious lives—this return is to be viewed only with extreme reluctance. Still, return they must. Why? Because they must create a society in which the wise man—Socrates—will not be put to death? Or because *only* the State can give that education which makes men capable of virtue and wisdom, and the grasp of reality which alone gives moral and intellectual security and satisfaction? These are different answers and not consistent with one another; but what they have in common is the view that men cannot and should not live outside the State.

It is true that Socrates kept out of things, on the whole: he obeyed the laws and performed his military service with exceptional distinction, but he kept out of politics, if we are to believe those who wrote about him, because Athenian democracy was too corrupt and no man who knew where the truth lay would seek the tawdry prizes which a vicious society offered. Nevertheless, one of the charges against him was that he was too close to Critias, chief of the tyrants who seized power and instituted a reign of terror and butchered a good many democrats. Socrates was accused not of turning his back upon civic life, but of "corrupting the young men" and of sowing scepticism about the values that preserved the social texture, and, no doubt, of being a friend of Alcibiades, who was a traitor, and of other young men of good birth who looked down upon the grocers and tanners who formed the bulk of the Athenian electorate; in other words, of preaching doctrines which made for the rule by an élite, a rational élite perhaps, but still, superior persons raised above the ordinary citi-

2. *Politics* 1253a2–3.

3. Plato *Apology* 41d1.

4. Plato *Republic* 613a.

zenry, oligarchs who believed in their own superior values and not in equality or majority votes.

This is not political detachment but active subversion of a particular type of political life. In the *Crito*, where the laws are speaking to Socrates before his approaching death, they tell him that he is a child and slave of the laws. He was among those who passed the laws. Once they are set up it is the duty of the citizen to obey—there is no question of opting out of such a commitment. The citizen owes more to the laws than to his physical parents.[5] Socrates takes this for granted; he does not dispute it: morality integrates you into society, and above all you must not destroy the laws by disobeying them because they are unjust, because you suffer unjustly under them. The claims of the social texture are supreme. The proposition that Plato was interested solely or even principally in creating conditions in which the minority gifted enough to discover the truth would have conditions in which they could pursue their studies is not really tenable. However the *Republic* may be interpreted, the *Politicus* is a treatise not about means, but about ends—how the only life which, according to him, men can lead while remaining men, namely the life of the city, should be conducted by those who are responsible. Virtue for Plato is the fruit of State-directed education. A bad State must be reformed or abolished, but not in favour of a loose association of individuals. There is nothing which Plato is more bitterly opposed to than "a society in which men are allowed to do whatever they like."[6] The most violent statement of this is in the famous passage in the *Laws* where, after earlier criticising Sparta as a militarist State—a mere "army camp"[7]—he declares, a good many pages later:

the principal thing is that none, man or woman, should ever be without an officer set over him, and that none should get the mental habit of taking any step, whether in earnest or jest, on his own individual responsibility. In peace and in war he must live always with his eye on his superior officer, following his lead and guided by him in his smallest actions. . . . In a word, he must train the mind even to consider acting as an individual or know how to do it.[8]

No doubt this was written in his embittered old age, after the failure of the Sicilian experiment, when his passionate belief in human reason may have been weakened by his experience of human vice and folly. Still, in a milder version, this is the note struck by Plato whenever the question of political organisation arises. The reduction of social life to a single rigorous pattern inspired by logic or mathematics may argue a latent hatred of human association as such and of the problems of reconciling the variety of men and purposes, or blending them

5. Plato *Crito* 50c–51c, esp. 51a.

6. *Republic* 557b5.

7. Plato *Laws* 666e.

8. *Laws* 942a–c.

into some viable form of life worthy of human beings, in which the art or science of politics may be held to consist. Be that as it may, Plato clearly thinks of men in a social context. In his image man is among other men. His morality is a social morality, even though not to the extent of Aristotle's—for whom morals were deducible from politics, We discover what men should do by asking ourselves what functions nature has designed them to perform in the pattern for which they were created. The Greek city is derived from this pattern. Where the association is too big, as, say, in Persia, or too crude, as it is among the barbarians, or does not exist at all—when disintegration sets in and men find themselves on their own—that causes degeneration, abnormality. The norm is the equilibrium of forces and characteristics embodied in the city. The worst and most corrosive of vices—injustice—is the upsetting of this equilibrium. The best constitutions are those which keep things in balance, preserve the pattern, and create the framework within which men can socially—and, therefore, morally and intellectually—realise themselves. Men's characters are defined in terms of the kind of society for which they were created by nature. There are the democratic, the oligarchic, the plutocratic man: bricks defined in terms of the building into which they naturally fit. This is a celebrated Greek ideal of life at its most articulate.

Is there no opposition to this? What about Antigone, who defied the laws of the State in order to bury her brother? She defies Creon's laws, but not in the name of some individual conviction or the values of private life: she appeals to the unwritten laws, not of today or yesterday, to which all mankind is subject, laws valid for any human society, but not for individuals unrelated by social links. It is an appeal from one social morality to another, not from a social morality to an individual one.

And the Sophists? Here we reach an important, but unfortunately insoluble, problem. For we do not know too much about what the Sophists taught. Perhaps they did not write books on any large scale; or perhaps what they wrote perished—for we know at least some titles of books by the opponents of Socrates and Plato that have not survived. But our main authority for what Protagoras, Prodicus, Hippias, Thrasymachus believed is what Plato and Aristotle tell us. We know a little more about other figures, for example, Antiphon. But the bulk of what we know comes from enemy sources, the caricatures of a man who hated them as much as Aristophanes—except that Aristophanes included Socrates as well—and painted satirical portraits of genius. The true facts about those he described are for ever obliterated. To this point I intend to revert later, for it is highly relevant to my entire argument. But for the moment let me say only that the Sophists, like the orators and the dramatists, give evidence of sharp disagreements about what kind of State is the best, but not of opposition to the supremacy of the social institutions.

Lycophron thought that the division into classes was artificial, a work not of nature but of the human will or prejudice. Alcidamas (and in some degree Euripides) thought the institution of slavery artificial, for nature meant all men to be alike—and likewise the distinction between Greeks and barbarians. Antiphon said: "None of us is by definition barbarian or Greek, for we all breathe out into the air by mouth and nostrils."[9] Being barbarian or Greek is a human arrangement which, presumably, humans could at will undo. Archelaus thought the distinctions between justice and crookedness were the results of human arrangements, not of nature; Phaleas thought this about the qualities of property. Critias thought God an invention for the purpose of keeping men in order, for unless they were taught that there was an ever-watchful eye upon them, even when no men saw them, marking their conduct and prepared to punish for transgressions, they would behave badly when they thought no one was looking, and society would be subverted.

The Sophists are relativists, egalitarians, pragmatists, atheists, but for the most part, at any rate towards the end of the fifth century, they are not individualists. They want to alter society, not concentrate attention upon the individual and his character and needs. They differ about what kind of society is the most rational. They wish to eliminate mere traditional survivals. They criticise institutions for which they see no good reason, but not institutional life as such. Some appear to be democrats, some are not. It is one of the great paradoxes of history that the democracy that is Athens' greatest political glory was defended by so few that almost every writer who has survived is in some degree an enemy or a critic of it. The ideal is *isonomia*, equality before the laws—"the most beautiful of all names," as Herodotus makes Otanes call it[10]—or *eunomia*, good order, a conservative slogan. Equality is defended against tyranny and arbitrary rule. Aristotle thinks that a State is satisfactory in which men rule and are ruled in turn,[11] while the cynical Antiphon wonders whether any man would not prefer to rule unjustly rather than be ruled justly by others.

There is no trace here of genuine individualism, the doctrine that there are personal values—pleasure, or knowledge, or friendship, or virtue, or self-expression in art or life—to which political and social arrangements should be subordinated: for which they create a pedestal, a means however indispensable, but still only a means. The assumption is, on the contrary, that all these values can be realised only within and as part of the life of the Greek *polis*. To ignore social arrangements, to profit by them, is not a normal frame of mind. Even Thrasymachus, who thinks that justice is the interest of the stronger, does not imply that life outside the intimate association of masters and slaves is conceiv-

---

9. Diels-Kranz, 6th ed., 87B44, B2.24–34 (ii 353).

10. Herodotus 3.80.6.

11. *Politics* 1317b2.

able. Callicles in Plato's *Gorgias* speaks for the bold, unscrupulous, self-seeking, gifted egoist who sweeps aside the institutions of the city like cobwebs and tramples on them and does as he likes—that is, might is right: nature demands despotism, not individualism. Lactamius is right in thinking Socrates does not win the argument against Thrasymachus and his like; the common opinion which he marshals against him is not enough against violent individualism of this type. But Plato evidently thought that he had refuted the claims of the egomaniacs, with their distorted view of the facts, which would cost them dear in the end.

At this point it may be asked whether I have forgotten the greatest of all professions of political faith, the funeral speech of Pericles as reported by Thucydides, incomparably the greatest statement of its kind in the whole of our history. Certainly, Pericles says, Athens differs from Sparta in that "we live as free citizens, both in our public life and in our attitude to one another in the affairs of daily life; we are not angry with our neighbour if he behaves as he pleases, we do not cast sour looks at him, which if they can do no harm nevertheless can cause pain."[12] There is a similar remark, less nobly expressed, in the speech of Nikias to the dispirited, defeated Athenian troops in Sicily in 416 B.C.[13] Euripides also speaks up for freedom of speech,[14] and Demosthenes says: "In Sparta you are not allowed to praise the laws of Athens, or of this State or that; far from it, you have to praise what agrees with their constitution";[15] whereas in Athens free criticism of constitutions is evidently permitted.

What does this come to? Pericles says that some States are more liberal than others: not, as he has all too often been interpreted, that in Athens individuals have rights, natural or State-conferred, to speak as they please or act as they please within certain limits, with which the State has no right to interfere. This is the view advanced by Gomme, but he seems to be mistaken. No doubt the individual did "have ample freedom in private life,"[16] no doubt there were protests from the conservatives, such as Aristotle's disapproval of men "who live as they please"—as Euripides says, "each according to his fancy"[17]—or Plato's disgust with the city that has so much variety, so many foreigners, women and slaves who get above themselves and presume to behave almost like citizens. The pseudo-Xenophontic *Constitution of Athens* launches a diatribe against resident foreigners and slaves. Isocrates complains that there is not enough moral control over private lives, that the Areopagus should reassert its ancient authority in these matters. All this implies that life in Athens was a good deal freer, that there was

---

12. Thucydides 2.37.

13. Thucydides 7.69 (Nikias "reminded them of their fatherland with all her great freedom and the uncommanded liberty of lifestyle for all").

14. Euripides *Hippolytus* 421–22; Ion 672–75; *Phoenissae* 390–93; *Temenidae* fr. 717 Nauck.

15. Demosthenes *Against Leptines* 20.106.

16. Herbert J. Muller, *Freedom in the Ancient World* (London: Secker & Warburg, 1962), 168.

17. Aristotle *Politics* 1310a33; Euripides fr. 883 Nauck.

more variety, perhaps more chaos than in totalitarian Sparta or perhaps other more tightly organised, more militarised States. But what Pericles is saying, in effect, is what any headmaster proud of the spirit of his school, any commander proud of the spirit of his army, might well say: We do not need compulsion. What other States have to force their citizens to do, ours perform because they are truly devoted to their city, because they are spontaneously loyal, because their lives are bound up with their city, in which they all have faith and pride.

It is a far cry from this to the assertion of the rights of the individual. Schoolboys, however lightly ruled, have no rights against the masters. The school may take pride in the fact that it does not need to threaten or bully, punish or intimidate, but it is the collective spirit of the school, the solidarity of its members, that is being praised: the Athenian State was the object of its own worship and upon its altar men were, if Pericles is to be believed, ready to sacrifice themselves. But to sacrifice oneself freely is still to sacrifice oneself, uncoerced surrender is still surrender; and vice and error are still defined in terms of each man pulling in his own direction, satisfying his own individual nature. Thucydides likes Pericles and does not like Cleon. Demosthenes believes in political freedom, freedom from rule by other States—say, Macedon—and so does Pericles, and all the great Athenians. Some believe in a loose texture, some in a tight one, but there is no note of individualism here, of the value of the State consisting in what it contributes to the individual satisfactions of its individual members. They are to lay down their lives for it; it has no duties, only claims; they have no claims against it, only duties. But in a well-organised, harmonious State, such as Pericles tries to represent Athens as being, claims are not pressed; they are satisfied spontaneously, and no one scowls at his neighbour for being different from himself. Variety versus uniformity, spontaneity versus coercion, loyalty versus tyranny, love instead of fear: these are the Periclean ideals. However attractive they may be found, they are not identical either with individualism or (a much later stage of human development) with the notion of the right of the individual against encroachment by the State—the staking out of a claim to the sacrosanct area within which he literally can do as he pleases, however foolish, eccentric, outrageous his conduct.

That is the testimony of the major authors. There are some dissident voices; they are few and far between, and I shall have occasion to mention them later. Aristotle may have been an old-fashioned conservative towards the end of his life, but it is his view of the nature of society—the harmonious social whole, pursuing goals implanted in it by nature herself, to which every element must be subordinated, so that ethics and politics are wholly social and educational, as explained in his treatises on what the relationships are between the natural purposes of the various constituents of society, and how they may be made to perform their functions, their natural functions, as effectively and richly as possible—it is that vision that has bound its spell on the ancient world, the middle ages, and on a good many modern societies since his day.

At this point there is a most surprising development. Aristotle died in 322 B.C. Some sixteen years or so later, Epicurus began to teach in Athens, and after him Zeno, a Phoenician from Kition in Cyprus. Within a few years theirs are the dominant philosophical schools in Athens. It is as if political philosophy had suddenly vanished away. There is nothing about the city, the education of citizens to perform their tasks within it, bad and good constitutions—nothing at all about this.[18] Nothing about the need for hierarchies or their dangers; nothing about the value of small organised communities, of extrovert social life as the mark and criterion of human nature; nothing about how to train specialists in governing men, or about the organisation of life so that unequal gifts are appropriately rewarded, with the explanation that different constitutions place different emphasis on different types of gift and character. Personal ethics are no longer deduced from social morality, ethics are no longer a branch of politics, the whole no longer precedes the parts, the notion of fulfillment as necessarily social and public disappears without a trace. Within twenty years or less we find, in place of hierarchy, equality; in place of emphasis on the superiority of specialists, the doctrine that any man can discover the truth for himself and live the good life as well as any other man, at least in principle; in place of emphasis on intellectual gifts, ability, skill, there is now stress upon the will, moral qualities, character; in place of loyalty, which holds small groups together, groups moulded by tradition and memories, and the organic fitting-in of all their parts and functions, there is a world without national or city frontiers; in place of the outer life, the inner life; in place of political commitment, taken for granted by all the major thinkers of the previous age, sermons recommending total detachment. In place of the pursuit of grandeur, glory, immortal fame, nobility, public spirit, self-realisation in harmonious social action, gentlemanly ideals, we now have a notion of individual self-sufficiency, praise of austerity, a puritanical emphasis on duty, above all constant stress on the fact that the highest of all values is peace of soul, individual salvation, obtained not by knowledge of an accumulating kind, not by the gradual increase of scientific information (as Aristotle taught), nor by the use of sensible judgement in practical affairs, but by sudden conversion—a shining of the inner light. Men are distinguished into the converted and the unconverted. There are to be no intermediate types—they are either saved or not saved, either wise or stupid. One either knows how to save one's soul or one does not. One can be drowned as easily in a foot of water as in many fathoms, said the Stoics. One is either in

18. This is almost certainly an overstatement, if only because of Zeno's *Republic*, a response (of which only fragments survive) to Plato's work of the same title. See Mal-colm Schofield, *The Stoic Idea of the City* (Cambridge: Cambridge University Press, 1991). H.H.

Canopus or outside it: to be an inch outside and many miles outside are equally not to be in Canopus—all or nothing. It is something like the sudden puritanism following the Elizabethan Age.

For the older of the two teachers, Epicurus, the State hardly exists. The problem is how to avoid being hurt, how to escape misery. Reality—nature—is governed by iron laws which men cannot possibly alter. You cannot destroy or avoid nature, but you can avoid colliding with it unnecessarily. What makes men unhappy? Fear of the gods, superstition, fear of death, fear of pain—whence all the elaborate ritual, propitiation, obedience to the infernal powers that is called religion. But what if the gods, even if they do exist, take no interest in men, but live blissfully in their own remote world, unconcerned with affairs on earth? If fear of the gods goes, the burden is much lightened. As for pain, skillful management will diminish that too, both for me and for my neighbours. If the pain is intolerably intense it will not last long and death will release me; if it lasts it cannot be intense, and by living carefully, following the prescriptions of nature, one can avoid pain and disease. What remains of life? Happiness, peace, inner harmony. How may it be obtained? Not by seeking wealth, power, recognition, for these expose you to competition and all the sweat and toil of the arena. Public life brings more pains than pleasures; its rewards are not worth having, for they merely multiply your anxieties. Avoid situations in which you become liable to pain. All men are vulnerable: they must contract the vulnerable surface that may be wounded by other men or by things and events. This must be done by avoiding all forms of commitment. Epicurus preaches passionately, as a man who wishes to suppress all passions as sources of pain and trouble, against what today is called an *engagé* attitude to politics. *Lathe biosas:*[19] get through life as obscurely as you can. Seek to avoid notice and you will not be hurt. Public life holds out rewards that are only a painful delusion. Be like an actor.[20] Play the part that has been set up for you, but do not identify yourself with it. Above all, no enthusiasm, *pas trop de zèle*. Pay taxes, vote, obey orders, but withdraw into yourself. "Man is not by nature adapted for living in civic communities."[21] "Confront every desire with the question: What do I gain by gratifying it, and what shall I lose by crushing it?"[22]

Should one be just? Yes, because if you cheat—break rules—you may be discovered, and others may, because they are not dispassionate sages like you, punish you or at least hate you; and if you are haunted by the fear of being exposed, this will ruin your pleasures. There is no value in justice as such; justice is only a means of avoiding too much friction with others, of getting along. The reason for it is utility: all society is founded upon a social contract whereby arrangements

19. Epicurus fr. 551 Usener.

20. Bion fr. 16A Kindstrand.

21. See under Epicurus fr. 551 Usener (p. 327, lines 9–10).

22. Epicurus fr. 6.71 Arrighetti.

are made which make it possible for human beings not to get in each other's way too much.

And knowledge? Is that desirable? Certainly, for only in this way will you know what to do and what to avoid if you are to attain to peace and contentment. "Vain is the word of the philosopher which heals not the suffering of man."[23] This might well be the motto of the Rockefeller Foundation today. Knowledge is not an end in itself; nothing is an end in itself except individual happiness, and this is to be obtained by reliable goods—the love of friends, which is a positive source of pleasure, the joys of private life.

Should wealth be sought? Not as such, for that leads to fears, conflicts, but if it comes your way it is unreasonable to reject it. The wise man should be able to do with bread and water, but if luxuries come his way, why should he not accept them too? Public life is a snare and a delusion, and you should participate in it only if you need to—to avoid pain—or if you happen to have a restless temperament, or enjoy it: that is, if it offers some kind opiate to you which other things do not. You cannot obtain all that you want: to want and not to get is to be a slave to desires, to be tossed about by forces stronger than yourself. Since you cannot get what you want, you must try to want only what you can get—you cannot manipulate the universe, but you can manipulate your own psychological states, within limits. Try not to want something that may easily be taken away from you. "There is but one way to freedom: to despise what is not in our power."[24] What you cannot get is not worth striving for.

There are two ways of being happy—by satisfying desires and by eliminating them. The first can be achieved only on a modest scale, since we are neither omniscient nor omnipotent, and facts are as they are and cannot be changed much; the second way is the only way to peace and independence. Independence is everything: the two great Epicurean words are *autarkeia* and *ataraxia*—self-sufficiency and imperturbability. And social life? And the glory of the city? And great dangers bravely faced? And Alexander in his plumed helmet mowing down the slaves of the King of Persia? These are not roads to permanent happiness. They merely excite the desires and make you seek for more and more, and enslave you more and more hopelessly to vast unfulfillable ambitions, and expose you to hopes and fears which do not let you rest. The greatest achievement of a man is to teach himself not to mind. That is the lesson to be drawn from the life of Socrates, not social arrangements or the value of mathematics as a path to metaphysical truth. You have not long to live and might as well arrange yourself as comfortably as possible in your own corner of the world. If you do not interfere with others, or envy or hate them, or seek to alter their lives against their wishes, or try for power, you will get by.

23. Ibid., fr. 247. 24. Epictetus *Encheiridion* 19.2.

This combination of belief in rationalism, which liberates one from fanaticism and anxiety, and belief in utilitarianism and personal relationships as the supreme good in life is a doctrine familiar whenever the stresses of life become too much for distinguished and sensitive persons. It is a form of retreat in depth, retreat into the inner citadel of the inviolable individual soul, so protected by fortitude and reason that nothing can upset it, or wound it, or throw it off its balance. Godwin believed something of the kind and imparted it to Shelley, in whose Platonism it plays a part. In our own day it constituted the morality of a good many English and, perhaps, some French and American intellectuals before and after 1914—rationalist, anti-clerical, pacifist, contemptuous of the pursuit of reputation or wealth—who believed above all in personal relationships and aesthetic enjoyment, friendship and the production and enjoyment of beauty, and the pursuit of the unvarnished truth as alone worthy of human beings. Virginia Woolf, Roger Fry, the philosopher G. E. Moore, in his earlier years Maynard Keynes, believed something of this kind. When E. M. Forster declared shortly before the last war, "if I had to choose between betraying my country and betraying my friend, I hope I should have the guts to betray my country,"[25] this was a militant expression of the Epicurean creed—a total reversal of previous Greek beliefs. "A study of the laws of nature creates men of haughty independence of mind [*sobroi* and *autarkeis*] who pride themselves on the goods proper to man [*idiois agathois*], not to circumstances."[26] Public life is part of circumstances, not of the individual. The state is an instrument and not an end. Personal salvation is all that matters. The doctrine is one of liberation through self-sufficiency. This is indeed a transvaluation of values.

The Stoics were, of course, more influential than the Epicureans. Zeno, who established himself in Athens at the turn of the fourth century, was a foreigner, a Phoenician from Cyprus who taught that wisdom consisted of inner freedom, which could be obtained only by eliminating the passions from one's constitution. The world was a rational pattern and order, and since man by nature was a rational creature, to understand this order was to recognise its beauty and its necessity—the laws of reason were graven in deathless letters upon our deathless reason.[27] If only you could rid yourself of the influences that ruined you—errors about the world, induced by stupidity or ignorance or a bad and corrupt condition—you would become invulnerable to that which made other men vicious and unhappy. To understand the world truly is to understand that everything in it is necessary, and what you call evil is an indispensable element in a larger harmony. To achieve this understanding is to cease to feel the common desires, fears, hopes of mankind, and dedicate yourself to a life led in accordance with reason or

25. E. M. Forster, "What I Believe," in *Two Cheers for Democracy* (London: E. Arnold, 1951), 78.

26. Epicurus fr. 6.45 Arrighetti.

27. *Stoicorum veterum fragmenta* (hereafter SVF) iii 360.

nature—which to Zeno are the same, for nature is the embodiment of the laws of universal reason. The Stoic sage observes that reason governs the world. If pain is part of the design, it must be embraced; your will must be adjusted to it. "Do your worst, Pain!" exclaimed the Stoic Posidonius when racked by mortal disease: "Nothing you do will make me admit that you are evil."[28]

Since any man can grasp the rational necessity of whatever occurs, there is no need to achieve harmony, stability, peace of mind for that minimum of material health and wealth that Aristotle admitted to be necessary for happiness. King Priam, however brave and good, could not achieve happiness, according to Aristotle, because his misfortunes were too great; according to the Stoics, he could. The only thing that is real is the basic reason that goes through nature and men. Why collect details of 257 constitutions in order to find out what suits what kinds of men, where, in what climates, with what traditions—when all men are fundamentally the same, and we can discover a priori, by training the reason within us to grasp the eternal laws of the world, what we must do to be at harmony with ourselves; and the external world, rather than learn this by the uncertain inductive path chosen by the Peripatetics? How do we know what is certain? Because sometimes something "almost takes hold of us by the hair . . . and drags us to assent."[29] Some truths are incorrigible and irresistible. It is easier to be harmonious and at peace in some circumstances than in others: if gold had not been dug up or luxuries brought by ships from abroad, there would be more simplicity and peace, but even in the sophisticated and corrupt Athens of the beginning of the third century, discipline over emotion can be obtained, and one can make oneself impervious to the evil will of men or the blows of fortune. The ship must be wholly sealed from leaking—allow the faintest crack through which feelings might seep through and you are sunk.

The ideal is *apathia*—passionlessness. The Stoic sage is impassive, dry, detached, invulnerable; he alone is king, priest, master, god. Like the Pharisees to whom Josephus compares them, the Stoic sages were accused of coldness, hypocrisy, pride, disdain, pretentiousness. The movement had its martyrs: since misery resulted only from deviation from reason, from over-attachment to persons or things, if circumstances became too evil or the tyrant too brutal and menacing, you could always escape the consequences by freely taking your own life. The Stoics did not advocate suicide, but neither did they preach against it. A rational man dies when life according to reason becomes impossible, because his faculties have decayed too far or life can be bought at too irrational a price. Man is a dog tied to a cart; if he is wise he will run with it. (That is called following nature—being rational and wise. If he is unwise it will drag him and he will run with it willy-nilly.)

---

28. *Posidonius* T38 Edelstein-Kidd.

29. Sextus Empiricus *Adversus mathematicos* 7 (*Adversus logicos* 1).257.

What are the political doctrines of the early Stoics? Only the wise can live in peace and concord. They can live in any city; it doesn't matter where, for being passionless they will feel no special attachment to any body of men. The ideal dwelling-place will have no temples to the gods, no statues of them, no law courts, no gymnasia, no armies or warships or money, for the wise do not need these things; if you live in the light of reason, the conflicts, the fears and hopes that lead to the erection of these institutions will melt away. Zeno advocates total sexual freedom; all children shall be children of all the inhabitants. In the proper human life, according to Zeno, "We should not live by cities or demes, severally divided according to our own idea of what is just, but should consider that all men are demesmen and fellow citizens; there should be one life and one world, just as of a herd feeding together, nurtured by a common pasture."[30] This is the world of good men; only they can enjoy love, friendship, inner and outer harmony.

This is what Zeno preached; and, Plutarch exclaimed enthusiastically, Alexander of Macedon achieved it. Tarn complains that, just as Aristotle divided men into those who are free and those who are slaves by nature, so Zeno divided them into the good and wicked, the saved and the sinners. But this is not just. Any man can be saved, but not any man can transform his Aristotelian, fixed nature from that of a slave to that of a free man. What is plain is that while Plato and Aristotle desired to organise, to create and preserve an order, Plato's communism is, principally, a means of breeding suitable citizens. Zeno wishes to abolish this; both Zeno and his disciples Cleanthes and Chrysippus advocated social freedom of the most extreme kind: sexual promiscuity, homosexuality, incest, the eating of human flesh, permission to do anything that is not forbidden by *physis*—nature—for all contrary rules and traditions and habits, when examined, will be found to be artificial and irrational. When you look into yourself, and only into yourself—for there is nowhere else to look (you should certainly not look at social institutions, which are a mere external, adventitious aid to living)—then you will find that some rules are graven upon your heart by nature herself, while others are mere human inventions, ephemeral and directed to irrational ends, nothing to the wise man.

Later Stoicism absorbed a much more Aristotelian doctrine into itself and adapted itself to the uses of the Roman Empire, abandoning its sharp anti-political tone and content—for in principle Stoicism is as anti-political as Epicureanism. True, Zeno impressed the Macedonian ruler of Athens, Antigonus Gonatas, as a teacher of civic virtue. He would not serve him himself, but supplied pupils who became court chaplains and personal advisers to Hellenistic kings, and sometimes generals and practical social reformers (as in Sparta).

30. *SVF* i 262. The Greek word for "pasture" also means "law."

Nevertheless the king, for the Stoics, is not a divine creature as he is for the Pythagoreans and even for Aristotle; he is a human being, and since it is desirable that life should be as rational as possible, the Stoic sage can give him advice and influence him in the right direction, which, although not the most essential duty—which is to put oneself in the right frame of mind and nothing else—creates conditions in which men can more easily save themselves by Stoic introspection, self-examination of the tasks that reason lays upon them.

It is sometimes said that Zeno believed in a world State, but this is a misinterpretation of Plutarch's text: he has no interest in the State at all. In sharp contradiction to Plato and Aristotle, he believes that wisdom is to be learned and exercised not in the ideal *polis*, but in a world filled with wise men. Society is fundamentally a hindrance to self-sufficiency. It is evident that men cannot avoid society altogether, and must make the best of it, but so far from ethics being deducible from politics, the private from the public, the proper route is the other way about: to regulate public affairs in accordance with the rules of private morality. The virtuous or wise man must learn not to mind the storms of public life, to escape into himself, to ignore that which, being public, is ultimately of small importance. The distance between the Epicurean *ataraxia*—imperturbability—and the Stoic *apathia*—passionlessness—is not great. Pleasure or duty, happiness or rational self-realisation, these were the opposed ideals of the Hellenistic world. Whatever their differences, they were as one against the public world of Plato and Aristotle and the major Sophists. The break is immense and its consequences great. For the first time the idea gains ground that politics is a squalid occupation, not worthy of the wise and the good. The division of ethics and politics is made absolute; men are defined in individual terms, and politics, at best, becomes the application of certain ethical principles to human groups, instead of the other way around. Not public order, but personal salvation is all that matters. To sacrifice salvation to public needs is the greatest, most fatal error a man can commit; the betrayal of all that makes him human, of the reason within him, that which alone confers dignity and value upon men. There is no need to speak of the influence of this conception in Christianity, particularly in its Augustinian and quietist traditions.

It is very odd. How could so sharp a break occur within two decades? At one moment all the major thinkers appear to be discussing social and political questions; less than twenty years later no one at all is doing so. The Aristotelians are collecting plants, accumulating information about planets, animals and geographical formations; the Platonists are occupied with mathematics; no one speaks of social or political issues at all—it suddenly becomes a subject beneath the notice of serious men.

The official explanation which almost all historians adopt is, of course, the destruction of the city-state by Philip and Alexander of Macedon. The conventional view, adopted by almost all historians on the subject (there are some honourable exceptions), is that the writings of the major thinkers reflect political conditions directly and unambiguously. Sophocles, the Thucydidean Pericles, Aeschylus, Herodotus are spokesmen for Athens during the highest peak of her power and creative achievement. Plato, Isocrates, Thucydides himself reflect the internal stress and strain of the beginning of decadence. Demosthenes is the last desperate stand of independent democracy. Then comes the battle of Chaeronea in 338 B.C. The *polis* is destroyed by the Macedonian phalanx. Aristotle—like Hegel's owl of Minerva[31]—speaks for the past, not the future, and is out of date by the time that he escapes from Athens in 323. The *polis* becomes insignificant. A great new world is opened by Alexander's armies, and the average Greek or Athenian (as the author chooses), deprived of the sense of intimacy and security provided by the walls of the small self-contained city, feels puny and insignificant in the vast new empire which stretches out to the East. There is no natural unit to which to give his loyalty, and in which he can huddle for security.

The bleak new atmosphere, with familiar landmarks gone, makes him feel frightened and solitary, and concerned with his own personal salvation. Public life decays. Public concerns seem irrelevant. Menander, the fellow citizen and contemporary of Epicurus, writes comedies about domestic personal issues. Naturalism succeeds the idealised painting and sculpture which represented common ideals of the entire *polis*—noble objects of social worship and admiration and emulation. Superstition fills the vacuum left by the disappearance of State religion. Men retreat into themselves. The social fabric disintegrates. All men are equal before the remote despot in Pella or Alexandria or Antioch. The organic community has been pulverised into dissociated atoms. Stoicism and Epicureanism are natural forms of faith for men in this condition.

What is unplausible about this account is that the catastrophic change—for it is nothing less—occurs too rapidly. Athens was of small account before Chaeronea, and did *not* cease to be a city-state in 337 B.C. It was defeated, but it had been defeated by the Spartans before, and yet it led a sufficiently intense life as a city-state in the fourth century, as the speeches of the orators, if nothing else, convey. There was a Macedonian garrison in the Acropolis; it was expelled. True, it returned to subdue the rebellious city. Still, civic feeling continued; men continued to vote, to elect to public office, to bear liturgies. The *poleis* were not dissolved by Alexander or his successors: on the contrary, new ones were created. The inscriptions do not show a slackening of public spirit. There was

31. Mentioned at the end of Hegel's foreword to *Grundlinien der Philosophie des Rechts*: see Georg Wilhelm Friedrich Hegel, *Sämtliche Werke*, ed. Hermann Glockner (Stuttgart: F. Frommann, 1927–51), 7:37.

no real collapse until Romans appear on the scene. No doubt the cities did lose their independent character, especially in the field of foreign policy. It would, of course, be absurd to deny that Alexander had transformed the Mediterranean world. Yet however firmly you may believe that the ideological superstructure faithfully follows changes in the social or economic substructure—in this case, political organisation—there was certainly no break in the history of the *polis* so sharp, to judge from the subjective experiences of the citizens, as to explain so abrupt, swift and total a transformation of political outlook.

That Alexander's conquests were a pertinent factor in the development is, of course, true; but it is difficult to suppose that it is alone sufficient to explain what occurred. It is as if one were to say that Napoleon's conquest of Europe totally transformed social and political thought; it did not. It modified it deeply, but there is not that gap between the writings of, say, Hume and James Mill, or Kant and Hegel, which marks the break between Aristotle and Zeno. Men do not say to themselves: "My old world is crumbling, I must turn my attention to other aspects of experience. The outer life has become dreary, frightening and flat—it is time to turn to the inner life." (And if the unconscious is, at this point, called to our aid, it is only reasonable to say that it does not work quite so fast underground.) Men did not say this, especially in the ancient world, where changes seem to have taken less abrupt and catastrophic turns than in our own time. It is only reasonable to assume, therefore, that Stoic and Epicurean individualism did not spring quite so fully armed from the head of this now defeated and humiliated Athena. And, indeed, the new thinkers had some predecessors, occasionally mentioned by the ancient historians of philosophy. Zeno was a pupil of Crates, who was a Cynic, and he, in his turn, belonged to the school of Diogenes, who flourished, if that is the proper term for his peculiar life, in the middle of the fourth century B.C. We know that behind him stand the figures of Antisthenes and Aristippus. Antisthenes, who was a personal pupil of Socrates and was known not to have taken an interest in public life or the State, who believed in independence, whose hero was Heracles, performer of great labours for the benefit of men, followed the narrow path of principle. Aristippus, who proclaimed himself a stranger everywhere, said that he wished "neither to rule nor to be ruled,"[32] and therefore went too far for Socrates. His device was *"Ekho all' oukh ekhomai"* ("I possess but am not possessed"):[33] I enjoy pleasures and seek them but they cannot make me their slave; I can detach myself from them at will. Antisthenes agreed with Plato about one thing, at any rate, that victory over oneself was the most difficult and most important of all victories. Aristippus was a Cyrenaic who came to Athens from a very different climate; he may have believed that pleasure, provided one is not

---

32. Socrates' formulation of Aristippus' position. Xenophon *Memorabilia* 2.1.12.

33. Diogenes Laertius 2.75.

enslaved by it, is the natural end of man, whereas the Stoics believed that it was the enemy and clouded the passions and obscured the truth and so made men stumble and lose their way and become enslaved by forces they could not control; but the ideal of both was the same—independence, self-possession, individual self-assertion. So far as most men were blind, enslaved, prey to irrational feelings, the sage was likely to be unpopular and in some danger; hence his interest in swaying the rulers to his own way of thought.

Behind Antisthenes, behind Socrates even, stands the enigmatic figure of Antiphon, the Sophist of the end of the fifth century, of whom at least we possess independent evidence in a papyrus. He believed that you can cheat men, but not nature. If you eat a poisonous food, you die; but if you commit what is called an injustice, then, if no one has seen it, you will not suffer for it. It pays you to practice justice only if there are witnesses of your act—human beings upon whom you can make an impression, if need be a false one. Anarchy is a painful state of affairs, so there is a reason to teach children to obey, but if you can get away with something condemned by the human rules which particular human beings have established, then why not do so? He was against lawsuits because in claiming justice you made enemies of those against whom you witnessed, however truthfully, and this might prove a source of grave disadvantage to you later. From what we gather, Antiphon was a pessimistic quietist who preached the need for self-protection. The world was full of violent, dangerous men ready to make the innocent suffer. He gives advice to the victims on how to keep out of trouble. This is the first audible voice in ancient Greece which says—what Epicurus and his followers later echoed down the centuries—that the only satisfactory life is lived by keeping out of the sight of those who can do you damage, by creeping into a corner of your own choosing and constructing a private life which alone can satisfy the deepest needs of man. This is what Plato set himself to refute—the view that justice, participation in public life, does not pay but leads to wounds and misery and frustrated ambition. How well he accomplished his task is an issue that is still argued to this day.

Diogenes went further than this. He declared that he had to alter the currency—to destroy the old values and substitute new ones. He boasted that he belonged to no city—for that is what the claim to be cosmopolitan means—in the sense in which the *Communist Manifesto* of 1847 declared that "The workers have no country. . . . The proletarians have nothing to lose but their chains."[34] Only the independent man was free, and freedom alone makes happy, by making invulnerable. He inveighed against the arts, the sciences and all external graces with deliberate rudeness to Alexander. The rough jokes attributed to him create

34. Karl Marx and Friedrich Engels, *Werke* (Berlin: Dietz, 1956–83), 4:479, 493.

an image of a man who deliberately set out to shock public opinion in order to call attention to the gratuitous falsity and conventional hypocrisies of civilised life. He advocated, so we are told, total disregard of the proprieties: sexual intercourse and every intimate function may be performed in public. What deters one from it? The fact that people are shocked? What of it? Why should one respect the reactions of fools or hypocrites, slaves of convention, men who do not understand that men can attain to happiness and dignity only by following nature, that is, by ignoring artificial arrangements when all their instincts urge them in the opposite direction? This is full-blown individualism, but represented by our authorities as eccentric and a little deranged.

Crates, a rich man, gave up his wealth and took a few possessions in a knapsack and became the missionary and the saint of life according to nature. He called on families made unhappy by fears or jealousies or hatreds, reconciled enemies, created harmony and happiness, and, pauper and hunchback that he was, won the love of a beautiful and aristocratic lady, who married him against all protestations and became his fellow missionary. Man must be free, his possessions must be few enough to be carried in a sack slung across his shoulders, the *pera* which became the symbol of itinerant preachers of the Cynic sect. Here are Crates' words:

There is a city, Knapsack is its name, in the midst of the wine-coloured sea of Typhos [illusion]. Fair and fruitful it is, exceedingly beggarly, owning nothing. Thither sails no fool nor parasite nor lecher delighting in harlots, but it bears thyme and garlic and figs and bread. For such men fight not one another, nor yet do they take up arms for petty gain, nor for glory. . . . Free are they from lust, the enslaver of men, they are not twisted by it; rather do they take pleasures in freedom and immortal kinghood.[35]

And again:

I am a citizen of the lands Obscurity and Poverty, impregnable to fortune, a fellow citizen of Diogenes who defied all the plots of envy.[36]

These are the true predecessors of the new individualism—not many; and represented by our major authorities as somewhat marginal figures in the development of Greek culture. But were they indeed marginal? We cannot tell, for the principal, the fatal difficulty of this entire account is that we simply do not know what doctrines and opinions were held either by ordinary Greeks or by the thinkers among them. The vast bulk of our information comes from the writings of Plato and Aristotle, and they do not trouble to conceal their bias. Aristo-

35. Lloyd-Jones-Parsons *Supplementum Hellenisticum* frr. 351, 352.2–5.   36. Diogenes Laertius 6.93.

tle is perhaps a little more detached, scholarly and objective than Plato, but his own views are very positive and he shows little charity to his opponents, neither more nor less than other philosophers have since the beginning of the activity. What we know about the Sophists of the fifth century, and the Cynics and Sceptics and other so-called minor sects, is about as accurate as it would be if all we knew about, say, the writings of Bertrand Russell and modern linguistic analysis came to us from Soviet histories of philosophy; or if our only source for medieval thought was Russell's own history of Western thought. It is difficult to represent one's opponents fairly, and Plato plainly did not even try, unless they were positively sympathetic to him, like Parmenides or, in part, Protagoras—while the thinkers of whom we speak were plainly bitter enemies, whose views were to be put down at all costs.

The only point I wish to stress is that it is intrinsically unlikely that Zeno and Epicurus, Carneades and the new academy sprang up fully fledged to take over ethics and politics from the failing hands of degenerate Aristotelians and Platonists. Other scholars have felt this and have made gallant efforts to derive Stoicism, at least, from Oriental sources. They point out, quite accurately, that every Stoic teacher of any note came from Asia or Africa. Grant and Zeller, Pohlenz and Bevan and a host of others think it no accident that Zeno and Persaeus came from the Phoenician colony in Cyprus; Herillus came from Carthage; Athenodorus came from Tarsus; Cleanthes from the Troad; Chrysippus from Cilicia; Diogenes the Stoic from Babylon; Posidonius from Syria; Panaetius from Rhodes; others from Sidon and Seleucia, Ascalon and the Bosphorus—alas, not a single Stoic was born in old Greece. It is implied that these men brought Oriental ideas for personal salvation, black-and-white conceptions of good and evil, duty and sin, the desirability of dissolution in the eternal fire, the attractiveness of suicide. And perhaps it is hinted that this is echoed, in however vague a form, in the Jewish Bible: in the notion of individual responsibility to God that is no longer communal in Jeremiah, in Ezekiel and in the Psalms.[37] Who knows? Perhaps Philo of Alexandria, who was always trying to persuade people that Plato was acquainted with the teachings of Moses, was saying something that had some substance in it.

These theories are more interesting as indications that there is something inexplicable in this situation than because they are intrinsically plausible. Epicurus, whose doctrines for these purposes come close to those of the Stoics, was of pure Athenian blood, even though he grew up in Samos. Diogenes had come from Sinope, but Crates came from Elis, and no one suspected Antiphon of foreign origin. There is nothing inherently un-Greek in Zeno's doctrines: the belief

37. Jeremiah 31:29–34; Ezekiel 18:20, 14:12–20, 33:1–20; Psalms 40, 50, 51.

in universal reason, in nature, in peace and inner harmony, self-mastery and independence, liberty and a calm detachment are not Hebraic values. He did speak of duty in terms of absolute rules, but this sprang from his conception of reason as providing *ends*, as in Plato—as a rigorous category admitting of no degree. There are no voices that thunder at human beings, no sublime and mysterious and terrifying divine presence whose nature it is impious to enquire into: on the contrary, everything is nearly too rational, too systematic, too neat and cut-and-dried, too positivistic. There is no element of mysticism in either Zeno or Epicurus. Cleanthes' profoundly religious hymn is not the utterance of a mystic but of a rationalist, a believer in cosmic reason. If these men were, indeed, foreign in origin and habits and appearance, they assimilated, if anything, too eagerly to the Greek model, like many a colonial in Imperial Rome or natives of the Levant or India in France or England in the nineteenth century. The movements are Greek through and through. Indeed Dodds complains that they were too rationalistic, so that the irrational impulses of the Greeks forced a return to superstition.

Yet the revolution is very great, and if it is not sudden—because the names of the thinkers who preceded it or the opposition to the philosophies of Plato and Aristotle have simply been suppressed or forgotten—that is no more than a conjecture, and rests on considerations of general plausibility, not on any hard evidence that we possess.

What did the revolution come to? Let me attempt to summarise it.

(a) Politics and ethics are divorced. The natural unit is now no longer the group, in terms of which men are defined as natural members of it—even if not limbs of an organism—but the individual. His needs, his purposes, his solutions, his fate are what matter. Social institutions may be natural ways of satisfying the individual's needs; however, they are not ends in themselves, but means. And politics, the discipline that deals with the nature and purpose of such institutions, is not a philosophical enquiry that asks about ends and the nature of reality, but a technological discipline that tells men how to obtain what they need or deserve, or should have or make or be—questions answered by ethical or psychological enquiry, not by treatises about the State or about kingship. There are many of these latter, but they are handbooks for Hellenistic rulers or loyal tributes and justifications of their conduct by tame court philosophers.

(b) The only genuine life is the inner life; what is outer is expendable. A man is not a man unless his acts are dictated by himself and not forced upon him by a despot from without or by circumstances which he cannot control. The only portion of himself that is within his control is his inner consciousness. If he trains that consciousness to ignore and reject what it cannot control, he acquires independence from the external world. Only the independent are free, and only the free can satisfy their desires, that is, attain to peace and happiness. Such independence can be obtained only by understanding the nature of reality. But whereas for Plato and Aristotle this reality contains public life—the State—as intrinsic parts of it, for the Hellenistic philosophers it does not; hence the decay of political philosophy until Roman needs and Roman practice cause a specious revival in it.

(c) The ethics are the ethics of the individual, but this is not the same—and this point is of some importance—as the notion of individual rights or the sacredness of private life. Diogenes did not mind whether you were disgusted by his mode of living, his rags, his filth, his obscenity, his insulting behaviour, but he did not seek privacy as such. He merely ignored social conventions because he believed that those who knew the truth would not be horrified, but would live as he did. There is more inclination to privacy in Epicurus, but even there there is no individual to keep others out of his particular corner—a right to a room of one's own. This is a much later idea, and those writers who, like Sabine and, indeed, Pohlenz, who is a far more genuine scholar, speak of the emergence of the new value of privacy, and in the case of Sabine go so far as to talk about the rights of man, misunderstand the ancient world profoundly. Not until a force that in principle resisted the encroachments of the civil establishment—the Christian Church in its early struggles against Rome, and, perhaps, before it, Orthodox Jews who fought the secularising policies of Antiochus Epiphanes—created a conflict of authority did the idea arise that frontiers must be drawn beyond which the State is not entitled to venture. Even then it took many centuries for the notion of individual rights to emerge, the notion defended so passionately by Benjamin Constant, that men need an area, however small, within which they can do as they please, no matter how foolish or disapproved of by others. The notion of freedom from State control which his contemporary Humboldt defended, and which found its most eloquent champion in John Stuart Mill—that notion is wholly alien to the ancient world. Neither Plato nor Xenophon nor Aristotle nor Aristophanes, who deplore the selfishness, rapacity, lawlessness, lack of civic sense, irresponsibility of Athenian democracy; nor Pericles, who defends the "open" society over which he presides; nor the Stoics and Sceptics and their successors, who thought of nothing but the self-preservation and self-gratification of individuals—none of these had any notion of the rights of man, the right to be left alone, the right not to be impinged upon within identifiable frontiers. That comes much later, and it is a gross anachronism to find it in the ancient world, whether Greek or Hebraic.

(d) But what happened was dramatic enough. One of the legs of the tripod upon which Western political philosophy rests was, if not broken, cracked. Individual salvation, individual happiness, individual taste, individual character emerge as the central goal, the centre of interest and value. The State is no longer what it was for Aristotle—a self-sufficient group of human beings united by *natural* pursuit of the good (that is, satisfying) life—but "a mass of people living together, governed by law" (so Chrysippus at the beginning of the third century defined it).[38] A man may serve the State "if nothing stops him,"[39] but it is not the central function of his life.

This is the moment that marks the birth of the idea that politics is unworthy of a truly gifted man, and painful and degrading to a truly good one. Of this attitude to politics there is scarcely any earlier trace, although perhaps the life of Socrates, as perhaps of original and interesting thinkers of earlier times of whom we know too little, bears witness to this too. At any rate, from now on this new scale of values haunts the European consciousness. Public and individual values, which had not been discriminated before, now go in different directions and, at times, clash violently. There is an attempt to patch up the situation by the Stoics of the Roman Republic and the Roman Empire: Panaetius regrets Zeno's violently anti-political attitude and tries to say that all this was written on the "dog's tail,"[40] that is, when Zeno was still under the influence of the Cynic, Crates. But once the seamless whole of the city-state in which the public and the private were not distinguished is torn, nothing can ever make it entirely whole again. In the Renaissance, in modern times, the notion of the separateness of moral and political values, the ethics of resistance, of withdrawal, of personal relationships, versus those of the service of mankind, is one of the deepest and most agonising issues. This is the hour of its birth.

It seems to have come to maturity, and to have begun to possess the minds of the intellectually most influential city that ever existed, somewhere between the death of Aristotle and the rise of the Stoics and the Epicureans. We know little about this intermediate period. Theophrastus reigned in the Lyceum in the place of Aristotle, and he believed in *oikeiosis*—kinship of all life—that there was a natural bond that united men to one another, a great solidarity, not service in a common cause, or the march towards a common purpose, or perception of the same truths, or union by some reciprocally accepted convention, or the claims of utility, but the sense of the unity of life, of the value of men as men, of humanity as a single family with world-wide frontiers. This is not a political idea, but a biological and moral one. Where does it come from? Not from Aristotle, who thought that neither barbarians nor slaves were even remote cousins to free men. But it is echoed by Zeno and by Epicurus. Where does it come from? That is a question to which we may never be able to discover the answer. Antiphon? Pythagoras? We do not know. Plato and Aristotle, if they knew, chose not to tell us.

(e) The new age of individualism is usually deplored as an age of decadence. Cornford says that after Aristotle "nothing remains but the philosophy of old age, the resignation of a twilight that deepens alike over the garden of Pleasure

38. *SVF* iii 329.

39. *SVF* iii 697. Cf. Zeno, *SVF* i 271.

40. Diogenes Laertius 7.4.

and the hermitage of Virtue."[41] Sabine observes that the result of the decline of the city-state was "a defeatist attitude, a mood of disillusionment, a disposition to withdraw and to create a private life in which public interests had a small or even a negative part."[42] Then follows a passage in which it is suggested that "the unfortunate and dispossessed" made themselves even more violently vocal against the city-state and its values and laid "stress upon the seamy side of the existing social order."[43] "To Plato and Aristotle," the same author goes on, "the values offered by citizenship still seemed fundamentally satisfying, or at least capable of being made so; to a few of their contemporaries and increasingly to their successors this appeared to be false."[44] How does he know that there were few? If Greek literature does not reflect the prevalent democracy, but, on the contrary, criticism of it, why should it record a perhaps widespread desire for private values and private salvation? Why should we consider Plato and Aristotle better witnesses to the general thought of their time than Prodicus or Antiphon? Are Burke and Hegel, because they possess more genius, more reliable witnesses of the thought of their own time than Paine or Bentham? If Goethe and Comte were the only authors that survived from their age, how accurately should we be able to deduce its political and moral outlook? As for the pessimistic note struck by Cornford or Sabine, why should we assume that the decline of the "organic" community was an unmixed disaster? Might it not have had a liberating effect? Perhaps the individuals who lived in greater and more centralised units felt a greater degree of independence, less interference. Rostovtzeff speaks of "buoyant optimism" in the cities of the Greek Diaspora.[45] The great leap forward in the sciences, and the arts as well, coincides with Cornford's theory of twilight and the disillusionment and defeatism of which Sabine and Barker speak. To every age its values: the individualism of the Hellenistic age is attributed by these thinkers to men's loneliness in the new mass society. Yet perhaps what they felt was not loneliness, but a sense of suffocation in the *polis*? First aristocrats like Heraclitus complained of it, then others. So far from being a sad, slow decline, it meant expanding horizons. The third century marks the beginning of new values, and a new conception of life; the condemnation of it by Aristotle and his modern disciples rests on assumptions which, to say the least, do not seem self-evidently valid.

41. Francis Macdonald Cornford, *Before and After Socrates* (Cambridge: Cambridge University Press, 1932), 109.

42. George H. Sabine, *A History of Political Theory*, 4th ed. (Fort Worth, TX: Holt, Rinehart, and Winston, 1973), 131.

43. Ibid.

44. Ibid., 131–32.

45. M. Rostovtzeff, *The Social and Economic History of the Hellenistic World* (Oxford: Clarendon Press, 1941), 1095.

LEFT-WING WITTGENSTEIN

Bernard Williams

The most powerful contribution to Anglo-American political philosophy in this century has been that of John Rawls, and like most people discussing this subject now, I shall start from his work. The central idea of Rawls's theory is to model the demands of a conception of social justice by the fiction of contracting parties making a rational choice under ignorance. We are to imagine people choosing a social system without knowing what particular role or position they will occupy in it. These people, in their assumed state of ignorance, are represented as dis-interested toward one another and as making what is roughly speaking a self-interested choice. This combination of self-interest and ignorance is equivalent, in effect, to impartiality on the part of an informed agent. If ordinary, informed people have a sense of social justice or fairness, they will be in effect willing to think about what they would choose behind "the veil of ignorance," as Rawls calls it, and willing to stick to those conclusions in actual life.

There are many deep analogies between these ideas and a characteristically Kantian approach to mortality. The willingness to take oneself behind the veil of ignorance and conduct this kind of thought experiment is analogous to the disposition which Kant identified as fundamental to morality, the disposition to

Originally published in *Common Knowledge* 1.1 (Spring 1992): 33–42. © 1992.

Common Knowledge 25:1–3
DOI 10.1215/0961754X-7299402

conceive of oneself as both a citizen and a legislator of a republic of equals. Rawls does not think, as Kant did, that the project of engaging oneself to this morality of justice is implicit in the very conception of being a rational agent. However, he does suppose that the dispositions of justice lie very close to a proper understanding of the self, and that a story of psychological fulfillment for the individual would embrace the dispositions of justice as his theory characterizes them. This is one way in which Rawls's theory, even though it insists that questions of what is right or just must come before questions of what is a good or satisfying human life, does have implications about what such a life will be. It will be a life shaped by a sense of justice, and the questions of justice are ones that it is natural for human beings living together to want to answer.

In his original book, Rawls did, very broadly, tend to agree with Kant in a further matter, namely that this was a universal theory of social justice: that is to say, that it was perfectly appropriate to think of any human beings anywhere as arriving at some such conceptions. This made the theory universalistic in a strong sense which associates it with the outlook of the Enlightenment. In more recent work, however, Rawls has rather moved away from this to a position well expressed by the title of one of his articles, "Justice as Fairness: Political not Metaphysical." Under this conception, he sees his idea of justice as particularly appropriate to a modern society, "a modern society" being conceived of as technically advanced, democratic, and, above all, pluralistic. This emphasis does not only limit the ambitions of the original theory. It also rewrites its basis. The idea of procedural justice was of course always contained in Rawls's theory, in the sense that the just society was defined in terms of what would emerge from a certain hypothetical discussion, namely that behind the veil of ignorance. But the new emphasis brings out a way in which the procedural aspects of the theory are not simply confined to a hypothetical discussion behind a fictional veil of ignorance. Under the new emphasis, the whole theory, the whole way of going about things—including the appeal to the veil of ignorance—recommends itself as a solution to a characteristically modern problem, namely that of negotiating fairly the conditions of coexistence of people who have very diverse conceptions of the good. The procedural motions of fairness no longer characterize merely the theoretical content of the theory (structuring, in particular, the situation behind the veil of ignorance) but apply also to the kind of social reality which is likely to embrace such a theory in the first place.

However, this new emphasis does at the same time still preserve, and indeed even underscores, the idea that living with a sense of justice is natural to human beings. It is very central to Rawls's more recent ideas that the adoption of the scheme of the well-ordered society by parties who have to live together with diverse conceptions of the good—the adoption, that is to say, of justice as fairness as an appropriate way of life under pluralism—this procedure is not merely a *pis aller*. (Here he emphatically differs from many other contractual theorists, such as Hobbes.) To live under some such system does itself express an important dimension of the human personality. This aspect of the theory throws an interesting light on the new developments which emphasize the idea that justice as fairness is a particular answer to some peculiar problems of modernity. If justice as fairness does particularly well express certain fundamental aspects of human personality; and if it is a characteristic response to the conditions of pluralism rather than a timeless demand on all human agents living in any society anywhere; then the right conclusion will be that the conditions of pluralism particularly well express fundamental aspects of the human personality. This view itself, interestingly, seems not so much Kantian as characteristic of some other liberal views, such as those of John Stuart Mill. If the idea is very strongly pressed—more strongly pressed than it has been by Rawls—then it would itself imply a certain conception of modernity to which Mill was well disposed: that at least so far as its pluralism is concerned, it represents a form of progress from societies which, in contrast to the typically modern condition, were held together by some more unifying and concrete conception of the good itself, and not merely by procedural arrangements for negotiating the coexistence of different conceptions of the good.

Rawls's enterprise has of course been criticized from many different directions. I shall leave aside criticisms from Utilitarians, which seem to me less interesting. More significant have been criticisms from what has been called, very broadly and perhaps not very helpfully, a communitarian direction. I have in mind here criticisms that have been made, among others, by Charles Taylor, by Alasdair MacIntyre, and (under the influence of Charles Taylor) by Michael Sandel in a book directly critical of Rawls's theory. Indeed I myself have been associated with some strains in these criticisms, though for reasons that I shall mention later, I am resistant to being classed with those who deserve in any strong sense the communitarian label. Some of the criticisms relate to the theory's conception of what human beings are like. It is said that the picture of the moral agent presented by Rawls is too resolutely abstract; the Rawlsian person is concerned in the first instance only with certain primary goods of a nonethical kind, and is capable of thinking of himself or herself in abstraction from any concretely given social or historical situation. Further, Rawls's emphasis on the primacy of the right over the good has been read as implying that a sense of justice is the primary moral sentiment. It is fair to say that Rawls himself in many places seeks to counteract the more severe consequences of this kind, but critics still insist that people who really fitted Rawls's conception would think of themselves, on the lines of traditional liberal theory, simply as individuals who were bearers of desires, individual projects and rights, to which in turn corresponded duties; other forms of bonds or social solidarity would be secondary to these.

These critics stand to Rawls much as Hegel and his followers stood to Kant. Their criticisms, like those of the Hegelians, have political and social consequences as well; but, again as with the Hegelians, it is not agreed what the consequences are. Charles Taylor tends to agree with certain things that Rawls says about modern society, including the value of certain aspects of pluralism and of the Enlightenment emphasis on individual rights, while holding that Rawls's explanation or understanding of this situation is too impoverished and does not allow enough for other aspects of the ethical consciousness. Alasdair MacIntyre, on the other hand, is certainly opposed to modern society in almost all its forms, and occupies a position radically opposed to liberalism. In the case of Michael Sandel, I must say that I find it quite hard to discover whether or not he believes that the ethical powers which he most esteems, and which he finds insufficiently honored in Rawls's theory, would be better expressed in a more homogeneous and traditional society. The rhetoric of his criticism is on the strongest Right Hegelian lines, but some of his political preferences seem distinctly to the Left of that.

It is easy to see why there should be a problem at this point. Rawls's theory, and particularly its more recent developments, directs itself to certain characteristics of a modern society, in particular its pluralism, and tries to give an account of how that pluralism might be related both to schemes of social justice, and to the moral capacities of its citizens. As I said, it has to tread quite a delicate path between thinking, on the one hand, that the pluralistic character of modern societies is in fact among their disadvantages, and that the conception of justice as negotiating a fair coexistence between different conceptions of the good represents a kind of second-best answer; and thinking, on the other hand, that the pluralism of modern societies brings out what is in fact the best in human beings, namely a capacity for impartial fairness and toleration, and therefore itself represents a desirable human social condition.

This ambivalence is not simply a difficulty for Rawls's theory. It is rather a very real ambivalence that faces all of us: these philosophical problems represent familiar disquiets of modernity. On the one hand, there are characteristics of modern societies, such as their pluralism, their ideology of toleration, and their emphasis on at least the ideal of justificatory discursive discussion, which are well expressed in a philosophy that emphasizes procedural justice and fair coexistence, rather than privileging any other substantive conception of what makes life worthwhile. On the other hand, such a philosophy seems untrue to a great deal of human experience, and tends to reduce the conception of the ethical powers of human beings to too thin a basis. This is so in at least two senses. The fundamental moral power, the sense of justice, is too abstracted from other affections, commitments, and projects that make people what they are or at least make their lives what they are. At the same time, it seems to introduce an element of dissociation or alienation at the social level, inasmuch as widely diverse conceptions of the good have to be seen under the sign of toleration, to such an extent that one has to be very deeply committed to one's own conception of the good, while at the same time regarding very different ones as tolerable within a framework that is held together by a form of citizenship motivated by the sense of fairness and not much more. Since these conflicting aspirations do act on many of us, the fact that they show up so strongly in current philosophy suggests the encouraging conclusion that philosophy is at least to this extent in touch with reality.

Rawls allows more than his critics sometimes admit to the other side of the argument, and gives an answer of very considerable fineness even if one does not entirely agree with it. The communitarians, on the other hand, find it difficult to avoid a simpler and more straightforwardly reactionary answer, to the effect that a culturally more homogeneous society, where fewer questions were asked and there was a higher degree of traditional social solidarity, would be a better state of affairs, and that the pluralism of modernity represents, in effect, varying degrees of disintegration. Taylor tries fairly hard to avoid that conclusion; MacIntyre on the other hand seems happy to embrace it.

My contribution to the philosophical debates has been to some extent that of making myself a nuisance to all parties. Inasmuch as I have tried to make a nuisance of myself to the Kantian, and also to the Utilitarian, party, I have found myself cast from time to time as a communitarian. I resist that description for political reasons, and because of the often undisguised element of nostalgia which seems to hang over its aspirations. The whole debate is, in a sense, rather too familiar. The responses of both Left and Right Hegelians to Kant in the nineteenth century already powerfully expressed the yearning (radical in the one case, conservative in the other) for a life that would have a greater ethical density, a more thickly shared sense of community, than was offered, it seemed, by modernity and its most progressive philosophy, critical liberalism. This yearning, at least in philosophy, hardly ever took simply the form of unqualified nostalgia for an imagined past of traditional solidarity. It was always associated in some way with a desire to preserve the reflective freedom and selfconsciousness that had issued in and from the Enlightenment; or, at the very least, associated with an assumption that at some level it would be preserved. The Left or radical tendency wanted a society that somehow would embody at once solidarity and criticism, tradition and freedom, familiarity and adventurous variety; the Right was happier to settle for a more traditional style of consciousness for most citizens, reserving the critical sense of the contingency of these arrangements to an elite, perhaps, or at the limit, to the theorist himself. Some of these nineteenth-century positions are being expressed again in the current discussions. Can we get beyond them?

The oppositions between (broadly) "Kantian" and (broadly) "communitarian" thinkers are often expressed, particularly by the Kantians, in terms of the possibility, and the basis, of critique. If there is some general and abstract framework of principles of justice, such as Rawls's theory, local practices and traditions can be criticized, at least to the extent that they stand opposed to toleration and the fair acceptance of diversity; but if we emphasize only the local significances of a densely structured traditional existence, there may seem to be no point of leverage for criticism. Particularly as things have recently gone, this form of controversy has been rather distorted by the fact that, faced with an Anglo-American consensus that has been in good part liberal, the various "Hegelian" theorists have themselves appeared in the role of critics, urging us to change our aspirations in a communitarian direction. (Indeed, this is not only a recent phenomenon: since all Hegelian positions represent to some extent the desire to recover something supposedly absent from modernity, they have always tended to be more oppositional than anyone would be in the world they themselves would best like.)

There is one important philosophical position which has been deployed for Right Hegelian purposes, in this contemporary sense, and which, taken in that way, makes it mysterious, not only how critique can be legitimate, but how it can even intelligibly exist. This is the later philosophy of Wittgenstein. This philosophy (which, together with Heideggerian and other influences, has contributed to the outlook of Richard Rorty) is very strongly opposed to foundationalism in every area of thought and experience. Whether in mathematics, in our ordinary language, or in ethics, everything equally is a matter of practice, of what we find natural. It is mistaken, on this picture, to try to ground our practices, whether ethical or cognitive; we must rather recognize that our way of going on is simply our way of going on, and that we must live within it, rather than try to justify it. This philosophy, in its rejection of the "abstract," may itself remind us of a kind of Hegelianism, though without, of course, Hegel's systematic pretensions or his historical teleology. But if so, it has been, up to now, very much of the Right variety: despite the efforts of some of his followers, the tendency of Wittgenstein's influence has been distinctly conservative.

The point may be put in a number of different ways. When the later philosophy of Wittgenstein has been applied to the social sciences, it has been thought to yield conservative conclusions because of its holism, which may have much the same consequences as the similarly holistic doctrine of functionalism did in social anthropology. Each practice, seen as part of a form of life, plays its own role in such a way that its suppression or criticism must involve the distortion of the functioning whole. Again, the point can be put in terms of gradualism. Even if you do not think that the Wittgensteinian picture encourages an extravagantly organic picture of the synchronic state of society, it certainly encourages the view that changes in our thought and practice must essentially be piecemeal if they are to be comprehensible at all, and not merely arbitrary: even if society as a whole is not one organic item, each conceptual tendril in the interwoven mass is itself a living thing and can be directed in a certain way only if that is the way in which, in that context of social vegetation, it finds it easy to grow. Or again, for those who dislike biological analogies, much the same point may be put in terms of consensus. On this picture of things, to understand anything is to share in understanding, and nothing sustains understanding or knowledge except a shared social practice. The redirection of an ethical term, or more generally, the radical departure from an ethical practice, looks as though it will be merely arbitrary unless it can carry at least a substantive body of agreement with it; indeed, some critics of the picture might say that even this is a kindly understatement, and that the consequence of the picture is that no change in practice can comprehensibly occur unless it has already occurred—that is to say, it cannot occur at all except by magic.

Yet another way in which the picture may seem to be conservative is that it involves an undiscriminating acceptance of whatever conceptual resources of the society actually exist. Moral philosophy, in its more radical moods, hopes to be able to put some existing ethical concepts out of business by showing that their implications are unacceptable from its preferred perspective; but if no such leverage can appropriately be applied, there seems no way in which any of the existing ethical ideas can be killed off. The most that might happen, perhaps, is that some might die out, but if this happens, it presumably does so for reasons that are, as it were, opaque to philosophy. The Wittgensteinian picture itself insists that conceptual change is likely to be closely associated with any social change there is, but it is unclear how an understanding of either could be particularly accessible to philosophy: even conceptual change is likely to be represented, in this perspective, as a matter of brute facticity.

It is at this point that a certain paradox in the view begins to emerge. If all social phenomena equally are just whatever they are, merely part of this interwoven net of practices, then all of them equally will be opaque to philosophical criticism. But the Wittgensteinian philosopher is himself criticizing something, if only the practices of ethical theorists and other philosophers who misunderstand the proper nature of our thought. In the case of Wittgenstein himself, this point does not really apply very directly, because so much of his later philosophy consisted of a criticism of himself, and of philosophy itself inasmuch as it had a hold upon him. But to those who regard Wittgensteinian ideas as making a contribution to an ongoing discourse of philosophy, the point does apply, and it applies even more to social philosophers of a conservative tendency who have taken up Wittgensteinian ideas in order to justify their conservatism. For they will wish to criticize not just the misconceptions of philosophy, but the aspirations of radicals, and there is a paradox in their doing so on the basis of such a philosophy. According to this philosophy itself, all that philosophy can do is to remind us how our ethical ideas are rooted in our ethical practice; but (as Ronald Dworkin has repeatedly emphasized) part of our ethical practice consists precisely in this, that people have found in it resources with which to criticize their society. Practice is not just the practice of practice, so to speak, but also the practice of criticism.

If we reject foundationalism, we have to recall (as Hegel did and Wittgensteinians typically do not) that our form of life, and hence, more particularly, our ethical concepts and thoughts, have a history, and that a society such as ours is conscious of that fact. Not every society can think about its ethical life in historical or social categories, but it is a salient feature of literate, and most particularly of modern, societies that they embody a conception of their own institutions and practices, and of the ways in which these differ from those of other societies.

The force of this point is not readily recognized by Wittgensteinian philosophers. This comes out particularly if one considers their use of the expressions "we" and "our." When Wittgensteinians speak of "our" form of life, they characteristically use that expression in what linguistics calls an inclusive rather than a contrastive way: the "we" represents not us as against others, but an "us" that embraces anybody with whom we could intelligibly hold a conversation. It is obvious why this should be appropriate to matters of meaning and of understanding, and why also it is plausible to say in those connections that we have no way of standing outside "us." But we cannot simply take this idea over into ethical and social thought, if "our" way of life is to be that way of life within which you and I live and find particular meaning in our lives; since that form of life is precisely not the form of life of other human beings who have lived within some ethical system or other. It is, for one thing, the life of a distinctively modern society, and that is very different from other lives that have been lived, and no doubt from other lives that will be lived in the future.

There are two points here that it is very important for moral philosophy to remember together. It must realize that we can understand from the inside, as anthropologists understand, a conceptual system in which ethical concepts are integrally related to ways of explaining and describing the world. At the same time, it must be conscious that there are alternatives to any such system, and that there is a great deal of ethical variety. A well-known feature of modern life—one that directly contributes to the disagreements between Rawls and his critics which I have discussed—is that it actually brings into the substance of ethical life the consciousness of this very diversity, and requires one to live some kind of ethical life while conscious not only that alternatives to it have existed in different social circumstances at different times and places, but also that alternatives to it may exist at our own door. Moreover, it is the case that our own ethical ideas come from very various sources.

Once we regard the ethical life we now have as a genuinely historical and local structure, one that is peculiarly self-conscious about its own origins and potentialities, we shall have less temptation to assume that it is a satisfactorily functioning whole; and we shall be more likely to recognize that some widely accepted parts of it may stand condemned in the light of perfectly plausible extrapolations of other parts.

The correct conclusion is not that foundationalism is necessary for social critique. What we are left with, if we reject foundationalism, is not an inactive or functionalist conservatism that has to take existing ethical ideas as they stand. On the contrary, once the resultant picture of ethical thought without foundationalism is made historically and socially realistic, in particular by registering in it the categories of modernity, it provides a possibility of deploying some parts of it against others, and of reinterpreting what is ethically significant, so as to give a critique of existing institutions, conceptions, prejudices, and powers.

So far as critique is concerned, there seems no reason why nonfoundationalist political thought, characterized in the way that Wittgenstein's philosophy suggests, should not take a radical turn. There could be, one might say, a Left Wittgensteinianism. The disposition of most of his followers not to go in this direction is due to their refusal to think in concrete social terms about the extent of "we." In Wittgenstein's own work, because of his principal preoccupation with problems of language, meaning, and knowledge, it may often not make too much difference whether the "we" refers to one cultural group or tribe as contrasted with another, or rather extends to everyone with whom we might intelligibly speak; or where it does make a difference, the correct understanding can be easily extracted. But in political and ethical matters of pluralism and community, these are the differences that matter to the exclusion of almost everything else, and the right understanding cannot be uncontentiously extracted. Once a realistic view of communities is applied, and the categories that we need to understand anyone who is intelligible at all are distinguished from those of more local significance, we can follow Wittgenstein to the extent of not looking for a new foundationalism, but still leave room for a critique of what some of "us" do in terms of our understanding of a wider "we."

The emphasis that this discussion has given to questions of toleration and critique of course accords with the traditional concerns of liberal theory; it also provides a familiar home for the labels, perhaps increasingly unhelpful, of "Left" and "Right." But any such discussion depends on an assumption, not only of liberal theory but of almost all political philosophy, that we are concerned with questions of how one society should be structured and ruled—of how people in one society, under a government, should live. With the exception of some considerations of global justice, third-world poverty and development, most political philosophy continues to address problems of justice and legitimacy within one society or state, and this concentration is taken for granted in formulating the issues of pluralism. It is not in the least surprising that this should be so, for both historical and theoretical reasons. More specifically, it is not surprising that American philosophers should think about these problems in terms of a large and complexly pluralist society with an elaborate system for identifying individual rights. They have already had their war to preserve the Union, a war that involved very obviously both the identity claimed for a local culture, and some definite individual rights. But in many other parts of the world, such as Eastern Europe and parts of what used to be Soviet Asia, what is at issue at the present time is precisely the integrity of states, and questions of what kind of society can reasonably claim a political identity. In relation to these problems, theories that tell us how to run a pluralist state simply beg the question.

It may be said, in admittedly very simplistic terms, that (whatever the practical difficulties) it is not impossible to extend pluralist theory to cover such cases. If a culturally homogeneous group within an existing state wishes to secede, and it could do so without severely damaging the interests of the others, then it should have the right to do so. Here, they may seem to be a benevolent alliance of liberal and communitarian opinion, the liberals resisting the coercion of these individuals, and the friends of community applauding their desire to live as a culturally individual society. But this happy agreement may be very fragile. First, the breakaway state is likely, in any real case, itself to include some minorities. It can be argued that those who claimed the right to set up the breakaway state did so in the name of a minority culture, and, in the merest consistency, must allow the expression of cultural identity by people who now form a minority among them. But apart from the well-attested fact that the previously persecuted are not often very sensitive to this kind of argument, the argument itself is not very strong. What the breakaway group claimed, after all, was the right to set up a culturally homogeneous state. This may commit the breakaway state to accepting the right of some minority to do the same thing, if they can; but if the minority cannot do that, it does not necessarily commit the new state to respect their rights to cultural self-expression, in the middle of what was precisely intended to be a culturally unitary state.

Another reason why the apparent accord between liberals and communitarians on the right of cultural secession may not be very robust is that pluralist liberals in the original formation may be concerned, not just with the rights of potential minorities in the breakaway state, but with the rights of individuals who belong even to the seceding culture: the culturally homogeneous society may contain people (women, for instance) whom the pluralist liberals see as disadvantaged by the separatist cultural system. Such a view would have put a strain on their pluralist toleration in the original situation; indeed, interference by a liberal government in the supposed interests of individuals who belong to the cultural group is just the kind of thing that could encourage the break from a pluralist state.

Faced with these conflicts, it is hard to see how political philosophy could attain some neutrally acceptable view of them. It is not even clear whether either liberal pluralist theory or its opponents can produce a clear answer derived from their own principles. The liberals will have to advance from the mere idea of fair coexistence in a society, to the stronger views that have been part of their Enlightenment legacy, which claim the absolute value of individual autonomy and self-determination against the values of traditionalist cultural homogeneity. It may be hard to support such a substantive conception of individual rights without taking the path which Rawlsian liberalism has resisted, of putting a conception of a desirable human life before, or at least on a level with, a theory of the right. The communitarians, on the other hand, will have to consider, more clearly than they have been disposed to do, how far their affirmations of the value of cultural solidarity can go once they are freed from the disapproved, but perhaps rather welcome, limitations imposed by a liberal consensus. In particular, they must consider how important it is to the affirmation of that solidarity that it is expressed in one society, and that that society should constitute one state. The Wittgensteinians, certainly, have nothing merely from their own resources that could help one to think about such issues—it is only too obvious that these are questions that involve who is to count as "we."

In the meantime, we have to look, as always, not so much to political theory, of whatever kind, as to the economic and political forces that surround these conflicts. The line between a politics of legitimate community, and blank tribalism, is going to be held, if at all, by the influence of a world commercial order and that of the only powers at the present time—themselves liberal powers—which are in a position, through international agencies, to enforce solutions. Writing as the smoke rises from Croatia, I see no great reason to suppose that the outcomes of these conflicts will be rapid, painless, or reasonable.

SUFFOCATION IN THE *POLIS*

Jeffrey M. Perl

However problematic the idiom or rhetoric of those who say "man is a social animal," it is hard to name an idiom that has been more successful.[1] As Isaiah Berlin once observed in these pages, "no argument seems" any longer "needed to establish this proposition, for it is evidently something that all sane men believe without question; it is part of the general notion of man. Solitude can be endured only by a god or a beast: it is subhuman or superhuman."[2] If so, the ideas entertained in *Common Knowledge* lately have not been those of "sane men" and sane women. "The only satisfactory life is lived by keeping out of the sight of those who can do you damage, by creeping into a corner of your own choosing" (208)— uncommon lives lived in accordance with that principle have been the subject of this symposium until now.

A life lived out of sight or in a corner may seem quietist or eremitic, hence vaguely Christian. But this passage about the "only satisfactory life" is Berlin's summary of teachings attributed to Antiphon, a Sophist of the fifth century BC. Standard histories represent such teachings as emerging later, rather suddenly, in the Hellenistic schools of the Stoics and Epicureans. But Berlin suggested that the

Originally published in *Common Knowledge* 13.1 (Winter 2007): 33–39, as part of the symposium "Unsocial Thought, Uncommon Lives, Part 3." © 2007 by Duke University Press.

1. Regarding the problematic and on occasion self-contradictory character of this rhetoric, see Perl, "Unsettling Others," *Common Knowledge* 12.2 (Spring 2006): 216, and "'A Diriment Anchorism'" 12.3 (Fall 2006): 379–80.

2. Isaiah Berlin, "A Turning-Point in Political Thought," *Common Knowledge* 7.3 (Winter 1998): 193. Article edited by Henry Hardy and published posthumously. Further references are given parenthetically in the text.

Common Knowledge 25:1–3

DOI 10.1215/0961754X-7299414

ancestry of these ideas—among the early Sophists, Cynics, Skeptics, "and other so-called minor sects" that may well have been major in their time—had been erased from history because their opinions had been "violently anti-political" (212).[3] Questioning if we should take for granted that, after Aristotle's time, "an age of decadence" followed the "decline of the city-state," Berlin wondered if, on the contrary, political decline had "had a liberating effect" on Greek philosophy. Intellectual historians tend to ascribe the unsocial values of Hellenistic thought to "men's loneliness in the new mass society." Berlin, on the other hand, asked if "perhaps what they felt was not loneliness, but a sense of suffocation in the *polis*?" (213–14).

"Suffocation" is, to say the least, evocative diction. The response to being choked or stifled is liable to be fierce. To imagine anarchists, misanthropes, antinomians, Scrooges, the chronically unemployed, nonvoters, and a range of criminals (from hackers and black marketeers to draft dodgers and tax evaders) as victims of asphyxiation may be an experiment worth enduring. For is it right to hold accountable for havoc those who have been deprived of air?

Antisocial is an adjective applied to forms of life each of which merits its own full description. Nathaniel Hawthorne, Emily Dickinson, Sir Vauncey Harpur Crewe, Joseph Cornell, Glenn Gould, and Pascal Quignard—previous subjects of discussion here—should not have to share an adjective with hooligans. Excusing themselves from company they saw as indelicate, each went up- or downstairs to a different safe haven. Etty Hillesum and Simone Weil present more problematic cases: what could *antisocial* mean if applied to Jews in the Nazis' stranglehold? In Europe, in the forties, would not *antisocial* be effectively an accolade (and *social*, a synonym for "inane")? Essays in this third and last collection of uncommon lives in *Common Knowledge* reflect positively on even harder cases: assorted chiliasts, adventurers in "uncanny psychic domain," and more routine saboteurs of public order; a theologian of *caritas* and *agape* who despised and offended nearly everyone he met; an aesthetic theorist who defined art as "the destruction of commonality through violence"; an architect who designed buildings and planned cities that impede social interaction. To feel empathy with these characters is not essential. But it is worth considering that the enduring desire to disrupt or outfox society may be evidence of what Berlin called "suffocation."

Societies do as a rule smother instinctive (along with distinctive) behaviors, but in the process they also as a rule incarnate the least respectable instincts with greater force than individuals can do independently. Freud depicted the work of society in the most repellent terms: "to help make everyone's wish—the wish to harm others—come true. . . . The primordial wish to do harm breaks out in

---

3. "Violently anti-political" is Berlin's characterization of Zeno.

war—in homicidal acts sanctioned by society as heroic or, in any case, legal."[4] The hermeneutics of suspicion, of which Freud's writings on war are exemplary, is a specialty of modern thought; yet the arguments that Freud, Sartre, Foucault, and the rest make seem always incomplete, veering off, as if inevitably, before reaching their logical terminus. If even heroism and altruism, let alone standard social conduct, are oblique expressions of aggression, cruelty, and the will to power (as the hermeneutics of suspicion maintains), then the obvious conclusion to reach is that human beings are not fit company for each other. Hence the best models for a decent relationship to society would be stylites, dendrites, and (on the hearty end of this spectrum) mendicants. The standard means of veering off from this conclusion is to blame one's own society, or aspects of contemporary society, and then to propose improvements. Historically, evidence suggests, efforts of this kind are (or else, become) opportunities for controversy and thus for exercise of the will to power. Social order is such that even the discussion of social order occasions conflict.

And even the most suspicious interpreters of society are themselves suspect. As Ronald Santoni has written of Sartre, he was "curiously ambivalent" about social violence.[5] Far from eliminating or controlling or rechanneling aggression, Sartre insisted, society is "the most immediate and constant form of Terror."[6] Societies not only direct aggression against neighboring societies; their violence is fratricidal as well, and expressed in the psycho- and sociopathology of everyday life. In Santoni's summary of Sartre's views, "*conflict* is indeed the core and 'original meaning' of our being-for-others. Indeed, everyone not oneself in one's vicinity is the projection of a refused self: 'the Other exists for consciousness only as a *refused self*.' Negation and counternegation are mutual; objectification and counterobjectification are reciprocal."[7] Thus conflict is in the first instance "internal" to the individual and, as such, for most people, intolerable. Societies form so that the individual, rather than face his or her conflicts *as* internal, may experience them "externally"—as marriage and sibling rivalry, politics, lawsuits, tennis, war, and competition in all its kinds. The illusion that my identity is unconflicted relies on the efficacy of projection. My "refused selves," in conflict

4. Tom McCall, "Society—'A Gang of Murderers': Freud on Hostility and War," *Common Knowledge* 12.2 (Spring 2006): 262.

5. Ronald E. Santoni, *Sartre on Violence: Curiously Ambivalent* (University Park: Pennsylvania State University Press, 2003). On Sartre's ambivalence about violence, see also Jeffrey M. Perl, *Skepticism and Modern Enmity: Before and After Eliot* (Baltimore, MD: Johns Hopkins University Press, 1989), 128–32. On a related subject, see Paul Berman, *Power and the Idealists; or, The Passion of Joschka Fischer and Its Aftermath* (Brooklyn, NY: Soft Skull Press, 2005).

6. Jean-Paul Sartre, *Critique of Dialectical Reason*, trans. Alan Sheridan-Smith, vol. 1 (1960; London: New Left Books, 1976), 440.

7. Santoni, *Sartre on Violence*, 16–17. For the internal quotation, see Sartre, *Being and Nothingness*, trans. Hazel Barnes (1943; New York: Philosophical Library, 1956), 284.

with my select identity, are dispossessed and repositioned in (or as) images that I construct of other subjectivities. Individual identity does depend on society, therefore, but not in the wholesome way that communitarians mostly assume.

Whatever the validity of this analysis—Sartre's analysis of social order, or my analysis of Sartre—the gambit of projection and negation that he described had no positive effects in his own life. In constant conflict with everyone around him, he remained internally conflicted as well. "Curiously ambivalent," his writings on violence comprise an exposé, but not a critique, of human belligerence. His anthropology was not calculated to inspire pacifism, generosity, or philanthropy. By 1939 he had come to view all human relationships as species of combat. In his army diaries, he replays straightforward exchanges with comrades as battle scenes: "He sees me, he speaks to me, at once he cuts into my very existence and I thrust myself like a knife into his."[8] Even relationships "with those I love," Sartre writes, are governed by "the desire . . . to hit at the Other in the Other's absolute freedom."[9] He admits to "a hint of fascism" or "an odd kind of imperialism" in such perceptions, but no change of mind followed on this revelation.[10] Given the nature of humanity, he concluded, there is no choice for any of us but to be armed and on guard. For man is not a social animal, if by "social" is meant "sociable" or "benignly involved with others." Humans are not naturally cooperative, gregarious, loyal, accommodating, and kind. But if the Aristotelian (or by now, the commonsense) definition of human nature understands "social" to mean "ensnared by, entangled with, and preying on others," then man is a social animal indeed.

Sartre's anthropology is a useful context in which to reconsider Aristotle's. Could Aristotle, in his famous phrase, have meant to stress his noun ("animal") as much as its modifier ("social")? In saying that man is more social (or "political") than bees, Aristotle was presuming a hierarchy of sociability among species. While biologists continue to make that assumption, in some form, they no longer compare humans and social insects. Aristotle was not an evolutionary biologist; and even had he noticed how intolerable social organization is to primates, he would not have considered the observation relevant to his characterization of "man." The classification of *Homo sapiens sapiens* as a "shy, murderous ape" would presumably have struck Aristotle—a taxonomist unacquainted with the premise of evolution, let alone the outlines of evolutionary history—as metaphorical, misanthropic, and misinformed:

Our everyday life is much stranger than we imagine, and rests on fragile foundations. This is the startling message of the evolutionary history of humankind. Our teeming, industrialized, networked existence is

8. *The War Diaries of Jean-Paul Sartre*, trans. Quentin Hoare (New York: Pantheon, 1984), 205.

9. Sartre, *War Diaries*, 256.

10. Sartre, *War Diaries*, 256, 146.

not some gradual and inevitable outcome of human development over millions of years. Instead we owe it to an extraordinary experiment launched a mere ten thousand years ago. . . . After the end of the last ice age, one of the most aggressive and elusive bandit species in the entire animal kingdom began to settle down. . . . The same shy, murderous ape that had avoided strangers throughout its evolutionary history was now living, working, and moving among complete strangers in their millions.[11]

These remarks, on page one of Paul Seabright's *The Company of Strangers*, explain its cover illustration—a great ape, wide eyed, hair standing straight up on its head; behind it, a darkened city skyline. Is this our last prehuman ancestor, recoiling from the unnatural future? Assuming so would attribute to the book's designer an optimism for which its author finds inadequate bases. The evolutionary corner turned "a mere ten thousand years ago" was not, Seabright maintains, turned once and for all. Nor was it turned for good:

the human capacity for cooperation is double-edged. It is not only the foundation of social trust and peaceful living but also what makes for the most successful acts of aggression between one group and another. Like chimpanzees, though with more deadly refinement, human beings are distinguished by their ability to harness the virtues of altruism and solidarity, and the skills of rational reflection, to the end of making brutal and efficient warfare against rival groups. . . . There are good reasons to think . . . that the coincidence of murderousness and intelligence is not accidental. On the contrary, the selection for murderousness and the selection for intelligence are mutually reinforcing. The more murderous the species, the greater the selective benefit of intelligence to individual members, and the more intelligent the species, the greater the selective benefit of murderousness to individual members. . . . So any evolution toward murderousness among our ancestors would have increased the speed at which intelligence evolved. . . . Whatever its fundamental causes, violence in primates, especially in the great apes, cannot be described as pathological. (7, 49, 52)

Seabright is an economist. His main interest is not in primatology (or anthropology or ethics) but in determining how the social collaboration required for complex economic orders emerged and developed. At no point does he find that human beings are naturally social and cooperative; nor does he find that humans have ever been as interested in material progress as we are in banditry and car-

11. Paul Seabright, *The Company of Strangers: A Natural History of Economic Life* (Princeton, NJ: Princeton University Press, 2004), 1. Further references are given parenthetically in the text.

nage. Seabright is unimpressed by "the popular modern view that trade between neighbors makes warfare less likely" (225)—that customers and vendors do not kill each other's children.[12] Given a choice between "peaceful trade" and "confiscation," human societies have tended, and still tend, to select the latter.

Furthermore, each step that human beings have taken toward altruistic or even selfishly motivated cooperation has entailed strong groups "preying on weaker neighbors." Human collaboration of whatever kind seems to be fundamentally martial:

> Agriculture raised the advantages to mankind of banding together for self-defense [and] . . . the result of devoting time, effort, and resources to defending yourself is not just to make you feel more secure. It usually also makes your neighbor feel *less* secure. . . . Once a community has invested in even a modest army . . . the temptation to encourage that army to earn its keep by preying on weaker neighbors can become overwhelming. (212)

Thus, "paradoxically, the more successful states have been in pursuit of strength through prosperity, the more they have been tempted to abandon it in pursuit of prosperity through strength" (213). Lest the reader conclude that war is an unfortunate by-product of higher social organization, Seabright explains how human society formed, to begin with, as "a team of fighters." Only for guerilla fighters, he emphasizes, "can it be an advantage to be fighting alone" (217).

This opposition, between fighting on "a team" and "fighting alone," helps to elucidate what distinguishes—and more unexpectedly, what unites—communitarian and individualist thinking. The word "team" is used more often of players than of warriors; and if Seabright did not intend his words "fighting alone" to echo the well-known phrase "bowling alone," he also should not object to readers' seeing a connection between them. Robert Putnam's influential article and book entitled *Bowling Alone* lament the decline of bowling in leagues—which, of course, is a metaphor for something consequential.[13] Seabright may be talking about that same momentous something when, as his book begins to conclude, he asks: "Has the great experiment launched by *Homo sapiens sapiens* ten thousand years ago reached its tolerable limits? And is it even conceivable to call a halt?" (232). These questions are rhetorical: the expected answers are "perhaps yes" (to the first question) and "perhaps no" (to the second). But what if "great experiment" is a bon mot rather than *le mot juste*? Substituting "great game" for

---

12. Seabright contends that this view "has no reliable basis in history" (225).

13. Robert D. Putnam, "Bowling Alone: America's Declining Social Capital," *Journal of Democracy* 6.1 (January 1995), expanded as *Bowling Alone: The Collapse and Revival of the American Community* (New York: Simon and Schuster, 2000).

"great experiment" in Paul Seabright's first question will return us to Robert Putnam and enlarge, at the same time, our sense of possibilities. We appear to have, roughly, two ways of looking at or dealing with society—communitarian and individualist. The communitarian bowls on a team in a league; the individualist bowls alone. (Though individualists, at least theorists of individualism, are as much a team as the communitarians are, and they play against each other in the same academic leagues.) These opposed options, as is often the case with artificial distinctions, are fundamentally in accord: bowl alone or bowl in company, they are agreed that we must bowl. A third option exists, however, categorically distinct from the other two—and the third has been, for the past year in *Common Knowledge*, the subject of this three-part symposium. "Unsocial Thought, Uncommon Lives," which now takes its bow and disappears, has concerned the choices and the rationales, the conduct and the moral vision, of those who do not bowl at all.

CALLS FOR PAPERS

Excerpts

Paul Feyerabend

I

Reading articles about deconstruction, correlations in quantum mechanics, or the terrible curse of irrationalism, I frequently ask myself: "What has this got to do with what I just saw or heard about people dying from government-imposed sickness in the Sudan, cholera in Peru, suppression in Iraq and Israel, and unkindness to refugees in Austria, Switzerland, and other 'civilized' countries? And would it not be excellent to remind these sublime minds from time to time of the really unpleasant future of the world in which they live and about which they claim to have knowledge?"

Asking this question does not mean giving up intellectualism; Fanon did not. What it means is a sign in every issue of *Common Knowledge* that—over ideas, over narrow intellectual issues—our fellow human beings have not been forgotten. Words are weak in this respect; human concern too often evaporates in "humanitarianism," in humanitarian intellectualism. I call for photographs and other pictorial work that remind intellectuals of disease, starvation, the ravages of war, and the ruthless exploitation of the environment for the sake of luxury and "progress."

We need a continuous wake-up call.

Originally published in *Common Knowledge* 1.1 (Spring 1992): 8–10. © 1992.

Common Knowledge 25:1–3

DOI 10.1215/0961754X-7299426

II

I call for papers on the historical, theoretical, and personal meaning of "poverty" and "economic growth." How are economic growth and poverty, as defined by major economic indicators, connected with the personal experience of the people said to be poor or economically retarded?

I also call for papers on the development of communist regimes in Eastern Europe and elsewhere. Is capitalism the only alternative to a totalitarian economy?

III

I would like to see *Common Knowledge* publish essays on various aspects of modern Catholicism. What I mean, more specifically: articles such as those commenting on Cardinal Ratzinger's speech (March 15, 1990) in Parma, responding to the strength of faith revealed in the newly liberated countries in Eastern Europe; and articles on the modern social teaching of the church, i.e., John Paul II's encyclical *Centesimus Annus*, the encyclical *Rerum Novarum* (issued by Leo XIII on May 15, 1891) on which *Centisimus Annus* is a commentary, and the encyclical *Quanta Cura* of Pius IX with its "syllabus of errors" (errors like naturalism, liberalism, rationalism, etc.). Considering the power of the Catholic church and the many problems created by its social teaching as well as by the "errors" of the syllabus, it would be well for economists and other social scientists, philosophers, theologians, and, above all, nonintellectuals to examine the economic and political principles of the modern Church.

LOVE AND MONEY

Richard Rorty

Howard's End asks whether it is sufficient to "connect," whether love is enough. "Only connect" has been taken as E. M. Forster's last word, but at various points in the novel he notes that connection is possible only when there is enough money. The heroine, Margaret Schlegel, wonders whether "the very soul of the world is economic, . . . [whether] the lowest abyss is not the absence of love, but the absence of coin." Speaking in his own voice —a voice that mingles pity with self-disgust—Forster says, "We are not concerned with the very poor. They are unthinkable, and only to be approached by the statistician or the poet. This story deals with gentlefolk, or with those who are obliged to pretend that they are gentlefolk." At the novel's end, one of the people who has been obliged so to pretend, Leonard Bast, dies as a result of being caught up in the struggle between the Schlegels, the people who are good at loving, and the Wilcoxes, the people who know how to make money. But even if he had not died, he would have become unthinkable—because he had been reduced from pseudo-gentility to grinding poverty.

As long as Bast had enough money to keep up the pretension to gentility, he was conversable; Margaret and the others could make connections with him. But when he lost his job and had no money left he became unconversable. This was

Originally published in *Common Knowledge* 1.1 (Spring 1992): 12–16. © 1992.

Common Knowledge 25:1–3

DOI 10.1215/0961754X-7299438

not because of the snobbery of the gentlefolk but because Bast himself, obsessed with the need to feed himself and his wife, could think and talk of nothing else. No money, no conversability and no connectability. No money, no chance for love. The very poor, those in the lowest abyss, the people whom Brecht called "the ones who live in darkness," can afford neither love nor conversability. "Only connect" has no relevance to them, for they cannot afford any disinterested actions. The light shed by novels does not reach them.

In *Aspects of the Novel* Forster distinguishes "the development of the novel," which is the same as "the development of humanity," from the "great tedious onrush known as history." The latter includes "trifles" which "belong to history but not to art"; Forster's examples of such trifles are the taming of the atom, landing on the moon, and abolishing warfare. The former is "a shy crablike sideways movement" toward tenderness, the tenderness which connection makes possible. Of tenderness Forster says:

Far more mysterious than the call of sex to sex is the tenderness that we throw into that call; far wider is the gulf between us and the farmyard than that between the farmyard and the garbage that nourishes it. We are evolving, in ways that Science cannot measure, to ends that Theology dares not contemplate. "Men did produce one jewel," the gods will say, and saying, will give us immortality.

Forster sometimes seems on the brink of saying that the very poor, the people who cannot afford love or friendship because every moment of every day is filled with anxiety for the next bit of food, are more like the farmyard than like gentlefolk, more like garbage than like us. Wells and Shaw sometimes did say things like that. But Forster was too decent to agree with them. Instead, he hopes, as all us liberal gentlefolk hope, that eventually the Wilcoxes will produce so much money that, when shared out as it should be, there will be nobody left who is very poor. He knows that the very soul of the "great tedious onrush known as history" *is* economic. He knows that tenderness only appears, that the shy crabwise movement only continues, when there is enough money to produce a little leisure, a little time in which to love. His decency consists in his confidence that tenderness *will*, in fact, appear when there is money enough. But he shares enough of Wells's and Shaw's realism to admit that money is the independent, and tenderness the dependent, variable.

Forster's hope that eventually there will be enough money to go around, enough so that its redistribution will make connection and tenderness ubiquitous, runs through liberal thought from the French Revolution to our own time. Every top-down liberal initiative, from the abolition of slavery through the extension of the franchise to the establishment of the International Monetary Fund and the World Bank, has been driven by the hope that someday we shall no longer need to distinguish us gentlefolk from those others, the people who live like animals. The cash value of the Christian ideal of universal brotherhood has, for the last two centuries, been the conviction that once science and technology have produced enough wealth—and enlightened, unselfish political initiatives have redistributed it—there will be no one left who is incapable of tenderness. All human beings will live in the light; all of them will be possible characters in novels.

Seen from this Forsterian vantage point, the distinction between Marxism and liberalism was largely a disagreement about whether you can get as much, or more, wealth to redistribute by politicizing the marketplace and replacing the greedy Wilcoxes with government planners. It turned out that you cannot. Liberals of Forster's time knew as well as the Marxists that the soul of history—if not of the novel or of humanity—is economic, but they thought that history had to be guided from the top down, by the gentlefolk. The Marxists hoped that once those on the bottom seized control, once the revolution turned things upside down, everything would automatically get better. Here again, alas, the Marxists were wrong. So now Marxism is no longer of much interest, and we are back with the question of what top-down initiatives we gentlefolk might best pursue.

This question looks manageable as long as we confine our attention to the Northern Hemisphere. If that part of the planet (suitably gerrymandered so as, for example, to include Australia and exclude China) were all we had to worry about, it would be plausible to suggest that there is, or soon will be, enough money to go around—that our problems are simply those of redistribution. All we need to do is to formulate effective Schlegelian appeals of the tenderness of the gentlefolk who make up the electorates of the rich nations, appeals which will overcome Wilcoxian greed. There seems to be enough money sloshing around the Northern Hemisphere to make it practicable, eventually, to raise the East European standard of living to that of Western Europe, that of Yorkshire to that of Surrey, and that of Bedford-Stuyvesant to that of Bensonhurst. There are relatively plausible scenarios for the working-out of top-down initiatives, scenarios which end with the life-chances of the Northerners roughly leveled out. Liberal hope, the hope for a decent world, a world in which Christianity's promises are fulfilled, nourishes itself on such scenarios.

The fear that is beginning to gnaw at the hearts of all us liberal gentlefolk in the North is that there are no initiatives which will save the Southern Hemisphere, that there will never be enough money in the world to redeem the South. We are beginning to be at a loss for scenarios which cross the North-South border, largely because of the scary population-growth statistics for countries such as Indonesia, India, and Haiti. This part of the planet is becoming increasingly unthinkable. We are more and more tempted to turn it over to the statisticians, and to the sort of poet whom we call "the ethnologist."

This temptation was brought home to me when, during my first trip to

India, I met a fellow philosophy professor who is also a politician. Starting as a young M.P. in the sixties, anxious to bring Western thought and technology to bear on India's problems, and especially on the Indian birthrate, he had risen, in the course of thirty years, to various high offices, including that of Minister of Health. He was in a very good position to dream up concrete and optimistic scenarios, but had none to offer. After thirty years' work on the part of people like himself, he said, it was still the case that the only rational thing for parents in an Indian village to do was to try as hard as they could to have eight children. It had to be eight because two would die in childhood, three of the remainder would be girls and thus require dowries, and one of the remaining boys would run off to Bombay and never be heard of again. Two male children working desperately hard, all their lives, with no time off for tenderness, would be required to insure that their sisters' dowries were paid, and their mother and father kept from starvation in their old age.

In the course of this trip, I found myself, like most Northerners in the South, not thinking about the beggars in the hot streets once I was back in my pleasantly air-conditioned hotel. My Indian acquaintances—fellow-academics, fellow-gentlefolk, honorary Northerners—gave the same small percentage of what they had in their pockets to the beggars as I did, and then, like me, forgot about the individual beggars when they got home. As individuals beggars were, just as Forster says, unthinkable. Instead, both of us thought about liberal initiatives which might eliminate the beggars as a class. But neither of us came up with any initiatives which inspired any confidence. The country, and perhaps the world, did not seem to have enough money to keep the number of Southerners who will be alive in the middle of the twenty-first century from despair, much less to open up to them the possibility of joining in the slow crabwise movement which has been taking place in the North. Of course, there might be enough money, because science and technology might once again come to the rescue. There are a few scientific possibilities—e.g., a breakthrough in plasma physics which makes fusion energy, and thus (for example) desalination and irrigation on a gigantic scale, possible and cheap. But the hope is pretty faint. As things stand, nobody who reads the statistics about the unthinkably poor of the South can generate any optimism.

I should like to produce a bracing conclusion to end these pessimistic reflections, but all I can offer is the suggestion that we Northern gentlefolk at least keep ourselves honest. We should remind ourselves, as Forster reminded us, that love is *not* enough—that the Marxists were absolutely right about one thing: the soul of history *is* economic. All the talk in the world about the need to abandon "technological rationality" and to stop "commodifying," about the need for "new values" or for "non-Western ways of thinking," is not going to bring more money to the Indian villages. As long as the villagers have enough Weberian means-end rationality to see that they need eight children, such talk is not to any point. All the love in the world, all the attempts to abandon "Eurocentrism," or "liberal individualism," all the "politics of diversity," all the talk about cuddling up to the natural environment, will not help.

The only things we know of which might help are top-down techno-bureaucratic initiatives like the cruel Chinese only-one-child-per-family policy (or, literalizing the top-down metaphor and pushing things one monstrous step further, spraying villages from the air with sterilizing chemicals). If there is a happy solution to the dilemma created by the need of very poor Brazilians to find work and the need of the rest of us for the oxygen produced by the Amazonian rain forest, it is going to be the result of as some as yet unimagined bureaucratic-technological initiative, not of a revolution in "values." The slow crabwise movement is not going to speed up thanks to a change in philosophical outlook. Money remains the independent variable.

I think that the sudden popularity of anti-technological talk among us Northern liberals, our turn over the last twenty years from planning to dreaming, and from science to philosophy, has been a nervous, self-deceptive reaction to the realization that technology may not work. Maybe the problems our predecessors assumed it could solve are, in fact, too tough. Maybe technology and centralized planning will not work. But they are all we have got. We should not try to pull the blanket over our heads by saying that technology was a big mistake, and that planning, top-down initiatives, and "Western ways of thinking" must be abandoned. That is just another, much less honest, way of saying what Forster said: that the very poor are unthinkable.

A REPLY TO PAUL FEYERABEND AND RICHARD RORTY

Frank Kermode

Answers to the question, what kind of knowledge can truly be called common, must take account of the global diversity of interest and concern. Paul Feyerabend, in the inaugural issue of this journal, wondered whether "sublime minds" occupied by such arcane topics as deconstruction, quantum mechanics, and so on, should not be reminded from time to time "of the really unpleasant future of the world in which they live, and about which they claim to have knowledge." He was of course thinking not only of the future but of the present, of the victims of "ethnic cleansing," of cholera, pollution, drought, and war. What can the "sublime minds" be expected to do about these difficulties? Feyerabend believes it possible for them to make a useful contribution. Richard Rorty doubts it. We can expect no revolution in "values" (his quotes); philosophy can do nothing for the sufferers except perhaps by endorsing "top-down" technological planning.

It is hard to imagine that there are contributors to, or readers of, this journal who doubt that if one can speak at all of ethical value it is ethically more valu-

These passages are taken from Frank Kermode's introduction to the symposium "Beyond *Post-*: A Revaluation of the Revaluation of All Values," *Common Knowledge* 1, no. 3 (Winter 1992): 10–12. His remarks on Paul Feyerabend and Richard Rorty refer to the pieces by them reproduced above. © 1992.

Common Knowledge 25:1–3

DOI 10.1215/0961754X-7299450

able to combat poverty, disease, war, the destruction of the environment, than from self-interest to sustain the state of affairs in which these manifest evils flourish, or even merely, from inertia, to acquiesce in their continuance. Yet, as Rorty's remark suggests, it is clearly a primary problem whether and how usefully one can speak of ethical value and expect some sort of useful agreement about what it is.

You have to cross a philosophical minefield to get to the point of being able to do so. Bernard Williams, in the first issue, threaded it with due delicacy. There is a respected view of the problem that runs rather like this: "widely diverse conceptions of the good have to be seen under the sign of toleration, to such an extent that one has to be very deeply committed to one's own conception of the good, while at the same time regarding very different ones as tolerable within a framework that is held together by a form of citizenship motivated by a sense of fairness and not much more." But Williams takes a less negative position, not accepting that ethical ideas are merely grounded in particular practices, so that there is, as it were, no common ethical knowledge. . . . An acceptance of antifoundationalism should not render social and ethical criticism impossible. . . . Other disciplines—theology, politics, anthropology—have necessarily to involve themselves, and confront that unpleasant future. The talk may seem rarefied, but the issues are horribly practical.

When I wrote my original call for papers on value, I had in mind the question as it has been engaged in recent literary criticism.[1] It would be easy to say of it what Albany, at the crisis of *King Lear*, says when news is brought of the death of Edmund: "that's but a trifle here." Yet it is intimately related to the ethical argument. As Williams, [Ronald] Dworkin, and others maintain, we cannot avoid reflection upon past values, and that reflection becomes, or should become, part of our practice, even in an antifoundationalist, antiessentialist epoch. Accordingly, I do hope to see the matter of literary value addressed in the broad context here provided for discussion of the philosophy of value. Precedence must obviously be given to a planet at risk; but to lose what has been valued in literature is a sure way of increasing the unpleasantness of the future.

1. See Frank Kermode, "Call for Papers IV," *Common Knowledge* 1, no. 1 (Spring 1992): 5–6.

THE POLITICAL ECONOMY OF HUNGER

On Reasoning and Participation

Amartya Sen

The modern age is not short of terrible and nasty happenings, but the persistence of extensive hunger in a world of unprecedented prosperity is surely one of the worst. Famines visit many countries with astonishing severity—"fierce as ten furies, terrible as hell" (to borrow John Milton's words). In addition, massive endemic hunger causes great misery in many parts of the world, debilitating hundreds of millions and killing a sizeable proportion of them with statistical regularity. What makes this widespread hunger even more of a tragedy is the way we have come to accept and tolerate it as an integral part of the modern world, as if it is a tragedy that is essentially unpreventable (in the way ancient Greek tragedies were).

Originally published in *Common Knowledge* 3.2 (Fall 1994): 1–9. © 1994.

An earlier version of this article was presented at a World Bank conference, "Overcoming Global Hunger: A Conference on Actions to Reduce Hunger Worldwide" (30 Nov.–1 Dec., 1993, Washington, D.C.).

Defeatism and Fear. I shall argue that not only is the problem of world hunger decisively solvable, but that one of the greatest barriers to achieving that solution lies in widely shared skepticism about such a solution—the defeatist and baseless fear that we will not succeed against so vast a challenge. Defeatism often masquerades as hardheaded realism, and the tendency to take that view has plagued the world for a long time. Malthus' dreary pessimism is a good example. It was aimed at the optimism of some of the leaders of European Enlightenment, such as Condorcet and Godwin, who saw social problems as being solvable by rational deliberation and cooperative action.

The rationalists did not assume, as is sometimes suggested, that unlimited population growth was no problem. Rather they believed, as Condorcet put it, that "the progress of reason" will make people recognize that "if they have a duty towards those who are not yet born, that duty is not to give them existence but to give them happiness," so that they will on their own choose to restrain family size, "rather than foolishly to encumber the world with useless and wretched beings."[1] In contrast, Malthus announced that "there is no reason whatever to suppose that anything beside the difficulty of procuring in adequate plenty the necessaries of life should either indispose this greater number of persons to marry early, or disable them from rearing in health the largest families."[2] He theorized that misery was therefore inevitable, that population would be persistently outstripping our ability to grow food, followed by famines and disasters that, in turn, would raise death rates and bring the population again to a smaller size.

Reasoning and Participation. The defeatist and cynical attitude reflected by Malthus and his followers continues to dampen the prospects of a reasoned solution of the world's problems, and the tendency by some contemporary writers to attribute greatness and vision to the Malthusian approach can misguide us in many different fields, from famine relief and economic development to population policy itself. The debate between the two sides was not one between smugness, on the one hand, and realism, on the other, as it is sometimes portrayed, but between working toward a reasoned and participatory solution of identified problems, on the one hand, and defeatism and compulsory hardship, on the other.

1. Marie Jean Antoine Nicolas de Caritat Marquis de Condorcet, *Esquisse d'un Tableau Historique des Progrès de l'Esprit Humain*, 1795. For later reprints of that volume, see *Oeuvres de Condorcet*, Tome Sixième (Paris: Firmin Didot Frères, 1847; Stuttgart: Friedrich Frommann Verlag, 1968). English translation by June Barraclough, *Sketch for a Historical Picture of the Progress of the Human Mind*, with an introduction by Stuart Hampshire (London: Weidenfeld & Nicolson, 1955).

2. T. R. Malthus, *A Summary View of the Principle of Population* (London: John Murray, 1830); in the Penguin Classics edition (Harmondsworth: 1982), 243. Elsewhere he argued that "the perpetual tendency in the race of man to increase beyond the means of subsistence is one of the great general laws of animated nature which we can have no reason to expect will change" (Malthus, *Essay on the Principle of Population*, chap. 17; in the Penguin Classics edition, 198–99).

In fact, it was Condorcet who had identified, before Malthus, the possibility of too rapid population growth, and Malthus quotes Condorcet in presenting his own theory of population. Where they differed was in Condorcet's belief, and that of many other rationalist thinkers of that period (such as Adam Smith), that by reasoning about the nature of solvable problems and by understanding the appropriate actions to be undertaken to avert these problems, we can prevent their occurrence, whereas Malthus saw no such hope and spoke instead of the need for obligatory suffering on the part of much of humanity. Indeed, Malthus went on to integrate his pessimism with his ruthless religiosity: "It seems, however, every way probable that even the acknowledged difficulties occasioned by the law of population tend rather to promote than impede the general purpose of Providence." In fact, "an uniform course of prosperity" would, he asserted, "degrade" rather than "exalt the character."[3] This is a fundamentally different attitude from that, shared by Condorcet and Smith, which seeks reasoned identification of problems and voluntary action to deal with them.

Development and Population Growth Rates. The history of the world since Malthus' time has not given much comfort to his harsh cynicism.[4] Population has risen very sharply since Malthus' days, and yet the availability of food per head has grown rather than fallen, death rates have steadily declined, average longevity has increased to levels very few could enjoy in the past, and, much as Condorcet expected, birthrates have come down with education (especially female education, on which Condorcet had particularly focused), and with economic development and the fall in death rates. While Malthus thought that population growth would speed up indefinitely with prosperity and had to be restrained by misery (and the compulsion of so-called positive checks), population growth rates are now very low indeed in countries with economic and educational development and remain high mainly in regions of misery and underdevelopment (such as sub-Saharan Africa and parts of south Asia). There are, of course, many problems still connected with population growth, but they do not arise from issues stressed by Malthus. Their solution clearly lies in bringing reason and cooperation to bear on them (including, as Condorcet noted, in an immensely farsighted reference, exploring "methods of preservation and economy").

Causes of Hunger. In Malthus' time, there was a great deal of hunger, combined with widespread general deprivation—proportionately much more than now—but Malthus' opposition to relief (and his hostility to Poor Laws and charitable hospitals) was based on his belief in the inevitability of—and some religious

3. Malthus, *Essay on Population*, chaps. 17 and 19; in Penguin Classics edition, 206 and 209.

4. On this general question, see Gerald Piel, *Only One World* (New York: Freeman, 1992).

merit in—sufferings of this type. While we should take some comfort in the fact that we live in a less terrible and morally less harsh world, I must now turn to the question of why there is so much hunger still, given the immense productive abilities and general economic prosperity in the contemporary world.

I have argued elsewhere that hunger is best seen in terms of failure of "entitlements" of people, that is, the failure to establish command over an adequate amount of food and other necessities.[5] A person may have few means of commanding enough food if he or she has no job, no other sources of income, and no social security; the hunger that will result can coexist with a plentiful supply of food in the economy and the markets. Famines have, in fact, occurred in situations of high food availability—sometimes even *peak* food availability.[6]

Famine Prevention and Science. Effective famine prevention has several distinct aspects. First, there is, as it were, the "science" of famine: the need to understand the real causes of famine, and not to identify the prospects of famine with the misleading figures of food supply per head. It requires understanding that famines result from particular sections of the population—typically some occupation groups—losing their ability to command food (for example, because of loss of employment, falling real wages, and so on). The Malthusian focus on food supply per head can be very misleading here in generating a false sense of security based on the belief that so long as food output per head is high enough, there is no problem. While we have tended to debate the merits and flaws of Malthusian pessimism, what may be called "Malthusian optimism" has killed millions: policymakers sticking to a false theory of famines have seen no necessity to take preventive action when food output per head is high and there is plenty of food in the market, while large sections of the population have been forced to starve because of their failure to command a part of the food that is there.[7]

The entitlement theory of famines does not deny the importance of food output—many people command food by growing it themselves and the price at which others can buy food is favourably affected by a larger food output. Scientific advances and changes in public policy in promoting more food production, especially in regions where it has stagnated or declined (such as sub-Saharan Africa), can be an extremely significant part of the protection of entitlements of the potential famine victims. Also, it is terribly important for famine relief to have some food available in public hands for distribution among victims or

5. Amartya Sen, *Poverty and Famines* (New York: Oxford University Press, 1981), and Jean Drèze and Amartya Sen, *Hunger and Public Action* (New York: Oxford University Press, 1989).

6. This occurred, for example, in Bangladesh in 1974; see my *Poverty and Famines*, chap. 6; see also Mohiuddin

Alamgir, *Famine in South Asia* (Cambridge, MA: Oelgeschlager, 1980), and Martin Ravallion, *Markets and Famines* (New York: Oxford University Press, 1987).

7. On this, see my *Poverty and Famines*, and Drèze and Sen, *Hunger and Public Action*.

for releasing it in the market to break spirals of rising food prices. One of the practical problems faced by relief organizations today is the decline in food made available for international relief as a result of programmed cutbacks in food production in Europe and America. The production of food and its availability in crucial areas are indeed important for any entitlement-based analysis of famines. What that approach does deny, however, is the *adequacy* of concentrating *only* on food output and availability. It is a fuller *economic* understanding of the process of commanding food on which sensible famine prevention policies depend.

Economics of Famine Prevention. In preventing famines, the economic policies needed to re-create the lost entitlements are not hard to identify. While direct food distribution has tended to be favoured in some regions of the world (and there is indeed a case for that in some situations), there is the possibility of much greater use of public employment programmes to generate income and security. By offering payment for jobs to the destitute in an area threatened by famines, the potential famine victims can be empowered economically to command food. They can then buy food in the market, and redress their loss of share of the total food availability. This can be combined with adding food to the market, but a more equal sharing of the available food itself—as a result of the regenerated purchasing power of the potential victims—tends to prevent famines.[8] Such policies have been tried with great success in many countries, including India. This kind of strategy involves a combination of state intervention and the market, and it is put together by an informed analysis of what causes famines and how these causes can be overcome by reasoned public programmes.

It is also worth emphasizing that such programmes need not be overly expensive even for very poor countries. The proportion of people threatened by famines rarely exceeds five percent of the total population, and their share of the national income (or of national food consumption) would typically be no more than two or three percent (given the fact that they are normally quite poor, even before the threatened famine). To re-create all their lost income and to offer them their normal share of the national food supply does not, therefore, require an inordinately large amount of economic resource, even for a very poor country. This is, of course, not an argument for other, richer countries to refrain from helping, but it is certainly an argument for the poor countries threatened by famines not to wait helplessly for aid from abroad.

8. On this, see Drèze and Sen, *Hunger and Public Action*, esp. chap. 8; also Jean Drèze, "Famine Prevention in India," and "Famine Prevention in Africa," in Jean Drèze and Amartya Sen, *The Political Economy of Hunger* (New York: Oxford University Press, 1990).

Politics of Famine Prevention. In addition to the scientific and economic aspects of famine prevention, there is also a political aspect. A government may be capable of undertaking an effective famine prevention policy and yet not do it. I have tried to argue that democracy and a free press are great forces in famine prevention, since a government has to respond quickly and convincingly if it has to face reelection, if it cannot censor out the terrible facts of starvation, disease, and death that go with famines, and if it has to face strong criticism from opposition parties and newspapers.[9] It is, in fact, not surprising that even though famines have happened in colonial economies and modern authoritarian states, never has a famine occurred in a democratic country with a relatively free press.

This observation applies not only to the richer countries in the world, but also to very poor ones that have a democratic state and a largely uncensored press. The contrast between India's avoidance of famines since independence in 1947 (the last famine there was in 1943, which killed between two and three million people) and the famine that occurred in China in 1958–61, which killed between twenty-three and thirty million people, is important to note in that context. The fact that China has been otherwise much more successful than India in expanding health care and social security makes this contrast even more significant. Similarly, democratic Botswana and Zimbabwe had very serious food shortages related to droughts in the early 1980's and nevertheless escaped without any famine due to quick public action, whereas dictatorial Sudan and Ethiopia, with much smaller declines in food output, suffered enormous famines over that period.[10]

Participation, Cooperation, and Criticism. The importance of political response based on democratic and pluralist critiques has to be seen in terms of the general importance of participation and cooperation in solving problems of hunger in the modern world. Participation needs to be interpreted at different levels in distinct ways. It involves working together, which can be extremely important, and I was happy to see that the statement of the Nongovernment Organizations to the World Hunger Conference has emphasized the significance of that route. But it also involves being politically active in influencing public policy in the right direction. Democracy and a free press open the way to that, but the opportunities created have to be actually seized, and thus political activism is ultimately imperative. Eternal vigilance is the price not only of liberty but also of conquering deprivation and hunger.

9. See my *Resources, Values and Development* (Oxford: Basil Blackwell, 1984); Drèze and Sen, *Hunger and Public Action;* and N. Ram, "An Independent Press and Anti-Hunger Strategies: The Indian Experience," in Drèze and Sen, *The*

Political Economy of Hunger. See also my "The Economics of Life and Death," *Scientific American,* May 1993.

10. On this, see Drèze and Sen, *Hunger and Public Action,* and *The Political Economy of Hunger.*

Markets and Cooperation. The role of politics in famine prevention opens the possibility that prejudices of one kind or another can stifle intelligent use of our available knowledge. This is indeed not an empty fear. Some organizations are well known for having, in general, a pro-market and a pro-capitalism bias; the World Bank has certainly had to listen to that charge. Other public bodies, not to mention political groups, are more inclined towards direct public intervention whenever possible. Both predilections have their pitfalls. On the one hand, there is plenty of evidence in recent experiences of how dreadfully wrong state intervention can sometimes be (the Khmer Rouge's Cambodia is an extreme example). On the other hand, there is also much evidence of suffering caused by excessive reliance on the market, by attempts to "adjust" too uncompromisingly to the supposed "right prices," and by the failure of the government to do those supportive things that it can do very well.

What is really needed is not to take a pro-market or a pro-state view, but to see the two types of institutions as having different functions and roles that can be mutually supportive and complementary. They both fit into a general view of participation and cooperation. It is not surprising that Condorcet and Smith, who argued in favour of social help in remedying individual misery (unlike Malthus, who was hostile to poorhouses and charitable hospitals), also saw the market as a great area of social cooperation. Indeed, it was that identification of coordinated mutual gains through market transactions that can be seen as one of Smith's principal contributions to the economics of market processes. The fecundity of market processes in generating economic growth and prosperity has been widely demonstrated across the world, not least in east and southeast Asia, and more recently in China. A reasoned solution of the problem of hunger in the modern world has to acknowledge the importance of well-functioning markets, without denying other forms of participation—through political and democratic process, through public action and influencing state policies, and through cooperation between individuals and social institutions of different types.

Family Planning and Compulsion. I turn finally to the issue of population policy. My focus on cooperation may be thought to be particularly unsuited to the need for forceful action to curb fast population growth rates in the developing world. There is much admiration in fact for China's policy of compulsion in holding down the growth rate of population, through such measures as the "one child policy" and through making basic social security and economic rights (such as housing) conditional on following government rules about the number of births. The birthrate has certainly fallen in China quite sharply; the last systematic calculation put it around nineteen per thousand—considerably lower than India's twenty-nine per thousand, not to mention the average figure of thirty-seven per thousand of poor countries other than India and China. It is very tempting to go on from there to recommend some forceful use of family planning to deal with the population problem.

But the comparison requires more scrutiny. For example, China's birthrate is not lower than that of the state of Kerala in India (a sizeable state of twenty-nine million people—rather larger than Canada). There are wide variations in the birthrate within India, related to diverse social and economic factors, including life expectancy and mortality rates, education (especially female education), health facilities, and availability of means of family planning and medical help. Kerala does well in all these respects, and the birthrate in Kerala has fallen sharply over the last few decades, from forty-four per thousand in the 1950's to eighteen per thousand by 1991.

While Kerala's per capita income is no higher than the Indian average, it has the highest life expectancy in India (more than 72 years, even higher than China's 69) and the highest rate of rural literacy in general and female literacy in particular (higher than that in China as a whole and also higher than *every* province in China in rural female literacy).[11] The Keralan birthrate of eighteen per thousand is certainly no higher than the Chinese rate of nineteen per thousand, and Kerala's fertility rate of 1.8 also compares well with China's 2.0 (and the United States' 2.1, Canada's 1.9, and Britain's and France's 1.8). Since "one child family" and related policies were introduced in China in 1979, the Chinese fertility rate has fallen from 2.75 to 2.0, whereas Kerala's fertility rate has declined (without any compulsion) from 3.0 to 1.8.

Kerala's achievements are not the result of compulsory birth control or the violation of any individual liberty in deciding on these matters, but are based on the voluntary exercise of the family's right to family planning. As the death rate has fallen and family planning opportunities have been combined with health care, and the desire of Keralan women—more educated as they are—to be less shackled by continuous child care has become more intense, the birthrate has tumbled. There is also a general perception in Kerala that the lowering of the birthrate is a real "need" of a modern family—a conceptualization in which public education and participatory discussion have been very effective.

The argument for compulsory birth control tends to be the result of pessimism about voluntary restriction of family size and the eagerness to institute state compulsion instead. That course can lead to deeply disturbing results. While China has almost as low a birthrate as Kerala, one result of the compulsion has been a much higher rate of infant mortality, especially for female children. The traditional "son preference" in China seems to have contributed

11. See Jean Drèze and Mrinalini Saran, "Primary Education and Economic Development in China and India: Overview and Two Case Studies," in K. Basu, P. Patta-naik, and K. Suzumura, eds., *Choice, Welfare, and Development* (Oxford: Oxford University Press, Clarendon Press, 1994).

to extreme reactions to compulsory birth control measures, including possibly infanticide and certainly a tendency to neglect female children. No such tendency can be seen in Kerala (Kerala's infant mortality rate for boys is 17, for girls 16, compared with China's 28 and 33, respectively).[12]

Gender bias is, of course, a widespread problem in India as well as China. The bias seems to be remarkably less in Kerala, possibly due to its long history of female education. In contrasting China with Kerala, it is instructive to note that the ratio of females to males in the population, which is substantially higher than unity in Europe or North America,[13] is still as low as 0.94 in China (rather like India's average 0.93), whereas the ratio in Kerala is 1.04, and even after adjustment for emigration, the ratio is still much higher than unity, roughly where the European ratio would be but for the lasting effects of higher male deaths in the last wars.

A Concluding Remark. Whether we look at ways of preventing famines, reducing undernourishment, promoting general economic development, or encouraging family planning, the advantages of policies based on reasoning, participation, and cooperation would seem to be enormous. Neither defeatism nor the use of forceful compulsion provides a viable alternative without the greatest of sacrifice.

I have argued that public action can help to eradicate the dreadful and tenacious problems of starvation and hunger in the world, but that for this to happen, we must see public action in a broad perspective—involving not just the government but also the public itself—in all its manifold economic, social, and political activities. The public is, above all, the agent of change, and not a patient to be looked after and ordered about. It makes a big difference how we see each other.

12. For further discussion of this issue, see my "Population: Delusion and Reality," *New York Review of Books* 41, no. 15 (22 Sept. 1994).

13. The average ratio is around 1.05 in Europe and North America, but this is somewhat inflated by higher male deaths in past wars. But even when that influence of wars is taken out the ratio still remains considerably higher than unity, and relates to systematically lower age-specific death rates of females vis-à-vis males.

THE CATHOLIC CHURCH VIS-À-VIS LIBERAL SOCIETY

Roger Cardinal Etchegaray

Translated by Mei Lin Chang

First I must situate the Church vis-à-vis society as a whole. I shall do so by quoting a few principles from Pope Paul VI's first encyclical, *Ecclesiam Suam* (6 August 1964), on the dialogue between the two:

Fully conscious of all that is new and remarkable in this modern age, it [the Church] nevertheless holds its place in a changing world with sincere confidence, and says to men: "Here in my possession is what you are looking for, what you need." Its promise is not one of earthly happiness, but it does nevertheless provide the best means for the attainment of earthly happiness, namely, light and grace; and it teaches men about their future life which transcends nature. In addition it speaks to them of truth, justice, freedom, progress, concord, civilization and peace. The Church well knows the value of these things. It knows them in the light of Christ's revelation. (no. 95)

Let us enter into this confidence together, especially since the Church seeks to express herself, as Paul VI said, "in the style of ordinary conversation" rather than

Originally published in *Common Knowledge* 7.3 (Winter 1998): 79-83, as part of the symposium "Outside the Academy." © 1998.

Common Knowledge 25:1–3

DOI 10.1215/0961754X-7299474

in an "extraordinary and dogmatic" way. Man, invited to this kind of dialogue, is man as defined by the Second Vatican Council, "man himself, whole and entire, body and soul, heart and conscience, mind and will" *(Gaudium et Spes,* no. 3, § 1).

It seems to me important also to underscore immediately the shift that has occurred lately from a Church-State dialogue to a wider Church-Society dialogue. Faced with a society that has become pluralist, one that renders convictions relative and references to authority banal, the Church and the State now have more common preoccupations than rival claims: they share the search for and defense of values without which there can be no stable and harmonious society. In refusing either to confront the State as an adversary or to call for its support, the Church preserves her own independence with respect to the ethical and religious dimensions of society. To be sure, the Church-Society dialogue creates no fewer tensions than the Church-State dialogue, but they are healthier, more real, because linked to the necessary and always fragile rapport between faith and history. A church that wanders among humanity, taking care to present her own original and evangelical face from amidst that caravan, is a church that can with some credibility hold her own in the great debates of society. She does not understand her role as limited to her members alone or merely to the private sphere of life; she assumes her own share of responsibility with regard to the common good of the whole of society.

In this spirit—of service and dialogue—what *does* the Catholic Church think of liberal society? And what, precisely, do we understand by "liberal society," an expression that lends itself to diametrically opposed interpretations. Depending on whether the portrait that emerges emphasizes light or shadow, the Church can either rear up or submit. It does seem easier today to speak serenely with a liberal society that is no longer subject to the game of brinkmanship since the fall of Marxist society. Six years ago, Pope John Paul II provoked some reactions when he affirmed in his encyclical *Sollicitudo Rei Socialis* that "the Church's social doctrine adopts a critical attitude towards both liberal capitalism and Marxist collectivism" (no. 21). Some saw, with astonishment or even indignation, a moral equivalence proposed between the two ideologies, whereas the pope was simply bringing a practical appreciation to bear on the development of individuals and of peoples—a severe appreciation, true enough, for in his eyes neither bloc was unscathed by the sources of backwardness, or even of waywardness.

It must be acknowledged that the Catholic Church, after 1789, showed a certain allergy to social movements that were inspired by the concept of liberty. This is surprising in a church that, throughout the vicissitudes of history, has never ceased to hone in its members a fierce taste for liberty as the most radical demand of the Gospel. But it is understandable in a church that has seen itself attacked by the protagonists of "libertarian liberty"—a liberty transformed into an idolatry of absolute rights, under whose regime the truth of Christianity was obscured. It is not generally realized how long and harsh a fight the Church has had, one that has sometimes been unjustly represented as a fight against modern society. It is true, however, that the Church has had difficulty freeing itself from nostalgia for the ancient régime, and true that the Church has not always surmounted its fears and avoided rigidity or maladroitness—that the Church has not known how to choose between the best and the worst elements that the liberal current has brought to troubled waters.

Three years ago, the Church commemorated the centenary of the *"Ralliement"* advocated by Pope Leo XIII: the word seems to express a tactical stance or resignation, and evokes the kind of cynicism evidenced by an impertinent commentator of the last century: "the thesis is to burn M. de Rothschild; the hypothesis, to dine with him." But no one can any longer doubt the sincerity of the Church, especially since 7 December 1967, the eve of the closing of the Second Vatican Council. On that day a vote was taken on the proclamation regarding religious liberty, a document laboriously formulated and fiercely debated. It is founded on the rights of the human person rather than those of the Church. Since 1967, the marriage of the Church to societal freedom has once more become a marriage of love after having been for too long a marriage of convenience. Today, full of confidence in its open and massive involvement on behalf of liberty, the Church feels more at ease in expressing all of its requirements to a "liberal" society that, by definition, thinks of itself too as founded on liberty. The principal difficulty in this dialogue stems from the fact that there are many dwelling places in the palace and one gets quickly lost in the maze of rooms, each bearing a variant of the word *liberal*. I shall not cite any theoreticians by name; they are many and diverse, and their works at times betray the rigidity of an ideology. But I imagine that none of them would wish to be imprisoned within a model, be it from the Rhineland or neo-American. Liberalism is an air that one breathes more than a system to apply, and, by and large, it lends itself to all sorts of pragmatic adjustments. In the overall decor, it is easy to spot those who preach liberalism like a religion, those who consider it capable of correction, and those who reject it in the name of those excluded. In face of this kaleidoscope, it is important for the Church to expose the major and constant tendencies of liberal society, to pass them under the lens of a freedom that permits the human person to be fully human. The social encyclicals of the popes, from Leo XIII to John Paul II, have proceeded in this way, with a burning discernment that, while appearing not to touch anyone, touches everyone in its courageous appeal to truth rather than to severity. To the varied advocates of a liberal society, the Church simply says: If you wish to build a society founded on liberty, let us test your words and especially your deeds by fire.

I am going now to hazard this delicate exercise myself, in light of John Paul II's encyclical *Centesimus Annus* (1 May 1991). The pope sometimes says "yes" to liberal society, and those affirmations are considerable; they are, however, almost all accompanied by "buts," and the reservations sometimes outweigh the affirmations:

- Yes, "[i]t would appear that, on the level of individual nations and of international relations, *the free market* is the most efficient instrument for utilizing resources and effectively responding to needs" (no. 34); but "there are collective and qualitative needs which cannot be satisfied by market mechanisms. There are important human needs which escape its logic" (no. 40).
- Yes, "[t]he Church acknowledges the legitimate *role of profit* as an indication that a business is functioning well" (no. 35); but profit is not its sole regulator—"*other human and moral factors* must also be considered which, in the long term, are at least equally important for the life of a business" (no. 35).
- Yes, "the *role* of disciplined and creative *human work* and, as an essential part of that work, *initiative and entrepreneurial ability* becomes increasingly evident and decisive" (no. 32); but, in many places, there are "situations in which the rules of the earliest period of capitalism still flourish in conditions of 'ruthlessness' in no way inferior to the darkest moments of the first phase of industrialization" (no. 33).
- Yes, John Paul II (like his predecessors) affirms forcefully "the natural character of the right to private property" (no. 30); but, with equal clarity he recalls that "the 'use' of goods, while marked by freedom, is subordinated to their original common destination" (no. 30), thus underlining the "social function" of private property.
- Yes, "[t]he Church values the democratic system inasmuch as it ensures the participation of the citizens in making political choices" (no. 46); but "[c]ertain demands which arise within society are sometimes not examined in accordance with criteria of justice and morality, but rather on the basis of the electoral or financial power of the groups promoting them" (no. 47).

One could extend this litany, but the passages from *Centesimus Annus* that I have quoted should suffice to make comprehensible the Pope's summary statement: "economic freedom is only one element of human freedom. When it becomes autonomous . . . then economic freedom loses its necessary relationship to the human person and ends up by alienating and oppressing him" (no. 39). Thus, paradoxically, the reservations of the Church concerning liberal society address its perception that this type of society does not show itself attentive enough to ensure liberty, full liberty, whether to the whole of the human person or to all persons. Too many facts bear witness that liberty is not pursued with the same intensity for each dimension of the human person in a society that mutilates the person by cutting him off from his divine source. Too many facts bear witness that liberty is not pursued with the same intensity for all categories of persons in a society where "the rich get richer and the poor get poorer." (The 20 percent who comprise the richest of the world's population now possess 150 times what the 20 percent who comprise the poorest can claim, and disparities are more glaring than ever between North and South. Moreover, what country, what city, on the planet does not have its own North and South?)

The demands of the Church vis-à-vis liberal society are made even more pressing by the unedifying spectacle presented today by countries that are liberalizing themselves to countries that are *liberating* themselves. The shams of liberty reflected in the eyes of those who emerge from the shadows of communism excite some to a frenzy but disenchant others, making them nostalgic. A disfigured liberty is more dangerous than a suppressed liberty, for idolatry conceals God more than does atheism. It would be a grave matter if liberal society, basking in its victory and settling lazily into "the end of history," did not draw all the lessons from the disintegration of Marxism, which was created in the last century to remedy the defects of liberalism. Liberalism too is capable of "totalitarian drift," as a recent book title has it, and only facile reassurance comes from saying that communism collapsed in a heap because it had no internal stabilizer while liberalism is blessed with a self-correcting system. If it is true that the same causes produce the same effects, it is not out of the question that a new collectivist society could be reborn from the ashes even where it seems most dead and buried. How stimulating in its harshness is the remark of Nicolas Berdyaev: "Marxism demasks a Christianity that has not realized its truth."

John Paul II dared to write in *Centesimus Annus:*

The Marxist solution has failed, but the realities of marginalization and exploitation remain in the world, especially in the Third World, as does the reality of human alienation, especially in the more advanced countries. Against these phenomena the Church strongly raises her voice. . . . The collapse of the Communist system in so many countries certainly removes an obstacle to facing these problems in an appropriate and realistic way, but it is not enough to bring about their solution. Indeed, there is a risk that a radical capitalist ideology could spread which refuses even to consider these problems. (no. 42)

The free market, the pope recently said to the bishops of the European Economic Community, should not be presented "as the panacea for all the ills suffered by the countries of Central and Eastern Europe" (11 October 1991). And he invited the responsible officials of the EEC to conduct "an examination of conscience" to verify if there is, on their part, full respect for those values that were repressed in the communist countries.

What, then, is required for liberal society to truly take hold of human liberty in its integrality and universality? First, I would say that liberty is too great and at the same time too fragile a thing to be borne by those who are not gods—it is realizable, as Bergson would put it, only by "heroes or saints." But liberty is far from being an elitist, Olympian design: God fixes the bar high before all, though very few will cross it. Every society is an effort to have humanity in extension and humanity in comprehension coincide.

This effort presupposes a climate of spirituality. In that concext, one is heartened to see the rise of ethical concerns in liberal society, in economics as well as in politics, even where they arise, as they have with an increasingly universal legitimacy, out of anxiety for success in business. We are a long way from the famous invisible hand of Adam Smith, who entrusted spontaneous market mechanisms the task of ensuring, almost automatically, both harmony and growth, equilibrium and equity. But where does this concern for the ethical lead? Is this a simple questioning of what values to promote and which ends to attain? Is it a substitute for morality, or a morality that dare not speak its name in a society that has become permissive? Each social engagement of the Church, particularly those of John Paul II, is meant to address the difficult choices that a banker, an industrialist, a politician are led to take—it is the moral imperative that above all mobilizes and binds a person to himself and to others; but to go the full distance, one must ascend, or descend, to God. De Tocqueville's *Democracy in America* still sounds fresh in this regard:

Despotism may govern without faith, but liberty cannot. Religion is much more necessary in the republic . . . than in the monarchy . . . and . . . in democratic republics than in any others. How is it possible that society should escape destruction if the moral tie be not strengthened in proportion as the political tie is relaxed? and what can be done with a people which is its own master; if it be not submissive to the Divinity?

A hundred and fifty years later, the general director of the International Monetary Fund, Michel Camdessus, addressing business leaders in Lille, straightforwardly says that "freedom is not the daughter of the world, but the daughter of the Kingdom of Heaven" (27 May 1992).

It takes considerable virtue to live in a collectivist society, but even more to live in a liberal society. With the enormous difficulties of installing among us more equality, more fraternity, the defense of liberties cannot be used as an easy alibi. It is a question of promoting in each individual and in each social group a liberty not only of protest but of responsibility. The responsibility lies in the fact of being fully able to recognize and recapture oneself in one's own acts; it is therefore the most authentic expression of liberty, especially as responsibility translates into solidarity at the point where one becomes truly free only through the freedom of others. As Dostoyevsky shows in the episode of the Grand Inquisitor, the natural drives of man incline him to consider freedom a "burden" that he seeks to free himself of by placing it into stronger hands. Against the Creons, the Antigones are rare. A society grappling with the logics of domination, of profit, and of violence will be able to accede to true liberty only through constant appeal to an internal self-mastery. As Emmanuel Mounier wrote,

those who have lost the passion for freedom become incapable of protecting concrete liberties. Freedom cannot be given to men from outside, like the social services or a reformed Constitution; they only drop asleep upon such liberties and wake up as enslaved as before. Our liberties can be no more than opportunities offered to the spirit of freedom. . . . Each new victory for freedom is turned against it and demands another battle: the struggle for freedom knows no end. (*Personalism*, trans. Philip Mairet [London: Routledge & Kegan Paul, 1952], 62–63)

With this citation from the master of Christian personalism, I write *finis* to my lecture. I have had trouble throughout taking stills of a society as fluid and on the move as liberal society is, and I have had to content myself with a kind of identikit picture. My theme has been liberty, for I wish to take seriously and at their word the denizens of a society that ceaselessly waves the flag of liberty, which is so often ragged. The Gospel that the Church carries in its human hands teaches us that God is man's freedom. If in society man is set as the foundation of man, then what we have is less a tautology than a hoax. If man is not anchored on the horizon of transcendence, which renders him incapable of being appropriated by the powers that be, the attempt of society to build a house of justice and of peace on earth is in vain. Such is the message, in all its vigor and its rawness, that the Church untiringly addresses to all of humanity— while at the same time trying herself to live it, "in spirit and in truth."

*—Paper delivered at the Institute for Human Sciences colloquium in Vienna,
in the "constant presence" of Pope John Paul II, 1994*

ON HOW POSTWAR GERMANY HAS FACED ITS RECENT PAST

Jürgen Habermas

It is difficult enough for us as individuals to come to terms with our own life histories; but at least we know what it means to face one's own biography more or less honestly. Søren Kierkegaard, for example, detailed a perspective from which one may scrupulously evaluate one's past and project one's future life. When opening one's mind to a critical examination and reflective appropriation of one's past in order to find out what kind of person one is and who one would like to be, one must first, in an almost counterfactual way, take full responsibility for the outcome of the processes that shaped one's identity and then discriminate those strands that one affirms and wants to continue from those to be rejected. But rejection as such is not sufficient. The painful episodes of failure and the appalling aspects of one's life that ought no longer to determine one's identity require more than just denial. If they are no longer to have an impact on the future, one has to face them consciously and work through them. Otherwise the past will unconsciously persist. The past loses its compulsory reign over the present only through the work of a truly faithful memory.

We have an intuitive knowledge of the intricate relations among past, present, and future where the individual is concerned; but it is far from obvious how

Originally published in *Common Knowledge* 5.2 (Fall 1996):
1–13. © 1996.

to apply that knowledge to a collective actor like a nation. Collectivities may have a historical fate, but entangled with it are many different people and generations, various social groups and subcultures, with distinct life patterns, diverging traditions, and forms of life. People occupy different places in social space and historical time. As contemporary members of the same political community they share, however, a common history. Even if those citizens experience, enjoy, and suffer the impact of their national history in so many different ways, most of them bear, in however indirect a way, a responsibility for the collective political decisions and policies that they either supported or tolerated by their lack of resistance. So also they share the liability for consequences of acts that they legitimated at the very least by tacit compliance—and this gives us some basis on which to draw parallels between individual and collective actors and to ask how a people, in view of its national history, may come to terms with its past—in particular, with a period of its recent history marked by unprecedented crimes. I am not going to write about the Holocaust, a task that goes far beyond whatever I could ever say; all that I can do is present my view of how Germany has faced a past whose outstanding feature is that event.

This is a subject for academic historians or political scientists. Being neither one nor the other, I cannot claim professional competence, or any special competence beyond that of a witness to contemporary history. The adult life of my generation happens to coincide with the political existence of the Federal Republic of Germany. For the sake of clarifying the context from which I am writing, I should note that I was fifteen years old when the war ended and finished high school four years later. Raised during the Nazi period in a politically more or less conformist family, it was only for accidental personal reasons that I did not fully identify with the spirit of the time. By the end of the war, I was in a rather confused state of mind, feeling a somewhat self-centered relief and the imminence of something totally new.

One afternoon in late summer of 1945, I visited, as I had many times before, the local cinema, the only one in our town. In this familiar surrounding, I was suddenly struck by images beyond the bounds of anything familiar, anything even imaginable, as I watched the documentaries of the incredible and unforgettable scenes when the liberators first entered the camps of Auschwitz and Birkenau. Owing in part to the receptiveness of adolescence, the shock of that afternoon was to structure my adult political life. A second event of lasting impact was, somewhat later, the broadcasts of the Nuremberg trial. Most of the private commentaries I heard in school and town did not concern revealed facts but procedures; the International Military Tribunal was denied legitimacy. I remember this as my first encounter with the kind of intellectual rationalization that was to become a typical reaction to the Nazi past in general. I am thinking here of the attitude of those who, with no personal involvement or guilt themselves, look for an interpretation of facts and situations that exculpates the guilty. This defense ironically confirms, again and again, the psychological reality that collective liability for a nation's poisoned past has, however manifestly denied. Karl Jaspers, in a famous speech in 1949, succinctly distinguished between collective liability and individual guilt; neither moral nor legal guilt, he held, may be collectively attributed. This important distinction between collective liability, which we should recognize, and collective guilt, which is incompatible with a postconventionalist understanding of justice, has been wilfully ignored in many public discussions. The confusion of one with the other serves particularly the purpose of those who wish to escape collective liability by rejecting the pretension of a wrongly imputed collective guilt.

At present, I am interested in the strange course of collective memory. For individual persons, it is often decades before repressed traumatic experiences surface from the unconscious. The documentary evidence from Claude Lanzmann's *Shoah* shows how long it takes to overcome obstacles and find an expression for the horrors of the past even within the intimate circle of the family. Memory evinces similar features, for different reasons, on the side of the perpetrators. As we know from psychological research, the psychohistory of the parents has been transferred to the next generation. Collective memory certainly works differently; among other things, it is shaped by public as well as private interactions between conflicting generations. Yet we observe here similar phases—at first, the long postponement of a public confrontation with a painful past, followed by an amplified and intensified concern with the return of the denied past under the pressure of the next generation. This explains the unexpected phenomenon that persistent reference to the Nazi period seems to block the normal flow of contemporary history.

The relevant discussions and corresponding manifestations in Germany's public culture over the last fifty years exhibit a discernible pattern. It took almost the span of a generation to overcome the ritualized exorcism of memories and selective perception of events that lay in the not very distant past; but, in the following period, younger generations were all the more occupied with the past of their parents and grandparents. This sequence resulted in a peculiar "time machine" effect: excited public attention to the annihilating energies of the national socialist period, stimulated by anniversaries and various incidents, seemed to slow down the flow of events, even to inhibit the past from passing away at its usual rate. The observation of this change in time consciousness was broadly shared until the acceleration of history after 1989, when the dramatic devolution of the Soviet empire appeared to speed up the pace of events. In recent years, there has been a reaction to the irritating phenomenon of a past that did not pass away.

If I am not mistaken in my perception of present trends in Germany, a debate—skeptical and sometimes denunciatory in character—about established procedures and policies for mastering an "unmasterable past" is now taking the place of the previously straightforward controversy about how to cope with this impossible task. As the discussion moves on to a reflexive level of discussions about discussions, the same neutralizing effect once brought about by an escape from discussion is now reached by its very means. In view of which, I will start with a sketch of the main responses prevailing in West German civil society. I will divide postwar history up to 1989 into four periods, then analyze the three issues that I regard as most important in the Historians' Debate of 1986–1987, and conclude with brief remarks on the present situation as it has developed since reunification in 1990.

Coping with an "Unmasterable Past"

There were four phases, before 1989, in the political attempt to accomplish the impossible task of mastering Germany's recent history: (1) the new beginning: the end of the war and the foundation of two German states in 1949, the Federal Republic of Germany and the German Democratic Republic; (2) the period of economic and social reconstruction, which is more or less coextensive with the Adenauer regime between 1949 and 1963; (3) the period of questioning and reorientation, which includes the protest movement of the late sixties and ends with the resignation of Willy Brandt in 1974; (4) the period of reaction, with its new conservative search for identity, which lasts until 1989.

(1) The traits of a national political culture reflect mentalities that continue over generations. But those orientations shift at turning points in history. Such shifts depend to some extent on generational constellations that indicate the clashing simultaneity of nonsynchronous biographical experiences. After 1945, even within peer groups there were divisions representing fateful differences in political biography. First, the Weimar generation was divided between those who supported the Nazi regime (such as Hans Globke and Martin Heidegger or Carl Schmitt) and those who were fortunate to escape its threats and dangers, either in marginalized acquiescence and mute opposition inside Germany (e.g., Konrad Adenauer and Karl Jaspers) or in the concentration camps (e.g., Kurt Schumacher and Eugen Kogon) or else in exile (e.g., most of the social democratic leaders, like Willy Brandt, Erich Ollenhauer, the Bavarian prime minister Wilhelm Högner, and many intellectuals such as Alfred Döblin and Bert Brecht, Max Horkheimer and Ernst Bloch). Immediately after the war, this oldest of the generations I am discussing could provide a link with, and to some extent a continuation of, the uncorrupted traditions of the Weimar period, in which these people had already acquired their competence, status, and reputation. The next generation did not grow up and begin careers before the Nazi takeover (as is the case, for example,

with Helmut Schmidt and Heinrich Böll). We usually term these the *Wieder-aufbau* or "reconstruction generation." Owing to the disciplined efforts of those in this age group, a defeated and destroyed country was soon rebuilt and quickly regained economic strength and social stability. Finally, there was the youngest generation (my own), which came of age after the war (today represented, if you like, by Hans-Jochen Vogel or Helmut Kohl on one side, Günter Grass or Hans Magnus Enzensberger on the other). This generational constellation provides the background for the first two postwar periods.

The four years between the end of the war and the foundation of the Federal Republic in 1949 were culturally shaped by a hungry, unprejudiced reception of hitherto repressed and excluded Western traditions, particularly in art, music, and literature, but also in political, social, and cultural criticism. Outside of press and broadcasting, vital public debates took place in many short-lived but highbrow cultural magazines circulating among the educated segments of the population. This was the soil for a widespread, yet illusionary consciousness of a clear break with the past. It was the time of enthusiastic welcome for a presumed "hour zero." There appeared the first biographical accounts of persecution during the Nazi period, above all Eugen Kogon's *Der SS-Staat*, Wolfgang Langhoff's *Moorsoldaten* and Annedore Leber's memoirs. It was, in any case, the time of a serious effort to examine critically traditions and mentalities that had contributed throughout the Nazi period to an enduring mass loyalty and that, moreover, might explain the embarrassing fact of active support for, or tacit complicity with, this regime by the academic elite, if not by the academic classes in general. Of the public intellectuals, during these first years, Thomas Mann, Karl Jaspers, Alfred Weber, and Walter Dirks enjoyed the strongest influence and highest reputation.

The prevailing moral attitude toward a more or less globally rejected past also marked the first attempts of German historians, who at that time had to work from a very few available sources, to give an account of the national socialist period. Returning emigrants, such as Hans Rothfels, presented a somewhat black-and-white picture, with Hitler in the almost mythical role of absolute evil, on the one side, and the assailants in the failed attempt of 20 July 1944 as heroes, on the other. In spite of the great merits of these attempts, it was realized in retrospect that the stark opposition between dark and light did not allow for much differentiation. Moreover, the focus on actors, bad and good, did not give sufficient attention to the annihilation of the European Jews and other groups, nor did it stimulate the readers' empathy with the fate of these victims.

(2) One might speculate that the general tendency to mythologize the regime as a criminal abyss had a double impact on public consciousness in Germany during the following, the second, period, from the fifties through the early sixties. The celebrated military opposition to Hitler, symbolized by the attempted coup d'état of the 20th of July, became a constitutive part of the offi-

cial self-understanding of the Federal Republic. This affirmative context allowed the government to assume legal responsibility for reparation claims, for example from Israel (though individual claims for compensation, mainly from Eastern Europe, are still pending). At the same time, however, generalizing a demonic segment of recent German history, which was rejected in toto, also released people from facing, let alone working through, a painful past that was part and parcel of their own.

Counteracting a denazification process that had more or less failed anyway, Adenauer and his governing party soon took all legal measures necessary to rehabilitate the rank and file of the former NSDAP, the Nazi Party. The fifties were the high tide of the *Wirtschaftswunder*, a relentless and efficient reconstruction of the damaged material conditions of life. These efforts aspired to restore a superior status quo ante; they absorbed, so it appears, all available energies for the pressing demands of a present that drew attention away from an uneasy past. As we shall see, however, the past that disappeared behind a façade of forced presentism kept the forgetting mind in its grip. The repressed memories would return.

From a retrospective point of view, the fifties have often been described as kind of a latency period, a "communicative silencing" (*kommunikatives Beschweigen*) of the past. In this context, Hermann Lübbe, a colleague of mine, has related the exemplary story of an émigré who, soon after his return from the United States, became rector of the university from which he had been expelled in 1933, and then grinned and bore it as he faced again those ever-compliant colleagues who remained as silent as before. The phrase "communicative silencing" is meant to describe a situation in which a tacitly acknowledged moral asymmetry between offender and victim is kept tactfully hidden beneath the surface of proceedings that pretend to business as usual. Yet most Germans were not required to share even this queer sort of tact with returning émigrés. Moving within the confines of a silent majority, they could afford to remember sufferings of their own rather than those of the victims. By the end of the fifties, the predominant feeling was relief. The manifest economic and social recovery, and the growing international acceptance of the new Germany, seemed to confirm that we had finally overcome the nightmares of an unhappy, more or less accidental, and more and more unreal—that is, derealized—past. Symptomatic of this mood was the tremendous outburst of public indignation among the readers of Günter Grass's piercing *Tin Drum*, a critical book that collided head-on with the self-delusions of the time.

(3) The public life of the Adenauer period was marked by a sharp division of labor between politics and culture—more specifically between, on the one hand, the policy of reconciliation with former Nazis and the preservation of a strong continuity in the personnel of government, academia, and higher management, and, on the other hand, the protests of a small but influential group of

writers and intellectuals who opposed the deep-seated continuities of an anti-Western mentality that had both nourished and survived the Nazi regime. The intellectual opposition was now reaching into the second and third generation. Protagonists like Theodor Adorno, Alexander Mitscherlich, Alfred Andersch, Heinrich Böll, and Peter Weiss were soon joined by younger writers like Hans Magnus Enzensberger, Martin Walser, and Uwe Johnson. Their publications paved the way for a shift in cultural climate, if not in public opinion, that can be traced back to the early sixties. The first Auschwitz trial under German authority not only attracted worldwide attention; within the national public sphere, this event symbolized the first conscious political effort to face the unique dimension and quality of what had happened in the death camps. It was also understood as a message addressed to the population at large—an attempt to stimulate consciousness of the particular responsibility we Germans bear for a genocide that depended on the supportive context of a community that once had prided itself on its civilizational standards and national traditions. It cost Fritz Bauer, the general prosecutor of the state of Hessen and himself an émigré, much effort to overcome the resistance of those who advocated a *Schlußstrich*—that is, putting an end to the public debate on this horrible chapter of recent history.

Since that time, a bitter struggle has continued between those who press for more debate and those who prefer to be done with it. The issue is whether we should recognize Auschwitz as an integral part of our national history and, if so, what that would mean for the critical reappraisal of, and discriminating choice between, received traditions. This struggle did not reach broader segments of the population, however, until it was taken up and reinforced by the student movement. Therewith a new generation made its appearance on the political scene, a generation born during and maturing only after World War II. The rebel students in Germany shared, of course, most of their motivations, goals, and rhetoric with the protest movement in the United States and in other European countries, except for one peculiar feature. In Germany the protest was immediately connected with the issue of repressed memories of the Nazi period. The students urgently demanded to know about the personal involvements of their parents, of their teachers, and of political, economic, and cultural elites in general. This was a time when many universities organized lecture series on the embarrassing pasts of their own departments. Certainly, these struggles were often fueled by the outrage and arrogance of adolescents who turned against their parents. But it was precisely due to the face-to-face nature of the confrontations that this vehement demand for disclosure, analysis, and enlightenment filtered down from the educated middle classes, penetrated into broader segments of the population, and had a long-term impact on mentalities.

(4) The following period, reaching from the mid-seventies to 1989, is marked by the interaction of opposing tendencies, both somehow linked with

the protest movement. The quest for unmasking had left wounds and polarizations, particularly in many cultural fields. This challenge in turn provoked resentments that furnished a psychological basis for harsh political measures; these were also prompted by the terrorism of the so-called Red Army Faction, which quite understandably poisoned the political climate even more. The antiliberal mood reached its climax in the fall of 1977, when the president of the Entrepreneurs' Association, Hans Martin Schleyer, was murdered in cold blood. This antiliberal trend did not last very long, but it reinforced the international turn toward neoconservatism on the level of manifest political debate. Beneath this level there was occurring, however, a less conspicuous and longer ranging change in political attitudes, In the late seventies, sociologists discovered a general shift from materialist to postmaterialist orientations in values, particularly among the younger generations and the more educated segments of the population. In combination with this general trend, the protest movement had obviously accelerated a process of cultural modernization that led to a remarkable spread of more liberal attitudes, in any case of attitudes that proved less susceptible to a rhetoric that combined the modernism of a market economy with the traditionalism of strong values, firm institutions, and quasi-natural identities.

These opposed trends, one of which was manifest while the other remained submerged, clashed when Kohl made his failed attempt to foster a kind of West German national identity on condition that the dark chapter of a no-longer-recent history was to be definitely closed. Kohl had invited President Reagan to join him in a military ceremony at a soldiers' cemetery in Bitburg, a small Eifel town. The ceremony was to enact a peculiar kind of historical reconciliation. The American president was supposed not just to endorse the German-American friendship, which was stable in any case; more importantly, he was expected to exculpate and officially rehabilitate a former enemy and present ally, so that for us Germans the present would be definitively unburdened of liabilities for a criminal past. This was to pave the way for rebuilding a national identity that seemed requisite for securing the reliability of a predictable NATO partner. Moreover, for Germans the ceremony contained a delicate subtext, which the *Frankfurter Allgemeine Zeitung* did not hesitate to uncover weeks in advance. The handshakes between veteran generals of the Second World War could wishfully be understood as a retrospective recognition that the Germans had always been fighting against the real enemy, communism.

But, you will recall, past realities soon overtook the escapist present. The whole idea was put into question by the accidental discovery that former members of the *Waffen-SS*, the Nazi elite branch of the armed forces, had been buried in that same place. While the ceremonial program was indeed carried through, large segments of the population, particularly among the young, had inconspicuously assumed a mentality different from that expected by Kohl. So the polls showed that people were not pleased by the transparent maneuver of cleansing the collective identity through the ritualized repression of bad memories.

Another indicator of a growing sensitivity to the moral challenge of the Holocaust was the title of an article that appeared in the *Frankfurter Allgemeine Zeitung* a little more than a year after Bitburg: "A Past that Does Not Pass Away." Ernst Nolte, the author, complained about the fact and offered historical arguments that were supposed to do what the military ceremony of Bitburg had failed to achieve. That article launched the Historians' Debate, a polemic among academics that nevertheless gained the attention of a much wider public.

The Historians' Debate

The name is misleading inasmuch as it was a political debate rather than a controversy about historical facts and their interpretation. Most of the participants were indeed historians, and the issues at stake did have an impact on how we Germans should understand our recent history. But no special competence was required to make reasonable contributions to this debate, at least as regards two of the three major issues. As one of the participants, I am not going to reconstruct and analyze the controversy or its outcome. A partisan's view can hardly match the brilliant historical accounts of Richard J. Evans (*In Hitler's Shadow: West German Historians and the Attempt to Escape the Past*, Pantheon, 1989) or Charles Maier (*The Unmasterable Past*, Harvard University Press, 1988), to say nothing of Dominick LaCapra's ("Reflections on the Historians' Debate," *Representing the Holocaust*, Cornell University Press, 1994). I can only explain the three main issues in debate: (a) the issues of uniqueness (or singularity), (b) normalization, and (c) historization.

(a) I agree with LaCapra that the central issue was whether public attention was being diverted from the Holocaust in a manner that decreased the chances of working through this most painful part of a history of which we are still part (45). Whether and to what extent the analytical process of "working through" is at all possible in view of such a catastrophic break with the civilizational underpinnings of any human mode of life remains, of course, an open question. Insisting on the uniqueness of the systematic annihilation of the European Jews does not imply an opposition to comparisons, e.g., between Nazi and Stalinist terror. The insistence is directed, rather, against the political attempt to use historical comparisons for the purpose of setting off one crime against another, thereby relativizing, even minimizing, the ethical implications of crimes emerging from and embedded in one's own history. This was the case with Nolte's intimation that what happened in the death camps was no different from other mass killings "but for the sole exception of the technical procedure of gassing." Eberhard Jäckel gave the correct response to that disturbing statement: "The Nazi extermination of the Jews was unique because never before had a state, under the responsible authority of its leader, decided and announced that a specific group of human beings, including the old, the women, the children and the infants, would be killed to the very last one, and implemented this decision with all means at its disposal." One might add that the specific group was delimited by ascribed criteria on the basis of a pseudoscientific, in fact paranoid, worldview.

Let me in this context briefly anticipate a discussion about the comparability of the Holocaust with Hiroshima that arose only a few months ago on the occasion of the fiftieth anniversary of the Japanese defeat (*Der Spiegel* 31 [1995]: 14.6 ff.). Again, the incommensurability of the two crimes is obvious: the Allies never had the intention of eliminating a particular people as a whole, and merely because of their Japanese descent; the declared goal was to force an enemy, with all means available, to surrender. There is no doubt that the suffering of any human being and the unjust fate of every individual victim deserves the same empathy and equal moral concern. But from the similarity of unjust suffering and from the equal moral worth of every victimized individual one must not conclude that the different historical contexts of such crimes and misdeeds are of similar type and equal weight, such that they might be reckoned against one another.

(b) False comparisons meant to relieve the German nation of a burdensome past highlight aspects of the intentional "normalization" of its citizens' historical and political self-understanding. The neoconservative idea that historical narratives may serve as compensation for the loss of traditional collective identities that have been uprooted by modernization reminds us of the twin phenomena of nationalism and historicism in nineteenth-century European nation building. But this example makes it all the more questionable whether an academic discipline such as history may and should be "instrumentalized" for the political purpose of projecting and promoting the shared ideas of a collective self-image. For this would require a purposefully selective presentation and integration of those valuable aspects of the past that would meet with an affirmative response from present generations. In the case of postwar Germany, such an affirmative approach could succeed only at the price of a leveling normalization. It would deprive people of the possibility of discriminating and choosing between those traditions worthy of conscious appropriation and those traditions that should not be continued. This critical attitude is necessary, however, if we who inherit this German past are not to betray the Benjaminian legacy of an anamnestic solidarity with the suffering and denigration of innocent victims. Without it, their children and grandchildren would no longer be able to breathe in our country.

In view of the cultural pluralism of complex modern societies, the idea of a fixed national identity has generally become problematic. Now, the political self-understanding of civil society is discursively shaped by different accounts of constitutional essentials, which compete in the light of different historical narratives and different projections of the future. To the extent that historians and academics in general participate as citizens in these debates of a political-ethical nature, they have to be careful not to confuse their roles. There are different requirements for the academic profession, on the one hand, and for the public intellectual, on the other.

(c) The most intricate issue of the debate was that of historization: whether a past will become ever more neutralized in its moral charge the more we view it through the objectivizing lens of historical research. There is an inevitable dialectic built into the flow of time itself. Once the generations of perpetrators and survivors, of their immediately affected children and grandchildren, and of those growing up during the period, like my generation, have passed away—once all contemporaries of the events are dead—historical research provides the only resource for keeping memories alive, and it can do so only by a cool and demythologizing representation of critically assessed facts. We do not know for sure, but it is not unreasonable to expect that it will become more and more difficult to connect these sober and detailed descriptions with the life, personal experience, and self-understanding of future generations. At the core of this question there looms even the doubt that it is at all possible to "understand" the Holocaust or to "represent" its horrors. If this is the premise, one might come to the radical conclusion that the incommensurabilty of Auschwitz cannot be captured by any historical account, but should be left to a ritualized remembrance, to a liturgy or at least to a quasi-religious practice of anamnestic memory.

In the context of the Historians' Debate, this question of historization was discussed from a specific point of view, namely in relation to an ongoing methodological controversy about the shortcomings and merits of oral history and *Alltagsgeschichte*—the local history of everyday life. Martin Broszat, the late director of the Munich Institute for Contemporary History and a man of political and personal integrity beyond doubt, had approached the Nazi period in just this way. Shifting perspective from the main political actors (and from the structural features of the system) to the local impact that political forces and processes had on individual life histories and everyday behaviors, Broszat had studied personal and social life in small Bavarian communities with the intention of replacing what he called the "mythical memory" of strange events with an historical account that would bring those days back into the reach of later generations. Saul Friedlander, the well-known Israeli historian and himself a victim of Nazi persecution, criticized this approach for its unintended apologetic implications. Friedlander suspected that *Alltagsgeschichte* would render too harmless a reading of the monstrosities of the age. That kind of historization "could mean not so much a widening of the picture as a shift in focus. From that perspective, the insistence on *Alltag* . . . could indeed strongly relativize what I still consider as the decisive historiographical approach to that period, an approach which considers these twelve years as a definable historical unit dominated, first of all, by the 'primacy of politics'" ("A Controversy about the Historization of National Socialism," *New German Critique* 44 [1988]: 104).

A Double Past and Present Ambivalences

My concluding remarks concern a situation determined by the fact that the unified nation now inherits a double past, including the political crimes and human rights violations of the post-Stalinist regime in East Germany. For quite a while our mass media were largely occupied with the stumbling disclosures of the extensive and pervasive machinations of the Stasi, the political police, who had been so incredibly successful in carrying on an almost panoptic supervision of the whole population by engaging a considerable part of it for its own projects. These revelations were accompanied by mutual accusations among East German intellectuals. The polemics between the dissidents and those who had remained in the East without manifest resistance appeared only to replicate the famous discussion after World War II between Thomas Mann, on one side, and Frank Thiess or Walther von Molo on the other—that is, between the émigrés and those who had remained in Nazi Germany. The tempting parallels between the GDR and Nazi Germany, and the general inclination to put both in the same box, soon revived, however, a still burning issue from the Historians' Debate—the question of singularity.

In the first years following 1989, there was a strong tendency to appeal to the presumed (in fact, highly selective) antitotalitarian consensus, which at one time only reflected the anticommunism of the cold war period. It was no surprise that Ernst Nolte felt encouraged to reaffirm his views concerning the purely reactive and imitative nature of the Nazi crimes. And many people found the uncritical and disburdening comparison between Hitler's and Stalin's terror now more attractive than before. This attempt to make good for a lost battle immediately met a forceful and in the end successful rebuttal from historians such as Eberhard Jäckel. An antitotalitarian consensus that is no longer selective in favor of one regime or the other must be based on a fair comparison between the two German regimes, which neither assimilates one to the other nor plays down existing similarities. In spite of its totalitarian and criminal character, the GDR had neither launched a world war nor committed genocide; and due to the sheer extent of its forty-year rule, it developed a kind of post-Stalinist normality that the short-lived national socialist regime could never enjoy.

Since its reunification, postwar Germany has experienced its most intense upsurge of right-wing radicalism, both in violent political action and on the intellectual scene. The expected growth of radical parties and splinter groups was accompanied by an unexpected outburst of spontaneous terrorist acts against the homes of asylum seekers, against the houses and shops of Turkish guest-workers—most of whom had been established in Germany for decades—against synagogues, and against the Jewish barracks in the former concentration camp of Sachsenhausen. Violent attacks were also directed against individual foreigners in streets and subways, mainly Ghanian and Vietnamese workers invited by the former GDR, but also handicapped people, homosexuals, and so on. Numerous people were killed. Fewer and fewer of these incidents are now reported since the conservative parties decided no longer to exploit the issues of immigration, *Ausländerhaß*, and *Überfremdung*. The heated and polarizing debate on the *Ausländerfrage* has died down since the parliament decided on a controversial change in the constitution that nearly abolished the right to political asylum and allowed the government to close the national borders to immigrants. A grand coalition of Christian and Social Democrats has paid a high price, I think too high a price, for taming rightist violence and keeping the right-wing Republican Party out of parliament.

During the last five years, the intellectual scene has changed as well. Besides a general shift in favor of all kinds of conservatism, there has formed, for the first time since the end of the war, an audible, even almost respectable New Right. The publications of a group of younger historians, political scientists, and journalists presently appear in a series, edited by Rainer Zittelmann for the Ullstein Verlag, once a renowned Jewish publishing house, now controlled by a neo-Nazi. It was here that the manifesto of the New Right appeared—a collection of essays by writers, historians, filmmakers, philosophers, and political analysts, published under the title *Die selbstbewusste Nation*. The essays were arranged in the format of commentaries on a piece by Botho Strauss, a poet of high reputation, an earlier publication by whom in *Der Spiegel* had stirred up sweeping polemics.

The ideas of this New Right are far from new; they are a weak echo of the nationalist and elitist aspirations of the young conservative intellectuals of the Weimar period, some of whom became prominent Nazis. The two most influential of these were, of course, Martin Heidegger and Carl Schmitt. The present group is held together by a protest against what it perceives as a left and left-liberal cultural hegemony. These people complain mainly about the postwar Westernization of German culture; they denounce in particular the lasting influence of a reeducation that is supposed to have been inspired and implemented by returning Jewish émigrés. The straightforward quest for normalization has led to a recapitulation of themes related to the earlier Historians' Debate. The main aims of the New Right are either to rewrite the history of the "Third Reich" in the spirit and the context of an old-style national history or to interpret the period from 1917 to 1989 in the light of Carl Schmitt's idea of a *Weltbürgerkrieg*—a globalized civil war, originally waged by Wilson and Lenin.

The conservative trend is conspicuous but has only limited importance. This became obvious when the New Right failed in its attempt to launch, with the help of a nationwide advertising campaign, a revisionist reading of the 8th of May, the fiftieth anniversary of which was celebrated this year. Ten years ago, President von Weizsäcker had reminded the nation of the liberating consequences of unconditional surrender, which not only sealed the defeat of Germany but that of the Nazi regime. The New Right tried to mobilize public opinion against the definition of the 8th of May as a day of liberation, an interpretation that in the meantime had also been accepted by the Kohl government. This controversy had the delicate complication that the liberal reading was not totally free from apologetic connotations. The contest led, however, to a satisfactory outcome. It became clear after all that in 1945 the overwhelming majority of the population did not immediately welcome the end of the war as a liberating transition to democracy. It took decades of public debate until the mass of the population retrospectively accepted this interpretation. That learning process was in fact dependent on the struggle for a public acknowledgment of our particular liability for the consequences of the moral catastrophe of Auschwitz.

In today's Germany there is still an ambivalent mood. It is not yet clear whether the New Right will succeed in one of their goals: to ridicule any effort to keep memory alive as a revealing sign of "political correctness." In Germany, the metacritique of political correctness more and more concentrates on this issue. But ambivalences are themselves a part of history and no reason not to hope for the better.

"THE PERIOD AFTER 1989"

Václav Havel and Adam Michnik

Translated by Clare Cavanagh

Václav Havel, about to become editor in chief of *Hospodárske Noviny*, the leading Czech business newspaper, put a set of questions to Adam Michnik, editor in chief of *Gazeta wyborcza*, a leading newspaper in Poland. The questions and replies were as follows.

Havel: In a recent essay, "Praying for Rain," you described the situation in contemporary Poland as a "creeping coup d'état."[1] Does this mean that it is not just a government that has changed but the system itself? Have the Kaczynski brothers established a Fourth Republic in Poland? And if so, does it differ fundamentally from the Third Republic—that is, "the period after 1989"?

Michnik: The coalition of three parties—the PiS, Samoobrony, and the LPR—has altered the system itself.[2] Poland has gradually become a different country from what it was in the aftermath of 1989. The state has also become

Originally published in *Common Knowledge* 15.3 (Fall 2009): 319–23. © 2009 by Duke University Press.

1. Adam Michnik, "Praying for Rain," wyborcza.pl /1,82049,4351018.html?as=1&ias=2&startsz=x (accessed February 12, 2009).

2. PiS is the Law and Justice Party, Samoobrony the Self-Defense Party, and LPR the League of Polish Families.

Common Knowledge 25:1–3

DOI 10.1215/0961754X-7299498

different; it is not what the democratic opposition spent twenty-five years fighting for. In 1981, I defined my ideal of a "Solidarity Poland" in these terms:

A self-governing Poland, tolerant, heterogeneous, founded on Christian values, socially just, a Poland well disposed to its neighbors, a Poland open to compromise and moderation, to realism and real partnerships, but resisting slavery, spiritual submission; incapable of spiritual subjugation. A Poland full of the conflicts typical of modern societies but also imbued with the principle of solidarity. A Poland where intellectuals defend persecuted workers and workers' strikes seek cultural freedom. A Poland that speaks of itself with both pathos and mockery, that has been defeated time and again but never beaten, conquered; never subjugated. A Poland that has now recovered its identity, its language, its face.

That was how I imagined our Third Republic in 1981; this was the Poland I supported after 1989. Of course, there were many things I had not foreseen, among them mass privatization and the harsh logic of the market economy. But privatization and the market do not mean renouncing "a shared Poland, a Poland free of the lethal logic of revenge or permanent cold war on the home front." I cannot support a situation in which the state security archive is considered a basic source of information about us all. The Third Republic has been a country of shared concern about Poland's freedom and the worth of every person in Poland; it has been a state governed by the presumption of innocence. The Fourth Republic — which is, I believe, the project of Jaroslaw Kaczynski and his entourage — is a country in permanent "moral revolution," where the secret service and state prosecutor organize the harassment of unworthy citizens; where wiretapping and accusation are our daily bread. The Fourth Republic is a state governed by suspicion and fear, in which we must all consider ourselves suspects. The Fourth Republic is a state in which we daily await our summons to the prosecutor's office. We used to describe the communist way of life in this way: "give me anybody, and we'll find him an article in the penal code." I have the feeling, every day now, that someone is trying to find the right penal article for me.

Havel: You recently wrote, apropos of Churchill's famous comment, that, in today's Poland, if someone rings the doorbell at six in the morning, no one can be fully sure that it's the milkman. What evidence is there? — apart from the dramatic detention of Janusz Kaczmarek.[3]

3. Janusz Kaczmarek was Polish minister of internal affairs from February to August 2007.

Michnik: My dear Václav, in today's Poland—alas—there is always someone being arrested in the glare of television cameras: doctors, businessmen, politicians from opposition parties. For example, Emil Wasacz, the former treasury minster, was arrested, filmed, taken by police car across half of Poland, and immediately released when a judge ruled that the arrest was illegal. The former minister of construction, Barbara Blida, was awakened at six in the morning, an event that was filmed by police cameras. During the search, she committed suicide—shot herself—in a bathroom. The cameras did not catch *that* part, and the public still has not uncovered the whole truth about this tragedy. . . . Some well-known doctors have been arrested in front of cameras and accused of corruption (one was almost accused of murder). Visits at 6:00 a.m.—the minister of justice has explained at a press conference—are the norm in Poland, just as they are throughout the civilized world.

Havel: But the Polish judiciary is still independent of the government, is it not? Kaczmarek *was* released the next day. And the Constitutional Tribunal more or less eviscerated the Kaczynski government's lustration law. Bronislaw Geremek and the others who called for civil disobedience with respect to that law were vindicated.

Michnik: I do think the courts remain independent, and that clearly distresses Premier Jaroslaw Kaczynski and Justice Minister Zbigniew Ziobro. Hence they continually attempt to revoke judicial autonomy, interfere in staffing courts, restrict judicial immunity—and they have also brutally attacked the Constitutional Tribunal and blackmailed its judges with material drawn from the archive of the communist secret police. I view all these matters with revulsion, since I remember the courts' subservience under the dictatorship, when all verdicts were subject to the wishes of the reigning communists. At least *that* is, fortunately, not the case today, though prosecutors' offices are subject in almost every way to political pressures.

I will pass over the peculiarity of Ms. Fotyga's qualifications to head the MSZ, the foreign ministry, since we Poles are chivalrous to the ladies. But when her nomination was announced, Jaroslaw Kaczynski said, "we've taken back Foreign Affairs." To which, for my part, I would add: they have also taken back the prosecutors. They have not taken back the judges, which means that Poland continues to have judges with the courage to defend the spirit and letter of the law, despite the brutal attacks and insinuations of the political authorities. Both the prime minister and president have descended to such attacks—and the both of them are lawyers, which lends a piquancy to the proceedings. Neither of the Kaczynski brothers seems aware that they are turning, slowly, into caricatures of party functionaries who considered it a mandate of the proletarian revolution to do away with judicial independence. The "moral revolution," in the Kaczynskis' variant, is a caricature of those times; so far it has been comparatively toothless, but it is just as vile and contemptible. The lustration law was overturned by the Constitutional Tribunal. So all praise to the Tribunal's judges. But it is enough to study the content of that law to recognize the intentions of the current coalition, which forced that law—anticonstitutional and despicable—through parliament. The state to which Jaroslaw Kaczynski's party aspires is an authoritarian one in which—I must repeat—each citizen would feel threatened and under suspicion. The judges of the Tribunal were subjected to a stream of insults from the premier; these were accompanied by an announcement that the Tribunal's powers would be curtailed. Such things do not bode well for the future.

Havel: How do you explain the high level of support for the PiS, the League of Polish Families?

Michnik: The Kaczynski brothers' party enjoys real support from one sector of society; all the public-opinion polls tell us as much. How has that come to pass? In your last book, Václav, you recall a speech of your own, given in February 1990, and "the shouts of protest from a crowd otherwise favorably disposed to [you] when [you] announced that [you] were going to abolish the death penalty; for some reason, people are very fond of the death penalty."[4] And *there* is the key to answering your question. Premier Jaroslaw Kaczynski has mastered to perfection the art of summoning up everything frightful, primitive, and base. His politics of permanent war and of baiting the pseudoelite and the educated has proved shockingly effective: he has managed to convince many people that Poland is governed by a "secret order" that must be hunted down and eliminated. A large part of our society—I say this with fear, sorrow, and shame—has been persuaded by this conspiratorial vision of the world. It has been persuaded that repression, capital punishment, wiretapping, and police harassment might heal an ailing Polish democracy. These things do not bode well either.

Havel: Do you regard the current Polish situation as exceptional in Central and Eastern Europe, or could it be situated within a larger, regional context? Do you see similar tendencies at work in other countries of the region?

Michnik: Poland is not an exception, although it may be in the avant-garde of some ominous tendencies. Similar threats have appeared throughout postcom-

---

4. Václav Havel, *To the Castle and Back*, trans. Paul Wilson
(New York: Knopf, 2007), 143–44.

munist Europe—including the Czech Republic. Allow me to quote from your recent book again:

Shortly after the revolution and the arrival of freedom, a very special kind of anticommunist obsession established itself in public life. It was as though some people—people who had been silent for years, who had voted obediently in communist elections, who had thought only of themselves and had been careful not to get into trouble—now felt the sudden need to compensate in some aggressive way for their earlier humiliation, or for the feeling or suspicion that they might have been found wanting. And so they took aim at the people who least held it against them, that is, the dissidents. They still felt, unconsciously, that the dissidents were the voice of their bad conscience, living proof that you didn't have to completely knuckle under if you didn't want to.

It's interesting that, at the time when dissidents appeared to be a tiny group of crazy Don Quixotes, the aversion to them was not as intense as it was later, when history, as it were, had proven them right. . . . Ultimately, many a new anticommunist vented more anger against the dissidents than against the representatives of the old regime.[5]

When Jaroslaw Kaczynski says that he represents the ordinary people and not the elite, he invokes a similar stereotype. He is not, after all, speaking the truth, which is that we are all ordinary people. Kaczynski is appealing to whatever is most petty and spiteful in each of us ordinary people. He appeals to these qualities very effectively. And we both know—you, Václav, no doubt better than I—that there are times when the winds favor what is worst in us, rather than what is best.

So I repeat: Poland is not an exception. I could multiply examples from other nations: the Slovak coalition (Fico, Mieczar, and Slota), Václav Klaus's Euroskeptical rhetoric, the radical anticommunism of Victor Urban, or the post-communist radicalism of Wiktor Janukowycz. But the real model is the consistent, effective authoritarianism of Vladimir Putin. We need only look at Putin's practice to understand the nature of the threats to democracy in the countries of postcommunist Europe.

Havel: Are there as many as three Polish politicians whose names are worth remembering?

Michnik: Three names worth remembering might be Zbigniew Ziobro, Roman Giertych, and Father Tadeusz Rydzyk. Each of these names is a symbol of tendencies on the rise, and each represents the worst side of Polish tradition and Polish politics. Authoritarianism, mendacity, ethnic exclusionism, fanatical devotion

5. Havel, *Castle and Back*, 115–16.

to religious homogeneity—I think of these as amounting to the Polish version of nationalist Catholicism à la General Franco. . . .

So, Václav, these are my answers to your questions, to which let me add one typically Polish reflection. This is a country in which filth never has the last word. In Poland, anything is possible—not excluding changes for the better.

COSMOPOLITAN

A Tale of Identity from Ottoman Alexandria

Maya Jasanoff

July 20, 1767, Alexandria, Egypt: a muggy season, when haze mutes the sun and the sea sits flat. Around noon, Etienne Roboly walks to the old port, northwest along the great curve of the harbor. He is the chief dragoman, or interpreter, for the French consulate, and has lived in Egypt for some thirty years. He knows the place about as well as anyone. As dragoman, Roboly not only interprets between French, Turkish, and Arabic (the word *dragoman* is derived from the Arabic verb "to translate") but often conducts negotiations with Ottoman and Egyptian authorities himself. Well-versed in local protocols, and deeply acquainted with the customs agents, Roboly also dabbles in private commercial ventures of his own: trading, and sometimes smuggling, through Alexandria with the help of collaborators in other Mediterranean entrepôts.

This has been a difficult summer in Alexandria. Fever, which visits the city with nearly annual regularity, is rife. Demands and extortionate taxes (known as "avanias") from the port officials are becoming more frequent and more appalling. Westerners are moving cautiously. All this the dragoman knows. But in his long Turkish-style robes, the usual clothing for men of his profession, Roboly attracts no notice. He, at least, should be safe. Then suddenly there is a hand on

Originally published in *Common Knowledge* 11.3 (Fall 2005): 393–409, as part of the symposium "Imperial Trauma, Part 2." © 2005 by Duke University Press.

his shoulder. It is the hand of a well-dressed Turk, who knows Roboly's name, his business, and some of his acquaintances in Constantinople. Is the man a friend of a friend? Roboly walks on further with him. Within minutes, catastrophe is upon him. The Turk, it turns out, is an officer of the sultan, armed with an order issued by the grand vizier to arrest the dragoman. Roboly is beaten, abused, and dragged on board the Ottoman ship *Reala*, where he is imprisoned in chains.

I read about this incident in a letter from the French consul in Alexandria to his superiors in Versailles, bound up in a volume of diplomatic correspondence in the Archives Nationales in Paris.[1] I was researching cultural exchange on imperial frontiers; I had encountered Roboly earlier in my readings, and my curiosity had been piqued by this character who seemed (not least because of his occupation) the very type of a "marginal" European, seeking out overseas opportunities. Before I could read on, the archive closed for the day, and I was on tenterhooks wondering about the rest of the story. Why was the dragoman arrested? What happened to him next? I would soon discover that his life story held greater relevance to questions of nation, empire, and identity than I had anticipated.

I had been drawn to these volumes in the first place because I was curious about the origins of European imperial desire in Ottoman Egypt. Inspired in part by Edward Said, who famously identified the French invasion of Egypt (1798–1801) as the launchpad of modern Orientalism, I wanted to turn the page back to the period *before* the French invasion. Looking to these decades, when European ambitions were only beginning to take shape, and when Europeans constituted a small and relatively weak minority in Ottoman domains, helped to frame questions of culture and power in different terms. In the dispatches and memoranda of French diplomats—documents rarely consulted by cultural historians—I found not so much the foreshadowings of Orientalist discourse as repeated evidence of the cross-cultural relations that formed part of daily life for French nationals living in an Eastern, Muslim, imperial domain. The consular records were a treasure trove of incidents and encounters: adultery, madness, murder, apostasy, antiquities, the drunken escapades of French sailors on shore, or the regular avanias levied against French commerce by Ottoman authorities. The lines between empowered and powerless, even East and West, did not always seem clearly drawn; nor did individuals' allegiances necessarily fit neatly within the borders between cultures or nations. Roboly's story in particular, as it unfolded in the dispatches, cast the ambiguities of national versus imperial identity into relief. It underscored the point that empires—while they develop

1. Etienne Fort to the ministry of foreign affairs in Versailles, July 23, 1767, Archives Nationales de France, Paris (hereafter cited as AN): AE B/I/109.

hierarchies and rhetorics of difference—also contain considerable potential for crossing and cosmopolitan mixing.

Alexandria, Roboly's home, had been a hub of cosmopolitanism since ancient times. The city was perhaps history's first melting pot, and was inhabited in antiquity by Egyptians, Greeks, Jews, Romans, and such a wealth of Christian sects—Orthodox, Arian, Monophysite, Gnostic—that "Christians," a baffled Emperor Hadrian wrongly concluded, must be "those who worship Serapis," or Jupiter.[2] You can still descend directly into the cosmopolitan world of the ancients, in the labyrinth of tombs that winds beneath the streets. In the catacombs of Kom ash-Shuqaffa, you can see Egyptian figures, standing with fists clenched, one foot before the other—but their heads are Roman portrait busts. There are bodies of Roman legionaries, wearing sandals, armored skirts, and breastplates—but they are topped with the animal heads of the Egyptian gods: jackal, ibis, and hawk. Crowned, knotted serpents, and Apis bulls, figments of the weird pantheon of Ptolemaic Egypt, join Medusa and Horus on the walls. This is a place of fusions and mixtures, survivals and innovations.[3] And well into the twentieth century, when approximately a third of its residents were non-Arab or non-Egyptian, Alexandria remained a byword for diversity. The city's greatest poet, C. P. Cavafy, was Greek; the city's best-known prose memorialist, Lawrence Durrell, managed to write four novels about Alexandria without including a single major Muslim character.[4] The Italian poet Giuseppe Ungaretti was born in Alexandria in 1888, to a father who had emigrated from Tuscany to work on the Suez Canal. The historian Eric Hobsbawm was also born there, to British and Austrian Jewish parents in 1917. The same year, another Briton in Alexandria, the novelist E. M. Forster (working for the International Red Cross), enjoyed a freedom he had not experienced in Britain by beginning a love affair with a tram conductor named Mohammed el Adl.[5]

Alexandria's status as a haven for foreigners, entrepreneurs, and outcasts may come as no surprise considering the crosscurrents of trade, culture, and migration that have always linked the shores of the Mediterranean. But the city's age-old cosmopolitanism owes as much to its history as it does to geographical setting. For, during most of its past, Alexandria was an imperial city. Founded by the Greeks, conquered by the Romans, ruled by the Arabs and the Ottomans, occupied briefly by the French and later by the British, Alexandria has flourished (and not) within empires extending over such far-flung regions as Algeria, Bul-

2. Anthony Sattin, *The Pharaoh's Shadow: Travels in Ancient and Modern Egypt* (London: Indigo, 2000), 40.

3. Jean-Yves Empereur, *A Short Guide to the Catacombs of Kom el Shoqafa, Alexandria*, trans. Colin Clement (Alexandria, Egypt: Sarapis, 1995). Cf. William Dalrymple, *From the Holy Mountain: A Journey in the Shadow of Byzantium* (London: Flamingo, 1998), 382–84.

4. On cosmopolitanism in modern Alexandria, see Robert Ilbert and Ilios Yannakakis, eds., with Jacques Hassoun, *Alexandria, 1860–1960: The Brief Life of a Cosmopolitan Community*, trans. Colin Clement (Alexandria, Egypt: Harpocrates, 1997), 18–88.

5. Michael Haag, *Alexandria: City of Memory* (New Haven, CT: Yale University Press, 2004), 28–53.

garia, Australia, and Jamaica. Modern Alexandria boasted an international aura, with Europeanizing architecture and a grid street plan, laid out in the nineteenth century by Egypt's ruler Muhammad Ali Pasha (himself an ambitious imperialist) and his successors; with an economy built on trade in wider imperial networks; and most conspicuously with a population marked by Greek, Italian, Syro-Lebanese, Jewish, and British communities, among others. As long as Alexandria was a city of empires, it was a city of many cultures. Today so much attention is paid to the way that empires divide people against each other that it is easy to forget how empires have also brought populations together, forcibly at times, yet often with enduring effects. The cosmopolitan possibilities of empire, as opposed to nar-rower definitions of national belonging, would shape the life of Etienne Roboly for good and for ill—just as they would shape the city in which he lived.

Alexandria was not bustling in Roboly's time. By the mid-eighteenth century, a combination of frequent plague epidemics and bad water supply had reduced Alexandria's population to five thousand or so residents, while nearby Rashid (Rosetta) was a flourishing town three times the size. Alexandria remained significant, however, as the only port in Egypt capable of harboring large ships and as the busiest port in the southeastern Mediterranean. Maritime trade was its lifeblood, exporting cotton, coffee, rice, and untanned leather, while importing textiles, paper, iron, silver, and gold. Power rested locally in the hands of Janissary governors and Jewish customs agents. (The latter would lose their offices, violently, to Syrian Christians in 1768.) Muslim merchants, particularly from the Maghreb, dominated Alexandria's commerce, but there were merchant houses from every European Mediterranean region with the apparent exception of Spain; and Austria, Holland, Sweden, and (sporadically) Britain were all repre-sented there by chargés d'affaires.[6]

In addition to running a permanent consular establishment in Alexandria, France maintained a resident population of civilians with it. They lived in an *oquelle* (English *okel*, derived from the Egyptian Arabic word *wikala*), a multi-story compound with a central courtyard, which was divided into fifteen sepa-rate dwelling units, shops, offices, and a chapel.[7] The community called itself *la nation*, and each year, the consul sent his superiors at Versailles a list of its members, almost all of whom were from Provence: eight or ten businessmen and clerks, a few domestic servants and carpenters, an innkeeper, and, for a time, a

---

6. Michael J. Reimer, *Colonial Bridgehead: Government and Society in Alexandria, 1807–1882* (Boulder, CO: Westview, 1997), 25–41; Michael Winter, *Egyptian Society Under Ottoman Rule, 1517–1798* (London: Routledge, 1992), 26. On the customs revenue of Alexandria, which was jointly collected with Rashid's, see Stanford J. Shaw, *The Financial and Administrative Organization and Development of Otto-man Egypt, 1517–1798* (Princeton, NJ: Princeton University Press, 1962), 109–10.

7. Vallière to ministry, December 16, 1769, AN: AE B/I/108. The Alexandria *okel* was in present-day Anfushi, on the eastern harbor (the only one open to European ships), and near the customs house. A *wikala* is a caravan-serai or rest house; many can still be seen in Islamic Cairo.

wigmaker from Grenoble.[8] In outline, the French in Alexandria seemed to be a modest little nation of secluded, busy, God-fearing folk.[9] But the tidiness of this picture is misleading. Contemporary lists of French subjects and protégés drawn up for other Near Eastern ports give a much more complete image of the kinds of communities these often were.[10] The Alexandria consuls only listed the males of *la nation*, but their wives often would have been Greek or Italian, and quite possibly Ottoman subjects. Consular lists for Alexandria also (unlike those for Smyrna, for instance) excluded non-French residents of the *okel*, as well as people under French protection living outside it. The likely reality is that most of these French men were married to non-French women, sharing their compound with non-French neighbors—and, of course, conducting all their daily business with non-French merchants and officials, in languages, more likely than not, other than French. The streamlined "French" community that Alexandria consuls described may suggest a certain anxiety about how "national" it really was.

Never were the boundaries of *la nation* more obviously threatened than when a Frenchman decided to "turn Turk" (*se faire turc*) or convert to Islam. Consuls did not say, and perhaps did not know, how often Frenchmen slipped through their net, settling down with Muslim women, or taking jobs on Turkish or Maghribi ships. But the cases in which the consuls intervened were frequent, striking, and poignant. There was the young monk from Languedoc who turned up in Egypt with a declaration of Islamic faith in his pocket. "Happily," the consul "was able to arrest him at the very moment at which he apostatized," and he was sent back to his parents by the next available ship.[11] More shocking was the case of Rashid's French priest, who decided to convert after suffering years of ill treatment from his father superior. The priest took refuge with the aga of the Janissaries, where the consular officials were "frozen with surprise" to see him, "still clothed in the habit of his Order, and with the cord of St. Francis, but having on his head a white turban of an ordinary Janissary."[12] There was Honoré Olivier, the leather buyer, who "went mad in consequence of a love affair" and insisted on turning Turk. "Since he would not stop crying out in Arabic that he wanted to apostatize," he too was saved from himself and packed off to Livorno on a Dutch ship.[13]

8. See, e.g., "Liste des françois qui Resident à Alexandrie, et qui s'y sont etablis avant le premier Janvier 1758: Dans laquelle sont compris ceux qui sont venus s'y etablir, et qui ont discontinué de resider pendant le cours de la dite année," and similar lists for 1762, 1766, and 1771, AN: AE B/III/290, ff. 23, 130, 160, 197. There had been a French baker in Alexandria (as in Cairo) until the early 1750s, but he was forced out of business when French sea captains started patronizing cheaper Egyptian bakers instead. (Sulause to ministry, February 1, 1753, AN: AE B/I/107.)

9. For an overview of French life in Egypt at this time, see Raoul Clément, *Les Français d'Égypte aux XVIIe et XVIIIe siècles* (Cairo: Institut Français d'Archéologie Orientale, 1960), 149–69.

10. See lists in AN: AE B/III/290. The records for Aleppo are especially thorough and revealing.

11. D'Evant to ministry, July 25, 1756, AN: AE B/I/108.

12. Chaillan to ministry, August 18, 1769, AN: AE B/I/970.

13. Vallière to ministry, December 15, 1760, AN: AE B/I/108.

And then, there was Etienne Sauvaire, womanizer, gambler, and pimp, who was on the verge of converting to Islam with his grasping Greek mistress, when the consul clapped him into chains: "I spared his family and *la nation* the discomfort of seeing him turn Turk."[14]

These and other less extreme crossings were part of daily life for the French community in Alexandria—and regulating them was part of Etienne Roboly's job as interpreter. Yet this invaluable servant to the interests and security of the French *nation* was himself, of course, a professional go-between, living on cultural borders. Many of the dragomans used in the various courts of the Ottoman empire were European renegades and converts; by the eighteenth century, most came from the Greek community in Constantinople's Phanar quarter. European embassies in the Ottoman empire generally recruited their dragomans from various Eastern Christian communities.[15] But France, unique among European nations, trained its own dragomans beginning in 1669. In Roboly's day, many French dragomans began their careers as young boys, when they were sent off to Constantinople or Smyrna to learn Turkish and Arabic under the watchful eyes of Capuchin friars. Others were born in the Near East, often into mixed French-Ottoman families, and also often into veritable dynasties of interpreters. The Fornetti family, for instance, whose scions could be found manning French Levantine consulates well into the nineteenth century, had been producing dragomans since about 1600.[16] The Robolys seem to have been something of an interpreting clan too, furnishing dragomans in Smyrna, Salonika, and Egypt.[17]

Raised partly in foreign lands and trained to speak (among other languages) Turkish, French, and Arabic with almost equal ease, a dragoman was the quintessential cosmopolitan—an insider and outsider rolled into one. As such, he was both an asset and a liability to his employers. On the one hand, dragomans had a native understanding of the local customs and rituals at the heart of diplomacy. More than the consul's tongue and ears, a dragoman served as his eyes and hands too—especially, as was often the case, when the dragoman had lived in the region much longer than the consul himself. It was not unusual for France's dragomans, for instance, to pay official visits and conduct negotiations without the consul even present. On the other hand, these were men of mixed, possibly suspect, loyalties. The French king was their master, and they lived in compounds with fel-

14. Vallière to ministry, October 27, 1758, and January 10, 1759, AN: AE B/I/108.

15. Bernard Lewis, *The Muslim Discovery of Europe* (New York: Norton, 1982), 78–79. A fascinating book remains to be written on dragomans; but see the catalog for an exhibition organized by Jean-Michel Casa, François Neuville, Emile Mantica, and Stéphane Yerasimos, *Enfants de langue et Drogmans* (Istanbul: Yapı Kredi Yayınları, 1995) for some useful remarks.

16. *Enfants de langue et Drogmans*, 17–50; "Mémoire envoyé par M. le Cte. De St. Priest Ambassadeur à la Porte sur les Officiers du Roy en Levant," AN: AE B/III/241.

17. Names drawn from index entries in AN series AE B/III.

low "French" subjects and protégés. Yet their strongest ties were not to France—where many had hardly been—but to their homes in the Ottoman empire, where they were rooted by family and job, pragmatism and preference. Until 1806, for instance, French dragomans were given the choice between wearing "Oriental" dress and Western uniforms; nearly all opted for turbans and robes, in place of hats and tight trousers.[18] In short, these were men for whom, as one of Louis XVI's ambassadors in Constantinople put it, France "is a fatherland in name only, and to which they have no desire to return."[19]

Like many dragomans of his time, Roboly seems to have maintained at best a distant connection to France. By his own account, he had been in Egypt since 1735 (we must take his word for it, because too many Robolys appear in the French records to allow one to track his early career precisely), which meant that when a new consul, Etienne Fort, came to take over the Alexandria office at the end of 1762, he found in Roboly a chief interpreter with nearly three decades' service in Egypt.[20] He also found, as his reports reveal, a dragoman deeply enmeshed in local business and politics—and a man who might be more capable of running the consulate than he was, which both of them knew.

The new consul relied heavily on his veteran dragoman as an emissary, informant, and adviser. There were Turkish officials to be wooed, French sailors to be bailed out of trouble, and European commercial rivals to be outdone. Most important, there were the unpredictable customs officers of the port, whose fluctuating demands regularly had to be confronted and appeased. Fort entered the consulate at a particularly difficult time for foreign trade in the city: the "wicked, cruel and seditious" behavior of Alexandria's governors, he said, had reached "unheard-of excess." They demanded payments from French ships, refused to allow cargoes to be unloaded, and generally obstructed the flow of commerce. Roboly was more necessary than ever. Using his friendships with high-ranking officials, and especially with Alexandria's Jewish customs agents, Roboly was able to help set French commerce back on an even keel by 1764.[21]

It did not hurt that Roboly had a vested interest in facilitating trade. Dragomans were not, on the whole, well rewarded for their work. In supplement to their small salaries, it was customary for them to receive a portion of *ancrages*, a tax paid by incoming ships. It was also common, albeit officially prohibited, for them to engage in private trade—which Roboly certainly did. A one-off venture

18. *Enfants de langue et Drogmans*, 53–60.

19. "Mémoire envoyé par M. le Cte. De St. Priest," 6.

20. Roboly to ministry, March 24, 1766, AN: AE B/ I/109.

21. See Fort's letters from these years in AN: AE B/I/109. The commercial resurgence that he observed was due more generally to the ending of the Seven Years War. For

a slightly later Ottoman critique of extortionate behavior among the Egyptian beys, commissioned for the Porte in 1785 from the governor of Syria, Cezzâr Ahmed Pasha, see *Ottoman Egypt in the Eighteenth Century: The Nizâm-nâme-i Misir of Cezzâr Ahmed Pasha*, ed. and trans. Stanford J. Shaw (Cambridge, MA: Harvard University Press, 1962).

of his (and there must have been more) involved shipping tobacco from Salonika to Genoa, in conjunction with a local French merchant and with Jewish traders in Greece. But his chief business seems to have been exporting rice and coffee, staples of Egyptian trade, to Salonika and Smyrna. It was a veritable multinational concern, which took advantage of all his cosmopolitan connections: kinsmen could probably help Roboly in Smyrna and Salonika, while his partners in Alexandria were Muslim merchants hailing from Crete, Persia, and Greece.[22]

Another, more unusual, endeavor was Roboly's collecting of antiquities. Though the catacombs of Kom ash-Shuqaffa were only discovered in 1900—by accident, when a donkey slipped through a hole in the ground—Alexandria's denizens had long known about the buried ancient tunnels beneath the city. Roboly certainly did, and he also knew about the high social value his European contemporaries placed on antiquities. He intended to make the most of it. In a 1751 letter to Versailles, the French consul reported:

I have read to Sieur Roboly the response with which you honored me, Monseigneur, on the subject of his statues and antiques. Since M. de Tournehem does not deem it appropriate to acquire them for the King . . . this dragoman . . . will profit from the first occasion that presents itself to dispose of them advantageously. I have nothing to add to the wise and judicious observations of M. de Boze; he is able to judge the merit of these sorts of monuments more surely . . . than I.[23]

It is a brief passage, but a very tantalizing one, not least because it presents an early documented example of European antiquities-collecting in Egypt. It also suggests Roboly's considerable powers of self-promotion.[24] Here was an obscure functionary in a second-tier French consulate who had managed to attract the attention of the Parisian elite (Le Normand de Tournehem was Mme. de Pompadour's guardian, and Monsieur de Boze a noted book collector and connoisseur) and even to make propositions to the king himself. This was no small achievement.

In 1763, Roboly's interest in antiquities-collecting was enhanced when he made a fascinating, influential new friend: Edward Wortley Montagu (or as one French diplomat rendered the name, "Edoüard d'Owertlay Chevalier de Mon-

---

22. Fort to ministry, September 11, 1767, AN: AE B/I/109; January 26, 1768, AN: AE B/I/110.

23. Sulause to ministry, December 8, 1751, AN: AE B/I/107.

24. But see the equally tantalizing unfootnoted quotation from Sulause in Leslie Greener, *The Discovery of Egypt* (New York: Dorset, 1966), 77: "The great stir this discovery has made in the country, in spite of all the precautions taken to keep it secret, prove beyond anything one could say, how much these three statues verily smell of antiquity. The authorities, indifferent to this kind of thing, of which they take no notice ordinarily, have become so annoyed at not possessing them themselves, that they wanted to take them by command from sieur Roboly . . . and it is only by the use of tact, manouevre, and money that he managed to calm their envy."

taigu"), the irresistibly eccentric son of the celebrated Eastern traveler Lady Mary Wortley Montagu.[25] The French consul in Rashid, where Montagu settled, could not believe his eyes when he encountered this bizarre Englishman. Not only had Montagu come to Egypt simply "for curiosity"—already unusual enough, at a time when few Western Europeans ventured even as far as Greece. Within weeks, he had "abandoned the rank of a person of his station, and became friends with all manner of Turks . . . adopting all their ways be they hard or soft, of eating, drinking, dressing, etc. . . . He knows Arabic well enough to be understood and he is studying to make it perfect." Montagu was also "a great friend of the French, enchanting them (*leur fascinant les yeux*) with his manners." And Etienne Roboly had ample opportunity to fall under his spell: Montagu made a three-week trip around the delta "to see and find antiquities there," and Roboly went with him.[26] The ambitious dragoman could only have been inspired by this charismatic collector, living proof that antiquarianism was a sport of gentlemen (even strange ones). Statues were in his reach. Consul Fort was in his debt and easy to manipulate. The time was ripe to approach the king of France again.

On the first day of spring in 1765, an eerie season, when the city bolted its doors tight against the plague, Fort wrote off to Versailles. "Sieur Roboly," he said, has acquired "a statue of white marble, which was found in the ruins of ancient Alexandria by the Catacombs. This piece . . . is provoking here, Monseigneur, the admiration of everybody, and especially those who have some knowledge of drawing and sculpture. It seems truly worthy of being . . . placed in some Palace of the King or in one of His Majesty's gardens." He went on to make a diplomatic proposition: "Some people have expressed to M. Roboly the desire to buy this statue from him, but I do not think that this officer will let himself be seduced by self-interested motives to [sell it to] . . . foreigners . . . without first knowing what your Grandeur's thoughts about the object might be."[27]

This "magnificent fragment of antiquity" was virtually undamaged and stood some seven feet high. The following month, Fort sent along an accomplished pencil sketch of it by the Austrian consul, Agostini, "who possesses the art of painting and drawing."[28] The drawing answers one question straight away: Roboly's statue was nothing like the sculpture from pharaonic Egypt most familiar to museumgoers today—sleek, crowned rulers, squatting scribes,

25. Though the eldest son of a hugely rich family, Montagu had been left with what he felt to be the unfairly small sum of £2,000 per annum on the deaths of his parents in 1761 and 1762. He spent 1762–64 in the Near East, and parts of 1769–75 in Egypt, where he owned a house "thirty feet" from the French *okel* in Rosetta (Chaillan to ministry, August 8, 1772, AN: AE B/I/970). The original *Dictionary of National Biography* concluded that "there is little doubt that he was more or less insane" (Leslie Ste-

phen and Sidney Lee, eds., *Dictionary of National Biography*, 66 vols. [London: Smith, Elder, 1885–1901], 13:686).

26. Vaugrigneuse to ministry, October 26, 1763, AN: AE B/I/970.

27. Fort to ministry, March 22, 1765, AN: AE B/I/109.

28. Fort to ministry, April 22, 1765, AN: AE B/I/109.

and stiff-armed gods. This statue was a Roman Egyptian or Ptolemaic grande dame, enthroned on a winged chair, full-bosomed, high-browed, thin-lipped, and proud. She represented Egypt as metropolitan, Enlightenment Europe liked to see it (and primarily *did* see it until 1798, when the French savants traveled to Upper Egypt and brought back detailed descriptions and drawings of the fantastic pharaonic monuments there). "All the connoisseurs," said Fort, including the visiting duc de Picquigny, a sprig of one of France's most distinguished families, thought her excellent.[29] She conformed beautifully to prevailing European tastes, as exalted in Winckelmann's *History of Ancient Art*, published just the previous year.

Agostini's drawing was excellent, and it worked. Versailles expressed an interest in the piece by return of post. What did Roboly hope to gain from the transaction? Not money, for sure—at least not explicitly, since between gentlemen, that expectation would be crude. "It is enough that your Grandeur seems to want this piece of antiquity for him to sacrifice it," said Fort. No, Roboly looked for his rewards in the intangible currency of prestige. By "sacrificing" his statue for his king, he showed himself, in a single stroke, to be discerning, capable, generous, and loyal—all of which, naturally, he made sure the consul spelled out: "Sieur Roboly has had to spend a great deal here to procure the statue . . . and it still costs him a lot of trouble, care and work. I doubt that anybody other than this Dragoman, who is as well-known in the area as he is esteemed, could have succeeded in getting this piece, and I dare say . . . that this is one of the most upstanding people to be found in these parts." "Embellishing the King's antiquities Cabinet," continued Fort, was Roboly's only goal, "and he expressed to me several times his ardent desire to be able to have this honor."[30]

In September 1765, Roboly's wish was at last fulfilled. The statue was packed up, permission obtained from the authorities to export it (which was itself a tricky task, requiring all Roboly's manipulative skills), and it was loaded onto a Marseilles-bound ship. On the whole, the episode was a splendid piece of self-promotion for Roboly—and a splendid example of how marginal figures could use collecting as a device to advance themselves in European society.[31] The statue opened doors, just as Roboly had wished. Within six months, timing that was surely not accidental, he wrote directly to the minister to protest the suspension of anchorage fees—the only legal supplement to a dragoman's salary—and to

29. Fort to ministry, September 15, 1765, AN: AE B/I/109. Picquigny, later duc de Chaulnes, had fled for Egypt the day after his wedding in 1758. The marriage was eventually dissolved; and the duke went on to write treatises on acids.

30. Fort to ministry, September 15, 1765; Roboly to ministry, September 15, 1765, AN: AE B/I/109.

31. For parallel cases in contemporary India, see my "Collectors of Empire: Objects, Conquests, and Imperial Self-Fashioning," *Past and Present*, no. 184 (August 2004): 109–35.

demand compensation.[32] A direct address to the top brass by a low-ranking officer was most unusual, and only Roboly's recent coup with the statue could have emboldened him to make it. He also requested and received special permission to get married, a rare privilege for somebody of his rank. In March, 1766, "without noise and ceremony," Roboly wed Maria de Sommo, daughter of a Neapolitan merchant based in Alexandria.[33]

It was no small irony that Roboly's patriotic gesture toward France hinged on his intimate local knowledge of Egypt—on his close contacts with Alexandria's scavengers and port authorities alike. According to a visiting Briton, "when any of the Bedouins (the people who spend their time in searching among the ruins) find any [antiquities], they generally offer them first to him."[34] Perhaps this was Roboly's greatest talent. For while his position as dragoman made him almost by definition a man of the margins, a permanent go-between, it also gave him the wherewithal to make his mark on a European elite and to assert his loyalty to France. Collecting paved a way from the cosmopolitan to the metropolitan, from Egypt to France.

And his arrest by the Turks, on July 20, 1767, would show just why he had been so concerned to prove his "Frenchness" all along.

At one o'clock in the morning after Roboly's capture, the officer who seized him, Ali Capitan, Ottoman vice admiral, barged into the French compound, calling for the consul. He demanded a substantial bail for Roboly and spelled out the charges against the dragoman. Fort, bewildered and terrified, took up a quivering pen to convey the news: "All that I have been able to learn up till now is that enemies he has in Constantinople gave the Grand Vizier to understand that this dragoman is not French, but Armenian, a *raya* [subject] of the Grand Seigneur; that he never paid the *Karach* [tax] . . . [and] that . . . he loaded French boats with all kinds of products, and under the pretext of sending them to Smyrna, Salonika, and other countries under Ottoman rule, he sent them to Christendom."[35] This stunning set of allegations was all "an abominable lie if ever there was one," he insisted, and a gross violation of the "capitulations"—the agreements outlining European privileges in the Ottoman empire—that shielded French subjects from Ottoman law.[36] But the more Fort pleaded for Roboly, the more they abused him. Egyptians who saw the dragoman down in the harbor reported that the Turks treated him worse than a slave. It would be a miracle if he reached Constantinople

32. Roboly to ministry, March 5, 1766; March 24, 1766, AN: AE B/I/109.

33. Fort to ministry, March 10, 1766, AN: AE B/I/109.

34. James Haynes, *Travels in Several Parts of Turkey, Egypt, and the Holy Land* (London, 1774), 40.

35. Fort to ministry, July 23, 1767, AN: AE B/I/109. Ali Capitan wanted 1500 patacoons (pieces of eight) for Roboly, but Fort was unwilling to pay more than 700.

36. Fort to ministry, July 23, 1767, AN: AE B/I/109.

alive. Fort was hysterical with fear. They might be coming for him next! "No Frenchman is safe in this country."[37] And without a dragoman, he was of course paralyzed, unable to communicate.

Vergennes, the French ambassador in Constantinople, protested personally to the grand vizier about this outrageous abuse of diplomatic conventions. France's chief dragoman in Cairo went to the pasha of Egypt and actually showed him the article of the written capitulations that forbade the arrest of a French subject. Yet these efforts to free Roboly were to no avail. In Alexandria, French trade was in ruins; merchants, customs officials, and the consulate's Jewish dragoman fled in fear for their lives. And on the *Reala*, Roboly continued to "groan in chains," sometimes up to twenty-five hundredweight of them, lashed to the slaves down in the sordid bowels of the ship.[38]

What of the allegations against him? "Calumny," insisted Fort. But that Roboly was up to his ears in tricky business nobody could deny. Even Fort never confidently said that Roboly did not smuggle rice out of the Ottoman empire; he merely said that the accusations were unproven. And what about Roboly's Frenchness? This was the crux of the case: if Roboly really was Armenian, as the Turks alleged, then the rest of their charges were justified; he had indeed dodged his taxes for forty years and had entered French service without the sultan's permission. If, on the other hand, he was really French, then his arrest was an absolute and inexcusable violation of the capitulations—a casus belli, should France choose to make it so. (In 1830 France would invade Algeria on a lesser pretext, in retaliation for an incident three years before, when the dey of Algiers struck the French consul with a fly whisk.) Fort and his superiors in Cairo and Constantinople referred again and again to the capitulations in their attempts to free Roboly, insisting that he was French. But one piece of evidence is conspicuously absent. Not once, in over twenty documents on the subject, does anybody say *where Roboly was born*. This single fact could have proved the point beyond doubt—if, that is, Roboly had been a native-born Frenchman.

Roboly must have known things could only get worse when the ship set sail, bound first for Syria, then on to the imperial capital. A tiny scrap of his writing, scrawled on a quarter-sheet of paper, slanted and nearly illegible, survives to tell of his torment. It took the ship an arduous thirty-three days from Syria, tossed on the swell of autumn storms, to reach land again. He arrived in Constantinople on December 22, five months and two days from the start of his captivity on the ship. But land was no better. He was immediately loaded down with chains and flung into prison with the slaves, the sultan's dreaded *bagnio*, from which even a slip of paper would be lucky to get out.[39] Astonishingly, Roboly had survived the

37. Fort to ministry, July 25, 1767, AN: AE B/I/109.

38. Fort to Vergennes, August 7, 14, 31, and September 11, 1767, AN: AE B/I/109.

39. Roboly to Fort, September 2, 1767, AN: AE B/I/109; Fort to ministry, January 26, 1768, AN: AE B/I/110.

voyage, but the slave prison was too much. On April 15, 1768, "broken by suffering and worry," Roboly died, with the slaves, a captive of the sultan. After nearly a year of sustained torture, for him and for his employers, it must have been a kind of release.

Roboly's arrest and captivity were part of the greatest crisis in French-Egyptian relations for a generation—an indirect consequence of what, in retrospect, was also one of the biggest political upheavals in Egypt until the French invasion in 1798. And it was just this kind of explicit, traumatic, personal experience that helped formalize French imperial designs on Egypt. (The blueprint for Napoleon's invasion would be drafted by a prominent, long-term French expatriate in Egypt called Charles Magallon, who lost most of his fortune in 1786, when the Ottomans deposed the leading beys in an attempt to reassert authority.) It took at least two years for things to settle down in Alexandria. And it took nearly ten years for the whole truth about Roboly to come out. It appeared in a report written by the comte de Saint Priest, French ambassador in Constantinople from 1769 to 1784, which recommended wide-ranging reforms for Levantine consulates and for the dragoman service in particular. Speaking of the practice of choosing dragomans born in the Levant, Saint Priest said: "The Porte has never wanted to recognize French citizenship to children born in its states. . . . Sr. Roboly, Dragoman of France in Alexandria, born in Constantinople, was recently the victim of this principle."[40] *Born in Constantinople*—perhaps of mixed parentage, perhaps never having visited France at all. The French called Roboly French, and the Ottomans called him Ottoman. The likely truth, which neither of these competing definitions could accommodate, was that Etienne Roboly was both: claimed by an imperial identity, while laying claim to a national one.

Though Roboly "had the reputation for being rich," when Consul Fort turned to his estate in the fall of 1768, he found Roboly's affairs in shambles. His assets were "in the hands of Turks, Moors, and Greeks, dispersed around Egypt and the Levant, and for the most part now insolvent, or of bad faith"; his debts were greater.[41] Ambassador Vergennes arranged a pension of five hundred livres for his widow, Maria. Roboly's story ends with one last unconventional letter to Versailles. It is written in one hand and signed in another, clearly unaccustomed to the pen: "La Veuve Roboly"—the Widow Roboly. "The King's goodness," she said,

> will never be erased from my memory and [I] will . . . number among
> my most essential duties the obligation to pray to God for the prolon-
> gation and happiness of His Majesty's days. The sentiment of human-
> ity which has made Your Grandeur take an interest in my unfortunate
> plight, makes me look at the Grace that the King has been so kind as

---

40. "Mémoire envoyé par M. le Cte. De St. Priest," 6–7.   41. Fort to ministry, August 21, 1768, AN: AE B/I/110.

to offer me, as a good which I owe to the generous feelings of Your Grandeur, to whom I can only very feebly express the true recognition which I hold in my heart.[42]

Roboly would have approved of his wife's loyalty to the king of France. After all, he had died seeking acknowledgment of his own allegiance to France. In much the way that he had helped pull Frenchmen back from "turning Turk," he had been arrested for "turning French." He died, under Ottoman law, an Ottoman subject. But in death, with the belated interest of France in his affairs and the award of a state pension for his (Italian-born) wife, was he not also in some sense validated as French?

After more than a year of imagining Alexandria from the pages of crumbly archival volumes and literature, I finally visited the city in May, 2001. Since the eighteenth century, Western visitors to Alexandria, steeped in tales of Alexander and Cleopatra, have lamented the absence of visible ancient vestiges. Little remains standing of the ancient city but a single column, known as Pompey's Pillar, perched on a weedy ridge south of town. (Florence Nightingale, for instance, "went to the catacombs" in 1849, "which, after those of Rome, are rather a farce; to Pompey's Pillar, through a great dismal cemetery: I thought we were coming to the end of the world.")[43] But today the city invites reflections on a different set of absences.

It seems more than coincidence that Roboly's collision with identity and empire took place in Alexandria, since his experience eerily foreshadowed the postcolonial history of Alexandria itself. Had he been born a century and a half later, Roboly would have found himself wrong-footed for a different set of reasons concerning national and imperial identities. The nineteenth and early twentieth centuries had seen Alexandria's population reach its high-water mark of diversity, with up to 30 percent of its inhabitants hailing from non-Arab or non-Muslim ethnic and religious communities.[44] In 1956, President Gamel Abdel Nasser passed legislation nationalizing foreign-owned companies and encouraging (or in some cases forcing) foreign nationals and "non-Egyptians" to leave. Massive exoduses of Jews, Greeks, and other minority groups followed; and within a couple of years the city's population was, as it remains, composed almost entirely of people considered to be Egyptian.[45] Etienne Roboly had painfully experienced the

42. Maria Roboly to ministry, November 21, 1768, AN: AE B/I/110.

43. Florence Nightingale, *Letters from Egypt: A Journey on the Nile, 1849–50* (New York: Grove, 1987), 25.

44. It is hard to quantify these communities in part because of shaky definitions of "foreign" or "European" status. To give one example, however, according to an 1878 tally, there were almost 43,000 "Europeans" living in the city. The total population at that time was approximately 220,000. See Reimer, *Colonial Bridgehead*, 160, 110.

45. For a somewhat fictionalized, firsthand account of cosmopolitan Alexandria and its demographic transformation, see André Aciman, *Out of Egypt: A Memoir* (New York: Farrar, Straus, and Giroux, 1994).

potential dangers of an inclusionary, imperial definition of identity that claimed him as Ottoman within an imperial regime that included Armenians, like other minority groups (or *dhimmis*), among the taxable ranks of its subjects. But in the postcolonial era, as a non-Muslim, non-Arab, and non-"Egyptian," he would have been shunted out of Alexandria by a nationalist and fundamentally *exclusionary* definition of identity—one that completely transformed the city itself.

Only two generations ago, you would have been hard-pressed to find Arabic-speakers in certain parts of central Alexandria. Now it felt as if I was the only foreigner to spend more than a night there. Imagine London or New York without their ethnic communities: London's Edgware Road without the Lebanese eateries; Chinatown shop fronts without roasted ducks in the window; Twenty-ninth and Lexington without the smell of curry and spices. Imagine Spanish Harlem with the bodega signs faded out and only English on the streets; or Brick Lane without Bengali. That was a bit how Alexandria seemed now. "It's all changed," says an Alexandrian Greek in Naguib Mahfouz's novel *Miramar*. "My dear," ripostes her Egyptian friend, "it had to be claimed by its people."[46] The cosmopolitan cityscape remains, inhabited by a largely homogeneous "native" population.

I walked past art deco apartment blocks and peered into grand, decrepit foyers with rococo plasterwork and dust-caked elevator grills, marble stairs with dented brass railings. They were lit by bright, naked bulbs of irregular sizes, as if each had been hand-blown to order. My hotel also gave off the distinct sense of being a relic. In the lobby was a telephone the size of a cash register, with a crank on the side and cloth-wound wires, and a glass case filled with tatty stuffed birds, surmounted by a swan, frozen in takeoff or landing, it was unclear which. I sat in Western-style cafés, a novelty in a country where cafés are very much men's worlds, for smoking hookahs and playing dominos. Pastroudis, once the haunt of Alexandria's cosmopolitan elite, seemed like a set on an abandoned Hollywood lot. A whole wall of Sophianapolou's coffee store, with its big brass roasting machines, was covered with a poster of the Kaaba at Mecca by night. One afternoon, I was at a café on the Midan Saad Zaghloul, facing the sea, diligently plowing my way through Lawrence Durrell's *Alexandria Quartet*, when I heard another reminder of changed times: a throat clearing, a cough, and a tentative "*allahu akbar.*" Somebody had set himself up with a loudspeaker in the square to conduct prayers. Men crossed the street to join him; minibuses pulled over and drivers jumped out. And for ten minutes, in answer to this makeshift call amid the *azans* from area mosques, men prayed on plastic mats, twenty feet away from

46. Naguib Mahfouz, *Miramar*, trans. Fatma Moussa Mahmoud (Cairo: American University in Cairo Press, 1978), 8.

the Hotel Cecil—where Durrell had staged scenes in his rather chauvinistically non-Muslim, non-Arab tales of Alexandria past.

But the most vivid sense of what had vanished came when I wandered around the antique market in the Attarin district of town. Only a couple of stores had distinctively Middle Eastern items (octagonal tables, inlaid mirrors, antique brassware). Shop after shop was filled, instead, with European-style furnishings, heavy rosewood armchairs and bulbous little chests, garish crystal chandeliers. There were oil paintings of autumnal Western landscapes, Arab horsemen against lurid orange hills and skies, and women of indeterminate ethnicity, captured in states between posing, pouting, lounging, and contemplating. There were assorted metal cups, trophies, browned family photos in frames, cigarette cases, and trinkets so corroded it was impossible to tell what metal they were made of. Only gradually did it strike me what all this stuff was: the debris of the families who left Alexandria behind, after 1956. These were the true relics of the city's cosmopolitan past, now being bought up and absorbed into Egyptian homes, or bought for export and sent "back" to the West. Like Etienne Roboly, or like the families who had once owned them, these objects, at home in a cosmopolitan setting, now had to take sides.

Of course, one only needs to read Durrell, with his ethnocentric, neo-Orientalist perspective on Egypt, to see why the city needed to be reclaimed, as Mahfouz put it, by its people—just as one only needs to survey Egypt's modern history, in thrall to Western informal and later formal empire, to understand why Nasser nationalized the Suez Canal. And the prayers by the Hotel Cecil, or the antique objects changing hands, show that some forms of cultural juxtaposition, even mixing, remain part of the present-day Alexandrian scene. But one lesson from all this is obvious: nation-states, as the briefest glance at twentieth-century history will confirm, have often proved themselves to be hostile toward minority populations. Everybody knows that nationalism is not nice. Yet we have also been taught to see empires as evil things, which makes the second lesson—that empires have sometimes been more accommodating of difference than many independent nations—seem somewhat counterintuitive. Rather than looking at empire only as a force of division and control, segregating cultures according to racial or ethnic hierarchies, the history of Alexandria invites us to look at how empire may provide an umbrella of common security for people from a range of cultures to coexist, and at times even intermingle.[47] This is not to say, of course, that empires treat all people fairly, without prejudice. Nor is it to overlook the ways in which, for many postcolonial nation-states, imperial legacies have cursed

47. This argument is developed further, with reference to India and Egypt, in my book *Edge of Empire: Lives, Culture, and Conquest in the East, 1750–1850* (New York: Knopf, 2005).

the process of identity-formation from the outset. If anything, Roboly's story shows that neither nations nor empires can claim to possess the secret to harmonious cosmopolitanism per se. The larger question is whether and how inclusionary definitions of belonging can be made to outweigh exclusionary ones—and whether empires or nation-states can find ways of embracing human difference in tolerant, even congenial, forms.

Alan S. Milward, *The European Rescue of the Nation-State*
(Berkeley: University of California Press, 1992), 477 pp.

"Given the apparent similarity of political developments in the United Kingdom to those elsewhere in western Europe the question arises . . . Why, having entered the EEC . . . has [the UK] been so fiercely obstructive to any extension of integration beyond the limits of the Treaties of Rome?" Milward does not deal exclusively with Britain's role in Europe, but this tired British neurosis illustrates well the general sticking point which has long bedeviled the European project. That is to say, the problem of how to reconcile the objectives of European unification with the old notion of the sacrosanct nation state. This putative dilemma sets the scene for Milward's book. In a comprehensive analysis, of not merely how but, importantly, why the European Communities originally came into being, he aims to show that, far from being the antithesis of the nation state, the EU "has been its buttress, an indispensable part of the nation-state's postwar construction," without which Europe's peoples would not have enjoyed "the same measure of security and prosperity." This is a large book on a complex topic, but Milward's argument is always lucid and powerful.

—*Edward Heath*

DOI 10.1215/0961754X-7299522

Originally published in *Common Knowledge* 3.3 (Winter 1994): 170.

Steven Shapin, *A Social History of Truth:*
Civility and Science in Seventeenth-Century England
(Chicago: University of Chicago Press, 1994), 483 pp.

England has been an occupied country since 1066, the consequences thereof remaining visible to this very day. In the seventeenth century, the chasm between the gentlemen (less than five percent, who owned almost all the property) and the ungentle was absolute, though mobility across was possible. That absolute divide, so the gentry itself proclaimed, lay in the virtue for which freedom from want was a precondition, a virtue itself presupposed by any warrant for trust. Only the disinterested, free from external constraint, can be trusted to have this virtue—taught as the gentlemanly code—and only the wealthy can be thus disinterested. The non-English may be skeptical that this code portrayed the society's real values any more than has the rhetoric of honor and glory, or freedom and equality, elsewhere and elsewhen. The doubt is not necessarily about behavior under normal circumstances (when wealth is not threatened), but about our access thereby to the real norms and values. Yet in Shapin's extraordinary book we find a convincing argument that the code did inform actual value judgment in practice, enforced through social benefits and penalties, within the circumstances surrounding the development of science in that era, and indeed, made that development possible. The argument proceeds in part by thorough and detailed examination of Boyle's scientific work and collaboration both with other gentlemen scholars and with ungentle professionals. The main clue to this case is that the society avowing the code had needed to craft forms of amicable dissent and mutual criticism not impugning the honor of the addressee. One striking consequence, for example, was the development of probabilistic language to temper contradiction. Shapin's link of probability to "epistemological decorum" is convincing; yet it may also explain why it was the French rather than the English who created the mathematical theory of probability.

—*Bas van Fraassen*

DOI 10.1215/0961754X-7311997

Originally published in *Common Knowledge* 4.1 (Spring 1995): 81–82.

Baptiste Morizot, *Les Diplomates:*
Cohabiter avec les loups sur une autre carte du vivant
(Marseille: Wildproject, 2016), 320 pp.

In 1992, after almost a century of the species' absence from France, two wolves from Italy entered French territory. Since then, the population has multiplied: in 2015, France had more or less five hundred wolves. These animals pose a social problem not only because of their bad reputation (which is not totally baseless) for devouring humans, but also because they decimate flocks of sheep. One lupine behavior in particular perplexes the herders: these predators kill more sheep than they can eat ("*those animals are really barbaric!*"). Scientists call this phenomenon "surplus killing." There are two main techniques for managing wild animals, neither of which is useful in the case of wolves. The first is to hunt, but present regulations in France protect wild species, and moreover there are not enough hunters to implement such a program. Delineating sanctuaries is the other technique, but wolves do not stay within given territories; they tend to disperse and disseminate.

Baptiste Morizot, a professor at the University of Aix-Marseille, proposes a third way of managing wolves, which he calls "diplomatic." Diplomacy as a technique is grounded on the idea that neither wolves nor humans are essentially good or bad. Hence the first diplomatic step is to ask how the historical routes taken by humans and wolves have made the latter "barbaric" in Europe. (To stress that this outcome is peculiar to Europe, Morizot invokes ethnographic works on Amerindians who believe that wolves are not harmful to humans. The Tanaina of Alaska, at least in one of their tales, advise people lost in the forest to ask for help from wolves.) The author explains that wolves adapt the way they run to the capabilities of their intended prey. In general, animals are afraid when they see a wolf and swiftly begin to run, allowing the predator to learn how best to pursue them. But some animals, such as the mouflon (a wild sheep), have learned to be courageous and immobile. The wolf is less likely to attack when it cannot observe how its prey will run. When mouflons do run, moreover, they split up, and so, to deal with them, the wolves have acquired the habit of killing as many as they can (though the numbers have never been large). As breeders select sheep for docility and gregariousness, domesticated breeds have lost the courage of their wild ancestors and are unable to remain immobile when facing predators. Domesticated sheep also tend to run in groups, which enables the wolf to kill many at the same time. Wolves are not, by nature, surplus killers; they have become so in the course of their relations with mouflons and their domesticated counterparts.

Diplomacy seeks neither to demonize and justify the hunting of wolves nor to sanctify and protect them. Diplomacy seeks to work on relationships, and so it is important to invent means of communicating with the wolf. Morizot does not suggest negotiating and then signing a contract with French wolves. His idea is modest and practical. He makes a case, for instance, for the "biofences" tested by the American scientist David Ausband, who, in order to indicate to wolves that a certain territory belongs to humans, replicates the markers that wolves use to delineate the territory of their own packs. "Biofences" are only one example of communicative forms that use ethological patterns in order to construct new relations with animal species. Diplomats must take into account the perspective of the wolf; they must learn "to think like a wolf": how does a wolf know, for instance, where its territory ends? The author argues that by implementing communicative devices instead of using violence, compromises can be found to enable herders and wolves to live with one another. In any case, scientific research by John Shivik and others shows that nonlethal techniques are more efficient than lethal ones in managing wolves.

Morizot's style of writing is sometimes awkward due to an excessive use of neologistic jargon (*lupology, metaphorology, informational obstacle* . . .), though it may be that the originality and audacity of his work made this difficulty inevitable. *Les Diplomates*, after all, combines the interests and methods of three disciplines: anthropology (which exposes the variety of human-animal relations), evolutionary science (which redraws the trajectories of encounters between species, allowing for a better understanding of their different behaviors), and ethology (which permits us to improve our knowledge of animal perspectives and opens the possibility of a biosemiotics). The result is that Morizot can speak not only expertly but also respectfully of wolves, and that achievement should not be underestimated. It would have been interesting, however, to know as well what French herders think of his diplomatic proposition. And he fails, moreover, to take into account the perspective of the sheep.

—*Thibault De Meyer*

DOI 10.1215/0961754X-7312105

Originally published in *Common Knowledge* 24.1 (January 2018): 161–62.

Adam Kuper, *Culture: The Anthropologist's Account*
(Cambridge: Harvard University Press, 1999), 298 pp.

A lively historical critique of the way anthropologists use the very idea of culture. Kuper is a British anthropologist of South African origins who did his first field work in the Kalihari desert, and who has become a major theorist. He does not like the way in which *culture* is so often invoked, especially by American anthropologists, as a term that picks out everything that defines a group, and to which all patterns of behavior and activity are relativized. The idea enters anthropology in 1871 and matures with Talcott Parsons. Kuper's early genealogy of the concept is quite mild, but his critique of later uses is devastating. Everyone should read the assault on Clifford Geertz; even if it makes you admire his work more than ever, you will have had to answer a lot of questions along the way. David Schneider and Marshall Sahlins are treated more gently. This is a provocative essay, clearly written and a good read.

—*Ian Hacking*

DOI 10.1215/0961754X-7312117

Originally published in *Common Knowledge* 8.1 (Winter 2002): 208.

Hilary Putnam, *The Collapse of the Fact-Value Distinction and Other Essays*
(Cambridge: Harvard University Press, 2002), 224 pp.

Putnam is at his best when puncturing the balloons of philosophers who think of natural science as the area of culture that uncovers "hard facts," as a paradigm of rationality, and as a source of metaphysical truth. In this book he targets economists who (unlike Amartya Sen, one of Putnam's heroes) try to make their discipline value-free by keeping it at arm's length from ethics. But he also gets in some good licks at materialist reductionists—people who think that if you can't say it in the language of physics, you probably shouldn't be saying it at all—and at rational choice theorists.

Putnam's dislike of science-worship is just one example of his distrust of all philosophies that stray too far from common sense, from what he sometimes (like his friend Stanley Cavell) calls "the ordinary." He thinks of moral philosophers like Habermas and Christine Korsgaard as too infatuated with Kant to be willing to combine, as common sense does, Kantian insights with Aristotelian ones. He sees people like me as jumping from the frying pan of foundationalism into the fire of cultural relativism. Using a strategy pioneered by Dewey, Putnam shows how his opponents have turned commonsensical distinctions into philosophical dichotomies (fact vs. value, objective vs. subjective, mind vs. matter) and then, typically, tried to eliminate one side of the dichotomy in favor of the other.

From Aristotle to Dewey, philosophers who have been dubious about the posturing and paradox-mongering of their flashier colleagues have been dismissed as tedious trimmers, too shortsighted to glimpse the new intellectual world that gleams on the horizon. But the gleam has often faded, and middle-of-the-roaders like Putnam have often enjoyed the last laugh.

—*Richard Rorty*

DOI 10.1215/0961754X-7312129

Originally published in *Common Knowledge* 10.1 (Winter 2004): 151.

Edward O. Wilson, *The Meaning of Human Existence*
(New York: Liveright, 2014), 208 pp.

David Bentley Hart, *The Experience of God: Being, Consciousness, Bliss*
(New Haven, CT: Yale University Press, 2013), 365 pp.

Recently a colleague drew my attention to *The Meaning of Human Existence* by my eminent Harvard colleague, the sociobiologist E. O. Wilson. This brief, general-audience treatise, a kind of intellectual memoir, encapsulates with simplicity insights refined over a lifetime about the "reason we exist," the "unity of knowledge," "other worlds," "idols of the mind," and the "human future." Given his strong ideas about the human as part of a larger bioecology, Wilson is a scientist of broad learning, interested in the humanities and in wider discourses on the human. It is not surprising, then, that comments on philosophy and religion appear throughout his book. Religion has its part to play, he concedes, since being religious, both as individuals and in groups, is inevitably part of the biological makeup of who we are: "The brain was made for religion and religion for the human brain." But, on the whole, religion does not fare well here, it being the second topic of part 4's "idols of the mind," placed intriguingly between "instinct" and "free will." In sketching his position on religion, Wilson mixes a few textual and historical references with sweeping comments that beg for greater precision. He touches on specific examples without developing them, as when he notes that "deeply religious people want to find a way to approach and touch [the] deity," by way of transubstantiation "in the Catholic manner" or at least through prayer. Most religious people, he states unequivocally, hope to pass after death into "*an astral world* where they will join in bliss those who have gone before."

In what may be an attempt at levity, Wilson recalls that the physicist Anton Carlson once said that, if the Virgin Mary was assumed into heaven, she would surely have passed out at thirty thousand feet. The judgment of Søren Kierkegaard that the idea of the Incarnation is absurd is enlisted here as evidence not that he wanted to push back against a reductive rationalization of Christian faith but, rather, as evidence that he wanted to attack "the core of the Christian creation myth." This remarkably abbreviated reading of Kierkegaard begs to be substantiated, but Wilson quickly moves on. So too his use of the words *theology* and *philosophy* is both novel and undefended: "The attempted resolution of [humanity's] mysteries lies at the heart of *philosophy*. The purest, most general form of religion is expressed by *theology*, of which the central questions are the existence of God and God's personal relation to humanity. . . . *Theological spirituality* . . . seeks the bridge between the real and the supernatural" (these are my emphases here and below). No one would look to *The Meaning of Human Existence* for theological precision, of course, but it is Wilson's indictment of religion that gives the chapter its energy, and it amounts to his own theology. Religion's "exquisitely human flaw is tribalism," he argues, a flaw "far stronger than [religion's] yearning for spirituality." Tribalism meets the human need for belonging, for not being alone, but it has dire consequences; unlike "pure religion," it "makes good people do bad things." Or, as Wilson repeats and develops the point a few pages later, digging in deeper: "The true cause of hatred and violence is faith versus faith, an outward expression of the ancient instinct of tribalism. *Faith is the one thing that makes otherwise good people do bad things*." All of this misery happens because the religious tribes—individual churches, whole religions—believe "that God favors them above all others" and "that members of other religions worship the wrong gods, use wrong rituals, follow false prophets, and believe fantastic creation stories." The consequences are dire, since "there is no way around the soul-satisfying but *cruel* discrimination that organized religions *by definition* must practice among themselves."

At the core of Wilson's animus is what he perceives as religion's insult to science. Religious groups define themselves by creation stories that stand "at the heart of tribalism." Indeed, "blind faith in supernatural creation stories" is said to be a hardened dogmatism dangerous even to argue against "in most parts of the world today." Wilson, confident in a sure and simple understanding of truth, has no doubt about the worth of such myths: "All of those invented by the many known thousands of religions and sects in fact have been *certainly false*." At book's end, Wilson reminisces that as a child he had been warned against the idea of evolution, since it was "invented by Satan and transmitted through Darwin and later scientists in order to mislead humanity." Wilson's solution is straightforward: "The best way to live in this real world is to free ourselves of demons and tribal gods" and to free ourselves of their absurd myths, cruel doctrines, and far-fetched views of creation.

David Bentley Hart's *The Experience of God: Being, Consciousness, Bliss*, also recently brought to my attention, is just the kind of book that Wilson should have read before writing his own chapter on religion. Throughout his book, Hart makes a case for the inevitability of the question of God, which he sees as written into the very stuff of being finite and yet self-transcending. Encountering God in the mystery of our finite but ecstatic consciousness is for Hart an essential feature of being human, evident once we understand what it means to be, to be conscious, and to experience deep joy.

Hart's writing, like Wilson's, has a sharp edge. Hart skewers religious simplifiers, as Wilson does, but Hart takes on as well their scientific cousins, who have no patience for what they do not understand about religion. Hart has no time for modern atheist warriors who demonstrate "an almost fantastic ignorance not only of remarkably elementary religious tenets, but of the most rudimentary psychology of belief." A. C. Grayling, Victor Stenger, and Richard Dawkins are singled out for their consistent ignorance of the theism that they attack, as they merrily "devise images of God that are self-evidently nonsensical" and then proceed triumphantly "to demonstrate just how infuriatingly nonsensical [those images] are." It is appropriate that Wilson is not mentioned in this context, since he has not made a career out of attacking religious beliefs. I suspect, though, that Hart would treat Wilson's chapter on religion more sharply than I have done.

The Experience of God should catch Wilson's attention because, while religious—Hart is an Orthodox Christian—the book is not tribal. Hart not only knows his own Christian faith but also thinks in a humane fashion about other religions and honors them for their intellectual and spiritual best. With lightly worn erudition, he draws on many traditions to make his points, since matters of faith pertain to who we are as human beings. Our humanity has no borders; in this context, there is no "us" and "them." Hart's subtitle indicates the real adventure here: *Being, Consciousness, Bliss*. That is, he has structured his book around the famed Vedantic triadic characterization of ultimate reality: *sat* (being), *cit* (consciousness), and *ananda* (bliss). He uses these terms from outside his tribal language, so to speak, because they offer "a particularly elegant summary of many of the most ancient metaphysical definitions of the divine nature." In the process, he makes a serious case for how our knowledge of the world, attentively understood, is always opening onto the greater realities signified by *sat, cit*, and *ananda*. Debates over science and religion tend to deal only with modern ideas expressed in English, so *The Experience of God* makes an especially welcome contribution to religious apologetics. Wilson and other scientists who venture to opine on religion from a distance would do well to read it. Despite his dogmatic views on religion, Wilson could well be a promising partner for conversation on the issues that Hart raises and, in particular, on his book's conclusion: "We shall then be able clearly to see how the contingency of finite existence directs our thoughts toward an unconditional and absolute reality, and how the intentional unity of rationality of the mind opens up to an ultimate unity of intelligibility and intelligence in all things, and how the ecstatic movement of the mind and will toward transcendental perfections is a natural awareness of an ideal dimension that comprehends and suffuses the whole of existence."

On a better day, in a better book, Wilson might even want to join Hart in this humane expectation. Wilson certainly makes it clear that he wants to learn from intellectuals who are not scientists and that he yearns for cooperation between the humanities and sciences. These are, after all, "complementary to one another in origin," arising "from the same creative processes in the human brain." Collaboration, Wilson writes, would be to the benefit of all: "If the heuristic and analytic power of science can be joined with the introspective creativity of the humanities, human existence will rise to an infinitely more productive and interesting meaning." Wilson is right to see better collaboration as essential to the human future, but he errs in his sweeping exclusion from the humanities of faith, theology, and even tribal religious formations.

This exclusion is neither necessary nor helpful to the conversation about the "meaning of human existence" that Wilson and I both hope to revive and deepen. Wilson is good at explaining some dire consequences of religion gone askew. But Hart reminds us why it is important to see how science, which likewise should take care not to wander off its terrain, does its best work in a world radiant with transcendental values: truth, goodness, beauty, bliss.

—*Francis X. Clooney, SJ*

DOI 10.1215/0961754X-7312141

Originally published in *Common Knowledge* 22.1 (January 2016): 125–28.

John Wortley, ***The Anonymous Sayings of the Desert Fathers:***
A Select Edition and Complete English Translation
(Cambridge: Cambridge University Press, 2013), 652 pp.

The tradition of "apophthegmata," maxims ascribed to the great spiritual teachers of the Egyptian desert, is probably best known to general readers through various collections of the fifth and sixth centuries—typically, very brief narrative scene setting followed by a memorable piece of counsel on prayer and the ascetic life. But the genre continued to develop, and the collection presented here shows something of what was happening to the tradition between roughly the sixth and the tenth centuries. Wortley disclaims any intention of offering a full critical text, chiefly because the nature of the manuscript tradition is so very complex; this is a collection with the most fluid boundaries, and any attempt at a "definitive" edition would misunderstand the nature of the texts themselves. So what is offered is a composite Greek text, with a basic but sound apparatus and a very serviceable English translation.

Quite a lot of the familiar sayings will be found here, but what is most striking is the significant number of enlarged narratives, edifying stories about monks and their neighbors. At their fullest and finest, some of these are real "short stories" from the pen of a Byzantine Kipling or Stevenson, spinning out narrative tension, displaying moral dilemmas, offering sketchy but strong characterization. A notable feature is how many show women positively—women who bring men back to their senses, who display a spiritual insight or courage denied to men in general and monks in particular. Many give a vivid picture of village and small-town life in the early Byzantine Middle East before the arrival of Islam, demonstrating very clearly how monastic individuals and communities were involved with the social life of their environment. Despite the "Anonymous" of the title, many of the stories are attached to the names of great monastic saints, but the overall sense is of an almost folkloric world of nameless governors, farmers, ascetics, soldiers, husbands, and wives. There is plenty more research to be done on what this family of texts brings to light, both theological and historical, and this handsomely produced volume is a welcome invitation to further study.

The introduction is minimal, and there could with advantage have been a word or two about some of the ways in which the conceptualities and vocabulary of earlier monastic tradition are altered in these stories—the most dramatic instance being that the word *logismos*, originally meaning a train of (usually distracting) thought and image that can upset spiritual equilibrium, has become a synonym for direct diabolical temptation, sometimes personified as an agent or speaker. But this book will be a valuable tool for anyone wanting to understand Byzantine society and the early evolution of Eastern Christian devotion at a popular level; valuable too for those who simply want to understand what the Desert Fathers and Mothers understood.

—*Rowan Williams*

DOI 10.1215/0961754X-7312153

Originally published in *Common Knowledge* 21.3 (September 2015): 510–11.

Daniel Defoe, *An Essay on the History and Reality of Apparitions*, ed. Kit Kincade (New York: AMS Press, 2007), 573 pp.

Daniel Defoe wrote his study of apparitions, angelic and diabolic, late in life, after the novels (not a term he used) for which he is famous: *Robinson Crusoe, Moll Flanders, Roxana*, and others. Apparitions were a lifelong interest of Defoe's: twenty years earlier he had published an account of how a respectable lady named Mrs. Bargrave is visited by an old friend named Mrs. Veal, only to discover later on that at the time of the visit, or visitation, Mrs. Veal was already dead.

Whether Mrs. Bargrave was visited by a supernatural messenger or haunted by a ghost or was simply dreaming the early Defoe does not venture to guess. The later *Essay* is much more searching in this respect. Here Defoe tries to steer a middle course between two radically opposed philosophical schools: on the one hand the rationalists, represented by Thomas Hobbes, who believe that, having created a self-regulating universe, God the clockmaker stands back and allows it to run itself; and on the other the angelologists, represented by the eccentric clergyman Joseph Glanvill, who believe that the air around us is thick with interfering supernatural presences (Edgar Allan Poe would later draw on Glanvill for his Gothic stories).

Defoe's mature position is that there are no such things as ghosts, that is to say, wandering souls of deceased persons. Much as we may want to believe that the souls of the departed linger on after death to watch over us, Scripture tells us that as of the moment of death the soul is rapt away into another realm. If souls did indeed have the power to stay behind—and this move in the argument is quintessential Defoe—we would see many more ghostly testators hovering around, making sure that we carry out the letter of their wills.

Defoe was a Puritan Christian and a providentialist, that is, someone who believes that God has a plan for each of us. Since they cannot be ghosts, apparitions can only be angels or devils. How can we tell the two apart, given that more often than not they appear in disguise? Answer: angels are the ones who guide us on the path God has prescribed for us, devils the ones who try to lead us astray. Where do angels reside when they are not visiting the sublunar earth? Answer: in the Void, that is, in that part of the universe not occupied by physical objects.

This more or less sums up the theoretical side of Defoe's *Essay*. The rest is taken up with case histories, a few drawn from the Bible, a few from the classics, the overwhelming majority from Defoe's England, narrated with an engaging art whose chief concern is to seem to be artless.

For those who think that angels belong to a superstitious age, and that Defoe's interest in them is merely quaint, Michel Serres' *Angels* (1993) may be a corrective. We are in transition, says Serres, from a cosmology that treats of physical objects to a cosmology of messages. The map of the universe is unceasingly being redrawn for us by angel-messengers. If we don't see them, that is because it is in the nature of the messenger to disappear in favor of the message.

In this new edition of the *Essay*, Defoe's text occupies 283 pages. In addition we are offered a useful 86-page historical introduction and 204 pages of scholarly apparatus. Whether the text is reliable I am not in a position to say. The fact that Kit Kincade has not proofread her own introduction does not breed confidence.
—*J. M. Coetzee*

DOI 10.1215/0961754x-7312165

Originally published in *Common Knowledge* 15.1 (Winter 2009): 92–93.

Stuart Clark, *Thinking with Demons: The Idea of Witchcraft in Early Modern Europe* (Oxford: Clarendon Press, 1997), 827 pp.

As an historian of early-modern European culture, Stuart Clark has always written in an interesting and innovative way. His early work on Francis Bacon's conception of history was pathfinding in its approach, and during the 1980's he produced some important historiographical articles about the *Annales* historians. But nothing in these earlier writings would have led one to expect that he was meditating a work so powerful in conception and so massive in scale as he has now produced. His *Thinking with Demons*, which runs to over eight hundred large, closely printed, and heavily annotated pages, suddenly places him at the forefront of cultural history.

Clark's study is most obviously remarkable for the sheer range and depth of the reading, in several languages, that has gone into it. But the truly novel character of his work stems from his demonstration of the multifarious ways in which demonological beliefs entered into the scientific as well as the religious and political assumptions of early-modern Europe. While this holistic approach is arguably the most original feature of *Thinking with Demons*, Clark also has a great deal of new information to offer, and is able in consequence to defend a number of sharply revisionist arguments. He stresses, for example, the extent to which the science of the period, rather than being straightforwardly opposed to demonology, worked within its intellectual framework. He shows that religious disagreements about witchcraft generally took place within rather than across the different sects. Perhaps most strikingly of all, he emphasises the sheer length of time during which scientific defences of witchcraft continued to appear. Belief in witchcraft was by no means killed off by the scientific revolution.

These findings not only present the background to the scientific revolution in a new light, but lead Clark to say some challenging things, in a more philosophical spirit, about the rationality of alien systems of thought. It is at this point that his historical-mindedness reveals itself most exhilaratingly. Rather than presupposing that there is one underlying body of truths that some systems of thought capture and others violate, Clark prefers to think of all such systems as constructions. He accordingly prefers to see the process of intellectual change more as a matter of one construction succeeding another than as the gradual unfolding of truth.

By contrast with so much scholarship that nowadays makes a stir, there is nothing in the least noisy or self-advertising about Clark's work. Many of his suggestions are nevertheless sensational, while the learning underpinning them is vast. For anyone interested in what we can hope to learn about ourselves from past systems of thought, this is a genuinely important book.

—*Quentin Skinner*

DOI 10.1215/0961754X-7312177

Originally published in *Common Knowledge* 7.2 (Fall 1998): 89–90.

Robert Bartlett, *The Natural and the Supernatural in the Middle Ages*
(Cambridge: Cambridge University Press, 2008), 170 pp.

In search of diversity and disagreement in medieval intellectual life, Bartlett finds them among the grandest conceptions of things—explanations of what causes what in the physical world, of what sorts of creatures inhabit it, and of what kind of agency they exert. Neither broad theological uniformity nor the other common-alities of (what Roger Bacon called) the *respublica Latinorum* precluded a range of opinions on these matters during the Middle Ages or the intellectual discomfort thereby produced. What was "natural" or "supernatural" or "monstrous," where magic and witchcraft were to be placed on any map of knowledge and practice, whether the world was more like a machine or a book, and how individual phe-nomena like eclipses or night flying or *cynocephali* were to be accounted for, were questions for debate and controversy. Yet both these issues themselves and the fraught, boundary-challenging consequences of debating them are familiar—familiar, in any case, to historians who have recently traced them through to at least the eighteenth century. Thus Bartlett's lecture series does not so much recruit the Middle Ages (and specifically, a naturalist like Bacon) for the world of intellectual diversity or for Max Weber's narrative of "disenchantment." Instead Bartlett reinforces a periodization increasingly used to identify the peculiarities of intellectual life during the long early modern age. From the thirteenth to the eighteenth centuries, it seems, knowledge issues of the sort traced in these lec-tures, rather than any straightforward trajectory of disenchantment, were char-acteristic of the republic of letters. Hence the answer to a rhetorical question Bartlett poses to his audience is contained in his own arguments: how does one reconcile the art of Leonardo, the science of Copernicus and Galileo, and the literature of Shakespeare with the witch craze? This question is no longer, as he terms it, "perplexing"; it is merely old-fashioned.

—*Stuart Clark*

DOI 10.1215/0961754X-7312189

Originally published in *Common Knowledge* 16.2 (Spring 2010): 290.

Nicholas Orme, *Medieval Children*
(New Haven, CT: Yale University Press, 2001), 400 pp.

Contradicting Philippe Ariès, Lloyd de Mause, and Lawrence Stone, Orme holds that childhood existed in the Middle Ages. Children, Orme observes, were regu-larly portrayed as children on tombstones and were indeed seen as individuals of consequence. By the thirteenth century, the killing of newborn children was treated as homicide, and as early as 1118 abortion was punished. (Mothers who aborted an embryo less than forty days old had to do penance for three years, and if the embryo was older, she had to do penance for seven.) Children said prayers written especially for them ("Matthew, Mark, Luke and John, / Bless the bed that I lie on") and adults addressed babies, according to one Bartholomew (thirteenth century), in a special language. It was only later, apparently, that some adults found fault with baby talk: Sir Thomas Elyot (T. S. Eliot's forebear) argued in 1531 that the language spoken to children should be "clean, polite, perfectly and articulately pronounced, omitting no letter or syllable"—which means that the opposite was by and large the case. As for schooling, William Horman in 1519 published an encyclopedia of English and Latin sentences that seems specifically directed at children since it contains a section in which a variety of games and toys are described. Some seventy-five games and toys are also reflected in the painting by Pieter Bruegel entitled "Children's Games" (1559), and some of these entertainments have survived down to the computer age. Rattles, for example, existed already in Aristotle's time; the English word *rattle* first appeared in Horman's book *Vulgaria* ("I will buy a rattle to still my baby for crying"), which, according to Orme, implies that rattles were mass-produced, a conjecture he supports with archaeological findings. He cites canon laws recognizing that children's moral responsibility began only at the age of twelve, and secular laws exempting children from adult punishment up until their teens. The evidence that Orme musters is convincing, not only that children existed in the Middle Ages, but that medieval and modern ideas of childhood were actually comparable or even similar. The question thus arises: Why did historians ever desire to argue otherwise?

—*Nadja Reissland*

DOI 10.1215/0961754X-7312201

Originally published in *Common Knowledge* 9.1 (Winter 2003): 160.

**James Robert Enterline, *Erikson, Eskimos and Columbus*
(Baltimore: Johns Hopkins University Press, 2002), 342 pp.**

It was the Eskimos who discovered America. That is more or less the message of this highly intriguing and remarkably speculative book. It was the Eskimos who had a cartographical way of looking at the world, who had cartographical memories, who were in touch with noncartographical but mapmaking Europeans through contact with the Norse of Greenland. There may even have been Eskimos who went to Europe to share their knowledge of the shape of the land west of Greenland, and that perhaps was how Baffin Island found its way onto the Vinland Map. Many years ago, just after the Vinland Map was first published, I lectured to six hundred first-year undergraduates along the lines of: Columbus knew where he was going. My most distinguished colleague—a Jewish American born in Berlin and educated as an Englishman at the school where *Goodbye, Mr. Chips* was filmed—remonstrated with me. After the Vinland Map was declared a forgery and my unhappy colleague had committed suicide, I was conscience-stricken: I had not told the truth to six hundred first-year undergraduates and I had thought gleefully of my colleague's reading as not up to the mark. Now the Vinland Map is back. It is just as likely to be genuine as not. I seem to be off the purgatorial rack.

Or possibly not. What Columbus knew when he set out westward into the Atlantic is an epistemological conundrum that may never be resolved. It seems, however, despite information from Bristol seamen (who, seeking "Brasil" and finding Newfoundland, may have had Eskimo-inspired charts in their cabins), that Columbus thought he was setting out eastward, or at any rate for the East. Old Europeans, Old Europeans of the dreamier sort, evidently prefer myths to maps, tall stories to cartography.

—*Colin Richmond*

DOI 10.1215/0961754X-7312213

Originally published in *Common Knowledge* 10.1 (Winter 2004): 160.

Steven Seegel, *Mapping Europe's Borderlands:*
Russian Cartography in the Age of Empire
(Chicago: University of Chicago Press, 2012), 384 pp.

When life came in three dimensions, power was asserted in two. Not so very long ago, most people, even people who mattered, spent most of their time outside. Whether seen or unseen, death like life came through the air or water, as projectile but more likely as microbe. The sources of death were either visible in three dimensions or invisible, but never in two-dimensional images, as they are today, when we can see a tumor on a screen. Making war was a matter of getting human beings across and through natural and artificial barriers without too many of them dying first of disease. Maps of the places one wished to reach were useful, as was discovered relatively recently: the Ottomans on their marches to Vienna did not use them, choosing instead to ask for directions. Now that maps exist, it is no longer manly to do so. Maps reduce three dimensions to two, with the side effect that all of the actual problems of exerting and exercising power seem, if not soluble, then at least visible. Maps also reduce the five senses to one, namely sight. A forest is no longer the buzz of flies, the smell of leaves, the shape of an edible mushroom, and the aching of muscles, but a bit of ink that recalls a leaf. None of the other senses lend themselves to abstraction and compression in the same way as sight. Some scholars of our own day confuse abstraction with mastery and the assertion of power with its presence, dwelling on the projects, gardens, and utopias of the "modern" state. These interpretations are copacetic because we ourselves deal in similar reductions. Seegel is more careful and more interesting, perhaps because the region of his very considerable expertise, Eastern Europe, can be presented neither as an overpoweringly "modern" state nor as an intellectually supine colonial possession of such. In the Russian and Habsburg empires of the nineteenth centuries, rulers knew all too well that their imperial maps were in competition with other imperial maps, not to mention with national maps. No one has taken up the subject of maps and power in Eastern Europe with as much energy and erudition as Seegel, and it is unlikely that anyone who reads his book will believe they can do better.

—*Timothy Snyder*

DOI 10.1215/0961754X-7312009

Originally published in *Common Knowledge* 20.3 (Fall 2014): 505–6.

Frances Stonor Saunders, *Hawkwood: Diabolical Englishman*
(London: Faber, 2004), 366 pp.

One is not allowed herein, the editor tells me, to express the white heat of incandescent rage. This Little Review will thus be littler than most.

The maps in Saunders's book are good.

—*Colin Richmond*

DOI 10.1215/0961754x-7312225

Originally published in *Common Knowledge* 12.3 (Fall 2006): 527.

Gordon M. Hahn, *Russia's Islamic Threat*
(New Haven, CT: Yale University Press, 2007), 349 pp.

Muslims probably make up a little over 10 percent of the population of the Russian Federation—a bit more than in France, and maybe a bit less than in India. In all three cases, current demographic trends imply that the percentage of Muslims will continue to increase, and in each case any realistic shortlist of the country's current policy headaches would include a Muslim problem (and by the same token, Muslims could be said to have a Russian, French, and Indian problem). But of course these problems differ in their genesis and character. One major difference relates to vulnerability to separatism. Since letting Algeria go, France has contained no Muslim-majority region that could form the basis of a Muslim state; by contrast, separatism among the Chechens and their Muslim neighbors of the northern Caucasus has been the cutting edge of Russia's Muslim problem, just as Kashmir is the most septic component of India's. Another major difference is that

France and India, whatever their political imperfections, are democracies in good standing, whereas Russia, after a chaotic postcommunist experiment with democracy and federalism, has effectively returned to a pattern of repressive centralism. The combination of these differences makes Russia potentially the most explosive of the three cases. Here the key issue is whether the relatively assimilated, not to say bourgeois, Tatars and Bashkirs of the Volga region could be swept into the jihadi maelstrom that in recent years has devastated the northern Caucasus.

A generation ago, Alexandre Bennigsen dreamed that the Muslims of the Soviet Union could play a central role in bringing down the edifice of communist power. Hahn now sketches a nightmare scenario in which the Muslims might do the same to the Russian Federation. My suspicion is that he is being unduly alarmist, just as Bennigsen was being unduly optimistic. One reason is that Islamism has not shown much ability to engender political unity in Muslim populations; another is that the Muslims of Russia may themselves be willing to accept a good deal of repression if the alternatives look even worse. But the tale Hahn tells is one of such unrelieved nastiness on all sides that it is hard to imagine a happy ending. The one moment of relief is a story about a policeman in the northern Caucasus who lost both hands when he intentionally absorbed the force of an exploding grenade and thereby prevented the outbreak of civil war between the Kabardians and the Balkars.

—*Michael Cook*

DOI 10.1215/0961754x-7312237

Originally published in *Common Knowledge* 15.2 (Spring 2009): 213–14.

Carlos Fraenkel, *Teaching Plato in Palestine: Philosophy in a Divided World* (Princeton, NJ: Princeton University Press, 2016), 240 pp.

Part One of this award-winning book takes us on an exploratory voyage through some of the most basic of philosophical questions as these are pondered in the least likely "corners" of the world. In Part Two, the "tour guide" finally lays out before us the intellectual map of this fascinating excursion. The purpose of this unique experience (which we signed on to, he as much as tells us, by reading the book) is to make us see the practical value of testing and introspecting our beliefs and ponderings through a congenial but sharp conversation with ourselves and others. Doing so essentially requires us to develop a disposition in ourselves to be open to such conversations, along with the analytical skills to carry them out. We are then part of what the author calls "a culture of debate." A programmed "habituation" of the young to these dispositions and skills, starting at the high school level, would guarantee over time a worthy life and better world, where varied convictions across cultures and religions would come to be grounded in good reasons for holding them but would not be blindly held on to or tightly sealed against possible alteration through a common search for truth.

Part Two of the book—a philosophical case for the culture of debate—shows us how to cope with each other in a world where we may share citizenship but at the same time be rooted in different cultures and hold different convictions, or where political borders may signal deep cultural or religious divides, often expressed in animosity and conflict. The "culture of debate" approach to dealing with such differences or divides stands to be far more conducive to a flourishing coexistence than alternatives grounded in a single set of liberal values. At the very least, the culture of debate accounts for and guarantees the achievement of the aims of these other accounts—from Mill to Rawls—while ensuring, through its mainstay of fallibilism, a *dynamic* promise of continued human betterment. An honest engagement with the "other" signals both respect for them as well as a readiness to be self-critical about one's beliefs: it is a positive engagement in civil life, rather than a de facto toleration for living under the same political roof with suspicious strangers.

A reader might get the wrong impression—corrected in the author's afterword to the second edition—that what is being "naively" proposed is a magical formula to end major world conflicts and problems in one fell swoop, from wars to religious fanaticism, or to resolve all ideological differences over what to regard as the best social or economic policies. But the author makes plain that, while "critical questioning" is necessary for human flourishing, it is neither sufficient nor appropriate as a mechanism to resolve differences or conflicts. Clearly, a violent assault will need the intervention of police officers, rather than philosophers. Even so, it is arguable that a state of war—such as that between Israelis and Palestinians, with which the author begins his first essay—has shown that force is by no means a guaranteed "resolving agent": force will not bring peace or deliver a better world. Of course, it is arguable too that one side or the other may prefer a state of war to peace (this being more suitable for its particular ends). Once again, however, Fraenkel's main message suggests itself: one must put to the test whether one's reasons for such a preference are worthy.

—*Sari Nusseibeh*

DOI 10.1215/0961754X-7312249

Originally published in *Common Knowledge* 24.2 (April 2018): 327–28.

Bruce Robbins, *Perpetual War: Cosmopolitanism from the Viewpoint of Violence*
(Durham, NC: Duke University Press, 2012), 247 pp.

If all human beings have an equal claim on the earth's resources, the claim is routinely ignored by rich and empowered nations like the United States, whose agricultural subsidies and drug-marketing rules cause damage to poor people in Bolivia and Angola. Bruce Robbins is an earnest and sensitive contributor to the increasingly robust debate on global justice. His intervention has a strong English department accent, focused on the ideas of Kwame Anthony Appiah, Edward Said, Noam Chomsky, Martha Nussbaum, Stefan Collini, Louis Menand, and W. G. Sebald. By sticking with this bunch, Robbins asks the concept of cosmopolitanism to do a huge amount of political work. There is an equally substantial literature produced by political scientists, economists, and legal academics, keyed by Charles Beitz's 1979 classic, *Political Theory and International Relations*. Samuel Scheffler long since distinguished between cosmopolitanism about culture (which is what Robbins engages, mostly) and cosmopolitanism about justice (which is what Beitz and his commentators pursue). Robbins parlays culture-centered cosmopolitanism into a wise protopolitics while delivering the most discerning commentaries I have yet to read on the theorists whose work he does engage (including my own). But the next step, surely, is to integrate the English department's idea of a cross-disciplinary conversation with what's doing next door, in law schools and social science departments. We are all in this together, as cosmopolitans should know.
—*David A. Hollinger*

DOI 10.1215/0961754X-7312261

Originally published in *Common Knowledge* 20.3 (Fall 2014): 497–98.

Robert B. Pippin, *Nietzsche, Psychology, and First Philosophy*
(Chicago: University of Chicago Press, 2010), 152 pp.

It has not been easy to accommodate what the philosopher Bernard Williams once called the "insistent continuities" between Nietzsche's concerns and our own while also acknowledging, as Williams certainly did, his challenge to the now-canonical understanding of philosophy in anglophone (and, increasingly, not only anglophone) countries. In line with such an understanding, Nietzsche has been read as a philosopher in the tradition of David Hume, an empirically minded thinker whose deep respect for science inspired him to try to explain all human behavior in the same causal, deterministic terms that explain the movements of inanimate objects. On this reading, when Nietzsche praises psychology as "the queen of the sciences," he is, if not actually thinking of, then at least anticipating the empirical science of today; and his extraordinary attacks on morality are squarely located within the terms of contemporary ethical debate. The trouble is that in this way Nietzsche's views turn out to be not just insistently but seamlessly continuous with ours. And so, little is made of his disdain for what passes as "reason" in philosophy, his startling charge that science (all science, including the humanities) is not the liberator of the spirit but the last stronghold of religious prejudice, and most everything else that makes reading him as disturbing as it is exhilarating. Impressed by the disturbing aspects of his thought, another approach—often influenced by the French "thought of '68"—finds in Nietzsche a wholesale rejection of traditional philosophy. This "first of the last metaphysicians" (in Ronald Hayman's apt phrase) breaks completely with everything "the West" has thought about Man, Nature, and God, and calls for a radically new language whose arrival is supposed to be as imminent as its nature is unpredictable.

Robert Pippin situates himself between these two extremes, and it is no accident that he dedicates his book to Williams's memory. Psychology is for Pippin not today's empirical science but the thought of the French moralists, especially Montaigne. He takes Nietzsche's fundamental questions regarding the grounding of values in modernity to be continuous—but his answers in fundamental tension—with our own concerns. The norms that govern human behavior change through history and, with them, so does what counts as "the human soul." We can neither decide to adopt these norms through a purely rational process nor is that something that merely happens to us through a causal mechanism over which we have no control: the two alternatives in play in contemporary philosophy, "the exclusive categories of 'event *or* action,' do not help us understand the phenomenon."

For Nietzsche, our most basic commitments depend on our historical position and have an affective component, which Pippin connects (not quite convincingly, in my opinion) with Platonic *erôs*. But his focus on the question of commitment directs him toward an understanding of human action, self-knowledge, and self-formation that does not fit easily within current philosophical orthodoxy. Pippin's is one of a small but growing number of works that, working through Nietzsche, recognize that orthodoxy is often little more than a heresy that has, for the moment, won the day.

—*Alexander Nehamas*

DOI 10.1215/0961754X-7312273

Originally published in *Common Knowledge* 18.2 (Spring 2012): 361–62.

Sanford Budick and Wolfgang Iser, eds.,
The Translatability of Cultures: Figurations of the Space Between
(Stanford: Stanford University Press, 1996), 348 pp.

All men are others. They might have been brothers, but now that they're sisters and half of them misters, there's no more convention, but only invention: A one-handed fable transmitted from Babel. For tongues in confusion attempt no trans-fusion. Give blood for the ghosts to the Lord and his hosts.

  This grumble is not directed against a well-edited and interesting book, but against the contemporary multiverse it presupposes. Alterity offers us a Hobbes-ian state of nature in which every act of speech is an act of power, directed first against the other, secondly against the speaker's self. To replace it by the state of civil society, we need to establish some elementary power sharing in the politics of language. Leviathan being neither acceptable nor available, it is likely that we shall have to reenact Enlightenment, and certain that we must try—though not that we shall succeed in the attempt—to renew power over ourselves, before we can share it with others. Long way to go.
—*J. G. A. Pocock*

DOI 10.1215/0961754X-7312285

Originally published in *Common Knowledge* 6.1 (Spring 1997): 144.

Jenny Davidson, *Hypocrisy and the Politics of Politeness:*
Manners and Morals from Locke to Austen
(Cambridge: Cambridge University Press, 2004), 252 pp.

Davidson romps through the eighteenth century as if it were her own private pre-serve. Her vast command of its literature and history, itself a source of pleasure to this reader, is put to use in demonstrating that politeness and manners served hypocritical aims, principally the subjugation of servants and women. Davidson places greater emphasis on dissimulation than on breach of trust in her definition of hypocrisy, and she seems to follow Machiavelli's view that in power (depen-dency) relationships honesty is not to be found on either side. This premise leads her to interesting perspectives on manners and to complex illustrations of the way society develops language to deal with the problem that telling the truth can be uncivil. Point counter point, Davidson pits one text against another to display the eighteenth-century arguments, with Mary Wollstonecraft's shining so brightly that it illuminates gender discrimination even today. This book does not shed any light on hypocrisy itself, however, or why, despite its long-standing bad reputation, it has proven to be so durable and so necessary.

—*Anton O. Kris*

DOI 10.1215/0961754X-7312297

Originally published in *Common Knowledge* 12.3 (Fall 2006): 526.

Joseph Dunne, *Back to the Rough Ground:*
"Phronesis" and "Techne" in Modern Philosophy and in Aristotle
(Notre Dame: University of Notre Dame Press, 1993), 492 pp.

Several years ago, Stephen Toulmin and I attempted, in our *Abuse of Casuistry*, to rehabilitate Renaissance casuistry as a legitimate mode of ethical analysis. We somewhat succeeded and flocks of neocasuists appeared, particularly in bioethics. However, we also stirred up swarms of countercasuists who, like postmodern Pascals, picked at casuistry's weaknesses, especially its insouciance about moral theory. But Dunne's book should cheer the hearts of neocasuists. While not directly about ethics, it studies the notion that is at the core of casuistry—Aristotelian *phronesis* as the key to practical rationality—and it both deepens and broadens the philosophy of practical knowledge, long distorted and emaciated by instrumentalist and technical reasoning. The title of the book comes from an observation of Wittgenstein's, that theorists walk on slippery ice where conditions are ideal, but "we need friction. Back to the rough ground!" Discourse about religion, art, politics, textual interpretation, and social structures must acknowledge, Dunne contends, that in real life there is friction. Although only when Aristotle appears does the conversation concentrate on ethics, readers interested in the epistemology of ethics will find in this book a formidable defense of casuistic reasoning. Neocasuists will move now on more solid ground, and countercasuists will have rougher ground to travel on their way to criticism.

—*Albert R. Jonsen*

DOI 10.1215/0961754X-7312309

Originally published in *Common Knowledge* 4.2 (Fall 1995): 123.

Donald Davidson, *Truth and Predication*
(Cambridge, MA: Harvard University Press, 2005), 180 pp.

The ideas of the late Donald Davidson are beginning to be appreciated beyond their origin in Analytic philosophy of language. Davidson doesn't make appropriation easy. He was an Analytic philosopher's philosopher, intricately technical, indifferent to questions outside a narrow specialization. As prose, Davidson is elegant, spare, subtle, and indirect. A great deal is left unsaid. If Quine were H. L. Mencken, Davidson would be Henry James. To follow Davidson's argument carefully, you need a course in logic, maybe more than one. The effort is worth it. It's been a long time since there was a really new idea about truth. Philosophers have recycled between Plato and Protagoras for two thousand years. Davidson credits logician Alfred Tarski, but without Davidson the ideas would have been lost, for Tarski himself didn't see the most important thing and would have learned as much from Davidson as the rest of us have. Before Tarski it seemed inevitable to think of truth in terms of relations extending beyond language. With Tarski truth becomes an artifact of the logic of language. The only way to explain what it is for a sentence to be true is to show how it relates to an infinite set of other sentences. The account never strays from relations of language to language. The result is an idea of truth that's as unconditional as any purist could ask for yet supports no metaphysical interpretation. Instead, metaphysical ideas of truth stand exposed as extravagantly superfluous. Davidson's question in these lectures is the point of *is*. What's this particle doing in language? There's no obvious answer. He decides that we never know exactly what *is* means because we never know what *is true* means. We would know both if only we knew what our language is, but we never will.

—*Barry Allen*

DOI 10.1215/0961754X-7312321

Originally published in *Common Knowledge* 14.1 (Winter 2008): 158–59.

Hans Blumenberg, *Care Crosses the River*, trans. Paul Fleming
(Stanford, CA: Stanford University Press, 2010), 157 pp.

Hans Blumenberg, *Paradigms for a Metaphorology*, trans. Robert Savage
(Ithaca, NY: Cornell University Press, 2010), 152 pp.

An important moment in the history of the United States took place in early 2011 when the government cited Aristotle's *Poetics* in a call for proposals on the topic of metaphor. Someone in Washington appears, moreover, to have been reading

Hans Blumenberg. The Department of Defense and the Office of the Director of National Intelligence invited scholars to submit proposals "that will exploit the fact that metaphors are pervasive in everyday talk and reveal the underlying beliefs and worldviews of members of a culture." Or, in Blumenberg's words, metaphors "indicate the fundamental certainties, conjectures, and judgments in relation to which the attitudes and expectations, actions and inactions, longings and disappointments, interests and indifferences, of an epoch are regulated." One of the studies in *Paradigms for a Metaphorology* demonstrates how metaphors have influenced the direction of astronomical research and ruminations, the ways in which thinkers and scientists have adjusted their thinking to accommodate metaphorical "needs."

Paradigms consists of ten studies exploring the relationship between metaphorics and conceptual thought. Robert Savage, the talented translator who navigates nimbly through Blumenberg's Teutonic abstractions, regards *Paradigms* as a beginner's guide to the Victorian home-sized works of Blumenberg's that bear correspondingly capacious titles: *Work on Myth*, *The Legitimacy of the Modern Age*, *The Legibility of the World*, and *The Genesis of the Copernican World*. Blumenberg is to philosophy what Proust is to literature. Generally, people acknowledge their works as important, absorbing, even essential—yet few people have taken the time to read their work, since the books are enormous and complex. Still, as the author in the 1960s of *An Intellectual History of Technology*, Blumenberg perhaps anticipated the appeal of more Twitter-sized chunks of prose for a different kind of audience. *Care Crosses the River* is a wonderful example of that genre (and a companion to the only other example available in English, *Shipwreck with Spectator*). Which is not to say that this reader-friendly genre is less intellectually impressive than the larger works. Heideggerian philosophy is a frequent topic in *Care Crosses the River*, particularly in a piece entitled "The Narcissism of Care," where Blumenberg laments that no one pays attention to the crucial fable about Care in *Being and Time*. Care (Cura) is an allegorical figure who crosses a river for reasons left unexamined in Heidegger's text. Blumenberg connects the allegorical figure to a Gnostic myth, the upshot of which is that Cura makes the crossing "so that she can see herself mirrored in the river." Blumenberg interprets the story in a manner that wounds Heidegger's philosophy in the heart of *Dasein*, then wonders in an arrestingly lighthearted way about the future deaths of Heidegger's followers.

—*Bruce Krajewski*

DOI 10.1215/0961754X-7312333

Originally published in *Common Knowledge* 18.2 (Spring 2012): 358–59.

Pierre Bouretz, *D'un ton guerrier en philosophie: Habermas, Derrida & Co.* (Paris: Gallimard, 2010), 592 pp.

Pierre Bouretz's story begins in 1977, when the first volume of the journal *Glyph* published a translation of "Signature événement contexte" by Jacques Derrida, to which John Searle replied in the second volume. The apple of discord was J. L. Austin, whose work Derrida had addressed *à la Derrida*, contesting the metaphysical character of the exclusion by Austin of utterances judged as "parasites" on the normal use of language. Searle affirmed that Derrida misunderstood Austin to the point that the confrontation with Austin "never quite takes place" and claimed that the generalized theory developed by Austin's successors included what Austin's strategy of research had provisionally neglected. The philosopher was thus rather contemptuously expelled from what was now a perfectly well-defined rational field of inquiry or, in Bouretz's terms, a family business.

Searle now disappears from Bouretz's narrative landscape, while new protagonists enter it, mostly American ones, such as Gilbert Harman, Richard Rorty, and Stanley Cavell, but also—back to the continent—Jürgen Habermas, who reconstructed Searle's position, linking it with his own theory of communicative rationality. Derrida is no longer an object of contempt but of denunciation; he is a destroyer of the Aufklärung, which it was Habermas's self-assigned mission to save.

Bouretz's book is an interesting, sometimes absorbing, cross between an inquiry that uses the thread of Derrida's reception, to explore milieus that usually ignore each other, and a sometimes overlong but always enlightening commentary on Derrida's and Habermas's texts. Habermas does not change, but Derrida's growing distance from "irresponsible" deconstructionism, along with the messianic (without a messiah) ethics that he developed in the 1990s, progressively blurred the figure of the nihilist destroyer of Reason whom Habermas had feared and attacked. On September 22, 2001, upon receiving the Adorno Prize, Derrida played a master card, relating in his acceptance speech the ethic of discussion, which Habermas had accused him of betraying, to a reworked concept of "misunderstanding," under the aegis of the negative dialectics of Adorno, the founder of the Frankfurt school. The war was over. Upon Derrida's death, Habermas declared that "his oeuvre can also have an enlightening impact in Germany, because Derrida appropriated the themes of the later Heidegger without committing any neopagan betrayal of his own Mosaic roots."

Is this, as Bouretz claims, a story of war and peace in philosophy? Opinions may diverge, since peace with Habermas can also be seen as a nonevent, the logical outcome of Derrida's becoming, as barbarity threatened, the defender of (a resolutely nonpagan) civilization to come.

—*Isabelle Stengers*

DOI 10.1215/0961754X-7312021

Originally published in *Common Knowledge* 19.3 (Fall 2013): 551–52.

David A. deSilva, *The Jewish Teachers of Jesus, James, and Jude:*
What Earliest Christianity Learned from the Apocrypha and Pseudepigrapha
(Oxford: Oxford University Press, 2012), 343 pp.

As a gentile attending the Passover seder one year in the home of friends, I was asked what I gathered was an old chestnut of a question: With whom did Jesus study Torah? I knew that in the New Testament Paul had boasted of studying with Rabbi Gamaliel, the grandson of Rabbi Hillel the Elder (Acts 22:3). But I had never heard the answer that my host gave that night to his own question—namely, that Jesus had studied with Hillel himself. That he did so is folklore at best, but it is chronologically possible. Hillel would have been about seventy, Jesus about ten. Nazareth and Jerusalem are not neighboring towns, but the Gospel of Luke (2:41–52) does report Jesus's parents traveling to Jerusalem at Passover, losing track of the boy, and then discovering him with elders in the Temple "both listening to them and asking them questions." Luke makes the Son of the Most High a prodigy of *talmud torah*. This is the scene imagined in Hieronymus Bosch's *Jesus among the Doctors of the Temple*, reproduced on the jacket of deSilva's book. DeSilva imagines this scene in reverse, however, turning Jesus from the prodigious little teacher that Bosch imagined into (with Jesus's brothers) a dutiful little learner. This is rhetorical synecdoche rather than historical reconstruction, but Jesus did have brothers or "half-brothers," as deSilva perhaps piously calls them. Three are named in the Gospels, along with unnamed sisters, to a minimum total of six children for Mary. Two of the brothers, James and Jude, are the authors of letters included in the New Testament. What deSilva offers, to put it less catchily than he does, is an admirably close intertextual study of links between, on the one hand, the "voice" (his term) heard in these letters and in the words of Jesus in the Gospels and, on the other hand, the voice heard in selected works of Jewish literature from the last pre-Christian centuries. This aspect of deSilva's serious and careful study is its major merit and principal claim to originality.

The literature of rabbinic Judaism was all produced in the Christian era. The "Apocrypha and Pseudepigrapha" of deSilva's subtitle thus refers to nonrabbinical Jewish literature chronologically prior to both the Christianity and the Judaism that were to be. The irony here, inasmuch as the author wishes to stress Christianity's debt to Israel, is that Christianity preserved the books in question, while Judaism eventually repudiated them. Some of them began as part of the Bible read by Grecophone Jewry both in Palestine and in the much more populous Western Diaspora. That Bible became (and remains) the Old Testament of Greek Christendom. Translated into Latin, it became the Old Testament of Latin Christendom until the Reformation, after which it has lived on as the Bible of Roman Catholicism. By the sixteenth century, however, this Bible had long since been repudiated by rabbinic Judaism as it had become the citation text for the emergent Christian scriptures. Nothing in it that was not extant in Hebrew made it into the emergent Palestinian Jewish canon, the *Tanakh* of today's Judaism.

Martin Luther declared the contested works apocryphal, and "apocrypha" they remain in most Bible scholarship to this day. Yet the Greek word *apocryphon*— meaning "hidden," it should be noted—carried initially a note of excitement and discovery rather than of inferiority or deception. Think of the hidden-and-then-discovered Dead Sea Scrolls in the twentieth century. Exegetical continuity existed between the habit, growing steadily stronger in Second Temple Judea, of discovering hidden, revolutionary meanings in received scriptures and the composition of purportedly lost-and-recovered scriptures (apocrypha), sometimes fictitiously attributed to hallowed names from earlier Jewish literature (pseudepigrapha). The fabrications may have been transparent even at the time, and yet the works were effective vehicles for new thinking. After such thinking led rebellious Judea into two catastrophic defeats, however, rabbinic Judaism turned away from most of the literature written in so fatally excited a mood. Pacifist early Christianity, by contrast, having displaced victory to the afterlife, could afford to remain scripturally apocalyptic and revolutionary without risking outright military conflict with Rome. And so it happened that Christians not only retained the full Greco-Jewish canon but also preserved extracanonical works from the agitated centuries before the destruction of the Temple, not all of which, in any case, were apocalyptic.

From among the (Greco-Judaean) canonical works, deSilva considers Ben Sira (Sirach or Ecclesiasticus), the Book of Tobit, and 2 Maccabees. These are the apocrypha of his subtitle. From among the pseudepigrapha, he considers the Book of Enoch, the Psalms of Solomon, the Testament of Job, the Testaments of the Twelve Patriarchs, and the Lives of the Prophets. The apocrypha and pseudepigrapha belong broadly to the once open-ended category of *ketuvim*: any of them could, and some of them did, become part of the Jewish biblical canon. As a body of work for study in English, they have been grouped together since at least 1913 when R. H. Charles published the two volumes of *Apocrypha and Pseudepigrapha of the Old Testament* with the Clarendon Press. James H. Charlesworth (who contributes a generous jacket comment to deSilva's book) published a major update and expansion of Charles, again in two volumes, with Doubleday in 1983–85. DeSilva is not bringing new works to light, then, but too many who have written on these works link them to Christianity with broad strokes. DeSilva is a pointillist, patiently and revealingly comparing the target works of Christian Jews in the first century, down to individual verses, with the works to which, no less than to the canonical Jewish scriptures, they were intellectual heirs.

—*Jack Miles*

DOI 10.1215/0961754X-7312345

Originally published in *Common Knowledge* 21.3 (September 2015): 513–15.

Norman Cohn, *Cosmos, Chaos and the World to Come:*
The Ancient Roots of Apocalyptic Faith
(New Haven: Yale University Press, 1993), 271 pp.

This book reads like a prequel to Cohn's still unnerving *The Pursuit of the Millennium: Revolutionary Millenarians and Mystical Anarchists of the Middle Ages,* first published in 1957. There Cohn argued, with extreme lucidity and drama, that much of the mystificatory power of Nazism, Marxism, modern anarchism, and European nihilism per se lay in the extreme distance between the twentieth-century killing grounds of these apocalyptic movements and their original, long-forgotten formations as heretical medieval sects. Now Cohn has gone back to the beginnings of recorded history, to Egypt, Mesopotamia, and India, to trace this same eruptive tendency to the Zoroastrian innovation: sometime between 1500 and 1200 BC, in what is now eastern Iran, a worldview that saw the cosmos as a permanent war between good and evil was replaced by a prophecy of the final defeat of evil (chaos, corruption, and suffering) by absolute good. Cohn argues that this once bizarre, altogether localized heresy ultimately shaped what he neatly names the Jesus sect, and thus the course of much of history ever since.

As with most prequels, *Cosmos, Chaos and the World to Come* seems lacking in a certain energy, at once too long and too short. While Cohn takes only a little more than seventy pages to get to the Zoroastrians, those seventy feel like hundreds, describing a world-without-change without change; his analysis of the Book of Revelation, though admittedly tailored to his particular thesis, is sketchy and hurried, and against such explosive, unstable material, Cohn's purposeful selectiveness calls itself into question. Instead of the brooding momentum of an impassioned search for the secret at the heart of a mystery, Cohn insists baldly on the mystery itself: "Coincidence or influence?" You be the judge.

All that said, there are moments when the essential strangeness of a confrontation with unacknowledged, perhaps unwanted ancestors comes through whole. Locating an origin for our world—a first body for our body politic—in the marginalized, impotent, conquered kingdom of Judah, which, while "a mere 25 miles long and with a population of perhaps 20,000," was so far from being the center of the cosmos it thus insisted that it was, Cohn tells more about the tiny levers that move the world than a shelf full of reasonable histories in which nothing is ever a surprise.

—*Greil Marcus*

DOI 10.1215/0961754X-7312357

Originally published in *Common Knowledge* 4.1 (Spring 1995): 84.

G. W. Bowersock, *The Throne of Adulis: Red Sea Wars on the Eve of Islam*
(Oxford: Oxford University Press, 2013), 208 pp.

429

Little Reviews

In the thirty-fourth canto of Ariosto's *Orlando Furioso*, the brave Duke Astolfo climbs the fiery sky up to the moon in Elijah's chariot, in order to recover Orlando's wits. The moon is the "place wherein is wonderfully stored / Whatever on our earth below we lose. / Collected there are all things whatsoe'er, / Lost through time, chance, or our own folly, here." Under the knowledgeable guidance of Saint John the Baptist, Astolfo takes an edifying walk on the moon among all the things that get lost on earth: fame, vows and prayers, lovers' tears and sighs, variously wasted time, vain designs, but also "old crowns of the Assyrian land / And Lydian—as that paladin was taught— / Grecian and Persian, all of ancient fame; / And now, alas! well-nigh without a name." Among these ancient crowns, one might find as well those of Aezanas and Kaleb of Axum, were it not for this book by Glen Bowersock, in which he illuminates the story of the martyrs of Najran, its background, and its consequences.

Out of three Chinese boxes the author unfolds a centuries-long drape of history that, it transpires, was the backdrop for the rise of Islam. A Ptolemaic basalt stele, extolling the conquests of King Ptolemy III Euergetes, was placed behind a fourth-century celebratory throne, commissioned by the Axumite negus Aezanas. Both carried inscriptions in Greek, which caught the attention of a sixth-century Ethiopian king, Kaleb (or Ella Asbeha), who had them copied by the Byzantine merchant Cosmas Indicopleustes just before launching an overseas campaign against the Jewish king of Himyar, guilty of savagely persecuting the Christians under his rule. The marble throne, which then stood in the port city of Adulis on the shore of the Red Sea, long lost, lies now neglected in some remote marsh of Ariosto's moon, but Cosmas reported the texts of the two inscriptions in his *Topographia Christiana*. Entering Cosmas's pages under Bowersock's knowledgeable guidance means abandoning some of our most cherished idées reçues: what we ultimately learn is that a massacre of Christians at the hands of Arab Jews inaugurated the challenge to the old order that led to the emergence of Islam. Retrieving from Ariosto's moon the most recondite pieces of historical truth is no quest for a fainthearted historian.

—*Maria Conterno*

DOI 10.1215/0961754X-7312369

Originally published in *Common Knowledge* 21.2 (April 2015): 328–29.

Arlette Farge, *The Allure of the Archives,*
trans. Thomas Scott-Railton, foreword by Natalie Zemon Davis
(New Haven, CT: Yale University Press, 2013), 152 pp.

As always, the problem lies partly with the definite article and the question of sin-gular or plural nouns: "The Allure of the Archives" is not quite the same as "The Allure of Archives" or "The Allure of the Archive," and none is quite the same as "Le Goût de l'archive," the title under which Farge's book was first published in 1989. It is made up of four discursive chapters and three narratives of daily life in the *fonds*. Its translator is faced with the same issue that confronts those trying to render *l'histoire du livre* into English. The uncertainty runs throughout the book. The reader is told at the start of sentences that "The archive": "was not compiled with an eye toward history"; "lays things bare"; "preserves these moments"; "imposes a startling contradiction"; "shines a light on the people of the city"; "is born out of disorder"; "always preserves an infinite number of rela-tions to reality"; "is an excess of meaning"; "speaks of the Parisian woman"; "is not simple"; "complicates the approach to these questions." At the same time, "the archives": "do not necessarily tell the truth"; "also shed light"; "find her not just caught in these circumstances"; "once again, surprise us"; "bring forward details that disabuse, derail, and straightforwardly break any hope of linearity or positiv-ism"; "are not a stockpile." The granting of agency to the archive(s)—they "reject any ready-made tropes"—is characteristic of the book's overheated and solemn prose. The documents allow the reader to "make out a long limping procession of baroque silhouettes," but the archive also "pins them down like trembling butterflies" (they have already been cut and cemented); it is "like a kaleidoscope revolving before your eyes," but one that produces a "whirlwind." When she reports directly on what she has found in the archive(s), Farge is always interest-ing, but the more portentous parts of the book are as irritating as the archivist's "high heels clicking crisply on the floor."
—*H. R. Woudhuysen*

DOI 10.1215/0961754X-7312381

Originally published in *Common Knowledge* 22.1 (January 2016): 129.

The Letters of T. S. Eliot, ed. Valerie Eliot and John Haffenden,
vol. 3 (1926–27), 954 pp., and vol. 4 (1928–29), 826 pp.
(London: Faber and Faber, 2012).

Punctilious, industrious, resolutely polite, and shrewdly diplomatic, the Eliot of
these letters is the perfect editor of a small and prestigious journal and the discerning partner of a small but influential publishing firm. *The Criterion* (first a
monthly, thereafter named *The New Criterion* and then, once more, *The Criterion*,
but a quarterly) consumed that part of his every working day not consumed by
his labors at Faber and Gwyer, soon to become Faber and Faber. In each case, the
mission was the same. As Geoffrey Faber put it to another partner of the small
house, it was "to bring grist to the mill." That meant soliciting writers for both
establishments and reviewers for the journal. It meant lunches and afternoon teas,
hundreds of them, letters, thousands of them; it meant reading the submissions of
"a boy named Auden" and corresponding with William Empson, I. A. Richards,
Walter de la Mare, Edmund Wilson, and myriad others. It meant continued
close association, through the mail, with Joyce, with Pound, and with Wyndham
Lewis. It meant liking some, but not all, of D. H. Lawrence. And it meant telling Edwin Muir, late in 1928, "I should be very glad indeed to see your essay on
Kafka. I know the name, but that is all."

Eliot was paid £400 a year by Faber (some $32,000 in current dollars) and
from January to June in 1928 earned, in the currency of the time, $38.20 in royal-
ties for his poems. When he was not ill, and he was ill again and again, he worked.
He did so without belief that his industry would have any immediate results: "*The
Criterion*, of course, must allow always about twenty-five years to elapse before
any of its ideas can reach the general public."

Only intermittently, and by sudden breaks in the industrious monotony,
does the reader get a glimpse of another Eliot: the one who wrote *The Waste
Land* and "Prufrock" and who, in these and other poems, created a landscape
of desolation, neurasthenia, and blocked hope that served to shape one generation of poetry and poets, if not several. That Eliot is rarely seen, and even then
he must be seen by ignoring his disguises: when we learn that he "has taken up
dancing" or that "he is learning to drive an automobile" or that his real special-
izations are "detective fiction and ecclesiastical history," we know we are being
misled. The Eliot of the poems, the person with an internal existence, is to be
discovered only when, abruptly, we come upon not his letters but those of his wife,
Vivien. Perpetually distraught, at odds with herself, at odds with her husband
("he simply hates the sight of me"), and forever suffering from medical problems
(pleurisy, headaches, influenza, restless fatigue), she was sufficiently disturbed to
cause Pound, Conrad Aiken, and Virginia Woolf, as well as his brother Henry, to
recognize Eliot as a man in distress. In "Tradition and the Individual Talent," he
had claimed that the poet undergoes a "continual surrender of himself." But the

troubled Eliot of these letters could no more surrender himself than he could jettison his perfectly correct manners. A decade after writing that essay, he wrote to E. M. Forster that, "as for the 'impersonality' doctrine, it has its personal motives of course, and is neither more true nor more false than its opposite doctrine." By 1928, he was seeking not a surrender of himself, but a form of religious discipline that would hold that self in the tightest of bonds: "I feel that I need the most severe . . . the most Latin, kind of discipline, Ignatian or other. It is a question of compensation. I feel that nothing could be too ascetic, too violent, for my own needs."

The religious practice that would provide that discipline had, for Eliot, its own peculiarities. It was indeed a form of ritualistic Christianity, but with certain key elements ignored or abandoned. When Richard Aldington wrote him saying, "I don't really like the gospels, and I don't much like Christ. I really think Paul was more interesting. He appears to have been a man. I have suspected that . . . Christ is an invention," Eliot responded by writing, "I agree with you about Christ and I do not disagree with anything else." To H. J. C. Grierson, he confided, "Of course there is the Immaculate Conception, which I cannot swallow," and to an American Jesuit he wrote that "what I really regret . . . is the intellectual break-up of Europe and the rise of Protestantism." Out of this distillation of likes and dislikes, needs, and surrender, Eliot fashioned the self that, in 1928, he would present to the world. In the preface to *For Lancelot Andrewes*, he had become "classicist in literature, royalist in politics, and anglo-catholic in religion."

Yet beneath that persona, constructed for reasons that these many letters make clear, emerges another:

Some day I want to write an essay about the point of view of an American who wasn't an American, because his America ended in 1829; and who wasn't a Yankee, because he was born in the South and went to school in New England as a small boy with a nigger drawl, but who wasn't a southerner in the South because his people were northerners in a border state and looked down on all southerners and Virginians, and who so was never anything anywhere and who therefore felt himself to be more a Frenchman than an American and more an Englishman than a Frenchman and yet felt that the U.S.A. up to a hundred years ago was a family extension.

That essay never got written. Perhaps his editorial labors, of which these two superbly edited volumes are a record, were too many; perhaps being what he called "a very slow and costive writer" disabled him; perhaps "impersonality" got in the way. And then, of course, he thought himself old. At age forty, he wrote to Harold Monro, "I am getting on in years." Eliot died thirty-seven years later.
—*William M. Chace*

DOI 10.1215/0961754X-7312393

Originally published in *Common Knowledge* 20.1 (Winter 2014): 145–47.

Serena Vitale, *Shklovsky: Witness to an Era,*
trans. Jamie Richards (Champaign, IL: Dalkey Archive, 2012), 120 pp.

In deep winter 1978–79, six years before his death, the enfant terrible of Russian formalism and its longest-living survivor, Viktor Shklovsky (1893–1984), granted a series of interviews to the Italian Slavist Serena Vitale. Her little book tells two stories. The first is the interviewer's own. There wasn't a glimmer yet of glasnost, and, during her second week in Moscow, Vitale was run down on the street by the KGB thugs assigned to trail her, leaving her badly bruised and with two cracked ribs. Shklovsky urged her to return promptly to Italy with her precious tapes; seventy years in literary harness had taught him how to bend so as not to break. The second story is an oral memoir, eased out of an eighty-six-year-old man with flexibility and tact, and full of marvelous things. Amid praise for Tolstoy and Pushkin, Shklovsky recalls his friendship with Mayakovsky, Khlebnikov, Pasternak, Meyerhold, Eisenstein. The master of montage did not care for the object in itself, we learn: "What interests him is the reciprocal interaction of objects and ideas." The poet Mayakovsky "wanted to be liked right away," most of all by the Revolution. And although Bulgakov was an "incomparable writer," the end of *The Master and Margarita* was a disappointment, because Christ and the Master have nothing to say to each other: "Christ is better informed, he has all the news, he's more interested and involved in the problems of the world."

Through every ghastly Soviet freeze and thaw, Shklovsky never withdrew from the world's problems. But by 1978, he did have some anxieties about the profession. He feared for language. Technology (that is, television) was distorting the living word. Critical jargon (in this case, that of Structuralism) was distorting discussions of literature ("The language of professors is always ugly"). Shklovsky was an unusual revolutionary formalist. He wrote pathbreaking studies of Sterne, Conan Doyle, Dickens, and Cervantes without knowing English or Spanish (and in Vitale's book we learn that he also "worked a lot on Boccaccio," thus adding Italian to the literary traditions on which he worked but whose language he did not know). Shklovsky as a formalist scholar and critic was dependent on forms not belonging to their authors. What he studied, of course, was less formal verbal structure than devices for waking up the reader ("estrangement") and for the pacing and dynamics of plot. But even plot, he confessed, was constraining: "Talking about a beginning, middle, and end has nothing to do with art. . . . I myself, with all the love I have for novels, I prefer to doze off before the denouement." Shklovsky did just that, dying four years before the end of the Soviet era that had defined his life.

This timely memoir, which passed from Russian conversation through Italian into English, is wonderfully rendered by Jamie Richards into the rambling, aphoristic, suddenly profound voice we recognize as that of Soviet Russia's most cosmopolitan monolingual critic. It took work to survive. To support himself, Shklovsky worked for everyone: editing banned film scripts to get them through the censorship, ghostwriting whole books for ungifted colleagues. Only two things, he remarked, he never wrote: "Poetry, and denunciations."

—*Caryl Emerson*

DOI 10.1215/0961754X-7312405

Originally published in *Common Knowledge* 21.2 (April 2015): 327–28.

G. L. Hagberg, *Meaning and Interpretation:*
Wittgenstein, Henry James, and Literary Knowledge
(Ithaca, NY: Cornell University Press, 1994), 183 pp.

Hagberg applies the investigative method and concepts of Wittgenstein's philosophy of language to an examination of the "meanings" of various works of art, and especially to what he calls a new sort of "close reading" of four short stories by Henry James. Hagberg's ideas and readings are not entirely new, for they serve to redescribe, in Wittgensteinian terms, existing concepts in the variegated history of literary and aesthetic criticism. Even his basic explicative frame—that a work of art is an expanded "microcosm" of a self-bounded "language game" that determines from within the possible authorial "moves" and implicates an "imagined form of life"—is closely concordant with aesthetic claims that, in the mid-eighteenth century, Baumgarten extrapolated from Liebniz's proposal that there exist an infinity of possible worlds, each a unique structure of "compossible" elements and interrelations. Baumgarten's conclusions, in parallel with Hagberg's, are that a literary work is a "heterocosm," or imagined "other world," subject only to its own compossible laws, organized around a particular theme, and related to this actual world not by mimetic correspondence but by analogy. But of course the thrust of Wittgenstein's way of thinking is against the expectation of unprecedented discoveries with regard to such familiar activities as looking at a painting or reading a novel. And these days, when so much academic critical activity is grounded in the extrahuman paradigm of the self-conflicting nature of language-as-such, or the ideological constitution of discourse-in-general, it is heartening to read Hagberg's demonstrations that our literary experiences can be enhanced and subtilized by recourse to a Wittgensteinian variant of the humanistic paradigm presupposed by major critics beginning with Aristotle: that a literary work is authored by a purposeful human being, for human beings, and about matters of human concern.

—*M. H. Abrams*

DOI 10.1215/0961754X-7312417

Originally published in *Common Knowledge* 4.1 (Spring 1995): 82–83.

Regina Ullmann, *The Country Road*, trans. Kurt Beals
(New York: New Directions, 2015), 160 pp.

Regina Ullmann's writing was highly praised in her time by writers of impressive stature—Herman Hesse, Rainer Maria Rilke, Thomas Mann, and Robert Musil ("Genius."). Yet only now, nearly one hundred years after it first appeared in German, has this valuable collection of stories become available in English, lucidly and sensitively translated by Kurt Beals with what seems to be close faithfulness to the original. The reason for the delay is not really clear to me—it is probably, as so often, due primarily to the unpredictable play of chance. True, these are not obviously "easy" stories. But other remarkably individual writing has found its way into English much sooner.

A few facts about Ullmann which are interesting without explaining how the flower of her writing came to blossom: she was born in Switzerland in 1884. Her birthplace, St. Gallen, was a town familiar to another Swiss writer and fellow eccentric, Robert Walser. Her Jewish-Austrian father was in the embroidery business. She was wall-eyed and squinted, slow in school, slow at everything. She lost her father when she was four. As an adult, she attempted and failed to earn a living at writing, and took up beekeeping.

I am trying to imagine how her background and life produced such an unusual and fine sensibility, along with the strength of character to write in direct response to her odd way of seeing the world. One commentator has drawn a connection between her conversion to Catholicism in 1911 and her habit of looking closely and patiently at real or imagined life and finding within each thing a kind of sacred mystery. The scope of the stories is not wide, yet their subjects somewhere between worldly and otherworldly—children's theft of strawberries, a dying wife who lies there "like a distant ancestor," a pregnant and vagrant girl kindly adopted by an old man. The writing goes at its own pace, pausing for reflection. In this, it has something in common with Proust's long novel: we cannot expect to be seized by any quick action, as from the first sentence of a Patricia Highsmith crime romance. An apter comparison might be to the stories of Brazil's Clarice Lispector. In the experience of reading Ullmann, one's expectations change, within the rarity of her vision and the precise beauty of her prose.

—*Lydia Davis*

DOI 10.1215/0961754X-7312429

Originally published in *Common Knowledge* 24.2 (April 2018): 318–19.

Raymond Carver, *Carnations: A Play in One Act*,
***Common Knowledge* 2, no. 3 (Winter 1993): 152–59.**

I tell my students—I teach playwriting at the University of Houston—that they shouldn't even consider a career in the theatre unless they feel they will be incomplete without it, that the theatre is a tough and unfair business where honor and talent don't carry much weight—rather like life, I suppose. I tell them that the theories of playwriting can be taught, that I can instruct them how to write like other people, but that only if they are playwrights by nature can I nurture.

If I had been teaching in 1962 (I was not, for I had just begun writing plays myself) and had Raymond Carver submitted *Carnations* as entrance evidence to my class, I imagine I would have taken him on; though with some misgivings. I prefer student work that is wild to that which is tame, chaotic to too-well-ordered, messy to neat, adventuresome to timid, and semicoherently alive to safely comatose. I think I would have been taken by Carver's stylistic jumble—expressionism cheek to jowl with surrealism; I'm sure I would have been impressed by the sudden startlements of the text, by the two or three moments I was suddenly and inexplicably moved; I know I would have been pleased by the unknowing of the stage technique, its crude and probably unsatisfiable demands.

As I say, I like the wild, the chaotic, the messy, the semicoherent, and I'm almost certain I would have taken Carver on, if for no other reason than to discover the mind and talent responsible for such work.

I'm not certain, however, I would have encouraged Carver to pursue playwriting, for I'm not sure I would have been convinced that it was there his quirky and undeniable talent could blossom best. I think I would have encouraged him to try other forms, to find where the possible turned into the inevitable—poetry, perhaps?—the novel, maybe?—short fiction, even?
—*Edward Albee*

DOI 10.1215/0961754X-7312441

Originally published in *Common Knowledge* 2.3 (Winter 1993): 151.

Péter Nádas, *Burial: Comedy without Intermission*,
trans. Imre Goldstein, *Common Knowledge* 8, no. 1 (Winter 2002): 218–68,
originally published 1982 in Hungarian.

Péter Nádas has written in a variety of forms since his first book, a collection of stories published in 1965; anglophone readers had to wait until 1997 to discover him, when *A Book of Memories* (1986), his maximal masterpiece, finally appeared in English. To start one's reading of a major writer with that writer's most ambitious, most accomplished, bulkiest book is bound to foster misreadings. There are sizable peaks surrounding this Everest. But it will take time to take their measure.

Burial (1982), the last and best of the plays Nádas wrote in the late seventies, is often described as the third part of a trilogy, of which the first two parts are *House Cleaning* (1978) and *Meeting* (1981). All three plays came after the first novel, *The End of a Family Novel*, which was written between 1969 and 1972, but not cleared for publication by the Hungarian censorship until 1977.

For those reading *Burial* in English translation, a drama with two nameless characters wandering around a barren stage is likely to evoke Beckett, behind whom stands that Symbolist tradition exemplified in, for instance, Maeterlinck's *Les aveugles*. This is not, I think, Nádas's genealogy. The roots of Nádas's imagination as a dramatist are thoroughly German: the work with which *Burial* is best compared would be the encounter-dramas of Pina Bausch and the declamatory plays of Thomas Bernhard.

Much of *A Book of Memories* takes place in the Brecht-dominated theatre world of the former East Berlin in the 1970s. (This, of course, draws on Nádas's own experience.) But it is one thing to be interested in theatre as a world, as a metaphor, as a system of meanings; in Nádas's great novel, thinking about theatre is a way of making reality more complex, more layered. Making a work for the stage engages a quite different idea of theatre; in *Burial*, theatre is a technique for peeling away, stripping down, exposing the layers of reality with which we clothe ourselves. "Despite all our social conventions," he once said in an interview, "we are all naked in front of each other. And theatre is perhaps nothing other than the perception and the demonstration of this nakedness."

For Nádas, theatre, the domain of actors, is not a branch of literature, at least not in the sense that a novel, which has characters, is literature. The novel describes, but theatre *performs* intensity, carnality. "What interests me in the theatre is not the story," Nádas has declared. Nor is it so-called ideas. That is a matter for literature and philosophy. In theatre it is the system of relations emerging between live bodies that is my interest."

In contrast to the plays of Beckett, but also unlike the plays of Bernhard, Nádas's plays are about sexual desire. Characters are above all bodies, agents of sexual desire. His master subject is the complexity and insatiability of desire, which finds its most original expressions in the heroically detailed, mesmerizing pages in *A Book of Memories* devoted to describing the possession, part by part, of the body of a desired other. Desire is a form of hysteria. Desire is a mania of possession. Desire is insistence. Reading *Burial*, one is struck by the obsessional specificity of the instructions for producing the play, with their raging exclusions—no change in the lighting, no music, no curtain call, no acknowledgment of the audience—and the rich punctuation throughout, by silences of different lengths.

Sexual dueling drives Nádas's narratives. Usually, it is a duel *à trois*—a child and his parents, two boys and a girl—with the desire agitating Nádas's principal character, who is invariably male, eventually veering from the Mother, the girlfriend, to the Father, the boyhood comrade or boyfriend of the girl. *Burial* depicts the more classic duel of two, female versus male. Still, much of the old ambiguities of attraction, the perennial conflict in Nádas's narratives about which kind of body is desired that is conveyed by a triad of characters, is retained here by stipulating that the two characters, MAN and WOMAN, aka ACTRESS and ACTOR, be dressed exactly alike. Ideally, he says, they are Twins . . . the oldest trope for fusing heteroerotic and homoerotic desire.

This is an opera of words, a ballet of movements. The only criterion is intensity. Again and again, the characters work themselves toward the ecstatic, the incorporating. They speak, they spar, they dance, they chant their engorging, their entering of each other, their exchanges of identity, their pauses, their frustrations. A whole lifetime, a whole relationship is enacted, parodied. Breathing, clutching, avoiding, declaiming, the two characters attempt to exhaust every permutation of their merging and their estrangement.

It seems to me a limitation in *Burial*, unlike Nádas's great novel, that the outcome is so logical, even predictable. Two characters called Actors emerge at the beginning of the play and take possession of the stage. Their exchanges rise to a rapturous account of desire. At the end, there is a leave-taking. Why? Perhaps because the play must end. The woman is banished by the man, and the man buries himself. More precisely, he takes up residence in his death.

"Of course," Nádas instructs us at the end (perhaps unnecessarily, but this is a writer who takes nothing for granted), "ACTOR and ACTRESS do not come out to take a bow."

—*Susan Sontag*

DOI 10.1215/0961754X-7312453

Originally published in *Common Knowledge* 8.1 (Winter 2002): 215–17.

Lincoln Kirstein, *Mosaic: Memoirs*
(New York: Farrar, Straus & Giroux, 1994), 270 pp., 16 pp. photographs.

When Mr. Kirstein said to me at lunch near Lincoln Center (named for him's the local joke) that he and I were "in agreement about *everything*—and we are *WRONG!*," I assumed he meant wrong in the eyes of the most judgmental of third parties, Everyone Else; and I laughed. But it seems he meant this: "the salvation of consciousness, a continual awareness of the precise quality of shifting situations by the process of self-questioning [is] the sole stern pursuit." The title of his memoir is both an adjective ("pertaining to Moses' Law") and noun ("a tableau of scraps"), implying that even prophet-kings are bricoleurs and that collage projects authority. Laying bare the vanities, "barbaric provender," and wandering of his early years on Earth only makes Kirstein's profile stronger. He was brought on stage at the climax of the Balanchine Festival to be served his vodka on a tray by Baryshnikov—a gesture of real grandeur that the audience found moving, that Kirstein appeared to find too-much, and that in poring over his autobiography I find myself finding inadequate tribute to a diffidence so absolute.

—*Jeffrey M. Perl*

DOI 10.1215/0961754X-7312033

Originally published in *Common Knowledge* 4.2 (Fall 1995): 120.

Vincent Descombes, *The Institutions of Meaning:*
***A Defense of Anthropological Holism*, trans. Stephen Adam Schwartz**
(Cambridge, MA: Harvard University Press, 2014), 360 pp.

A still room where one hears the clock ticking, a quiet voice speaking with great clarity. A sense of privilege accompanied my reading Descombes, a sense that I was being invited to share something rather rare and fine—and the translator's exquisite rendition of this text, first published in Paris in 1996, must be part of that impression. A nonphilosopher reading the book is reminded of the virtues of scrupulous analytic reasoning; an anthropologist, of anthropology's enduring premise about the contextualizing power of social life. How to account for what we take for granted when people apparently understand one another? Given the endless argumentation surrounding this question and its variants, there is much to consider and much to dispose of. The author does raise his voice at times, of course, as for example when dissipating the mirage of social totalities imagined as indivisible collections of elements—as collectivities that are more than the individuals who compose them. Descombes instead favors the complexity of structural holism (following in the path of Louis Dumont), which requires a specification of relations and their logic. Thus, one of Descombes's excursions takes in "the gift" and the fallacy of rendering interaction as a question of dyadic relations. Without the third term of an institution or law of giving, there could be no gift. The realism of triadic relations is a holism, he writes, reducible neither to the positivism of dyadic relations nor to the atomism of monadic terms. Anyone writing the history of British social anthropology might wonder what the effect of this argument might have been had this book appeared in English in (say) 1956 or 1966. But then, that was the very time when Dumont's writing was gathering force, and for myself I take from Descombes the thought that Dumont's criticism of A. R. Radcliffe-Brown's British legacy (collective representations and dyadic relations alike) deserves reappraisal. The hands of the clock keep coming around to the same hour; this book is highly pertinent to the way much anthropology is still being written.

—*Marilyn Strathern*

DOI 10.1215/0961754X-7312465

Originally published in *Common Knowledge* 22.2 (April 2016): 321.

William Weber, *The Rise of Musical Classics in Eighteenth-Century England: A Study in Canon, Ritual, and Ideology* (Oxford: Clarendon Press, 1992), 274 pp.

Lévi-Strauss doubts that an anthropology of high culture is possible, and trains attention on meals and marriage. But a few recent studies, emerging from backstage of the canon agon, have worked out terms for an anthropology of the arts in modern Western societies. Weber's book examines the "harvest festivals" (the concert schedule) of the English county elite and townsfolk in the eighteenth century and—with a density of detail worthy of the antitheorists to whom he makes a discreet nod—Weber arrives at something like a theory. Shy of statement, he describes its embodiment, the Handel Commemoration of 1784: "the reunion of Tory and Whig within a new political community," "a ritual solution to divisions created by the Civil War," "a celebration of the end of crisis." A canon of approved art is less aesthetic in motive than political—but not political in the sense we have presumed.

—*Jeffrey M. Perl*

DOI 10.1215/0961754X-7312477

Originally published in *Common Knowledge* 2.3 (Winter 1993): 145.

Gundula Kreuzer, *Verdi and the Germans: From Unification to the Third Reich* (Cambridge: Cambridge University Press, 2010), 382 pp.

Reception history is all the rage among scholars of music. This form of research takes as its principal material writings in a country about a composer's work and often pays little heed to the works themselves and their own history. Interest lies primarily in how critics and scholars *receive* what they take to be the music. In this world, where scholars frequently show extreme ignorance both about what is being performed and to what political or aesthetic camp the critics and scholars belong, Gundula Kreuzer's *Verdi and the Germans* is a remarkable achievement.

Professor Kreuzer has set out to demonstrate no less than what Verdi meant to the German peoples and how their vision of his operas and his persona changed from the period immediately preceding German unification of the mid-nineteenth century to the traumatic, post-Nazi, post–World War II period. Unlike many of her peers, she knows the works themselves thoroughly (although she seems to have little patience for what she refers to as an approach that insists upon *Werktreue*) and speaks precisely about just what German performers and theaters presented as Verdi's operas. She eloquently talks about the model of the "two cultures" (Germanic and non-Germanic) made familiar recently through the writings of Carl Dahlhaus but based on a contrast between Rossini and Beethoven already present in the writings of Raphael George Kiesewetter in the 1830s; she tackles the Wagner/Verdi axis that pervaded European thinking in the latter part of the nineteenth century; she forces a thorough revaluation of the so-called Verdi Renaissance that took place in Germany particularly during the Weimar period (but actually dates back to an earlier period of the twentieth century); she demonstrates how Verdi's operas were used by the Nazis, particularly in terms of their deepening involvement with Mussolini's Italy; and she indicates in a more sketchy fashion what a history of post–World War II movements, including *Regietheater*, might teach us.

Because Kreuzer knows the Verdi works well, she can demonstrate just how any given opera was "adapted" and "modified" in German theaters, making clear in the process that, when she (and her sources) talk about a work, they are always talking about what they know as *Nabucco*, *La forza del destino*, or *Don Carlos*, rather than what the composer and his librettists wrote. When Kreuzer strays from Verdi, however, her knowledge becomes more limited. It is fine to write about German reactions to Rossini, but nowhere are we told that what the Germans knew as *Il barbiere di Siviglia* was a score worked out in Vienna in 1818. When Germanic critics wrote about Rossini, they did so in utter ignorance of his Neapolitan serious operas, since these could not be performed by theaters that did not sport two major tenors to assume parts written for Andrea Nozzari and Giovanni David. In Paris, Stendhal knew these matters well and was able to indicate when French revivals of some of these operas were wretched. No wonder, then, that German critics despised an art they did not and could not know. Rossini's fame and reputation in Italy seemed utterly incomprehensible to the Germans, except as an indication of faults in the Italian character.

Fortunately this kind of problem, which continually dogs reception history, falls away when Kreuzer turns to operas that she knows much better. And she is very sensitive to the political persuasions of those whose writings she quotes. They are not abstract names but writers (for example) for newspapers that are pro- or anti-Nazi and belong to specific sectors of opinion. She does not cite the writings of a Herbert Gerigk or a Wolfgang Boetticher without informing us who they were and under what auspices they were writing. In doing so, she largely escapes what Leon Botstein has called "The Perils of Method in Reception History."

—*Philip Gossett*

DOI 10.1215/0961754X-7312489

Originally published in *Common Knowledge* 18.2 (Spring 2012): 359–61.

Maria Bloshteyn, *The Making of a Counter-Culture Icon: Henry Miller's Dostoyevsky* (Toronto: University of Toronto Press, 2007), 261 pp.

Professor Bloshteyn's book is a lively and erudite investigation of a little-known aspect of how Dostoevsky's life and works were accepted and assimilated outside Russia, primarily in the United States, but also with side glances at England and France. The American reception is focused on Henry Miller and two other authors, Anaïs Nin and Lawrence Durrell. In the early 1930s, all three lived together on the rue Villa Seurat in Paris, sharing Miller's friendship, his view of Dostoevsky and, in the case of Nin, also his bed. As Bloshteyn remarks of their common conception of Dostoevsky, "few other writers have been subjected to such radical misreadings and had their ideological credo distorted to such a dramatic extent."

Any reader of Dostoevsky's letters, notebooks, and his *Diary of a Writer* knows that he began as a Utopian, pre-Marxist Socialist in the 1840s, whose early work gave a sympathetic depiction of the victims of a caste-ridden bureaucratic society. After being arrested, experiencing the ordeal of a mock execution, and spending four years in a prison camp followed by six in the Russian army, he emerged a changed man, whose convictions, as he wrote himself, had been "regenerated" by his encounter with the Russian people. He then became a faithful, if not uncritical, supporter of the czarist regime. When Alexander II liberated the serfs in 1862, this "regeneration" was strengthened, because the existence of serfdom had been one of the major causes for Dostoevsky's radicalism of the 1840s.

All through the major post-Siberian novels that made him famous, Dostoevsky was thus inspired by his opposition to the radical ideas that became influential among the Russian intelligentsia in the 1860s. How could it have happened, Bloshteyn asks, that such a writer (she calls him a "Russian Orthodox monarchist," terms not inaccurate but that need some qualification) could have become the idol of "so many left-wing, irreverent, anarchically minded groups?" Among such fringe groups that took Dostoevsky as their prophet, she lists the Surrealists, the Existentialists, and the Beats.

In searching for an answer to this question, Bloshteyn goes back to the early history of Dostoevsky's introduction to Anglo-American readers. The famous Madame Blavatsky, for example, of Russian origin and the founder of Theosophy, published in 1881 her translation of the Grand Inquisitor chapter of *The Brothers Karamazov* without reference to the rest of the novel; and she wrote that this chapter was Dostoevsky's "cutting satire on modern theology." The well-known anarchist agitator Emma Goldman, who also published a magazine entitled *Mother Earth*, printed a story in 1910, "The Priest and the Devil," supposedly written by Dostoevsky on the wall of his cell during his imprisonment to protest against the exploitation of the working class. To raise funds for her own propaganda work, as Goldman recounts in her memoirs, she decided to follow the example of Sonya Marmeladova in *Crime and Punishment* and walk the streets for a worthy cause. Luckily, Goldman was given some money by a kindly passerby she accosted and told to return home. The name and writings of Dostoevsky thus became associated very early with attacks on the reigning social and moral-religious pieties.

In the very year of Dostoevsky's death (1881), a secondhand translation of *Notes from the House of the Dead* was published (it is not clear from what language; probably German, given the name of the translator). This text was replaced seven years later by an "authorized" translation with the title *Buried Alive or Ten Years of Penal Servitude in Siberia*. Dostoevsky's own text is basically an autobiographical account of his four years in the prison camp, living among peasant convicts, many of whom had committed murders; but his own story is introduced by a fictional narrator supposed to have murdered his wife. Nobody knew why Dostoevsky had been "buried alive," and readers simply associated him with all the others in what was largely the story of his life. His fictional narrator was thus taken as a self-portrait (Dostoevsky complained later, though this is not mentioned by Bloshteyn, that many readers thought he had actually murdered his wife).

Another image of Dostoevsky was given in the important French book *The Russian Novel*, written by the Vicomte Eugène-Melchior de Vogue and available in English since 1886. This work introduced non-Russian readers for the first time to Turgenev, Tolstoy, and Dostoevsky, and the image given of the last also had a considerable influence on how Dostoevsky's work was perceived. Having met Dostoevsky personally, the vicomte depicted him as a perennial outsider in Russian society, awkward and clumsy in good society, unlike the two other novelists, who came from an aristocratic, Western-educated milieu. The vicomte also spoke of Dostoevsky's books as being mainly autobiographical and insisted they could not be understood except as "incarnations of his own soul." The characters of his novels, who commit all sorts of crimes and are obsessed with feelings of guilt, or who, like the Christ-figure Prince Myshkin in *The Idiot*, are still indirectly responsible for murder, thus become identified with the author himself, who became a cult figure for later authors like Miller.

Bloshteyn is well aware that this interpretation has little to do—indeed, is a total distortion—of the meaning that the historical Dostoevsky intended his work to have and was based on a complete misunderstanding. "A reader attempting to make sense of Miller's reflections on Dostoevsky," she writes, "will often find them vague, muddled, tendentious, hyperbolic, and, on occasion, simply inaccurate. Miller substitutes Dostoevsky's characters for Dostoevsky himself, confuses Dostoevsky's novels one with another, misattributes words spoken by various Dostoevsky characters, and obfuscates his earlier arguments." Nonetheless, this is the basis on which Dostoevsky is constantly invoked as the inspiration for such a work as *The Tropic of Cancer* and numerous others by Miller, Nin, and Durrell.

The remainder of Bloshteyn's book examines the writings of all three in relation to their connection with various Dostoevsky novels, pointing out echoes, resemblances, and extravagant extensions of his supposed creative intentions. She has done an extremely useful job in the historical investigation and uncovering of this falsified, self-created, pseudo-Dostoevskian world, which, for all its misapprehensions, still had the effect of inspiring new creations. As the veteran Dostoevsky scholar Robert Belknap paradoxically writes in his jacket blurb, the book offers "a lesson in the psychological and cultural benefits of misreading."
—*Joseph Frank*

DOI 10.1215/0961754X-7312501

Originally published in *Common Knowledge* 18.2 (Spring 2012): 374–76.

Boris Groys, *The Total Art of Stalinism:*
Avante-Garde, Aesthetic Dictatorship, and Beyond,
trans. Charles Rougle (Princeton: Princeton University Press, 1992), 176 pp.

This book attempts a revision not only of totalitarian art, but of the very phenomenon of Soviet totalitarianism, claiming it to be an avant-garde project brought to life by the greatest artist of all time and all nations, comrade Stalin. If only the artist Malevich and the poet Khlebnikov, while challenging the classic tradition with their "Black Square" and "transrational language," had imagined that their ultimate artistic ideals were to be realized in the transrational style of Soviet newspapers and in the black holes of concentration camps in the fabric of Soviet society. . . . In his book, Groys does not polemicize any particular author so much as he does the stereotypical Soviet assumption that socialist realism is fundamentally opposed to any "rotten bourgeois" avant-garde or modernist movement. What Groys succeeds in arguing is that socialist realism is the most faithful, though thankless and forgetful, heir to avant-garde utopianism. The radicalism of Groys's conflation of totalitarianism and the avant-garde may be as one-sided as the stereotype he is attempting to dispel. Nevertheless, an extreme reaction is somehow preferable to its extreme antecedent, since it restores the balance.

—*Mikhail Epstein*

DOI 10.1215/0961754X-7312513

Originally published in *Common Knowledge* 6.3 (Winter 1997): 149.

Frank Dikötter, *Mao's Great Famine:*
The History of China's Most Devastating Catastrophe, 1958–1962
(New York: Walker, 2010), 448 pp.

As one of the many who personally lived through the fearful years from 1960 to 1962 in China, I would like to thank Frank Dikötter, whose book reliably exposes the details of the largest famine in Chinese history. A few tens of millions of people died of starvation during the catastrophe known as the "Great Leap Forward," a product of Mao's insane and cruel utopia, which was based, in turn and in part, on the so-called science of Marxism. One acre of land, Marxist science determined, could produce 5 million kilograms of grain; this and other statements of the kind could be found almost every day in the *People's Daily*, the most important newspaper of communist China. Dikötter's book describes an omnipotent leader so ignorant, rash, and reckless as to apply the adulatory word *science* to such stupidity and, on its basis, to make policy decisions that would affect the lives of 1 billion people. Certainly, many with common sense knew the mendacity of the "Great Leap Forward," even at the time. China was, however, and remains a country that suppresses speech. That anyone who ever queried Mao's policies was silenced and punished is a fundamental cause of the great famine.

—*Fang Lizhi*

DOI 10.1215/0961754X-7312525

Originally published in *Common Knowledge* 18.2 (Spring 2012): 373.

**Hans Joas and Wolfgang Knobl, *War in Social Thought: Hobbes to the Present*
(Princeton, NJ: Princeton University Press, 2013), 336 pp.**

Let us start with three observations, the most moving by a writer who fell victim to war, Simone Weil: "Death is the most precious thing which has been given to man. That is why the supreme impiety is to make bad of use of it." Has anything more profound been said about war—its waste, or its glory? The reality of both has been conveyed for centuries through philosophy and literature. A book, wrote Kafka, any book "must be an ice-axe to break the seas frozen inside our soul." But those seas have intimidated most social theorists from diving very deep. It was Freud who wrote that frightening and threatening experiences are the ones that the conscious mind is likely to shut out, though without robbing them of their potency—an explanation, perhaps, for the failings of even the most renowned social theorists (not excluding Marx and Weber) to come to terms with the phenomenon of war.

Joas and Knobl are sociologists, and they are commendably honest in taking their own discipline to task for this failure. They have also in this book produced a substantial work of contemporary social theory that ranges widely—from Hobbes and Rousseau to present-day social thought—and that in focusing on European writers offers a welcome antidote to the strategic community's Anglo-American bias. War still has its votaries and probably always will have. Whether this generalization extends to the new players—the criminal cartels, jihadists, pirates, and militias of the world—is a moot point. Is war itself like the Borg Collective, appropriating every social phenomenon in its path? And is our two authors' patent unwillingness to face this question (which they themselves pose) another case of suppressing war within the social sciences?
—*Christopher Coker*

DOI 10.1215/0961754X-7312537

Originally published in *Common Knowledge* 20.3 (Fall 2014): 500.

**Evelyn Fox Keller, *The Mirage of a Space between Nature and Nurture*
(Durham, NC: Duke University Press, 2010), 120 pp.**

Why are we obsessed with nature and nurture—or, more precisely, with nature *versus* nurture? In this short, lucid book, historian and philosopher of science (and erstwhile mathematical biologist) Evelyn Fox Keller explains why the opposition is not only wrong—nature and nurture work hand in hand—but also wrong-headed, since to frame the problem in this way obscures the real questions we should be asking about evolution, genetics, and development. As she readily acknowledges, neither of these points is new to most biologists. It is their research that has exploded older doctrines of genes as particulate units of inheritance and even newer doctrines of genes as the sequences of DNA that code for a protein. Yet the old opposition of nature versus nurture stubbornly persists, and not only in the popular press. Why?

Keller's answer is: slippages of language. Our habitual ways of speaking about heredity, development, and traits routinely conflate individuals and populations, traits and trait differences, mutations with mutants. She recognizes that politics also plays a muddling role but contends that language is the chief villain. Can linguistic hygiene alone exorcise metaphysical demons? If so, then this is the book to do it.

—*Lorraine Daston*

DOI 10.1215/0961754X-7312549

Originally published in *Common Knowledge* 20.2 (Spring 2014): 365–66.

Anne Toner, *Ellipsis in English Literature: Signs of Omission* (Cambridge: Cambridge University Press, 2015), 255 pp.

This book offers a history of English literature under the species of a history of typographical marks of omission. Such marks are ellipsis, editorial or not; dashes, dramatic or otherwise; ellipsis points; stars and asterisks; and a few minor others. The author discusses "early printed drama" (late sixteenth-century translations of Terence, Ben Jonson, Shakespeare); the eighteenth-century novel, non-Gothic (Defoe, Sterne, Richardson, et al.); the Gothic novel (with a backward glance at Chaucer); the nineteenth-century novel (Austen, Eliot, Dickens, Meredith, Collins, et al.); the so-called modernist novel (Conrad, Ford, Woolf); with a passing nod to twentieth-century drama (Pinter, Beckett). There is a considerable amount of erudition; mention is made of grammars. What is remarkable is how much the history offered resembles your average history of English literature: parochial, gentle, and unsurprising; lots of novels and no poetry. One finds the usual periods and epochs; a correct estimation of the importance of English drama; a slightly exaggerated admiration for the pyrotechnics of the eighteenth-century English novel; a fully justified awe for Jane Austen; and a calculated approbation of Virginia Woolf. Thus, one is left with the impression that the book was ultimately not affected by being a study of signs of omission in English literature: under this sort of description, ellipsis in English literature looks exactly like English literature.

—*Miguel Tamen*

DOI 10.1215/0961754X-7312561

Originally published in *Common Knowledge* 23.3 (September 2017): 547.

Janet Malcolm, *Two Lives: Gertrude and Alice*
(New Haven, CT: Yale University Press, 2007), 229 pp.

The three essays that constitute Malcolm's book appeared in earlier form in the *New Yorker*. A mix of anecdote, gossip, and biographical detective work, they provide an enjoyable read: Malcolm is a shrewd analyst of personal relationships, and she writes tellingly—if maliciously—about such issues as Stein's failed love affairs or her friendship, during the German occupation, with the young French surrealist poet Bernard Faÿ, who turned out to be a Nazi sympathizer, quite willing to help deport Jews from France. Malcolm is, for that matter, shocked that Stein and her companion Alice B. Toklas stayed on in their country house in the Bugey during World War II (they could have escaped across the border to Switzerland) and that they repeatedly failed to own up to their Jewishness. Only in the late *Wars I Have Seen* (1945), about which Malcolm writes discerningly, do Stein's wartime fears and anguish come out into the open.

It has, in recent years, become fashionable to "out" Stein as a Pétain sympathizer (she translated some of his speeches during the war) and an anti-Semitic Jew. Stein and Toklas were able to stay in the Bugey, Malcolm posits, because they colluded with Faÿ, who adored Stein, and with others like him. "What was in it for Faÿ?" Malcolm asks. "What drew the Royalist anti-Semite to the Jewess in funny clothes?" It never seems to occur to her that, however awful his politics, Faÿ genuinely admired Stein and recognized her genius. But then Malcolm—and this is what makes her book finally so unsatisfactory—has no use for the bulk of Stein's writing. She dismisses it early in *Two Lives* as "unreadable," making a sharp distinction between the "experimental writing" of *Tender Buttons* or the *Portraits* and nonfiction of the twenties and "conventional" work, like *The Autobiography of Alice B. Toklas*, written in the thirties to attract a larger public. I find this distinction dubious: even *Alice B. Toklas* uses a panoply of modernist devices, and certainly it has little or no plot or "rounded" characters.

The one work Malcolm does tackle, evidently on the suggestion of the leading Stein critic Ulla E. Dydo, whom Malcolm consulted, along with Dydo's fellow scholars Edward M. Burns and William Rice, is *The Making of Americans*. Gritting her teeth and making her way through this long and daunting early masterpiece, mainly so as to find out what made Stein tick, Malcolm concludes that Stein is incapable of "invention" and hence of writing a novel: "The characters . . . resemble shades. You never see them." It never occurs to Malcolm that perhaps this is the case because what began as a novel becomes something quite different. Modernist literature, after all, is full of such cases: *Finnegans Wake* has no "real" characters either.

Never granting that the limitation may be her own, not Stein's, Malcolm, in her third chapter, tells a long story about Leon Katz, the Stein scholar who has evidently deciphered the "Rosetta stone" for *The Making of Americans*—namely, a set of notes in the Beinecke Library that "decodes" the novel—but has refused to share his research with anyone. Although Malcolm flew to Los Angeles to meet with him, he backed out at the last minute. If only we had these notes, Malcolm suggests (although we do have Katz's PhD dissertation on the subject on file at Ann Arbor), we would know what Stein was *really* alluding to in *Making*, how she felt about her Jewish background, her family, Alice, and so on. As it is, Malcolm has to resort to gossip and hearsay: she relays, for example, Hemingway's oft-told nasty story about an overheard argument, replete with unpleasant sexual references, between Alice and Gertrude.

The Stein that emerges from Malcolm's double portrait (and why include Alice in the first place, such equal time rarely being given to the wives or husbands of Stein's heterosexual fellow modernists?) is a self-centered, dismissive egomaniac, unable to face her own shortcomings. Malcolm has little truck with what must have been the painful marginalization that Stein, as a gay, Jewish, exiled woman, living in Paris (a Paris she chose because it was more tolerant of sexual deviance), must have experienced. Yes, everyone loved to come to her Rue de Fleurus salon, but it has been shown again and again that the artists Stein loved and admired, especially Picasso, had no use whatever for her *writing*. No wonder she accepted the adulation of young men like Carl Van Vechten and then Bernard Faÿ.

As for the perfidy of wanting to stay on in France during the war, who would have benefited if Stein and Toklas had in fact fled to Switzerland? Remember that Stein died of cancer in 1946, just a year after war's end. And remember how badly many Frenchmen, even those later associated with the Resistance, behaved during the early war years. André Malraux, for one, went into retreat in the south, acquiring a Riviera villa (La Souco), where guests like Jean-Paul Sartre were served gourmet meals by a butler wearing white gloves. In Monte Carlo, Malraux and his second wife saw a good deal of the then-convicted traitor Drieu la Rochelle, compared to whom Bernard Faÿ was surely small potatoes.

It is within this French context that we should try to understand Stein's wartime behavior. More important, it is Stein's groundbreaking *writing*, rather than her everyday village life, that deserves our attention. Despite its sprightly writing and vivid portraiture, *Two Lives* is, finally, a reactionary piece of criticism, wedded as it is to the notion that one reads fiction or poetry in order to gain access to the mind of its author. Stein herself knew better. "Remarks," she warned her readers, "are not literature."

—*Marjorie Perloff*

DOI 10.1215/0961754X-7312573

Originally published in *Common Knowledge* 15.1 (Winter 2009): 93–95.

Pascal Khoo Thwe, *From the Land of Green Ghosts: A Burmese Odyssey*
(New York: HarperCollins, 2002), 320 pp.

This is a classic coming-of-age, my-life-as-parable story with a strange and shattering cross-cultural twist. Pascal Khoo Thwe is a Burmese tribesman—a Kayan Padaung from the hills south of Mandalay, where the women wear brass coils around their artificially elongated necks, demons are captured by seizing their testicles with bamboo tongs, and opium poppies keep the economy going. Baptized a Catholic (hence the "Pascal") by an itinerant Italian missionary, he is raised in a magical world of ghosts and goblins, the famous "nats" that animate and infest the jungled landscape, his grandfather a powerful, charismatical, anti-authoritarian regional chief. After several years in the local government school where he seems mainly to have been instructed in the virtues of Ne Win, the blood-drenched Burman dictator, and then several more years preparing to be a priest in a makeshift local seminary, where he soon loses his vocation, he goes off to national university in Mandalay to study English, the first of his village to do so.

Working there as a flunky in a Chinese restaurant, he encounters a passing-through Cambridge don who has heard-tell of him in Rangoon as a tribesman unaccountably devoted to the work and example of James Joyce, and he starts to dream of England and its scholastic gardens. As the brutality of the military regime is increasingly felt in the university, a shambling, dispirited place at the best of times, and his activist lover, a laughing Buddhist beauty with a rebellious streak, is arrested, raped, and murdered, he becomes himself inflamed and disappears into the jungle to join the guerrilla resistance. There he survives numerous long marches into Thailand and back and several set-to battles with government forces. Ill, wounded, and, most of his comrades killed or captured, near despair, he pulls out the scribbled address of the Cambridge don he has been carrying about with him and writes to the man in the hope that he can somehow rescue him and bring him to England. The don, a somewhat elusive, hard-to-read figure—he is eventually banned from Burma—shows up somehow in northern Thailand and does indeed cart him off to Cambridge. There, after three years of struggle and confusion as "the only oriental reading English in the whole university" he gets a narrow third (he wrote on tragedy, Aeschylus to Chekhov), dresses up in native costume to receive his degree, gets drunk with his mates at the local pub, and returns to visit his left-behind family. Beautifully written, exactly felt, immediate, and genuine, Thwe's book is indeed a contribution to English literature, worthy of its Irish model. And, more importantly, a contribution to Burmese witness.

—*Clifford Geertz*

DOI 10.1215/0961754X-7312045

Originally published in *Common Knowledge* 11.1 (Winter 2005): 349–50.

Walter Burkert, *Babylon, Memphis, Persepolis: Eastern Contexts of Greek Culture* (Cambridge, MA: Harvard University Press, 2004), 192 pp.

Research into classical antiquity is no longer the specialist mug's game—yet another edition of a book of Homer or Herodotus, or the quest for the origins of the Peloponnesian War. Now that the Internet and Google have tied up the problems of collecting the evidence, the main effort has to be in making further connections, in being highly critical of all evidence, in making coherent sense of it all, and then telling the rest of us all about it; the step from the traditional PhD to serious scholarship has become much more than a formality.

Walter Burkert could not have made it more difficult for himself than by embarking on a career studying Greek religion, which requires deep familiarity with every branch of antiquarian study, even outside "Classics," none barred. His success has been remarkable, far outpacing the dedicated philologist, philosopher, or analyst of ancient art. His writing is seldom (well, not often) difficult. In this short book he seems to summarize the results of many of the more taxing subjects he has covered in a long career, those involving the identification and explanation of Greek beliefs and practices paralleled in other, older cultures, and deciding whether there is a case for borrowing or simply of coincidence when things seem to match near perfectly. Of course, they never quite match perfectly, and then the volume of evidence and plausibility have to be weighed. He tends to be optimistic in seeing connections. Looking at Greece and the East, the case has by now been made, although it can still be overargued in some essentials and depends almost more on detecting literary devices than on beliefs; but with Zarathustra and the magi, and to some degree Orpheus and Osiris, we may begin to feel that the pace is being forced a little faster than the flow of incontrovertible evidence might allow. Of course, in antiquity, despite travel problems, everyone was in everyone else's pocket, and it was not only that great minds thought alike but that people at large, faced with comparable problems of survival, found comparable remedies and dressed them in imaginative literature and a nexus of cult practices recognizable in any age and place, whatever the differences of emphasis. In these matters, the Greeks were seldom the passive receptors of the ideas of others, but rather translators. Even a little reading in the religion of Oriental and early American and African peoples teaches us not to expect that Greece, or Greece plus the Near East and Egypt, are in any way special in their treatment of the numinous. Globalization of scholarship hardly starts here, but it could not easily find a more rewarding, if often frustrating, subject. The cover picture of Burkert's book is of a first-century BC head of a god of mixed Greek and Eastern identity, at a site in east Turkey. The god looks perplexed, as well he might be in his role, poised between West and East.

—*John Boardman*

DOI 10.1215/0961754X-7312585

Originally published in *Common Knowledge* 12.3 (Fall 2006): 523.

T. J. Gorton, *Renaissance Emir: A Druze Warlord at the Court of the Medici*
(Northampton, MA: Olive Branch Press, 2014), 248 pp.

For a few decades in the early seventeenth century, the Druze warlord Fakhr ad-Din (1572–1635) ruled a sizable portion of today's Lebanon and Syria, forging his own trade agreements with the West under the nose of the Ottoman Empire. In 1613, threatened by the sultan, he used his agreements with the Grand Duke of Tuscany as a pretext to set sail for Livorno, where he began an exile that eventually lasted five years, split between the courts of the Medici in Florence and of the Spanish viceroy in Naples. In 1618 he returned home, with unprecedented knowledge of Western ways, as one of the more remarkable figures to bridge the gap between Islamic East and Christian West. Praising Italy as a model of efficiency, he then challenged the sultan's self-image as a beneficent ruler. A remarkable story, well told, but the moral is disheartening. For his independence of mind, Fakhr ad-Din was assassinated in 1635.
—*Ingrid D. Rowland*

DOI 10.1215/0961754X-7312597

Originally published in *Common Knowledge* 22.2 (April 2016): 319.

Mary Ting Yi Lui, *The Chinatown Trunk Mystery: Murder, Miscegenation,*
and Other Dangerous Encounters in Turn-of-the-Century New York City
(Princeton, NJ: Princeton University Press, 2005), 298 pp.

On June 18, 1909, New York City Police Officer John Reardon uncovered the putrid body of Elsie Sigel in a trunk, with a rope wound round her neck. The room where her corpse was found bore thirty-five love letters addressed to William L. Leon, a "Chinaman" also known as Leon Ling. Sigel, a young Protestant missionary and the granddaughter of a prominent Civil War general in the Union Army, had written the letters. Soon, papers around the country were abuzz with the news of her death and the disappearance of her alleged killer and lover.

Responses to the brutal event become emblematic, in *The Chinatown Trunk Mystery*, of attitudes toward the Chinese and other immigrants in the United States. Juridical and popular accounts of "Chinatowns" often enforced the sense that the Chinese immigrant community was hermetic. But the cultural and geographical boundaries that were thought to separate Chinatown from the rest of Lower Manhattan's immigrant neighborhoods were permeable: only 4,000 Chinese were estimated to have lived in Chinatown in 1898. The rest, numbering 13,000, were scattered throughout metropolitan New York. According to Lui, social reformers such as Elsie Sigel, the city's police force, and Chinese and non-Chinese residents contended daily for dominance over Chinatown.

The death of Sigel and the implication of Leon Ling dramatized the sense of danger in encounters across perceived ethnic boundaries. The public learned that white middle-class women, like Sigel, ventured voluntarily into Chinatown; and census surveys revealed that an overwhelming number of interracial marriages existed there. The capture of Leon Ling came to mean effective regulation of Chinese movement, but the sweeping manhunt for his capture was doomed to failure from the start. "With police and civilians doubling their efforts to scrutinize every Chinese person in the country, these efforts," Lui writes, "demonstrated the problems derived from executing a search for a man that ultimately depended on the illusion of racial differences and classifications for success." Leon Ling could not be captured, precisely because he was thought—despite every indication to the contrary—to be fixed and locatable in one place.
—*Charlie Samuya Veric*

DOI 10.1215/0961754X-7312609

Originally published in *Common Knowledge* 22.2 (April 2016): 319.

T. J. Clark, *Picasso and Truth: From Cubism to Guernica*
(Princeton, NJ: Princeton University Press, 2013), 344 pp.

In the spring of 2009, I was a member of the standing-room-only audience for four of Tim Clark's six A. W. Mellon Lectures in the Fine Arts on "Picasso and Truth," at the National Gallery of Art in Washington, and I can testify that the present volume, closely based on those lectures, conveys much of the experience of being in his presence on such an occasion. Clark is an electrifying lecturer in addition to being a superb writer on art, and the combination gives *Picasso and Truth* a cumulative force that is nothing short of remarkable. Naturally, I cannot summarize his argument here. Suffice it to say, though, that he approaches Picasso (not all of him; the story really gets under way in the wake of the initial Cubist revolution, which Clark earlier treated in a memorable chapter in *Farewell to an Idea: Episodes from a History of Modernism* [1998]) from a Nietzschean perspective, posing a question extrapolated from the *Genealogy of Morals*: "What will art be, . . . without a test of truth for its findings, its assertions; without even a *will* to truth?" Clark's relentlessly original book offers one answer—or rather, considering its intense and detailed encounters with a wide range of paintings from the master's oeuvre, many answers—to this unexpected question.
—*Michael Fried*

DOI 10.1215/0961754X-7312621

Originally published in *Common Knowledge* 20.3 (Fall 2014): 499.

F. W. Kent, *Lorenzo de' Medici and the Art of Magnificence*
(Baltimore, MD: Johns Hopkins University Press, 2004), 230 pp.

Kent's book is a remarkable biography of a remarkable man, and also a biography of fifteenth-century Florence. But does the city's persona reflect off Lorenzo de' Medici as a personification of Florence, or is Lorenzo's persona a condensation of Florence as a Medicean city? Consider such expressions as The Alexandrian Empire or The Augustan Age or Elizabethan England—each a person fused with an era: the whole in a detail, or the other way around. Kent's venture of seeing the desert in a grain of sand is so skillfully performed that I doubt if the reader's naked eyes can make out the risks. At what point in a geological process does a desert make its own grains of sand? Out of what circumstances in the fifteenth century did Florence create Lorenzo? Can one reverse the signifiers?

Kent tries to synthesize Lorenzo with his *imago*, but Lorenzo as *magnifico* and Lorenzo as *maestro della bottega* resist fusion. Even in Lorenzo's time (he became head of the Medici family in 1469), this synthesis was difficult to anneal. Machiavelli, whose opinions were cautious against rhetorical adulation, saw two Lorenzos in one body. Imagine one of them as an ultrarefined patron of the arts, a connoisseur of taste and decorum, a wise and munificent new Solon. Think of the other as a city manager or a trade union boss who distributes jobs and acts as a broker of political influence. As Machiavelli acutely observed: "If in Lorenzo you saw two distinct persons, then they were more or less made one by an impossible fusion."

Intellectual snobs have been unable to tolerate the combination. And since the 1960s, young scholars who could barely differentiate between grain and chaff have been cutting down and harvesting the reputations of great men and great books, finding what every carpenter knows: it is easier to demolish than to build. The mature and renowned art historians Ernest Gombrich and André Chastel led the assault, however—armed with claims that Lorenzo did not demonstrate the active and catholic patronage of the arts with which historians deferentially credit him, his record much less laudable than his grandfather Cosimo's over the previous decades. But hard evidence for justifying demystification is as difficult to come by as hard evidence in support of myths. The Lorenzo myths were appropriate to Lorenzo's time, as was the flattering hyperbole that survived the downfall of the Medici dynasty in the 1490s. And who is to say that the Lorenzo myth is inappropriate for our time? The 1992 observances of the five-hundredth anniversary of Lorenzo's death generated several publications recreating the superman portrayed in Renaissance rhetoric. Kent admits that the myth of Lorenzo as the Magnificent has not lost its seductive allure. My question is, why should it?

Kent comes clean about his own skepticism—his dismissals of the mythological Lorenzo that, he now admits, tainted his earlier scholarship. Following a long paragraph of self-laceration for impulsive judgments now corrected, Kent takes on Asconio Condivi and Giorgio Vasari, who asserted in the mid-sixteenth century that the all-marble library Lorenzo planned to build within the Palazzo Medici was a mythic library. Kent offers "hard evidence" that Lorenzo did indeed love learning and that the library was not mythical. From about 1472, Lorenzo began collecting ancient Greek and Latin manuscripts for this project; and while construction on the library started late in Lorenzo's life, it was half-built when he died at the early age of forty-three.

Efforts to persuade skeptics that the Lorenzo de' Medici persona as fashioned by flattery and adulation was the real Lorenzo is not to justify hero worship or succumb to what Kent calls "florentinitis." Still, the innocent scholar is left to transact moral business with *that other person*: Lorenzo the shop boss. Lamenting that he had too many holes to fill and not enough money, Lorenzo diverted public funds for himself, making use of trusted agents in the government finance office to cook the books. It was no secret that, having married into the family of Innocent VIII, Lorenzo used his influence at the papal curia to lease and purchase land at very low rates. In the summer of 1477, he set to expanding one of his many properties, a dairy farm a few miles from Florence, and prevailed upon the nearby town of Prato to allow him to appropriate some ecclesiastical lands that bordered on his pastures. That sort of corruption, with public institutions made to serve private interests, raised eyebrows and at times great wrath. The stonemasons' guild alleged that Lorenzo had acquired its property for his wife neither legally nor for a just price, to which accusation the document adds: "as was the custom in similar cases concerning the family and house of the said Lorenzo."

Academics in the humanities tend to have a problem dealing with worldly subjects. Even professional historians find it difficult to know what it is like to live in history: operating farms, developing commercial housing for rental income, performing civil and public service—acting as a shop boss while mediating between secular and religious interests. Lorenzo was not a philosopher, poet, artist, or for that matter an intellectual whose work one can isolate as an extant whole and put on display in a museum or on a book shelf. If Lorenzo needs cutting down to size, to whose size should one make "the real Lorenzo"? My opinion on this matter is more immoderate than Kent's. The real Lorenzo was who he was in the context of his time and place—his self-representation and how his contemporaries represented him. His cast of representors changed over time. But the changes were of the changes, not of Lorenzo as he was before historians began working him over.

—*Wayne Andersen*

DOI 10.1215/0961754X-7312633

Originally published in *Common Knowledge* 14.1 (Winter 2008): 161–63.

**Marisa Bass, *Jan Gossart and the Invention of Netherlandish Antiquity*
(Princeton, NJ: Princeton University Press, 2016), 222 pp.**

The Renaissance got its name from a rebirth of classical antiquity occurring largely in Italy. Inspired by the achievements of ancient Rome, Italian humanists, artists, and poets styled themselves as inheritors of a lost tradition, and they labeled the benighted millennium that intervened a "dark" or "middle age." By this historical scheme—still operative today—northern Europe is imagined as remaining "medieval" much longer than Italy. And indeed modern art historical textbooks often term Netherlandish and German art of the fifteenth-century "Gothic," even though, during the Renaissance itself, the great Flemish masters Jan van Eyck and Rogier van der Weyden were deemed—by *Italian* humanists— more revitalizing than any of their contemporary Italian counterparts. A Florentine, Giorgio Vasari, surveyed in 1550 the previous two centuries of art history to prove the actuality of a Renaissance and did so, chauvinistically, with reference only to *Italian* art, but he was preceded in this effort by a northerner. Some thirty years earlier, the German painter and printmaker Albrecht Dürer referred to an epochal "regrowth" (in his German, a *Widererwaxsung*) of art occurring all around him. Dürer's epochal trips across the Alps to Venice, his classically influenced style and repertoire, his theoretical interests, and his modern-seeming sensibility allowed him to inaugurate (conveniently at 1500, a century after the Italians) what the textbooks awkwardly term the "northern Renaissance." It remained unclear, however, what exactly Dürer revived: the "classical" antiquity renewed by the Italians or something different, perhaps something distinctively northern or Germanic.

Dürer was not the only northerner of his period to attempt, self-consciously, to assimilate the styles, motifs, and ambitions of a classical past. In 1508, the Netherlandish painter Jan Gossart, who called himself Jan Mabuse (after his birthplace, Maubeuge), set off for Rome, probably in the company of his patron Philip of Burgundy, the powerful illegitimate son of Duke Philip the Good. In Rome, Gossart produced several remarkable sketches of Roman antiquities, including drawings of the Colosseum and the Spinario statue. These "from life" impressions of the distant past were firsts in the northern tradition, but in Gossart's art they joined other retrospective glances back in history, including ones directed toward his native northern tradition, embodied in the supreme art of Jan van Eyck. More intriguing, Gossart's mythological paintings, while derived from classical literature and art, referred to an imagined *local* antiquity. Philip of Burgundy, it turns out, was obsessed by a Hercules inscription washed ashore in Zeeland, where he had one of his residences, and this fragment spurred research into, and fantasy about, the prehistory of the region dubbed "Batavia" by Roman authors.

This invented past, based on classical and local lore, is the subject of Marisa Bass's lively and beautifully produced new book. Gossart has long been regarded as a highly polished, stylistically forward-looking, if also rather eclectic master, absorptive like Dürer but without the Nuremberg master's power to make his influences his own. In Gossart's "invention" of a Netherlandish antiquity, Bass discerns a consistent purpose behind the artist's varied output. It is a project Gossart shares with the greatest (and least classicizing) Netherlandish painter of his century, Pieter Bruegel the Elder. And it is a project, too, that will return, three centuries later, in Romanticism's paradoxical "renaissance" of the Middle Ages.
—*Joseph Leo Koerner*

DOI 10.1215/0961754X-7312645

Originally published in *Common Knowledge* 23.3 (September 2017): 532–33.

Willard Spiegelman, *Majestic Indolence:*
English Romantic Poetry and the Work of Art
(Oxford: Oxford University Press, 1995), 221 pp.

Once, sloth was a sin: how did indolence—for aesthetes and artists, at least—become a duty and an ideal—the "majestic indolence" of Wordsworth's recommendation in *The Prelude*? Spiegelman locates the turn in the Kantian emphasis on the freedom of the imagination and describes its appearance in Romanticism through the work of Wordsworth (play), Coleridge (the anxiety of torpor), Keats (receptivity), and Shelley (utopian pastoral), with an epilogue on Whitman, Frost, Bishop, and Merrill. It is interesting to see the "contamination" of Spiegelman's criticism by the hostile attacks recently made against poetry (as oppressive, hermetic, antipopulist, mystificatory). I doubt that it is either necessary or useful to "answer" such attacks in asides; the asides will not convince the attackers, and they distract from Spiegelman's central interest in the impulses of both guilt and delight attached to "wise passiveness." The book gives many famous poems a new life by bringing them within the sphere of "indolence": but are we enlightened by being told—by Spiegelman in New Historicist mode—that Wordsworth's "golden daffodils" are "the equivalent of money in the bank," as Wordsworth "reaps the rewards of his capital investment . . . later, when the accumulated interest of his capital returns to him in a flash?"
—*Helen Vendler*

DOI 10.1215/0961754X-7312657

Originally published in *Common Knowledge* 5.3 (Winter 1996): 62.

The Translation of Lucretius, vol. 1 of *The Works of Lucy Hutchinson*,
ed. Reid Barbour and David Norbrook
(Oxford: Oxford University Press, 2012), 960 pp.

The earliest surviving complete translation in English of Lucretius's great philosophical epic *De rerum natura* came from a surprising source: Lucy Hutchinson
(1620–81), the wife of the parliamentarian and regicide Colonel John Hutchinson.
Lucy Hutchinson was on multiple grounds an implausible conduit for Lucretius's
Epicureanism. Though there were other learned women in her age, few if any
possessed the linguistic skills and the tenacity to render Lucretius's demanding
Latin hexameters into English rhymed couplets. The challenge was compounded
by her having, to borrow Virginia Woolf's phrase, no room of her own. Rather,
as she made clear in her dedicatory epistle, she grappled with her task "in a roome
where my children practizd the severall qualities they were taught, with their
Tutors, & I numbred the sillables of my translation by the threds of the canvas I
wrought in, & sett them down with a pen & inke that stood by me." Moreover, by
the time she made her translation public, she professed that she hated its central
principles as so much "Pagan mud." In a remarkable two-volume edition, Barbour and Norbrook subtly explore the paradoxes of Hutchinson's achievement
and assess its significance. Their long introduction, learned commentary, and
notes comprise by far the best resource available for understanding the strange
conjunction of radical Protestantism, Epicureanism, and an exceedingly complex,
brilliant woman.

—*Stephen Greenblatt*

DOI 10.1215/0961754X-7312669

Originally published in *Common Knowledge* 20.3 (Fall 2014): 495.

Paul Feyerabend, *Philosophy of Nature*,
trans. Dorothea Lotter and Andrew Cross, ed. Helmut Heit and Eric Oberheim
(Cambridge: Polity, 2016), 260 pp.

"Anything goes," Feyerabend famously quipped in his controversial 1975 classic,
Against Method, making the point that there is no universal, rational method by
which science advances and that, consequently, scientific knowledge cannot be
regarded as better than any of the alternative systems of knowing the world that
are incommensurable with science. Feyerabend remained at the time under the
influence of Karl Popper, with whom he had worked in the 1950s, believing that
theoretical pluralism was the path to scientific progress. But the strongly negative criticism of *Against Method* ultimately led to Feyerabend's radicalization, to

his development from critical rationalist to epistemic anarchist. Many failed to understand this change: was it merely a sociocultural idiosyncrasy, due to time spent at Berkeley?

Twenty-two years after his passing, a clue to the puzzle presents itself in *Philosophy of Nature*, the first part of a planned but unexecuted trilogy, the typescript of which was discovered providentially in 2004 at the University of Konstanz, in a folder hidden under Feyerabend's dissertation, and then published in 2009 in German. Here is a historical account of the ways in which prehistoric art and mythology represent fully worked-out worldviews, holistic and context-sensitive and sensual, as opposed to the abstract, context-independent metaphysics that followed. The Homeric-mythical worldview, Feyerabend contends, set out to describe the cosmos, rather than simply to convey logical relations, as Lévi-Strauss and classical structuralism would have it. Myth ultimately was defeated not by arguments but by history, *logos* replacing *mythos* by happenstance, rather than by reason on its imagined path to cultural and moral progress. Only by carefully exploring myths, archaeology, and early Greek art could Feyerabend demonstrate the idea that even the putative rules of reason are unable to make any essential distinction between science and nonscience. History had come to the philosopher's rescue, but the rise of rationalism in Greek antiquity emerges, in this account, as a disastrous development.

His unfinished project nearly drove Feyerabend crazy: "Damn the *Naturphilosophie*," he wrote in a letter to Imre Lakatos. Feyerabend's radicalization, which led the journal *Nature* in 1987 to dub him "the Salvador Dali of academic philosophy and currently the worst enemy of science," is now established as clearly less a sociocultural quirk and more the result of sustained, serious (though not faultless) historical research. Feyerabend was and is a force to contend with, and in the "post-truth" environment of the present day more so than ever.

—*Oren Harman*

DOI 10.1215/0961754X-7312681

Originally published in *Common Knowledge* 24.3 (September 2018): 452–53.

Amir D. Aczel, *The Artist and the Mathematician:*
The Story of Nicolas Bourbaki, the Genius Mathematician Who Never Existed
(New York: Basic Books, 2007), 256 pp.

Aczel takes the vagaries of Bourbaki as an emblem for those of structuralism as a whole. A group of French mathematicians set out in the 1930s to produce a final synthesis of all of mathematics based on set theoretical foundations—all to be published under the collective pseudonym of N. Bourbaki. The group did issue impressive work, but it now appears in retrospect like a dead end. Bourbaki was founded, and then judged, on the false criterion of finality. If you aim for a theory of everything, so as to end all theory, you will fail and put in question the quest itself. But is that quite fair? It is not that theories of everything do not exist, any more than Bourbaki does not exist. What they are is nonunique. There are *plenty* of such theories. We should not expect any particular theory of everything to be the last one: the infinite richness of the mathematical universe demands not one theory of mathematical everything, but many. The same, of course, is true for the infinite richness of humanity. We should therefore have many theories of human everything: many structuralisms.

Works of popular science must decide on a balance between intellectual weight and accessibility. Aczel chose accessibility, to the point where one no longer can tell just what it was that was meant to become accessible. The name-dropping of terms like *cohomology* and *algebraical geometry* resonates and titillates, leaving no knowledge in its wake. What remains are mostly biographical vignettes . . . which brings to mind a paradox. Why are the biographies of modern academics so boring, while the genre of the academic novel is so full of charm? It appears that the modern research university has constructed the most predictably boring form of life. It sets up the perfect setting for the comedy of bourgeois boredom—while academic biographies remain as interesting as the CVs on which they are patterned.

—*Reviel Netz*

DOI 10.1215/0961754X-7312693

Originally published in *Common Knowledge* 16.2 (Spring 2010): 287.

Denys Turner, *Thomas Aquinas: A Portrait*
(New Haven, CT: Yale University Press, 2014), 312 pp.

Professor Turner believes that Aquinas was one of the few minds in history large enough to contain a coherent universe of thought. "Thomas," he writes, "is in that company to which Dante, Plato, Shakespeare, Homer, and perhaps a few others belong." Turner's enthusiasm for his subject infects the reader, and the vivacity of his style makes the reading easy. He brings out the contemporary relevance of Aquinas's thought, and he avoids encumbering his text with scholastic terminology. Not that Turner ignores the medieval context of Aquinas's ideas—far from it. He constantly contrasts the saint's thought with that of his Christian contemporaries. While others, Platonically, regarded human beings as souls imprisoned in bodies, Aquinas, materialistically, insisted that human persons were animals of a particular kind and that a disembodied soul would no longer be a person.

While other theologians, following the Song of Songs, described the relationship between God and man in erotic terms, Aquinas, following Aristotle's *Ethics*, took friendship as the guiding concept.

Turner sums up accurately key elements of Aquinas's philosophy, wisely avoiding the topic of Being. In theology he is not afraid to present a full-frontal view of the most difficult theses, such as the claim that the persons of the Trinity are subsistent relations (pure relations that are not relationships *between* anything) and the claim that divine grace, though irresistible, does not constrain human freedom. Despite the genius of Aquinas and the skill of Turner, only those who are already believers are likely to find these sections convincing. Turner is at his most persuasive when discussing Aquinas's character. He points out that the great *Summae* are completely devoid of ego. In other philosophers (such as Descartes and Kant) and other saints (such as Augustine and Bernard), the author's personality constantly intrudes. Not so with Thomas: he is a teacher, invisible, standing out of the light that others may see. It is fitting that he was canonized not for working miracles but for writing the *Summa*. The Saint's sanctity shows itself above all in his silence about himself.

—*Anthony Kenny*

DOI 10.1215/0961754X-7312057

Originally published in *Common Knowledge* 21.2 (April 2015): 339–40.

John Lynch, *New Worlds: A Religious History of Latin America*
(New Haven, CT: Yale University Press, 2012), 384 pp.

It is not uncommon to see in some remote church in Mexico or Peru a solitary Indian worshiper gazing up in a fervor of devotion at the image of an elaborately dressed Virgin Mary or a suffering saint. What exactly is the nature of popular religion in the Latin America of today? How did a few thousand Spaniards, brusquely intruding in the sixteenth century on an alien world, succeed in converting millions of lost souls to their faith, and how closely did that faith, as it took root in its new surroundings, conform to the beliefs and practices brought by the intruders from their native Christendom?

These are questions that have long occupied historians of the European conquest and colonization of central and southern America and students of Latin American religion, both past and present. There is an enormous literature on what was once known as the "spiritual conquest" of the New World, but it now tends to be seen more as a process of persuasion, coercion, and mutual adaptation leading to the development of hybrid religious forms. Similarly, much has been written about the development of the institutional church in the societies of colonial Iberian America, its clashes with the secular power, and its legacy to the new nations that emerged from the independence movements of the early nineteenth century. Surprisingly, however, there has been no adequate English-language survey covering the history of religion in Latin America during the five centuries between the arrival of the Europeans and the present day. This is what John Lynch, formerly professor of Latin American history in the University of London, has set out to provide.

He has done so with great efficiency, synthesizing a vast body of literature while offering trenchant observations of his own. Inevitably, parts of the story will be familiar to many readers, but even the more familiar parts are enlivened by well-chosen contemporary quotations. We are told, for instance, how the eighteenth-century Indian keeper of a toll bridge shouted abuse at a friar who forced his way through at gunpoint. His choice of words—"Hey Friar, you Spaniard, you Jew, you renegade!"—vividly captures the complexities of a confusing colonial world. As Lynch comments: "Indians of South America caught the virus of anti-Semitism from colonists from Spain."

A central argument of the book is that "religion and culture are not the same thing. And a society can acquire a new religion without abandoning its previous behavior, language, customs, works of art, and traditions." The story thus becomes one of juxtaposition, in which "Spaniards preserved their religion without surrendering to cultural relativism, and Indians clung to reserves of their own culture without challenging Christian beliefs." I am not convinced that this summary adequately explains the complex processes at work. The book unfortunately has nothing to say about the religious art and architecture that developed in these colonial societies and that suggest a degree of mutual adaptation to an evolving ethnic and social environment that goes rather further than mere juxtaposition. Lynch is surely right, however, when he goes on to say that "the association of old and new gave popular religion a Latin American identity—and a diversity—not easily classified and not immediately recognizable to Spanish newcomers in America."

The later part of the book traces both this distinctively Latin American popular religion and the relationship between the church and governments, including the government of the church itself in Rome, from the advent of independence to the coming of liberation theology in the later twentieth century. Given the diversity of Latin American states and societies, this undertaking requires an examination of developments in each Latin American nation in turn, as priests and hierarchy wrestle with ways of responding to the succession of challenges presented by liberal regimes, social oppression, economic development, and the rise of the twentieth-century dictators. There is much interesting material here, and several suggestive points of comparison, but readers may well find themselves flagging in the course of this extended ecclesiastical tour. Even so, however, they can be grateful to have been placed in the hands of such an expert tour guide, whose book will be consulted as an essential compendium of information on Latin American religion for a long time to come.

—*J. H. Elliott*

DOI 10.1215/0961754X-7312069

Originally published in *Common Knowledge* 19.3 (Fall 2013): 159–60.

Rohan Bastin, *The Domain of Constant Excess: Plural Worship at the Munnesvaram Temples in Sri Lanka* (New York: Berghahn, 2002), 254 pp.

Every undergraduate who has taken a "world religions" survey course has heard the cliché that Hinduism is the most successfully syncretistic of the major religious traditions. Hindu iconography, theology, and ritual are well known for absorbing and integrating aspects of other religious traditions and coexisting with multiple and manifold layers and versions of "the sacred." But it is a very useful exercise to look carefully into the messy details of how the process of syncretism actually operates in contemporary Hindu social reality. It is particularly useful in a time when we have all been invited by inescapable global realities to look seriously at how competitive religious ideologies too often interact with consequences that are anywhere from difficult to disastrous.

Bastin's book is a detailed ethnographic analysis of the social reality surrounding a prominent Hindu temple complex in western Sri Lanka. His research was conducted in the mid-1980s to the mid-1990s, during the height of the Sinhalese-Tamil conflict on the island. A significant ritual and social site to both Sinhalese Buddhists and Tamil Saivites, Munnesvaram is portrayed by Bastin as an architecturally, ritually, socially, aesthetically, theologically, and politically functional model of the sacred as a multilevel "blossoming or unfolding" of complexity, diversity, and multivocality. In opposition to characterizations of the sacred as univocal, static, and transcendentally oriented, the Munnesvaram temple complex is a real-world demonstration of a "religious" institution that functions as a model of the sacred as inherently dynamic. A core notion in Bastin's analysis is that it is the often imperfect embrace of diversity, complexity, and contradiction—rather than the purified yearning for unity, simplicity, and order—that provides the social power of Hinduism and the Hindu temple. Through careful descriptions of bathing rites, flag-hoisting rituals, firewalking, trance possession, and ritual processions, Bastin's book describes how the ability to integrate and recognize multiple and competing societal voices without a need for ultimate synthesis, consensus, or reconciliation enables social order even in the midst of religious conflict and other serious disorders. For those of us who lean toward reading "theoretical" texts, the combination of delicacy and crudity that this kind of ethnography brings to ideologically based social problems is like a cleansing of the palate. One can easily forget, in the midst of too much abstract speculation, that human social reality runs happily roughshod over most carefully developed political and philosophical distinctions.

—*Andrew P. Tuck*

DOI 10.1215/0961754X-7312081

Originally published in *Common Knowledge* 10.1 (Winter 2004): 159–60.

Robert B. Pippin, *After the Beautiful:*
Hegel and the Philosophy of Pictorial Modernity
(Chicago: University of Chicago Press, 2014), 184 pp.

A felicitous conjunction of Hegel and Manet in the philosopher Robert Pippin's book *After the Beautiful* has confirmed my belief that chance determines the order in which objects, categories, and constructs receive our critical attention. Nothing necessitates the choice of Manet as primary modernist other than a fait accompli. As Pippin would have it, this is "the usual way." Just as the status of Hegel is our intellectual inheritance, our historical chance and fate, so is the status of Manet on the sensory side. If art, philosophy, culture, and the social order have a history (singular or multiple), we can only hope that things are going somewhere better than here and now. And even if it were a turn for the better, the route from our present unease to our future satisfaction can be neither predicted nor logically reconstituted, yet Pippin refers to "the trajectory of modernist art" as if the course were set. Chance events lead to contradiction if we insist on sorting them out. Luckily (ironically), we have a concept of chance at hand, as well as allied concepts of tragedy and comedy; these rational notions dissuade us from applying reasoned analysis to chance itself. Those who accept chance leave explanation aside and get on with life as best they can.

After the Beautiful is a beautiful—that is, an artfully elaborated—thought experiment, a grand hypothetical. Without fulfilling the aim, Pippin argues for the value of applying Hegelian discourse to the morass of our "conflicting commitments in intellectual, cultural, and political life." He notes that analogous conflict marks the "aesthetic experimentation that seemed to begin with Manet," which critics have labeled "modernist painting." Manet's experiment in painting (and its aftermath in Picasso, Pollock, and others) is Pippin's would-be target of, and partner in, his experiment in critical philosophy. I say that Pippin does not actually do what he proposes because he remains on a theoretical plane, never identifying the particularity or historicity of our conditions of moral conflict or laying claim to a specific definition of "modernism." He is nearly mute on such matters, yet inconsistently so. At the start of his introductory chapter, he states that the characterization or periodization known as "modernist" is "highly contested"; at the end of the same chapter, he refers to "the usual way in which all modernist art is characterized." Which is it? Both statements are passive, leaving the reader in want of sources to check. On the topic of modernism, Pippin implies that a broad consensus as well as its utter lack constitutes our situation—a fine Hegelian contradiction.

According to Pippin, a Hegelian sense of the inherent contradiction in all identities—the tension, say, between the body-self in itself (perceived as sensation, emotion, feeling, *existence*) and the mind-self for itself (perceived as intellection, conceptualization, discourse, *meaning*)—has the potential to ameliorate, or at least alter, the vexed situation of modernism. "What is the meaning of existence?" a modernist asks, with little expectation of a definitive answer. Pippin asserts what few would dispute: whatever else it may be, modernism is a process of change. He prefers to use Hegelian discourse in a process-oriented way, rather than directing it to a "triumphalist" end. Hegelian discourse may not change the world of modernity any more than it terminated conflict in the philosopher's own era, but it will affect the way we negotiate our course *through* modernity, and the resulting habits of thought may well amount to historical change. Our thinking alters our art, if not our existence, just as our art affects our thought. Neither changes chance.

Pippin has selected painting, a concrete rhetoric, as the primary modernist art. For the same role, he could have chosen philosophy, an abstract rhetoric, but he did not. Beyond or beneath the discursive thought associated with it, a painting is a material thing. So when critical thinking uses pictorial art as its medium, it must not only change itself but also affect something physical, or at least change the relation of thought to the physical and sensory. Hence Pippin's attraction to and adaptation of Michael Fried's art history, which has a strong phenomenological basis. Modernism puts the lie to Hegel retrospectively, to the Hegel who believed that the project of sensory, physical art had run its course, having become "a thing of the past." But, again, what is this modernism that we find pictured or exemplified in "modernist painting"? Everyone acts as if everyone knows, though no one is talking, least of all Pippin. (I suspect that he could venture a definition if he were so inclined.) For his art-historical modernism, Pippin relies on only two figures, Fried and T. J. Clark; their modernism is the painting lineage fathered by Cézanne and grandfathered by Manet. Manet is crucial to both Fried's phenomenology and Clark's social history—two bodies of academic study that Pippin regards as recto and verso of a viable modernist critique. But why does he trouble himself with Cézanne, who is not central to the analysis presented in *After the Beautiful*?

It is Heidegger, whom Pippin introduces primarily as a philosophical foil to Hegel, that motivates Cézanne's inclusion. Although the evidence is sketchy, Heidegger appears to have appreciated Cézanne for his radically earthy art. "Earthy" is my colloquial way of referring to Cézanne's dogged pursuit of the most fundamental sensations. Of course, "earthy" resonates with "Heidegger," and one of Pippin's best insights pertains to Heideggerian elements he perceives in Cézanne: "If there is something to the notion of a struggle, or *Streit*, between earth [existence] and world [meaning] in painting, then in Cézanne's paintings of bathers . . . earth is 'winning.'" There may be more "history" realized here than Pippin would imagine, for the notion that in Cézanne "earth is winning" was the opinion of the painter's most astute observers around 1900. Cézanne's art was earth, matter, sensation, existence. The compelling rhythms of his marks caused commentators to wonder what this turn from refined conceptualization to brutish materiality might signify. Cézanne's turn displaced the theme of beauty by the sensation of beauty—beauty that remains *after* "the beautiful," after the concept of the beautiful ceases to function—and it occurred in the art of a well-educated, affluent, high-bourgeois individual. In short, Cézanne was a Manet who was not acting like one. The material beauty of Cézanne's painting, off the scale of cultural norms, spurred critics to imagine what the moral value to society might be when a practice of painting becomes amoral.

Hegelian philosophy may have once celebrated its own triumph, but Pippin applies it now to a different end. We creatures of the twentieth and twenty-first centuries have found our triumph in accepting indeterminacy—that is, endless contradiction. So there is nothing perversely anti-Hegelian in extending Hegelian discourse beyond the era during which it should have fulfilled itself and expired. Every generation is triumphalist, even if its triumph consists in concluding that tensions in the human soul never attain resolution: to live is to be unfulfilled and unresolved. We continue living, nevertheless. Similarly, every generation finds some degree of adequacy in its art, and even some beauty; such discoveries are not mistaken, despite a following generation's exposure of inadequacies and failings in the art that it inherits. Each new generation desires a more satisfying form of communicative expression, the "social intelligibility" that Pippin (along with Fried and Clark) discovers in the incompleteness of modernist art. The notion of "social intelligibility" is attractive, yet the circularity of Pippin's intellectual confection nags at me. Was not modernism—identified with social contradictions and pictorial ironies—a Hegelian construct to begin with? Has not modernist art history been inhaling Hegel all along, even if only second hand?

I stumble backward over what Pippin calls "practical contradictions," or (as I might say) logical tragedies, our indeterminate troubles with our words. Pippin features a certain Hegelian principle, directing it from the logical toward the pragmatic: "All things are in themselves contradictory." As an example, consider that existence is not the meaning of existence. From a pragmatic perspective, there ought to be more to life than mere existence. Putting it as a logical abstraction: though A must be the same as A (A is A), A cannot be the same as A (A is not A), if only because one A is displaced from the other, analogous to the way that meaning is displaced from existence. The more we think, the less we know. Can I imagine my nonexistence? I do not know. Whatever sits on the other side of a sign of equivalence or translation (the word *is*, the symbol =), whatever has been carried across this copulative breach in language, must have become different in either existence or meaning; otherwise, we face the contradiction constituted by a thing existing and the same thing being meaningless (as it were, meaning nothing, that is, not existing). Wittgenstein writes in the *Tractatus*: "To say of *one* thing that it is identical with itself is to say nothing at all." One A is the thing as it is, as we feel it; the other A is the same thing in its meaning, as we conceive of it (perhaps nonexisting). With sensory feeling being personal and with conceptual meaning being social, the one cannot be the other. This lack of equivalence is reality—a practical political dilemma as well as a logical contradiction.

Pippin's book leaves me wondering what kind of society I might be living in if I were no longer to find contradiction, negative equivalence, nonexcluded middles, and every variety of change so very familiar, at-home, assuring, comforting. Would I be a nonmodernist living under modernism—a social misfit, a nonentity, a nonexistent? I suppose that, from a Hegelian perspective, contradiction indicates my intellectual freedom, if not some sensory freedom. An ideologically rigid society would tolerate no contradiction. Yet such conclusions come all too easily. I fear that our collective academic enterprise has become stuck in its beloved, but invariant, principle of change. The alternative is not stasis but chance. Academics: loosen up.

—*Richard Shiff*

DOI 10.1215/0961754X-7312093

Originally published in *Common Knowledge* 22.1 (January 2016): 1–4.

Stéphane Hessel, *Time for Outrage!* trans. Damion Searls with Alba Arrikha (London: Quartet, 2011), 40 pp.

... then, maybe, Nap Time and—when we grow up—Happy Hour?

—*Jeffrey M. Perl*

DOI 10.1215/0961754X-7314537

Originally published in *Common Knowledge* 18.2 (Spring 2012): 381.

LITTERAE HUMANIORES

Belle Randall

"Hello," she called out breathlessly, pulling off her wide-brimmed hat, setting on the mantlepiece the baby wrapped in green tissue-paper and fern, not noticing until she spun around that the room behind her was infested with angels. An angel lounged on the Victorian sofa. Another stood, arms crossed, beside the mantle mirror. Still another loitered in the doorway of the dark vestibule, leaning on the handlebars of a bicycle.

All were identically dressed in the manner of a boy she had known in school whose phobia of germs had caused him to wear only white. They wore white cotton shirts and white denim pants fastened at the ankles with bicycle clips. Each had a black leather band strapped around one wrist. All wore dark glasses the color of a river in the shade. Their handsome, muscular faces were somehow too clean-shaven.

The bicycle clips recalled another kind of angel—not these handsome young men, but the cupie with wings who rides the back of playing cards. Someone had once told her the name of that angel. Remembering it, she went to the one who stood at the mirror, his body poised in an attitude of perpetual readiness, like a cardboard cutout in an advertising display.

"Hermes," she said, holding out her hand; immediately he sprang to life.

Originally published in *Common Knowledge* 3.1 (Spring 1994): 10. © 1994.

DOGS

Aldo Buzzi

Translated by Ann Goldstein

The bells of St. Paul's Basilica rang without interruption, anything at all was good for distraction—chatter, the radio, the newspaper. When the hairdresser entered for a moment, to get something, or simply to be seen, her pink smock, unbuttoned in the back, had the effect of a gust of wind: all the trees tossed, the leaves rustled, dry branches fell to the ground.

A dog came in, hesitating, and looked around. Perhaps he was searching for something or . . . It's not easy to understand what a dog is thinking, perhaps he was simply deafened by the bells. The barber carefully put down his razor, went over to the dog, and, with his arm outstretched, showed him the door. And when the dog did not obey quickly enough he gave him a kick. Weeping, numbed, the dog flew out of the shop and everyone smiled with satisfaction.

As soon as the dog was outside, he disappeared among the buses carrying tourists to the basilica—vanished, forgotten. What had driven him to enter the shop, who or what he was looking for, what he would have done if he had found the object of his search, where he was going now, yelping, were questions destined to remain without answers. The tourists, descending from the buses by the

Originally published in *Common Knowledge* 3.1 (Spring 1994): 186–88. © 1994.

Common Knowledge 25:1–3

DOI 10.1215/0961754X-7299546

hundred, had probably buried him under the avalanche of their light-heartedness. Because for them everything is fine: the bells ring joyously, and we are the extras who, for nothing, animate the background of the basilica—one cutting hair, one giving kicks, one weeping, one gesticulating in the Italian fashion.

It was Saturday, I had to fill out the coupon for the soccer pool.

I go to eat up on the Volpi hill, I'll do the coupon afterward. A dog passes me, walking at a good pace—he knows exactly where he's headed. In order not to deviate from his precise direction, he just grazes me, and now, suddenly, he stops, one paw raised off the ground as if he were posing for a photograph. What is he thinking? What could have come into his mind to make him stop?

The dog remained on three paws for only a few seconds. His brain had worked—had reflected, pondered, and come to a decision: he made an about-face and returned quickly, retracing his steps and grazing me again, and I could look him in the face, a face not only intelligent, compared to the louts I meet in the bar, but also amiable.

The carabiniere signaled me to stop. Inside the little shop was the tailor: he had slid off the chair in an unseemly way and was being supported under the armpits by a friend. He was staring at me with his eyes wide open. He was looking at me but he did not see me, he was looking *beyond*. "He's in a bad way," they said. "You'll have to take him to the hospital." "But can't you see that he's dead?" I said. A woman who had come over let out a cry, the carabiniere nodded to me to go, immediately . . . to play the soccer pool. Ah, if only dogs could speak, or man could bark!

But why not play the pool the other days of the week, in tranquillity, without seeing anyone? The old dog in the trattoria, sitting to my left, looked at me as if he were ready to tell me something. I threw him a piece of bread. He followed the trajectory of the bread with his eyes but did not move. He wasn't hungry, he wanted to speak to me.

The fruit arrived. The dog continued to hang on my words, he wanted to make contact. The poor old . . . animal had in his life received innumerable kicks, plus beatings, pans attached to his tail, attempts to poison him with meatballs, to burn him alive with gas, as they do in China during the carnival. He, perhaps precisely because of the kicks and all the rest, had a look so penetrating that there was no need to speak. If I made the least nod with my chin he repeated it to show that he did not miss anything I did. Perhaps in the end it's a dog's life that gets the best results.

The bill arrived. The money went whistling out of the wallet, leaving in the air a trail of the scent of new money. I had to return to the bar, to do my duty, to play the soccer pool.

The bells of the basilica were ringing very loudly.

The barber put down the brush, picked up the razor with three fingers, and began to shave. He had before him the most docile client that had ever come between his hands: stretched out in the easy chair, immobile; of his face, all covered with soap, only the nose and eyes could be seen. The eyes were closed . . . forever. It was the tailor.

The barber took an old soccer coupon, cleaned the lather off the razor with it, and threw it into the wastebasket.

The row of street lights, seen in prospect, seems infinite. But if you follow the rule of walking under street lights without paying attention to them you reach the end of the row in a flash.

Reaching the end I realize I've simply been daydreaming. I remember now having met an old man so dark and wretched that he seemed to be only his shadow. He was walking in a hurry, on the edge of the sidewalk, stumbling, clutching to his chest a tattered lawyer's briefcase, and waving his right arm in all directions. When he passed close by, without seeing me, I realized that he was speaking out loud, arguing, fighting against a powerful enemy . . . hitting him.

I stopped and followed him with my eyes while he went away as if dragged by the fluttering of his arm, until he disappeared into the darkness.

FIFTY-SIX GUINEA PIGS
OVER THE GARDEN

(A Novella)

Péter Esterházy

Translated by Marianna Birnbaum et al.

In conclusion, I give an example. If it is not possible to speak openly about the '56 revolution, then the number 56 develops another meaning; it begins to shimmer and glow, or to pale and tremble; it takes on mythical overtones. So if the 56 guinea pigs appearing in the title take flight over the garden of our novel, then the poor understanding reader already pricks up his ears and takes up the scent like a hunting dog: surely we have reached something forbidden! Because of this, one is likely to forget, from time to time, the dreamy, sad, disillusioned lady in the garden.

By now the number has lost its force, its mystery, but if truly our novel *was* good . . . , before, . . . it wouldn't suddenly have become *bad* by the present

Originally published in *Common Knowledge* 1.1 (Spring 1994): 128. © 1994.

"Fifty-six Guinea Pigs Over the Garden" was jointly translated by Gloria Caris, Martha Cowan, and Sarolsa Takács under the supervision of Marianna Birnbaum at the University of California, Los Angeles.

Common Knowledge 25:1–3

DOI 10.1215/0961754X-7299606

time—just a little different. *Our novels have become historical novels.* And then the guinea pigs elegantly soaring above the garden can mean something now, too. . . . In all likelihood they call attention to this: that the woman is sad because of us, that we are the ones who have disillusioned her.

A MOUNTAIN FROM THE NORTH

Chapter XIV

László Krasznahorkai

Translated by George Szirtes

The stone they used to render the perfect surface of the courtyards and which, for a long time, they called *kogetsu* was not local but excavated at specially selected flint mines in mountainsides a good hundred nautical miles from here in picturesque Takagaso province, as well as at ever less significant sites, and it was there they ground it into tiny pieces using enormous millstones driven by mules, running regular trade trips to Kyoto, a city that cast its spell on the whole nation, the stone hauled to the grander monasteries by means of small carts, just as they did here in Fukuine district, tipping the small stones out behind the monastery on a neglected patch of ground somewhere between commercial buildings and the vegetable gardens, where specially designated young novice monks would bring heavy masonry hammers and set to reducing the stone to the requisite uniform size before carrying it into the courtyards and spreading it out so that after a storm or major downpour, or maybe just one dawn, as an act of gratitude for the arrival of spring, they might take their wide iron rakes and shape the white rubble

Originally published in *Common Knowledge* 20.3 (Fall 2014): 562–63. © 2014 by Duke University Press.

into parallel waves so it was no longer simply an idea but a true embodiment of a paradisal perfection which is like a representation of the restless western sea and the waves that here and there swirl about the ragged cliffs but is really the dream of a simple undifferentiated beauty that says we have everything and nothing, that the incomprehensibly terrifying speed that comprises objects and processes locked into an apparently necessary endless cycle of flashes and cessations may nevertheless persist with a brilliance that is as profound as the incapacity of language before an indescribably beautiful meaningless landscape, like myriad waves exactly like each other on the vast distances of the ocean, like a courtyard in a monastery where an even and serene surface sprinkled and carefully raked with white rubble might calm a pair of deeply startled eyes or an expression plunged into madness and a few precariously stable minds, and experience the way an ancient, now somewhat foggy idea can simply come alive, so it is suddenly obvious that there are no parts, only the whole.

BETWEEN WARS

Colin Richmond

Day One

The small party sailed out of Stralsund and through the Strelasund into the Kubitzer Bodden anchoring off Rudenhof for a light lunch. In the afternoon they sailed through the strait between Ummanz and Lieshow into the Koselower See anchoring for the night immediately off Teschvitz. The evening was spent at a gasthof in Gingst. There was a late return to the boat.

Day Two

Negotiating the narrow Gahlitzer Strom in the light of a misty dawn was not easy but they made the Udarser Wiek without incident. Taking provisions on board at Schaprode and purchasing a new night lantern at nearby Poggenhof they sailed northward to Seehof and then eastward into the Rassower Strom until passing the Wittower Fähre they sailed into the Breetzer Bodden. That evening they were off Breege where they made anchor. After supper aboard they walked along the Shaabe to Kegelinberg.

Originally published in *Common Knowledge* 9.2 (Spring 2003): 355–58. © 2003 by Duke University Press.

Day Three

In the morning they sailed south into the Grosser Jasmunder Bodden as far as Lietzow then turned west to lie up at Ralswiek where they went ashore to eat in the hotel at Buchberg. It was a lively lunch and all agreed that they had got to know one another much better after two days aboard. Was it the wine talking? After a siesta they set sail northward and explored the Tetzitzer See until the sun began to go down. They anchored off Grubnow and turned in early after the lightest of light suppers.

Day Four

They were away before daybreak retracing the route of Day Two as far as the Rassower Strom. They departed that stretch of water without entering the Buger Boden as some had wanted to do and with the Buker Hagen to starboard entered the Libben resolved to make the circuit of Hiddensee before the sun went down. This they only three-quarters achieved and were obliged to call it a day when they reached Plogshagen. Here they dropped anchor and somewhat wearily consumed the remainder of the beer and the remnants of sausage they had brought with them from Stralsund.

Day Five

Rising late they weighed anchor and with a refreshing breeze sailed into the Libben. They were too early at Dranske and somewhat regretfully agreed not to make a call there for provisions. It was a mistake as arriving at Kap Arkona in midafternoon they found that it was a strenuous walk to Putgarten in order to replenish their store of food and drink. The museum at Arkona and the cliffs of Jaromarsburg were their compensation. In the evening they sailed to Juliusruth and anchored there so that they might dine at a recommended hostelry in Altenkirchen. This they did once again overdoing both eating and drinking. The hike back to the boat was long remembered by them all as hilarious not to say gleeful.

Day Six

They sailed southeast during the morning giving both Glowe and Lohme a miss even though both villages looked inviting. Dropping anchor off the Grosse Stubbenkammer they partook of a quick lunch. Afterward they explored both Grosse and Kleine Stubbenkammer roaming inland as far as Herthaburg and the Kollicker Ort. Tired by their exertions and after some differences of opinion they sailed on southward to anchor for the night off Sassnitz where they enjoyed a late supper.

Day Seven

After an enormous breakfast at a *wirthaus* on the seafront at Klocker Ufer they hired a car and drove to Sagard which they looked around before driving on to Borchtitz. Here they left the car and explored on foot the railway sidings at Wostervitz and the ferry port of Neu Mukran. They watched while a boat from Memel came in and another left for Trelleborg. Returning to their car and driving back to Sassnitz it was after seven before they sat down to dine. Having missed lunch they were famished and did justice to all that was heaped before them at what they had been told was the best hotel in the place.

Day Eight

They once again rose later than they had anticipated. They sailed close along the shore of the Prorer Wiek lying up for lunch off Ostseebad Binz. In the afternoon they took their leisurely way southward passing Ostseebad Sellin and Ostseebad Baarbe. If they had been better informed they might have looked out for Kurt Schwitters at Sellin where he was busy making a hole on the Südstrand for his son Ernst to sit in. As it was they sailed blithely by. Making the Nordperd in the early evening they dropped anchor off Lobbe and walked into Middelhagen for dinner.

Day Nine

They weighed anchor at sunrise and were beyond Thiessow and into the Griefswalder Bodden before breakfast. At Gager they ate lunch at an inn near the summit of the Bakenberg. They climbed the hill in the afternoon before returning to the boat by making the circuit of the Gross Zicker. Sailing the short distance to Mariendorf in the evening they had their supper aboard. It had been a long and tiring day.

Day Ten

Rising late they agreed upon a relaxing day. They sailed into the Rüggischer Bodden between the Muglitzer Ort and Insel Vilm taking all morning to do so as the wind was light. Anchoring at Seglerhafen they packed what belongings they needed and took the train the short distance to Bergen. Here they lunched at the hotel they had booked into immediately on arrival and for the rest of the day wandered somewhat disconsolately around Rügen's principal town. They all said they missed the sea and went to bed early only partially consoled by an excellent dinner at their hotel.

Day Eleven

After a hearty breakfast they took the train back as far as Putbus where they descended because one of the party was reading Proust and wished to see a place whose name that writer had used for an importantly erotic character: Madame Putbus's maid. The little town pleased them so they stayed to lunch there. They were back on the boat at Seglerhafen before four so decided to sail to Zudar for supper. The Schoritzer Wiek was duly made by seven and they dropped anchor where they had intended. Having eaten supper aboard they played bridge until eleven.

Day Twelve

The trip was nearing its end. Everyone felt downcast. They sailed out of the Schoritzer Wiek with the lethargy that never fails to arrive on the last day of a holiday all have enjoyed. By lunchtime they were back into the Strelasund and they hove to off the Wussitzer Haken to finish off the last of their supplies. In the afternoon they sailed on past the Prosnitzer Schanze and Steinort arriving at Stralsund in good time for dinner. Goodbyes were exchanged that evening as most of the party were leaving early the following morning for Berlin. They drank schnapps until midnight when they fell into their bunks but not before promising one another that they would repeat the trip in 1924.

BIHAR COUNTY HOMECOMING

György Konrád

Translated by John Bátki

I have never known a girl more beautiful than Magda. As a little boy, I was in seventh heaven when she let me cuddle next to her sweet-smelling body on the guest bed at the Hotel Gambrinus in Hajduszoboszló. The first thing I did when I woke in the morning was to take a peek and see who would make that telltale movement that would let on they were only pretending to be asleep, trying to hide their presence in the waking world. Ever since I can remember I've always woken at six, while the others slept on, snoring slugabeds dug in like carrots and potatoes underground, waiting for the sun to shine on their bellies, not the least ashamed for being such sleepyheads, but in fact treasuring this prolonged bit of morning sleep—as did my sister Eva, and later in life, my wife. I could crow like a rooster, and they would dig in all the more, burrowing into the pillow those faces whose smiles one would so much like to see. This creates a little hiatus, a brief spell of time waiting to be filled.

So there's nothing finer in the morning than taking up diplomatic relations with someone, anyone who happens to be nearby—one of a succession of governesses: Annie, Hilda, or Livia, or best of all cousin Magda, the fairest of them all, blood of our blood, whose languorous application of suntan lotion one

Originally published in *Common Knowledge* 4.2 (Fall 1995): 154–57. © 1995.

Common Knowledge 25:1–3
DOI 10.1215/0961754X-7299582

could watch all day long; but this is not yet sunbathing time, this time smelling of dreams, when we love to inhale the scent of Magda's underarm, and sense the warmth of her motionless body, the stuff that dreams are made of. The two of us get along charmingly in the dawn, facing the splendid prospects of breakfast followed by the beach. However at night on the terrace of the Hotel Gambrinus I cannot help but notice that Magda has lost all interest in her veal cutlet and asparagus and ignores the curtain of sound provided by the famous jazz band from Budapest. She absentmindedly listens to my words and would much rather gaze at the man wearing yellow pants and a blue silk shirt. His pencil mustache, broad shoulders, soft shoes, and cloud of pipe-tobacco aroma all fill out the picture suggested by the unfamiliar designation of his profession that I overheard at table talk: "entrepreneur." I do not know what that means, but suspect it is something dubious. His name was Mr. Flóra, with his sportsman's air and strut, and he took Magda for rides in his sportscar over the great Hungarian plain.

Up in the hotel room Magda became subdued. Had this Flora been any good for her, she would have shared her happiness with me; singing the man's praises, but she never said a word about him. "I adore Roquefort cheese," Magda announced on the hotel terrace, and she placed her long, suntanned legs across my chair, wiggling those toes resplendent with nail polish. A napkin dropped to the floor, and Magda wrinkled her brow in concentration as she picked it up with her toes. There was something provocative in this newfangled enthusiasm of hers. "The riper the better," she concluded. Back home in Berettyóujfalu I had never eaten Roquefort, although I had heard that the real thing was consumed ripe and wormy. "Do you eat the worms?" I asked. Oh yes, she did; in fact the worms were the best thing about it! Having thus tossed the gauntlet at me, Magda regally turned away.

As for me, I loved that jazz band, I couldn't take my eyes off the band leader's elegantly tapping foot. At dinnertime I was deemed worthy of a dash of wine in my glass. The multicolored wicker lampshades swung in the breeze that had suddenly arisen. There's going to be a storm, said I, as Mr. Flóra asked Magda to dance: Stepping up with a self-confident swagger, he simply pulled her away from our table, forcing Magda off balance, making her dip forward as if bowing to this cheeky entrepreneur. He didn't even bother to join us at our table, or make an effort to ingratiate himself with me—after all, I did claim a share in Magda's affections, and I felt he should have consulted me. In which case I would have deigned to give the matter some thought, and decide the right thing to do.

The wind came roaring through the trees, snapping at the blue and white awning, and caught streaming strands of Magda's hair. She floated away from us, as if entering a different current. As she leaned back in the white sportscar she cast a parting glance at the neon sign of the Hotel Gambrinus above its lit-up menu. Mr. Flóra, having promised marriage, eventually abandoned her.

The small-town girl was not a particularly spectacular catch, although Uncle Dolfi's hardware store in Nagyvárad was a decent little business and would have provided a respectable little dowry. Then again, Flora must have been put off by the onus of her Jewishness: why should he become involved with a member of an undesirable minority? A few months after he jilted Magda, the girl, whose wisdom, alas, did not match her beauty, swallowed a fatal dose of sleeping pills.

And now it was Magda's brother, cousin László, coming to Nagyvárad from Bucharest in a black Chrysler Imperial for my sister and me. The automobile came complete with chauffeur when László purchased it from the previous owner, the former Queen of Romania. The driver was taciturn, reserved, unsmiling. I wouldn't say that he detested us, but his behavior indicated that he felt the measure of reverence owed to his new employer was far less than that due to the royal family. In other respects we found it natural that our cousin László was the new owner of the Romanian queen's former vehicle; why, given the opportunity he would have bought the throne, the crown, the royal palace itself. A former swimming champion, he was a robust forty-year-old with an assertive voice, had little patience with silly, petty matters, but displayed a thorough and sound judgment regarding important issues. He would have made a rather suitable king.

He did not put up with insults. The housewarden during the previous war year could testify to that. Cousin László had three downed American pilots hiding in the back room of his apartment, trusted to his care by the resistance movement. The housewarden, a man appointed by the authorities, whose role included that of police informer, somehow got wind of this and rang the doorbell one day. Cousin László hated to be interrupted at dinner. Here was the housewarden inquiring if there were any extra occupants in the apartment, such as houseguests perhaps. László replied in the negative. The housewarden insisted on seeing for himself. "Are you implying I am a liar?" Cousin László asked, standing in the doorway. The housewarden repeated his request. The response was a resounding slap in the face that knocked the man back to the banister on the stairway landing. László locked the door and resumed his dinner. The pilots, who witnessed the scene, expressed concern about whether they should move on. After a moment's thought László said, "That man is no fool. The slap he received conveys to him the balance of power. A slap of that magnitude signifies for him that the Germans will not be around much longer. That is the way his mind works. Ergo, he will not report us. After the war he will show up for his payoff and I will give him an amount of money. And he knows perfectly well that while he will get nothing in advance, his eventual reward is guaranteed."

And that is precisely how matters took their course. László stayed true to form; he ran his factory, and this involved frequent trips to Nagyvárad in the royal automobile. He saw to it that his business affairs linked his native town with Bucharest, and large shipments proceeded back and forth under his direction. For him the additional incentive of Nagyvárad was that his mistress resided there. She looked remarkably like his wife. Both were excellent women, ladies of the Jewish middle class, complete with a multitude of intricate rules and regulations, both of them confirmed believers in their modernity and enlightenment, in their ability to leave old-fashioned customs and conventions behind. The automobile suited them to a T, and so did László, who addressed them in the familiar mode (the equivalent of *tutoyer*), while they deferred to him by using the more formal manner of address. My head was big for my age, but when he placed his hand over me, it covered me like a cap. That great big car gave a groan and a bounce when Cousin László heaved himself into it.

It was as if my father had grown a foot taller and ten years younger, which would have been miracle enough. But the real miracle, the breathtaking one, was that here he was, tangible and loud, and not in a mass grave, or slumping on a concentration camp bunk, or wielding a pickaxe in some ditch, but here, radiant, holding out to me a larger-than-life hand covered with reddish-blond down from the height of his full stature—even though I knew full well that this wasn't my father, but Cousin László, only son of his sister Sarolta, László the engineer and cello player, horseman and factory owner, who would now take us under his wing and would from now on be in charge of our fate.

I don't think we even kissed each other: it seems he extended his big hand and pressed mine down a tiny bit. A great chief had entered the room and sat me down facing him. I asked him what was I to do, what was expected of me. He mused a bit and reached into his pocket to pull out a handful of large banknotes, far more money than I could have realistically needed at the time. "Keep reading, explore the place, and be sure to spend this. In a month, I'll be back for the both of you. I can't tell you much more right now." And he pointed at the bookcase.

So I was to live my life fancy-free. Yes, here at last was an offer I couldn't resist. Oh, I wouldn't be bored in Nagyvárad. In the evenings, when I sat in the empty apartment by the French windows opening on the balcony, it was the ecstasy of freedom that I tasted sipping my thimbleful of walnut liqueur, accompanied by fond thoughts of my cousin László.

SUCKLING PIG

A. L. Snijders

Translated by Lydia Davis

I often think about a photo that I've never seen. It was taken on New Year's Eve in 1926 in Yugoslavia. A man in a tuxedo is enjoying himself in a night club with two beautiful women in low-cut evening dresses. Under his arm he is holding a suckling pig. The women are laughing and he is too, the pig is not laughing, it is holding its mouth wide open, it is probably squealing. Now that I write it down, I realize that this is an expression: "to squeal like a pig." And I also realize that I never hear this expression anymore. The boy next door to us was often struck by his father, the walls were thin, at these times my mother would say: "He's squealing like a pig again." There was no television, she did not yet know which authority she should notify. Time slips away and takes language with it. The man in the tuxedo would become, in 1938, the father of the poet Charles Simic. He had acquired the pig through his dexterity. At midnight the lights went out, and to celebrate the new year a suckling pig was released. In the rising chaos within the fault zone of 1926/27 he was able to capture the little creature. The lights went on again, he was congratulated and got a piece of rope which he tied around the pig's foot. After that, the party went on till daybreak and ended in a nondescript bar where a drunken priest was uniting a young pair of lovers in matrimony. He crossed a knife and a fork to bless them. Charles Simic's father gave them the little pig as a wedding present.

Originally published in *Common Knowledge* 21.3 (September 2015): 541–44.

Common Knowledge 25:1–3

DOI 10.1215/0961754X-7299594

THIRTEEN POEMS

Wisława Szymborska, Jee Leong Koh, Yusef Komunyakaa,
Samuel Menashe, Gunter Eich, Thom Gunn, Miroslav Holub,
Darrel Alejandro Holnes, Luis Garcia, Ewa Lipska,
Grzegorz Wróblewski, Belle Randall

Foraminifera

Well then, let's take the Foraminifera.
They lived, since they were, and were, since they lived.
They did what they could since they were able.
In the plural since the plural,
although each one on its own,
in its own, since in its own
small limestone shell.
Time summarized them later
in layers, since layers,
without going into details,
since there's pity in the details.
And so I have before me
two views in one:

Originally published in *Common Knowledge* 16.1 (Winter .
2010): 137–38. © 2010 by Duke University Press.

Common Knowledge 25:1–3
DOI 10.1215/0961754X-7299618

a mournful cemetery made
of tiny eternal rests
or, rising from the sea,
the azure sea, brilliant white cliffs,
cliffs that are here because they are.

—*Wisława Szymborska*
Translated by Clare Cavanagh

Pull the drawstring to close the sea into a lake

Pull the drawstring to close the sea into a lake.
The sea is wild but one can walk around the lake.

This small country is famous for its new bird park.
Wings clipped, the pink flamingoes flower on the lake.

These birds of paradise are trimmed to map the walks
so that their orange flames direct you to the lake.

A naked flame is dangerous. Replace the candle
with a lightbulb and hang the lantern over the lake.

The eye sees everything else at a proper distance.
The weathered sign says twenty miles more for the lake.

The lover stands in no location but his feet.
He is close to the lake. The lover is the lake.

To see flamingoes, flowers, flames as forms of sea,
you must strip to the skin and enter, Jee, the lake.

—*Jee Leong Koh*

Originally published in *Common Knowledge* 16.3 (Fall 2010): 566. © 2010 by Duke University Press.

In the Blood

Like Rimbaud in Ethiopia,
He slips his hands into doeskin gloves
Before touching barrels & trigger housings.
Cold steel burns Cosmoline & cerecloth,

As if to ignite the gunpowder
In his genes. "My great-granddaddy
Was at The Alamo," he loves to say.
But that never explained his lost twin brother,

The name his mother never stopped
Calling in her sleep, the one now ten miles away
In the same desert, surrounded with bullion
& automatic rifles. If they met

They'd slap each other on the shoulder,
Call the buyers barbarians, have caviar
In Monte Carlo, talk about Alma in Rio,
Facing each other like mirrors someone forgot to silver.

— *Yusef Komunyakaa*

Originally published in *Common Knowledge* 2.2 (Fall 1993):
103. © 1993.

Common Knowledge 25:1–3
DOI 10.1215/0961754X-7299642

Snide
Sly and Snide
Live in one house
When Sly comes in
Snide goes out
To snipe, deride—
No virtues win—
Nor can one hide
Vices from him

More to Come
A piece of your mind
Is no more than that
To give your all
You must call back
With yet another
Piece of your mind—
Unchanged, intact.

—*Samuel Menashe*

Originally published in *Common Knowledge* 11.3 (Fall
2005): 532–33. © 2005 by Duke University Press.

Names

Names with i
or names with o,
the effort to remember
consonants
seems beyond me.

It all hisses by
like the hiss on the phone,
like like.
I listen hard.
A lot of conversations
in the year 1200
concern me
but the pronunciation is different,
which throws me off.
Someone with a
is addressing me now,
a particular pressure of the hand
that I don't return,
a sip of wine
baked dry,
a leftover u,
an unavailing y.

—Gunter Eich
Translated by Michael Hofmann

"Namen," from: Günter Eich, Gesammelte Werke in vier
Bänden. Band 1: Die Gedichte. Die Maulwürfe. Herausgegeben von Axel Vieregg. © Suhrkamp Verlag Frankfurt am Main 1991. All rights reserved by and controlled
through Suhrkamp Verlag Berlin.

Common Knowledge 25:1–3
DOI 10.1215/0961754X-7299666

Ghost Neighbors

The uncomplicated joy
Of a Monday evening date:
After a meal together,
A flick that won't end late
—With special effect, wisecrack,
And Nazi spy to boot.
(We found the villain cute.)
Call it escape. I do.
And later riding back
Snugly behind my boy,
I touched his hips, my cheek
Grazing his shoulders too,
Solid beneath the leather.

But then I felt it change:
Climbing the streeted ridge
We met the ocean wind's
Perpetual attack.
And when it bit my knee,
Like a reviving pain,
I found my trap again,
My anger and cold dread
That my own home should be,
As I could picture, strange,
The upper unit's line
Of windows blanketed
Behind the lowered blinds,
Where they were getting ready,
My neighbors, to smoke crack.

Call it escape. They do.
From theirs I had made mine.

Originally published in *Common Knowledge* 1.3 (Winter
1992): 157. © 1992.

I held my temper steady
For the long night ahead
Of sleep broken by noises:
A fuss above my ceiling,
Something done in a hurry,
A sudden heavy tread,
Outbreak of squabbling voices,
Any old kind of feeling
—Laughter or sobs—a flurry
That rises to subside.

So Robert dropped me off.
Here is the house I love,
Top-heavy from outside
While blacked-out thus above
In the attempt to hide
All detail of a need
They try to fill—they try
And cannot satisfy,
Till it has turned to greed:
For, getting what they want,
It won't last long enough,
And so they must replace
It with itself, or face
Their busy emptiness
With which they occupy
This upper floor they haunt,
Bored with their own excess.

— *Thom Gunn*

The British Museum

To the tune of "Bolero,"
any ark
will be ruined
once, the trilingual
Rosetta Stone will be broken, steles of Halicarnassus
will turn to dust, sandstone Assyrian spirits
with eagle heads will take off shyly,
the carved man-head lions of Ashursirpolis will croak,
the last red-granite hand of the Colossus of Thebes
will drop off, the Indian supergod Harikaru
will cover his onyx eyes, the Rhind mathematical scrolls
will catch fire, the suspended Zen poems will evaporate,
and the green hellish judge from the Ming dynasty will whine.

For the time of stone is meted out
and so is the time of myth.

Only genes are eternal,
from body to body,
from one breed to another breed,
on Southampton Row
in fact
you find walking genetic codes of Egyptian mummies,
deoxyribonucleic acid of the man from Gebelin,
hereditary traits of the man from Lindow,
whose bodily receptacle, cut in half by a bulldozer,
successfully swells under a glass bell,
in Bloomsbury, in fact, you find
all the eternity of the world rushing around
buying black flowers
for the Last Judgment, less Last
than a midnight hotdog.

Originally published in *Common Knowledge* 1.2 (Fall 1992):
24. © 1992.

Common Knowledge 25:1–3
DOI 10.1215/0961754X-7299690

So the British Museum is not to be found
in the British Museum.

The British Museum is in us,
quite in the middle,
quite at the bottom.

—Miroslav Holub
Translated by David Young and Dana Hábová

Millennial

I didn't start this war or die in those towers
nor sweep into urns what remained.
I never bit the fruit, never swallowed its pit,
nor even wished for peace upon a thimble.
Yet like it even does to the mountains, this world's gravity
pushes me out of its nest. I'm afraid of flying, or falling
so a mental magic carpet will have to do as I search
for Neverland. I'm a lost boy tallying antiquity's thread count.
I'm a lost boy weaving million dollar textiles for minimum wage
and snorting the carpets' Disney—
Some *whole new world*, new hole world, old world new.
I'm a lost conquistador sailing the stars,
freewheeling through an endless diamond sky
beyond the open door to fishes as big as little boys' heads
filled with stories of flying I believed were true
back when hunger was just the name of a child on television
in commercials in between cartoons and cereal on a Saturday afternoon.
Fairy dust is the path back to Peter Pan.
I'm a lost boy loving Band-Aids and bruising others,
I'm a lost boy learning how to make blood spill itself,
I'm a lost boy staring at the television. Can't find the remote,
or find the Jolly Roger, and I've got to kill Cook,
got to sail past the sea of butchered bodies in our video game
somehow. I can't stop pulling the trigger
on the controller. A lost boy, I can't read
without my gun turning the page. A lost boy I can't
watch death tolls dance across the TV news headlines
without wanting to shoot the screen, without wondering
how I could post it on Facebook, without trying
to color it vintage on Instagram. A lost boy I can't stop googling
and tweeting myself. I break my own world news
and in the wonderland west of Sudan I can't stop clicking as if it's touching,
out west I can't stop social networking as if it's fucking. Breathe in
these poppers, link to my link, and blow an electronic fire

Originally published in *Common Knowledge* 21.3 (September 2015): 533–34. © 2015 by Duke University Press.

onto the abandoned car. Not even rain can wash us of our sins
or at least put out the flames. I drink but never drown
because my daddy owns the water park
and a lifeguard taught to me how to swim, hours late,
lights and trunks off, only our bodies and the stars.
We lost boys love drowning then saving each other.
We lost boys know how to bring back the dead.
We lost boys can't stop sleeping with fishes,
can't stop drinking like whales, swallowing men
like worms at the bottom of our shot glasses.
¡Pa 'rriba, pa 'bajo, pal centro, pa 'dentro!

—*Darrel Alejandro Holnes*

The Stranger

He comes to lend the sky
to a feather, to angels eating frost
and clowns eating stone.

His tongue is wet
with the saliva of bees
and his veins are filled
with a tulip's blood.

There are people who say
that he sleeps
in the bones of bad weather
or the secret places
where the water kneels.

The birds that lay their eggs
in the goblets of dawn
are perched on his fingers.

—*Luis Garcia*

Originally published in *Common Knowledge* 1.3 (Winter
1992): 173. © 1992.

God Asks

2001, dear Mrs. Schubert, is not only the beginning
of the new century, but also the number of my imagination.
As you know, for some time now my fiction
has resented my flirting with reality,
consorting with useless time.
I therefore inform you that the dead season is coming,
which, as usual, I am spending
on the short-term list of missing persons.

—Ewa Lipska
Translated by Robin Davidson

Common Knowledge 25:1–3
DOI 10.1215/0961754X-7299726

The Other Side

First there will come your parents and old
friends
Joyful they will stand in a circle around you
asking you to tell them about everything
in detail

When you are finally ready
they will leave to take a well-deserved rest
You will take their place then and you will
patiently wait
You will be joined by several other
people well-known to you

And then?
Then you will see the one who is going to replace you in the end
Joyful you will stand in a circle around him
asking him to tell you about
everything in detail

When he is finally ready
you will go to take a well-deserved rest
With you several other
people well-known to you
And thus it will all happily
come to an end . . .

— *Grzegorz Wróblewski*
Translated by Adam Zdrodowski

Originally published in *Common Knowledge* 13.2–3 (September 2007): 484. © 2007 by Duke University Press.

Dear Reader

Riffling backward through these pages seeking
an arresting image, a memorable line,
I feel you hovering outside my door.
Come in. Put down your pack. Rest a while.

How did I know you were lurking here?
Did I "used to be some kind of 'seer'"?
If you're asking did I ever hang a sign
with a diagram of an open palm—

You're standing under it.
Am *I* myself perhaps some kind of *reader*?
For you, the Lazyboy. Just lean back
And press the lever. There!

Can I bring you something?
Pepsi-Cola, bologna on white?
Oh I forgot, you've been to college.
My Wonder Bread's not good enough for you.

So tell me, how can I,
a tragic old woman, delight you?
Why should you linger
amid the bric-a-brac with me?

Give me your palm. I'll show you
a thing I learned in the Old Country.
                    Oh my God

Wherever you purchased this book,
take it back. Shut it at once and keep
it shut. Don't make me tell you
                what I see.

—*Belle Randall*

Originally published in *Common Knowledge* 10.3 (Fall
2004): 564–65. © 2004 by Duke University Press.

Common Knowledge 25:1–3
DOI 10.1215/0961754X-7299750

TWO HUNDRED YEARS TOGETHER

Alexander Solzhenitsyn

Translated by Jamey Gambrell

Throughout a half century's work on the history of the Russian Revolution, I have touched on the question of Russian-Jewish relations many times. Doing so has often served as a way into events and into human psychology, but the question has elicited heated passion.[1]

I have long hoped that some writer, before I myself had the opportunity, would shed light for us all on this difficult topic, and in a manner that is thorough, two-sided, and equitable. But mostly what we find are one-sided reproaches. On the one hand are accusations of Russian guilt, even of ancient Russian depravity, with respect to the Jews—these claims can be found in abundance. On the other hand, Russians who have written about this mutual problem have done so for the most part vehemently, with bias, and with no desire to see what might be tallied to the credit of the other party.

Originally published in *Common Knowledge* 9.2 (Spring 2003): 204–27, as part of the Seriatim Symposium "Peace and Mind." This material was originally published as "Vkhod v temu" and "Evreiskoie i russkoe osoznanie pered mirovoi voinoi" in the author's book *Dvesti let vmeste (1795–1995)* (Moscow: Russkii put', 2001).

1. I wrote the volume [from which this article is taken] in conformity with no dictate but that of the historical materials and [of my] search for benevolent decisions [that might be taken in] the future. It should be kept in mind that the condition of Russia [since I finished the Russian text in 1995] has changed so drastically in the last few years that the problem studied here has been forcefully thrust aside and has faded in comparison with other contemporary Russian problems. [Note added by Alexander Solzhenitsyn, 2000.]

Common Knowledge 25:1–3

DOI 10.1215/0961754X-7579425

The problem is not a dearth of journalists. There are many, especially among Russian Jews—many more than among ethnic Russians. However, for all the brilliant array of minds and pens, there has not appeared, to date, a representation or elucidation of our mutual history that could be met with mutual understanding.

Still, we must learn not to stretch the taut threads of this interwoven history to the tearing point.

I would be happy not to try my energies again on so sensitive a problem. But I believe that this history—the attempt to comprehend it—should not remain "forbidden." The history of the so-called Jewish question in Russia (and is it only in Russia?) is first and foremost *rich*. To write about it means to hear new voices and convey them to the reader. (In this work, Jewish voices will be heard more abundantly than Russian ones.)

To approach the problem, depending on the press of social currents, can feel like walking along a razor's edge. On both sides you experience every possible, impossible, and still developing reproach and accusation.

The feeling that carries me through this work on two hundred years of the Russian and Jewish peoples' lives together is the search for every point of common understanding and every possible route—cleansed of the bitterness of the past—into the future.

Like every other people, like all of us, the Jewish people is both an active subject of history and its suffering object; and it has often fulfilled, sometimes quite unconsciously, major tasks imposed on it by history. "The Jewish question" has been interpreted from many perspectives, always passionately, but often self-deceptively as well. After all, what happens to any people in the course of history is defined, not simply by that people itself, but also by the peoples who surround it.

The excessive vehemence of the two sides in this matter is humiliating for both. Though no earthly question can be unsuitable for thoughtful discussion, popular memory has, alas, accumulated many reciprocal offenses. Still, if we remain silent about events, then how will we heal the memory? Until popular opinion has found lucid expression, it will remain an indistinct (or worse, a threatening) hum.

We cannot turn our backs on the last two centuries. And the planet has grown so small that in any sector we are again neighbors.

I postponed writing this book for a long while and would be pleased not to assume the burden; but my time in life is growing limited, and I have had to take it on.

I have never conceded anyone's right to conceal events that have occurred. I cannot call for an accord based on unjust witness to the past. I call on both parties, Russian and Jewish, to engage each other with tolerant mutual understanding and in recognition that each has its share of sin. Though it would be so much easier to turn aside and say: Well, it was not *our* fault . . .

I am sincerely trying to understand both sides. To do so, I study events rather than [engage in] polemics.[2] My attempt is to *report*. I enter into arguments only in those unavoidable cases where justice is covered by layers of untruth. I dare to expect that I will not meet with the fury of the most extreme and irreconcilable; my hope is, on the contrary, that this work will serve mutual accord, that it will find well-disposed interlocutors among Jews and among Russians.

This writer understands his ultimate task as follows: to do all in his power to consider, on behalf of the future, mutually accessible and benevolent paths along which Russian-Jewish relations may proceed.

Jewish and Russian Identity before World War I

In Russia, during the single decade [of the twentieth century that] it was saved from destruction, the best minds among both Russians and Jews had time to look back, judge the essence of our common life from various perspectives, and give serious thought to the question of each people's culture and destiny.

The Jewish people had moved through the unsettled contemporary world with the comet's tail of its three thousand year diaspora. Jews never lost their constant awareness of themselves as a "nation without language and territory but with its own laws" [Solomon Lurie], and they preserved, through the strength of their religious and national intensity, their separate and distinctive nature in the name of a higher, suprahistorical idea. Did Jewry of the nineteenth and twentieth centuries strive to identify with and merge with the surrounding peoples? Russian Jewry actually preserved its self-isolation longer and later than its brethren elsewhere, concentrating on its religious life and consciousness. Yet, from the end of the nineteenth century onward, it was Russian Jewry in particular that grew stronger, multiplied, and blossomed—and thus "the entire history of Jewry in the new era developed under the sign of Russian Jewry," which possessed "an intense *sensitivity to the course of history*."[3]

2. Bracketed material in this article has been added, with the assistance of Naphtali Pratt (editor of the Russian-language *Jewish Encyclopedia*), where a non-Russian reader unused to the author's allusions and allusive style may require clarification or information. [Editor] In the text, Russian names are given according to commonly accepted spellings (Tolstoy, Dostoevsky, Soloviev, Gorky) or in order to make pronunciation easier for the reader of English. Citations of original publications in the notes, however, are given in the Library of Congress transliteration of the Cyrillic alphabet in order to convey historical sources accurately. In the text, for example, the reader will find the spelling Jabotinsky, while in the notes the same name is spelled Zhabotinskii. [Translator]

3. B. Ts. Dinur, "Religiozno-natsional'nyi oblik russkogo evreistva" [The religious-national face of Russian Jewry], in *Kniga o russkom evreistve: Ot 1860-kh godov do Revoliiutsii 1917* [Book of Russian Jewry: From the 1860s to the 1917 Revolution], ed. Jacob G. Frumkin, Gregor Aronson, and Alexis Goldenweiser (New York: Soiuza Russkikh Evreev [Union of Russian Jews], 1960–68), 319, 322, hereafter referred to by English titles.

Russian thinkers were confounded by Jewish segregation and, in the nine-teenth century, the question for them was how to *overcome* it. Vladimir Soloviev, who was deeply sympathetic to the Jews, proposed doing so through Russian love for them.

Earlier in the century, Dostoevsky had observed that a disproportionate animosity greeted his hurtful, though negligible, remarks on the Jewish people: "This animosity testifies vividly to how the Jews themselves view Russians . . . and [testifies] that among the causes of our separation from the Jews, perhaps the Russian people is not alone guilty . . . causes have of course accumulated on both sides, and it is still not clear on which side there are more."[4]

Ya. L. Teitel, from the same end of the nineteenth century, gives us the benefit of his observation:

> Jews are materialists for the most part. Their striving to acquire mate-rial goods is robust. But what disdain we see for these goods when their internal "self" or national dignity is at issue. One would think, why doesn't the mass of Jewish youth, which doesn't observe any rituals and often doesn't even know its national language—why don't they convert to Russian Orthodoxy, at least for appearances' sake: a move that would open wide the doors of all institutions of higher learning and would ensure all earthly blessings? *At least for the sake of education?—after all*, scholarship and higher knowledge are valued more highly among them than financial riches.[5]

But they have held, [Teitel continues,] to the idea of not abandoning their fellow tribesmen, who have lived in straitened circumstances. Teitel moreover says that Europe was not a happy alternative for Russian Jews: "Young Jewish students have felt uncomfortable in the West . . . German Jews have looked on them as an undesirable element, unreliable, noisy, untidy"—and the "French and Swiss Jews . . . have followed [German Jews] closely" in this opinion.[6]

Daniel Pasmanik, on the other hand, reminds us of a category of Jews who were forced to convert and thus held an even more bitter grudge against the authorities and feelings of hostility to them. (From 1905 on, the transition to Christianity was eased: conversion to Russian Orthodoxy was no longer the only option, and Protestantism seemed more acceptable in spirit to many Jews. Moreover, in 1905 the prohibition on reverting to Judaism was lifted.)[7]

4. Fedr M. Dostoevskii, *Dnevnik pisatelia* [Diary of a writer] (1876–1881; reprint, Moscow; Leningrad: GIZ, 1929), 78, chap. 2.

5. Ya. L. Teitel', *Iz moei zhizni za 40 let* [Forty years of my life] (Paris: Y. Povolotskii, 1925), 227–28, hereafter referred to by its English title. The italicized passage, interpolated by Alexander Solzhenitsyn in the quotation from Teitel, appears to be the former's paraphrase of the latter's argument. [Translator]

6. Teitel', *Forty Years*, 227–28.

7. *Evreiskaia Entsiklopediia* [Jewish encyclopedia], 16 vols. (St. Petersburg: Obshchestvo dlia Nauchnykh Evreiskikh Izdanii i Izd-vo Brokgauz-Efron [Society for Scholarly Jewish Publications and Brokgauz-Efron Publishers], 1906–13), 11:894, hereafter referred to by its English title.

Another writer concluded with bitterness in 1924 that, during the pre-Revolutionary decades, not only did the "Russian government . . . definitively count the Jewish people among the enemies of the fatherland," but "what is worse is that many Jewish politicians counted themselves among such enemies as well, hardening their hearts and ceasing to distinguish between 'the government' and the fatherland—Russia. . . . The indifference of the Jewish masses and the Jewish leaders to the destiny of Great Russia was a fateful political mistake."[8]

Needless to say, like any social process, this one—especially in an environment as diverse and dynamic as that of the Jewish people—did not follow a single course, but split; in the hearts of many educated Jews, it splintered. On the one hand, "belonging to the Jewish tribe gives the individual a certain specific position in the Russian environment."[9] But on the other hand, there is "a marvelous duality: the customary emotional attachment of quite a number [of Jews] to the surrounding [Russian world], their rootedness in it, and, at the same time, their rational rejection, their abhorrence of it across the board—infatuation with a hated environment."[10]

So tormented and ambivalent an approach could not help but bring tormented, ambivalent results. At the Second State Duma in March 1907, I. V. Gessen, denying that the bloody momentum of the [1905] revolution would continue and thus undercutting the right-wing pose of defending culture from anarchy, asserted [about Russian Jews that] "we [are] teachers, doctors, lawyers, statisticians, writers . . . you call us enemies of culture? Who will believe you, gentlemen?" And the answer shouted from the right was: "Of Russian culture, not of Jewish!"[11] Not enemies, the Jews, no, why use such extreme terms?—the Russian Right asked—but are you truly our wholehearted friends? The difficulty for [Russian-Jewish] intimacy was this question: how could these outstanding lawyers, professors, and doctors not have profoundly, preferentially Jewish sympathies? Could they feel themselves thoroughly Russian in spirit? And from this question arose a more complex one: could they take the interests of the Russian state to heart in full measure and depth?

In these same decades, the Jewish middle class moved its children from a religious to a secular education, specifically in the Russian language. Simultaneously, a strong print culture, which had not previously existed, developed in

8. V. S. Mandel', "Konservativnye i razrushitel'nye elementy v evreistve" [Conservative and destructive elements in Jewry], in *Rossiia i evrei* [Russia and the Jews] (Berlin: Osnova, 1924; reprint, Paris: YMCA Press, 1978), 201, 203, hereafter referred to by English titles.

9. D. O. Linskii, "O natsional'nom samosoznanii russkogo evreia" [On the national self-awareness of the Russian Jew], in *Russia and the Jews*, 142.

10. G. A. Landau, "Revoliutsionnye idei v evreiskoi obshchestvennosti" [Revolutionary ideas in Jewish society], in *Russia and the Jews*, 115.

11. Gosudarstvennaia Duma—Vtoroi sozyv [State Duma—second session], *Minutes*, Session 2, Meeting 9, vol. 1 (St. Petersburg: March 13, 1907), 522.

Yiddish, and the term *Jewishness* emerged, implying: let the Jews be Jewish and not assimilate.

An unusual path to assimilation, far from widespread but not insignificant either, was mixed marriage. Another, more superficial stream of assimilation was the adoption of artificial pseudonyms in the Russian style. (But *by whom*!—the Kiev sugar manufacturers "Dobryi" [Kind] and "Babushkin" [Grandmother's], who during the war were brought to trial for doing business with the enemy; the publisher "Yasnyi" [Clear], whom even the Cadet [Constitutional Democratic Party] paper *Rech'* [Speech] described as an "avaricious speculator," a "shameless, profiteering shark";[12] or the future Bolshevik David Goldendakh, who considered "all of Russia lacking in unique [qualities]" but himself assimilated as "Ryazanov" [from the town of Ryazan], and under that name, as a fixatedly Marxist theoretician, clouded readers' brains until his imprisonment in 1937.)

It was during these decades that Zionism developed, most powerfully of all in Russia. The Zionists harshly ridiculed assimilated Jews, whose heads were swelled with the idea that the destiny of Russian Jewry was inextricably tied to the destiny of Russia.

And here, we must turn above all to the brilliant and rather dramatic journalist Vladimir Jabotinsky, whose lot it was in the pre-Revolutionary years to express, not just aversion to Russia, but also words of despair. Jabotinsky thought of Russia as no more than a wayside inn for Jews on their historical circuit; he felt they had to move down the road to Palestine.

Jabotinsky wrote passionately: we [educated Jews] do not have dealings with the Russian people—we know Russia through its culture, "primarily through its writers . . . the highest, purest manifestation of the Russian spirit," and then we apply our judgment [of Russian high culture] to the entire Russian world. "Many of us, the children of the Jewish intelligentsia, are madly and humiliatingly in love with Russian culture . . . with the demeaning love of the swineherd for the tsarevna," whereas we know Jewry only in its commonness and narrowmindedness.[13]

Jabotinsky is merciless to assimilated Jews: "A multitude of slavish habits developed in our psychology during the russification of our intelligentsia," [he writes. We] "have lost the hope or desire to preserve Jewry untouched and are causing its disappearance from the stage." The average Jewish intellectual forgets about himself, thinks it better not to pronounce the word *Jew*: "It's not the right time." He is afraid, [Jabotinsky says,] to write "we Jews," and so writes, "we Russians" or even "our brother *rusak*": "A Jew can be a Russian citizen of

12. "P. G.," "Marodery knigi" [Marauders of the book], *Rech'* [Speech], May 6, 1917, 3.

13. Vladimir Zhabotinskii, *Fel'etony* [Feuilletons] (St. Petersburg: Gerold Tipografiia, 1913), 9–11, hereafter referred to by its English title.

the first order, but only a second rate *Russian*."[14] "From the moment when the Jew declares himself Russian, he becomes a second-class citizen," but all the same he "preserves a distinctive 'accent' of the soul." There was, [according to Jabotinsky,] an epidemic of conversion for profit, often for things far more trivial than a diploma: "thirty silver pieces of equality." On abandoning their faith, [he concludes, Jews] should not remain in their nationality either.[15]

The position of Jews in Russia (not at all times, but specifically after 1905–6) Jabotinsky viewed as hopelessly gloomy: "The objective advantage of all we associate with [living in] a foreign land has now turned against our people, and we are powerless and helpless." "We knew before that we were surrounded by enemies," [he wrote, but now Russia] "is a prison," "a barking kennel," "the prostrate and wounded body of defenseless Russian Jewry, persecuted and surrounded everywhere by enemies." "Six million [Russian Jews, he continued,] swarm in a deep pit . . . it is an era of slow torture, of a drawn-out pogrom." It even seemed to Jabotinsky that "newspapers supported by Jewish money" did not defend the Jews "in this era of unprecedented persecution." Then, at the end of 1911: "For the last few years, Jews in Russia have been sitting firmly in the dock"—we are not revolutionaries, [he said,] we "did not sell Russia out to the Japanese," and we are not like Evno Azef and Dmitri Bogrov.[16] Indeed, concerning Bogrov, Jabotinsky wrote: "Whatever he may have been personally, at the hour of his amazing end, this unhappy young man was abused by those ten boors from the cesspool of Kiev's Black Hundreds" who wanted to assure themselves that the murderer [of Pyotr Stolypin] had been executed.[17] ("Bogrov's *amazing* end"?!)

Over and over, turning his gaze on Jewry, [Jabotinsky wrote]: "We are culturally impoverished now, our hut is joyless, our way is stifling." "Our main illness is self-contempt, our basic need is to develop self-respect. . . . Scholarship

14. The words used here are, respectively, *rossiianin* (Russian citizen) and *russkii* (ethnic Russian). The adjective *rossiiskii* refers to the territory of Russia and/or the Russian state and citizenship; in addition to Russian ethnicity, *russkii* refers to the language, literature, and culture. Both are often translated into English as *Russian*, but the distinction is important, particularly in this context. Generally, where *rossiiskii* is used as distinguished from *russkii*, I have tried to translate the word or phrase as *Russian state* or *Russian citizen*. [Translator]

15. Zhabotinskii, *Feuilletons*, 16, 62–63, 176–80, 253–54.

16. Evno Azef, a Jew, was an exiled member of the Social Democratic Party, who was recruited as a spy for the Okhrana, the Russian internal security police. Asked to join the Socialist Revolutionary Party so that he could inform on its members as well, he was eventually exposed as an informer and fled to Germany, where he died during World War I. Dmitri Bogrov, a Jew and member of the Socialist Revolutionary Party, was also recruited as an Okhrana spy. But in 1911, possibly as an act of penance, he assassinated Pyotr Stolypin, minister of the interior, and was hanged the same year. [Editor]

17. Zhabotinskii, *Feuilletons*, 26, 30, 75, 172–73, 195, 199–200, 205. The Black Hundreds was a reactionary party that chose the Jews as scapegoats for the 1905 edict by which Nicholas II established the rudiments of a constitutional government. The Black Hundreds perpetrated major pogroms against the Jews in Kiev, Odessa, Yekaterinoslav, and Bialystok (and assassinated several important Russian liberals). [Editor]

on Jewry should become the heart of scholarship for us. . . . Jewish culture has become the only safe harbor of salvation for us."[18]

And this view can well be understood and shared (especially by us Russians today. . . .)

Jabotinsky did not judge those who assimilated in the past: in history, [he said,] "there are moments when assimilation has undoubtedly been desirable, when it has been a necessary stage of progress." A moment of that kind arose after the 1860s, when the Jewish intelligentsia was nascent and was absorbing its surroundings, a mature culture. At that time, [according to Jabotinsky,] assimilation was "not a rejection of the Jewish people, but on the contrary, the first stage of Jewish national initiative, the first step toward the renewal and renaissance of the nation." It was necessary to "assimilate what was foreign in order to develop one's own [self] with renewed strength." But half a century had passed, much had changed drastically, both without and within Jewry. The thirst for general education had become powerful, in any case; now the zeal for it was unparalleled. Now was the time for *Jewish* principles to be inculcated in the younger generations, [for] now there was a threat of tracelessly dissolving into a foreign culture. "Our sons are leaving with every passing day," [Jabotinsky wrote,] and "are becoming alien to us": our "educated children are serving every people on earth, except us; no one labors for any Jewish causes. . . ." "The surrounding world is too magnificent, spacious, and rich," [he continued;] we will not allow it to lure Jewish youth from the "unsightliness of Jewish existence. . . . Immersion in the national values of Jewry must become the main . . . element of Jewish education." "Collective responsibility . . . is the only thing a nation can hold on to" and renegade behavior slows down the struggle for Jewish rights. "Recently"— ah, so there was an exit [from responsibility]—young Russian Jews "have been leaving . . . in droves . . . with such cynical ease."[19] ("Collective responsibility . . . is the only thing a nation can hold on to"—would that we Russians had such an awareness!)

And most strikingly, [Jabotinsky concludes]: "The majestic spirit [of Israel] in all its might, its tragic history in all its colossal magnificence . . ."—"Who are we that we should justify ourselves to them? Who are they to interrogate us?"[20]

This last formulation also commands full respect. But its application should be two-sided. No one nation or faith is given to *judge* another.

These appeals to return to Jewish *roots* did not fall on deaf ears in pre-Revolutionary Petersburg: "One could observe a sharp rise in interest in Jewish history among circles of the Russian-Jewish intelligentsia."[21] In Petersburg

18. Zhabotinskii, *Feuilletons*, 15, 17, 69.

19. Zhabotinskii, *Feuilletons*, 18–24, 175–77.

20. Zhabotinskii, *Feuilletons*, 14, 200.

21. "Pamiati M. L. Vishnitsera" [In memory of M. L. Vishnitser], in *Book of Russian Jewry*, 8.

in 1908, the Jewish Historical-Ethnographic Commission expanded and transformed itself into the Jewish Historical-Ethnographic Society, headed by Maxim Vinaver.[22] The society began actively and successfully collecting an archive on the history and ethnography of Jews in Russia and Poland—nothing like it had been created by Jewish historical scholarship in the West. Under the editorship of Simon Dubnov, the journal *Jewish Antiquity* began to appear.[23] At the same time, the sixteen-volume *Jewish Encyclopedia* (which I use abundantly in this work) and the fifteen-volume *History of the Jewish People* were prepared for publication. True, in its final volume, the encyclopedia complains [that] "the leading circles of the Jewish intelligentsia . . . displayed indifference to the cultural tasks of the encyclopedia" (they were engaged in the struggle for more open manifestations of Jewish equality).[24]

Still, in other Jewish heads and hearts, a contrary conviction grew: that the future of Russian Jewry was inextricably bound with the future of Russia. [In I. M. Bikerman's words:] Although "dispersed across vast expanses, living sprinkled here and there in a foreign element . . . Russian Jewry was in fact, and conceived of itself as, a single entity. For the environment surrounding us was one and the same . . . a single culture. . . . We absorbed that culture throughout the entire country."[25]

[Or as Stephan Ivanovich made the point:] "Russian Jewry has always known how to connect its interests to those of the Russian people as a whole. And this is a result, not of noble character or feelings of gratitude, but a good sense of historical realities." Continuing the argument peremptorily, as if in direct contradiction of Jabotinsky, [Ivanovich added]: "For the millions of Jews that inhabit her, Russia is not a chance way station in the historical peregrinations of the Wandering Jew. . . . The Russian paths of world Jewry have been and will remain the most significant historically. We cannot escape from Russia, just as Russia herself cannot escape from us."[26]

O. Ia. Pergament, a deputy in the Second and Third State Dumas, described this inability to "escape" even more categorically: "No improvement of Russian internal life is [itself] possible without the simultaneous emancipation of the Jews from the lack of civil rights that weighs them down."[27]

Another significant voice that cannot be ignored is that of Genrikh Sliozberg, a Jewish lawyer who had close dealings with the Russian state for decades, as assistant oversecretary of the Senate and as legal adviser to the ministry of

22. *Jewish Encyclopedia*, 8:466.

23. *Jewish Encyclopedia*, 7:449–50.

24. *Jewish Encyclopedia*, 16:276.

25. I. M. Bikerman, *Rossiia i russkoe evreistvo* [Russia and Russian Jewry], in *Russia and the Jews*, 86.

26. Stephan Ivanovich, "Evrei i sovietskaia diktatura" [Jews and Soviet dictatorship], in *Evreiskii mir: Ezhegodnik na 1939* [The Jewish world: Almanac for 1939] (Paris: Ob'edinenie russko-evreiskoi intelligentsii, 1939–40), 55–56.

27. *Jewish Encyclopedia*, 12:372–73.

internal affairs, a man whom many Jews reproached for *requesting* rights from those in power, when the time had come to *demand* Jewish rights. In his memoirs, Sliozberg says: "From childhood I was accustomed to thinking of myself as a Jew first and foremost. But from the very beginning of my adult life, I felt myself to be a son of Russia as well. . . . To be a good Jew doesn't mean not being a good Russian citizen."[28] [He continues:] "In our work, we did not have to overcome obstacles of the kind that the Poles put up for Polish Jewry every step of the way. . . . In Russian government life, we, Jews by nationality [ethnic origin], did not constitute an alien element, since many nationalities inhabited Russia, unified in Russian statehood without attempts on the part of the dominant nationality to swallow all others. . . . The cultural interests of Russia did not conflict in the least with the cultural interests of the Jews. One culture in effect complemented the other."[29] Indeed, Sliozberg goes so far as to joke that, given the incoherence and contradiction of Russian laws about Jews, he was in the 1890s "supposed to begin development of a distinctively Jewish jurisprudence, employing purely talmudic methods."[30]

And moreover [from another source, D. O. Linsky, we find]: "The softening of the national yoke in recent years, not long before Russia entered a tragic streak in her history, created in the souls of all Russian Jews the hope that gradually the consciousness of Russian Jewry would follow the path of filling that consciousness with the creative content of reconciling Jewish and Russian aspects in a synthesis of higher unity."[31]

And can we forget that, of the seven authors of the incomparable *Vekhi* [*Landmarks*: a collection of anti-intelligentsial, antiradical essays], three were Jews—M. O. Gershenzon, A. S. Izgoev-Lande, and S. L. Frank?[32]

Despite which, on the other side [of the political divide], Russian Jews of the pre-Revolutionary decades enjoyed as well the powerful, unified support of social progressives. It may well be that this support developed against a background of constraint and pogroms; nevertheless, in no other country (perhaps

28. Genrikh Borisovich Sliozberg, *Dela minuvshikh dnei: Zapiski russkogo evreia* [Affairs of days gone by: Notes of a Russian Jew], 3 vols. (Paris: Imprimerie Pascal, 1933–34), 1:3–4, hereafter referred to by its English title.

29. Sliozberg, *Affairs of Days*, 2:302.

30. Sliozberg, *Affairs of Days*, 1:302.

31. Linskii, "On the National Self-Awareness," in *Russia and the Jews*, 144.

32. *Landmarks: A Collection of Articles on the Russian Intelligentsia* (in Russian) (Moscow, 1909; published in English translation as *Signposts*, ed. and trans. Marshall S. Shatz and Judith E. Zimmerman [Irvine, CA: Schlacks, 1986]).

In Gary Saul Morson's description: "Here is one case where it is entirely justified to call a publication a scandal: *Landmarks* dissected, indeed tried to bury, the intelligentsia's self-image, psychology, mores, etiquette, and unquestioned values and assumptions, most of which *Landmarks* described as destructive. Generally liberal in their views, the contributors criticized the intelligentsia's automatic habit of radicalism. Still more iconoclastic, *Landmarks* refused to consider politics the solution to all problems, not even to political problems": Morson, "Prosaic Bakhtin: *Landmarks*, Anti-Intelligentsialism, and the Russian Counter-Tradition," *Common Knowledge* 2.1 (Spring 1993): 38.

even in all of world history up to that time?) had support [for Jews] been so extensive. The high-minded, freedom-loving intelligentsia of Russia placed anti-Semitism entirely beyond the bounds of society and humanity. Anyone, moreover, who failed to offer clear and voluble support for the Jews, especially in their struggle for equal rights, was immediately branded a "dishonorable anti-Semite." The excruciatingly conscientious, acutely sensitive Russian intelligentsia tried to heed and assimilate fully the specifically Jewish understanding of political priorities: whoever protests the oppression of the Jews is progressive, all others are reactionary. Russian society not only staunchly defended the Jews in relationship to the government, but forbade both itself and everyone else to express even the faintest shadow of criticism regarding the behavior of individual Jews: what if suddenly, in my annoyance [at a particular Jew's behavior], anti-Semitism should reveal itself in me? (The generation that grew up at that time retained this attitude for decades.)

In his memoirs, V. A. Maklakov recounts a characteristic episode that took place at the Zemstvo congress of 1905, after the recent pogroms against the Jews and intelligentsia, and when pogroms against the landowners were gathering force: "E. V. de Roberti proposed that the amnesty [demanded by the congress] not be extended to crimes involving violence against children and women." His amendment was immediately suspected of "class bias"; that is, that he was concerned about the landowning families that had suffered. [As Makhlakov tells the story, Evgeny] "de Roberti hastened . . . to calm everyone: 'I wasn't thinking of the gentry's estates at all. . . . If 5–20 estates burned down, that is insignificant. I meant the many Jewish estates and homes that were burned and pillaged by the Black Hundreds.'"[33]

In the terror of 1905–7, Mikhail Gertsenshtein (who had been so ironic about the burning of the landowners' estates) and Boris Iollos—but none of the thousands of murdered innocents—were recognized as martyrs [because they were Jews].[34] In the satirical journal *Poslednii samoderzhets* [The last autocrat], which Russian liberals published abroad, it is even said that, under the portrait of the general whom the terrorist Girsh Lekkert failed to assassinate, was the caption: "*Because of him*, the tsar executed . . . the Jew Lek[k]ert."[35]

33. Vasilii Alekseevich Maklakov, *Vlast' i obshchestvennost' na zakate staroi Rossii (Vospominaniia sovremennika)* [Power and society at the sunset of old Russia (Memoirs of a contemporary)], Prilozhenie k "illiustrirovannoi Rossii" [Supplement to "The illustrated Russia"], no. 3 (Paris, 1936), 466.

34. Mikhail Gertsenshtein, a Constitutional Democratic Party (Cadet) delegate in the First Duma, was assassinated by members of the Black Hundreds in Finland in 1906.

Boris Iollos, likewise a member of the First Duma and an enemy of the Black Hundreds, was assassinated in 1907 by the "Union of the Russian People." [Editor]

35. Italics added by Alexander Solzhenitsyn. Viktor Petrovich Obninski, *Poslednii samoderzhets: Ocherk zhizni i tsarstvovaniia imperatora Rossii Nikolaia II-go* [The last autocrat: Sketches of the life and reign of the Russian emperor Nikolai II] (Berlin: Eberhard Frowein Verlag, 1912), 58.

Not only the opposition parties, but also the large midlevel bureaucracy, trembled at the thought of appearing "unprogressive." One had to be entirely independent financially or possess outstanding spiritual freedom to have the courage to withstand the pressure of the general current. In the legal, artistic, and scholarly worlds, any deviation was immediately ostracized.

Only Lev Tolstoy, by virtue of his unique social position, could allow himself to say that *for him* the Jewish question occupied eighty-first place.

The *Jewish Encyclopedia* declares that the October 1905 pogroms "provoked among the progressive intelligentsia no special protest [no opposition specifically to the persecution of Jews], but only protest of a general nature, directed against all manifestations of 'counterrevolution' in general."[36]

Russian society would have ceased to be itself if every question was not exacerbated by tsarism, tsarism, tsarism.

On that account, "concrete aid to Jewish victims after the October events [the 1905 pogroms] was given exclusively by the Jews of Russia and other countries."[37] To which [spectacle] Nikolai Berdiaev responded: "Do you feel the soul of the Jewish people? . . . No, your struggle . . . is for an abstract person."[38]

Sliozberg confirms [Berdiaev's observation]: "In the eyes of certain politically developed circles," the Jewish question "at that time did not have the significance of a political issue in the broad sense of the term. Society was preoccupied with thoughts about manifestations of [tsarist] reaction [against the 1905 revolution] in general."[39]

To correct this miscalculation on the part of Russian society, an unusual collection of essays was assembled. An intervention on the Jews' behalf, *Shchit* [Shield]—while comprehensively and exclusively devoted to Jews—included no contributions from Jewish writers. Every contributor was Russian or Ukrainian, and to be sure all the names most resonant at the time were represented, some forty altogether.[40] The entire anthology is dedicated to the single theme of "the Jews in Russia"; it is unequivocal in its resolution of the problem and sometimes selfless in its articulation.

Among the views expressed [in the anthology] is that of Leonid Andreev: the solution to the Jewish question is already within reach [and its result is] a feeling "of joy, close to awe"—of deliverance "from the pain that has accompanied me all my life," from something resembling "a hump on my back." I have,

36. *Jewish Encyclopedia*, 12:621.

37. *Jewish Encyclopedia*, 12:621.

38. Nikolai Berdiaev, *Filosofiia neravenstva* [The philosophy of inequality], 2d ed. rev. (Paris: YMCA Press, 1970), 72.

39. Sliozberg, *Affairs of Days*, 1:260.

40. Leonid Andreev, Maksim Gorkii, and Fedr Sologub, eds., *Shchit: Literaturnyi sbornik* [Shield: A literary anthology], 3d ed. (Moscow: Russkoe Obshchestvo dlia izucheniia evreiskoi zhizni [Russian Association for the Study of Jewish Life], 1916), hereafter referred to by English titles.

[Andreev adds,] been "breathing poisonous air." Maxim Gorky's [opinion] is that the Jew, as a psychological type, is considered, by "the major thinkers of Europe, to be culturally higher, more comely than the Russian." (And Gorky expresses satisfaction with both the growth of the Sabbatarian sect in Russia and with the "New Israel.") Pavel N. Maliantovich, [a minister of justice, offers this assessment]:

The horror of the Jew's lack of legal rights in Russia is a shameful blemish on the name of the Russian people. . . . The best Russians experience it as a disgrace from which there is no escape throughout their lives. . . . We are barbarians among the cultured people of humanity . . . deprived of the precious right to be proud of our people. . . . The struggle for Jewish civil rights is, for the Russian . . . genuinely a national affair of the first importance. . . . The Jew's lack of rights dooms the Russian people to powerlessness in the work of attaining their own happiness."

[And Maliantovich concludes:] if we [Russians] do not concern ourselves with the emancipation of the Jews, "then we will never determine our own affairs." [As for] K. K. Arsenev, [his contribution to *Shield* argues that,] if all barriers are removed for the Jews, there will be "an increase in the mental riches of Russia." A. N. Kalmykova [adds that, while,] on the one hand, we [Russians] have "close spiritual ties with Jewry in the area of higher spiritual values," on the other hand, [Russians] "consider contempt and hatred for Jews permissible." Andreev [returns]: we Russians "are ourselves *the Jews of Europe*, our *border is that very same Jewish Pale*." D. S. Merezhkovsky [also has his say]: "What do the Jews want from us? Moral indignation?" "That indignation," [he replies to his own question,] "is so strong and simple that . . . one can only shout out loud with the Jews. And we are shouting." By some misunderstanding, Berdiaev was not included [among the contributors] to *Shield*. But he said [elsewhere that, for his part,] he had broken with his circle of early youth and preferred to keep company with Jews.

All the authors in *Shield* characterize anti-Semitism as a vile sentiment, "an illness of consciousness, distinguished by obstinacy and contagion" ([I am quoting] Dmitry Ovsianiko-Kulikovsky, an academic). But several contributors note that "the means and techniques . . . of [Russian] anti-Semites are of foreign origin" (P. N. Miliukov). "The new anti-Semitic ideology is the product of the German Spirit industry . . . the 'Aryan' theory . . . was taken up by our nationalistic press . . . M. O. Menshikov [echoes] the ideas of Gobineau" (Fyodor Kokoshkin). The doctrine of the supremacy of the Aryan over the Semite "is German handiwork" (Vyacheslav Ivanov).

Yet what does this [point—that anti-Semitism is not Russian in provenance—] matter to those of us [like Andreev] with "a hump on [our] back"?

In the "Progressive Club" at the end of 1916, Gorky "devoted his two-hour speech to every possible form of slur against the entire Russian people and to an immoderate praise of Jewry"—so recounts the progressive Duma member S. P. Mansyrev, a founder of the "Club."[41]

Alexander Voronel, a Jewish author in our time, writes about this phenomenon objectively and with insight: "there occurred a reeducation of educated Russian society, which took the Jewish problem much closer to heart, alas, than might have been expected. . . . Sympathy for the Jews became almost the same kind of imperative as 'God, Tsar, and Fatherland'"—and individual Jews "used these social tendencies in accordance with their level of cynicism."[42] [The phenomenon to which Voronel refers,] V. V. Rozanov referred to at the time as the Jews' "hunger to have it all."[43]

In the 1920s, Vasily Shulgin held the following view of the situation: "Over this period [the quarter century before the 1917 Revolution], Jewry took the political life of the country into its hands . . . it seized political Russia. . . . The brain of the nation (if one doesn't count the government and government circles) turned out to be in Jewish hands and was accustomed to thinking according to Jewish orders." "Despite all the 'limitations'," [Shulgin wrote,] "Jews had captured the soul of the Russian people."[44]

But—had the Jews *captured* it? Or did the Russians not know what to do with it [themselves]?

In the same issue of *Shield*, Merezhkovsky tried to explain that Judeophilia is created by Judeophobia and ends in the affirmation of a nationality that is just as blind [as the rejection that preceded it]. In the place of an absolute "no," [Merezhkovksy wrote, there is now] an absolute "yes!"[45] Professor Jan Baudouin de Courtenay expressed [similar] reservations: "Many people, even in the camp of the Jews' 'political friends,' actually feel a certain aversion to them and will acknowledge this face to face. In that case, of course, there's not much you can do. Feelings of sympathy and antipathy . . . do not depend on us." One should be guided, in any case, "not by affect, [but] by reason."[46]

In 1909, Pyotr Struve articulated, with great depth and social significance,

41. Prince S. P. Mansyrev, "Moi vospominaniia" [My memoirs] in *Fevral'skaia revoliutsiia* [The February revolution], comp. S. A. Alekseev (Moscow; Leningrad: GIZ, 1925), 259.

42. Aleksandr Voronel', "22," *Obshchestvenno-politicheskii i literaturnyi zhurnal evreiskoi intelligentsii iz SSSR v Izraile* [Sociopolitical and literary journal of the Jewish intelligentsia from the USSR in Israel] 50 (1986): 156–57.

43. "Perepiska V. V. Rozanova i M. O. Gershenzona" [Correspondence of V. V. Rozanov and M. O. Gershenzon], *Novyi mir* [New world], no. 3 (1991): 239.

44. Vasily V. Shul'gin, "*Chto nam v nikh ne nravitsia . . .*": *Ob Antisemitizme v Rossii* ["What we don't like about them . . . ": About anti-Semitism in Russia] (Paris: Izd-vo Russia Minor, 1929), 58, 75.

45. Andreev, Gorkii, and Sologub, *Shield*, 164.

46. Andreev, Gorkii, and Sologub, *Shield*, 145.

the ambivalence of [Russian] social psychology. All his life, Struve fearlessly overcame barriers and other taboos along the spectrum from Marxism to right-wing statism. A historically important polemic appearing in the liberal newspaper *Slovo* [Word] in March 1909—it is now utterly forgotten—reported with an immediate bang throughout the entire Russian press.

[The controversy] began with the overblown, widely discussed "Chirikov episode": a furious explosion in a narrow literary circle, involving abrupt accusations of anti-Semitism against Evgeny Chirikov, the author of an extremely sympathetic play titled *The Jews*. [The furor followed on Chirikov's] remark, dropped at a literary dinner, that most Petersburg reviewers were Jews, and were they really capable of appreciating fully the themes of everyday Russian [life]? The incident hit a sudden nerve in Russian society. (S. Liubosh, the journalist, referred to it at the time as "the one-kopeck candle that burned down Moscow.")

Jabotinsky felt that he had not, in his first article, sufficiently expressed himself on the [subject of] the Chirikov episode; and so on March 9, 1909, he published a second article in the *Word*, titled "Asemitism." In it he expressed alarm and indignation that most of the progressive press had sought to suppress [information about] the incident with Chirikov and Konstantin Arabazhin, [and] that even a certain leading liberal newspaper (he was alluding to *Russkie Vedomosti* [Russian gazette]) had supposedly for twenty-five years written nothing "about the terrible persecution of the Jewish people. . . . Since that time, hushing up is considered the highest chic of progressive Judeophilism." [Jabotinsky argued, moreover,] that the most harm is done by purposely suppressing the Jewish question. (And one can indeed agree with [Jabotinsky on this last point].) When Chirikov and Arabazhin "assert that there was nothing anti-Semitic in their remarks, they are both absolutely right," [Jabotinsky concluded]. Because of our [the progressives'] traditional silence, "one can end up being marked an anti-Semite for simply using the word 'Jew' or for the most innocent remark about Jewish particularities. . . . Only the Jews have been transformed into this sort of forbidden taboo [group], about which even the most mild criticism may not be made, and it is the Jews who lose the most from this custom." (And again, one can only agree with [Jabotinsky].) "The impression," [he continued,] "is created that the very name 'Jew' is an unprintable word": here [we have the] "echo of a certain common mood that has made headway among the progressive Russian intelligentsia. . . . There's no documentary evidence—the presence of such a mood can thus far be established only by feel." But [the vagueness of] this [mood] is precisely what causes alarm: [proceeding] by feel and without documents, Jews will not hear the approaching thunder; they will be caught unaware. At the moment, [Jabotinsky foretells,] "a sort of cloud is forming, and from far away one hears an indistinct, still faint, but already inhospitable murmur." This [approaching cloud] is not anti-Semitism, it is still only "asemitism"—but it is no more allowable, and neutrality cannot be justified. After the Kishinev pogrom, when reactionary newspapers are spreading the "burnt hemp of hatred," the silence of the Russian progressive press "about one of the most tragic questions of Russian life" is impermissible.[47]

In the same issue, in its editorial preface, the *Word* expressed reservations [about Jabotinsky's article]:

The accusations that the author directs toward the progressive press do not, in our view, correspond to the reality of the situation. We understand the feelings that dictated his bitter lines, but to attribute to the Russian intelligentsia the almost premeditated tactic of suppressing the Jewish question is unjust. In Russian life, there are so many unresolved problems that relatively little space can be devoted to each of them. . . . And after all, the positive resolution of many of these problems has enormous real significance also for Jews—as citizens of our common homeland.[48]

Would that the *Word* had asked Jabotinsky why he did not defend the three simpletons who had made the "most innocent remarks about Jewish particularities." Did Jewish society pay any attention to or defend such people? Or did it only watch as the Russian intelligentsia cleansed itself of these "anti-Semites"? As far as "forbidden taboos" are concerned, it must be said that Jews were no less guilty than Russians.

And the newspaper accompanied [Jabotinsky's] commencement of its discussion [of the Chirikov incident] with one other article, [titled] "Accord, but Not Coalescence," by Vasily Golubev. [His argument is that,] yes, the Chirikov incident "comprises a far from private occurrence" [since] "the national question . . . at the present time . . . concerns our [Russian] intelligentsia as well." In recent years, [Golubev continues,] especially in the year of the revolution [1905], our intelligentsia "sinned woefully" in its cosmopolitanism, but "not without trace has the struggle proceeded within society . . . and among the nationalities inhabiting the Russian state." Like other nationalities as well, during these years "the Russian people also had to think about their national tasks . . . when the stateless nationalities began to define themselves, it became necessary for the Russian to define himself as well."[49] Even with respect to our history, "we, members of the Russian intelligentsia, are in practice less informed" [about Rus-

47. Zhabotinskii, "Asemitism," *Slovo* [Word], March 9 (22), 1909, 2 (hereafter referred to using English titles); see also *Feuilletons*, 77–83.

48. *Word*, March 9 (22), 1909, 1.

49. See note 14 above. It should be observed as well that the word for *nationality* in Russian [*natsional'nost'*] is dis-

tinct from the word for *citizenship* [*grazhdanstvo*], and is often closer to and interchangeable with contemporary English use of the word *ethnicity*. Thus, "nonterritorial" or "stateless" nationalities refers in this context to the many non-Russian ethnic groups that inhabited the Russian empire. [Translator] sian] than about European history. "Common human ideals . . . have [always] been . . . far more important to us than our own creations." But in the opinion of even Vladimir Soloviev, who was far removed from any sort of nationalism, "we must, before becoming the bearers of common human ideals, raise ourselves to a certain national height. And that feeling of self-elevation, it seems, is beginning to reach even the circles of the intelligentsia." Until now, [Soloviev wrote,] "we have suppressed the particularities . . . of the Russian people." And there is no anti-Semitism in recalling [Russian particularities]. [Recalling them] means in no sense oppressing other nationalities, but [only that,] among nationalities, there should be, [in Golubev's phrase,] "accord but not coalescence."[50]

Perhaps the *Word* expressed its reservations so strongly because another article had passed its typesetters, colliding by chance with Jabotinsky's but arriving independently of it—an article also dealing with the disturbance surrounding the Chirikov incident. Pyotr Struve's article, "The Intelligentsia and the National Countenance," appeared in the *Word* the day [after Jabotinsky's appeared], on March 10.

Struve wrote: "This incident," which would "soon be forgotten," "showed that something has arisen in peoples' minds, has awakened, and will not be calmed. What has awakened demands to be taken into account." "The [ethnically] Russian intelligentsia," [Struve continued,] "grows colorless in the intelligentsia of the Russian state . . . needlessly and fruitlessly covering its national countenance," which "should not be hidden." "Nationality is something far more undeniable [than race or skin color,] and at the same time it is subtle. It consists of spiritual affinities and aversions, and in order to become aware of them, one need not have recourse to either anthropometric techniques or genealogical research. [These spiritual qualities] live and tremble in the soul." One can and should struggle, [Struve argued,] to prevent these affinity-aversions affecting the legal system, "but 'state' justice does not require of us an indifference to 'nationality.' Affinities and aversions belong to us, they are our own property"; [ours] "is an organic feeling of nationality. . . . And I do not see the least grounds . . . for rejecting this property on behalf of anyone or anything."

Yes, Struve repeats, it is necessary to define [national] borders—the lawful territory of the government—and the territory where [national] feelings are alive in us. [Then he adds that,] "especially regarding the Jewish question, this [demarcation of territory] is both very simple and very difficult": "the Jewish question," [Struve argues,] "is formally a legal one," and for that reason it is simple, natural, to resolve. Give the Jews equal rights—why, of course! But to resolve [the question is also] "very difficult, because the strength of aversion to Jewry in the most varied layers of the Russian population is actually quite great,

50. V. Golubev, "Soglashenie, a ne sliianie," [Accord, but not coalescence], *Word*, March 9 (22), 1909, 1.

and significant moral and logical clarity are required in order irrevocably to resolve the legal question despite the aversion." However, [Struve continues]:

for all the strength of the aversion to Jewry among a broad section of the Russian population, the Jews are closest to us of all "foreigners"; they are most closely tied to us. This is a cultural-historical paradox, but it is true. The Russian intelligentsia has always counted Jews [among] its own, [considered Jews to be] Russians—and not accidentally, not without reason, not by any sort of "misunderstanding." The conscious initiative of rejecting Russian culture, affirming Jewish "national" particularities, belongs not to the Russian intelligentsia, but to the Jewish movement known by the name of Zionism. . . . I have not the least sympathy for Zionism, but I understand that the problem of "Jewish national identity" exists and is even growing.

(It is significant that [Struve] puts the words "Jewish national identity" in quotation marks, so hard is it for him to believe: do the Jews, [he wonders,] really think of themselves as apart?) "In Russia," [Struve says,] "there are no 'foreigners' other [than the Jews] who have played such a role in Russian culture. . . . And there is yet another difficulty: they play this role while remaining Jews." You cannot, [Struve adds,] deny the role of Germans in Russian culture and science; but Germans, upon entering Russian culture, dissolve into Russian culture completely. "Not so the Jews."

And [Struve] concludes: "It is unbecoming for us to dissemble [about Russian national feeling] and hide our face. . . . I, and every other Russian, have the right to these feelings. . . . The more clearly this is understood . . . the fewer misunderstandings there will be in the future."[51]

Which is true: if only we had all come to our senses several decades earlier. (The Jews did so much earlier than the Russians.)

Meanwhile, it was as if all the newspapers had been waiting [for this debate to at last occur]! The next day a whirlwind ensued, both in the liberal *Nasha Gazeta* [Our newspaper] (*"is this the proper time to say so"*?—the classic question) and in the right-wing *Novoe Vremia* [New time]. In the quintessentially Cadet [liberal] Petersburg paper *Speech*, Miliukov could not help but gasp: Jabotinsky, [he wrote,] "has managed to make the silence end, and all the terrible and threatening things that the progressive press and intelligentsia tried to hide from the Jews have finally been drawn in their true proportions." But further along, Miliukov, with his invariably reasonable coldness, moved on to [issue] his verdict. The most important element [of it] was the warning [question]: *Where are we being led, [and] to whose advantage is it?* "A national countenance," one

51. Petr Struve, "Intelligentsiia i natsional'noe litso," [The intelligentsia and the national countenance], *Word*, March 10 (23), 1909, 2.

that "should not be hidden"—is that not reminiscent of far right-wing bigotry? (The "national face," apparently, *should* remain hidden.) Thus, [P. N. Miliukov concludes,] the intelligentsia, "descending the slippery slope of aesthetic nationalism," will quickly die out and descend into the "genuinely tribal chauvinism" generated "in the rotten atmosphere of contemporary social reaction."[52]

But the forty-year-old Struve, with almost youthful agility, bounced back to counter Miliukov's "instructive words" in the March 12 issue of the *Word*. "Where are we being led, to whose advantage?" was the turn of phrase that, above all, he challenged. (*Whose grist for whose mill?* . . . they will still be shutting mouths with that one—on any theme—a hundred years from now: a twisted choice of words, betraying no awareness that words can in themselves be honest and profound.) "Our views have not been fundamentally refuted," [Struve wrote,] "but [merely] juxtaposed polemically with a 'forecast' of 'where they lead'."[53] The *Word* [itself] commented several days later: "The tried and true way of discrediting both an idea that you don't share and the person who professes it is with a nasty hint that this fellow would meet with complete sympathy in the *New Time* and *Russian Banner*. This procedure, in our view, is entirely unworthy of the progressive press."[54] But the heart of the matter [for Struve was that] "at the present time, strong, stormy feelings often adhere to the nationality question. These feelings, since they express awareness of one's own national individuality, are completely valid, and . . . extinguishing [them] is . . . a great perversion." If [national feelings] are driven inside, [Struve says,] they will break out in a perverted form. And [he continues]:

The most terrible "asemitism" is far more favorable soil for the legal solution of the Jewish question than the hopeless battle . . . of "anti-Semitism" versus "philosemitism." No single non-Russian nationality requires . . . Russians to love it without fail. Still less [does any nationality require] that [Russians] pretend to love it. And indeed, "asemitism," combined with a clear and sober understanding of well-known moral and political principles and . . . governmental requirements, is far more necessary and useful for our Jewish citizens than feeble, sentimental "philosemitism," particularly when it is simulated.

Moreover, [Struve argues,] "it is beneficial for Jews to see the open 'national face'" of Russian constitutionalism and democratic society: "For [the Jews], it is entirely useless to give in to the illusion that that sort of face belongs only to

52. Pavel Nikolaevich Miliukov, "Nationalizm protiv nationalizma" [Nationalism against nationalism], *Rech'*, March 11 (24), 1909, 2.

53. Struve, "Polemicheskie zigzagi i nesvoevremennaia pravda [Polemical zigzags and untimely truth], *Word*,

March 12 (25), 1909, 1, hereafter referred to by its English title.

54. *Word*, March 17 (30), 1909, 1.

anti-Semitic bigots." This [face] "is not a Medusa's head, but the honest and kindly face of the *Russian* nationality [*russkoi natsional'nosti*], without which the '*Russian*' [*rossiiskoe*] state will not stand."⁵⁵ And also, as the editors added: "Accord . . . means recognition of all the distinctive qualities of each [nationality] and respect for those qualities."⁵⁶

The newspaper polemics continued heatedly. "Over the last few days, an entire literature has been compiled," [Maxim Slavinsky wrote in the *Word*]. Something, [he continued,] is happening "in the progressive Russian press . . . something that would have been completely impossible not long ago: the question of Great Russian nationalism is being debated!"⁵⁷ But while the *Word* raised the argument to its full stature, other papers focused on "affinities and aversions."⁵⁸ With irritation, the intelligentsia attacked its recent hero, Struve, [and his] liberal journal *Osvobozhdenie* [Liberation].

Nor did Jabotinsky remain silent; he spoke out twice again. He hurled [an article,] "The Bear Leaves the Den," at Pyotr Struve. [Struve] had seemed so calm and evenhanded, but Jabotinsky was offended [just the same,] and referred to [Struve's] article and Miliukov's as "a brilliant appearance of the bigwigs": "Their affectionate declamation," [Jabotinsky wrote,] "is drenched in hypocrisy, insincerity, timidity, obsequiousness, and for this reason is utterly mediocre." [Jabotinsky] gathered from Miliukov that, [or so] it seems, in "the old Russian intelligentsia, holy and pure, there were anti-Jewish 'aversions'? . . . Curious." [Miliukov, Jabotinsky said, tongue in cheek,] had cursed "'the holy and pure' climate of this marvelous country" and the "zoological species *ursus judaeophagus intellectualis*" [intellectual Jew-eating bear]. (Maxim Vinaver, the peacemaker, came in for his share [of ire] as well: [Jabotinsky referred to Vinaver as] "the Jewish servant of the Russian mansion.") Jabotinsky furiously rejected the notion that Jews should wait "for the moment when larger state tasks had been resolved" (that is, the overthrow of the tsar): "[We extend] our thanks for such a flattering opinion of our willingness to assume canine selflessness" [and for such a flattering opinion] of "the efficiency of the loyal subject, Israel." [Jabotinsky] even concluded [on the subject of the Jews of Russia] that "the exploitation of a people by another people has never before avowed itself with such innocent cynicism."⁵⁹

It must be acknowledged that the extreme vehemence of [Jabotinsky's] tone did not serve his point of view well. Furthermore, the very near future made clear that it was indeed the tsar's overthrow that would open previously incon-

55. Struve, "Polemical Zigzags," 1.

56. Golubev, "K polemike o natsionalizme" [Toward a polemics on nationalism], *Word*, March 12 (25), 1909, 2, hereafter referred to by its English title.

57. Maxim Slavinskii, "Russkie, velikorossy, i rossiiane" [Ethnic Russians, great Russians, and Russian citizens],

Word, March 14 (27), 1909, 2, hereafter referred to by its English title.

58. *Word*, March 17 (30), 1909, 1.

59. Zhabotinskii, "Medved' iz berlogi" [The bear leaves the den], in *Feuilletons*, 87–90.

ceivable positions for Jews—would [make possible for Jews] even more than they had already achieved—and in so doing would pull the rug out from under Zionism in Russia. Thus Jabotinsky turned out, in addition, to be essentially wrong.

Much later, another witness to that era, a member of the Bund, recalled coolly: "In Russia, during the years 1907–1914 a certain epidemic of 'asemitism,' if not exactly open anti-Semitism, would occasionally take hold of some liberals in the Russian intelligentsia, and disappointment with the maximalist tendencies of the first Russian revolution gave others an excuse to place responsibility for those tendencies on the conspicuous participation of Jews in the revolution." And during the prewar years, [this witness continued,] "the growth of Russian nationalism could be observed . . . in particular circles where, it seemed, the Jewish question had quite recently been viewed as a Russian question."[60]

In 1912, Jabotinsky himself, quite calmly now, recounted an interesting observation of a well-known Jewish journalist: as soon as Jews are interested in some cultural phenomenon, it becomes alien, as it were, for the Russian public, which is [then] no longer drawn to it. [This response is] a variety of invisible *aversion*. Yes, [Jabotinsky wrote,] a line of national demarcation will be inevitable, [and] Russian life organized "without admixtures from outside, which in such quantity are obviously unacceptable for [Russians]."[61]

All considered, it would be most correct to conclude that two processes were simultaneously at work among the Russian intelligentsia (as is often the case with historical phenomena), and that, with regard to the Jewish question, [intellectuals] were distinguishable largely on the basis of temperament rather than degree of goodwill. But the [view] that Struve expressed was not very loud, was unsure of itself, and was muffled, [while the view] that was stridently declared by the philosemitic publication *Shield* turned out to be dominant in terms of publicity and social custom. One may still regret that Jabotinsky did not appreciate Struve's point of view, did not see its virtues.

The 1909 debate in the *Word* was not limited to the Jewish theme, but grew into a discussion of Russian national consciousness, which, after our country's eighty-year deafness, is today fresh and edifying for us as well. [The contribution of Pyotr Struve, in this context, was to say]: "Just as one shouldn't be involved in 'Russifying' those who do not wish to 'Russify,' so should we not 'Russianize' *ourselves*"[62]—should not drown and lose our individuality in the Russian state's multinational expanse.[63] Golubev protested against the "monopoly on

60. G. Ia. Aronson, "V bor'be za grazhdanskie i natsional'nye prava: Obshchestvennye techeniia v russkom evreistve" [In the struggle for civil and national rights: Social movements in Russian Jewry], in *Book of Russian Jewry*, 229, 572.

61. Zhabotinskii, *Feuilletons*, 245–47.

62. Again, the distinction here is between "obruset'," to Russify, and "obrossiivat," a neologism meaning "to become *rossiiskii*." [Translator] See also note 49.

63. Struve, *Word*, March 10 (23), 1909, 2.

patriotism and nationalism held by reactionary groups": "We have," [he wrote,] "disregarded the fact that the Japanese victories had an oppressive effect on popular and national feeling. Our defeat humiliated not only the bureaucracy," as [Russian] society had desired, "but indirectly the nation as well." (Oh, [I would say] far from "indirectly!"—[the national humiliation was] quite direct.) "The Russian nationality," [Golubev continued,] "effaced itself"; "neither is the defamation of the very word 'Russian,' transformed as it has been into 'authentic-Russian,' any laughing matter."[64] Progressive society let both concepts slide, handing them over to the [political] Right: "after all, we understood patriotism only in quotations marks," though "one must compete against reactionary patriotism with popular patriotism. We just stopped and went no further than a negative attitude to Black Hundreds patriotism, and if we countered it with anything, it was not patriotism, but common human ideals."[65] However, [Golubev concluded,] we see that all our cosmopolitanism has still not allowed [Russian society] to make friends with Polish society.[66]

A. L. Pogodin recalled [that it was] after Vladimir Soloviev's threatening rebuke to N. Ya. Danilevsky's [pan-Slavist work] "Russia and Europe," [and] after G. K. Gradovsky's article [appeared, that Russia experienced] "the first emergence of the consciousness that awakens in peoples, like the instinct of self-preservation, in moments when danger threatens." (As it happened, moreover, it was precisely during the time of this debate, March 1909, that the Russian state experienced a national humiliation: it was forced to recognize, with pitiful resignation, its "diplomatic Tsushima"—the Austrian annexation of Bosnia and Herzegovina.) "In a fateful way," [Pogodin wrote,] "we are moving toward this question [of Russian nationality], which not long ago was utterly alien to the Russian intelligentsia, and now is set forth so abruptly by life [itself] that there's no getting around it."[67]

The *Word* concluded [its own remarks on the Chirikov debate as follows]: "A chance incident has served as the catalyst for an entire newspaper storm." [In the aftermath,] "the need for national self-knowledge is felt in Russian society." Russian society in earlier years "was ashamed not only of that false antinational politics . . . but of genuine nationalism as well, without which state-building is unthinkable." A creative people, [the editorial continued,] "invariably has its own face": "[Kuzma] Minin was obviously a nationalist."[68] Constructive state

64. Golubev, "Toward a Polemics," 2.

65. Golubev, "O monopolii na patriotism" [About the monopoly on patriotism], *Word*, March 14 (27), 1909, 2.

66. V. Golubev, "Ot samouvazheniia k uvazheniiu" [From self-respect to respect], *Word*, March 25 (April 7), 1909, 1.

67. A. L. Pogodin, "K voprosu o natsionalizme" [On the question of nationalism], *Word*, March 15 (28), 1909, 1, hereafter referred to by its English title.

68. *Word*, March 17 (30), 1909, 1. Directly in front of St. Basil's Cathedral, Moscow, is a statue that honors Kuzma Minin and Dmitry Pozharsky, who defeated the invading Polish army in 1612 and drove the Poles out of the Kremlin. [Editor]

nationalism is characteristic of *living* nations, and that is precisely [so Pogodin argued,] the kind needed [in his time].[69] "Just as it did three hundred years ago, history demands an answer from us" [the editors wrote in 1909. History] "demands that, during the terrible days of our trials, we answer whether we have, as a unique people, a right to autonomous existence."[70]

Clearly, something imminent could be felt in the air!—though the year 1909 seemed relatively peaceful.

But the [participants in this growing debate] did not overlook the truth [that, as Slavinsky wrote,] "the attempt to Russify, or more accurately, to Great Russian-ize all of Russia . . . has turned out to be deadly for those national features, not only of all the nonterritorial peoples of the empire, but first and foremost, of the Great Russian people [itself] . . . the cultural strength of the Great Russian people turned out to be too weak [to sustain this effort]."[71] For the Great Russian nationality, [in summary:] only intensive internal development, normal circulation of the blood, is useful—a lesson (it is a shame to say) that has not been assimilated by Russians even now. "There must," [Pogodin argued,] "be a struggle against physiological nationalism, [when] a stronger people strives to impose a form of government alien to them on weaker peoples."[72] After all, [the editors added,] such an empire should not be created with physical strength alone but with "moral strength" as well. And if we [Russians] have that [moral strength, the editors said,] then the equality of peoples, whether Jews or Poles, will not threaten us in the least.[73]

In the later decades of the nineteenth century—and at the commencement of the twentieth, even more so—the Russian intelligentsia felt itself already on a plateau of one-worldly, all-humanitarian cosmopolitanism or international-ism (these terms were interchangeable at the time). In many senses, [the Rus-sian intelligentsia] had almost, even then, completely rejected everything that was Russian. (From the tribune of the State Duma a joke was heard about the "Patriot, Iscariot.")

But the Jewish intelligentsia did not reject the question of nationality. And even the most extreme Jewish socialists tried to somehow combine their ideol-ogy with their national feeling. Still, at the same time not a word was heard from the Jews—from Dubnov to Jabotinsky and Vinaver—to indicate that the Russian intelligentsia, which had supported its oppressed [Jewish] brethren with all its soul, might not have to reject its *own* national feelings. In all justice, this opinion should have been heard. No one understood at the time: by *equal rights*, the Jews meant something *greater*.

69. Pogodin, "On the Question," 1.

70. *Word*, March 17 (30), 1909, 1.

71. Slavinsky, "Ethnic Russians," 1.

72. Pogodin, "On the Question," 1.

73. *Word*, March 17 (30), 1909, 1.

And the Russian intelligentsia—it stepped into the future alone.

The Jews did not receive equal rights under the tsar, but—partly because that was so—they received the hand and loyalty of the Russian intelligentsia. The strength of [the Jews'] development, perseverance, and talent *took up residence* in the Russian social consciousness. Our notions of our goals, our interests, the impulses behind our decisions—we merged all these with their principles. We accepted their view of our history and of the possible ways to shape it.

And it is more important to understand this [aspect of our mutual history] than to count how many Jews stirred things up in Russia—we all did—or made the revolution or participated in the Bolshevik regime.

ROMANIA—BETWEEN CONTINUITY AND CHANGE

His Majesty King Michael of Romania

Michael of Romania is the last king of the Hohenzollern dynasty and the last surviving head of state from the era of the Second World War. He ascended the Romanian throne in 1927, at age five, on the death of his grandfather King Ferdinand, a consistent supporter of the Liberal Party. Michael was removed by his father, King Carol II, in 1930 but was restored to the throne in 1940, when Carol was exiled by a government intent on alliance with Hitler and on war with the Soviet Union. On 23 August 1944, King Michael led a palace coup in which General Ion Antonescu, the fascist head of government, and several of his ministers were arrested, and the Nazis were ousted from Romania. Michael was twenty-three when he transferred his country's allegiance from the Axis to the Allies, for which he was awarded the Legion of Merit by the United States and the Order of Victory by the Soviet Union. From 1945 to 1947, King Michael opposed and obstructed the Soviet-backed communist government of Romania; and for several months, in an action called the Royal Strike, refused to sign government bills and decrees. On a visit to London in 1947 for the wedding of his cousins Princess Elizabeth and Prince Philip (Michael's grandmother was a granddaughter of Queen Victoria and his mother was a princess of Greece and Denmark), the British government advised against his returning to Romania; and, on his return to Bucharest, the king was forced to abdicate. After he was exiled in 1948, Michael declared his abdication void. His next appearance in Romania, after the

Originally published in *Common Knowledge* 4.2 (Fall 1995): 158–83. © 1995.

Common Knowledge 25:1–3

DOI 10.1215/0961754X-7579437

overthrow of the Ceauşescu regime, was at Christmas 1990, when Michael and his party were forced at gunpoint to leave the country. In 1992, Michael was allowed his only visit to Romania since 1948. Vladimir Tismaneanu termed the visit "a sea-change political event" and, subsequently, President Ion Iliescu has refused King Michael entry, most recently in October 1994, when his aircraft was turned back upon landing in Bucharest. At a 1994 news conference in New York, Iliescu said that Michael "is contesting Romania's public constitutional order." King Michael, for his part, contends that, despite the 1989 revolution, his country is "obviously still controlled by a dictatorial regime."

—Editor

With crowds storming barricades and dictators fleeing from palace rooftops, the so-called Romanian revolution of 1989 appeared both curiously old-fashioned and thoroughly modern; it provided the best television pictures in what was already a remarkable year. But real political change remained confined to appearances rather than realities. To this day, nobody knows who shot whom during those December events and for what purpose. Romania's uprising did not spring from years of dissidence; it was a rebellion born out of desperation, and the country's rulers are still in power because they were able to redefine a popular revolution to suit their needs. Yet, despite all that has gone wrong in Romania, it is my fervent belief that my country will ultimately join the family of democratic European nations. Romania is an example of how deep the scars of communism can be, and for how long the agony of a nation can he prolonged.

My country was the only Eastern European state to experience a violent uprising in 1989. Yet, instead of signifying a complete break with the communist past, the Romanian revolution has created a hybrid of democracy and authoritarian rule. Romania is ruled by a curious combination of communists turned "democrats" who, although still able to prevent opposition forces from assuming power, are not powerful enough to suppress dissent. The country is now in a legal and political limbo: it possesses ostensibly democratic institutions, a new constitution, a free press, and a liberalized media sector (its radio is probably the most vibrant in the former communist bloc). However, those who protest against the current regime can do so to their heart's content, but they cannot change anything in the current political structure. And the gulf between realities and appearances in state institutions is as wide as it has always been.

With the exception of the Czech Republic, former communists have returned to power in every other East European state. But Romania nevertheless remains an exception even in this respect: former communists are not only in power; they never left it to start with, even for a brief period of time. A country ruled by probably the harshest communist regime in Eastern Europe is still headed by a president who was a notable functionary under the old regime. As a result, the internal political fight in Romania is not merely between personalities and parties. Instead, it continues to be a confrontation about the very nature of the state and its character. Everything, from Romania's form of government and national composition to the country's economic policies, remains in a seemingly perpetual state of flux.

Throughout the long years of Nicolae Ceaușescu's rule, Western observers noted the paucity of internal opposition, the absence of social dialogue, the disappearance of a "civil society." And, since all these factors were inherently not quantifiable, general analysis increasingly relegated Romania to clinical observations: Ceaușescu was assumed to be an unbalanced despot, and Romanians were portrayed as a "traditionally" fatalistic and meek people who actually welcomed the "strong hand" that he provided. The reality, however, was different: the dictator operated an ingenious system of control that manipulated people's fears and aspirations.

The Specific Features of Communist Rule

The small Romanian Communist Party—established in the early 1920s—had little place in the country's political life before the war. The party, advocating a policy of the dismemberment of the state, guided by leaders appointed, dismissed, or murdered on Moscow's behalf, and claiming to represent the "workers" in a country that was overwhelmingly agrarian, fervently nationalistic, and devoutly religious, had little chance of winning power through democratic means. Indeed, even in the widely falsified elections held under Red Army intimidation after the Second World War, the communists, suitably camouflaged with other "progressive" parties, still failed to win any substantial support. The people that I had to face when the Red Army arrived in Bucharest (and broke all the conditions that were placed on their being stationed in Romania) were virtually unknown, drawn from Romanian citizens who had left their country of birth decades earlier in order to serve in the Moscow-based Comintern.

This dilemma faced by the Romanian communists was also experienced by communists in other East European states. However, while the Bulgarian and Hungarian parties claimed some "credit" for having organized rebellions in their own states, and the Czechoslovak and Polish parties could point to some serious parliamentary activity before 1945, the Romanian communists had nothing: their party failed to benefit from the substantial economic and social progress that followed the achievement of Romanian unity in 1918 and, despite their subsequent efforts to exaggerate their role in some industrial disputes, they had no contacts at all with the country's working class. In short, the Romanian communists represented little more than themselves and, of course, Moscow. This feeling of detachment from the nation had important consequences: it spurred Romania's communists to pursue their social engineering policies with a speed rarely encountered among their East European counterparts.

At the beginning, the lack of national roots mattered little, for the rule of Romania's communists was overwhelmingly based on Soviet control. However, once the interests of the Romanian party started to diverge from those of Moscow, the establishment of a truly national support base became a question of political survival. All East European communists experienced a split between a "Muscovite" faction, formed by those nurtured and propelled to power by Stalin in 1945, and an "internal" faction comprising those who—for one reason or another—remained to fight for their cause in their own state. The Romanian party had no less than four factions and only one, entitled the "Workers' Group" (led by Gheorghe Gheorghiu Dej), was relatively homogenous. Most of its members shared a similar experience, and most had served many years in jail, usually in the same prisons. The fact that this group of home communists succeeded in wresting control from the "Muscovite" faction well before Khrushchev's de-Stalinisation polices were imposed on Eastern Europe ultimately decided the future of the country. When the clash of interests with Moscow took place, the Romanian party, ruled by a tightly knit circle of leaders who were very much aware of what was at stake, managed to resist any change. And they continued to resist change until 1989.

The country's rift with Moscow started precisely because of its leaders' refusal to accept any digression from industrialization-at-all-costs. For the Romanian communists, pursuing heavy industrialization was not only a matter of sound economics and ideological rectitude; it was seen as a question of political survival, for there was only one other option: the perpetuation of the country's agricultural base. Like most urban-based political movements, the Romanian Communist Party equated the peasantry not merely with economic backwardness, but also with superstition and opposition to "progress." If the transformation of society was to take place at all, it could only come from destruction of traditional social structures—thus the breakdown of rural communities—from the dismantling of the old and the reassembling of a new Romania. The small clique of Ceaușescu supporters who remained loyal to their leader until his death in December 1989 never deviated from this course. Again, similar policies were pursued elsewhere in Eastern Europe, but the Romanian communists were conspicuous by the sheer scale and speed with which they implemented them.

Most investment was diverted into vast steel mills and heavy engineering projects with little attention paid to the country's industrial infrastructure or, indeed, patterns of capital formation. As early as the mid-1950s, it was clear that Romania's electricity supplies, raw material reserves, and transport could not keep pace with such growth, but the priorities never changed. The disappearance of Moscow's explicit support, however, meant serious difficulties for the Romanian Communist Party. Most East European communist regimes ultimately had to face the question of accommodation with their own people. They usually opted for two courses of action: "consumerism," the deliberate attempt to buy popular acquiescence through the maintenance of a steadily rising standard of living, and nationalism, the effort to anchor an essentially alien ideology to their country's historic traditions. The mixture between these two approaches varied from country to country, but both consumerism and nationalism were used in this process of legitimation. Romania's example remains unique, however, for the Communist Party under Ceaușescu relied almost completely on only one ingredient: nationalism. Given the disagreement with Moscow and the priorities of the party, this was a predictable course; consumerism would have meant the diversion of resources and consumption to "nonproductive" sectors; in short, it could have resulted in the postponement of the radical transformation of the state.

The Pillars of Ceaușescu's Regime

The aberrant traits of Ceaușescu's character and personality cult should not obscure the fact that he was also a tactician. Unlike his predecessor, who initiated the policy of differentiation from Moscow, Ceaușescu did not simply respond to Soviet *diktat* (usually by attempting to limit its impact on Romania) but initiated his own aggressive foreign policy of opening up to the West, ostensibly in order to escape the Kremlin's control. This policy allowed access to Western technology, raw materials, and markets. It also raised the price that Moscow would have had to pay for forcing Romania into submission. But the third internal reason for forging better ties with the noncommunist world was equally important. As a country, we are strongly "westward leaning." We are a Latin people speaking a Romance language. Nothing was more resented in my country than the communists' subservience to Russia, an explicit connection with an inherently "inferior" East. Ceaușescu's flirtation with the West in general promised a change and, as such, was initially quite popular with most Romanians. This westward orientation in foreign policy was thus also part of the president's strategy for achieving internal legitimacy through the subtle manipulation of nationalist symbols. Those within the party who finally rose against Ceaușescu in 1989 were his most loyal supporters when the policy of opening to the West was initiated. For many of them, the president stood accused not so much for his cruel despotism (with which, incidentally, many of them did not particularly disagree), but for failing to combine the maintenance of communism with the anchoring of Romania to "the West."

Initially, Ceaușescu's policies registered considerable successes. In the

West, he was praised and feted as a brave defender of his country's independence. He was offered substantial financial credits and trade benefits: alone and without the aid of any congressional lobby, Romania retained pride of place among America's commercial partners in Eastern Europe until the end of the 1970s. No matter what or where the conflict may have been—in the Middle East, China, between the superpowers, Africa—the Romanian president offered mediation and his offers were not always derided as irrelevant. In multilateral negotiations, Ceauşescu was praised for setting forth arms control proposals that were often different only in wording from those of his Warsaw Pact allies. In the West, Romania became renowned for "standing up" to Moscow.

At home, the Romanian president revealed a different face. As Romanian society became more diverse, as sons of peasants migrated to the towns and flocked into factories, it was clear that the party had to accommodate their interests and articulate their aspirations in some way. Ceauşescu's response was incorporation without representation: during his first years in power, almost half of all university professors and academics were made to carry a party card and, in the armed forces, 80 percent of all officers were co-opted into the party. Throughout Ceauşescu's rule, the constant enlargement of the party served two specific purposes: the penetration and neutralization of any alternative power base and the increasing equation of the state with the party. But these control techniques went even further: Ceauşescu not only neutralized any alternative power bases, but he perpetuated a conflict among them, maintaining a constant state of tension that assured his position as supreme arbiter.

The treatment to which Ceauşescu subjected the armed forces, Romania's biggest alternative source of power, is a case in point. He appealed to their patriotism and professionalism by assuming the nationalist mantle. This allowed him to sever the umbilical cord between Romanian and Soviet officers and strengthened his security against any foreign challenge. The fact that the president's initial archenemy was the head of the internal security service—the Securitate—also reinforced Ceauşescu's image as that of a man who would rely on the armed forces rather than the party's own instruments of coercion. Nothing could have been further from the truth. Having secured his power base, Ceauşescu moved to control the armed forces through a method that he applied throughout his life: their deprofessionalization. Immediately after the invasion of Czechoslovakia, Romania adopted a military doctrine of territorial defense that envisaged that the entire nation would repel any invader. This doctrine set up a parallel military body, the Patriotic Guards, that was placed under the control of the party rather than the general staff. Having established two levels of command, Ceauşescu then proceeded to unify them under a defense council that was intended to supervise all military and economic activities. In practice, Patriotic Guard officers (who were promoted from among party members rather than military personnel) were put in command of all armed forces including the army itself—whose importance was automatically diminished by the formation of additional paramilitary organs. In the end, the army was reduced to being a pool of cheap labour, digging canals or helping with the agricultural harvest. The Securitate, however, was allocated vast resources, and large investments were also channeled into the air force and the navy. Ceauşescu therefore perpetuated a four-cornered fight: between the armed forces and the Securitate; between the army and the navy and the air force; between the Securitate and the Interior Ministry (which was supposedly in charge of most paramilitary forces); and between the Patriotic Guards and the regular troops.

The imposition of draconian measures ensured a perpetual conflict in the countryside and therefore prevented local leaders from assuming too much power. At the national level, this policy was reinforced by a system of rotation of cadres with the explicit aim of preventing the promotion of professionals. Some officials were dismissed in order to take the blame for the failure of policies that they had not devised; others were replaced for no reason. The sheer pace of this musical chairs game defied the comprehension of most Western experts, yet it served a purpose: it isolated people and set one party official against the other. As many of Romania's current leaders testify, demotion did not necessarily signify disgrace or permanent oblivion, for Ceauşescu was also aware of the dangers inherent in the creation of a large group of discontented officials. Army generals who changed positions with Central Committee secretaries and county officials who donned the hat of a scientist or a planner were often reprimanded and punished for mis-demeanors but they usually reappeared, sometimes within a matter of months, under different guises. Blind loyalty to the leader and the readiness to perform any task were the only requirements, which were just as important when in a position of power as during a period of temporary disgrace. The result was the complete atomization of society and the deprofessionalization of all Romanians.

The system was sustained by two additional levers of control: the president's family and the security police. No fewer than fifty relatives of Nicolae and Elena Ceauşescu controlled the most strategic positions in the state: central planning, the capital city, the army, security services, foreign intelligence, the party cadres and its youth movements. The promotion of the family also created a sophisticated advance warning mechanism quite outside party structures and the security services: the Ceauşescus and the Petrescus (Elena Ceauşescu's maiden name) ensured that threats to the survival of their mafia's chieftain were identified and eliminated well before they became dangerous.

It is important to note that Ceauşescu's aim was never to rely on sheer terror for his survival. Instead, he sought to control Romanian society through the encouragement of nationalism, the fusion of the state and party, and the destruction of any alternative power base. Rather than the first line of the system's defense, the Securitate remained more an instrument of last resort. The Securitate employed informers and intercepted communications but it gained additional strength by the very fact that it operated in a country that became identified with the capriciousness of one man. Throughout the last two decades, most East European dissidents who dared speak their minds usually knew what to expect from the authorities. Not in Romania, where some opponents simply disappeared, others were exiled, and many more (especially the ones within the party) were merely demoted to harmless but nevertheless still seemingly important positions. The Securitate's tactic was one of continuous deterrence through the sheer unpredictability of the potential punishment.

The Collapse

How is the demise of Ceaușescu's regime to be explained, given the fact that all the instruments of control were in place by the late 1970s? Essentially, through four cardinal mistakes. The first was the belief—implicit in all of the president's policies—that Romanians would bear any suffering, however great, without a murmur. The second was the assumption that the geopolitical interests of both East and West would remain immutable and Romania would retain its special position. The third was the conviction that nationalism was an infinite commodity, capable of galvanizing people even at the expense of great personal hardships. And the fourth was Ceaușescu's miscalculation in assuming that the perpetual conflicts that he created within Romanian society would neutralize any opposition to his regime. With the benefit of hindsight, it is clear that the seeds of the Romanian revolution were sown in the early 1980s, when the policies of the Communist Party started unraveling one by one. The process followed a neat sequence: the first to fail was the country's economic experiment. Then followed Romania's foreign policy, then the utilization of nationalism, and finally—in the fury of the December rebellion—Ceaușescu's coercion *apparat*.

Ceaușescu's foreign policy aim was not integration in the world economy. In his characteristically contradictory manner, he forged closer cooperation with the West in order to create a "fortress Romania" that could, one day, be independent from both East and West. Yet Ceaușescu's follies—such as the continued buildup of the country's steel industry and the creation of a gigantic petrochemical capacity—relied on imports of coal and oil, thereby merely compounding the country's exposure to those world market forces that he never understood but always mistrusted. The creation of an industrialized, prosperous Romania through policies of import substitution proved, not surprisingly, to be a total failure.

Yet Ceaușescu would not admit defeat and, when Western credits dried up, he decided to repay his $10 billion worth of foreign debt as quickly as possible in order to avoid any of the strictures that foreign creditors regularly impose on defaulting debtors. As a result, exports were maximized and imports strictly forbidden even when they entailed the purchase of new machinery. A vicious cycle therefore set in. Antiquated machinery produced goods that failed to find markets. This forced Romania to rely more and more on exports of food and semifinished products in order to obtain hard currency. But, since resources devoted to agriculture were minimal, exports of food could be sustained only through further reduction in local consumption. By 1982, rationing was introduced; by 1985, most food products were persistently unobtainable; and by 1987, the population was subjected to serious malnutrition. Worse still, every industrial branch continued to apply the dictator's "precious indications." The gigantic machine was spinning out of control: steel production outpaced power generation and the electricity grid collapsed; coal extraction exceeded transport facilities and the rail network disintegrated. Unable to increase productivity, the president continued to resort to extensive growth: in an obscene policy, Romanian women were forced to produce more children in order to satisfy the thirst for labour in unautomated factories and, since agricultural production failed to live up to the president's absurd targets, he resolved to destroy thousands of villages, partly in order to erase the last vestiges of private agriculture, partly in order to eliminate the peasants as a social group, and partly simply in order to increase the surface of arable land. All these inhuman policies were pursued with the presumption that Romanians could be whipped into harder work and would endure every privation. In reality, however, a veritable social time bomb started ticking. Between 1966 and 1976, birth rates were 40 percent higher than might otherwise have been expected. Yet, even with the highest infant mortality rate in Europe and the most inefficient employment policy, a labour market of such a magnitude simply could not be absorbed. The heirs of this baby boom were those who set up the December 1989 barricades and became the revolution's cannon fodder.

Ceauşescu's foreign policy represents yet another case of the difference between tactics and realities. Goading Moscow and enhancing Romania's independence could succeed only as long as the Soviet Union chose to rise to the bait and as long as the West was prepared to encourage such wayward behaviour. Yet tactics could not change strategic facts: Romania remained important as long as Europe remained a chess board between East and West. Once Gorbachev arrived in the Kremlin, Romania's circumstances changed. Moscow's genuine interest in disarmament reduced the importance of individual pawns on the chess board, while the Soviet leader's tolerance of diversity in Eastern Europe transformed Ceauşescu's objections to Soviet hegemony from an act of defiance into a historical irrelevance.

At the beginning, Ceauşescu responded by ignoring the Soviet reforms. However, when it became clear that the thaw in East-West relations would last, Romania proceeded to complicate the process of disarmament and multilateral negotiations as far as possible. When this tactic failed, Ceauşescu abruptly abandoned all claim to independence and started calling for the Warsaw Pact's intervention against "imperialists" and "renegades" in the communist camp. And, when this failed to elicit any response, Ceauşescu retreated into a hermit's existence, hoping that the wind of change that was sweeping from power every one of the colleagues whom he had annoyed for so long would spare him; so tight was his control over the country that many Western observers genuinely believed him to be immune. But changes were on the way, for by the end of 1989, an exasperated nation was ruled by an exasperated president.

"Revolution" and the Beginnings of a New Regime

One by one, countries promised the "golden future" of socialism, as Ceauşescu used to refer to his preferred ideology, turned away from this mirage. The Romanian dictator was well aware of what was happening in Europe: as the doctored transcripts of the party meeting that decided to crush the Timisoara riots in December 1989 with force indicate, Ceauşescu went into battle convinced that he would win and that this confrontation with the people would ultimately decide the future of communism in the country. He also knew who his potential successor might be: Ion Iliescu, a man touted for years as Moscow's ally and Ceauşescu's deadly enemy. The fact that Mr. Iliescu managed to survive unharmed until the end is yet another mystery in a string of unexplained events that surround the so-called Romanian revolution.

Interpretations of this "revolution" usually concentrate on two conflicting scenarios: either that Ceauşescu's overthrow was the result of a coup d'état or that it was due to a popular rebellion. This is a false contradiction, for the December 1989 events represented both a palace putsch and an uprising at the same time. There is some circumstantial evidence that alarmist reports about thousands of deaths in Timisoara brought the crowds onto the streets of Bucharest and other cities. And there is proof that certain segments within Ceauşescu's own Securitate— eager to save themselves—were keen to replace him with a more flexible figure. Yet even if the Securitate itself did encourage the demonstrations, it is unrealistic to believe that hundreds of thousands of people would have braved bullets and potential death unless they were convinced that living under Ceauşescu was worse than not living at all. The problem of the Romanian revolution is different. The crowds that poured onto the streets knew what they were opposing. They were against the man and the woman who had destroyed their lives; they were against the economic privations (especially the lack of heat and electricity, as well as the food rationing); they were against the entire communist system itself. They shouted for a democracy, which so many of them had never experienced in their lifetime, and for a new government formed by people whom they did not yet know. The revolution was a prime candidate for hijacking from the beginning and it is here that theories of a plot gain more substance.

Romania's First Postrevolutionary Institutions

In the immediate chaos after the revolution, such considerations were not of primary importance. Romania's new leaders were all former communist notables. The National Salvation Front, which seized power, was chaired by Ion Iliescu, Ceauşescu's party youth leader in the late 1960s and subsequently a dissident, but always within the Communist Party. The Front was supposedly formed out of 145 personalities from "different walks of life" and set up as a temporary ruling body, intended to govern Romania in the lead-up to free, multiparty elections that were promised from the outset. In its first proclamation, the Front also dissolved all the country's institutions and assumed complete control over all state affairs. The press was freed from party control; all political movements were liberalized; and the country was promised a free and impartial judiciary, a rule of law and order, and above everything else, freedom from travel restrictions, cold, hunger, and fear. Yet, right from the start, concerns about the Front's real intentions surfaced. First, the full list of the Front's membership was not published and the biographies of those included were never released. It subsequently emerged that some—such as the courageous dissident Doina Cornea—were included without their prior consent. Furthermore, the full body of the Front had no powers: instead, the mythical 145 members "delegated" their powers to a "council" that also appeared to do nothing, just as Ceauşescu's Central Committee never supervised party affairs. This council, in turn, established an executive body that was the real power in the land. And, just as happened with Ceauşescu's own Political Executive Committee, control remained concentrated in the hands of a few.

More disturbing was the fact that these leaders decreed the separation of powers but continued to hold both executive and legislative functions. Government ministers were made responsible to the Front, rather than to the newly appointed prime minister (Mr. Petre Roman), and "decree-laws" were issued without any reference to the cabinet. It was Mr. Iliescu—and not the prime minister—who solved industrial disputes and who expounded on the country's new policies. The Front professed the importance of the independence of the media, yet appointed the head of radio and television as its spokesman; it promised that all political parties would be allowed to function freely, but at the same time suggested that the very notion of a political party was "surpassed by history" and no longer relevant to Romania's present conditions, which supposedly required "consensus" within the Front (a notion, incidentally, not very different from Ceauşescu's "democratic centralism"). Crucially, leading members of the Front vowed to abolish all vestiges of Ceaușescu's twenty-five-year dictatorship. Nothing was said about the forty years of communist rule. Instead of encouraging the yearning for freedom, the postrevolutionary authorities proceeded to provide justifications for holding onto power. They tried to blame everything on Ceaușescu, claiming that the revolution was not against the communist regime but against him and his clique. The signs were certainly not good, yet many Romanians still believed their leaders, and many intellectuals still assumed that a government born in a revolution had to exist within a certain legal vacuum. Not for long, however, for the postrevolutionary honeymoon lasted for only two weeks.

The first worrying sign was the Front's insistence on "consensus." In the name of this concept, new mayors and county leaders were appointed, almost invariably from the ranks of the Communist Party and without any consultation with the local population. This was followed by a nonevent that at the time appeared inexplicable: nobody wanted to talk about the face of the Communist Party—its vast organization, its funds and structures, stretching back to the smallest village, simply "disappeared." Within weeks after the uprising, dissidents such as Doina Cornea left the Front, accusing the government of being dominated by communists and Securitate officers. As the suspicions multiplied, the country's new leaders continued to give interviews—especially in the Soviet press—in which they denied attempts to restore communism in Romania but refused to answer any of the specific accusations made against them.

Meanwhile, other political parties were created. These parties were initially revivals of the political movements that had existed before 1945. The National Peasant Party was revived at the beginning of January 1990; the National Liberal Party, immediately thereafter. These two parties had dominated Romanian political life before the war. The newly established political parties immediately asked to share power with the Front. Yet the Front's members, many of whom were responsible for sentencing the leaders of the Peasants and Liberals to long-term imprisonment decades earlier, prevaricated for as long as possible by promising "roundtable" discussions that never materialized. Within days, those who fought for the revolution started receiving anonymous telephone death threats and the opposition parties were increasingly intimidated. And, very soon, Romanians learned that the Front, which had originally been established as a temporary institution intended to guide the country toward free elections, had decided to take part in the parliamentary elections as a political party, with all the advantages of representing the new state authority.

This prevarication, coupled with the more subtle moves of the Front and compounded by the absence of any dialogue between government and opposition, led to the first postrevolutionary outbreak. On 12 January 1990, only twenty-one days after Ceaușescu's overthrow, thousands came onto the streets, demanding the abolition of the Communist Party, an inquiry into the events surrounding the revolution, and the reinstatement of the death penalty (abolished by the Front in a move widely regarded as shielding former communists from criminal responsibility). The Front leaders, startled by this challenge that went to the heart of deliberately maintained political ambiguity, swiftly published a series of proclamations outlawing the Communist Party and confiscating its property, instituting a special committee to investigate previous communist crimes, and calling for a referendum on the question of the death penalty. Convinced that they had obtained everything that they had demanded, the crowds dispersed. Yet immediately thereafter, the Front changed its mind: instead of banning the Communist Party, outright (as they had promised), they called for a referendum on the issue, scheduled to be held a few days later. Needless to say, neither the referendum on the death penalty, nor that called in order to decide the fate of the Communist Party, was ever held. Although the party assets were confiscated by the government, what became of these riches has never been discovered and the entire issue simply disappeared from the agenda never to be mentioned again, just as Romanians never got an explanation about who was responsible for the killings during the revolution. Obviously these maneuvers merely led to further trouble, and opposition parties vowed to take to the streets again. Their platforms included not only a demand that elections should be postponed so as to allow all political movements time to organize after forty years of dictatorship, but also advocated the creation of a government of "national unity" in order to guide the country until the elections.

Surprised by the speed of the challenge to their newly established rule, Romania's leaders went on the offensive. They used the only instruments they were familiar with: mass mobilization and violence. A meeting of Bucharest factory workers was called at the behest of Iliescu, the Front's president. In an atmosphere that reminded many Romanians of Ceauşescu's rallies, the participants duly asked Iliescu to stand in the forthcoming election. The Front offered a new poisoned chalice to the opposition: ostensibly at the latter's behest, the Front postponed the parliamentary elections for a short while—to 20 May 1990. This was hardly a concession for parties that had been banned for over four decades. At the same time, the Front prohibited all other political formations from obtaining financial support from abroad (just about the only possible source of funds for the newly created movements) and restricted electoral rallies to weekend days only, to be held in specific public parks. Yet on the matter of sharing power with the opposition or allowing an impartial team of administrators to govern the country in the lead-up to the elections, there was no compromise: the Front asserted that it was itself the revolution's creation and its only keeper.

This series of decisions led to more riots, which continued on the streets of Bucharest throughout the last week of January 1990, defying the ban imposed by the government. The demonstrations culminated in a large rally on 28 January, when crowds besieged the Front's headquarters in Bucharest. Not for the first time, it appeared that the Front's rule was doomed. Yet the government implemented an abhorrent strategy that was subsequently destined to become Romania's original contribution to Eastern Europe's postcommunist history: the use of so-called miners. Transported by the state-owned railways, miners descended on defenseless demonstrators with chains and sticks. The police and the army did nothing, and the miners proceeded to opposition party headquarters, where the Peasant Party's leader Corneliu Coposu had to be saved from the mob by the personal intervention of the prime minister. The television started broadcasting urgent appeals from the Front to "save the revolution" and Mr. Iliescu assured citizens that Romania would never again become a "bourgeois democracy." The Front had therefore come full circle: from representing the opposition to the communist regime, it had become the newly contested state power. Octavian Paler, one of Romania's foremost commentators, penned a lament on his country's illusions with democracy ("which lasted only a month").

In every sense, Paler's obituary on Romania's democratic promise was apt. Within weeks after a revolution that appeared to have swept aside an entire communist structure, all the state's institutions had reappeared. More importantly, the country's new rulers exhibited the same contempt for democratic procedures as their predecessors and the same lack of compunction about the use of mob rule in order to silence opposition. Almost everything that followed this first tumultuous month of the new Romania is scarred by the episodes of that time. The mistrust between those governing and those governed, the personal confrontation between political partners, the heavy mist of suspicion that permeates Romanian society, all have their causes in the events of December 1989 and January 1990. The country's new leaders laid the foundations of a new political game that will, I am convinced, ultimately sweep even them from power. And they have virtually guaranteed the country's isolation from its European neighbors. The Western media, feeling deceived by a state in which the distinction between the lie and the truth was invisible, eventually lost interest. By the spring of 1990, Romania had faded from the world's attention and remained synonymous with violence, duplicity, and desperate poverty.

Over one hundred parties were registered for the May 1990 elections. In the period after the elections, the number of parties continued to grow, reaching more than one thousand by 1991. The entire exercise in democracy became a farce. Parties were promised a state subsidy in order to compete in the elections. They were also entitled to priority allocation of houses, ostensibly in order to use them as offices. And they were promised a national platform through membership in the Provisional Council for National Unity, an organization tasked with acting as a replacement parliament in the run-up to the 1990 elections. From the Front's viewpoint, the more parties that were established, the more divided the opposition would become. In the Council, the Front reserved half of the seats for itself. With the aid of other parties—many of which were established with the government's support or connivance—the Front continued to retain an absolute majority. The Council therefore became an instrument for Front rule under a new guise. Yet there was a difference: decisions could now be taken with the semblance of a democratic debate, and the Front co-opted the opposition by its actions in a manner not dissimilar from those I remember the communists taking during the late 1940s. In practice, the Council confined itself to voting on the electoral law; the country continued to be governed by the Front's leaders, who very seldom even debated their decisions in Romania's rudimentary parliament. The tightly controlled state television broadcast the Council's proceedings, yet what most Romanians saw was a parody of democracy. These sessions of the Council had a serious impact. Romanians concluded that—apart from the Front's leaders, who enjoyed constant exposure on television and who, through their state positions, could appear to speak with some knowledge—no one else was fit to govern. The electoral law that the Council adopted contained all the usual safeguards of any democracy. In practice, the law was irrelevant, for Romania's future rulers were already chosen after the first televised Council session.

The Front itself, however, was undergoing some transformations. Having realized that any attempt to retain the overt signs of communism would be forcefully resisted and could create a severe reaction in the West, the governing party changed its strategy. This is how the period of the "salami tactics" began. The aim, obvious with the benefit of hindsight, was the prevention of any recrimination against former communist notables by the smooth transformation and adaptation of old institutions in the new political context. Few Romanians were aware that when the communist regime was toppled, the Front decided to change the country's name from the Socialist Republic of Romania to, simply, Romania. Yet for the Front, this choice (not adopted anywhere else in Eastern Europe, where states remained "Republics," although they changed and dropped the ideological connotations of their names) had some importance. It avoided the thornier issue of whether Romania should revert to its monarchical traditions. A strictly legal interpretation of the country's situation in December 1989 would have suggested that the monarch should be restored, as the existing and last legitimate head of state before the illegal communist coup of 1947. Yet the Front feared that any discussion about the return of the monarchy could trigger a wider process of reckoning with former communist officials and galvanize the opposition. In public, government officials claimed to pay no attention to the issue and suggested that I could return for a visit, as "a private citizen" or a "tourist." My daughters were allowed into the country, but, when I expressed an interest in coming, I was refused entry in March 1990 and actually deported twelve hours after my arrival on Christmas Day of that year.

Instead of confronting the issue of the monarchy directly, the Front tackled it piecemeal. The avoidance of the word *republic* in Romania's name neatly bypassed the issue, and the distribution of posts immediately after the revolution maintained this careful silence: thus, Ion Iliescu was merely the "president of the Front" and, although he fulfilled the functions normally attributed to a head of state, he was not usually referred to as such. The Front's real intentions were revealed only during the deliberations in the Provisional Council for National Unity, when the government tabled an electoral law, calling for the election of a two-chamber parliament and a president. By envisaging the creation of a 387-member Chamber of Deputies and a 199-member Senate, the Front appealed to the Romanians' sense of history, since these names were used in the country's parliament before the war. And at the same time, by calling for the election of a president, the Front hoped to kill off the issue of the monarchy once and for all, without ever discussing it openly. Thus, with most of the deputies not even realizing what was happening, the Council adopted an electoral law that created institutions anchored in no other legislation. Romanians were asked to vote for deputies, senators, and a president, with little idea of their functions, responsibilities, or powers. The electoral law was presented as the first step toward the creation of a parliament that would draft a new constitution, a curious procedure that was not followed in any other East European state saddled with communist legislation. Deputies who objected at the time were told that the electoral law was merely a temporary stopgap, a necessary device in order to set Romania on its democratic course. In practice, the very same legislation was subsequently used in order to prove that Romania had already opted for a set of institutions and was already a republic. Furthermore, the fact that the president was elected through direct popular ballot—rather than indirectly, through parliament—was advanced as the best proof that Romanians wanted a presidential, rather than a parliamentary, democracy. Romania's current constitution therefore traces its main features to a supposedly temporary electoral law, adopted by an assembly that ultimately represented no one. The government claimed that this was an unavoidable outcome, given the fact that the country's revolution erased all previous constitutional contracts. In fact, as Romanians learnt later, the 1965 constitution imposed on them by Ceaușescu was not abrogated until 8 December 1991 when their new constitution supposedly replaced it.

Mr. Iliescu and Prime Minister Roman were aware of the West's insistence on free elections as a precondition for extending much-needed economic aid. Elections were held in 1990, and a triumphant Front now expected a flood of aid and loan packages. None of them understood that, even given optimum political conditions, Romania would still have had an uphill struggle in attracting Western investment. The government frequently asserted that, alone in Eastern Europe, Romania did not have any outstanding foreign debts. The debt had been cleared in an erratic manner by Ceauşescu, mainly by depriving the country and the people of bare necessities. Yet by wiping out this debt, the Romanians had no leverage on their former creditors who, by 1989, were free to consider loan propositions without the burden of rescheduling previous loan agreements. Thus, paradoxically, heavily indebted Poland, Hungary, and Bulgaria were accorded more attention than a supposedly solvent Romania. Since Eastern Europe offered plenty of other investment opportunities, Western bankers had little interest in becoming embroiled in a country ruled by a party that made the rejection of foreign-capital involvement one of its cardinal planks during the election campaign. Two years after the revolution, Romania had still failed to obtain any commercial loans.

After exhausting their hard currency reserves in less than six months during a pre-election spending spree, the Romanian authorities attempted to obtain aid and credits only to find that they had to compete with other former communist states in a much better position to attract foreign capital. The Gulf War in 1991 restricted Romania's ability to collect its unpaid bills from Iraq or engage in oil barter deals, and the growing economic recession in the West completed the picture of desolation. Increasingly exasperated, the government looked for scapegoats. It accused the opposition of deterring Western investors. Investment legislation was changed no fewer than four times in two years, and the privatization regulations were amended three times during the period in order to facilitate the flow of foreign capital. Each time, these efforts failed to elicit a strong response, for the government that had sown so much suspicion was now reaping the consequences. A catastrophic drop in industrial production; followed by a huge inflation rate as the authorities strove to keep Romania's industries in business, and spiraling retail prices ultimately drove Premier Roman from office sixteen months after securing one of the largest parliamentary majorities in Eastern Europe's postcommunist history.

Roughly a month before the 1990 elections were held, a group of students disillusioned and unable to exercise any influence on a government that claimed to represent the country's "youth" decided to display their anger in the only way they could, by taking over one of the main squares in the center of the capital (University Square), the scene of much bloodshed during the revolution. The police tried to disperse them during the first day but, faced with determined opposition and still unwilling to use force, immediately withdrew. The demonstration continued to grow, leading intellectuals and dissidents joined the students, similar demonstrations of support were held in other towns. But after a month, conditions became very difficult. The demonstrators did not manage to galvanize the nation against the authorities and found little support among Bucharest's population.

Having obtained their electoral mandate, the government decided that it was no longer risky to move against the University Square demonstrators. On 13 June 1990, heavily armed police moved in and violently dispersed the sit-in. Yet the demonstrators came back and the tragic events that followed only added to the web of lies and mystification that began with the revolution and the emergence of the National Salvation Front. According to the authorities, groups of students set fire to the police headquarters nearby, attacked the television station, and rioted in other parts of the capital. Mr. Iliescu quickly accused the demonstrators of initiating "an organized attempt, prepared for a long time, to overthrow by force and violence the government democratically elected on 20 May." Indeed, Bucharest dailies immediately reported that the Legionaries, Romania's prewar fascist bands, appeared "in uniform" on the streets of the capital. Everything followed a now-familiar pattern. Thousands of miners arrived in chartered trains from the country's north and west. For two days, they were fed in specially created centers. They wreaked appalling violence. They beat anyone who appeared to be an "intellectual." The university was devastated, headquarters of political parties were ransacked, and shops were looted. Throughout, the police took no action. The miners were supplied with specially printed maps and directed by individuals who, when asked by journalists to identify themselves, started attacking the foreign press as well. Rumors abounded: it was reported that weapons had been found at the opposition parties' headquarters, together with forged currency notes and drugs. Pictures of these items were reproduced in the press and appeared on television, only to forever disappear immediately thereafter. And nobody was ever arrested or held to account for the death of six people and the wounding of 555 more. A parliamentary committee of inquiry was eventually appointed. With a delay of one year, it filed two reports: one supported by the government and absolving the authorities of any responsibility; the other authored by the opposition and pointing an accusing finger at the government. Yet the most eloquent evidence of what really happened that June was presented by none other than Iliescu, when he thanked the miners for their deeds. During an emotional rally, he congratulated them for their "workers' solidarity" in opposing this "fascist coup." He also told them that the coup was engineered by "foreign forces," who supported "with dollars and drugs" an attempt to "divert the Romanian revolution to the right and take over power." Having spent five months in redefining the essence of the Romanian revolution, Mr. Iliescu was now enacting his own revolution. Any opposition could come only from the "right" and had to be portrayed as an instrument of "foreign powers," tarred with the brush of national treason. Those unwilling to adhere to theories of "democratic centralism" and still prepared to challenge him after his overwhelming victory in the May elections had to be crushed. Yet Mr. Illescu's victory was a pyrrhic one. He achieved complete control at the price of isolating his country for years to come. For more than a year, Romania was shunned by the entire world community. And what had happened once happened again in September 1991, this time with the result of Prime Minster Roman's removal from office.

Yet despite the violent crushing of the University Square demonstration, the opposition to the regime persisted. It ultimately included all the country's intellectuals, as well as a large share of Romania's youth and, more generally, urban population. Bereft of funds and with their meager resources scattered by the miners, the opposition parties continued to struggle in Romania's parliament. The Front, with its crushing majority, did as it pleased, but the opposition enjoyed one last political forum. Parliament's primary task was the drafting of a new constitution and the elaboration of legislation for fresh local and parliamentary elections immediately thereafter. In fact, the local elections were postponed for one year, and a short bill, introduced in direct contravention of the Deputies' own regulations and actually applied before its final approval by parliament, enabled the government to appoint prefects and mayors throughout the country without any popular consultation. Once again, a state institution in operation before the communist takeover of power was revived without any legislation regulating its functions; and very soon, Ceauşescu's practice of instructing local deputies over the telephone was revived. In a rare display of parliamentary powers, deputies demanded the right to elaborate a law regulating the operation of government ministries and their spheres of competence. Yet, while the two chambers were attempting to iron out their differences on the subject, the government ignored parliament altogether and proceeded to create new ministries without having the appropriate legislation. The freshly appointed ministers (initially barred by the electoral law from being members of parliament) made few appearances in the legislature. A year later, a change in the legislature's internal regulation, allowing ministers to retain their parliamentary seats, was announced after, and not before, deputies were already made ministers, while continuing to vote in parliament. During Prime Minister Roman's administration (which lasted for sixteen months), no cumulative state budget was presented, no debate about the budgets of specific ministries was undertaken, and members of parliament had no idea of just how much the country was spending on defense. Meanwhile, the president created his own staff, grouped in separate departments closely shadowing the responsibilities of government ministries. In the absence of any legislation, nobody took the trouble to inquire what the presidential departments would do and, despite rampant inflation, their budget remained ostensibly unchanged for more than a year. More significantly, most of those appointed to the presidential staff were old Securitate officers or Communist Party ideologues, and not one came from the opposition, despite the fact that the presidency was supposedly above all parties and ostensibly neutral.

The two chambers in a united session quickly agreed on the regulations governing the drafting of a new constitution. A drafting committee was established, reflecting the balance of power in parliament. However, while the protocols of the committee's deliberations remained secret, voting on each article was declared open, mainly in order to ensure that all the Front's deputies would toe the party line. From the start, Iliescu was sure of what his parliamentary allies would want: a republic with a strong presidency and a relatively weak legislature. The drafting committee presented its constitutional "theses" in December 1990. These were then submitted to a discussion in the two chambers which for this purpose operated in unison. Once the theses were adopted, they were returned to the committee with suggestions for further drafting and then presented to parliament for a final vote. The government remained determined to push through the constitution at whatever cost, especially since the Front's popularity was constantly falling. Thus, although the elaboration of the constitutional provisions took quite some time, the actual voting was rapid and the final provisions were, in the words of a local observer, "marched" through the chambers. Out of a total of more than 1,100 proposed amendments (of which thirty-nine, or less than 4 percent, came from opposition parties), 145 were incorporated into the final text. Furthermore, since voting was by show of hands, the counting was often defective. On a number of occasions, a particular article was rejected, only to be suddenly approved after a second counting. And toward the end of the procedure new regulations were introduced that called for repeated votes on the same article until it was passed. Finally, the last vote on the entire text was made compulsory for every deputy (in order to defeat any attempt at filibuster and bypass regulations about the legislative quorum); a senator who defied this obligation forfeited his seat, in a procedure unprecedented in the annals of most parliaments.

Thus against the wishes of the opposition and less than two years after toppling the most personalized dictatorship in Eastern Europe, Romania became, according to its new constitution, a presidential republic. The Front was careful to characterize the country's political system as "semi-presidential." Yet, to all intents and purposes, a combination of badly drafted provisions coupled with deliberate ambiguities resulted in a potentially dangerous concentration of power in the hands of one man. More importantly, the Front's majority refused to write into Romania's constitution the principle of the separation of powers that, although not present in many other democratic constitutions, would have helped to calm the opposition's fears. Indeed, by enshrining a Supreme Council for National Defense chaired by the president and tasked with organizing the entire array of Romania's "security"—a wider concept than merely defense—the Front had already created a fusion of different government departments, legislature, and head of state. And to complete the picture, the constitution entrusted legal supervision not to a supreme court of irremovable and impartial judges but to a council of legal experts, appointed for a fixed period of time by the president and parliament.

Parliament allowed the government additional powers that may thwart democratic guarantees. Thus, the government may rule by decrees and ordinances under parliament's specific delegation. The government may also enforce "emergency ordinances" by merely presenting them to the legislature, rather than obtaining their approval. A constitutional referendum was performed hurriedly, in what became another mockery of democratic procedures. Giving a further indication of just how much the Front feared the monarchy, the government argued that a simple "yes" vote to the new constitution that defined the state as a republic settled the issue forever. To the surprise of all parties (including the Front), the "campaign" for the constitutional referendum was declared to have begun on the date the fundamental legal text was finally approved by the legislature. Within two days (one of which was a weekend), returning officers had to be appointed. Two days thereafter, parties had to nominate, if they wished, representatives in no less than 14,000 ballot stations and had an additional forty-eight hours to query electoral rolls and ballot procedures. The entire campaign was scheduled to last exactly six days. A high abstention rate was predicted, especially given the season's harsh climate. Yet, once opposition parties called for a boycott of a referendum whose results were known in advance, the authorities did everything possible to ensure a respectable turnout. Ballot rules were flouted. Ignoring the law that prohibited any campaigning a day before the referendum, Mr. Iliescu himself appealed to Romanians to vote for the constitution. More importantly, after the vote, the country learnt that the electoral roll, which stood at seventeen million in May 1990, had been reduced to just over fifteen million in sixteen months. The attempt to boost the turnout figures by reducing the number of those eligible to vote was so haphazard and poorly coordinated that the total declared figure did not even tally with the number of the electorate as reported by each county. Significantly, one of the members of the Central Electoral Bureau reported instances of fraud during the vote, but her evidence was never even considered—by either government or opposition. According to the official figures, 77.3 percent of the ballots cast were for the new constitution and 20.4 percent against. The government claimed a complete victory. However, this was far from being the case. The turnout was 69.1 percent according to the "revamped" electoral roll and, therefore, it is evident that even if the authorities' figures are to be believed, only 53.5 percent of the electorate opted for Romania's new constitution. Although abstentions cannot be equated with outright opposition, it is also clear that the constitution did not obtain the popular legitimacy that the authorities so craved.

Despite the reputation of being run by Eastern Europe's most heinous communist regime, Romania was showered with praise by the West throughout much of the Cold War, though only because the country seemingly dared to stand up to the Soviet Union. Many ordinary Romanians, who had to suffer Ceaușescu's dictatorship, feel genuinely distressed that soon after their December 1989 anticommunist rebellion, they were shunned by the West. Yet unfortunately for my country, circumspection about the people who took over after Ceaușescu's overthrow remains warranted. Romania has most of the trappings of a Western democracy, with less of its substance. Appearances still matter more than realities. Ultimately, the government aped Romania's historic institutions, seeking to legitimize its existence by appeals to nationalism, but emptying these institutions of any meaning. The two chambers of parliament were revived, but no definition of responsibilities was offered. Romania has many scores of political parties, but not one is able to gain power; it has thousands of publications, all of which are starved of funds and readers; the security services are ostensibly accountable to parliament but, in practice, remain a law unto themselves. In 1990, the tally of votes cast exceeded the number of people on the electoral roll by one million; in 1992, no less than 13 percent of the votes cast were declared invalid. Even with a plethora of political parties, none of Romania's three postrevolutionary prime ministers came and left power as a result of a fully transparent democratic process. The West's greatest fear in Eastern Europe has been a coalition between former communists and fanatical nationalists, yet this is precisely what Romania's government has been since 1992.

The fact that Romania is run by former communist officials is unremarkable: the same situation exists in many other East European countries. But there is a difference, for Romania is governed by people still determined to legitimize the communist inheritance. This is particularly apparent in the government's privatization policy. From 1992, all Romanians were issued with privatization vouchers but, as nothing happened, most people disposed of their certificates. In 1994, however, the government proposed to issue a fresh set of vouchers, at once dispossessing those who had bought the first voucher issue and discrediting the concept of privatization altogether. The problem is not one of plain ignorance but, rather, one of deliberate policy pursued by people who want to avoid the creation of a propertied middle class, so important to any functioning democracy. The result was to be expected: investors are wary. Foreign direct investment into Romania totaled only five dollars per person last year, the lowest in any former communist state. And Romania's condition is also proof of the fact that the choice between a slow or rapid pace of economic change really does not exist: the country suffers now from all the pains of economic reform (including huge inflation rates) with few of the benefits.

There is a tight interdependence between the progress of economic reform and the state of democracy and social stability in a country. The powers that be in Romania have displayed a lack of political will for change and this has badly hampered the economic reconstruction of my country. Moreover, a government that is not seen to be legitimate can hardly be expected to implement economic reform effectively. Legitimacy is not simply a technical matter of ballot papers and electoral boxes, but is also a matter of trust between those ruling and those ruled. The basic mistrust between Romanians and their rulers is at the root of my country's problems.

By Way of a Prescription

The governments of all European states are grappling with immense problems for, indeed, everything is now back on the drawing board: the pace of European unification, the continent's security structures, the future of European-American relations, and, most importantly, the chance of making democracy triumph.

Many of these questions will, no doubt, take years to work out. Yet a few tentative conclusions can already be offered. First, the age of the monolithic single-party communist state on our continent is now over. Wherever applied and in whatever form—from the Goulash variety of communism in Hungary to the Gulag variety in the Soviet Union—it has failed to ensure either economic prosperity or social equality. Ultimately, it was not the West but the people of Eastern Europe—my country included—who relegated this system to the dustbin of history. Second, the collapse of totalitarian communism has unlocked a whole host of problems that have remained unsolved for the last forty years. These include ethnic disputes and territorial demands, but also serious social injustices and questions of national identity. Third, it is clear—as I have outlined in my survey of Romania—that the collapse of one totalitarian system is no guarantee of the triumph of democracy.

The countries that used to be grouped together under the common heading of the "Eastern bloc" are ancient states with rich histories and traditions. As they find their feet and re-create their national institutions, they will diverge. Therefore, the task today is not to impose uniformity but, rather, to make sure that the basic ingredients of a democracy will always survive. Finally—and most importantly—it is also clear that what we witnessed in 1989 throughout Eastern Europe were, to a certain extent, revolutions directed from above, by intellectuals, dissidents, and a number of courageous politicians. Before us lies the much more difficult task of encouraging a revolution from below, a radical transformation in peoples' mentalities and expectations. A true democracy is sustained by a social contract between those ruling and those ruled, and cannot be achieved by simply imposing an ostensibly democratic constitution from above.

A democratic government should start by encouraging democracy to grow from the bottom up, rather than seek to maintain a political experiment controlled from above. It should offer people the truth, and nothing but the truth, including a realistic estimate of the pain associated with inevitable economic reform and dispelling any notions that, somehow, the supposedly comfortable certainties of the communist past can be preserved. Yes, all these are easier said than done, but without the creation of trust between those governing and those governed there will be no prosperous future. The trust is established not only by refusing to lie any longer, but also by becoming engaged in the process of dialogue between those ruled and those ruling.

The leaders of Eastern Europe therefore bear the heavy responsibility of creating this social contract, very often from scratch. The leaders of Romania may have done less than others, but a civil society is now being recreated from below. Much time has been wasted, but in the long course of Romanian history, the current travails may, I hope, yet be just a transitional phase.

My country probably represents the best example of the contradictions, difficulties, and ironies of Eastern Europe's current predicament. In terms of territory, Romania is second only to Poland in the region; however, it is also now one of the poorest countries on the continent. Before the Second World War, the Romanian Communist Party was probably the weakest in Europe. Yet my country experienced one of the most cruel of communist regimes, governed by essentially two Stalinist rulers who went to their graves both unreformed and unrepentant. Furthermore, these rulers, who espoused a supposedly internationalist ideology of the working class, were also responsible for unleashing the most vicious nationalism imaginable. And to add to all this, Romania was also the only East European state to experience a violent revolution in 1989, yet for all that remains a country in which the fight for democracy is still far from won.

I have never accepted the view that Romanians are somehow incapable of or still unprepared for democracy. Democracy can certainly flourish with economic prosperity; but, at the same time, without democratic institutions, the true benefits of economic prosperity can seldom be enjoyed by all people. The two notions reinforce each other and—to my mind—are inseparable. Thus, no East European country should have any illusion that it can somehow achieve prosperity without political freedoms: this supposed middle road does not exist, as Romania's postrevolutionary experience indicates. Romania has both economic and political decay in equal measures. And there is another lesson: there is now no middle road between freedom and dictatorship in Europe. Instead of "democratization," the people of the continent expect democracy pure and simple. The old ruling communist system must be swept from power, together with its apparatus of repression, its network of secret surveillance, its privileges, and its supposed planned economy. The transformation must be total, or it will ultimately amount to no transformation at all.

By calling for radical measures, I do not intend to advocate a witch-hunt or a policy of recrimination. It is another one of the ironies of my country that the Romanian Communist Party increased to a membership of millions, yet few were those who ever believed in the system or in its ideology. As one of our intellectuals remarked, for the majority of Romanians membership of the Communist Party was very similar to obtaining a driver's license: a necessary document for social mobility and advancement. These millions of people should not be victimized, and I know of no responsible party in Romania that advocates such a measure.

At the same time, however, no democracy can survive without popular accountability and, more importantly, truth. To be sure, the fear instilled by almost forty-five years of dictatorship will take a long time to wear off. However, it will never be dispelled completely if it is replaced by a hazy world of half-truths and semi-falsehoods, a state that is neither democracy nor dictatorship. Since the revolution, I have maintained contacts with many Romanians, from all walks of life and political persuasions. And it is with sorrow that I often still encounter the same fear of the authorities, the same suspicions and apprehensions as in the past.

Obviously, much has improved in Romania since the dark ages of communism. Yet it is now time to stop comparing our time with our lowest historical point; we must look forward to a better future. I will not pretend that Romania was a perfect democracy in the interwar period. Yet the 1923 constitution, which I restored in 1944, guaranteed the rights of the individual and of ethnic minorities as groups. And under this constitution, Romania flourished. None of Romania's prewar intellectuals were meek or spineless people, none tolerated dictatorship, none composed songs of praise to Ceauşescu. There are many like them in Romania today, and more will come forward given the right environment. Democracy is not merely a system of government: it is a way of life that must be based on truth, tolerance, and respect for the rule of law. It is an ideal that always needs further improvement. It is these ingredients, rather than the formal trappings of a state of law and order, that my country still needs today. Without these ingredients, any constitution—however perfectly drafted and solemnly proclaimed—will hardly be honored or applied.

Our continent is facing another major challenge: the specter of unrestrained nationalist movements, coupled with territorial demands and general instability. The situation, of course, varies from country to country, and my suggestions must be confined to the one place I know best. First, there is nothing inherently wrong in expressing pride in one's own country and its achievements. The West must understand that, after over forty years of a totalitarian regime that perverted all history and glorified nonentities, an outburst of national pride—and the re-creation of symbols and history—is necessary and positive. The states of Eastern Europe are reviving their true identities and the process need not be destabilizing.

Second, it is important to remember that our historical experience is different from that of Western Europe. While Western European states were created gradually, through the enlargement of kingdoms over a relatively lengthy period of time, our states were created often suddenly, out of the breakup of multinational empires. It is therefore only natural that Romanians should feel sensitive about their national unity, about according some ethnic groups specific rights and creating separate entities within their state. This is not to say that ethnic minorities should be ignored or that their justifiable demands for the protection of their traditions, languages, and religions should not be met. However, we would do well to remember that this task requires patience, determination, and not a small amount of negotiation. I would like the Romanian people to understand that only when the legitimate aspirations of all citizens are respected, only when ethnic minorities are made to feel equal, will territorial disputes be banished from Europe. A new democracy that starts with racial hatred ultimately ends as a dictatorship, and Romanians will remember that the violent individuals who launched the anti-Semitic campaign in the late 1930s finished by destroying Romania's parliamentary democracy and assassinating the country's best politicians.

What can therefore be done now? First, it is important to realize that, despite all the errors (both those deliberately committed and those unintentionally applied), a civil society is being created in Romania. This is of fundamental importance, and certainly no easy task to undertake in a country used to totalitarianism and centralism. This concept, civil society, has now become a mass slogan, yet it is critical for the success of democracy and prosperity in the whole of Europe. Only civil society can provide a solid infrastructure for political and economic success, which implies the generation of that creative plethora of organizations and institutions that intervene between isolated individuals and powerful governments. It is the emergence of civil society, or the lack of it, that will be the decisive factor in determining whether the twin revolutions of democracy and prosperity succeed or fail, by remaining vulnerable to personalized or central power. But hand in hand with political and economic renewal, a moral renewal must take place. Above all else, the transition to a truly democratic society is, and must be seen to be, an act of moral regeneration.

The task is formidable, but we must tackle it and must succeed. This entails a moral reconstruction of society, the restoration of civic awareness, the renewal of democratic debate, and the crystallization of political plurality in the broadest sense. It entails the rehabilitation, in my country, of such values as honesty, trust, openness, solidarity, love, personal responsibility. And it entails the establishment of a new spirit of community and shared purpose, and an awareness that, in spite of our differences, we all belong to the same moral universe.

Equally important is the fact that, despite their authoritarian methods of control, the only ideology that the country's current leaders can adopt is still that of the market economy and democracy. Democracy may be honored more in word than in practice. Nevertheless, sooner or later, democratic aspirations will bury authoritarian leaders. Signs of this are already apparent: uniquely among the former communist states, trade unions in Romania are demanding more, rather than less, economic reform, and only the government now stands in their way. It will not be able to do so for much longer.

And here the West has an important role to play. Having isolated Romania during its first two postcommunist years, the West was right to switch its tactics. Romania signed its association treaty with the European Union in 1994 and was admitted as a member of the Council of Europe. I have supported and encouraged both these moves, for Romania's incorporation into European institutions can be a critical factor in promoting change within the country. And embracing Romania has given the West some useful levers for applying pressure: The Council of Europe reports twice yearly on Romania's human rights performance, and the Council's latest study has uncovered a list of problems, ranging from the casual arrest of journalists for "bringing into disrepute" the "presidential institution" to an inadequate and still politically influenced judiciary. This critical approach must continue and should intensify; only persistence and patience on the part of the West could serve notice on the country's leaders that European standards of human rights, to which Romania now officially subscribes, are applicable throughout Europe without exceptions.

But ultimately, it will be for the Romanians, including myself, to re-create our own country. Even the best government, with the best intentions and policies, will need years to bring economic prosperity to any East European state. Clearly, the task cannot be accomplished without Western aid and, clearly, this aid must be tied to democratic progress, as well as to a coherent economic program. The West must not squander the opportunity of promoting democracy in the East. Therefore, the West must not offer economic help simply to prevent radical change, simply because it fears what may happen. Change, radical change, is necessary and inevitable, and must start in Eastern Europe itself, among its people.

In pursuing this task, the institution of the monarchy may offer a few important advantages, such as unity, stability, national legitimacy, and managed but radical change, all at the same time. An analysis of Romania's present conditions shows that these ingredients are the ones that are most lacking. Romanians doubt that they have really made the transition from communism to democracy;

the present authorities are contested not only because of their policies but, very often, because of who they are and what they did in their communist past. The essence of Romania's problem is a lack of faith in its present and in its future. Young Romanians often tell me that their social experience has taught them that, as they put it, "nothing is worth trying." I know from my conversations with them how frustrated and disillusioned they are. Romania deserves better than second best. Hope must be returned to the tens of thousands of young people whose only desire now is to abandon ship. These are the very people without whom the reconstruction of the country—arduous and painful, in any case—will be even more difficult. The monarchy would represent a decisive break with the troubled past. It would act as an ultimate arbiter between political parties. And it would reassure ethnic minorities in our country that they will no longer be used as pawns in wider political struggles. Anyone who believes that a monarchy is a thing of the past had best look at events in Spain during the last two decades, as well as in Belgium, where monarchy represents a moral authority capable of transcending specific historical and cultural identities. Of course, every country is different: Spain's problems were not as vast in 1975 as Romania's are today (and the challenges facing my country are not comparable to those of Yugoslavia). Nevertheless, I am convinced that the monarchy, which contributed so much to the building of modern Romania from independence, and guided the country throughout its adulthood, still offers the best point of unity. Our aim must be unity not division, reconciliation not retribution, selfless dedication to our country and its people and not narrow political gain and self-advancement. Unity in political diversity: that was the dream of the fathers of the European Community, and that is my dream for Romania today.

—*March 1995*

THE BIRTH OF PEACE

A Ballet

René Descartes

Translated and with an afterword by André Gombay

AT 5, 616

Ballet Danced in Stockholm's Royal Palace on Her Majesty's Birthday
December 19, 1649

Words sung before the ballet

Let us stand here in silence
And revere the presence
Of the Goddess who rules in these lands:
She wants to draw us away from the hazards of war,
And, unlike some other Gods,
Wants peace to return upon earth.
Let us hail that peace
As the greatest of her bounties.

Originally published in *Common Knowledge* 20.2 (Spring 2014): 371–86. © 2014 by Duke University Press.

Common Knowledge 25:1–3
DOI 10.1215/0961754X-7579449

Thanks to her prudence
And the secret influence
Of the generous commands that she has given us,
We have fought to such advantage

That large stunned nations have come under our rule
And to us now pay homage.
But the birth of peace
Is the greatest of her bounties.

So let us celebrate that birth
And declare in this dance,
Where war and peace each display their strength,
That Pallas is right in thinking
That war, even the best one can have,
Strips away much beauty from the earth;
And so, bringing us peace
Is the greatest of her bounties.

Verses of the ballet

First dancing entry: MARS

I want to make every corner of the earth tremble,
And show mortals that no other God
Has ever in this world had as much power as I have,
Not even he who discharges thunder.
His flashes of lightning, his fires, cause only minor fear
Whereas my cannons and other machines,
My mortars, my pistols, fires and mines,
Bring everywhere death along with terror.
I crush rocks, flatten mountains,
Fill moats, destroy castles,
Bloody the seas, burn vessels
And litter with corpses the fairest of lands.

Second dancing entry: FOUR LARGE MEN,
two from cavalry, two from infantry,
Representing an army corps led by Pallas.

Mars must not credit himself
With the top honors of war.

618

The sky, the sea, the air and the earth,
It is Jupiter's Daughter
Who alone deserves those honors.

It is Pallas, whose prudence
Is so tied to valor
That excess assurance
Never gives her excess ardor.
She is wise, vigilant,
Courageous, and constant.

So she is in our body
The head without which it cannot live;
And we make every effort
For the honor of escorting her.
Without her, that severed body
Despised by all would be.

When it pleases her to lead us,
All lands to us are open,
Nothing can harm us,
We can vanquish the universe,
And often have the glory
Of here bringing victory.

Third dancing entry: PANIC

It is wrongly that Pallas and Mars
Boast that in hazardous straits
Their power has no match:
Mine is much more fearsome.

They need hard labor,
Grand decorum:
Gunpowder, horses, and arms,
And men who rush to alarms
To fight just one battle
Which, even though they look good
And their breed is godly,
They lose often enough.

619

But I, who make much less noise
I, who am a daughter of the night,
Who am cold, pale, and trembling,
When I want to bestow terror
Upon one million fighting men
And trample on their laurels,
All I need is a fantasy,
A dream, a light shadow
That I send into their brain.
They then tremble like calves,
They turn ashen, they flee
And often throw themselves
Into evils more to be dreaded
Than the ones they think they have avoided.

Fourth dancing entry: Some RUNAWAY SOLDIERS whom panic has led to
defect from the army before the battle.

To Ladies:

We have defended ourselves well;
But we were sold:
Our leaders did nothing of any worth.
All fields are littered with corpses,
On our side everyone is dead.
We have lost the battle.

The enemies are close.
We have come running,
For the express purpose to defend you.
If they come we shall show them

That we have the puissance
To punish their impudence.

Dear beauties, fear not
That our hearts be missing,
Even though you keep them captive.
We shall be lionhearted enough,
And also most joyful
If your own hearts you deign to give us.

620

Fifth dancing entry: VOLUNTEERS, going to the camp
as the battle is about to begin.

We go with courage,
With no fear of fire or sword,
So as to help capture
A most beautiful and rich lady.
We only go for the sake of the battle,
Since the lady herself is not for us.
Our highest expectation
Is to perhaps enjoy
The favors of her young maid.
To gain that prize,
We are not afraid
To risk our own demise.

Hearing that this is our aim,
If you doubt our courage,
You may think that we are not very wise,
That our minds are unhealthy;
And perhaps also that our fair companions
Will view us as unfaithful.

But when we tell you
Who your maid is
That pleases us all,
You shall no longer be surprised:
That maid is Glory,
And her mistress is Victory.

Sixth dancing entry: VICTORY

Even though this Court only houses ladies
That are beyond esteem,
And that the noblest souls
Are bound to love,
I still surpass in beauty
The most beautiful of them.
Proof is that
For every lover who sighs for them,
A thousand die for me.

621

Seventh dancing entry: CRIPPLED SOLDIERS

Whoever sees what we are like,
And thinks that war is beautiful
Or worth more than peace,
Is crippled in his brain.

Eighth dancing entry: LACKEYS, about to engage in pillage.

Our fate is thought to be
The cheeriest in the army,
For we are never exposed to blows:
Our masters fight the battle for us,
And when they gain the advantage,
We, ahead of them, go for pillage.

Still, whatever our booty,
Whatever profit we gain from it,
We never get rich,
For we know not how to be niggardly:

What we have gained so swiftly
We always squander thoughtlessly.
In affluence one day,
In penury the next,
We have so much ill time,

So little contentment,
That in truth
None of us can find the war any good;
Its crop is all quite nasty;
And since our life is thought
To be the blithest in the army,
Peace is what everyone must desire.

Ninth dancing entry: RUINED PEASANTS

Without an oath,
We can assure you
That war to us brings harm.
Still, as you see us dancing here
You may think
That our hearts have but sparse feelings.

622

Consider, though, that in our extreme misery,
We have no oxen, no horses
To labor for us;
No hens, no eggs, no butter,
To carry and sell outside our village.

Poverty, as we all know,
Teaches idleness.
Having nothing left to worry about,
We need spend no time complaining;
And so are void of all care.

Tenth entry: EARTH, dancing with the other three Elements.

Seeing fire amid water,
When vessels are burning there;
Feeling it in my chest
When a shell that has hit me,
Tears me up
And blows limbs of mine into the air;
Seeing this air filled with gunpowder
And with fires worse than lightning;

In short, seeing that battles
All earthly bodies perturb,
I fear that in a short while
Earth will perish or be disarrayed
And become chaos—
Unless to these lands the Gods send peace.

TALE sung in the sky before the *Eleventh entry*, where Pallas dances alone.

People: even though war abuses you
And Mars seemingly persists
In wanting to ruin you all,
Do not lose courage.
Pallas can compel fate
To soon bring war to an end.

623

Victories are assured
When it pleases her to seek them.
But much dearer to her is your own good.
She is weary to see your sorrows,
She can compel fate
To bring them soon to an end.

So thank her benevolence,
In the fine goals that she has devised.
As for the ills that have come,
Suffer them with forbearance:
She can compel fate
To bring them soon to an end.

Twelfth entry: JUSTICE, dancing with Pallas, for the sake of Peace.

Pallas always orders me
To accompany her armies,
For without my help,
They would be overblamed.

But she also orders me
To be a faithful companion

Of the peace that hither has come,
And wears a crown with her.

And from this moment on,
I hope to be so constant
In maintaining this peace,
That it will blossom and flourish.

Thirteenth entry: all the GODS—debating with Peace.

Our interests are so diverse
That we are not to be believed about what is glorious
And good in the universe.

Mars, for example, would be blamable
If he didn't love war.
And on the contrary, if Earth loved it,
Astonished we should be.

Pallas alone is both
A war- and a peace-lover;
So let none of us take it upon himself
To control her judgment.

Fourteenth entry: MERCURY, to RENOWN, dancing with it
as he comes to publicize Peace.

Stay close to me, RENOWN.
For, when you march first
You are so prone to telling lies
That the wise often
Take as true
Just the contrary
Of what you seek to make them believe.

RENOWN's answer

Are you any more than me believable?
Are you less than me reproachable?

624

You, who are the God of merchants
And of the wickedest thieves?
You, whose cheatings
Have duped many virginities?
Still, when you announce Peace,
May you never be a liar.

Fifteenth entry: APOLLO, dancing with Pallas.

Now that Peace has come
And Mars has turned his tail,
Pallas can use me,
In the states under her rule,
To repair in scant years
All the sites that have been ruined.

625

I can with very good reasons
Assure her that my songs
Will not be useless to her:
For, like ancient Amphion,
I have, through the mere sound of my voice,
Power to erect cities.

Sixteenth dancing entry: the NINE MUSES

Ladies, we have come to invite you
To walk in the footsteps of Pallas,
Your most learned mistress,
Who is ignorant of nothing,
And whose supreme virtue
Is wisdom.

If you only perceive
What sex we are,
And how great our knowledge is,
To no man will you want to give
The glory of owning all the arts.

Even if you don't care
To surpass them by very much,
You will have no excuse —
Given where we live:
For one Apollo, nine Muses we are.

Seventeenth entry: the EARTH, dancing with the three Graces.

Be not surprised to see me young and fair —
I, who not long ago, looked so different.
My nature is such that I become novel
As soon as I feel contentment.

When my forests are gashed, my towns ruined,
My fields all abandoned, my castles destroyed,
It is fair to say that I am time-worn,
And that my dead limbs are almost buried.

626

But with the return of peace, my towns are healed,
New forests are sown, new castles are built,
My fields are plowed to make them prosper:
Thanks to them I have limbs that are all new.

Eighteenth entry: JANUS, closing the door of his temple.

You must not be surprised
To see me with two visages:
I have become a sage,
Thanks to those who gave them to me.

The givers believed
That the memory of what is gone
Helps to make one know
What is to come.

And so I have two foreheads:
One is at the back and pictures
All the life that is past;
The other is geared to the future.

It is common belief
That these two foreheads are similar.
But times being changeable,
We must think differently.

Having till now seen nothing
But a very long war,
And Peace arriving on Earth
To rescue us from anguish,

One need not be much learned,
Or think extravagant thoughts,
To believe that my rear visage
Is less handsome than the one at the front.

627

Nineteenth entry: KNIGHTS dancing a grand ballet.

Adorable Pallas, whose godly powers
Govern in war as in peace
All the acts that go against vice,
Could any follower of yours fail to do his duty?

We, who have the honor of being your knights,
Wish to follow you on Mount Parnassus
As well as on the powder fields of Thrace's mighty God,
So that we appear next to you and gather laurels.

But we do not hope to climb as high as you:
The Mount has levels: the higher each of us gets,
The more knowledge and grace he is thought to have.
You alone have climbed to the highest.

It is enough for us that we live in a body
Whose arms we are, and you the divine flame
That by itself directs all and is called the soul.
Arms need only be supple and strong.

Words sung before the Ladies' grand ballet
In which PALLAS, PEACE, and JUSTICE dance with
the Muses and the Graces.

Humans, what do you think as you behold
All the marvels that dazzle your eyes?
They are unlike anything seen so far on this earth:
Think that your minds have been ravished into the skies.

You are about to see Pallas, the Muses, and the Graces;
Justice and Peace, also.
Won't you deem, as you look at their faces
That all that graces heaven is here?

Through Pallas we hear eternal wisdom.
It is Pallas who reigns in these lands.
Justice and Peace reign with her:
Yet we have only one Queen, and one God.

Afterword

At the end of a letter sent from Stockholm on December 18, 1649, to a Parisian diplomat, the Vicomte de Brégy, Descartes writes that he is appending "the verses of a ballet that will be danced here tomorrow night."[1] Descartes says no more, but it is generally believed, following his biographer Adrien Baillet, that the verses he appended were his own.[2] Apparently, Queen Christina had asked him to dance at the celebration of her twenty-third birthday; he pleaded physical incapacity and instead wrote verse in honor of the event—verse also meant to celebrate the recent signing of the Treaty of Münster that ended the ultramurderous Thirty Years' War. The title of his piece was *La Naissance de la Paix*. Descartes died a few weeks later. The *Naissance* was lost, and not found again until around 1920: it now graces the standard edition.[3] There is of course no certainty that what we have here are the lines that Descartes appended to the Brégy letter and, even if they are, that it was he who wrote them. Question: can we perhaps find Cartesian motifs in this *Naissance* as it has reached us?

Motif is perhaps a strong word, but we certainly meet in the poem por-

1. AT 5, 457 [= vol. 5, p. 147, of the *Œuvres de Descartes*, ed. Charles Adam and Paul Tannery, 2nd ed., 11 vols. (Paris: J. Vrin, 1964–76)]. This is the standard mode of reference to Cartesian texts.

2. Adrien Baillet, *La Vie de Monsieur Des-Cartes*, 2 vols. (Paris: Horthemels, 1691), 2:395.

3. AT 5, 616–27. I have put the page numbers on the left-hand margin of the text.

trayals of a conduct that figures prominently in the philosophical work, namely, duplicity. Remember, the *Meditations* begin with Descartes worrying that God might constantly deceive him, even in his most assured beliefs. It turns out (next meditation) that there is one belief about which there can be no deception—the certainty that he, Descartes, has of having a mind. This is the *Cogito.* Two meditations later, we learn that it is not possible that God should *ever* deceive, which brings about an inculpating query: why has God so created us that we are so often mistaken? Answer (*Meditation Four*): it is we who deceive ourselves; our mistakes occur because we misuse an immense and positive faculty that God has given us, free will. Readers may accept this verdict, but it does not end the matter as far as Descartes and delusion are concerned. On the final pages of the sixth and final meditation, he points out that not all our mistakes come about in the *Meditation Four* way—for example, the lapse of the man suffering from dropsy who craves drink even though drinking is deadly for him; or the fault of the young woman who feels pain in a finger even though, unknown to her, the hand whose finger it is has been cut off from her body. The man and the woman *are* deceived—not by themselves, not by God, but by *nature.* These are perhaps uncommon cases, yet Descartes returns to them more than once in the published work, for instance, in the *Reply* to the second set of *Objections* (AT 7, 143), or in one of the final articles (bk. 4, no. 196) of his final metaphysical opus, the *Principles of Philosophy.* Why this persistent attention? Answer: "deception by nature" is used by Descartes to introduce an important doctrine about human beings—that in them mind and body are *united.*

Mind, free will, mind-and-body—these are major philosophical topics, and Descartes approaches them all through the lenses of deception. Turn now to *La Naissance*: are its viewers not offered that path too, at two perhaps important moments? The first is the commonplace story that cowardly soldiers tell in the fourth entry (619) of having fought bravely, when they have actually run away—we shall soon see that this is more significant than it looks. More immediately puzzling is the dialogue, ten entries later (624), between Mercury and Renown (*Renommée*), where each accuses the other of being apt to lie (*mentir*). Mercury is the god of trade, so there is no mystery in the charge. But why *renommée?*

That indictment brings us, I think, to Descartes's deepest reason for writing the poem at all—hatred of war. The *Naissance* is an emphatic paean to pacifism. Perhaps the starkest utterance of that creed is the pronouncement of the seventh entry's *crippled soldiers* (621):

Whoever sees what we are like,
And thinks that war is beautiful
Or worth more than peace,
Is crippled in his brain.

Again and again, the poem stresses the horror of war—the wounds, the deaths, the destructions. So why do human beings, why does the goddess Pallas (= Queen Christina), engage in it so profusely? The lure cannot be the material gains that victory brings: they end up being squandered, as we are told by warfare's prime profiteers, the plundering lackeys of the eighth entry (621):

What we have gained so swiftly
We always squander thoughtlessly.
. . . In truth
No one can find the war good;
Its fruit are all very bad; . . .
Peace is what everyone must desire.

Why does everyone, then, not preserve constant peace?

The answer is that the plundering lackeys have overlooked *one* fruit they have not plucked. Fighting in battles, we learn in the fifth and sixth entry (620), attracts thousands of volunteers, who are ready to risk their lives. Why this readiness? Because by winning, they will gain the favors of a marvelously attractive young woman, a servant-maid of Victory:

When we tell you
Who the maid is
That pleases us all,
You shall no longer be surprised:
That maid is *Glory*.

We have just met the big word, one that blossoms in late Descartes—*la gloire*. Without the impersonation, we find it elsewhere in the *Naissance* (in the second, thirteenth, and sixteenth entries); and, more important, the word appears about a dozen times in a treatise that our philosopher had been writing for the previous few years and that came out in Paris just as he arrived in Sweden: *Les Passions de l'Âme* (*The Passions of the Soul*). Glory, we are told there, is a *passion* (article 27)—a personal sentiment or emotion—aroused (article 66) by "the good that is or has been in us, related to the opinion that others may have of it." This characterization is expanded in article 204: *gloire* "is a kind of joy based on the love we have for ourselves and resulting from the belief or hope we have of being praised by some other people." So, as a fighting soldier of the *Naissance*, I may gain *gloire*, which (according to Descartes) would involve in me two mental events. The first is a kind of joy at having fought (in English, we probably would call it "pride"), and the second, a belief that others admire me for doing so (and so, here, the English word *glory* works as a translation, as does the synonym we meet in entry 14 of the poem: *renommée* or, in English, "renown"). Cartesianly, belief in renown is vital to pride. On a desert island, I could not feel proud of having climbed a perilous 5,000-meter peak, for *renommée* would not be obtainable there.

Renown is one of the parties in entry 14 (624), and there we take note of a new factor. *Renown* is not always a synonym of *glory*; it can be an antonym—there can be *bad* renown. Suppose I am one of the soldiers in entry 4 (619) and have not fought the enemy but have run away, and my doing so becomes known: my renown will now be that of a renowned coward. I shall accede to *renommée* but not to *gloire*; rather, I shall merit the opposite—*honte*, shame, "a kind of sadness also based on self-love, which proceeds from the expectation or fear of being blamed" (*Passions*, article 205). To avoid that fate I may well not avow my run but seek to conceal it, telling the ladies that I was sold (*vendu*) by my officers' military ineptitude and, having lost the battle, had to take to my heels. Fear of bad and wish of good renown make me lie (which is the charge made in entry 14). Indeed, I may even be lying in a more complex manner: to myself! I might regard my run as having issued not from the vice of cowardice but from the virtue of prudence. This sort of substitution is what vanity (*vanité*) involves—so Descartes says in article 206 of the *Passions*, adding that it occurs "in quite a few people."

Entry 14 of *La Naissance* ends with Renown voicing the hope that Mercury may never lie when he announces peace. Fear of a deceiving god—are we not entitled to suppose that the author of the *Meditations* also wrote the verse of our ballet?

M. H. Abrams (1912–2015) was a recipient of the US National Humanities Medal and of the American Academy of Arts and Sciences Award for Humanistic Studies. A professor of English literature at Cornell University for nearly forty years, he was the founding editor of *The Norton Anthology of English Literature* and the author of *The Mirror and the Lamp*, which was included on a Modern Library list among the most important books of the twentieth century. His other writings include *Natural Supernaturalism*; *The Correspondent Breeze*; *Doing Things with Texts*; and *The Fourth Dimension of a Poem*, edited by his student Harold Bloom.

Edward Albee (1928–2016) received three Pulitzer Prizes and seven Tony Awards, including one for lifetime achievement, as well as the US National Medal of Arts, recognition at the Kennedy Center Honors, the Gold Medal in Drama of the American Academy and Institute of Arts and Letters, and the PEN/Laura Pels Theater Award. His plays include *Who's Afraid of Virginia Woolf?*; *A Delicate Balance*; *Three Tall Women*; *Seascape*; *The Zoo Story*; *The Sandbox*; *The Play about the Baby*; *The Goat, or Who Is Sylvia?*; *Tiny Alice*; and *The Ballad of the Sad Café*.

Barry Allen is distinguished university professor of philosophy at McMaster and a fellow of the Royal Society of Canada. He is the author of *Truth in Philosophy*; *Knowledge and Civilization*; *Artifice and Design*; *Vanishing into Things*; and *Striking Beauty*.

Wayne Andersen (1928–2014) was a painter, corporate art consultant, architect of the King Khaled Mosque in Riyadh, and professor of art history and architecture for more than twenty years at the Massachusetts Institute of Technology. His many books include *The Youth of Cézanne and Zola*; *Manet: The Picnic and the Prostitute*; *Gauguin's Paradise Lost*; *Picasso's Brothel*; *Marcel Duchamp: The Failed Messiah*; *German Artists and Hitler's Mind*; and *The Ara Pacis of Augustus and Mussolini*.

Kwame Anthony Appiah is professor of philosophy and law at New York University and Laurance S. Rockefeller University Professor of Philosophy Emeritus at Princeton. Among his books are *Cosmopolitanism*; *The Ethics of Identity*; *As If: Idealization and Ideals*; *The Honor Code: How Moral Revolutions Happen*; *Experiments in Ethics*; and *In My Father's House: Africa in the Philosophy of Culture*. He delivered the BBC's Reith Lectures in 2016 on the theme of "mistaken identities."

Sir Isaiah Berlin (1909–97) taught philosophy and intellectual history at Oxford University for sixty-five years, mainly as a fellow of Wolfson College, of which he was the founding president, and as Chichele Professor of Social and Political Theory at All Souls College. Appointed to the UK Order of Merit in 1971 and to the presidency of the British Academy in 1974, he received the Jerusalem Prize in 1979 for contributions to "the freedom of the individual in society." His books include *The Hedgehog and the Fox*; *Four Essays on Liberty*; *The Age of Enlightenment*; *Three Critics of the Enlightenment*; *Against the Current*; *The Magus of the*

North: J. G. Hamann and the Origins of Modern Irrationalism; *Vico and Herder*; *The Crooked Timber of Humanity*; *Russian Thinkers*; *Karl Marx: His Life and Environment*; *Concepts and Categories*; *Historical Inevitability*; *Personal Impressions*; and four volumes of correspondence.

Sir John Boardman is Lincoln professor of classical art and archaeology emeritus at Oxford University and a fellow of the British Academy, which awarded him its Kenyon Medal in 1995. Editor of the *Oxford History of Classical Art*, his other books include *The Greeks in Asia*; *The Diffusion of Classical Art in Antiquity*; *The Greeks Overseas*; *The Triumph of Dionysos*; *The History of Greek Vases*; and *The Relief Plaques of Eastern Eurasia and China*. He received the inaugural Onassis International Prize for Humanities in 2009.

G. W. Bowersock, an honorary fellow of Balliol College, Oxford, and professor emeritus of ancient history at the Institute for Advanced Study, Princeton, is the author of *Empires in Collision in Late Antiquity*; *The Throne of Adulis*; *The Crucible of Islam*; *Mosaics as History*; *Interpreting Late Antiquity*; *Roman Arabia*; *Greek Sophists in the Roman Empire*; *Augustus and the Greek World*; *Julian the Apostate*; and *Gibbon's Historical Imagination*.

Aldo Buzzi (1910–2009) began his career as an architect, then turned to filmmaking (alongside Federico Fellini, among other directors) and, in his seventies, emerged as a writer of fiction. Among his books are *A Weakness for Almost Everything*; *The Perfect Egg*; *Journey to the Land of the Flies*; and, with his friend Saul Steinberg, *Reflections and Shadows*. **Ann Goldstein**, who received the Poggioli Award from PEN for her translation of *Journey to the Land of Flies*, is best known for her translations of Elena Ferrante's *Neapolitan Quartet*.

Caroline Walker Bynum, professor emerita of medieval European history at the Institute for Advanced Study, Princeton, and University Professor Emerita at Columbia, is the author of *Christian Materiality*; *Wonderful Blood*; *The Resurrection of the Body in Western Christendom, 200–1336*; *Holy Feast and Holy Fast*; *Fragmentation and Redemption*; *Metamorphosis and Identity*; and *Jesus as Mother*. She was a MacArthur Fellow from 1986–91 and, in 1996, served as president of the American Historical Association.

Anne Carson has received a MacArthur Fellowship, Lannan Award, T. S. Eliot Prize, Pushcart Prize, and Griffin Trust Award for books of poems and essays that include *Decreation*; *Economy of the Unlost*; *Autobiography of Red: A Novel in Verse*; *Nox*; *Red Doc>*; *Float*; *Plainwater*; *Glass, Irony, and God*; *Men in the Off Hours*; *Eros the Bittersweet*; and *The Beauty of the Husband: A Fictional Essay in 29 Tangos*. She is also a distinguished translator of Sappho and the Greek tragedians. Formerly a professor of classics and comparative literature at the University of Michigan, she is now artist-in-residence at New York University.

Cornelius Castoriadis (1922–97) was an economist at the Organization for European Economic Cooperation, director of studies in political philosophy at the École des hautes études en sciences sociales, practicing psychoanalyst, and cofounder of the journal *Socialisme ou Barbarie*, which contested every trend in French intellectual life from existentialism in 1948 to poststructuralism in 1967. The journal's critique of both capitalism and communism was credited by Daniel Cohn-Bendit with inspiring the May 1968 uprising in Paris. Castoriadis's books in English translation include *The Imaginary Institution of Society*; *Political and Social Writings* (in three volumes); *Philosophy, Politics, Autonomy*; *World in Fragments*; *Crossroads in the Labyrinth*; and *On Plato's Statesman*. *A Castoriadis Reader* appeared in 1997.

Stanley Cavell (1926–2018) held the Walter M. Cabot Professorship of Aesthetics and the General Theory of Value at Harvard University for more than thirty years and a Mac-Arthur Fellowship from 1992–97. A recipient of the Morton Dauwen Zabel Award in Criticism from the American Academy and Institute of Arts and Letters, he served as president of the American Philosophical Association in 1996–97. His many books include *Must We Mean What We Say?*; *The Claim of Reason*; *Conditions Handsome and Unhandsome*; *Disowning Knowledge in Seven Plays of Shakespeare*; *Themes Out of School*; *In Quest of the Ordinary*; *A Pitch of Philosophy*; *This New yet Unapproachable America*; *Emerson's Transcendental Etudes*; *The Senses of Walden*; *Philosophy the Day after Tomorrow*; *Little Did I Know*; and several volumes of influential film criticism. "A Taste for Complexity: Ten Nondisciples of Stanley Cavell" appeared as a symposium in the fall 1996 issue of *Common Knowledge*.

William M. Chace is president emeritus of Emory University and honorary professor emeritus of English at Stanford University. His books include *One Hundred Semesters*; *Lionel Trilling: Criticism and Politics*; and *The Political Identities of Ezra Pound and T. S. Eliot*.

Stuart Clark is professor emeritus of history at Swansea University and a fellow of the British Academy. His books include *Vanities of the Eye: Vision in Early Modern European Culture*; *Thinking with Demons: The Idea of Witchcraft in Early Modern History*; and (as editor) *Languages of Witchcraft*.

Inga Clendinnen (1934–2016) is the author of *Dancing with Strangers: Europeans and Australians at First Contact*, which received the Kiriyama Prize for nonfiction; *Ambivalent Conquests: Maya and Spaniard in Yucatán, 1517–1570*, which received the Bolton Memorial Prize for Latin American studies; *Reading the Holocaust*, which was a *New York Times* "best book of the year" in 1999; *True Stories*, originally delivered as Boyer Lectures for the Australian Broadcasting Corporation; and *The Cost of Courage in Aztec Society*, which received the Hodgins Memorial Medal. She was appointed an officer of the Order of Australia in 2006 and received the Dan David Prize in 2016.

Francis X. Clooney, SJ, Parkman professor of divinity at Harvard University and a fellow of the British Academy, is the author of *His Hiding Place Is Darkness: A Hindu-Catholic Theopoetics of Divine Absence*; *The New Comparative Theology: Interreligious Insights from the Next Generation*; *Learning Interreligiously*; *Beyond Compare: St. Francis and Sri Vedanta Desika on Loving Surrender to God*; *Theology after Vedanta*; *Thinking Ritually: Retrieving the Purva Mimamsa of Jaimini*; *How to Do Comparative Theology*; *The Future of Hindu-Christian Studies*; and *The Truth, the Way, the Life: Christian Commentary on the Three Holy Mantras of the Srivaisnava*.

J. M. Coetzee has received the Nobel Prize for Literature, the Booker Prize (twice), and the Jerusalem Prize. His many works of fiction and nonfiction include *Disgrace*; *Life & Times of Michael K*; *The Childhood of Jesus*; *The Schooldays of Jesus*; *Foe*; *Diary of a Bad Year*; *Slow Man*; *Elizabeth Costello*; *Waiting for the Barbarians*; *Age of Iron*; *The Master of Petersburg*; *Dusklands*; *In the Heart of the Country*; *White Writing*; *The Lives of Animals*; *Giving Offense*; *Inner Workings*; *Stranger Shores*; and three volumes of fictionalized memoirs (a chapter of the first, *Boyhood*, appeared in the fall 1996 issue of *Common Knowledge*).

Christopher Coker is professor and head of the Department of International Relations at the London School of Economics. His books include *Barbarous Philosophers: Reflections on the Nature of War from Heraclitus to Heisenberg*; *Humane Warfare*; *War in an Age of Risk*; *War and Ethics in the Twenty-First Century*; *Warrior Ethos*; *Warrior Geeks*; *The Future of War: The Re-enchantment of War in the Twenty-first Century*; and *Waging War without Warriors*.

Maria Conterno, lecturer in history at the University of Ghent, is the author of *La 'descrizione dei tempi' all'alba dell'espansione islamica: Un'indagine sulla storiografia greca, siriaca e araba fra VII e VIII secolo* and *Temistio orientale: Orazioni temistiane nella tradizione siriaca e araba*.

Michael Cook is university professor in Near Eastern studies at Princeton, a fellow of the American Academy of Arts and Sciences, and a recipient of the Mellon Foundation Distinguished Achievement Award. His many books include *Commanding Right and Forbidding Wrong in Islamic Thought*; *Early Muslim Dogma*; *Population Pressure in Rural Anatolia, 1450–1600*; *A Brief History of the Human Race*; and (with Patricia Crone) *Hagarism: The Making of the Islamic World*.

Lorraine Daston, director of the Max Planck Institute for the History of Science, held the inaugural Humanitas Professorship in the History of Ideas at Oxford University in 2013 and is honorary professor at Humboldt University in Berlin. She has been awarded the Dan David Prize, the Pfizer Prize in history of science, and the German Order of Merit. Her books include *Classical Probability in the Enlightenment*; *Objectivity* (with Peter Galison); and *Wonders and the Order of Nature, 1150–1750* (with Katharine Park).

Lydia Davis received the Man Booker International Prize in 2013 and, from 2003–8, was a MacArthur Fellow. Professor of creative writing at the State University of New York, Albany, she is a member of the American Academy of Arts and Sciences and a Commander of the Order of Arts and Letters in France. Her books include a novel (*The End of the Story*) and seven story collections, as well as translations of *Madame Bovary* and *Du côté de chez Swann*.

Natalie Zemon Davis, a recipient of the US National Humanities Medal, the Holberg International Prize, and the Toynbee Prize in Social Science, was appointed a companion of the Order of Canada in 2012. She is Henry Charles Lea professor emerita of history at Princeton University; professor emerita of history, anthropology, medieval studies, and comparative literature at the University of Toronto; and a fellow of the American Academy of Arts and Sciences. Her books include *The Return of Martin Guerre*; *Fiction in the Archives*; *Trickster Travels: A Sixteenth-Century Muslim between Worlds*; *The Gift in Sixteenth-Century France*; *Society and Culture in Early Modern France*; *Women on the Margins*; and *Slaves on Screen*.

Thibault De Meyer is a PhD candidate at the University of Liège, writing under the supervision of Vinciane Despret on the relationship between perspectivism and contemporary scientific practice in ethology and animal psychology.

René Descartes (1596–1650) was tutor to Queen Christina of Sweden during the final year of his life.

Gunter Eich (1907–72) was among the leading poets of postwar Germany and received the George Buchner Prize in 1959 and the Schiller Memorial Prize in 1968. His poetry and radio plays have been translated into numerous languages, including Korean and Thai. His collected works were published in four volumes in 1991. **Michael Hofmann** has received the Schlegel-Tieck Prize and the Independent Foreign Fiction Prize for translation.

Sir John H. Elliott, Regius professor emeritus of modern history at Oxford University and a fellow of the British Academy, has received the Prince of Asturias Prize for the Social Sciences and the Balzan Prize for History. Among his many books are *Empires of the Atlantic World: Britain and Spain in America, 1492–1830*; *The Old World and the New, 1492–1650*; *The*

Revolt of the Catalans: A Study in the Decline of Spain, 1598–1640; *Richelieu and Olivares*; *The Count-Duke of Olivares: The Statesman in an Age of Decline*; *Spain and Its World, 1500–1700*; and *History in the Making*.

Caryl Emerson is A. Watson Armour III university professor emerita of Slavic and comparative literatures at Princeton. Her books include *The First Hundred Years of Mikhail Bakhtin*; *The Life of Musorgsky*; *Boris Gudonov: Transpositions of a Russian Theme*; *All the Same Words Don't Go Away*; and (with Gary Saul Morson) *Mikhail Bakhtin: Creation of a Prosaics*.

Mikhail Epstein, Samuel Candler Dobbs professor of cultural theory and Russian literature at Emory University and founder of the Center for Humanities Innovation at Durham University in England, is the author of more than thirty books and seven hundred articles, published in English or Russian and translated into eighteen other languages. He is a recipient of the Liberty Prize for Russian-US Cultural Relations and of the International Essay Prize of Weimar for "Chronocide," which appeared in the spring 2003 issue of *Common Knowledge*.

Péter Esterházy (1950–2016) received the state-sponsored Kossuth Prize in Hungary, as well as international awards in France, Austria, Germany, Slovenia, and Poland, for novels that have been translated into twenty-four languages. These include *Celestial Harmonies*, about the Esterházy dynasty; *A Novel of Production*; *A Little Hungarian Pornography*; *Helping Verbs of the Heart*; *The Transporters*; *The Book of Hrabal*; *The Glance of Countess Hahn-Hahn (Down the Danube)*; *Revised Edition*; *Pancreas Diary*; and *She Loves Me*. **Marianna Birnbaum** is professor emerita of Germanic languages at the University of California, Los Angeles.

Roger Cardinal Etchegaray, emeritus archbishop of Marseilles, retired as vice dean of the College of Cardinals in 2017. He had served in the Roman Curia for nearly half a century, as president of the Pontifical Council for Justice and Peace; president of Cor Unum, the Vatican council for humanitarian relief operations; and personal envoy of Pope John Paul II on missions to Rwanda, Iraq, Cuba, and China. His book *J'ai senti battre le coeur du monde: Conversations avec Bernard Lecomte* was published in 2007. **Mei Lin Chang** is a former managing editor of *Common Knowledge*.

Fang Lizhi (1936–2012) was vice president of the University of Science and Technology of China when he was named "most wanted counterrevolutionary criminal" by Chinese authorities in 1989. Following a year's refuge in the US embassy in Beijing, he was permitted to emigrate and then held positions at Cambridge University, the Institute for Advanced Study in Princeton, and the University of Arizona. Recipient of the Nicholson Medal of the American Physical Society, the Freedom Award of the International Rescue Committee, and the Robert F. Kennedy Human Rights Award, he wrote more than 230 scientific papers and authored, coauthored, or edited twenty books, including *Bringing Down the Great Wall: Writings on Science, Culture, and Democracy in China*.

Paul Feyerabend (1924–94) was professor of philosophy at the University of California, Berkeley, for more than thirty years and, concurrently during the 1980s, at the Swiss Federal Institute of Technology in Zurich. His books include *Against Method*; *Farewell to Reason*; *Science in a Free Society*; *Conquest of Abundance: A Tale of Abstraction versus the Richness of Being*; *The Tyranny of Science*; *Three Dialogues on Knowledge*; *Naturphilosophie*; *Killing Time: The Autobiography of Paul Feyerabend*; *For and Against Method* (with Imre Lakatos); and four volumes of *Philosophical Papers*. As the *Stanford Encyclopedia of Philosophy* accurately reports, "a surprisingly large number of papers in the 1990s . . . appeared in a new journal, *Common*

Knowledge, in whose inauguration he had a hand, and which set out to integrate insights from all parts of the intellectual landscape": "[there were] signs of an increasing unhappiness with relativism in Feyerabend's publications around this time. But [he was] still vigorously opposed to objectivism." Despite his reservations about scientific method, Asteroid Feyerabend (22356) was named in his honor.

Joseph Frank (1918–2013) received the National Book Critics Circle Award, the James Russell Lowell Prize of the Modern Language Association, and the Christian Gauss Prize of Phi Beta Kappa for his five-volume biography of Dostoevsky, written while he was professor of comparative literature at Princeton University and professor of Slavic and comparative literature at Stanford University.

Manfred Frank, emeritus professor of philosophy at the University of Tübingen and an officer "dans l'Ordre des Palmes Académiques," is the author of *The Philosophical Foundations of Early German Romanticism*; *What Is Neostructuralism?*; and *The Subject and the Text: Essays on Literary Theory and Philosophy*, as well as untranslated books on the problem of time in German Romanticism and on Hegel, Schelling, and Marxist dialectic. **Ruth Morris**, formerly a staff interpreter for the European Union, lectures in the department of translation studies at Bar-Ilan University.

Michael Fried, J. R. Herbert Boone professor of humanities and art history at Johns Hopkins University, is a fellow of the American Academy of Arts and Sciences and a corresponding fellow of the British Academy. He received the Andrew W. Mellon Foundation Distinguished Achievement Award in 2004 and, in 2006, the American Academy of Arts and Letters Award in Literature. He is the author of *Art and Objecthood*; *The Moment of Caravaggio*; *Absorption and Theatricality: Painting and Beholder in the Age of Diderot*; *Realism, Writing, Disfiguration: On Thomas Eakins and Stephen Crane*; *Flaubert's "Gueuloir"*; *Courbet's Realism*; *Menzel's Realism*; *Manet's Modernism*; *Why Photography Matters as Art as Never Before*; *Four Honest Outlaws*; and four volumes of poetry.

Luis Garcia's first book of poems, *The Calculated Lion*, was published in Santiago, Chile, in 1963, where he had gone, from Berkeley, to study with Nicanor Parra. Subsequent volumes include *The Handle*; *The Token*; *A Place of Morning*; *A Gift from the Darkness*; *Even Steven*; *More than Naked*; *Poems for Dinner*; *Snowbird*; *Two Pears*; *Beans*; *A Blue Book*; *The Mechanic*; and *Mr. Menu*.

Clifford Geertz (1926–2006) was the first and founding professor in the School of Social Science at the Institute for Advanced Study in Princeton. His book *Works and Lives: The Anthropologist as Author* received the National Book Critics Circle Award, and his collection *The Interpretation of Cultures* (which comprises theoretical essays of wide influence on historiography and the humanities as well as on the social sciences) was included on the *Times Literary Supplement*'s list of the hundred most important books published since World War II. His other works include *Local Knowledge*; *Available Light*; *Life among the Anthros*; *The Religion of Java*; *Agricultural Involution*; *The Social History of an Indonesian Town*; *Peddlers and Princes*; *Islam Observed*; *Negara: The Theater State in Nineteenth-Century Bali*; *Person, Time, and Conduct in Bali*; *Kinship in Bali* (with Hildred Geertz); and *After The Fact: Two Countries, Four Decades, One Anthropologist*.

Carlo Ginzburg's International Balzan Prize was accompanied in 2010 with a citation noting that "the impact of Professor Ginzburg's scholarship has been immense. His book on

Menocchio (*The Cheese and the Worms*), everywhere recognized as a classic, is available in twenty-four languages, while his book on myths and clues (*Clues, Myths, and the Historical Method*) has been translated almost as widely." His other books include *The Night Battles*; *Ecstasies: Deciphering the Witches' Sabbath*; *The Enigma of Piero*; *No Island Is an Island*; and *History, Rhetoric, and Proof*. He is professor emeritus at the University of California, Los Angeles, and professor of history at the Scuola Normale Superiore di Pisa.

André Gombay (1933–2014), emeritus professor of philosophy at the University of Toronto, was chief editor of the *Oeuvres complètes de René Descartes* and coeditor (with Byron Williston) of *Passion and Virtue in Descartes*.

Philip Gossett (1941–2017) was professor of music at the University of Chicago for more than forty years and received the Mellon Foundation Distinguished Achievement Award and the Italian government's highest civilian honor, the Cavaliere di Gran Croce. General editor of *The Works of Giuseppe Verdi* and *The Works of Gioachino Rossini*, he also wrote *Divas and Scholars*, which received the Kinkeldey Award of the American Musicological Society, and *"Anna Bolena" and the Maturity of Gaetano Donizetti*. A fellow of the American Academy of Arts and Sciences and the American Philosophical Society, he served as president of both the American Musicological Society and the Society of Textual Scholarship.

Stephen Greenblatt, Cogan University Professor of the Humanities at Harvard, has won both the Holberg International Prize and the Mellon Foundation Distinguished Achievement Award. He received the Pulitzer Prize, the National Book Award, and the James Russell Lowell Prize of the Modern Language Association for *The Swerve: How the World Became Modern*. His other books include *The Rise and Fall of Adam and Eve*; *Shakespearean Negotiations*; *Renaissance Self-Fashioning*; *Will in the World*; *Learning to Curse*; *Marvelous Possessions*; *Hamlet in Purgatory*; *Shakespeare's Freedom*; and *Tyrant: Shakespeare on Politics*.

Thom Gunn (1929–2004) was a key figure among "The Movement" poets in Britain until his move in 1958 to California, where he taught at Berkeley for more than forty years. He was a recipient of a MacArthur Fellowship (1993–98), the Shelley Memorial Award of the Poetry Society of America, the Lenore Marshall Prize of the Academy of American Poets, and awards from the Arts Council of Great Britain and the Rockefeller Foundation. His books include *My Sad Captains*; *The Man with Night Sweats*; *Fighting Terms*; *The Sense of Movement*; *Touch*; *Moly*; *To the Air*; *Jack Straw's Castle*; *The Passages of Joy*; *Sidewalks*; *Undesirables*; *At the Barriers*; *Frontiers of Gossip*; *Boss Cupid*; *Selected Poems, 1950–1975*; and his *Collected Poems* of 1994. He also published two books of autobiographical and critical essays, *The Occasions of Poetry* and *Shelf Life*.

Jürgen Habermas, professor emeritus of philosophy and social theory at the University of Frankfurt, is perhaps the leading public intellectual in Europe today. He has received the Holberg International Prize, Prince of Asturias Award, Erasmus Prize, John W. Kluge Prize, Kyoto Prize in Social Science, and numerous other honors globally. Among his major works are *The Structural Transformation of the Public Sphere*; *The Theory of Communicative Action*; *Moral Consciousness and Communicative Action*; *The Philosophical Discourse of Modernity*; *Toward a Rational Society*; *Between Facts and Norms*; *The Inclusion of the Other*; *The Postnational Constellation*; *Time of Transitions*; *The Future of Human Nature*; *The Crisis of the European Union*; *Faith and Knowledge*; *Religion and Rationality*; and (with Joseph Cardinal Ratzinger) *The Dialectics of Secularization*.

Ian Hacking is professor emeritus of the philosophy and history of scientific concepts at the Collège de France and university professor emeritus of philosophy at Toronto. A Companion of the Order of Canada and a fellow of the Royal Society of Canada, the American Academy of Arts and Sciences, and the British Academy, he has received the Holberg International Prize, the Killam Prize for the Humanities, the Pierre Janet Prize, and the Prix Psyche. His many books include *Historical Ontology*; *The Social Construction of What?*; *Mad Travelers: Reflections on the Reality of Transient Mental Illness*; *Rewriting the Soul: Multiple Personality and the Sciences of Memory*; *Representing and Intervening*; *The Taming of Chance*; *The Emergence of Probability*; *The Logic of Statistical Inference*; and *Why Does Language Matter to Philosophy?*.

Oren Harman chairs the graduate program in science, technology, and society at Bar-Ilan University and is a senior fellow of the Van Leer Institute in Jerusalem. His books include *The Man Who Invented the Chromosome*; *Evolutions: Fifteen Myths that Explain Our World*; and *The Price of Altruism: George Price and the Search for the Origins of Kindness*, which received the *Los Angeles Times* Book Award.

Václav Havel (1936–2011) was president of Czechoslovakia and then of the Czech Republic from 1989–2003. As the *New York Times* reported in its obituary, his "moral authority and his moving use of the Czech language cast him as the dominant figure during Prague street demonstrations in 1989 and as the chief behind-the-scenes negotiator who brought about the end of more than 40 years of Communist rule and the peaceful transfer of power known as the Velvet Revolution." In addition to nineteen plays in the absurdist tradition, he wrote seminal essays on politics and individual conscience, including *The Power of the Powerless*; *Living in Truth*; *Disturbing the Peace*; and *Letters to Olga: June 1979–September 1982*, produced while he was a political prisoner. Samuel Beckett's play *Catastrophe* (1982), written around the same time, was dedicated to Havel.

Sir Edward Heath (1916–2005) was prime minister of the United Kingdom from 1970–74 and leader of the British Conservative Party from 1965 to 1975. It was under his government that the United Kingdom joined the European Economic Community.

Albert O. Hirschman (1915–2012) was professor of social science at the Institute for Advanced Study in Princeton, from 1974–2012, and played important roles in projects for the World Bank, the Marshall Plan, the US Federal Reserve, the Emergency Rescue Committee, and the National Planning Board of Colombia. His many honors include the Talcott Parsons Prize for Social Science of the American Academy of Arts and Sciences, the Thomas Jefferson Medal of the American Philosophical Society, the Toynbee Prize, the Lippincott Award of the American Political Science Association, and the Kalman Silvert Prize of the Latin American Studies Association. Among his most influential works are *Exit, Voice, and Loyalty*; *A Propensity to Self-Subversion*; *The Strategy of Economic Development*; *The Rhetoric of Reaction*; *Essays in Trespassing*; *The Passions and the Interests*; and *A Bias for Hope*. In a review of Jeremy Adelman's biography, *Worldly Philosopher: The Odyssey of Albert O. Hirschman*, the *New Yorker* appraised Hirschman as "one of the twentieth century's most extraordinary intellectuals."

David A. Hollinger is Preston Hotchkis professor of history emeritus at the University of California, Berkeley. A former president of the Organization of American Historians and a fellow of the American Academy of Arts and Sciences, he is the author of *Postethnic America*; *Protestants Abroad*; *After Cloven Tongues of Fire: Protestant Liberalism and Modern American History*; *Cosmopolitanism and Solidarity*; *Science, Jews, and Secular Culture*; *In the*

American Province: Studies in the History and Historiography of Ideas; and *Morris R. Cohen and the Scientific Ideal.*

Darrel Alejandro Holnes teaches poetry, playwriting, and screenwriting at New York University and at Rutgers. His poems have appeared in *Best American Experimental Writing 2014*, *Poetry*, *Callaloo*, and *The Caribbean Writer*, among other venues. He is coauthor of *PRIME: Poetry and Conversations* and coeditor of *Happiness, The Delight-Tree: An Anthology of Contemporary International Poetry.*

Miroslav Holub (1923–98) was a Czech immunologist, after whom Asteroid Miroslavholub (7496) was named, and a poet, translated into more than thirty languages. In English, his *Selected Poems* (1967) appeared in the Penguin Modern European Poets series, with an introduction by Al Alvarez and enthusiastic reception by Seamus Heaney and especially by Ted Hughes, on whose collection *Crow* of 1970 readers have discerned Holub's influence. Among Holub's books in English include *Vanishing Lung Syndrome* and *The Rampage*, cotranslated by **David Young** and **Dana Hábová**, as well as *Intensive Care*; *Poems Before and After*; *Shedding Life*; *The Fly*; and *Supposed to Fly.*

Maya Jasanoff is Coolidge professor of history at Harvard University and a recipient of the National Book Critics Circle Award for Nonfiction, the Windham-Campbell Literature Prize, the George Washington Book Prize, and the Duff Cooper Prize for Nonfiction. Her books include *The Dawn Watch: Joseph Conrad in a Global World*; *Edge of Empire: Lives, Culture, and Conquest in the East, 1750–1850*; and *Liberty's Exiles: American Loyalists in the Revolutionary World.*

Albert R. Jonsen is emeritus professor of ethics in medicine at the University of Washington School of Medicine and codirector of the Program in Medicine and Human Values at California Pacific Medical Center in San Francisco. In 2017 he received the Beecher Award of the Hastings Center. Among his books are *The Birth of Bioethics*; *The New Medicine and the Old Ethics*; *Clinical Ethics*; *Responsibility in Modern Religious Ethics*; and (with Stephen Toulmin) *The Abuse of Casuistry.*

Stanley N. Katz, president emeritus of the American Council of Learned Societies, received the US National Humanities Medal in 2010. Founding director of the Princeton University Center on Arts and Cultural Policy Studies, he has also served as president of the Organization of American Historians and of the American Society for Legal History. Editor-in-chief of the *Oxford International Encyclopedia of Legal History*, he is coauthor of *Mobilizing for Peace: Conflict Resolution in Northern Ireland, South Africa, and Israel/Palestine*. He has chaired the *Common Knowledge* editorial board since 2008.

Hugh Kenner (1923–2003) wrote some thirty books, among them *The Pound Era*, for which he received the Christian Gauss Award of Phi Beta Kappa. "Kenner has earned a well-deserved reputation as our pre-eminent expert on modernism in English," as Michiko Kakutani, former chief book critic of the *New York Times*, has written, but he also published seminal works on the animator Chuck Jones, the futurist Buckminster Fuller, a variety of modern painters, and the Heath-Zenith Z-100 computer. He held the Andrew Mellon chair in the humanities at Johns Hopkins University from 1973 to 1990.

Sir Anthony Kenny has been the master of Balliol College, Oxford; the warden of Rhodes House; and the president of both the British Academy and the Royal Institute of Philosophy. He is the author of more than forty books on philosophy of mind, philosophy of religion, and the history of philosophy, with emphasis on Wittgenstein (of whose literary estate he is an executor), Frege, Descartes, Thomas More, Aquinas, and Aristotle.

Sir Frank Kermode (1919–2010) was a fellow of the British Academy and held various chairs in literary studies at Cambridge University, University College London, and Columbia University, along with the Charles Eliot Norton Professorship at Harvard. Among his many books are *The Sense of an Ending*; *Shakespeare's Language*; *Romantic Image*; *The Genesis of Secrecy*; *Forms of Attention*; *The Uses of Error*; *The Art of Telling*; *History and Value*; *An Appetite for Poetry*; *Pleasure and Change: The Aesthetics of Canon*; *The Classic*; *Modern Essays*; *Wallace Stevens*; and *Not Entitled*.

Joseph Leo Koerner, a recipient of the Mellon Foundation Distinguished Achievement Award and a fellow of the American Academy of Arts and Sciences, is Thomas Professor of the History of Art and Architecture at Harvard University. He is the author of *Caspar David Friedrich and the Subject of Landscape*, which received the Mitchell Prize for art history; *The Moment of Self-Portraiture in German Renaissance Art*; *The Reformation of the Image*; and *Bosch and Bruegel: From Enemy Painting to Everyday Life*. He wrote and presented a three-part series, "Northern Renaissance," for BBC Television, as well as a BBC documentary, "Vienna: City of Dreams."

Jee Leong Koh is the founder of the literary nonprofit Singapore Unbound, which organizes the biennial Singapore Literature Festival in New York City. His books—which have been translated into Japanese, Chinese, Malay, Russian, and Latvian—include *Steep Tea*, which was named a Best Book of the Year by the *Financial Times*; *Payday Loans*; *Equal to the Earth*; *Seven Studies for a Self Portrait*; *Shadows of Japan: Images and Words*, which is a collection of haiku and photography; and *The Pillow Book*, a collection of Zuihitsu.

Yusef Komunyakaa, who has received the Pulitzer Prize for Poetry and the Wallace Stevens Award, is distinguished senior poet in the New York University graduate program in creative writing. Chancellor of the Academy of American Poets from 1999 to 2005, he is the author of *Neon Vernacular*; *Dien Cai Dau*; *Dedications and Other Dark Horses*; *Lost in the Bonewheel Factory*; *Copacetic*; *I Apologize for the Eyes in My Head*; *Talking Dirty to the Gods*; *Thieves of Paradise*; *The Chameleon Couch*; *Testimony: A Tribute to Charlie Parker*; *Emperor of Water Clocks*; and *Gilgamesh: A Verse Play*.

György Konrád, former president of PEN-International and of the Berlin Akademie der Künste, is the author of *Antipolitics*, widely regarded as the key manifesto of dissidents during the years preceding the 1989 revolutions in the Soviet bloc. Among his novels in English translation are *The Loser*; *The Case Worker*; *A Feast in the Garden*; and *The Stone Dial*. His essay collections include *The Melancholy of Rebirth* and *The Invisible Voice*. He is a recipient of the Goethe Medal, the Herder Prize, the Hungarian state Kossuth Prize, the Charles Veillon Prize, the Hans Werfel Human Rights Award, the European Essay Prize, the National Jewish Book Award, the Maecenas Prize, the Manès-Sperber Prize, and the highest state distinctions awarded by France and Germany. **John Bátki** has received the O'Henry Award for Short Fiction.

Bruce Krajewski is the author of *Traveling with Hermes: Hermeneutics and Rhetoric*; the editor of Gadamer's *Repercussions*; coeditor of *The Man in the High Castle and Philosophy: Subversive Reports from Another Reality*; and cotranslator of *Gadamer on Celan*, for which he shared the Modern Language Association's Scaglione Prize. He is professor of English at the University of Texas, Arlington.

László Krasznahorkai, recipient of the Man Booker International Prize, the Best Book of the Year Award in Germany, and the Hungarian state Kossuth Prize, is the author of *War and War*; *The World Goes On*; *Satantango*; *The Last Wolf and Herman*; *Animalinside*; and *The Melancholy of Resistance*. "The universality of Krasznahorkai's vision," W. G. Sebald wrote, "rivals that of Gogol's *Dead Souls* and far surpasses all the lesser concerns of contemporary writing." George Szirtes, poet and translator, has received the Geoffrey Faber Memorial Prize, the T. S. Eliot Prize, the Bess Hokin Prize, and the Poetry and the People Award of Gwangzhou.

Anton O. Kris, MD, clinical professor of psychiatry at the Harvard Medical School and a training and supervising analyst at the Boston Psychoanalytic Institute, is the author of *Free Association: Method and Process*. He is a member of the editorial board of the *Journal of the American Psychoanalytic Association* and of *Psychoanalytic Quarterly*.

Julia Kristeva, who received the first Holberg International Prize in 2004, is professor emerita of linguistics at the University of Paris Diderot and a practicing psychoanalyst. She has received the Hannah Arendt Award for Political Thought as well as the Vision 97 Prize of the Havel Foundation, and she is a commander of the French Order of Merit and of the Legion of Honor. Her more than thirty books, which have appeared in ten languages, include *New Maladies of the Soul*; *Desire in Language*; *The Revolution in Poetic Language*; *About Chinese Women*; *Powers of Horror*; *Time and Sense*; *Black Sun*; *Nations without Nationalism*; *Strangers to Ourselves*; *Hannah Arendt: Life Is a Narrative*; *Tales of Love*; *Hatred and Forgiveness*; *The Severed Head*; the trilogy *Female Genius*; and (with Philippe Sollers) *Marriage as a Fine Art*. One of her five novels, *The Old Man and the Wolves*, was excerpted in the inaugural issue of *Common Knowledge*.

Bruno Latour, emeritus professor in the Medialab and in the program in political arts at the Institut d'études politiques de Paris ("Sciences Po"), is currently a fellow of the Zentrum für Media Kunst and a professor at the Staatliche Hochschule für Gestaltung, both in Karlsruhe, and professor-at-large at Cornell University. His many awards include the Holberg International Prize, Prix Bernard, Prix Roberval, Siegfried Unseld Prize, appointment to the French Legion of Honor, and election to the American Academy of Arts and Sciences. His books in English translation include *An Inquiry into the Modes of Existence: An Anthropology of the Moderns*; *We Have Never Been Modern*; *Laboratory Life: The Construction of Scientific Facts*; *Science in Action*; *Aramis, or the Love of Technology*; *The Pasteurization of France*; *Pandora's Hope*; *Politics of Nature*; *Facing Gaia*; *On the Modern Cult of the Factish Gods*; *Rejoicing: Or the Torments of Religious Speech*; *The Making of Law*; *Reassembling the Social: An Introduction to Actor-Network Theory*; *Iconoclash*; and *War of the Worlds: What about Peace?*.

Ewa Lipska has written some twenty volumes of poetry (which have appeared in fifteen languages), as well as a novel, *Sefer*, published in 2009. The recipient of awards from PEN-Warsaw, the Kościelski Foundation of Geneva, and the Jurzykowski Foundation of New York, she has three books in English translation: *The New Century*; *Pet Shops and Other Poems*; and *Poet? Criminal? Madman?*. Robin Davidson, herself a poet, is cotranslator of Lipska's *The New Century*.

Greil Marcus, formerly Anschutz Distinguished Fellow at Princeton University, is the author of *Lipstick Traces: A Secret History of the Twentieth Century*; *The Dustbin of History*; *Invisible Republic*; *Mystery Train*; *The Old, Weird America*; *Dead Elvis*; *Double Trouble: Bill Clinton and Elvis Presley in a Land of No Alternatives*; *When that Rough God Goes Riding*; *The*

Shape of Things to Come; and *Ranters and Crowd Pleasers*. His *New Literary History of America* was coedited with Werner Sollors, and *The Rose and the Briar: Death, Love and Liberty in the American Ballad* was coedited with Sean Wilentz.

Steven Marcus (1928–2018), a fellow of the American Academy of Arts and Sciences and cofounder of the US National Humanities Center, taught at Columbia University throughout his career, beginning in 1956. With Lionel Trilling he coedited an abridged version of Ernest Jones's three-volume biography of Freud and then, as a lay psychoanalyst, wrote *The Other Victorians: A Study of Sexuality and Pornography in Mid-Nineteenth-Century England.* His other primary interest, explored in his books *Dickens from Pickwick to Dombey* and *Engels, Manchester, and the Working Class*, was in the Victorian social context out of which Marxism emerged. *Doing Good: The Limits of Benevolence* was coauthored with a psychoanalyst, a social historian, and the director of the New York Civil Liberties Union.

Samuel Menashe (1925–2011) was the first recipient of the Neglected Masters Prize of the Poetry Foundation, and Christopher Ricks's *Samuel Menashe: New and Selected Poems* was published by the Library of America in conjunction with that award. Menashe's first book, *No Jerusalem But This*, published in 1971, was praised by Stephen Spender for "language intense and clear as diamonds."

H. M. King Michael (1921–2017) was the head of the state of Romania from 1927 to 1930 and 1940 to 1947.

Adam Michnik cofounded the 1976 Workers' Defense Committee, the earliest dissident institution in Eastern Europe, and has been editor-in-chief of *Gazeta Wyborcza*, the largest circulation newspaper in Poland, since its inception in 1989. His books in English translation include *Letters from Prison*; *Letters from Freedom*; *The Church and the Left*; *In Search of Lost Meaning: The New Eastern Europe*; and *The Trouble with History*. He has received the Robert F. Kennedy Human Rights Award, the World Press Freedom Hero Award, the Freedom Award of PEN-Paris, the Organization for Security and Cooperation in Europe Prize for Journalism and Democracy, the Goethe Medal (awarded by the German government), and the highest Polish decoration, the Order of the White Eagle.

Jack Miles received a Pulitzer Prize in 1996 for his book *GOD: A Biography*. Formerly a MacArthur Fellow, his other books include *Christ: A Crisis in the Life of God*; *God in the Qur'an*; and (as general editor) the *Norton Anthology of World Religions*. He is Distinguished Professor of English and Religious Studies at the University of California, Irvine, and Senior Fellow for Religious Affairs at the Pacific Council on International Policy.

Alexander Nehamas, a recipient of the Mellon Foundation Distinguished Achievement Award, is Carpenter Class of 1943 Professor in the Humanities at Princeton University and a member of the American Academy of Arts and Sciences. His books, which have appeared in ten languages, include *Nietzsche: Life as Literature*; *The Art of Living: Socratic Reflections from Plato to Foucault*; *Virtues of Authenticity: Essays on Plato and Socrates*; *Only a Promise of Happiness: The Place of Beauty in a World of Art*; and *On Friendship*.

Reviel Netz, professor of ancient science in the Stanford University department of classics, is coauthor (with William Noel) of *The Archimedes Codex*, which has been translated into twenty languages and received the inaugural Neumann Prize of the British Society for the History of Mathematics. Coeditor (with Nigel Wilson) of a critical edition of the Archimedes Palimpsest for the British Academy, he is also the author of a three-volume translation of the works of Archimedes. His other publications include *The Shaping of Deduction in Greek Mathematics*, which received the Runciman Award of the Anglo-Hellenic League; *Ludic Proof: Greek Mathematics and the Alexandrian Aesthetic*; *The Transformation of Early Mediterranean Mathematics*; and *Barbed Wire: An Ecology of Modernity*.

Sari Nusseibeh, formerly president of al-Quds University in Jerusalem, now holds the UNESCO professorship in freedom of expression there. He founded, with Ami Ayalon, The People's Voice, a Palestinian-Israeli peace initiative, and was corecipient (with Amos Oz) of the Siegfried Unseld Preis. A Commander of the Order of Léopold, the highest order of knighthood in Belgium, he is the author of *The Story of Reason in Islam*; *What's a Palestinian State Worth?*; *No Trumpets, No Drums*; and *Once upon a Country: A Palestinian Life*.

Jeffrey M. Perl is the founder and editor of *Common Knowledge*. His books include *Skepticism and Modern Enmity: Before and after Eliot*; *The Tradition of Return: The Implicit History of Modern Literature*; and (as editor) *Peace and Mind: Civilian Scholarship from "Common Knowledge."* He taught for many years at Columbia University and the University of Texas and is currently professor of English literature at Bar-Ilan University in Israel and a member, at Durham University in England, of the Center for Humanities Innovation.

Marjorie Perloff, Sadie Patek professor emerita of humanities at Stanford University, is a fellow of the American Academy of Arts and Sciences and former president of the Modern Language Association. Her many books include *The Futurist Moment*; *Unoriginal Genius*; *Radical Poetics*; *Poetic License*; *Poetry on and off the Page*; *The Poetics of Indeterminacy*; *The Dance of the Intellect: Studies in the Pound Tradition*; *Wittgenstein's Ladder*; *Edge of Irony: Modernism in the Shadow of the Habsburg Empire*; and *The Vienna Paradox: A Memoir*.

J. G. A. Pocock is Harry C. Black professor emeritus of history at Johns Hopkins University and author of the six-volume study *Barbarism and Religion*, for which he received the Jacques Barzun Prize in Cultural History of the American Philosophical Society and the Lippincott Award of the American Political Science Association. His other books include *The Ancient Constitution and the Feudal Law*; *Virtue, Commerce, and History*; *Politics, Language, and Time*; *The Machiavellian Moment: Florentine Political Thought and the Atlantic Republican Tradition*; and *The Discovery of Islands*. A fellow of the American Academy of Arts and Sciences and a corresponding fellow of the British Academy and Royal Historical Society, he was appointed an officer of the New Zealand Order of Merit in 2002.

W. V. Quine (1908–2000) held the Edgar Pierce Chair of Philosophy at Harvard University from 1956–78. He received the first Rolf Schock Prize in Logic and Philosophy and the Kyoto Prize in Arts and Philosophy. A member of the US National Academy of Sciences and the American Academy of Arts and Sciences, he was the author of *Mathematical Logic*; *From a Logical Point of View*; *Word and Object*; *Set Theory and Its Logic*; *Ways of Paradox*; *Ontological Relativity and Other Essays*; *The Roots of Reference*; *Theories and Things*; *Pursuit of Truth*; *From Stimulus to Science*; and *Quiddities: An Intermittently Philosophical Dictionary*. In an obituary for Quine in the spring 2002 issue of *Common Knowledge*, Hilary Putnam wrote that "the process of thinking and rethinking what we mean by *translation* (and by *meaning* and by *understanding what somebody means*) that Quine has forced upon the philosophical world will, I predict, go on for a very long time—perhaps for centuries."

Belle Randall has been poetry editor of *Common Knowledge* since its inception. Her poem "A Child's Garden of Gods" is included in the anthology *The Open Door: One Hundred Poems, One Hundred Years of "Poetry" Magazine*. Her books include *101 Different Ways of Playing*

Solitaire and Other Poems; *The Orpheus Sedan*; *Drop Dead Beautiful*; and *The Coast Starlight*. She is coeditor (with Richard Denner) of *Exploding Flowers: Selected Poems of Luis Garcia*. A recipient of the Inez Boulton Award of *Poetry* magazine and the Anthony Hecht Prize of Waywiser Press, she has taught in several creative writing programs, including Stanford University's, where she was a Wallace Stegner Fellow.

Nadja Reissland, associate professor of psychology at Durham University, is the author of *The Development of Emotional Intelligence* and coeditor (with Barbara Kisilevsky) of *Fetal Development: Research on Brain and Behavior, Environmental Influences, and Emerging Technologies*.

Colin Richmond, professor emeritus of medieval history at the University of Keele, is the author of *John Hopton: Fifteenth-Century Suffolk Gentleman* and a three-volume history of the Paston family in fifteenth-century Norfolk.

Richard Rorty (1931–2007) went from being professor of philosophy in an Anglo-analytic department (at Princeton) to professor "of the humanities" (at the University of Virginia) to professor of comparative literature at Stanford. What he accomplished thereby, as Alasdair MacIntyre wrote in a memorial published here in 2008, was "to step back and ask whether . . . the question 'What is philosophy good for?' did not need a better answer than those customarily given or presupposed" by Anglo-Americans. Thus, as János Boros wrote, also in these pages, "In his own generation, Rorty had only two colleagues of comparable stature, both of them Europeans—Jürgen Habermas and Jacques Derrida." His principal academic distinction was the MacArthur Fellowship that he held from 1981 to 1986. Among his most influential works are *The Linguistic Turn*; *Philosophy and the Mirror of Nature*; *Consequences of Pragmatism*; *Philosophy and Social Hope*; *Contingency, Irony, and Solidarity*; *Achieving Our Country*; and two volumes of *Philosophical Papers*.

Ingrid D. Rowland, fellow of the American Academy of Arts and Sciences and a professor at the Rome campus of the University of Notre Dame School of Architecture, is the author of *The Place of the Antique in Early Modern Europe*; *From Pompeii: The Afterlife of a Roman Town*; *Giordano Bruno: Author/Heretic*; *The Culture of the High Renaissance: Ancients and Moderns in Sixteenth-Century Rome*; *The Scarith of Scornello: A Tale of Renaissance Forgery*; *From Heaven to Arcadia: The Sacred and the Profane in the Renaissance*; and (with Noah Charney) *The Collector of Lives: Giorgio Vasari and the Invention of Art*.

Hanna Segal (1918–2011) held the Freud Memorial Chair at University College London in 1987–88 and was president of the British Psychoanalytical Society and vice president, twice, of the International Psychoanalytical Association. In 1992, she received the Sigourney Award for her contributions to psychoanalysis. She wrote a number of seminal papers (notably, "The Clinical Usefulness of the Concept of the Death Instinct"; "Silence Is the Real Crime," "Notes on Symbol Formation," and "A Psychoanalytic Contribution to Aesthetics"), as well as books, including *Dream, Fantasy, and Art*; *Psychoanalysis, Literature, and War*; *Yesterday, Today, and Tomorrow*; and two books on Melanie Klein, with whom she did her psychoanalytic training.

Amartya Sen, a recipient of the Nobel Prize in Economics, is Lamont university professor at Harvard and emeritus master of Trinity College, Cambridge. Former president of the American Economic Association, the Indian Economic Association, and the International Economic Association, his books, which have been translated into more than thirty languages, include *Commodities and Capabilities*; *Poverty and Famines*; *Growth Economics*; *Collective Choice and Social Welfare*; *On Economic Inequality*; *The Standard of Living*; *On Ethics and Economics*; *Development as Freedom*; *Rationality and Freedom*; *The Argumentative Indian*; *Identity and Violence: The Illusion of Destiny*; and *The Idea of Justice*. He is a Companion of Honor in the UK and has received the US National Humanities Medal, the Eisenhower Medal, the George Marshall Award, the Johan Skytte Prize in Political Science, and the highest civilian award of India—the Bharat Ratna.

Richard Shiff, a fellow of the American Academy of Arts and Sciences, holds the Effie Marie Cain Regents Chair in Art at the University of Texas, Austin, where he also directs the Center for the Study of Modernism. His publications include *Doubt*; *Between Sense and de Kooning*; *Cézanne and the End of Impressionism*; and *Ellsworth Kelly: New York Drawings, 1954–1962*.

Quentin Skinner is Regius professor of history emeritus at Cambridge University and Barber Beaumont Professor of the Humanities and codirector of the Center for the Study of the History of Political Thought at Queen Mary University of London, as well as a fellow of the British Academy. He has received the European Balzan Prize, the Wolfson History Prize, the Sir Isaiah Berlin Prize of the British Political Studies Association, the Lippincott Award and the David Easton Award of the American Political Science Association, and the Bielefelder Wissenschaftspreis. His books include the three-volume *Visions of Politics*; the two-volume *Foundations of Modern Political Thought*; *Machiavelli*; *Liberty before Liberalism*; *Rhetoric and Reason in the Philosophy of Hobbes*; *Hobbes and Republican Liberty*; *From Humanism to Hobbes*; *Ideas in Context*; and *Forensic Shakespeare*.

Barbara Herrnstein Smith is Braxton Craven professor emerita of English and comparative literature at Duke University and the founder of its Center for Interdisciplinary Studies in Science and Cultural Theory. She has received the Christian Gauss Award of Phi Beta Kappa, the Explicator Literary Foundation Award, and the Lifetime Achievement Award of the Society for Literature, Science, and the Arts. Her many books include *Contingencies of Value*; *Belief and Resistance: Dynamics of Contemporary Intellectual Controversy*; *On the Margins of Discourse*; *Scandalous Knowledge*; *Poetic Closure*; and *Natural Reflections: Human Cognition at the Nexus of Science and Religion*.

A. L. Snijders, the author of some fifteen-hundred very short stories, which he circulates to an e-mail list and publishes occasionally in Dutch collections, has been a columnist for *Het Parool* and several regional newspapers in the Netherlands.

Timothy Snyder is the Housum professor of history at Yale University and a permanent fellow of the Institute for Human Sciences in Vienna. His book *Bloodlands: Europe between Hitler and Stalin*, which has been translated into thirty-three languages, received the Emerson Prize in the Humanities, the Literature Award from the American Academy of Arts and Letters, the Leipzig Award for European Understanding, and the Hannah Arendt Prize in Political Thought. His most recent book, *Black Earth: The Holocaust as History and Warning*, will appear in twenty-four foreign-language editions. His other books include *Nationalism, Marxism, and Modern Central Europe*; *The Reconstruction of Nations: Poland, Ukraine, Lithuania, Belarus, 1659–1999*; *Sketches from a Secret War: A Polish Artist's Mission to Liberate Soviet Ukraine*; and *The Red Prince: The Secret Lives of a Habsburg Archduke*.

Alexander Solzhenitsyn (1918–2008), recipient of the Nobel Prize for Literature in 1970 and the Templeton Prize in 1983, was the author of, among many other works, *One Day in* *the Life of Ivan Denisovitch*, *The First Circle*, *Cancer Ward*, *Warning to the West*, *The Oak and the Calf*, and the three-part historical novel *Red Wheel*. Expelled from the Soviet Union in 1974 after publication of *The Gulag Archipelago*, he returned to Russia in 1994. After Solzhenitsyn's death, Mikhail Gorbachev said that the writer had "changed the minds of millions of people, making them rethink their past and present." **Jamey Gambrell**, who has published translations of works by Marina Tsvetaeva, Joseph Brodsky, and Tatyana Tolstaya, has received the Thornton Wilder Translation Prize from the American Academy of Arts and Letters.

Susan Sontag (1933–2004) was a MacArthur Fellow from 1990 to 1995 and received the National Book Award in 2000 for her novel *In America*, a chapter of which appeared in the fall 1998 issue of *Common Knowledge*. (Her play *Alice in Bed* had appeared in the spring 1993 issue.) Her other novels are *Death Kit*; *Benefactor*; and *The Volcano Lover*. Among the most influential of her essay collections are *Against Interpretation*; *Styles of Radical Will*; *On Photography*; *Illness as Metaphor*; *AIDS and Its Metaphors*; *Under the Sign of Saturn*; *Where the Stress Falls*; and *Regarding the Pain of Others*. She was named a Commander of the French Order of Arts and Letters in 1999 and received the Jerusalem Prize in 2001. She was a citizen of the intellectual world whose capital, she took as given, was New York. "Without her New York City seems a colder place," *The New Yorker* wrote on her passing.

Isabelle Stengers received the grand prize for philosophy from the French Academy in 1993. Professor of the philosophy of science at the Free University of Brussels, she is the author of *Cosmopolitics* (in two volumes), which won the Ludwik Fleck Prize in 2013; *Thinking with Whitehead*; *Power and Invention: Situating Science*; *The Invention of Modern Science*; *Capitalist Sorcery: Breaking the Spell*; *In Catastrophic Times: Resisting the Coming Barbarism*; and (with Nobel Prize laureate Ilya Prigogine) *Order out of Chaos*; *The End of Certainty*; and *La Nouvelle Alliance*.

Dame Marilyn Strathern is life president of the British Association of Social Anthropologists, William Wyse professor of social anthropology emerita at Cambridge University, and a life fellow of Girton College. A fellow of the British Academy and an honorary foreign member of the American Academy of Arts and Sciences, her many books include *The Gender of the Gift*; *Kinship, Law, and the Unexpected*; *Partial Connections*; *After Nature*; *Women in Between*; *Reproducing the Future*; *Property, Substance, and Effect*; *Kinship at the Core*; and *No Money on Our Skins: Hagen Migrants in Port Moresby*.

Wisława Szymborska (1923–2012) received the 1996 Nobel Prize in Literature. Her many other honors include the Goethe Prize, the Herder Prize, and the Polish PEN Club Prize. Collections of her poems translated into English include *People on a Bridge*; *View with a Grain of Sand: Selected Poems*; and *Monologue of a Dog*. A selection of her reviews was published in English under the title *Nonrequired Reading: Prose Pieces*. **Clare Cavanagh**, Frances Hooper professor in the arts and humanities at Northwestern University, is the author of *Lyric Poetry and Modern Politics: Russia, Poland, and the West*, for which she received the National Book Critics Circle Award in Criticism.

Miguel Tamen is professor and director of the program in literary theory at the University of Lisbon, and he has been visiting professor since 2000 at the University of Chicago. His books include *What Art Is Like, in Constant Reference to the Alice Books*; *Friends of Interpretable Objects*; *Manners of Interpretation: The Ends of Argument in Literary Studies*; and *The Matter of the Facts: On Invention and Interpretation*.

G. Thomas Tanselle, who was vice president of the John Simon Guggenheim Memorial Foundation from 1978 to 2006, is coeditor of the recently completed *Northwestern-Newberry Edition of the Writings of Herman Melville*. His other publications include *A Rationale of Textual Criticism*; *Textual Criticism and Scholarly Editing*; *Textual Criticism since Greg*; *Bibliographical Analysis: A Historical Introduction*; *Essays in Bibliographical History*; and *Literature and Artifacts*.

Sir Keith Thomas, professor emeritus of modern history at Oxford University and Distinguished Fellow of All Souls College, is the author of *The Ends of Life: Roads to Fulfillment in Early Modern England*; *Man and the Natural World*; and *Religion and the Decline of Magic*, for which he received the Wolfson History Prize in its inaugural year. He was president of the British Academy, from 1993 to 1997, and president of Corpus Christi College, Oxford, from 1986 to 2000.

Stephen Toulmin (1922–2009) was professor emeritus in the Committee on Social Thought at the University of Chicago and Henry R. Luce Professor at the Center for Multiethnic and Transnational Studies at the University of Southern California. His writings include *Cosmopolis: The Hidden Agenda of Modernity*; *Quantum Mechanics: An Empiricist View*; *Human Understanding: The Collective Use and Evolution of Concepts*; *Knowing and Acting*; *The Return to Cosmology*; *Return to Reason*; and "A Dissenter's Story," his 1997 Jefferson Lecture to the National Endowment for the Humanities.

Anna Lowenhaupt Tsing is Niels Bohr professor at Aarhus University, in charge of the university's research project on the Anthropocene, as well as professor of anthropology at the University of California, Santa Cruz. A recipient of the Huxley Memorial Medal of the Royal Anthropological Institute, the Gregory Bateson Book Prize, and the Victor Turner Prize in Ethnographic Writing, she is the author of *The Mushroom at the End of the World*; *Friction: An Ethnography of Global Connection*; and *In the Realm of the Diamond Queen: Marginality in an Out-of-the-Way Place*.

Andrew P. Tuck, a founding partner of ARC Research in New York, is the author of *Comparative Philosophy and the Philosophy of Scholarship: On the Western Interpretation of Nāgārjuna*. He has taught Western philosophy and South Asian religion at several universities, including Columbia, Princeton, and the New School for Social Research.

Michiko Urita, associate professor of ethnomusicology at Kogakkan University in Ise, Mie, Japan, has received a four-year grant, from the Japan Society for the Promotion of Science, for research on the history and future of the imperial enthronement ceremony. Her article "Transreligious and Intercommunal: Hindustani Music in Classical and Contemporary North India" appeared in the May 2016 issue of *Common Knowledge*.

Bas van Fraassen is McCosh professor of philosophy Emeritus at Princeton University and distinguished professor of philosophy at San Francisco State University. A fellow of the American Academy of Arts and Sciences and the Royal Netherlands Academy of Arts and Sciences, he has received the Lakatos Award of the London School of Economics and the Hempel Award of the Philosophy of Science Association. His books include *Scientific Representation*; *The Empirical Stance*; *Quantum Mechanics: An Empiricist View*; *Laws and Symmetry*; *Formal Semantics and Logic*; *The Scientific Image*; and *An Introduction to the Philosophy of Time and Space*.

Marina Vanzolini, professor of social anthropology at the University of São Paulo, is the author of *A Flecha do Ciúme: O parentesco e seu Avesso Segundo os Aweti do Alto Xingu*, an eth-nographic analysis of sorcery and kinship in Aweti social life. **Julia Sauma** is a researcher in the University of Bergen Egalitarianism Project.

Gianni Vattimo, a former member of the European Parliament, is professor emeritus of the-oretical philosophy at the University of Turin. He is coauthor—with René Girard, Jacques Derrida, and Richard Rorty, respectively—of books titled *Weak Faith*; *Religion*; and *The Future of Religion*. His monographs in English translation include *Weak Thought*; *Nihilism and Emancipation*; *The Adventure of Difference*; *Beyond Interpretation*; *The End of Modernity*; *The Responsibility of the Philosopher*; *The Transparent Society*; *Art's Claim to Truth*; and *After Christianity*. "Beyond Despair and Conflict: A Reading of Nietzsche's Positive Nihilism" was serialized in *Common Knowledge* in the spring and fall of 1998.

Helen Vendler, A. Kingsley Porter university professor at Harvard, is a recipient of the National Book Critics' Circle Award for Criticism, the Modern Language Association's James Russell Lowell Prize, the National Institute of Arts and Letters Award, the Truman Capote Prize, and both the Thomas Jefferson Medal and the Moe Prize of the Ameri-can Philosophical Society. She is a fellow of the American Academy of Arts and Sciences and delivered the 2004 Jefferson Lecture ("The Ocean, the Bird, and the Scholar") to the National Endowment for the Humanities. Her many books include *The Art of Shakespeare's Sonnets*; *Dickinson: Selected Poems and Commentaries*; *On Extended Wings: Wallace Stevens's Longer Poems*; *Our Secret Discipline: Yeats and Lyric Form*; *Poets Thinking*; *The Music of What Happens*; *Last Looks, Last Books*; *Invisible Listeners*; *Coming of Age as a Poet*; *Soul Says: On Recent poetry*; and *The Given and the Made*.

Charlie Samuya Veric teaches literature and cultural theory at Ateneo de Manila University in the Philippines. His books of poems include *Boyhood: A Long Lyric* and *Histories*. In 2018, he was a Writing Fellow at the Johannesburg Institute for Advanced Study in South Africa.

Eduardo Viveiros de Castro is professor of anthropology at the Museo Nacional Univer-sidade Federal in Rio de Janeiro and has held the Simón Bolívar Chair in Latin American Studies at Cambridge University. Editor of the journal *Mana: Studies in Social Anthropology*, he is the author of *Cannibal Metaphysics*; *From the Enemy's Point of View*; and *The Inconstancy of the Indian Soul: The Encounter of Catholics and Cannibals in Sixteenth-Century Brazil*.

Sir Bernard Williams (1929–2003) was Knightbridge professor of philosophy at Cambridge University from 1967 to 1987, White's professor of moral philosophy at Oxford University from 1990 to 1996, and Monroe Deutsch professor of philosophy at the University of Cali-fornia, Berkeley, from 1988 to 2003. A fellow of the British Academy, he was the author of *Moral Luck*; *Ethics and the Limits of Philosophy*; *Problems of the Self*; *Shame and Necessity*; *Truth and Truthfulness*; *Making Sense of Humanity*; *In the Beginning Was the Deed*; *Philosophy as a Humanistic Discipline*; and (with Amartya Sen) *Utilitarianism and Beyond*.

Rowan Williams (Baron Williams of Oystermouth) was, from 2002 to 12, the one hundred-fourth archbishop of Canterbury and is currently the thirty-fifth master of Magdalene College, Cambridge. A member of the UK Privy Council and House of Lords, he is also chancellor of the University of South Wales, a member of the British Academy, a fellow of the Royal Society of Literature, and formerly Lady Margaret professor of divinity at Oxford University. His many books include *Peacemaking Theology*; *The Truce of God*; *Faith* *and Experience in Early Monasticism*; *Arius: Heresy and Tradition*; *Faith in the Public Square*; *The Edge of Words: God and the Habits of Language*; *Dostoevsky: Language, Faith, and Fiction*; and *The Poems of Rowan Williams*.

H. R. Woudhuysen is the rector of Lincoln College, Oxford, and a fellow of the British Academy. He is the author of *Sir Philip Sidney and the Circulation of Manuscripts, 1558–1640* and coeditor (with Michael Suarez, SJ) of the *Oxford Companion to the Book* and *The Book: A Global History*.

Grzegorz Wróblewski's writings have been translated into ten languages. He has published eleven volumes of poetry and four collections of short prose pieces in Poland; three books of poetry, a book of poetic prose, and an experimental novel in Denmark; and selected poems in Bosnia and Herzegovina. He is also the author of six plays. **Adam Zdrodowski**'s own collections of poetry include *Przygody, Etc.* and *Jesień Zuzanny*.

Santiago Zabala is Catalan Institute for Research and Advanced Studies Professor at Pompeu Fabra University in Barcelona and the author of *The Remains of Being*; *Only Art Can Save Us*; *The Hermeneutic Nature of Analytic Philosophy*; and (with Gianni Vattimo) *Hermeneutic Communism*. He has edited several books by or on Vattimo and one, *The Future of Religion*, cowritten by Vattimo and Richard Rorty. **Yaakov Mascetti**, lecturer in comparative literature at Bar-Ilan University, is an associate editor of *Common Knowledge*.

DOI 10.1215/0961754X-7313689

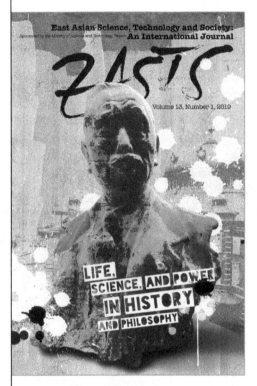